THE DOODLEBUGS

Books on the Second World War

How We Lived Then
If Britain Had Fallen
The Real Dad's Army
The GIs
Air Raid: The Bombing of Coventry
When We Won the War
The Bombers
The Home Front (*editor*)
Hitler's Rockets

Other Social Histories

King Cholera
The Waterdrinkers
The Workhouse
The Hungry Mills
The Breadstealers

In Preparation

Defending the Island

THE
DOODLEBUGS

The Story of the Flying Bombs

Norman Longmate

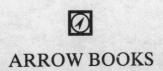

ARROW BOOKS

Arrow Books Limited
62–65 Chandos Place, London WC2N 4NW

An imprint of Century Hutchinson Limited

London Melbourne Sydney Auckland
Johannesburg and agencies throughout
the world

First published by Hutchinson 1981
Arrow edition 1986

© Norman Longmate 1981

Made and printed in Great Britain
by Cox & Wyman Ltd, Reading

ISBN 0 09 929020 0

To P.E.S. and S.R.S.
who also lived through them

CONTENTS

ILLUSTRATIONS

ACKNOWLEDGEMENTS

Grateful acknowledgement is made for the use of the copyright material as follows: to Ian Allan Ltd for Arthur Reed and Roland Beamont, *Typhoon and Tempest at War*; to the editor of the *American Journal of Orthopsychiary* for Adolf G. Woltman, 'Life on a Target'; to the Executive Officer at Birkbeck College for Professor E. H. Warmington, *A History of Birkbeck College during the Second World War*; to the editor of the *British Medical Journal* for R. C. Bell, 'An analysis of 259 of the Recent Flying-Bomb Casualties'; to Cassell Ltd for Lord Tedder, *With Prejudice* and A. B. Hartley, *Unexploded Bomb*; to Chatto & Windus Ltd for James Lees-Milne, *Prophesying Peace*; to William Collins Sons & Co. Ltd for Sir Arthur Bryant, *Triumph in the West*; to J. M. Dent & Sons Ltd for Mrs Robert Henrey, *The Siege of London*; to Dennis Dobson for Vere Hodgson, *Few Eggs and No Oranges*; to Mrs G. W. Eyre for the late A. H. Eyre, *Perpetual Target*; to Faber & Faber Ltd for William Sansom, *Westminster at War*; to John Farquharson Ltd for R. V. Jones, *Most Secret War* published by Hamish Hamilton; to the editor of *Glaxo Group News* for extracts from the former *Staff Bulletin*; to the editor of the *Hastings and St Leonards Observer*; to Her Majesty's Stationery Office for various official documents; to William Heinemann Ltd for Charles Graves, *Women in Green* and Jane Gordon, *Married to Charles* and Richard Hough, *One Boy's War*; to Jeremy Howard-Williams for *Night Intruder* published by David & Charles Holdings Ltd; to David Irving for *The Mare's Nest* published by William Kimber & Co. Ltd; to Wil-

11

liam Kimber & Co. Ltd for Prudence Hill, *To Know the Sky*; to London Transport for Charles Graves, *London Transport Carried On* (now published as *London Transport at War*); to Macdonald Futura Publishers Ltd for George P. Thompson, *Blue-Pencil Admiral*; to Laurence Pollinger Ltd and the Estate of the late H. E. Bates for *The World in Ripeness* published by Michael Joseph Ltd; to Sidgwick & Jackson Ltd for Hugh Trevor-Roper (editor), *Hitler's War Directives*; to A. P. Watt Ltd for A. P. Herbert, *Light the Lights* published by Methuen & Co. Ltd; to George Weidenfeld & Nicolson Ltd for Dusko Popov, *Spy Counterspy*; to Joseph Angell, Jr, for 'Guided Missiles Could Have Won' in *The Atlantic Monthly*; to Howard Baker Publishers Ltd, William Heinemann Ltd and Hutchinson Publishing Group Ltd for A. P. Herbert, *Independent Member*; to Roland Beamont for *Phoenix into Ashes* published by William Kimber & Co. Ltd; to Geoffrey Bles (Publishers) Ltd for Elizabeth Sheppard-Jones, *I Walk on Wheels*; to Chatto & Windus Ltd for Pierre Closterman, *The Big Show*; to A. D. Peters & Co. Ltd for Constance Babington Smith, *Evidence in Camera*; to Harper & Row for G. H. Arnold, *Global Mission* published in the UK by Hutchinson Publishing Group Ltd; to The Bodley Head for Hanna Reitsch, *The Sky My Kingdom*; to Doubleday & Co. Inc. and the Estate of the late Dwight D. Eisenhower for *Crusade in Europe* published in the UK by William Heinemann Ltd; to George G. Harrap & Co. Ltd for General Sir Frederick Pile, *Ack Ack*; to William Heinemann Ltd and the Estate of the late John Lehmann for *I am My Brother*; to Hutchinson Publishing Group Ltd for E. K. Bramsted, *Goebbels and the National Socialist Propaganda*, published by the Cresset Press; to Interpress Publishers, Warsaw, for Bohdan Arct, *Poles Against the V Weapons*; to the editor of the *Kent Messenger*; to E. P. S. Lewin and Partners for Edward Lanchberry, *Against the Sun* published by Cassell Ltd; to the Ministry of Defence for Air Vice-Marshal Gell, 'Balloons v Flying Bombs' in the *Royal Air Force Journal*; to the editor of the *Oldham Chronicle*; to the editor of the *South London Press*; to Stedehill Publications for R. H. Goodsall, *A Third Kentish Patchwork*; to the Borough of Lambeth for *Streatham's 41*.

Acknowledgements for illustrations

BBC Hulton Picture Library: 31, 32, 33
British Aerospace: 17
Bundesarchiv, Koblenz: 4
Imperial War Museum: 1, 2, 3, 5, 7, 8, 9, 10, 12, 13, 14, 15, 16, 18, 19, 20, 21, 24, 25, 26, 27, 30, 34, 38, 39, 40, 42
Mr Brian Johnson: 6, 11
Photo Source: 22, 28, 41
London Transport: 37
Popperfoto: 29
Mrs J. Rendell: 23
St Helier Hospital: 35
Syndication International: 36
Ullstein Bilderdienst, Berlin: 5

FOREWORD

The flying-bomb has a unique place in the history of the Second World War. Work on designing it did not begin until 1942; it presented a menace for only ten weeks; and when, in March 1945, the last one was fired in anger it ceased to have any military significance, in contrast to the rocket, the shadow of which hangs over the world to this day. Few weapons have been so brilliant in conception, so swift in development, or had so brief an operational life.

The idea of writing about this brief-lived invention attracted me for several reasons. It was by its nature an indiscriminate weapon, highly relevant to my own special interest in civilian experience during the Second World War. It made an extraordinary and lasting impact on all who lived in Southern England in 1944, although the majority of the population of the British Isles never even heard one. And almost everything so far written about the subject has concentrated on the intelligence and military aspects of the subject and has ignored those at the 'receiving end'. There was available, too, thanks to the 'thirty year rule' an enormous wealth of official material denied to earlier historians.

The sheer volume of the documents on the subject almost defeated me, indeed had I known the vast amount of research involved I would never have started on the project. I was also overwhelmed by the response – nearly 2000 replies – when I appealed for reminiscences in the press. Indexing, extracting, collating and finally selecting extracts for quotation from the millions of words these letters represented proved laborious,

if at the same time fascinating and rewarding. A further difficulty was provided by the self-contradictory nature of many
contemporary documents. Partly because of censorship, partly
because the first casualty figures and other details often proved
to be inaccurate, the normal rule that the nearer one gets back
to the original date the more accurate a written source is likely
to be did not apply.

Secret contemporary records are even more confusing than
published ones since the same incident is regularly referred to
by several different names and it is rare for two accounts to
agree on even the most basic facts. One eminent biographer's
book confuses (as he generously admitted to me) the date of
arrival of the first flying-bomb and the first rocket. Another,
justifiably popular, writer clearly misread the official casualty
figures for the 'Barnet' factory incident (which in any case
occurred in New Southgate), and quoted as the number of
dead the total of *dead and seriously injured*, an entirely different matter. A third, normally most reliable, attributes the
official history by Basil Collier to a mythical figure called Kelly.
Another writer, Angus Calder, on the same page of *The People's War* (Cape, first edition, p. 559) states both that the first
flying-bombs were fired on 'the night of August 12th/13th', and
that the attack began in earnest on the night of 15 June, while
a photograph in the same book purports to show a 'flying-
bomb crashing into a side road off Drury Lane . . . in May
1944', a totally false date. I make these comments in no superior spirit, knowing how easily such mistakes can slip into
print, but they clearly make the task of later writers no easier.
It would be surprising if in a book on this scale there were no
factual errors, but the present book undoubtedly contains more
information about the flying-bomb offensive than has appeared
in print before.

The Doodlebugs was also originally intended to cover the
V-2s, on which I also collected information from contributors,
but it eventually appeared that this would make it inordinately
long, and would have delayed its completion, perhaps by another year. I hope those who sent me material on the V-2s will
understand why it does not appear here. The V-2s were
covered in *Hitler's Rockets*, which was published in May 1985.

The present book could not have been written without the

Foreword

cooperation of the many newspapers which printed my appeal
for recollections. I must also thank all those who responded,
and who have so patiently waited for the present book to be
published. Even where I have not quoted from them directly,
all the contributions I received have been valuable in helping
to paint a comprehensive picture. I must acknowledge a special
debt to the following: Mr R. G. Auckland, who drew my
attention to the use of the V-1s to carry leaflets; Mr Brian
Johnson, of the BBC Science and Features Department, to
whom I was able in return to provide some material for his
television series, *The Secret War*; Dr Bernard Donoughue, who
kindly provided some additional details about Herbert Morrison; Mr Clem Leslie, who supplied some personal recollections
about Morrison's attitude to the V-1s; Mr David Irving, who
generously made available to me confirmatory evidence on the
same subject which does not appear in his own book, *The
Mare's Nest*; the staff of the Metropolitan Borough of Wandsworth, and especially the Reference Librarian at Battersea;
the Director of the Central Library, Oldham, the District Librarian, Southampton, the sub-Librarian of the Local History
Library, Manchester, and the Divisional Librarian, Gloucester;
the editor of the *Hastings and St Leonard's Observer*, who
provided some press cuttings on the 'guns' controversy described in chapter 33; and Professor R. V. Jones, who answered
a series of questions which the official sources had left unre-
solved. I am also grateful to Mr William H. Cunliffe, Colonel
William Strobridge and Mr Tom Lockwood, of the Historical
Services Division and Historical Records Branch, of the Department of the Army, Washington DC, for providing me with
information about the effect of the V-1s on the American
forces. The chapter 'At the Factory Gate' could not have been
written without the enthusiastic help of Standard Telephones
and Cables Ltd, particularly Mr Peter Earl, Director of Public
Relations, Mr David Robertson, Public Relations Manager,
Mr John Eve, Editor of *STC News*, and Mr A. R. Byford, Site
Archivist at New Southgate. Finally I must acknowledge my
appreciation of the tireless research of Miss Idina Le Geyt in
the Public Record Office and elsewhere; and of the support
and forbearance of Mr Anthony Whittome of Hutchinson. I

hope the result may stand as a belated memorial to all those who died or suffered injury or loss because of the flying-bombs.

For this edition I have made one or two small changes in the original text and have corrected some minor errors kindly pointed out by readers.

N.R.L.

1

A WEAPON WHICH CANNOT BE
USED AGAINST US

There are serious indications that Germany has been developing bacterial warfare, gases, flame weapons, glider bombs and pilotless aircraft . . . and it is recommended that necessary precautions should be taken.

Report by the Scientific Adviser to the Secret Intelligence Service, 11 November 1939

When, on Tuesday, 19 September 1939, Hitler made a speech in Danzig it attracted unusual attention in Great Britain. The British public, keyed up to expect great events on the outbreak of war, had been disappointed, or relieved, when nothing had happened, except that Hitler had advanced into Poland far faster than even the most pessimistic had predicted. Hitler himself, however, was disappointed, as the American radio journalist William Shirer learned that day from a Nazi acquaintance. Having hoped to broadcast from Warsaw, he had, after waiting 'three or four days outside the Polish capital', had to settle for the Danzig Guild Hall, a beautiful but singularly inappropriate setting for Hitler's entourage, who to Shirer's hostile eye, resembled 'a pack of Chicago gangsters'. As for the Führer himself, 'when he spoke of Britain his face flamed up in hysterical rage'.

Hitler had, he insisted, no further quarrel with Britain or France, but if they insisted on continuing the war, 'We have,' the translation used by the British press ran, 'a weapon which cannot be used against us.' The German News Agency, reflecting more accurately Hitler's tortuous prose, put it slightly differently. 'The moment might very quickly come, for us to use a weapon with which we ourselves could not be attacked.'

With news scarce, 'Hitler's secret weapon' made headlines

everywhere, although as the weeks passed and no sign of it appeared it became a national joke. In government circles, however, there was no disposition lightly to dismiss what he had said, and when the Intelligence Services were asked by the Prime Minister to identify the mysterious secret weapon, they assigned to the task Dr R. V. Jones, an ex-Oxford physicist, aged only twenty-eight, a former pupil of Professor Lindemann, Winston Churchill's confidant and Scientific Adviser. Dr Jones had been evacuated to Harrogate with the Scientific Branch of the Air Ministry, but was now recalled to London and the less imposing surroundings of Number 55 Broadway, headquarters of the Secret Intelligence Services, where he was to spend the rest of the war. While, after a marvellously sunny autumn, the nation settled down to endure the black-out and the hardest winter of the century, Dr Jones was investigating even worse horrors:

I went through the files and they were sometimes pathetic, sometimes amusing. I found the Secret Service had got mixed up with trying to get a death ray going, all kinds of rather wild ideas. There was also some quite good stuff in the files, although one had to look for it. But I was in the end convinced that there was no secret weapon at all, in the sense that Hitler was speaking about it. And so when one gets to that stage one tries to go back and find out what it was the man actually said.

With the help of the BBC recording, and the Professor of German at King's College, London, who 'came back absolutely indignant at Hitler's grammar', Dr Jones reached the conclusion that 'it is . . . very probable that the weapon to which reference was made was neither intentional bluff nor a novelty. It is submitted that Hitler was speaking of his Air Force.' But in the same report, Dr Jones summarized the results of his inquiries into all the relevant intelligence so far collected:

A search of S.I.S. files has been made for possible novel weapons. . . . Apart from the more fantastic rumours such as those concerned with machines for generating earthquakes and gases which cause everyone within two miles to burst, there are a number of weapons to which general references occur, and of which some must be considered seriously. They include:
(1) Bacterial warfare.
(2) New gases.

(3) Flame weapons.
(4) Gliding bombs, aerial torpedoes and pilotless aircraft.
(5) Long range guns and rockets.
(6) New torpedoes, mines and submarines.
(7) Death rays, engine-stopping rays and magnetic guns.

From this depressing list Dr Jones rapidly eliminated (6) as already in use, and (7) for lack of evidence. But none of the others could be dismissed so lightly.

We know from experience that pilotless aircraft are feasible technically and that we could have made such weapons ourselves had we devoted sufficient effort. If these small aircraft be used for the legitimate aim of ramming hostile bombers, they are likely to prove an economic proposition. It is somewhat more probable that these aircraft are intended as long range projectiles, but it is unlikely that they would be accurate, even with wireless control and would therefore be very inefficient against military objectives. It might be thought by the Germans that such weapons would have a serious effect on our morale, if launched indiscriminately against England in a manner similar to that in which they sprayed Paris with the long range gun in 1918.

A detailed analysis of all the fourteen 'references to gliding bombs and pilotless aircraft' followed, going back to March 1937, when a 'reliable source' had reported the existence of 'about 1000 . . . small aircraft, fuselage about 9 ft long, 21 ft span, range 600 miles'. More alarming, and more recent, was the message from a 'source untried' on 22 September of a 'pilotless aircraft W/T [Wireless] controlled carrying ½ ton of explosive . . . 10'–15' in length, launched by catapult', and the last report of all, on 20 October 1939. This stated that the Director of the great Junkers factory had indiscreetly remarked in a letter that 'We are working feverishly on a new weapon to destroy England.' Dr Jones summed up the fourteen close-packed foolscap pages of his survey with a solemn warning:

There are serious indications that Germany has been developing bacterial warfare, gases, flame weapons, glider bombs and pilotless aircraft, and long range guns, and it is recommended that necessary precautions should be taken.

This paper, *The Hitler Waffe*, was completed on 11 November 1939, just about the time that the bundle of documents known

21

collectively as 'The Oslo Report' appeared on Dr Jones's desk. This three-inch-thick parcel, from a benefactor who described himself as a 'well-wishing German scientist', had been left in the porter's lodge of the British Legation in Norway in the middle of a heavy snowstorm a week earlier. On the subject of pilotless aircraft the Oslo Report was silent, but it asserted that the Germans had launched a major programme of long-range rocket development and were carrying out secret research of some kind at a place called Peenemünde on the island of Usedom in the Baltic, the first time this later famous name had appeared in the records. We now know why the Oslo Report made no mention of pilotless aircraft: in November 1939 none was under development. The basic idea, however, had been known for years. During the First World War a French artillery officer, René Lorin, had suggested that an unmanned aircraft, propelled by a ram-jet or pulse-jet, stabilized by gyroscopes, and guided to its target by radio control from another aircraft, should be developed for the long range bombardment of Berlin. Lorin's proposal was published in 1919 and made clear that the essential requirement for any pilotless aircraft was a simple propulsion unit which could operate without human control. Lorin favoured a pulse-jet, operated by means of pumping an explosive mixture into a combustion chamber, where it was ignited by a sparking plug. The resulting explosion briefly cut off the fuel supply so that the machine progressed by a series of explosions which provided a continuous thrust. This, however, was only an idea. The real pioneers in working out the details of the pulse-jet system were another Frenchman and a Belgian. The former, Victor de Darvodine, had lodged a specification for such an engine as early as 9 April 1906 and had patented it a year later, while on 17 February 1909 a Belgian engineer, George Marconnet, had applied for a similar patent in Belgium, and on 10 February 1910 in Paris, describing the unit as particularly suitable for aeroplanes and airships. Neither engine, however, seems to have been built.

The first pilotless aircraft actually to fly was in fact American and powered by a conventional petrol engine. A full-size prototype, made by the famous Sperry company, tested in the spring of 1918, had an impressive performance, coming down within a hundred yards of its target after a flight of forty miles, but it was too complicated for mass production. A second prototype, developed by Charles F. Kettering ('Ket') of the go-ahead firm of Delco, later of General Motors, was far cheaper, being made of papier-mâché, reinforced with wood. Although it had a wing-span of less than twelve feet, it could carry a bomb-load equal to its own weight, three hundred pounds. Nicknamed 'The Bug', the machine was extraordinarily cheap – no more than $400 (about £80), of which the 40 horsepower engine, built by Henry Ford, cost about $50 (£10). The device used to limit the distance flown consisted of a 'cam', a little like a milometer, set to a specific number of engine revolutions. When this figure was reached the cam dropped downwards, drawing back the bolts supporting the wings, so that, in the graphic phrase of one observer, they 'folded up like a jack rabbit's ears, and the Bug plunged to earth as a bomb'.

Despite some embarrassing mishaps during its trials as when, during its first major demonstration, it dived suddenly on 'the group of brass hats below scattering them in all directions', the design proved basically sound and plans were drawn up 'to launch thousands every day against German strong points, concentration areas, munition plants, etc.' The war ended, however, before production really got under way, and though development work continued 'the economy wave of the mid-twenties caused it to be shelved.'

Great Britain's record was even worse. In 1926 the chief designer of Gloster Aircraft, Mr H. P. Folland, offered plans for 'a petrol-driven pilotless aircraft' to the Air Ministry. They were, one of his wartime staff later learned, 'not impressed and informed Mr Folland that they could see no future for such a revolutionary plane.'

Between the wars interest in pilotless flight centred on radio-controlled conventionally powered aircraft. The Germans successfully test flew in 1939 a prototype intended for photographic reconnaissance. The British were further ahead with the De Havilland DH82b, or Queen Bee, a pilotless version of the famous Tiger Moth, the RAF's basic trainer. The Queen Bee had a ceiling of 17,000 feet and a range of 300 miles, while its spruce and plywood fuselage made the airframe cheap to manufacture. Between 1935 and September 1939, 210 Queen Bees were built as target aircraft, and another 380 were turned out during a second production run between October 1943 and July 1944. No one, however, seems to have contemplated using the machine for offensive purposes and with its 130 horsepower Gipsy Major engine producing a top speed of only 104 miles per hour it would have been hopelessly vulnerable in action.

The Germans had during the 1930s experimented with two types of pulse-jet on the lines of that suggested by Lorin back in 1919. Work on the first, the Schmidt duct, had begun at Munich in 1929, and by about 1935 its inventor, Dr Paul Schmidt, had made sufficient progress to suggest that it might be used to propel a 'flying torpedo' or to serve as a supplementary source of power for gliders. Meanwhile a second type of engine, based on a very similar principle, was being developed by the Argus Motorenwerke under the direction of Fritz Gosslau. His design, the Argus duct, was demonstrated in 1939, but not put into production and when, shortly before the outbreak of war, the firm was invited to draw up plans for producing a pilotless missile with a range of 350 miles, they suggested that it should be powered by a conventional piston engine.

Aircraft technology had made enormous strides since 1918 and an improved version of the First World War 'Bug', which flew in the United States in December 1939, achieved a range of 200 miles, with the promise of further improvement both in range and accuracy. Radio control had now been added and General Arnold, commanding the US Air Force, was impressed by the machine's potential:

The pilotless Bug was . . . already a modern military weapon. . . . It would cost, per unit, between $800 and $1,000 as compared to . . . $400,000 for a single heavy bomber and could be produced quickly in large numbers. For the price of one Flying Fortress with a bomb load of 6,000 pounds, we could send 500 of these little Bugs over enemy territory, each carrying about 800 pounds of explosive. . . . More important than any monetary factor was the possible saving in human life.

General Arnold later concluded that had a decision to go ahead been taken after Pearl Harbor in December 1941, 'we could probably have had this assault in full swing by late 1942 or early 1943', but a high-level meeting decided that the machine's range was too limited to justify mass production. As Arnold explained, 'even with the most improved type of Bug the best we could do from England would be to hit Paris, or some of the other large cities in France, Belgium or Holland. We could not get at the real heart of our enemy – interior Germany itself.'

In Germany both the Army and the Luftwaffe had, in the first heady months of Nazi rule, become interested in developing the Argus duct, though the Luftwaffe withdrew in 1934 – partly perhaps because pilotless aircraft would render redundant their cherished skill. The Army's enthusiasm for new weapons was increasingly directed to plans for a long-range rocket, on which preliminary work had begun as early as 1930 under the direction of a young artillery officer, Captain Walter Dornberger of the German Army Weapons Office. In 1932 Dornberger recruited an even younger scientist, Dr von Braun, and at von Braun's suggestion the Army, in 1936, with some financial help from the Luftwaffe, bought a large part of the remote island of Usedom on the Baltic, seventy miles from the nearest city, with 300 miles of open water to provide a firing range. Here, at a spot called Peenemünde, a huge research establishment was erected in great secrecy. Its director, Werner von Braun, was by 1942 the leading authority on rocket propulsion in the world and the Army eagerly welcomed the development of what it regarded as essentially another form of artillery.

For the Luftwaffe meanwhile the situation had changed. Everywhere its squadrons were being forced back on the defensive, and the devastation of Lübeck by Bomber Command on 28 March 1942 marked the real opening of the offensive against German cities. The old restraints on using indiscriminate weapons against civilians were clearly disappearing and Hitler, on 24 April, ordered 'attacks of a retaliatory nature' on non-military targets. The search was on for a cheap and simple type of aircraft making few demands on industry, with accuracy of minor importance. But the decisive argument was inter-service rivalry. The German Air Ministry knew that the Ger-

The Doodlebugs

man Army was working independently on a major project of its own, a long-range missile of totally new design, also designed to bombard London. 'The German Air Force,' in the words of Hitler's Minister of Munitions, Albert Speer, 'was disturbed that the Army alone would be bombing London. . . . They protested that the Army was sprouting wings.'

Thus when, in March 1942, the Argus company asked the Air Ministry in Berlin if it was still interested in pilotless aircraft it was warmly encouraged to continue work on the project. The idea particularly appealed to Field-Marshal Erhard Milch, Inspector-General of the Luftwaffe and deputy to Reichsmarschall Hermann Göring, its Commander-in-Chief. More than any one man, Milch was to be responsible for the decision to produce a flying-bomb. The concept of indiscriminate slaughter delighted Milch, a ferocious Nazi – he complained in 1942 that there were not nearly enough death sentences on suspected traitors – but the whole project might never have got off the ground had Milch not chanced to meet at the crucial moment a man who could turn his dreams into reality. Robert Lusser, to whom Milch was introduced on 28 May 1942, was a talented aircraft designer who had – like Milch himself – fallen foul of both the Heinkel Company and Professor Messerschmitt, head of the great concern which bore his name. The airman and the engineer took to each other immediately. Within a few days of Milch outlining his plan for an Argus-tube-propelled pilotless aircraft, Lusser returned with calculations proving it to be practicable and some rough drawings. The new machine met Milch's needs to perfection, for it would make no demand on the aluminium industry, being made of thin steel plate, and would burn cheap low-grade petrol instead of scarce and costly high octane aviation spirit. The labour needed would be extremely small, only 550 man hours, excluding the explosive and auto-pilot.

From the moment Lusser produced his designs the idea of a self-powered flying-bomb made rapid headway. By 9 June 1942 its main outlines were already settled. It was realized, for example, that keeping its wings short, to facilitate handling, would mean a high stalling speed and the need to launch it by catapult. On that day the idea became a firm project, with a codename, *Kirschkern* or 'Cherry-stone'.

A Weapon Which Cannot Be Used Against Us

Work on the catapults involved no great new breakthrough, since they were already under development for other purposes and selecting a company to develop the airframe presented even fewer problems. Fieseler Flugzeugbau, of Kassel, makers of the famous 196 or Storch, a small high-wing monoplane powered by an Argus engine, was outstanding in the production of light aircraft. In June 1942 the company received a formal specification for the new aircraft, which was, they were told, to be able to carry a warhead of around 2000 lbs and to be driven by a pulse-jet engine. Argus and Fieseler, having already cooperated so successfully, were natural partners in the new project, and the Air Ministry appointed one of its own engineers, to coordinate it, and brought in a third firm, Askania, to develop the control mechanisms. The early work done by Dr Paul Schmidt in the jet propulsion field also at last came into its own, as it was decided to combine the valve mechanism he had devised with the existing Argus duct.

The next key date in the development of the flying-bomb was 19 July 1942. On that morning representatives of both the main companies concerned attended a meeting in Berlin under Milch's chairmanship. The leading role was played by the Argus representative, who made a deep impression, drawing a sketch of the proposed aircraft on the spot. He proved such an effective advocate that the meeting decided that, as soon as development work was completed, the missile should go straight into production with the highest priority. It was hoped that it would be ready for action in eighteen months time, i.e. around the end of 1943, a remarkably short period for a totally new type of machine.

The only difficulty came from the Army. The former Captain Dornberger was by now a colonel at the War Ministry in Berlin, and on 9 October 1942, his department, the Army Weapons Office, wrote to von Braun asking for a report on the Luftwaffe's project, with a hint that criticism of it would not be unwelcome. Von Braun replied a week later with a scrupulously accurate description. The missile, he explained, was 'powered by a so-called "Argus duct" developing 670 pounds thrust', and would be launched by being 'catapulted from a 230 foot long ramp'. Von Braun forecast that the aircraft would fly at a steady speed of 470 miles per hour, at a height between 700 and 6500 feet, and that flight trials would begin around 10 November. Already, however, it seemed unlikely that the production target, of 1000 missiles a month, would be met by the summer of 1943, since many problems were still unsolved, especially concerning the launching mechanism. On the credit side, von Braun pointed out that since it would not be steered by radio the guidance mechanism could not be jammed, and that, once development was complete, production should present no great problem as three companies, Argus, Fieseler and Rheinmetall, were already equipped to manufacture it. On cost von Braun warned, quite correctly, that the rocket would be far more expensive than the pilotless aircraft, though his actual estimates were wildly amiss. Each pilotless aircraft, he thought, might cost about 10,000 Reichmarks (£1000), each rocket about 30,000 Rm (£3000).

The ground-launching procedure seemed likely for a long time to prove the Achilles heel of the whole scheme, since the machine could not take off unaided at a sufficient speed to stay airborne. The necessary acceleration could be provided by release from an aircraft, and though this had many disadvantages for operational use, it was safe enough at Peenemünde, a long way from the nearest Allied fighters. Early in December 1942 a prototype of the proposed production model flew for the first time, after being lifted into the air by a Focke-Wulf 200. On board the latter was Gerhard Fieseler, head of the firm building the missile, and he ceremonially pulled the lever which released the bomber's 'passenger'. Although unpowered, the latter glided to earth exactly as predicted. A little later came another landmark. On 24 December a powered Fi.103, short for Fieseler 103, as the aircraft was now known, was launched from a ramp pointing out to sea. This missile, too, behaved perfectly, soaring off into the winter sky exactly as intended and offering promise that by the following year its successors would be scattering death and destruction wholesale among British civilians.*

---

*A diagram showing the construction of the V-1, as later issued by the British Government, is reproduced on page 210.

2

SUSPICIOUS ERECTIONS
OF RAILS OR SCAFFOLDING

*We should therefore be grateful if you would keep a close
watch for any suspicious erections of rails or scaffolding.*

Military Intelligence to Major Norman Falcon, Central
Interpretation Unit, Medmenham, 13 February 1943

For a long time after the Oslo Report had first mentioned
long-range rockets and Peenemünde, though not linking them
together, little more was heard in Britain of either subject. It
was not until 15 May 1942 that a Spitfire reconnaissance pilot
photographed the area around Peenemünde while carrying out
another mission. Soon afterwards the prints were sent to RAF
Medmenham, home of the Central Interpretation Unit. The
CIU occupied a large Victorian country house, Danesfield, 'a
pseudo-Tudor . . . pretentious edifice', according to one of its
occupants, 'of whitish grey stone with castellated towers and
fancy brick chimneys', between Marlow and Henley, but the
impressive high-ceilinged rooms were now filled with filing
cabinets, box files and plain deal tables laden with magnifying
glasses, rulers and stereoscopes, the tools of the photographic
interpreter's still novel trade.

The interpreters, who worked in shifts round the clock, were
drawn from many backgrounds, with the academic predomi-
nating. Hamshaw Thomas, the wing-commander in charge of
'Third Phase' work, which looked for long-term trends in enemy activities, was in peacetime a classical scholar, as was the
flight lieutenant, E. J. A. (André) Kenny, in charge of 'D'
Section, which concentrated on industrial as distinct from purely military intelligence – he was an authority on the hydraulic
engineering of ancient Greece.

Another of the Unit's most experienced, and subsequently

its most famous, interpreters was Constance Babington Smith, a young WAAF officer, who specialized in enemy aircraft. It was in May 1942 during a purely routine Third Phase scrutiny of the pictures mentioned earlier, that for the first time, as she later wrote, she 'noticed the name Peenemünde', and was struck by the sight of 'some extraordinary circular embankments' but these 'mysterious rings' were clearly no concern of hers and the photographs were filed away.

Apart from photographic reconnaissance, the intelligence authorities in London relied largely on intercepting German messages, including those – exceptionally secret – classified as 'Ultra' when deciphered, and on reports from agents and Allied sympathizers. Despite its remoteness, Peenemünde was vulnerable to penetration for it depended on slave labour, and the chief problem of Allied intelligence was soon not a lack of information but an embarrassing and contradictory flood of reports. As Constance Babington Smith commented, 'nothing seemed to tally with anything' – because, of course, information was arriving, not about one weapon but two.

The first apparently reliable news of a secret weapon to arrive in London, in December 1942, referred to a long-range rocket under development on the Baltic and in February 1943 a similar story named Peenemünde – its first appearance on the files since the Oslo Report three and a half years before. The rocket, it was assumed, would have to be fired from fairly close at hand and so, on 13 February 1943, Branch MI14 (h) of the War Office sent its orders on the subject to the chief Army photographic interpreter at Medmenham.

There have recently been indications that the Germans may be developing some form of long-range projectors capable of firing on this country from the French coast. There is unfortunately little concrete evidence on the subject available except that the projector may be similar in form to a section of railway track. It is obviously of great importance to obtain the earliest possible warning of the existence of any such device, and we should therefore be grateful if you would keep a close watch for any suspicious erections of rails or scaffolding and consult M.I.10 through us, on any doubtful cases.

Further clues now came from another classic intelligence source. Two captured generals, in a 'bugged' room, revealed

30

in conversation on 22 March 1943 that huge rockets had reached the testing stage and were likely soon to be in use.

When all this information reached Dr R. V. Jones, suggesting that the 'secret weapon' might at last be about to become a reality, he advised against raising the alarm at that stage but the Air Ministry, on 19 April, warned Medmenham to look out for signs of a long-range rocket gun, a rocket-powered aircraft and some new type of missile, such as 'a rocket launched from a tube possibly in a disused mine'. Dr Jones's opposite numbers in the War Office, meanwhile, insisted on informing the Director of Military Intelligence, who in turn told the Vice-Chief of the Imperial General Staff. Through the Vice-Chief of Staffs Committee the news passed on 15 April 1943 to the Prime Minister, along with the suggestion that Churchill's son-in-law, Duncan Sandys, should undertake a special investigation.

There were good reasons for this choice. Sandys, as Parliamentary Secretary to the Ministry of Supply, was familiar with such rocket development as Britain was undertaking; he was, though still a Member of Parliament, an experienced artillery officer and a man of dynamic energy. But his appointment had one unforeseen result. Lord Cherwell, as Professor Lindemann had now become, was affronted that his own protégé, Dr Jones, had not been appointed, and, with the small-mindedness so typical of him, from henceforward poured scorn on the whole venture, declaring that a long-range rocket was scientifically impossible, and through a policy of guilt by association, arguing that this meant that a pilotless aircraft did not exist either.

Happily, although Cherwell's voice was powerful it was not decisive and in spite of his scepticism (perhaps indeed, since so many people detested him, partly because of it) the search for secret weapons went ahead. The investigation was code named 'Bodyline', perhaps by some cricket-enthusiast, who regarded this style of bowling, made notorious by Harold Larwood during the British Test Team's tour of Australia in 1932, as unfair and un-English.

Easter 1943, like Christmas 1942, was a landmark in the flying-bomb story. On that Sunday, 24 April, the two RAF officers leading the photographic interpretation team at Medmenham, met the two civilians appointed to assist Duncan Sandys, Mr William Cook, an authority on projectile development from the Ministry of Supply, and Dr H. J. Phelps, a specialist from the Ministry of Economic Warfare. After puzzling over photographs of the mysterious earthworks which had defeated Constance Babington Smith, and an equally inexplicable construction, apparently machinery, at one end of the airfield, one of the officers made an ingenious guess; the construction, he suggested, was a pumping plant, sucking up mud from the sea bed as the site was extended. It was a sensible and imaginative explanation; it was also disastrously wrong.

Other identifications were more successful, however, and Duncan Sandys returned to London convinced that the secret weapon threat was a real one. He immediately commissioned further surveys of Peenemünde from the reconnaissance squadron based on RAF Benson, in Oxfordshire. The first full report on the site was circulated on 29 April and that same day Flight Lieutenant Kenny went to London for a further meeting at the Ministry of Supply Headquarters in Shellmex House. The panel assembled to assess Kenny's findings included some of his former academic colleagues from Cambridge and the meeting went swimmingly. Before it broke up it had been agreed that Peenemünde was probably an experimental station and that the 'earthworks' were 'probably for the testing of explosives and projectiles'.

Two weeks later, on 9 May, Duncan Sandys was back at Medmenham, where he questioned Constance Babington Smith, as she later wrote, 'whether I had seen any aircraft at Peenemünde which I could not identify, but at this point . . . none of the existing covers was sharp enough or of large enough scale to give the sort of information that was needed.'

On 17 May 1943 Mr Sandys reported his interim findings to the War Cabinet. The evidence, he advised his colleagues, pointed to research and development being in progress on a long-range rocket 'probably . . . proceeding side by side with the development of jet-propelled aircraft and airborne rocket torpedoes.' He went on to recommend an intensification of the intelligence attack from all directions, including a search for 'any suspicious works in the coastal region of North-West France.'

And now at last the pressure on British agents to produce evidence about a secret weapon began to pay off. The first hard information seems to have come from Dusko Popov, a self-confessed 'playboy' recruited by the Germans to spy for them under the name of 'Karl'. He had immediately offered his services to the British, and the 'Twenty' ('XX' or 'Doublecross') Committee, which operated turned-round agents, christened him 'Tricycle'. Tricycle in turn recruited 'Artist', a German friend called Johnny, whose first findings were puzzling:

Johnny combed the Greater Reich from one end to the other, yet he couldn't find the monster weapon. He did unearth two German firms, Argus and Fieseler Flugzeugbau of Kassel, which were receiving large orders and credits for the development of a new weapon, but both firms specialised in the construction of light aircraft and didn't have the facilities to produce something in the way of seventy tons. British Intelligence insisted we were on the wrong track, and Johnny went doggedly back to the task.

Perhaps what Dr Jones later described as 'the rocket's red glare' blinded those concerned to a totally different danger; perhaps the fact that Popov worked for the counterespionage department, MI5, made MI6, which was responsible for intelligence gathering overseas, reluctant to accept his findings. Whatever the reason, this first firm evidence about the possible existence of another type of missile seems to have been ignored or dismissed as a deliberate German attempt to cover the real threat.

Fortunately, however, MI6 had informants of its own, including one 'quite unusually well-placed and hitherto most reliable source', a disgruntled officer in the Weapons Department of the German War Office. On 22 June he reported the existence of 'winged' rockets, operated by remote control, to be launched against London by catapult, of which thirty had already been constructed. 'We had,' Dr Jones, has since commented, 'no means of judging the reliability of this report, which was typical of many that now flooded in generated by . . . ill-considered questionnaires being sent out to all parts of our agent network.'

Other sources of information also existed. If, calculated Dr

Jones, the Germans were 'developing any long-range missile' they 'would almost certainly try to plot it by radar. . . . They would want pretty skilled radar operators and I knew the very best . . . were in two particular radar companies, the 14th and 15th companies of the German Air Signals Experimental Regiment. So, as a very long shot I asked my sources at the codebreaking establishment to follow those two companies . . . let me know what they were doing, and especially if either of them moved up to the Baltic coast and began to string itself out in a series of detachments along that coast.'

But the main source of intelligence at this stage – all the more valuable because it was necessarily objective – was the series of photographs of Peenemünde taken by the RAF. In high summer the secret duel between the German scientists and the British photographic interpreters grew more intense. The experts at Medmenham were asked to look afresh at German factories, experimental establishments and possible launching sites, but it was on Peenemünde that the search was concentrated.

The weather, for once, favoured the British. In June alone four reconnaissance sorties were flown in brilliant sunshine, resulting in a flow of sharp new covers arriving on Constance Babington Smith's desk in the former hall of Danesfield, through the high windows of which she could make out 'a mass of mauve wisteria'. Her brief was to look for 'anything queer' on this mysterious airfield 600 miles away.

Both in London and at Medmenham it was a time of frustrating confusion . . . a time of groping in the dark. . . . It was as though the parts of two or three jigsaw puzzles had been jumbled together, and it was sorely tempting to try to find only *one* answer – only *one* weapon. It seemed a triumph when two or three bits of puzzle fitted together . . . and it was all too easy to ignore the bits which did not fit in with these.

Almost all the doubters were now convinced – all but Lord Cherwell. But, precisely because he rejected the idea of a rocket, Cherwell was prepared to concede, as few others were, that the Germans might be up to something totally different. After explaining to the Prime Minister in a minute on 11 June 1943 his reasons for questioning the existence of a seventy-ton rocket, he suggested an alternative possibility. 'The old scheme of unmanned radio-directed aeroplane, jet propelled or otherwise, would seem more feasible, though even this was shown to be less efficient than straightforward bombing.'

On 28 June Duncan Sandys circulated his Third Interim Report to the Cabinet Defence Committee (Operations) and on the following evening the committee discussed the whole question at great length. The rocket dominated the proceedings but Lord Cherwell still remained unconvinced, as the minutes recorded:

His suggestion was that the whole story bore the marks of an elaborate cover plan to conceal some other development. . . . He had no definite views as to what the real plan was. As an example, he suggested that possibly the Germans might intend to use pilot-less, perhaps jet-propelled, aircraft. . . . In any event he felt that we should not confine our efforts to, and focus our attention on, the rocket and thus blind ourselves to the possibility of other developments. . . . He quite agreed that our action should be to bomb Peenemünde, to scrutinise most carefully the areas in Northern France where projectors might be erected and to keep a radio watch. At the same time, we should not neglect to search for other devices, especially for signs of radio developments which would indicate preparations for the use of the pilot-less aircraft.

The Committee took two decisions of crucial importance:

It was agreed . . . That the most searching and rigorous examination of the area in Northern France within a radius of 130 miles of London should be organised and maintained, no step being neglected to make this as efficient and thorough as possible. . . . That, as far as possible, plans should be prepared for immediate air attack on rocket firing points in Northern France as soon as these were located. . . . That the attack on the experimental station at Peenemünde should take the form of the heaviest possible night attack by Bomber Command on the first occasion when conditions were suitable, and that in the meanwhile, undue aerial reconnaissance of the place should be avoided.

Even more important in the long term was the belated acknowledgement that there might be *two* secret weapons under development.

The Joint Parliamentary Secretary, Ministry of Supply [i.e. Duncan

Sandys], should examine and report in a month's time on the state of development of pilotless and/or jet-propelled aircraft in Germany. Dr R. V. Jones should be closely associated with him in this enquiry, in view of the special interest of the Air Intelligence Staff in this matter.

3

ALL WILL BE REVENGED

When it's time to settle accounts, all will be revenged.

Völkischer Beobachter, 30 May 1943

The simultaneous development of the rocket and the flying-bomb, which was causing so much confusion in England, also created problems for the Germans, as the Army and Luftwaffe each became increasingly committed to its particular weapon. On 3 January 1943, Lieutenant-General Walter von Axthelm, commanding the anti-aircraft forces, which were part of the Luftwaffe, paid a visit to Peenemünde and wrote a glowing report to the Chief of the German Air Staff. The flying-bomb, he advised, was the ideal method of attacking targets up to a range of 225 miles. At a later meeting with the bomb's chief sponsor, Field-Marshal Milch, von Axthelm advocated scattering up to a hundred launching sites along the French coast, arguing that the RAF could not put them all out of action. Milch, however, favoured eight huge storage 'bunkers' with their own launching ramps, which would be easier to defend and operate and in the end it was agreed to leave the matter to Göring.

By April 1943 wind-tunnel tests were complete and on a fine, sunny day Milch flew down from Berlin to Peenemünde to watch a catapult launching. All went well and at 3000 feet the aircraft levelled off according to plan and roared rapidly into the distance. On 26 May Milch returned to Peenemünde with Albert Speer, Hitler's recently appointed and spectacularly successful Minister of Munitions. This time everything went wrong but fortunately for the Luftwaffe one of the rockets – now known as the A.4 – also failed to behave as intended and the delegation agreed to recommend that work on both weapons should go ahead.

At this stage fortune seemed to be favouring the flying-bomb. On 18 June, Göring was told that thirty-five out of fifty Fi.103s so far launched had worked perfectly, while the faults which had caused the failure of most of the remainder had been identified and rectified. By now a speed of 375 miles per hour had been achieved, and a range of forty-four miles – ample to get across the Channel, though not to reach London. Fuel consumption had been remarkably low: only forty gallons. Already an ambitious production programme covering an initial order of 24,500 flying-bombs had been drawn up. Beginning with a modest output of 100 in August 1943, the flow of missiles was intended to rise to 500 in September, 1000 in October, 1500 in November and 2000 in December; a total of 5100 during the year. Each month thereafter would show a further increase, to 2600 in January 1944, 3200 in February, 3800 in March, 4800 in April, the production graph finally flattening out at a monthly level of 5000 from May onwards.

Göring then settled by a compromise the disagreement between von Axthelm and Milch about the deployment of the bomb. The former's plan for a large number of launching sites was accepted, but scaled down from a hundred to ninety-six. Milch's plea for eight impregnable concrete bunkers was also agreed, but Göring ruled that only four should be started for the moment. Göring enthusiastically fired off telegrams to Munitions Minister Speer, and to Gauleiter Sauckel, responsible for the allocation of manpower, exhorting them to give the project full priority, and he was himself already talking of boosting production of pilotless aircraft tenfold to 50,000 a month.

At this point, things started to go wrong. On 19 June 1943, the very next day, the commanding officer of the flying-bomb research station at Peenemünde-West had to report that four out of five Fi.103s fired from a new type of catapult had been a failure. Another missile, launched from a bomber, misbehaved spectacularly, turning right round and crashing in woodlands inside the perimeter of the adjoining Army establishment at Peenemünde-East. The Army got its own back a few days later, on 28 June, when an A.4 rocket suddenly veered off course and plunged down on to Peenemünde-West, destroying three Luftwaffe aircraft and blowing a crater 100 feet across in the runway. It had, commented one watching officer, clearly justified the title of 'revenge weapon'. Another rocket fired that day, however, behaved perfectly, deeply impressing Heinrich Himmler, who was watching, and he returned that evening to Hitler's headquarters full of the wonders he had seen.

Both the rocket and the flying-bomb now had a powerful advocate in the highest circles, but the allocation of labour and factory space ultimately depended upon Albert Speer. At the end of June Speer dispatched his chief adviser on the chemical industry to Peenemünde to make an independent assessment and his report, circulated on 29 June, praised the Fi.103 but criticized the A.4, as 'inordinately complicated and expensive'. From a production, as well as a research point of view, the real problem lay in finding hydrogen peroxide for the launching catapults, if the simultaneous, but far heavier demands, of the A.4 were also to be met, since even 3000 Fi.103s a month would require 300 tons.

Hitler, in his lordly way, never paid much attention to such tedious restrictions as factory capacity and, after his imagination had been fired on 8 July by seeing a film of an A.4 being launched, he ordered that both projects should go ahead. Hitler also approved the building of Milch's four giant 'launching bunkers' by the Todt Organization, which handled all major construction projects in the occupied countries. There were, however, to be 'economies' in the use of concrete, of which vast quantities were currently required for the 'Atlantic Wall' on the French coast, though how these were to be achieved was not indicated.

Even Milch was beginning to come round in favour of von Axthelm's 'small site' programme since the sites would, he believed, prove irresistibly attractive to the RAF. 'This,' he told a conference, 'is where we will bury the British Air Force. We shall no longer need fighter defences in the rear; we can throw them right forward to the coast.' As for the Americans, who bombed in daylight, 'In a short time,' boasted Milch, 'we can tear them limb from limb And the aircraft and airmen we knock out over there cannot visit us in Germany any more.'

From the moment when, in March 1943, he first heard about

them, Josef Goebbels, Hitler's Minister of Propaganda and overlord of the Home Front, took an intense interest in the progress of the *Wunderwaffe*, or 'miracle weapons', but the first specific promise of revenge came from Speer. In the battered Ruhr on 29 May Speer roused his audience to a frenzy of applause with the declaration: 'Even if the German mills of retribution may often seem to grind too slowly, they do grind very fine.' 'When it's time to settle accounts – all will be revenged,' proclaimed the *Völkischer Beobachter* next day. Goebbels spoke in similar terms a few days later, in the Sports Palace in Berlin. 'The entire German people is only filled with one idea,' he declared, 'to retaliate in an equal fashion. . . . The British nation has no reason for triumph. It will have to foot the bill, which its responsible men have incurred here, by their guilt of blood.'

Everyone in Germany already favoured revenge, but the demand became even stronger when, on 24 July 1943, the devastating series of raids on Hamburg known as 'Operation Gomorrah' began. At a meeting on the following day, 25 July, his advisers fell silent as Hitler screamed, rather than pleaded, for retaliation. 'You can only force them to give up by getting at their people,' he declared. 'The only thing that will have any effect is a systematic attack on their villages and towns.' That afternoon, after repeating four times that 'You can only smash terror with counter-terror', Hitler eagerly signed a decree giving supreme priority to the production of the rocket. But any weapon offering the prospect of reprisals was now in demand and the Luftwaffe, which Hitler blamed for failing to stop the Allied air raids, was eager to vindicate itself. On the morning of 29 July a full-scale conference took place at the Air Ministry in Berlin of all those concerned with the development of the Fi.103. They included Fritz Gosslau, of Argus, Gerhard Fieseler, 'Group Leader' Kroger of Peenemünde-West and a new figure on the scene – Colonel Max Wachtel, commanding officer of the unit already being formed to fire the flying-bomb in action.

The meeting covered a great deal of ground. Group-Leader Kroger reported that of sixty-eight Fi.103s launched twenty-eight had been entirely successful, including one which had flown 152 miles, on only 133 gallons of fuel. Another had reached 375 miles per hour and an operational height of 4300 feet. But poor security was causing anxiety. The major commanding the troops at Peenemünde-West complained that even the servant girls in Berlin were talking about the flying-bomb, and that it was being openly discussed in the streets of Kassel. General von Axthelm had therefore that day issued orders to change its covername from Fi.103 to FZG 76, FZG standing for *Flakzielgerät*, or anti-aircraft artillery target apparatus, to suggest that the aircraft would act as a target for anti-aircraft gunners. (In fact the new abbreviation was widely interpreted to mean *Fernzielgerät*, or 'long-distance target apparatus', which gave at least a hint of its real purpose.)

The shadow of the rocket hung over a further conference, of Air Ministry officials and Luftwaffe officers, called by Milch on 3 August. Everywhere, those attending heard with horror, the army's emissaries, flourishing Hitler's last order, were seizing resources earmarked for the flying-bomb. One unnamed official, it was reported, had 'turned up at the Daimler-Benz factory and said that "all 103 production is being shut down and A.4 rockets will be manufactured instead".' Milch ordered that anyone practising similar tactics in future was to be arrested and a directive was issued by Speer on 17 August that 'The Air Force's manufacturing programme is *not* to be interfered with by the A.4 programme.'

That very evening the sirens wailed over Peenemünde and at ten minutes past midnight in the early morning of 18 August 1943, the first bombs began to fall. 'The heaviest possible night attack', decided on by the War Cabinet on 29 June, had come at last. The story of the great Peenemünde raid, 'Operation Hydra', belongs rather to the history of the rocket, work on which was set back by at least two months, than of the flying-bomb, which was hardly affected at all by its direct results, though some material and equipment destroyed had been earmarked for new launching ramps. The indirect results were more serious. The foreign labourers used to do the unskilled work were moved to the mainland and the Luftwaffe transferred the bulk of its training and testing effort to a naval establishment at Brüsterort in East Prussia. Some operations continued in the Peenemünde area, both on the main launching

site, and at a new one at Zinnowitz, a few miles further along
the coast.

The Peenemünde raid provided a convenient alibi for the
delays which occurred in bringing the flying-bomb into action,
but hardly held up production at all. Milch's old adversary,
Professor Messerschmitt, was now talking wildly of turning out
not a puny 60,000 flying-bombs a year but a million, though
Milch himself set his sights more modestly. 'I will be satisfied,'
he declared on 24 August, 'if the Fi.103 works at all.' Even an
output of 3500 missiles a month, well below the 5000 target,
would make it possible to fire one every twelve minutes. 'They
will never endure it,' he predicted. 'It will be the end of any
real life in the city.' Milch eagerly welcomed the suggestion
that the flying-bomb warheads should contain incendiary devices. Four days, he thought, would be enough to destroy
London – the time taken by the RAF to convert much of
Hamburg into rubble and ashes.

From August 1943 onwards work went ahead simultaneously
on the three plans needed to make the flying-bomb offensive
a reality: producing the missiles, training the crews to fire
them, and building the launching sites. The first presented the
greatest problem. There was no shortage of factory capacity,
for the vast Volkswagen plant at Fallersleben, north of Bruns-
wick, which in peacetime produced the 'people's car', had been
assigned the largest FZG 76 contract. Where the difficulties
arose was in the perfectionism of the engineers and scientists,
who between early August and the end of October called for
150 modifications in the original design, involving 131 new
parts.

As a result of these incessant changes, during September the
number of missiles reaching Peenemünde actually dropped and
by mid-November the monthly rate of output at the Volkswagen factory at Fallersleben was only twenty-five. At the end of
November the heroic decision was taken to scrap all the 2000
missiles already made by Volkswagen and to order instead only
the new models made to a far higher specification, though they
could not be ready till mid-February.

While 'the people's pilotless aircraft' was proving a sad disappointment at Fallersleben, the Fieseler Works at Kassel,
housing the other main production line, was suffering from

different problems. On 22 October 1943, as part of the RAF's regular strategic bombing campaign, Kassel had been subjected to a heavy attack. When the flames had died away, 5300 of the 228,000 population lay dead, 91,000 had been made homeless and the nine principal factories, including Fieseler, had suffered heavy damage. Much of the machinery had previously been transferred to the neighbouring town of Rothwesten, but 40 per cent of the work force failed to report there for duty, and those who did found the factory paralysed by lack of power. An Air Ministry engineer, sent to report on the situation, had a dismal tale to tell the conference called by Milch on 3 November. 'Because Kassel has been lost Rothwesten is . . . lost as well,' he told his superiors. 'The men live in Kassel and their homes and transport are wrecked.' The raid had cut off the supply of the missile's control-gear, diving mechanism, compass and other vital components, and much more than the attack on Peenemünde, represented Bomber Command's greatest contribution to delaying the flying-bomb offensive.

If the Germans could not yet attack, they could still threaten. 'The technical and organisational conditions,' Hitler promised in a broadcast on 10 September, 'are being created not only to break his [i.e. the enemy's] terror for good, but also to pay him back.' Goebbels took the same line, in even clumsier language, in a speech in Berlin on 4 October. 'As regards the theme of "revenge", discussed by the German people with such hot passion,' he boasted, 'I can for obvious reasons only say that the English commit an extraordinarily fateful error if they believe it was a mere rhetorical or propagandist slogan without any reality behind it. England will come to know this reality one day.'

Increasingly, however, it was becoming uncertain when that day would be. At a meeting on 1 November Lieutenant-General von Axthelm had told the chief of the German Air Staff with heavy Teutonic joviality, 'the aim up to now has been a "New Year present",' but only two days later he was hedging his bets and remarking that 'As far as we can now see, provided there are no major problems, trials will be complete by the beginning of February.' On 4 November Hitler circulated a directive to his most senior commanders announcing his intention to strengthen the defences along the Atlantic coast, 'particularly in the region from which we shall be opening our long-range bombardment of England,' and four days later, in a broadcast speech from the Beer Hall at Munich, he uttered on 8 November an explicit threat against Great Britain. 'Even if for the present we cannot reach America,' he declared 'thank God that at least one country is near enough for us to tackle and on that state we are going to concentrate.'

On everyone except Hitler some understanding of the real situation was now beginning to dawn. A week after the Munich speech the commander-designate of the launching units, Colonel Wachtel, was warned to expect only 1500 bombs a month at first, not 5000. In mid-November, when von Axthelm suggested to Hitler bombarding the South Coast ports to prevent the Allied invasion fleet setting sail, he met little encouragement. 'Don't concern yourself with warding off an invasion,' Hitler told him, 'Keep to the subject of our retaliation offensive. Get your bombs over there first. Then you will get the production you want!' How this was to be achieved, if not planned beforehand, Hitler failed to explain.

Worse was soon to come. On 26 November, accompanied by Himmler, Hitler for the first time inspected a flying-bomb, on the ground. The head of Peenemünde-West explained to Hitler how the missile worked and, in answer to a question about when it would be ready, named the end of March. This was not at all what Hitler wanted to hear. He fell silent and stumped off, visibly displeased.

Training the troops who were to fire the FZG 76 in action proved far easier than producing it. A small detachment of troops had long been stationed at Zempin, eight miles south of Peenemünde, and this Erprobungs und Sonder Kommando – Test and Special Purposes Unit – formed the nucleus of a large new regiment which began to be mustered on 16 August. It was to consist of small detachments at Zempin and Peenemünde and of the larger body posted initially to Brusterort, which was given the successive code names of *Windecke* (Wind-corner) and *Wiesengrund* (Meadow-land). The regiment's expansion proved a slow process. By mid-August very few of the 680 men due had actually arrived and only half of the further 400 supposed to be gaining experience by handling flying-bombs in the factories. Even if well below establishment, however, the organization of Flak Regiment 155 (W) was clear. In addition to eight supply and maintenance units, it consisted of four Abteilungen, or operational detachments, sub-divided into four batteries, each responsible for four launching platforms. In theory, therefore, the unit could carry on a bombardment from sixty-four positions, though extra ramps were planned to enable the firing locations to be varied. 'Flak', meaning 'Anti-aircraft', was incorporated in the regiment's title for security purposes, while 'W' stood for its commanding officer, Colonel Max Wachtel. A First World War artillery officer, Wachtel had worked in industry until 1936 when he rejoined the Army and rapidly made his name as a commander of technical development projects. By April 1943, when he learned of his new appointment, he was a lieutenant-colonel, in command of the Anti-Aircraft Artillery School.

Wachtel rapidly justified his reputation of being able to work well with both engineers and industrialists, and he tackled his new assignment with vigour. One recurring fault, the tendency of the flying-bomb to dive to earth after only a few hundred yards' flight, was rapidly overcome by fitting a baffle-plate to stop the blast from the motor upsetting the trim of the elevators, but trouble with the gyro controls, which sometimes caused the aircraft to turn through 180° and roar back towards the launching site, persisted. Wachtel pleaded that mass production should not start until all these teething-troubles had been overcome, but when he visited Paris in September he discovered to his great annoyance that the planners of Luftflotte 2, responsible for Northern France, still expected the attack to begin in December, and had even drawn up detailed target maps without consulting him. At this stage far too few missiles were reaching East Prussia to give his men experience in handling and firing them. During the whole of September only four arrived, in place of the hundred promised, and by 25 October the total was still only thirty-eight, many of which were of the earlier type, now abandoned. It was not till 16 October that the first Mark II bomb, to use a British Army term, soared skywards from Zempin and some specimens even of this improved model behaved erratically, flying as much as thirteen miles beyond the planned 125 mile cut-off point. But training, of a kind, was provided. The first of the four Abtei-

45

lungen left Germany on time, and the final part of the first contingent, bringing the total number of batteries in France to six out of sixteen, left the Baltic on 18 November, two days ahead of schedule.

Slotting Wachtel's troops into the German administrative structure in France presented no particular difficulties. For what the British Army called 'A' matters, i.e. manpower, Flak Regiment 155 (W) was served by Luftflotte 2, while its 'Q' needs – for accommodation and transport – were met by the Luftgau, or Air District, covering Belgium and Northern France. The real struggle came over operational control – 'G' Branch responsibilities in British parlance. Late in November Reichsmarschall Göring fought a determined battle to keep Flak Regiment 155 (W) independent of the Army, but he failed. The Regiment became part of Army Corps LXV, which came formally into existence on 15 December. The same Corps would also be responsible for the rocket units, when they finally arrived, and for the third secret weapon, known for security reasons as 'the high-pressure pump', an extremely powerful, quick-firing long-range gun, which was never to be fired in anger.

The Commander of Army Corps LXV was Lieut-General Erich Heinemann, a great authority on artillery matters but at sixty-seven past his prime; Wachtel's staff dismissed him as 'a good old man'. The real authority rested with Colonel Eugen Walter, Heinemann's Chief of Staff, a professional soldier fresh from the General Staff, but sadly ignorant of the needs and potential of the flying-bomb. Although the headquarters of Army Corps LXV interleaved members of the Army and the Luftwaffe, the result was to exacerbate traditional enmities rather than to remove them, and relations between Army Corps LXV, which established itself in pleasant surroundings at Saint-Germain on the outskirts of Paris, and Flak Regiment 155, which set up its headquarters at Saleux, near Amiens, nearer the coming battle-front, were also bad from the first. But, despite the shortage of missiles, preparations went ahead. A special meterological service was set up to provide detailed forecasts for the weather over London and the English Channel, to predict cloudy days rather than fine ones, and the construction of sites continued on schedule.

This proved in fact the smoothest of all the operations needed to get the flying-bomb into action. During the first half of 1943 a survey had been undertaken to find suitable locations in northern France and at the end of August 1943 a large-scale construction programme had begun. By 23 September 40,000 labourers and artisans had already been assigned to the work and it seemed that fifty-eight of the first sixty-four sites would be ready by the end of November. All told ninety-six were planned along the 140 miles of coastline between Calais and the river Seine. In addition, two giant bunkers designed for storage purposes were being built, at Lottinghem, ten miles south-east of Boulogne, and at Siracourt, another twenty or so miles further inland in the same direction. These 'large sites', as the British later described them, also contained launching ramps, and there was a third at Equeurdreville, close to Cherbourg, to serve the sites constructed in the Côtentin peninsula and its hinterland, which were aligned on Southampton and Bristol instead of London.

The Germans can have been under no illusions that activity on this scale, carried out in a hostile countryside, could be kept a secret but did what they could to make things difficult for British intelligence by inventing several new covernames. To the original FZG 76 and the innocent-sounding *Kirschkern* (Cherry-stone) was added the more minatory *Höllenhund* (Hell-hound), favoured by fire-breathing top Nazis, and *Maikaker* (May-beetle or cockchafer), which Wachtel's soldiers were ordered to use. Distinctly unofficial were the names used by the Poles near the German border who saw test missiles that went off course. Some, wrote a Polish historian, were 'too vulgar to be mentioned', but the printable ones included 'witchcraft', 'madman' and, most appropriate of all, 'window-buster', which sounded even more impressive in the original: *szybotluk*.

4

SINISTER ACTIVITIES

*Almost every day there were sinister new activities to be
examined.*

Former WAAF Officer, Constance Babington Smith,
recalling autumn 1943

As, from August 1943 onwards, more and more people became
involved in the Germans' plans, the flow of information about
the secret weapons, hitherto so scanty, increased to a flood.
Only with hindsight is it clear what was important and, applying
this test, a key date is 12 August, when a document arrived
from MI6's star informant in the German War Office explaining
that two separate missiles were under construction: a 'rocket
projectile officially known as A.4', and a 'pilotless aircraft
officially known as Phi.7'. Confirmation, if also confusion,
came from a French agent on 30 August, passing on what he
had heard from someone formerly stationed at Peenemünde.
A rocket was under development there, the latter had revealed,
which could reach a height of fifty miles, and 108 catapults to
fire it were being built in France, to be operated by a regiment
under the command of a Colonel Wachtel, which would ultimately be responsible for another 400. From internal evidence,
such as references to a unit, Kampfgruppe 100, often used in
experimental work, the authorities in London finally concluded
that the original informant probably did have 'an inside and
genuine contact with the German Air Force' and more information now arrived from a new source, Denmark, after, on 22
August, a flying-bomb crashed on the island of Bornholm. The
first Dane on the scene, a former naval officer, beat the Germans to it by ten minutes and eventually eight copies of his
drawings and descriptions, plus some photographs of the badly
twisted wreckage, were sent to London by various routes. By
31 August, at least one had got safely through.

On 10 September the Chiefs of Staff agreed that, while Mr Sandys should concentrate on studying evidence about the long-range rocket, the Air Ministry, whose job it would be to deal with it, should collect information about the flying-bomb.

Dr Jones, of the Air Intelligence Branch, wasted little time. On 14 September he circulated his first tentative 'appreciation', to the effect that a project known as the FZG 76, clearly regarded by the Germans as important, was under development, and that it was in fact a rocket-propelled pilotless aircraft.

The case for the existence of the flying-bomb was accepted by Sir Charles Portal, Chief of the Air Staff, but Lord Cherwell again challenged it, arguing that the machine which had crashed on Bornholm could carry only a 1000 lb warhead and that it would be uneconomic to build an aircraft to deliver so small a quantity of high explosive. Fortunately MI6 paid more attention to the reports of its own agents, including those passed on by Duskov Popov, in Portugal, from his friend Johnny, in Germany:

In September, after weeks of fruitless search for a seventy-tonner, Johnny came to me with definite information about a much smaller missile, the FZG–76. . . . His research showed that the two light aircraft manufacturers were constructing a small pilotless machine, a monoplane carrying a bomb of about one ton. It was in mass production at Fallersleben. . . . When I passed the information on to M.I.6. they came back with literally hundreds of detailed questions. What was the range, weight, speed, source of power, fuel: was it radio-controlled, etc? Johnny would go out and get the answers and then the British would think of more technical details they needed.

As such intelligence accumulated it grew increasingly clear that the Germans were developing several different weapons; indeed, as Dr Jones pointed out in his second report, what was more probable than that the German Army should be working on one missile and its old rival, the Luftwaffe, on another? By 25 September 1943 he felt confident enough to sum up his findings in a classic sentence, which at last dispelled the confusion which for nearly a year had befogged the whole secret weapons inquiry:

It is probable that the German Air Force has been developing a pilotless aircraft for long-range bombardment in competition with the rocket and it is very possible that the aircraft will arrive first.

Just about this time the results of the German construction programme begun in France during the summer became impossible to conceal. Here, happily, there was no shortage of agents, and many Frenchmen and Frenchwomen risked their lives to help the Allies at this period – none more constantly, or fruitfully, than Michel Hollard, a forty-five-year-old engineer whose wartime job, as salesman for a firm making producer-gas engines, gave him unlimited opportunities for travel around the Seine Department. Hollard had made contact with the British by the simple means of crossing into Switzerland and ringing the doorbell of the British Legation, where he got a cool reception – it was a Sunday morning – but eventually he operated a network of a hundred agents, many of them people like hotel-keepers and station-masters, well placed to keep track of German activities.

One of these, a railway engineer, who overheard two building contractors speculating in a café about the significance of a new German construction programme, first put Hollard on the track of the flying-bomb sites, but his contact in Lausanne was initially unimpressed: so many 'suspicious constructions' had later turned out to be the foundations for a field laundry or similar building. After, however, Hollard had passed to London another, apparently unconnected, piece of information, brought to him, in the best spy fiction tradition, in the heel of a workman's boot – a short account, in German, of a 'cigar-shaped missile with wings', fired over a range of 250 miles across the Baltic – the situation changed. Hollard was now urged to collect all the details he could about the new sites and fulfilled his commission spectacularly well. Many, by posing as a travelling evangelist interested in the workmen's welfare, he managed to visit himself, observing all he saw and even taking surreptitious bearings with a pocket compass; others were surveyed by members of his network, one of whom, a young draughtsman, was persuaded to 'borrow' the plan of the central 'concrete strip' seen on all the sites, while its German engineer was briefly absent in the latrine. The results of all this heroic activity were remarkable. Within three weeks sixty sites, all on the same basic pattern, had been located in an area 200 miles long and thirty wide; by the end of October the score had risen to a hundred. Bearing his rich haul of tracings and site plans Hollard once more visited Switzerland and when, four days later, the documents reached London by diplomatic bag – by a curious quirk of wartime travel they had had to cross enemy territory en route – a cable was dispatched to Lausanne: 'Booty received safely. Congratulations.' Hollard and his colleagues – plus the members of other networks, some of whom paid with their lives for their courage – also received a private accolade from the Prime Minister. 'We have,' Churchill wrote to President Roosevelt on 25 October 1943, 'an excellent system of intelligence in this part of Northern France and it is from these sources as well as from photographs and prisoners that the story is built up.'

One obvious source of information was the interception of enemy radio traffic. Because they came down over a wide arc at varying distances, Colonel Wachtel had tried installing radio in some flying-bombs so that the spot where they landed could be plotted by cross-bearings, but the sets proved unreliable. It was natural, therefore, that he should turn to the use of radar. Ultra, which had failed even to reveal that there were two weapons under development, did now provide some belated help, for an Ultra intercept confirmed that the 14th Company of the Experimental Signals Regiment, the unit most likely to be employed on such duties, had been moved to Zempin, just as Dr Jones had foreseen, and the results of every test were sent by radio in an easily broken code. By late autumn the performance of each flying-bomb test-fired was known in London almost as rapidly as in Berlin. The machine's speed, it was confirmed, was around 400 miles an hour, its height between 1000 and 6000 feet and its accuracy was steadily increasing.

On 21 September Winston Churchill made the first carefully worded reference to the new danger in the House of Commons. 'The speeches of the German leaders,' he commented, 'contain mysterious allusions to new methods and new weapons which will presently be tried against us. It would, of course, be natural for the enemy to spread such rumours in order to encourage his own people, but there is probably more in it than that.'

If it was an anxious autumn in Whitehall, at Medmenham it was a frantically busy one. In September the teams involved in the secret weapon investigation had been reorganized so that the Army interpreters, studying possible defence works on the French coast, and the RAF interpreters, concerned with Peenemünde and new types of aircraft, could work more closely together. Wing Commander Douglas Kendall was now in charge of the inquiry, and Constance Babington Smith has recalled, 'when evening came . . . always gravitated towards the Army Section, eager to see any new *Bodyline* finds.' Almost every day 'there were sinister new activities to be examined.'

On 28 October 1943 Duncan Sandys ordered that the whole area of North-West France within 150 miles of London should be rephotographed, a prudent precaution which involved 'a hundred separate sorties', yielding thousands of pictures. 'During the first week of November the full effects of this hit Medmenham. Each day the box-files stacked up in towering mountains around the Army interpreter whose job it was to "watch France". . . . Doggedly he ploughed through the piles of prints, searching for railway spurs and the scratchings and burrowings that had not been there before.'

Lord Cherwell had still not budged from his original conviction that a 70-ton rocket (the only type so far seriously considered) was a technical impossibility, and at a full-scale meeting of the Cabinet Defence Committee on 28 October, the division of opinion as to whether any secret weapon existed at all remained so sharp that the Prime Minister set up a special Committee of Inquiry to resolve the question. Its chairman, Sir Stafford Cripps, started work the following morning, when one of the first visitors to his flat in Whitehall Court, overlooking the Embankment, was Dr Jones. Cripps had not been involved in the Bodyline inquiry so Dr Jones's account came to him as a great shock. His interim report to the Prime Minister, on 2 November 1943, dealt mainly with the rocket, but did not rule out the possible existence of a second weapon and Churchill replied immediately, asking Cripps to examine the evidence further. In the previous week, aerial reconnaissance had been prevented by the weather but on the following day, 3 November, the skies cleared at last and sorties were flown over the area of northern France where one agent – probably Hollard – had reported seeing six suspect sites. On 4 November the resulting prints reached Medmenham. All six sites were partly located in a wood and contained nine apparently standard constructions, though none seemed to have any obvious connection with a long-range rocket. But as Wing Commander Kendall concentrated his attention on the site nearest completion, in a wood called Bois Carré, at Yvrench, ten miles north-east of Abbeville, it struck him that three of the buildings looked rather like a ski turned on its side, long and narrow, but curved gently at one end. Once pointed out, the resemblance struck the two Army interpreters working with him, and the 'ski sites', as they were promptly labelled, all had one alarming feature: a long platform pointing towards London.

With something specific to look for, the interpreters' task was vastly simplified. Two more ski sites were found by 5 November, and by the morning of 8 November, when Kendall attended a meeting presided over by Sir Stafford Cripps, the total was nineteen. Cripps adjourned the meeting while more photographs were examined and when, two days later, on 10 November, it reassembled the score had risen to twenty-six. Low-level oblique photographs of some of the sites confirmed the description given by the French agent, which suggested that the rest of his information, which could not be checked from a photograph, was also reliable. This had included the statement that each site included a square building which contained no metal, not even metal door hinges, and that this was connected to the London-orientated ramp by means of wooden rails and rollers. These precautions, the experts concluded, meant that whatever object the square building contained needed to be free from magnetism, which implied some form of sensitive compass steering.

The interpreters' findings seemed to rule out a large rocket, and Cripps's second report, circulated on 16 November, concluded that 'the order of probability' was first, glider bombs, second 'pilotless aircraft' and third a long-range rocket, size unknown; the giant 60–70 ton rocket so often derided by Cherwell was not ruled out, but came last.

Two days later, on 18 November 1943, the Chiefs of Staff officially endorsed this conclusion and their decision was accepted by the Prime Minister. The Bodyline inquiry was over. It was agreed that a new secret weapon might well be used against London in the near future, but it was a pilotless aircraft, not a rocket; a rocket did, it was believed, exist, but posed a less immediate threat.

Although by 22 November ninety-five ski sites had been positively identified the 'skis' themselves still held their secrets. Flat-roofed, windowless constructions, 260 feet long but only 10 feet wide, their purpose could only be guessed at, and though it would be difficult to manoeuvre a rocket round the curved section, it might just be managed, if it were no more than 38 feet long, with fins removed. The building was, however, far too narrow to accommodate a winged aircraft. And what was to be made of the rows of 'studs', apparently of concrete, in six pairs 20 feet apart, which looked, in Constance Babington Smith's homely phrase, 'like a set of buttons down the front of a double-breasted coat'? What, too, was the purpose of the small square building, with a door 22 feet across, directly in line with one end of the row of studs and orientated towards London? The argument raged back and forth and light dawned only slowly. From one of the Army interpreters came an ingenious suggestion: perhaps the 'ski' building housed aircraft with their wings removed, which were added to them in the square building. From Wing Commander Kendall came another. The 'studs' he wrote in a report towards the end of November, were probably to carry a sloping ramp, the square building could be used to set an automatic pilot, and the small but very strong building at the far end of the ramp might provide protection for the man firing the missile.

Kendall himself now believed that the object they were searching for was some form of aircraft, but so deeply had the idea of rockets and rocket-projectors been implanted that the argument about the sites continued. What was needed to settle it one way or another was a photograph of a pilotless aircraft, if one truly existed. Already thousands of photographs had been taken – the total number of exposures was ultimately to reach one and a half million – but so far not a single print had betrayed any such object. This was not for want of looking. Back in May Section Officer Babington Smith had been asked if she had seen any mysterious aircraft at Peenemünde, but as an aircraft specialist, she knew nothing about the ski sites, and by mid-November, after fruitless months of peering at somewhat fuzzy photographs, 'my interest in the secret weapon hunt,' she has since written, 'had been flagging a bit.' On 13 November, it was suddenly revived, for Kendall 'gave me something specific to look for: a very small aircraft, smaller than a fighter. This was the first time I had been briefed in these terms.'

Only an exceptionally clear photograph would show such a small object in detail and Constance Babington Smith's thought rapidly turned to the excellent set of pictures taken back in June, which she now retrieved from the picture library:

It was by far the best of the early covers and, sure enough, I did find a midget aircraft on those splendid photographs. The absurd little object was not on the airfield, but sitting in a corner of a small enclosure some way behind the hangars, immediately adjoining a building which I suspected, from its design, was used for testing jet engines. . . . I named it 'Peenemünde 20', as its span was about 20 feet, but there was precious little I could say about it. The midget aircraft had the aggravating cotton-wool look that all light-coloured or shiny objects acquire on aerial photographs, owing to the 'light-spread' that blots out shadow and prevents detailed interpretation.

Chance now again took a hand in the story. On 28 November a Mosquito pilot, sent to photograph Berlin, found it veiled in deep cloud and turned his aircraft instead towards his secondary targets, shipping around Stettin and Swinemünde and a suspected radar installation at Zinnowitz – the very transmitter in fact which the Germans were using to monitor the performance of their pilotless aircraft. He then turned homewards, having used up the last of his film just as he was flying over the airfield at Peenemünde.

While these pictures were still on their way to Medmenham, Constance Babington Smith began a new study of back covers, looking for another Peenemünde 20. On 1 December 1943 her eye was caught by the 'strange structures' which, several months before, she learned, 'had been looked at . . . and interpreted as something to do with dredging equipment.' The 'dredging equipment', she now suggested to Wing Commander Kendall, could instead be 'a catapult for pilotless aircraft'.

After an intensive study of the pair of photographs through

the stereoscope Kendall set off to consult the Army Section and during his absence the new pictures of Peenemünde taken three days before arrived.

My chief anxiety was as to whether the run over Peenemünde airfield started in time to include the launching place. Fortunately it did – just. Only the first print of the run showed it and . . . the quality of the photograph was poor, but even with the naked eye I could see that on the ramp was something that had not been there before. A tiny cruciform shape, set exactly on the lower end of the inclined rails – a midget aircraft actually in position for launching. . . . Late through that night I worked feverishly with Kendall to trace back the history of the 'Peenemünde Airfield Site'. We found that the first experimental ramp had been built late in 1942, during the interval between the earliest two covers of the area. Kendall himself measured and analysed the ramp and then started drafting an immediate report.

Meanwhile two interpreters of the Army Section 'had been searching the wooded shoreline' at Zinnowitz, photographed during the same sortie:

Almost at the same moment that I was asking myself what on earth the ramp near the airfield could be, they had found, between Zinnowitz and the village of Zempin eight miles away down the coast of Usedom, a launching site with firing points aiming out to sea, which also matched up with the foundations for ramps at the ski sites. Before daylight next morning [i.e. 2 December 1943] Kendall's report on both Peenemünde and Zinnowitz was on its way to London, with the news that the nature of the most imminent cross-Channel threat was at last established beyond doubt. It was going to be a flying bomb.

5

MYSTERIOUS TARGETS

*Early in November, we were briefed urgently on entirely
new and mysterious targets.*

Former Typhoon pilot, Richard Hough, recalling
November 1943

Once convinced that a real threat existed even Lord Cherwell
reacted vigorously. Having been shown the latest report from
Medmenham, he wrote instantly to the Prime Minister, who
was in Cairo, warning that the first missiles from the sites
detected in France might be launched during the next one to
three months and that the Director of Intelligence (Operations)
at the Air Ministry thought that a hundred sites could deliver
2000 tons of high explosive every twenty-four hours. On 14
December the Deputy Chief of the Air Staff submitted an even
more alarming report: 'If present rates of construction are
maintained,' he warned the Prime Minister, 'the work on some
twenty sites should be completed by early January 1944, and
the remainder by February. The launching points on the sites
in the Pas de Calais and Somme–Seine areas are oriented on
London, and those of some of the sites in the Cherbourg area
on Bristol.'

At this moment news arrived from France which suggested
that the expected offensive might begin at any moment. The
ubiquitous Michel Hollard had hardly got back from Switzerland after delivering the drawings of the Bois Carré site, when
he heard from the station master at Rouen that a goods wagon
carrying a number of unusually shaped crates had passed
through en route for Auffay, near the first 'mystery' site he
had reconnoitred. The wagon had been shunted into a closely
guarded requisitioned shed, but Hollard managed to slip inside,
peering about in the semi-darkness and measuring everything
in reach with a tape measure. He identified a long, cigar-shaped

body and two flatter sections, and managed to prepare a sketch of the object's likely shape and dimensions when assembled. Soon afterwards other agents began to report the arrival of similar objects, some of which were already secretly being assembled.

The original codename for the secret weapon inquiry, Bodyline, introduced on 26 July, was replaced from 27 November by 'Crossbow', a crossbow being a deadly weapon which had made earlier types obsolete. The Air Force, influenced by the same cricketing enthusiast who had selected Bodyline, chose to call their new targets 'No-Ball', a more optimistic choice, with a hint of unfairness – a 'no-ball' was one which, released too late, gave a run to the other side. The name aroused some ribaldry among the airmen involved, such as twenty-year-old Richard Hough of 195 Squadron, whose Hurricanes had recently been replaced by the powerful Hawker Typhoon:

Early in November [1943] we were briefed urgently on entirely new and mysterious targets – what appeared to be chalk white slits cut into the fields and woods of the Pas de Calais.

'These are No-ball sites,' the Spy [the station intelligence officer] told us, and blushed at the raucous guffaws which geeted this statement. Somebody told him to pitch his voice higher and the C.O. shut him up.

'They are secret weapon sites of some description,' Spy continued gamely. 'We're not quite sure what but we do know they are dangerous and are going to get top priority.'

To prepare for, and support, the invasion the Allied Expeditionary Air Force had recently been set up under Air Chief Marshal Sir Trafford Leigh-Mallory. It absorbed part of Fighter Command, the rest of which was renamed Air Defence of Great Britain. In command of ADGB was Air Marshal Roderic Hill, who had operational control of Anti-Aircraft Command, the Royal Observer Corps and Balloon Command as well as of forty-eight RAF squadrons. Fighters alone, however even those equipped to carry bombs beneath their wings, as many now were, could not destroy the massive concrete buildings now spreading like a rash across Northern France. Leigh-Mallory was, therefore, also ordered to attack the No-ball sites with bombers of the Allied Expeditionary Air Force, reinforced by heavy bombers of the US Eighth Air Force, when the weather ruled out attacks on Germany. At first five sites were allocated to RAF Bomber Command, but following opposition from Air Chief Marshal 'Bomber' (officially Sir Arthur) Harris, these sites, too, eventually became Leigh-Mallory's responsibility.

The involvement of their bombers in the attack on the secret weapon sites meant officially informing the Americans of what was happening. Already wild rumours were circulating in Washington, as one resident recorded, that 'the Germans were preparing to bombard London with huge containers bearing gruesome and fatal "Red Death" . . . to destroy every living creature in the British Isles' and constructing 'a gigantic refrigerating apparatus along the French coast for the instantaneous creation of massive icebergs in the Channel.' Even the Pentagon's scientific adviser thought that the Germans might plan to load the new missiles with bacteria or some form of radioactive liquid, to render uninhabitable an area two miles square – a suggestion which Winston Churchill genially described as 'very fruity'.

The American government reacted as seriously – and as generously – to the threat now developing as if it had been New York, not London, which was at risk. On 12 January 1944 General Marshall ordered the Army Air Forces to give top priority to working out the most effective method of attacking the launching sites, and the solution adopted was typically American: to build as many sites as were necessary and go on demolishing them until the airmen had a satisfactory answer. On 25 January 1944 General Arnold ordered Brigadier General Grandison Gardner, in command of America's Peenemünde, the Air Force test centre at Eglin Field, Florida, to get 'the job done in days not weeks'.

General Gardner immediately mobilized the full resources of the 800,000 acre Proving Ground and its thousands of personnel. With utmost secrecy the Army Air Forces duplicated in the remote pine barrens of the Florida Panhandle the activity so closely observed on the Channel coast of France. . . . Construction materials were rushed by air, train and truck and boat, into the secret ranges of Eglin Field. Working in twelve-hour shifts, thousands of civilian and military personnel assembled concrete, steel, lumber, brick and building blocks into a series of key target buildings and entire Ski Sites. Within minutes after the first concrete had hardened, every type of weapon available to the AAF [Army Air Force] was thrown against replicas of the German installations. . . . When it had been conclusively proved that one technique was superior to all others – minimum altitude attack by fighter aircraft especially equipped to pinpoint very heavy bombs on the most vulnerable point at each site – General Gardner and a team of Proving Ground officers flew to England to demonstrate the new method of knocking out the Ski Sites. A motion picture of the tests, prepared by top Hollywood experts, gave most of those to whom it was shown their first detailed view of the massive sites, as well as conclusive evidence of how they could most economically and efficiently be rendered useless.

The counter-attack had really begun on 5 December 1943 when fighter-bombers and light bombers of the second Tactical Air Force and the US Ninth Air Force raided three of the sixty-four sites so far identified. The results were disappointing. The concrete launching ramps and storage buildings made small targets and could be damaged only by a direct hit or very near miss but the heaviest bombs dropped were only 1000-pounders.

The sites also proved heavily defended, as Richard Hough's squadron, flying from Manston, rapidly discovered. With two 500-pound bombs beneath their wings the already weighty Typhoons became so vulnerable they themselves needed a fighter escort, but the pilots set off in a mood of cheerful confidence:

At first sight these ops looked like . . . 'a piece of cake'. The launching sites were only a few minutes' flying time from the Kent coast and you could almost glide back with a dud engine. We kept in very loose formation, the two squadrons of twelve planes each half a mile apart. High above us some top cover Spits sparkled in turn as they weaved alertly from side to side. To see their protective presence was half a comfort, half an affront: we husky Typhoons nannied by mere Spits! As it turned out, nothing came down on us. But plenty came up. None of us had seen flak like this before, even off the Dutch coast. In seconds the sky before and behind, above and below, and on both sides was scored with black puffs. . . . There was no doubt that the Germans regarded these innocuous-looking strips as highly important. . . .

Before I went down I saw two holes in my starboard wing, and I saw one of 3 Squadron enter, but fail to emerge from, a yellow cloud of what I was later told was phosphorous flak. . . . The only thing on one's mind after bombing was getting out as fast as possible, with survival as the first priority . . . going flat out for those friendly looking white cliffs of Dover.

The pilots of 602 Squadron, flying Spitfire Vs, with 'clipped' wings, and 182 Squadron, flying the outmoded Hurricane, both based on Tangmere, near Chichester, also did not greatly enjoy attacking No-ball targets. The famous French ace, Pierre Closterman, later described how the senior intelligence officer warned the pilots, 'Gentlemen, the situation is grave!', as he 'gloomily unveiled a large-scale map of northern France studded with little numbered flags' – the fourteen sites assigned to the two squadrons. There was good reason for gloom, especially among the Hurricane pilots, as Closterman, who flew a Spitfire, realized:

With their four 60 lb. rockets the miserable machines dragged along at 200 m.p.h. . . . We didn't laugh long at their expense. . . . On 4 December, 8 Hurricanes had just crossed the French coast when 10 Messerschmitt 109 G's attacked them. . . . Weighed down by their bombs the Hurricanes hadn't much hope of coming through. Six were brought down and the other two crashed on landing, their pilots both seriously wounded. . . . We laughed quite the other side of our faces when it was decided that in future the Hurricanes would be escorted at ground level by Spitfires.

A dangerous time now began for Closterman and his fellow pilots. Many who had survived the perils of high-level combat were shot down by ground fire, and because not a day could be lost, missions were flown even in poor visibility and pouring rain. This was a typical attack, on 20 December 1943, which seemed to show that Milch's dream of 'burying the British Air Force' alongside the launching sites was well founded:

Out of the corner of my eye I watched the Hurricanes about to launch their attack. The target, carefully camouflaged against vertical photography, was visible in every detail at this angle; the high tension cables to the transformer, the concrete block of the control room with its curious aerials. On either side, clearly hidden in the undergrowth, the low-ski-shaped construction . . . and, lastly, the launching ramp, 45 yards long, pointing straight at the heart of England. On the rails, a sinister cylinder, about twenty feet long, with two embryonic wings. Things seemed to be so devilishly advanced! All round the No-ball stretched a 20-yard wide barbed wire barrier and light flak posts – 15 in a radius of 800 metres, according to the interpretation of the latest photos . . . and on the roof of the control block were two 37 mm. The Hurricanes began their dive, slap into the machine gun bullets. The tracer bullets formed a wall of steel and explosive round the target.

The inevitable happened. Powerless, I watched the tragedy. Flight Lieutenant Roughead, just as he let go his salvo of rockets, was hit and killed instantly. . . . As in a nightmare I saw Warrant Officer Pearce's Hurricane literally mown down by a burst of 37 mm. The tail came off, the machine crashed in a wood, scything down the trees, scattering jets of burning petrol.

Whatever the research in peaceful Florida had demonstrated, quite clearly the fighter-bombers, for all their pilots' gallantry, were not going to knock out the launching sites unaided. With some reluctance, the Allies decided to use their medium and heavy bombers. Oddly enough, in urging, on 15 December 1943, that the US Eighth Air Force, with its self-defending Fortresses and Liberators, should be called upon, the Chief of the Air Staff, Sir Charles Portal, advanced the same argument as his opposite number, Erhard Milch. The American 'heavies', he suggested, were bound to bring the German fighters up to battle, when they would be outnumbered by the Allied Spitfires and Mustangs, and their destruction would help to pave the way for the coming invasion.

Events worked out according to Milch's scenario rather than Portal's. Very few German fighters ever appeared, but German ground fire proved lethal to large numbers of Allied aircraft. Most opposition to the use of the bombers, however, was on other grounds. There was, first, the 'Harris' argument, that the proper role for bombers was in attacking German cities, and the 'Leigh-Mallory' one that they would be better employed in softening up the defences in France before the invasion. But there was also a humanitarian reason for not letting the heavy bombers loose on the sites, as the novelist H. E. Bates, then working in the Public Relations Department of the Air Ministry, described:

Such small targets demanded a far greater degree of accuracy than was needed to knock out a factory. The Germans' favourite site was a small wood of five or ten acres close to a hard road, where trees in both summer and winter gave them perfect cover. In such woodland sites the Germans built hundreds of sites and supply depots. But they also chose more domestic sites. Orchards of apples and pears were favourite places. Nor had they any compunction whatsoever about putting them into the back-gardens of French peasants in remote villages. And on at least one occasion they built an entire launching site in a village street.

Bombing at night was less dangerous, but even more inaccurate than raids by day. The first serious attack, on the night of 16 December, had everything in its favour, for the target, near Abbeville, was marked by Mosquitoes of the Pathfinder Force, using the radar-navigational aid Oboe, and the main force, of nine Lancasters, was led by the famous Wing Commander Leonard Cheshire. Bombing from between 12,000 and 15,000 feet the Lancasters delivered all their bombs within 150 yards of the markers, and two were actually within 30 yards of the target, which measured only 300 by 250 yards, but even this was not close enough. On 21 December bombing by the American daylight squadrons began in earnest, rising to a climax on Christmas Eve, a year to the day since the flying-bomb had first taken to the air. In place of the 'New Year present' the Germans had planned, they received a Christmas box of 1700 tons of bombs, delivered by 672 Fortresses on twenty-four separate sites. Other attacks, by smaller aircraft, brought the number involved to 1300 aircraft – the largest single operation ever undertaken by the Eighth Air Force. The second Tactical Air Force and US Ninth Air Force attacked twenty-three more, and Bomber Command five. At first, the effects, as with all bombing, were greatly overestimated. By the end of December fifty-two sites had been bombed and the British believed that twenty-one had been very badly damaged and fifteen more had suffered some damage. The true picture was very different. Only seven sites had been destroyed, though the construction of some others had been held up, and thirty French civilian workmen – but no German soldiers – had been killed.

At this stage the Germans were still finishing sites faster than the Allies could destroy them, with, at mid-January, two new ones completed every three days. Then the increasingly heavy Allied bombing began to take its toll. Repairs to badly bombed sites, Allied intelligence discovered, were taking up to twenty-two days and in January more than half of the first hundred were abandoned and efforts were concentrated on finishing the rest. These could still prove sufficient to delay the invasion and on 17 February 1944, with the approval of the Combined Chiefs of Staff, the Air Ministry issued a new directive to Bomber Command. The destruction of the German Air Force remained its primary objective, but a series of 'other objectives' were now added, even taking priority over 'Berlin and other industrial areas'. 'Operations under all means available,' the directive laid down, 'will be taken to neutralise threats developing under Crossbow.' Three days later General Eisenhower issued a notably different directive to the US Tactical Air Force. In *his* list of priorities Crossbow came in paragraph 12, near the bottom, though the Air Commander-in-Chief, Allied Expeditionary Force, Sir Trafford Leigh-Mallory, could 'where necessary . . . call for assistance from the strategical air forces in the United Kingdom through the Deputy Supreme Allied Commander', Air Chief Marshal Sir Arthur Tedder.

Although the American Air Force Commander-in-Chief, General Arnold, argued that 'the Crossbow diversion may well make the difference between success and failure in accomplishing our pre-Overlord objectives', the commander on the spot, General Spaatz, loyally obeyed the orders to give the sites priority. In relation to its area each site sustained a far heavier bomb-load than Cologne or Hamburg. In December 1943 3217 tons were dropped, in January 1944 6726, in February 5532, in March 4211, in April, with longer days and better weather, 7248. In January 90 per cent of all the Tactical Air Force's efforts were devoted to secret weapon targets, including suspected rocket depots; by April, with pre-invasion targets, like railways and bridges, demanding even greater priority the total was still 30 per cent. The US Eighth Air Force made a smaller contribution: 23 per cent of its sorties in January, 17 per cent in April, but by 12 June 1944 it had flown 5950 sorties, mainly of B.17s (Flying Fortresses) and B.24s (Marauders), against Crossbow targets, out of a total of 25,150, during which 36,200 tons of bombs had been dropped. Bomber Command had contributed only 3900 sorties – but, even so, thanks to the demands made on it, the proportion of its bombs dropped on

Germany itself declined sharply, to 40 per cent in April and to 8 per cent by the end of June. The flying-bombs, even before a single one had been fired, had helped to give the German cities the breathing-space they desperately needed.

On one category of targets everyone could agree, factories in Germany engaged in flying-bomb production. The main works at Fallersleben, the former airship works at Löwenthal, near Friedrichshaven, and two hydrogen peroxide plants, believed to be manufacturing fuel to propel the flying-bomb, at Ober Raderach and Hollreigelskreuth, were all attacked by Bomber Command, while the Mediterranean Air Force was called in to bomb another plant at Wiener Neustadt in Austria. Whether any of these raids made any difference seems doubtful: the United States Strategic Bombing Survey later found that at Fallersleben, for example, production had not been affected at all.

But the weight of the Allied response, and the heaviest losses, came in the attacks on the sites, where – no doubt at the expense of the guns around other potential targets – the defences were rapidly thickened up. In mid-December the ski site belt, stretching from the Pas de Calais to Dieppe, was protected by about sixty heavy and another sixty light anti-aircraft guns. By the end of May, the numbers were 520 heavy guns and 730 of lighter calibre. The defences around Cherbourg, where a separate cluster of sites was believed to be aligned on Southampton, were also increased, from 120 guns to 200, until the area acquired among Allied air crews the same unenviable reputation as the Ruhr. In one attack near Cherbourg 160 out of 217 Marauders were damaged by flak, some seriously.

All told the flying-bombs had already cost the Allies 154 lost aircraft and 771 aircrew dead or missing – and at the heights at which most such raids were carried out the chances of baling out successfully were usually small. Of the planes lost, forty-one were single-seater fighter bombers, sixty-four medium and light bombers and forty-eight heavy bombers of the US Eighth Air Force, which, because of their larger crews, lost by far the largest number of men: 462.

What had all this effort achieved? By the end of May 82 of 96 ski sites believed to have been neutralized, about a third –

35 – were knocked out by the US Eighth Air Force, another third – 39 – by the US Ninth Air Force, and the rest – 33 – by the British Tactical Air Forces. The Americans had contributed more than half the total bombs dropped and lives given.

Many of the lost aircraft were fighter-bombers and eventually they were withdrawn when it became clear, as the Air Ministry confirmed, that the best results were achieved by 'the light bombers of the Tactical Air Forces – the Mosquitoes', which 'specialised in low level attacks' and 'averaged 39 tons of bombs per "ski" site neutralised as against the next best, 125 tons for the Fortresses.' Apart from the aircrew the real victims of the Crossbow campaign were the French, for, especially with high-flying bombers, the only sure way of destroying the target was to plaster the whole area with bombs. Some sites, no bigger than a forty-acre field, attracted as many as 4000 bombs, and H. E. Bates, who visited the Pas de Calais that autumn, was appalled at the destruction all around him:

The countryside of the launching site is bleak with tragedy. Its villages have crumbled into heaps of stone and plaster; its fields are like miniature alpine ranges, unploughable until an army of bulldozers can level the countless bomb craters; village streets are chains of ponds after heavy rain; gardens and orchards have been obliterated. For the night and day bombing which caused all this the French had a single and terribly expressive word – '*Effrayant!*' Yet again and again the observer talking to them in the days immediately after their liberation heard them say, 'We did not mind . . . however often you came and however much you bombed us. . . . We knew that it had to be done and that it had to be done to us.'

6

ANY TIME NOW

*There is at least a possibility of an attempt at a preliminary
use of the new weapon at any time now.*

Letter from Ministry of Home Security to Regional
Commissioners for Civil Defence, 7 April 1944

From the very beginning of the secret weapon threat one man
had taken it more seriously than any of his colleagues. Herbert
Morrison, Home Secretary and Minister of Home Security,
was the son of a Lambeth policeman who had risen to the top
through his work for local government in London. He had an
intuitive understanding of what the ordinary citizen expected,
and would tolerate, from his rulers, and an intimate knowledge
of how the mind of the average London councillor worked.
Morrison was concerned all along to counteract any tendency
to brush the danger from the pilotless aircraft and rocket to
one side. As long ago as July 1943 the Cabinet Civil Defence
Committee, of which he was chairman, had fought a losing
battle against proposals, in the words of the committee's minutes, 'to meet the demand for labour for the Forces and the
productive war effort by reducing the strengths of the various
Civil Defence Services.' He had finally agreed that the total
should come down to 293,000 by the end of 1943, to be followed by a further cut of another 50,000 during the first half
of 1944. Now he found himself called on to honour that promise, even though the situation had totally changed. What was
proposed, Morrison pointed out in two papers of 25 November
and 16 December 1943, meant the Civil Defence losing their
youngest and fittest wardens and firemen to the Forces and
having to look to inexperienced servicemen to fill the gap. Such
a policy, he urged, made no sense at all. The result was a
compromise. The cuts, it was decided, would stand, but would
be postponed until the six months beginning on 1 April 1944.

Morrison had more success over another precautionary measure, the manufacture and distribution of additional stocks of the excellent indoor table shelter bearing his name. In September 1943 additional Morrisons were sent to London, Portsmouth and Southampton, and another 100,000 were ordered, though by mid-March so few had arrived, due to the shortage of steel, that the contracts for the final 25,000 were cancelled.

The alternative to protecting people where they lived was to send them away, and the War Cabinet at one time contemplated a new evacuation scheme to cover not only London, Portsmouth and Southampton, but even Cardiff and Bristol. Here, however, Morrison was less alarmist than his colleagues. In a persuasive paper circulated on 28 December 1943 he argued against any such wholesale evacuation and suggested that even the evacuation of the 'priority classes', consisting of schoolchildren, infants with their mothers, expectant mothers, and the blind and crippled, should be restricted to London, Portsmouth (including Gosport) and Southampton.

The Cabinet accepted Morrison's advice and it was also decided not to evacuate government departments but to provide accommodation for them underground. Whitehall, as usual, showed every sign of looking after its own. The Ministry of Works, the Civil Defence Committee learned on 31 December 1943, considered that priority should be given to civil servants in the best shelters available, those built in former tubes, even though 'this course would be likely to lead to protests from certain sections of the civilian population'.

The disagreeable prospect remained of lesser mortals 'attempting to force their way in', but the Ministry of Home Security was equal to that. Its chief engineer, the same committee learned on 20 January 1944, 'was designing a simple method of blocking up entrances which could be put into use at short notice.' Other claimants for shelter space had now appeared on the scene. 'The London Regional Commissioners,' the Civil Defence Committee were told at the same meeting, 'were considering whether some of the unallocated deep tube shelter accommodation might be used for first aid posts and rest centres,' but in the end it was decided that it should all be reserved for the men from Whitehall. Plans were made to move some ministries into steel-framed buildings with strengthened basements, and the Ministry of Home Security itself also looked to its own position. Its war room, from which the whole Civil Defence effort was directed, really did need to be kept going and by April a reserve war room had been set up at Edgbaston Hall, Birmingham, which even the most pessimistic thought far enough away to be safe.

On 15 January 1944, on the grounds that even the newly adopted codename No-ball had become known to the Germans, two new codewords were added to the already extensive secret weapons anthology: 'Diver' and 'Big Ben'. Diver was expected to arrive first, and, as an official circular instructed, the dread news must be reported by scrambler telephone in a fixed form of words: 'Crossbow Diver reported from No. — Region at — hours.' (The long-range rocket, hitherto known as 'the LRR', would make its debut even more dramatically: 'This is Home Security War Room speaking. Big Ben has been confirmed.')

Opinion in London as to the likely scale of the coming attack now oscillated between excessive optimism and near despair. Early in the new year the Joint Intelligence Committee issued the most despondent estimate yet: the Germans might, by the end of March, be able to launch 45,000 pilotless aircraft across the Channel. Lord Cherwell's natural scepticism, which had earlier led him astray, now came into its own. Where, he asked, could the Germans possibly find the factories to produce such an aerial armada? One thousand five hundred a month was far more likely, and such a rate of fire meant 'that the average Londoner would be exposed to one explosion within a mile's distance once a week'. As for the threat to the D-Day embarkation, he added later, if 1500 flying-bombs were aimed at 1000 ships moored at Portsmouth and Southampton, only two would be hit. The Chiefs of Staff, influenced by Cherwell, agreed late in January that an attack need not be expected before 1 March and that, apart from some ten-hour blitzes involving up to 920 tons of explosive, the general level would be below 130 tons a day, and perhaps as little as 45 tons.

Herbert Morrison refused to accept this reassuring prediction. On 8 February he wrote to the Prime Minister reminding him that in addition to people in London, and possibly Bristol and Plymouth also, a large number of civilians living between the capital and the coast were also at risk in what had been casually dismissed as 'spillover areas'. As early as mid-October 1943 he had met selected newspaper editors to tell them, in the words of the Chief Press Censor, Admiral Thompson, that he had 'no objection to the publication of stories [about possible secret weapons] from neutral sources, for, if the secret weapon did materialise, they would prevent the public being taken completely by surprise.' In January 1944 Morrison met the editors again to warn them that 'the weapon was to be a large winged bomb with some form of jet or rocket propulsion . . . sufficiently large . . . to be shot at.' They should still not specifically refer to the secret weapon, but could carry such reports as 'The military targets now being bombed in France every day may well be . . . the rocket guns which have been reported from neutral sources.' This restriction remained in force even after 22 February, when the Prime Minister made a far more explicit mention of the subject in the House of Commons. 'There is,' said Churchill, 'no doubt that the Germans are preparing on the French shore new means of attack on this country, either by pilotless aircraft, or possibly rockets, or both, on a considerable scale. We have long been watching this with the utmost vigilance.'

Because it was hidden away in a long review of the whole war situation, this discreet reference seems to have passed unnoticed, although during the next few weeks thousands of people were let into the Diver secret. On 10 February Morrison's ministry addressed to the regional commissioners of the five Civil Defence regions most at risk a long letter warning that 'the main threat is now from pilotless aircraft'.

It is assumed that the Southampton, Portsmouth, Bristol and Plymouth areas will be subjects of Crossbow attack, but that a proportionate reduction may be made in scale . . . compared with Greater London. Because of the larger hinterland of lightly populated country behind these target areas, any spill-over due to inaccuracy of aim . . . should not prove beyond the resources of the Civil Defence Services within easy reach of the affected areas.

The Government was obsessed at this time with the fear that the first pilotless aircraft might be mistaken for ordinary bombs and the same letter laid down elaborate rules for letting the ministry know of any 'crashed aircraft' which might not be what they seemed. For the same reason the Civil Defence Committee five days later, on 17 February, considered draft instructions to newspaper editors to be issued as soon as the attack began. One version called for outright suppression of any suspicion incidents: 'It is suspected,' it ran, 'that the raid/incident which took place at ——— this ——— involved the use by the enemy of pilotless aircraft. . . . Will you please refrain from publishing any reference to this raid/incident, until you receive a further notification from Censorship.' The Ministry of Information, very sensibly, was in favour of the public being told what was happening, and won the right to issue, when the moment came, a somewhat more liberal note of guidance:

It is particularly important to deny to the enemy any information of the accuracy of his new weapons and for this reason the normal rule allowing general indications of the location of a raid or incident, i.e. Home Counties London or London area (including the term 'outskirts' and 'suburbs' of London), S.E., S., S.W. will, so far as raids in Southern England are concerned, be suspended for the time being and only the general term Southern England allowed in stories of raids or incidents, including the sounding of an Alert, in any of these areas.

Much thought was devoted to the question of whether a special warning system was needed, and this subject was to cause further anguished discussion later. Herbert Morrison was strongly opposed to making the existing system more complicated. 'Pilotless aircraft,' he pointed out in a paper submitted to the Civil Defence Committee on 28 December 1943, 'may travel somewhat faster than ordinary aircraft, but . . . the speed is not likely to be so great as to defeat the ordinary air raid warning system entirely. . . . It appears possible to give warnings for pilotless aircraft in the same way as for ordinary aircraft, by giving the national air raid warning and the special imminent danger warning for factories.'

During this time the volume of words generated by the flying-bombs was prodigious. The civil departments were the worst. *Civil Preparations for Crossbow*, which began life as a modest seventeen-page document in January, was soon expanding, and the flow of memoranda within and between departments was enormous. The service departments' Diver plans were, by contrast, distinguished by a soldierly directness and brevity, like these STANDING INSTRUCTIONS FOR DUTY GROUP CAPTAIN, AIR MINISTRY, drawn up on 7 March.

When pilotless aircraft attacks commence . . . the normal aircraft reporting and air defence machinery of A.D.G.B. [Air Defence of Great Britain] will be brought into action automatically. On receipt of information that pilotless aircraft have been detected by the radar chain, the Duty Group Captain at A.D.G.B. will inform the Duty Group Captain, Air Ministry.

What was to happen when this key figure was shaken respectfully from his slumbers by a subordinate? The plans for the military response had been evolved over weeks of discussion between Air Chief Marshal Sir Roderic Hill, Air Officer Commanding the Air Defence of Great Britain, and General Sir Frederick Pile, head of Anti-Aircraft Command. Originally approved in outline on 16 December 1943, *The Overlord Diver Plan* was finally circulated, in a drastically revised form, on 4 March 1944. Its contents, and how the plan worked out in action, will be described later. The immediate results were felt, however, by some members of Anti-Aircraft Command. One heavy AA battery, stationed in Wales, one of its warrant officers recalls, found itself ordered that winter to specialize in training to engage low-level targets, but the attempt was abandoned since 'the surrounding mountain ranges . . . interfered with radar and the pilot of the target towing plane was put too much at risk. . . . Diver was mentioned,' this informant remembers, 'but we thought this had connection with the Japanese suicide planes.' The gunners in a light AA battery in Dorset were not much better informed. One member of a Bofors gun crew remembers being told, not very comfortingly, that the expected missiles were obsolete Heinkels, radio controlled and packed with high explosive.

Members of Balloon Command, which was part of the RAF, also found themselves involved, for reasons not revealed to them, in constructing new anchorage positions in high-lying parts of Kent, an activity which caught the eye of many civilians. 'There was much speculation as to their purpose,' remembers one man living at Petts Wood, talking of the concrete blocks sunk into the surrounding hillsides on the North Downs.

The best informed section of the population was the Civil Defence services. No reader of *ARP News*, the unofficial Civil Defence house-journal, had any excuse for not anticipating what might soon happen, for as early as November 1943 the paper had warned of the 'repeated threats of reprisals by novel means against this country', and in January 1944 it returned to the subject with a cautionary editorial, reminding its readers of 'the possibility of their having to face in the future a period not unlike that encountered during the heaviest blitzes.'

Three months later, in March, the references in Churchill's speech, which the press as a whole failed to follow up, provided the text for another warning against complacency. 'There can be no further ground for scepticism at all,' the paper commented, adding a notably accurate forecast:

Neither rockets nor pilotless planes can be accurately aimed . . . to hit specific targets at a distance, so that the weapons must be used against some general objective such as a big city. We may, therefore, expect attack over a large urban field. . . . London is the most likely . . . but . . . by no means necessarily the only target. . . . Let it not be too readily assumed that other big industrial centres of the country . . . are out of range.

Up to this time very little information had been given officially to the rank and file of the Civil Defence services. The regional commissioners had been expressly told not to pass on the first warning sent to them, in February, beyond 'Controllers and Chief Constables', and a second alarming letter, on 7 April, was given an equally restricted circulation:

You ought to know, for your own 'Private information', that the Air Staff may no longer be in a position to give us much preliminary notice. . . . There is at least a possibility of an attempt at a preliminary use of the new weapon at any time now.

On 26 April regional commissioners were at last told that 'Police, Wardens and members of the Royal Observer Corps in the areas likely to be affected should now receive appropriate instructions   to prevent publication of any reports which would indicate to the enemy where his missiles have fallen' and a notice was enclosed 'for distribution to all Police Stations and Wardens Posts in the areas listed' – which covered virtually the whole southern half of the country, from Suffolk westwards.

The pilotless aircraft is believed to resemble a small monoplane having a wing span of about 20 feet and an overall length of about 18 feet. No pilot's cockpit will be visible. . . . The aircraft will be jet-propelled and consequently no propeller will be fitted. . . . The pilotless aircraft will probably cause a shallow crater. . . . Identification may be established by the presence in or about the crater of parts of light metal sheeting, pieces of wing or wing spars, tail unit, and metal control rods . . . small electrical units, insulated wire, gyroscopes, metal tanks, lengths of metal tubing and possibly small electric motors and/or parts of clock-work mechanism.

The first Diver reports were likely to come from the Observer Corps and its Operation Instruction No. 51, issued on 22 April, was even more detailed, thanks to the 'ringside seat' which MI6 had occupied at the trials in the Baltic:

Maximum Speed –	Is likely to exceed 400 m.p.h.

Average Speed –	Speed increases with range from launching point . . .
	Probable speeds are –
	    at 10 miles from launching point
	    230 m.p.h. . . .
	    at 30 miles from launching point
	    330 m.p.h. . . .

Operational Height –	Between 500 and 10,000 feet. 6,000 feet with a cruising speed of 330 m.p.h. is considered probable.
Flight Path –	Steady climb to about 6,000 feet for 25 miles and then level flight in both vertical and horizontal plane.

Curiously enough, the widespread communication of these alarming facts rarely had the expected results. As the historian of No. 17 Group, ROC, based on Watford, discovered, 'So engrossed were most Observers in the . . . impending attempt to land forces on the Continent . . . that the warning caused but a mild and temporary flutter. Some, indeed were of the opinion that this weird and doubtful aircraft was a thing of imagination deliberately conjured up for the express purpose

. . . of keeping all Observers on their toes.' The Home Guard, of course, took it seriously, as they did everything, and one in Walthamstow remembers his commanding officer calling his men solemnly together and then in hushed voice, 'as if a spy was listening at the keyhole', communicating the deadly facts. ARP workers were less easily impressed. A chief warden in Clacton who dutifully told his subordinates of the horrors to come was not pleased to be asked jocularly, 'Is Hitler getting short of pilots?'

Some of those in the secret faced agonies of conscience in trying to decide whether they could properly take private precautions. One Grenadier Guards officer longed to send his wife and fourteen-year-old daughter away from London, but felt he could not do so without offering an explanation he was not free to give. Others compromised by dropping hints. One woman from Clapton, staying at Goudhurst in Kent, was highly alarmed to receive from her husband, a post warden, a letter telling her that 'something' might happen at any moment, 'but he was not allowed to tell me what.' Another warden, in Notting Hill, could not resist blurting out the secret to a local resident. The latter laughed aloud, he now admits, declaring flatly that such an invention could not possibly reach Dover, let alone London.

Just as many in high places had become sceptical about the whole secret weapon story, so humbler citizens also rapidly got over the first shock of the Diver warning. 'My first reaction was one of awe,' recalls a woman part-time warden from Upton Park of a training lecture at her workplace, the Standard Telephones and Cables Company factory in New Southgate, where 'a pamphlet was passed round' with 'on the front cover . . . a sketch which looked like a Spitfire . . . named as the pilotless plane.' The wardens were warned that 'the blast was devastating . . . but as the weeks went by and we didn't get any I thought it must have been a rumour.'

It was not only among ordinary civilians that a spirit of unjustified optimism prevailed. The Air Ministry believed, late in March, that by the end of April even the remaining twenty ski sites would have been knocked out, but on 18 April, taking no chances, the Chief of Staff warned the Prime Minister that enough might still be repaired to interfere with the invasion.

On the following day, prompted by Churchill's Chief of Staff, General Ismay, General Eisenhower ordered that attacks by the Allied air forces on secret weapon targets should be given absolute priority over other operations. Still no attack came, and then suddenly, 'at the end of April 1944', while 'examining a new cover of the Cherbourg peninsula' one of the interpreters at Medmenham spotted a totally new development:

Near a village called Belhamelin something peculiar had been constructed between two farm buildings . . . a long concrete platform, with pairs of studs embedded in it. . . . And some way from it, in a field, was a heavily camouflaged square building. The two essential installations! It was a launching site of a new, much simpler variety, and the camouflage and dispersal was extremely subtle. . . . The new sites were horribly difficult to spot, but within a few days twelve had been identified. These finds sounded off a new Crossbow alarm, and for the fourth time a special flying programme was laid on. The whole area within 150 miles of London, Southampton and Plymouth was to be photographed yet again. At Medmenham, Kendall put fifteen more interpreters on to Crossbow work.

At first the discovery of what became labelled 'modified sites' caused irritation rather than alarm to the Allied commanders. 'The Allied Expeditionary Air Force,' Air Marshal Hill's Air Defence of Great Britain's headquarters was told, 'attaches little importance to the new sites,' although by 16 May the number detected stood at nineteen and was rising fast. The Chiefs of Staff placed their faith in knocking out the original sites, and on destroying eight so-called 'supply sites', which, we now know, the Germans had intended to use but had abandoned. Another 8000 tons of bombs were dropped on 'large sites', which the Germans called 'bunkers'. Their function was not known, but the Germans had in fact intended to use three of them as underground launching sites for flying-bombs. Thanks to the Allied forces, neither supply sites nor large sites ever came into action.

Between 5 December 1943 and 12 June 1944 more than 8000 tons of bombs were showered on the large sites; 300 more on two of the eight supply sites, and more than 23,000 tons on the ninety-six ski sites, a formidable total of nearly 32,000 tons. The modified sites, by contrast, built by General Heinemann following the first attacks on the ski sites, were largely ignored.

Only one was attacked, on 27 May, by Typhoon fighter-bombers, and the raid was a failure and not repeated.

While the Operations Branch of the Air Ministry was indulging in premature self-congratulation, the Air Intelligence Branch was still striving to fill in the few missing pieces of the flying-bomb jigsaw. One of the last arrived, publicly and spectacularly, on 11 May, when what the following day's British newspapers described as a 'radio bomber' and a 'Nazi mystery plane' crashed in Sweden.

The *Daily Sketch* reported that the machine was 'believed by those who saw it fall to be quite a new type, either radio or rocket driven', which had emerged from cloud 'at great speed with a buzzing sound unlike any usual aircraft engine drone.' Readers of the *Daily Mail* learned that the aircraft had been 'radio-governed, without crew' and had been 'carrying two magnetic mines'. The *Daily Express* explained that the machine was 'rumoured to be a radio-directed "flying bomb" ', the first occasion this famous name had appeared in print. Dr Jones and his colleagues knew well enough what the mysterious arrival was, and, thanks to a helpful Swedish Army officer, were able to obtain a specimen of its fuel. An officer sent from London returned clutching a bottle of blue fluid which finally ended speculation about the use of hydrogen peroxide, for analysis revealed it to be ordinary, low-grade petrol. Two British experts – a professor of engineering at the Royal Aircraft Establishment at Farnborough, and a peacetime engineer serving in the RAF – jointly worked out that the flying-bomb was probably powered by a pulse-jet. Final confirmation that the design was aerodynamically feasible came when the drawings they had prepared were put to Sydney Camm, chief designer of Hawkers. Could such a craft, he was asked, carry a sufficient payload to justify its journey? His answer became a classic: 'Can I have a contract for 10,000?'

The other major problem only solved late in the day concerned the flying-bomb's guidance system. The presence of aerials on the launching sites and persistent reports that some missiles carried radio equipment seemed to confirm that the machine must be radio controlled, making it vulnerable to jamming. Here, too, patient deduction, and intensive study of the evidence, led to the proper answer. If the flying-bomb had to be directed by radio, one wing commander suggested, it would be prepared for launching in an ordinary building. If it was to fly independent of ground control, then its compass would have to be pre-set in a non-magnetic building and the square building seen on every launching site fitted the bill precisely.

As D-Day drew nearer the interpreters at Medmenham noted with alarm the steady increase in the number of un-bombed, modified sites:

By the beginning of June sixty-eight* . . . had been found, most of them oriented to the 'London line'. But one rather puzzling thing came to light. Once the concrete bases for the ramp and the square building were laid, nothing more happened. . . . The answer to this was found not in France but at the training centre at Zinnowitz. New cover showed that an additional launching site, of the modified type, was being completed there. . . . Sections of rail six metres long were brought to the site, and there they were fitted together and erected; while prefabricated parts of the square building were also assembled on the spot.

The very day before D-Day Wing Commander Kendall broke this news to a Crossbow meeting in London. Its grave implication was . . . that the modified sites in France, and also perhaps some of the ski sites which had seemed to be abandoned, could be made ready for use within a matter of forty-eight hours.

Although, as a precaution, it was agreed that news of 'the arrival of components for the ramp and the square building . . . should immediately be sent to the Air Ministry,' the significance of the new development was not fully grasped, for reasons which Air Chief Marshal Hill, looking back, explained:

The threat from the 'modified sites' was under-estimated. . . . For many months past the 'ski sites' had been felt as a . . . diversion of effort. . . . The officers responsible would have been hardly human if they had not been . . . reluctant . . . to recognize that the neutral-isation of the 'ski sites' had not averted the menace after all. During the first half of June the Germans were able to press on with their preparations to bombard us with pilotless aircraft virtually unmolested.

---

*Other authorities give the figures as sixty-one by 9 June and sixty-six by 12 June.

7

OPEN FIRE!

The bombardment will open like a thunderclap by night.

Directive issued by Field Marshal Keitel, Chief of the
German High Command, 16 May 1944

The extent of the Allied response to their preparations to
bombard England came as a disagreeable surprise to the Germans. 'If allied bombing continues at its present rate for two
more weeks,' Colonel Wachtel confided on 7 January 1944 to
the War Diary of Flak Regiment 155 (W), with what later
proved unwarranted despondency, 'the hope of ever using the
system operationally will have to be abandoned.' The reaction
of his immediate superior, General Heinemann, was more robust. Heinemann decided, after touring the bomb-battered
countryside of the Pas de Calais, to make a virtue of necessity
and to allow work on the launching sites to continue specifically
to attact more bombs. Meanwhile, he ordered that new sites,
of a far simpler design, and heavily camouflaged, should be
built in woodland, to make them almost invisible from the air.
The new sites consisted only of concrete foundations for the
launching ramp and what Allied interpreters had labelled the
'square building', where the aircraft would have its compass
set. The ski building, so invaluable to Allied photographic
interpreters – it had in fact been given the shape as a protection
against blast – was scrapped altogether. The missiles were now
to be delivered to the site ready fuelled and dispersed among
the trees. Allied experts later calculated it took only 650
man-hours to build each modified site, compared to 1610
man-hours for the ski sites. Once pre-fabricated components
for the launching ramp and the square building had been delivered, a modified site could be made operational in six to
eight days. Flak Regiment 155 now became almost mobile, for

different sites could be used in turn and abandoned if they attracted unwelcome attention from the Allied air forces.

At the same time security and counter intelligence were tightened up. The assembly work on each site was confined to Germans, leave for Wachtel's men was cut, and no one was allowed near the genuine sites without a pass. But no effort was made to conceal the work continuing on the ski sites, which the German had no intention of using, and an elaborate cover plan was devised to suggest that the sites were nowhere near ready to open fire. The story was put about that Colonel Wachtel had returned to Zempin and been replaced by Colonel Martin Wolf – Wolf being in fact Wachtel himself, who, in the course of a taxi ride in Paris, put on a different uniform, and a false beard along with his new name. His staff suffered a similar transformation, leaving their headquarters at Saleux dressed as civilians and travelling to Paris. From here they returned wearing the uniform of supervisory staff of the Todt Organization Construction Office Schmidt, which set up in business at Auteuil. All this play-acting probably did little to confuse the British. Far more serious was the Germans' success in penetrating several resistance networks so that eleven British agents were captured in the first week of March alone.

Meanwhile the bombing of the ski sites went ahead and if the results were not as great as the Allies believed they were still very substantial. The War Diary of Regiment 155 (W) reported that between 15 December 1943 and 31 March 1944 9 sites had been totally destroyed, 35 badly damaged, 29 partly damaged and 20 slightly damaged, a total of 93. Only 11 of the 104 sites so far built by the Germans – some undetected by the Allies – had escaped. Heinemann's decision to abandon the permanent ski sites had been amply vindicated.

So, too, was the drastic simplification of the flying-bomb supply network which he now undertook. The Allies had been right in diagnosing the supply sites as the most vulnerable points in the whole system. The original plan had been for the factories to deliver their output to five large dumps inside Germany, each with room for 2000 missiles, from which they would be forwarded to three field munitions dumps in France, and from there to eight large depots – the supply sites – holding 250 bombs each. These would then provide sufficient missiles to keep up a steady barrage of seventy-two per site every twenty-four hours, and each site would have storage capacity for only twenty-one bombs. Heinemann had correctly reasoned that the Allies would try to strangle the offensive at source once it started by heavily bombing the supply sites. In fact they were attacked before it began and though work on some of them continued they ceased to be used to house flying-bombs. These were now to be stored instead in three new depots, far more difficult to detect, in caves and in a disused railway tunnel, of which more will be heard later. The eight massive concrete bunkers, the Allies' 'large sites', also ceased to play any part in the flying-bomb supply system, though work continued on them in preparation for the opening of the rocket offensive.

Efficient though the Germans were, they were the victims of over-optimism, and because no one was eager to pass on unwelcome truths, the High Command remained in the dark about the true position on the ground. Colonel Wachtel's original target date of 15 December for opening fire had already receded, when, on 23 December, General Heinemann was ordered to begin operations in mid-January, forcing him to reply that this was impossible. On 4 January 1944 Hitler ruled that the attack should start on 15 February, with a mass bombardment of London, supported by a few diversionary bombs fired at other cities. The ideal time, he suggested, would be 'eleven o'clock on a foggy morning'. Goebbels spent a happy morning with the Führer drawing squares on a map of London and calculating how many people each missile was likely to kill. Its inhabitants, he told his secretary, were in for a 'terrific awakening'. But mid-February came and went with little to mark its passing, except an embarrassing scene in which Milch had to tell Hitler the true facts and endure the customary tirade in return. On 1 March, still without a guaranteed flow of missiles, Army Corps LXV filled in time with a 'war game' designed to show up weaknesses in the command structure. The scenario, based on the supposed German response to a 'terror' raid on Dresden, was nothing if not sanguine; London was supposed to have been struck simultaneously by conventional bombers, rockets, flying-bombs and even the long-range gun now being constructed, the first joint salvo at midnight being followed by others during the next six hours. The subsequent 'inquest' confirmed that Wachtel should be able, with twelve hours' advance warning, to open fire within three hours of receiving the executive order, and to bombard London with between 672 and 840 bombs from fifty-six sites, while another eight could discharge 96 to 120 missiles at Bristol. The only difficulty was that the necessary missiles for such an attack did not yet exist. Two weeks after the war game Colonel Wachtel was told, on 17 March, that – even by 15 April – the new mid-month target date – the total stock of flying-bombs would still be only 3000; nothing like enough for a sustained bombardment. By 28 March the date had slipped back again, to the end of April, though Field-Marshal Milch suggested an opening salvo on 20 April, to mark Hitler's birthday. The Allied invasion, Milch pointed out, might come at any moment, and if, as expected, the main landing was in the Pas de Calais 'the launching zones may well become battlefields'.

Among those directly responsible, a sharp difference of opinion had by now developed about the first use of the new weapon. Army Corps LXV, supported by General von Axthelm, favoured what he described to Milch as 'a really sadistic bombardment', consisting of a series of separate salvoes with 'only very few shots . . . interspersed between the mass attacks'. This meant waiting, however, till more flying-bombs were ready, perhaps until June. Milch therefore favoured a continuous, though lighter, rain of flying-bombs, to deny all rest to the defences. 'Every half-hour or so a flying-bomb,' he suggested with relish. 'That will be enough to disrupt the life of this city over a very long period. . . . Twenty days of that will have them all folding at the knees.'

The plan finally recommended by the chief of the Luftwaffe's operational staff, General Koller, was a compromise. His suggestion, put to the Chief of the German Air Staff on 29 March, was for a *Grand Reveille* of 300 flying-bombs two hours before dawn on 20 April, followed by a midday *Salute* of another 100 at noon and ending with a *Grand Retreat* of a final 200 as evening fell. An alternative to the noon *Salute* would be to fire two or three bombs every hour throughout the day. But Hitler, it appeared, had other plans. 'The revenge bombard-

Open Fire!

ment,' he told Goebbels in May, 'is going to be synchronised with their invasion.'

The governing factor, as all along, was the supply of missiles. At the end of December 1943, LXV Corps had laid down a 'realistic' production programme, with 1400 flying-bombs to be completed in January 1944, 1200 and 1240 in February and March, followed by an increase to 3200 in April, 4000 in May and a maximum of 8000 in September.

The figures produced for the Führer's benefit on 5 January 1944 were even more promising. The Volkswagen works at Fallersleben alone, he was assured, would produce 1400 flying-bombs in January and 2000 in February, rising thereafter to the same 8000 a month. In practice there was no prospect of any of these targets being met. During January 1944 not a single missile came off the production lines at Kassel or Fallersleben, due partly to the shortage of skilled labour, partly to continuing problems with the steering gear and diving mechanism. When at the beginning of February Milch asked the Air Staff Engineer responsible 'What is your Fi.103 production now?' he received the frank but discouraging answer: 'Nil', and on the 5th of the month Colonel Wachtel was told that the most he could hope for was a supply of 1000 missiles by July. All now depended on the factories, Goebbels recognized. 'If only our production can meet the occasion!' he remarked to his press secretary in January. 'Thank God we still have Speer!' This was Hitler's attitude, too. 'You will put it right, as you did before,' he told his Armaments Minister. Contrary to widespread belief, Speer could not work miracles, but the final output of flying-bombs, though never as high as Hitler had hoped, did confound the pessimists. Only 400 were turned out in March, but the total rose to 1000 in April, 1500 in May and 2000 (some figures suggest 3000) in June.

As month followed month the failure of the secret weapons to appear became an increasing embarrassment to Goebbels. In his New Year Address to the German People on 31 December 1943 he was noticeably vague. 'The war in the air,' he told his countrymen, 'only gives pleasure to the enemy so long as it is one-sided; when it becomes bilateral the outburst of joy about it will soon cease in the London press.' Although not personally responsible, Goebbels believed that he would be

83

blamed if the wonder weapons proved stillborn. 'He is, so to speak, responsible for the "Revenge", ' wrote his adjutant in his diary, 'because he announced it. . . . The responsibility for retaliation or, rather, its failure to appear weighed like a nightmare on the mind of the minister.' Goebbels was particularly conscious that following one of the recent raids on Berlin he had given his personal word of honour to its citizens that they would be avenged, and he was much encouraged when visiting Hitler's headquarters early in 1944 to find that the Führer still had faith in the secret weapons. 'The English believe now that they have the victory in their pocket,' Goebbels told his adjutant. 'The greater a shock must our retaliation mean to them.'

In the meantime restraint was the order of the day. Early in 1944 Goebbels issued a directive forbidding the use of the term 'retaliation' by the press or radio, and his own references to the subject became increasingly guarded. 'In a not too distant time,' he promised the German people in March 1944, 'the initiative would be in the hands of the Germans again and they would not only match the temporary technical superiority of the enemy, but gain it for themselves.'

'It will not be long before . . . the British people will have to show that they possess the same stoicism as the Germans,' he added on 16 April. 'We have the hardest part of the war behind us, England has it still in front of her.' But the Führer's birthday four days later came and went without the hoped-for salute of flying-bombs. 'May,' wrote Goebbels later, 'passed in an intolerable tension. The retaliation is to be coupled with the beginning of the invasion, the Führer replied to my constant anxious enquiries.'

The Germany Army and Luftwaffe, despite their perpetual feuding, had now done all that could be expected of them. Vesting control of 5000 Luftwaffe men in an Army Corps headquarters, designed to command 40,000 soldiers, seemed absurd, as Colonel Wachtel had pointed out, but General Heinemann had in fact served the Reich well. The modified sites, undamaged, and mainly undiscovered, lay ready, needing only the last-minute addition of prefabricated components to make them operational. Colonel Wachtel, too, had justified his appointment. His men were fully trained and his organization as efficient as good staff work and constant rehearsal could make it. A second war game, on 11 April, had shown up some bottlenecks in the supply process, but these were being put right, and he could now do little more than await the code word *Rumpelkammer* (Junk-room), which had replaced its equally odd predecessor *Eis Bär* (Polar-bear). This was his signal to begin erecting the catapults on the selected launching sites and to bring up to them the first consignments of flying-bombs, to be assembled and prepared for firing. The whole process was expected to take six days, after which the final order to open fire would be received from General Heinemann at Corps headquarters.

On 16 May 1944 the Chief of the High Command – and one of the most servile of all Hitler's entourage – Field Marshal Keitel, issued his final orders in a grandiose directive:

The Führer has ordered:

1. The long range bombardment of England will begin in the middle of June. The exact date will be set by Commander-in-Chief West, who will also control the bombardment with the help of LXV Army Corps and 3rd Air Fleet.

2. The following weapons will be employed:
    (a) FZG 76.
    (b) FZG 76 launched from He.111.
    (c) Long-range artillery.
    (d) Bomber forces of 3rd Air Fleet.

3. Method:
    (a) Against the main target, London. The bombardment will open like a thunderclap by night with FZG 76 combined with bombs (mostly incendiary) from the bomber forces, and a sudden long-range artillery attack against towns within range. It will continue with persistent harassing fire by night on London. When weather conditions make enemy air activity impossible, firing can also take place by day. . . .
    (b) Orders will be given in due course for switching fire to other targets.

On 20 May 1944, with the Allied armadas massing across the Channel, Colonel Wachtel began unobtrusively to withdraw his men from the ski sites, where they had been ostentatiously filling in craters, and moved them to the still intact modified sites. Morale stood high, but Wachtel still wondered anxiously if the new weapon would be used in time. On 2 June 1944 he confided his uncertainty to paper:

These past months have seen a relentless, embittered struggle with the enemy. . . . In this brief lull before our zero-hour, the fight is entering its decisive phase. The big question is: Do we fire first? Or will the enemy by then be across the Channel?

Colonel Wachtel soon received his answer. News of the first Allied landings reached his headquarters at 1.30 a.m. on the morning of Tuesday, 6 June 1944, followed at 5.45 p.m. by the codeword *Rumpelkammer*. Wachtel's staff now stripped off their Todt Organization disguise and put on Army uniforms and, as night fell over the invasion beaches in Normandy, in the Pas de Calais the bulky launching catapults were dragged out of their storage depots and hurried towards the launching sites. Wachtel hoped that the first of the sixty-four modified sites would be ready by the evening of 12 June, and on 11 June he received orders to open fire at 11.40 p.m. on the following day. This first salvo was to be followed by a second at 12.40 a.m. and then by independent fire from all the sites until 4.45 p.m.

But the Germans had in the words of one of their own proverbs, reckoned without their host, or, more precisely their uninvited guest. The RAF's repeated raids had left the actual launching sites unscarred, but the general 'interdiction' programme launched in support of the invasion had wreaked havoc with the French railway system. Trains were held up or shunted into sidings all over Northern France, so that many of the catapults failed to arrive, or were delayed after being transferred to lorries for transport by road. Soldiers and technical staff alike stumbled about in the darkness, worn out from lack of sleep, and not much comforted, one suspects, by Colonel Wachtel's stirring Order of the Day:

After months of waiting the hour has come for us to open fire. Today your wait and your work will have their reward. The order to open fire has been issued. Now that our enemy is trying to secure at all costs his foothold on the Continent, we approach our task supremely confident in our weapons; as we launch them, today and in the future, let us always bear in mind the destruction and the suffering wrought by the enemy's terror bombing.

Soldiers! Führer and Fatherland look to us, they expect our crusade to be an overwhelming success. As our attacks begin, our thoughts linger fondly and faithfully upon our native German soil.

Long live our Germany! Long live our Fatherland! Long live our Führer.

Their long-sustained propaganda campaign had deceived even the Germans themselves. Even such hard-bitten professionals as Field Marshal Keitel and General Jodl, meeting at Berchtesgaden at 5.30 p.m. that afternoon, agreed that once the first flying-bombs were fired there was bound to be at least a diversionary attack in Artois, to relieve the pressure on Normandy, if not the still-awaited landing in the Pas de Calais itself. Wachtel, knowing how far behind schedule his preparations had fallen, would no doubt have preferred to open his offensive with little publicity, but Goebbels was not going to allow the great moment to pass unremarked. Thus into Wachtel's underground command post at Saleux crowded not merely Lieutenant-General Heinemann, eager to share any credit that was going, but also a flurry of senior officials from the Air Ministry, top-level scientists from Peenemünde and a group of eager reporters from the German press and radio. Amid the rising excitement of the 'first night' atmosphere only Wachtel failed to look expectant. The messages that poured in from the launching batteries told of exhausted men, waiting bleary-eyed beside catapults that could not be fired because the vital permanganate of potash needed to produce the explosive mixture was still missing.

Nor was the news from other Luftwaffe formations much more encouraging. It had always been planned to accompany the first flying-bombs with conventional bombardment from long-range sites and piloted bombers. The artillery did duly go into action early on the morning of Tuesday, 13 June 1944, but by 4 a.m., when it stopped, only some thirty rounds had been fired. Not a single German bomber, however, added to the supposed terror and confusion across the Channel, for most of the Heinkel 111s attached to Wachtel's regiment had been destroyed on the ground that afternoon by sheer chance when the Allies bombed their airfield at Beauvais-Tille. Even a Messerschmitt 410 reconnaissance aircraft supposed to report on the expected 'fall of shot' failed to materialize.

As the minutes ticked on towards 2315 hours, when the pilotless aircraft bombardment was now supposed to begin, Wachtel must have realized that he was on the edge of a monumental fiasco. Only eighteen sites of the sixty-four supposed to be operational had fired even a single trial shot, while almost everywhere safety equipment was lacking so that any rounds which were discharged would gravely endanger the launching crew. The full picture of the prevailing chaos only emerged slowly, for Allied bombing had crippled the communications network linking Wachtel's headquarters to his fifty firing positions spread over 5000 square miles. Fifteen minutes before firing was due to begin it became clear that more time was needed. Somewhat oddly, instead of consulting his superior, General Heinemann, who was on the spot, Wachtel telephoned Heinemann's Chief of Staff, Colonel Walter, who had been left behind at Corps headquarters at Maison-Lafitte, to suggest an hour's postponement. Walter refused, whereupon Heinemann took the telephone from Wachtel and countermanded his own Chief of Staff's decision. At 11.50 p.m., 2350 hours, with only twenty-five minutes to go to the new deadline, the start of the operation was postponed again. Instead the battery commanders were told to open independent 'harassing fire' as soon as they could after 3.30 a.m. on Wednesday, 13 June. This was at least a realistic deadline and, by truly heroic efforts, shortly after the appointed hour, ten flying-bombs were whisked forward on their catapults and hurled into the night sky in the direction of England. Half crashed almost at once and one vanished soon afterwards, presumably into the dark waters of the Channel, but four clattered noisily and triumphantly on towards the shores of England. The flying-bomb offensive had begun.

8

DIVER!

*We . . . could see nothing but a black shape with sheets
of flame spurting out behind it.*

Landgirl stationed near Romney Marsh, recalling the
early morning of 13 June 1944

The early morning of 13 June 1944 was cold for the time of
year and there was a threat of rain in the air. The quarter
moon gave little light, for the sky was heavily overcast between
two and five thousand feet, with five to nine-tenths cloud.
Black-out was not due to end till 5.13 a.m. and sunrise was
not till 5.43, but there were a fair number of people about in
Kent, for, after a lull in enemy activity lasting several months,
the Germans were proving unusually troublesome. Soon after
midnight their cross-Channel batteries had fired twenty-two
heavy shells at Folkestone, and, most unusually, there had
been a further eight aimed further inland, which had caused
damage as well as astonishment in Maidstone and the neighbouring village of Otham. At 3.50 a.m. the air-raid warning
sounded over most of Kent, followed just after 4 o'clock by
the all clear and then almost immediately by another warning,
which brought Civil Defence workers in the affected areas back
to a state of readiness.

Scanning the skies from their lonely watchtowers, even before the siren sounded, were the members of the Royal Observer Corps, an all-civilian, mainly unpaid, organization, with
34,000 members, on duty in pairs throughout the twenty-four
hours. Their 1500 observation posts were linked to a Group
Centre, which controlled up to thirty-six posts, the Group
Centre being connected in turn to Fighter Group and Fighter
Command headquarters. Other information for the defences
came from WAAFs and airmen staring unceasingly into the
cathode-ray tubes of the Chain Home network of radar sta-

tions. One of the key stations was high up on Beachy Head, on the Sussex coast, and its personnel included two former fighter pilots sent there as part of their training as future airfield controllers. On the cliffs outside, one of them has written, revolved unceasingly 'an enormous piece of . . . wire netting . . . called a T.1 . . . very hush-hush, very low-seeing. . . . "We're watching for the Hun secret weapon," ' the newcomers were told, as they huddled in the gloom of the dimly-lit bunker. ' "You'll recognise it when it comes – very, very fast, dead straight course, no pilot, just a lot of T.N.T. Code word is Diver." '

In the event it was the Observer Corps who spotted it first. At 4.08 a.m. two part-timers, a greengrocer and a builder, were manning post M.2, on top of a martello tower at Dymchurch on Romney Marsh, when they saw roaring towards them a strange shape, the size of a small fighter, surrounded by a red glare from the rear of the fuselage, and emitting a noise like 'a Model-T Ford going up a hill'. Although they were the first two people in Britain ever to see such a machine, they identified it instantly from the description circulated in April. While one followed the apparition through his high-powered American naval binoculars, the other called into the telephone the message that would soon be spreading through the highest reaches of Whitehall and Washington: 'Mike-Two, Diver! Diver! Diver! one four, north-west one at one.'

Much labour and thought had been devoted to ensuring that when the first flying-bombs arrived they should not creep in undetected and the reporting system worked perfectly. The plotter receiving the call from Dymchurch at Maidstone Observer Corps Centre reacted instantly and, strictly according to the book, shouted 'Diver! Diver! Diver!' across the Operations Room. The air-raid warning officer, on the balcony above, ordered the sirens to be sounded, and the 'tellers' repeated the message to No. 11 Fighter Group at Uxbridge, who were sceptical, believing that if a missile had appeared, one of their own radar stations would have reported it first. However, the suspect report was passed on to Air Defence of Great Britain headquarters at Stanmore. Meanwhile post Mike-Two, its duty done, handed over 'their' Diver, still heading north-west, to post Fox-Three at Pluckley, near Ashford, which passed it to

Easy-Three at Lenham, near Maidstone, who handed it on
again to the neighbouring group No. 19, with headquarters at
Bromley.

While the ROC were following the missile's movements with
professional interest, its clattering progress above the sleeping
countryside had also attracted the attention of many previously
sleeping citizens. Among them was a twenty-one-year-old landgirl, living on her parents' farm at Brenzett on Romney Marsh:

The noise was unlike anything we had heard before. At first we
thought it was a plane with engine trouble but on looking through
the window we could see nothing but a black shape with sheets of
flame spurting out behind it. . . . We all rushed downstairs and outside but it was too dark to see much more. The most amazing thing
was the reaction of the American soldiers stationed around the
area. . . . They let fly with anything that would fire, mostly small
weapons, and it was like a firework display.

These brave efforts left the target unscathed though it was later
rumoured locally that, with his comrades blazing enthusiastically away in all directions, one GI who 'climbed onto a hut
with his rifle' had 'been accidentally shot'. Some of the pre-
vailing excitement appears in the surviving signals sent by an
unidentified American unit to its headquarters that night:
'MOST PILOTS IN THIS THUNDERBOLT BASE CONVINCED THAT
ONE OF GERMANY'S LATEST SECRET WEAPONS PAID THEM
PASSING VISIT ABOUT FOUR A.M. TODAY WHEN PILOTS THEM-
SELVES SITTING IN PLANES WAITING TO TAKE OFF ON MIS-
SION AGAINST ENEMY' ran one message. 'AS PILOTS
CROUCHED INSIDE DEEP BELLIES THEIR THUNDERBOLTS
WAITING GO SIGNAL FROM CONTROL TOWERS THREE LIGHT-
ED OBJECTS WHICH RESEMBLED BALLS OF FIRE MOVED AC-
ROSS SKY ABOUT THREE THOUSAND FEET ABOVE FIELD . . .
OBJECTS GAVE OFF SOUND LIKE ONE LONG WASHING MACH-
INE.' To one lieutenant-colonel from Nebraska 'THEY LOOKED
LIKE SMALL BLADDERS WITH TINY ONE HORSE POWERED EN-
GINE,' while a major from Texas reported that 'ALL MADE
COUGHING CLATTERING SOUND LIKE DIESEL TRUCK!', and a
second-lieutenant from Wisconsin identified it as 'LIKE OLD
PEETWENTYSIX PURSUIT SHIP [i.e. the P–26 fighter] TRAMP-
ING SLAMPING SOUND.' The last word lay with a staff sergeant

from Yonker, New York: 'THEY CAN ONLY SAY SUBQUOTE
BY GOD WE THINK IT WAS SECRET WEAPON THEY ALWAYS
TALKING ABOUT.'

The RAF, as might have been expected, was more restrained
in its reactions. At Gravesend airfield the crews of the Mosquito wing based there were just making for their tents after
a night 'on ops' over Normandy when an exceptionally noisy
aircraft was heard approaching. His instinctive reaction, one
navigator remembers, was to 'comment that the clot couldn't
have realized he had left a light on somewhere'. The local
searchlight crews had also assumed the aircraft was British and
now began to go through the standard 'assistance' procedure,
'lighting the searchlight in a vertical position as near as possible
to the "lost" aircraft, waggling the beam about 15 degrees to
either side in the same vertical plane and then coming down to
a horizontal position indicating the track that the pilot should
follow. . . . As the plane took no notice, the searchlight crews
waggled their beams faster and faster.'

The first flying-bomb to land on British soil fell to earth at
4.13 a.m. on Tuesday, 13 June 1944, at Swanscombe, near
Gravesend, though the official record – starting that process of
identifying a single spot by several different names which was
to continue for the whole of the subsequent campaign – described it as 'Stone, near Dartford'. About the details of what
happened, as reported to the Ministry of Home Security that
day, there is no ambiguity:

The missile fell on agricultural land just to the NORTH of A2 ROCH-
ESTER–DARTFORD road. There was an extremely shallow saucer-
like crater some 15 to 20 feet in diameter with a smaller crater in the
centre . . . from 5 to 6 feet diameter by about 2 feet 7 inches to 3
feet deep. The land on which the missile fell had been covered with
various growing crops – young greens and lettuces – and for a distance
of approximately 80 yards around the crater the whole of the vegeta-
tion had been completely destroyed. . . . Some trees on the opposite
site of the A2 (large oaks) had had a great quantity of their leaves
stripped off. . . . A house nearby had been very severely damaged.

The second flying-bomb landed at 4.20 a.m. in Sussex. Among
those who saw it was Mrs Phyl Bowring, who had moved, just
after the Munich crisis, to this 'old sixteenth century cottage
. . . about one and a half miles from Cuckfield high on the

ridge which runs towards Handcross and some two hundred
yards from the main road down a narrow lane.' Mrs Bowring's
husband, a Territorial, was away in the army and she was
caring single-handed for her young family.

Sarah, then twenty-two months old, was in her cot in a corner of my
room, Caroline (aged six and a half years) and Michael (aged five
years) were sleeping in a large room nearby. . . . After a wartime of
responsibility for the children I slept very lightly and remember vividly
waking suddenly with prickles of fear all over and hearing this sinister,
eerie, grunting noise. . . . I sat up in bed and could see, coming from
the south-west across the night sky, what I took to be one of our
bombers, limping home with an engine on fire. It looked so low I
was sure it could never clear our house and flames were trailing from
it. It was nearly on us as I leapt from bed and flung myself on top of
Baby Sarah in her cot. . . . I can remember the uncanny silence when
the engine cut out and then the ear-shattering explosion, and the
house shaking and shuddering. . . . Terrified screams were coming
from Caroline and Mike. I ran out of my bedroom door and found
them standing crying on the landing, gathering them up on either side
of me in the double bed and tried to comfort . . . them. They kept
saying that they'd been knocked out of bed and I kept saying 'No,
you heard a big bang and were frightened and jumped out'. . . . On
getting up I discovered that the children's story of being 'knocked out
of bed' probably wasn't very far wrong. The windows in their room
were leaded, diamond-shape panes; these were all twisted and buckled and blown out of their frames; . . . and, on going outside, I
found a wide crack running up one chimney, and some dislodged
tiles, but nothing worse. Caroline and Mike looked a bit pale and
heavy eyed, but I reasoned they'd be much better off occupied at
school. . . . Once there, I gather, they soon perked up, especially
when they found their 'bomb story' was hot news and they were the
heroes of the hour.

Mrs Bowring, little knowing that her children's 'bomb story'
was even hotter news than they realized, settled down to clear
up, and to round up her livestock, for the blast had blown
open 'the doors of the pig-sty . . . and large and small pigs
were running everywhere'. She was not left long to herself,
however, for 'soon we had army personnel and police
everywhere'.

A number of very official top brass arrived at the front door wanting
to know where our 'bomb' had fallen and we had to direct them down

the lane to Mizbrooks Farm . . . which was some four hundred yards distant as the crow flies across the fields. A field behind the farm was sown with wheat. All eighteen acres were 'mown' by the blast. This stripped the whole crop to a uniform height. On the high land it was cut off to the ground; as the field sloped, correspondingly more of the stalk was left; at the lowest level only the ears were taken.

The fate of the third flying bomb to be fired that morning will be described in a moment. The fourth and last did not land until 5.06 a.m. at Platt, near Sevenoaks in Kent, a location also described, misleadingly, as 'Borough Green, near Wrotham'. According to the official Air Ministry report it caused 'slight damage but no casualties'. One man then serving with the RAF regiment at Seal, sent to guard the wreckage, 'found that the pilotless plane had landed in the back garden of a very large house. There were some dead chickens lying around and it had made a terrible mess of two rows of greenhouses.'

To some the arrival of the first flying-bomb came almost as a relief. A full-time ROC plotter at the Bromley centre, roused from sleep by her father – she had only come off duty at 11 p.m. – 'to look at this strange object in the sky', immediately identified it and at last felt free to tell him the secret she had hugged to herself for so long. More frustrating was the experience of a bomb disposal officer at the Air Ministry, who rushed downstairs in his pyjamas, eager to be 'the first to yell the secret word into the mouthpiece' as a flying-bomb – no doubt the one destined to land at Cuckfield – passed over his house in Sussex. The GPO telephone girl readily accepted his demand for a priority call but then 'her plaintive voice informed me that it was no use trying. "The switchboard operators at the Air Ministry are all taking shelter," she said.'

Only one pilotless aircraft of the first four to be fired reached London, but it did far more damage than the other three put together. The bomb landed at 4.25 a.m. on the bridge over Grove Road, Bow, which carried the four tracks of the main line between Chelmsford and the LNER (London and North Eastern Railway) terminus at Liverpool Street, in the City. The bridge, a solid late Victorian structure, built in 1871, stood up remarkably well to the impact of mid-twentieth-century explosives, though half of the brickwork just below the north-west parapet collapsed and the two tracks on the down side were torn up. The houses nearby, 'two and three storey terrace type with basements, old and in poor condition,' according to a Home Office report, proved less robust. Two, with nine-inch-thick walls, were demolished and several others up to 320 feet away badly damaged. It was in these houses that the flying-bomb claimed its first casualties.

One of the first Londoners to see the damage a flying-bomb could do was a ten-year-old girl then staying at her grandmother's house in Bow.

The engine stopped, then there was a sound of whistling . . . and the next thing was a tremendous bang and the front room windows came in. . . . After a while the all clear was sounded and then my mother, grandparents and aunt decided to go outside and see what had happened. . . . When we got near the bridge half was lying in the road. All the buildings around were badly damaged or knocked down with the blast. Alongside the railway line was a wall standing of what remained of a public house. The outline of the fireplace could still be seen on the second floor but above that there hung a large glass mirror, not scratched, slightly moving.

By pure chance, the bomb had landed, as a Civil Defence official explained, 'in that part of Stepney which is under the operational control of Bethnal Green' and both seemed eager to claim it as their own, as the group senior operations and control officer,* who arrived at 5.45 a.m., discovered:

Some confusion seemed to be apparent . . . as to which borough was to deal with the incident. . . . Two incident officers' posts were set up within four yards of each other and the deputy controller, Bethnal Green, . . . and deputy controller, Stepney, . . . consulted each other in my presence and seemed to have differences of opinion, as to the demarcation of boundaries in the area. In view of the nature of the incident, it was suggested to these officers that their respective parties should carry on with the work as quickly as possible to extricate the trapped persons and each went off to direct operations.

No one suffered as a result of the divided control, indeed the result was to provide far more helpers and vehicles than were required. 'Bethnal Green,' commented another official, 'are

---

*Each Civil Defence region was sub-divided into a number of groups, which were responsible for several boroughs and held reserves of equipment and specialist staff.

always liable to lose their heads in cases like this and they over-insured in ambulances. . . . There were fourteen . . . at the incident altogether and the total number of casualties is only 32 so far as is known, 4 being dead and 10 . . . detained in hospital.' Being overcautious, however, was a fault on the right side and it is clear that all the Civil Defence services worked smoothly.

Although there could be little doubt that the pilotless aircraft had arrived at last, a great deal of effort was devoted all through Tuesday to confirming its identity. The first two messages sent to group headquarters had referred respectively to a bomb and a crashed aircraft, and a technically qualified official was immediately sent to the site 'to confirm if possible from the bits and pieces' that they belonged in fact to a 'PAC', the abbreviation then in use. By 6.15 he was able to report that 'it was apparent that the missile which had fallen was not a bomb' and 'that there were portions of light metal sheeting on the site, one portion 7 ft 6 in long, being of tubular form, with other portions of small length and about 6 in diameter. Marking on the pieces read "*Nicht Anfassen*" [Do not remove].'

After another expert, a Royal Engineers bomb disposal officer, had confirmed the identification, a thorough search for fragments of the bomb began and every spare pair of eyes and hands was pressed into service. One wartime railwayman recalls seeing the burly men who normally worked in permanent-way repair gangs on their knees like so many charwomen, sorting through the rubble – a task enlivened by a 'good old Cockney voice' calling out: ' "Cor blimey! 'as Jock dropped his tea tanner again?" '

Hardly had the group staff left, than more senior officials from regional headquarters arrived, followed around 1.30 p.m. by an even more high-powered delegation from the Ministry of Home Security, who attempted, as one of them remembers, to 'measure the depth of the crater and the rough areas of blast damage' and to discover 'whether the point of impact was vertical', as it might be from a bomb or rocket, or 'at an angle' as with an aircraft diving into the ground at full power. He found little suspicion in the area as to what had really happened. 'We spoke to several people,' he remembers, 'who thought it was a German plane shot down because "it dropped like a stone" quite suddenly.'

During the next day Ministry investigators painstakingly collected a large volume of similar pieces of testimony, which offered a variety of estimates of the machine's speed – from 150 to 400 m.p.h. – and its height when it began to dive. Equally important was the weight of high explosive it carried. The preliminary report of the Research and Experimental Department of the Ministry of Home Security, produced the same day, estimated that this was 'greater than 1200 kg' of Trialen and less than 2000 kg, i.e. 2646 to 4410 pounds – serious enough but nothing like the ten-ton warheads once feared. The results, however, did provide cause for alarm. Six people, it finally emerged, had been killed, thirty seriously injured and 200 made homeless, while an important road and both local and mainline railway tracks had been blocked, though by heroic efforts the two down tracks were back in operation by 7.45 p.m. the following day, and the other two by 8 p.m. on Friday, the 16th. Tuesday's morning papers carried no reference to the raid but thousands of people knew that a major incident had occurred, for their morning trains were diverted to Fenchurch Street, or stopped short at Stratford and main line services were affected as far away as Bishops Stortford and Cambridge.

None the less, the prevailing reaction in official circles that morning was one of euphoria. The Germans' opening effort had been far more trivial than anyone had dared hope. Setting a lead in unjustified optimism, Lord Cherwell greeted Dr Jones with uncharacteristic jocularity when the latter hurried round to see him. 'The mountain,' boasted Cherwell, 'hath groaned and brought forth a mouse.' He was unimpressed when Dr Jones urged him, 'For God's sake don't laugh this one off,' and refused to persuade the Prime Minister to issue an immediate public statement, though he did go down to Bethnal Green next day to inspect the damage for himself.

The Chiefs of Staff also met Lord Cherwell and Duncan Sandys, and seem to have been infected by the former's complacency. Air Chief Marshal Leigh-Mallory was told that they were not 'unduly worried' by what had happened while Air Marshal Hill 'came to the conclusion,' as he later frankly admitted, 'that so small an effort did not justify the major redisposition of the anti-aircraft defences required by the Overlord/ Diver plan. . . . In the meantime the existing defences were authorised to engage pilotless aircraft on the same terms as ordinary aircraft' – in other words, to shoot them down on top of heavily populated areas, just as Anti-Aircraft Command was proudly claiming to have done a few hours before.

Although many rumours circulated that morning, only a few got near the truth. A fifteen-year-old girl in Greenwich was told by a friend that no trace of a pilot had been found in the wreckage of his plane because he had been blown to pieces. In an East London oil refinery the word went round – no doubt prompted by memories of the Hess mission three years before – that an empty aircraft had crashed because its occupants had previously parachuted to safety, being 'German peace emissaries . . . on their way to end the war'. Other reports spoke of a thwarted invasion attempt, while the biggest liar of the morning was the driver who assured one St John's Ambulance man who had hurried to Grove Road that 'a plane had crashed and . . . he had the remains of the pilot in the van'.

The Civil Defence services, their little local difficulty apart, had done all that could be expected of them, and even this 'frontier' dispute had done no harm. With the other government departments involved it was different. Neither AA Command, the Air Ministry nor the Ministry of Information had much on which to congratulate themselves and, looking back, it is clear that 13 June was an unlucky day on which a variety of things went wrong.

The routine report compiled by General Pile's headquarters, for example, even got the date wrong, attributing the raid to 'the night of 11/12 June' and claiming that 'Ju 88s', believed to be part of a force of 4E/A (enemy aircraft), had 'followed behind a target', i.e. a flying-bomb, 'for 2 or 3 miles' perhaps 'acting as observers'. All this, apart from the presence of the 'target', was mere fiction. The Ministry of Home Security's account based on 'information supplied by 1st A.A.H.Q.' referred to an enemy plane which had 'intruded with returning friendly aircraft' – also a ghost machine. Both AA Command and the Air Ministry believed, the Ministry of Home Security learned, that a solitary Me. 410 reconnaissance aircraft had flown over London until brought down in flames at Barking at

0346 hours. This was also nonsense. The Luftwaffe had intended to accompany its first flying-bombs with conventional bombers, but when the moment came none was available. The Junkers and Messerschmitts supposedly reporting on where the flying-bombs landed were non-existent.

Even the Cabinet, however, was misled by the report from the Chief of the Air Staff laid before it when ministers met at 6.30 p.m.:

Last night the enemy launched an attack by pilotless aircraft against this country. . . . It appears that up to 27 pilotless aircraft may have been employed. . . .

According to reports, the first wave of pilotless aircraft appeared off Folkestone between 0407 and 0440 hours and penetrated Kent, Surrey and Sussex, four penetrating as far as Greater London. The second wave, reported to consist of thirteen aircraft, appeared over the Channel between Dungeness and South Foreland between 0458 and 0520 hours. Nine of these operated over Kent, Surrey and Sussex. The third wave, about which there is still considerable uncertainty, is reported to consist of two to four aircraft, which made landfall between Lyme Regis and Bridport from 0501 to 0535 hours. There was some movement of our own aircraft in this area at the time, and since no incidents have been reported, it may turn out that the aircraft reported were not all pilotless.

Even by the time the meeting started the first estimates of the number of missiles had been scaled down, from twenty-seven to eleven, but the other facts collected about the missiles' appearance and performance were reasonably accurate.

The Cabinet was also reassured by the first details of the bombs' destructive power. 'The reports of the damage done,' Herbert Morrison told his colleagues, 'showed that the effect was no greater than a parachute mine and was rather less than an up to date 2000 lb bomb.' Morrison was concerned, however, about the need to deny the Germans any information as to where their first salvo had landed.

He [the Home Secretary] had arranged with the Ministry of Information that the press should publish no information about the attack on the previous night. . . .
The War Cabinet . . . agreed that no public statement should be made about the new form of attack until the enemy had made it

public or until the weight or extent of attack made a statement desirable. . . .

The War Cabinet also invited the Home Secretary and the Minister of Information to arrange that in future information published about air raids . . . south of a line from the Wash to the Bristol Channel would give no indication where the air raid had taken place, beyond saying that it had occurred in Southern England.

In reaching these decisions – which confirmed those arrived at long before – the Cabinet seem to have been unaware that the harm had already been done. Believing, as it did, that the defences had achieved a victory, the Air Ministry had that afternoon issued a communiqué which duly appeared in late editions of the *Evening Standard*:

RAIDER SHOT DOWN IN EAST LONDON

Two short alerts, the first since April 27, were sounded in London early today. Some districts had three warnings. A raider was brought down in the East End of London.

Several people were killed during the second alert, when bombs fell in a working-class area.

Other German aircraft operated over districts of East Anglia, South-Eastern and Southern England, as well as over the Thames Estuary.

They did not appear to be carrying out any well-defined attack.

Next morning's *Times* was even more explicit, not merely confirming that 'one raider was brought down in East London', but adding that 'part of the wreckage fell on the railway line and the L.N.E.R. announce that some passenger services are being diverted until the damage has been repaired.'

Many people subsequently blamed the authorities for letting the Germans know that at least one of their missiles had reached its target, though the communiqué did *not*, as some people imagined, state that no trace of the pilot had been found. 'A few weeks later,' remembers a then photographer in a Fleet Street news agency, 'the news was circulating that the British censors made a "boob".' And so indeed they had, as the Chief Censor himself candidly admitted.

A news agency report was . . . passed and broadcast on the BBC that a raider had been shot down in the London area and that the wreckage had fallen across the London North Eastern Railway line. Soon after the broadcast I was informed by the Air Ministry that the raider . . . had since proved to be a pilotless plane. . . .

This was most unfortunate. There was no reason now to assume that every piloted plane was not safely back at its base which meant . . . that the enemy knew that at least one flying bomb had reached the London area. I therefore asked editors to be most careful about what they published regarding the previous night's attack. . . . I also requested no reference to the sounding of an air raid alarm in London nor to the bringing down of an aircraft.

With hindsight it seems unlikely that the unfortunate slip, although it invalidated hours of painstaking planning and discussion, really affected the enemy's tactics. The Germans would have continued the bombardment whether they had heard the encouraging news about Bethnal Green or not. More serious was the fact that after all the months of anticipation and vigilance the enemy had achieved tactical surprise.

The interpreters at Medmenham were not to blame. Following a meeting in London on 5 June, the officers specializing in the search had been warned, in a note circulated on D-Day itself, to remain alert:

The main installations are probably pre-fabricated, and might well be installed in a matter of days, once the foundations had been laid. . . . It is therefore of great importance that the interpreters keep a watch for the first indication of a general attempt to put up the missing installations. . . .

But no watch could be kept without new photographs and it was not till 11 June, with the Allies safely ashore, that aircraft could be spared from the invasion and up-dating sorties were resumed with flights over nine of the modified sites. The resulting photographs reached Medmenham later that evening and very alarming they were. Rails had already been laid on four sites, while there was considerable activity at six others. Instantly the Diver signal was sent from Medmenham to the Air Ministry marked 'Immediate', but, owing to some unexplained misunderstanding, it was ignored.

The Secret Intelligence Service had also been doing its job. That same day, 11 June, it had passed on to the Air Ministry a report from an agent in Belgium that two days earlier, on 9 June, he had seen thirty-three railway wagons laden with 'rockets' passing through on their way to Northern France. This clue, too, was simply filed away by the Air Ministry and not passed to Air Chief Marshal Hill, though he later admitted that 'little or nothing would have been gained if I had received it earlier, for . . . I should not have ordered redeployment merely on the strength of these two reports.'

The true reason why the first attack had caught the British off guard was that those at the top had their thoughts and eyes elsewhere. Even when the first flying-bombs did arrive no one was anxious to see aircraft diverted to deal with this new danger. 'I am of the opinion,' Air Chief Marshal Portal told the Cabinet on 13 June, 'that in view of the present inaccuracy and light scale of the attack . . . the air effort diverted should . . . be limited to what can be spared without prejudicing in any way the urgent needs of the battle of France.' Less justifiably, Portal even asserted that 'it is not possible to state whether these pilotless aircraft attacks were delivered from the few "ski" sites which remain not completely damaged, or from the newly discovered modified sites.' His advice was that 'in view of the difficulties attending the attack at the small and well camouflaged sites . . . the supply sites which are suspected of constituting the servicing depots and rail heads of the modified launching sites . . . should be heavily attacked immediately.'

This solution, offering the maximum advantages for minimum cost, was accepted by the Cabinet. All that was done that day and on the two following days was an attack on three supply sites. Meanwhile, wrote Air Chief Marshal Hill, 'The "modified sites" still went unmolested, although it . . . was strongly suspected . . . that the missiles had been launched from sites of this class.'

9

TARGET 42: LONDON

Southern England and the London area were bombarded with very heavy high-explosive missiles of novel design during the last night and this morning.

German High Command communiqué, Friday, 16 June 1944

The Germans were well aware that the unveiling of the first of their terror weapons had proved embarrassingly different from their grandiose expectations. After the first ten flying-bombs had been launched the operation was abandoned, and the plan for a further salvo at 8 a.m., *General Reveille*, was dropped. Colonel Wachtel narrowly escaped being court-martialled, though the failure was not his fault, and it was decided to devote the next three days to ensuring that all the sites were properly equipped. By tremendous efforts fifty-five catapults were made operational within two days, not three, and on Thursday, 15 June, Wachtel sent new orders to his four subordinate commanders:

Open fire on target 42 [London] with an all-catapult salvo, synchronised at 11.18 p.m. (Impact at 11.40 p.m.) Uniform range 130 miles. Then sustained fire until 4.50 a.m.

This time all – or almost all – went well. The bombardment started on schedule and by noon next day 244 missiles had been fired, though forty-five crashed directly after launching, destroying nine sites and killing ten French civilians. Of the remaining 199, one fell in Sussex, near Chichester; one wandered off course, to Framlingham in Suffolk; a large number simply disappeared, but seventy-three got through to Greater London of which eleven were shot down on to the capital.

As each new intruder crossed the coast and roared on inland it left a trail of excited speculation in its wake. One man, then aged fifteen, recalls his next-door neighbour at St Leonards on

103

Sea telling him that aircraft were flying in with their lights on. 'When I heard the next one coming I ventured out of the shelter to watch. I couldn't believe my eyes when I saw the light coming in over the sea and the tracers from the Bofors guns pumping up to meet it.' A man then on duty at Dungeness signal station remembers reporting to his headquarters at Dover Castle that two Spitfires were returning from patrol on fire, only to be put right by the duty officer. Soon 'they were coming in wholesale. I could see about six coming towards us at Dungeness, but there were many more crossing the coast towards Dover and Romney Marsh.'

Astonishingly few people seem to have identified the aircraft correctly. At Eastbourne one warden returned from night duty to tell his wife: 'I think the boys on the guns went mad tonight. A poor devil was coming in with his belly light on and they let him have all they'd got!' At Chatham a sailor on board a destroyer in the dockyard, who had 'slung his hammock between two stanchions near the bridge', was 'awakened by . . . poms-poms and machine-guns going off all around and hundreds of tracer bullets going up.' When he spotted a 'plane . . . with a flame coming from its tail,' he decided 'that it must have been hit . . . I and my pals had not heard even a whisper about flying-bombs.'

This was also the first that H. E. Bates, who was to soon write the history of the flying-bomb, had heard of it – and 'heard' was the appropriate word. He was asleep at home in Kent.

I woke in the middle of the night to a great and hideous noise and the sight of what was clearly a burning aircraft flying low over the roof of the house. . . . Within minutes it was followed by another and then another and yet another. All were flying in the same direction . . . north-westwards, towards London, at the same height and with the same hideous racket. I was greatly mystified and, with four young children in the house, not a little frightened.

Another person thoroughly alarmed by this unexpected phenomenon was a woman staying at Addington with her seven-year-old daughter:

Being the guests of these particular friends was always something of a trial, partly because of their 'If-it's-got-your-name-on-it' attitude, and partly because they never gave me sufficient blankets. If I wasn't shivering with fright in an air raid through which they were sleeping soundly, I was shivering with cold. None of us had the slightest suspicion that another weapon was about to be hurled at England but when the onslaught began I knew at once that some new devilry was afoot. The tempo of it was so different from anything which had occurred before, and the nonstop clackety-clack-silence-BANG! rhythm gave one the impression that, whatever it was, it was unstopp-able. . . . I became so rigid with fright that I couldn't even shiver.

No group living in Kent and Surrey was more intrigued by this new presence in the sky than keen aircraft-spotters like the boys of Ashford Grammar School, among whom was one self-confessed 'aircraft recognition fanatic', aged sixteen.

It was a noisy night. I could identify the Merlin engines of Lancasters coming back from a raid, the odd Mosquito stooged around, Merlins, too, but a different sound. And then a new noise, coming rapidly from the coast, rattling over, with a flashing light . . . and heading toward Maidstone at a speed rarely seen. . . . I decided that they were bombers with 'rough' engines staggering home, but their speed gave the lie to this diagnosis.

Many of the intruders came up the Thames Estuary. Among those on the river that night was Petty Officer A. P. – later Sir Alan – Herbert and his famous motor-launch, the *Water Gipsy*.

On the night of 15–16 June we were lying in a favourite nest inside Tilbury Pier. . . . At 11.35 the sirens went. Something roared over, my mate went out and came back crying: 'Skipper, it's got a *light*.'
   That was the most colourful and crazy scene I remember in the river war. . . . We could see the little lights appearing, far off, like fireflies, over the Kentish hills, and the unprecendented monsters roared in procession over our heads for London. Everything in the river (except the *Water Gipsy*) let off everything it had – steamers, mine-sweepers, patrol boats, all. Sailing-bargemen fired their rifles and rockets. The river seemed to go mad in the face of this new madness. The Bofors battery on the north shore near to us made a noise like a destroyer in action, and the men were yelling. The red 'tracer' bullets chasing the pale green speeding lights from every part of the wide beach made a fantastic figure. . . . As the guns on the south side lowered their trajectory in pursuit of the fleeing targets they seemed to be shooting just over our heads, and I feared for our lives. . . . One of the things came down in, or near, the Tilbury Docks, and all the sailors cheered like mad.

A similarly misguided response occurred all over London that night. A warden in Thornton Heath remembers his fire-fighting squad becoming more and more excited as each distant machine, apparently on fire, dived to earth. 'Look,' one man exclaimed, 'they are shooting the bastards down like flies.' Gradually, however, the very scale of the defences' apparent victory caused doubts to creep in. One man, then an aircrew cadet, remembers how the members of his barrack room, which 'looked across the Rainham marshes . . . towards Kent, . . . began to wonder if there was a new radar system on the guns' as they saw one plane after another apparently on fire, until 'a few of us . . . began to think there was something very peculiar going on, because for three aeroplanes so close together to be hit by our guns was . . . almost miraculous.' But if the planes were not on fire why were they lit up? There was inevitably a 'little old lady' offering a cosy explanation. The lights 'in the cabin' she suggested to a fire officer at Hoo, Kent, clearly meant that these were ambulance planes bringing home the wounded from France: 'Isn't that nice?'

Many people felt, even when they did not know what was happening, a strange sense of foreboding. Among them was a woman living on Primrose Hill, in North-West London, who, as 'an Admiralty inspector of aerial torpedoes, could vaguely imagine all sorts of horrors.'

No one at the house had any sleep till the early morning. . . . The gunfire was terrific. There was a particularly heavy gun near us which we used to call 'The Dragon' because it lived in the railway tunnel. . . . When it fired, bits of stucco would fall into the garden. . . . The weather was very dark and close, [there was] a floating sensation from lack of sleep and a musical theme, left over from Sunday's concert, playing itself over and over in my head. It was Beethoven's Seventh Symphony, Fourth Movement.

Nearer Central London, in Gloucester Place, close to Baker Street, a wartime nurse, Jane Gordon, felt apprehensive as her husband, the journalist Charles Graves, insisted on singing 'Spanish Ladies' to celebrate beating some friends at bridge. 'The last line "And never, no never, will we meet again",' his wife wrote later, 'made a shiver run down my spine.'

After the dress rehearsal three nights before there was no

danger of the Royal Observer Corps being caught off guard. One member, whose post was on the roof of the telephone exchange at Eltham in South-East London, was just falling asleep in the adjoining bunk room when he heard his relief calling out 'Diver! Diver! Diver!'

I was out of bed like a shot and into the reporting zariba. . . . It was not long before our first pilotless aircraft passed over the post . . . the first of many to be seen that night. . . . Just after 0500 hours I took over the head and breast telephone set from Mr D. and he went into the post hut to make some tea. It was then I heard Zebra-Two post (Farnborough) reporting a Diver overhead, travelling north and that the engine had just stopped. . . . I looked south and . . . a small aircraft broke through the cloud, losing height in a shallow dive. I called to Mr. D. who emerged from the hut, teapot in hand. . . . We both realized what the object was at precisely the same time and . . . ducked. The bomb exploded in between North Park and Eltham High Street. . . . Making my way home at 0800 hours, Eltham High Street was without most of the shop windows.

The first of what were to be proudly described as 'Streatham's 41' also arrived that Friday morning, around 2 a.m.

It dived right into the old Empire cinema and a sheet of flame shot skywards as debris, glass and tiles crashed all around. The cinema was in use as an emergency food store, stacked high with tons and tons of tea, sugar and tinned foodstuffs of all kinds. Fire broke out and . . . the heart of the store was 'going nicely' by the time the N.F.S. got there. It was a tricky fire to fight, for it was deep-seated and the firemen had to clamber up tottering mountains of tins and packing cases, with a very real danger of collapse into the fire. The smoke, too, made movement risky. Wardens were to be seen up aloft holding the hose or shining torches to guide footsteps through the smoke.

This incident provided a foretaste for the Home Guard of what was to become their most common duty that summer, guarding damaged property. On this occasion, 'they set about their task,' the same local historian recorded, 'in a thorough manner by throwing a line of men across the width of the High Road and advancing with rifles at the ready, challenging everybody. This had the effect of removing from the scene all unnecessary sightseers and potential looters (if any). By mischance, some members of the Fire Guard were also eliminated by this military manoeuvre but that was "Just one of those things." '

Many Home Guards were by now actively engaging the enemy alongside regular troops. Among them was one man who spent his days in a government factory in Holloway and his nights with a 'Z' battery, of twin-barrelled rocket-launchers, near Jack Straw's Castle on Hampstead Heath.

At about 12.30 a.m. we were rudely awakened by our alarm sounding and . . . rushed back to the site and manned our projectors. Each . . . was fitted with headphones and I remember putting mine on and receiving my first shock. . . . A distant voice said, 'Seventy divers approaching the Kent coast.' I thought to myself, 'Good God. I only thought there would be about ten or twelve at a time, at the most.' . . . Within a few minutes another voice said, 'Approximately forty approaching from the east.' We were all straining our eyes towards central and south London. . . . . We did not have long to wait. The first thing we saw was a number of about twenty tiny flames in the sky, some of which were lit up by searchlights. Every so often there would be a terrific explosion either on the ground or in the air. We watched in awe as they slowly came nearer, but . . . by this time there were only about five or six left . . . right over central London. All of a sudden we saw around a hundred rockets go up together from what we assumed was our site at Battersea Park, about five miles as the crow flies, from us. There were now only three left and these all exploded on the ground around central London. . . . Everything went quiet as the last one exploded and out went the searchlights. . . .

This sequence went on throughout the night, but the intervals grew greater. . . . We did not stand down until after 8 a.m., and I was late for work.

Instead of bringing the customary sense of relief, the arrival of morning with the warning still in force left ordinary citizens more puzzled than ever. The father of one young girl, living in Barkingside, ruled that the authorities 'had forgotten to sound' the usual siren and insisted on her going to work, but 'As my train was pulling into Stratford Station the all clear sounded and everyone on the train cheered. By the time the train was arriving in Liverpool Street station the warning was sounding again. We all knew then that something different was afoot.'

Some people already knew precisely, like the duty driver with a Fleet Street photographic agency, whose rounds had taken him to the Ministry of Information in Malet Street. Deeply impressed on hearing that the aircraft now buzzing over London 'were . . . robots of some description', he woke his wife on his return home around 6 a.m. to suggest taking shelter but his concern was not appreciated. His wife 'turned on her side, . . . mumbled "Don't be bloody silly!" or words to that effect, and . . . was once more asleep.'

One of the first places to suffer from the flying-bombs had been Hastings and rumour was exceptionally active there that morning. 'I bet Phil B. half a crown that she was wrong when she said that a pilotless plane had crashed just by the Bull Inn on the Bexhill Road,' one local resident recorded in his diary for 16 June. 'I lost.'* The thirteen-year-old daughter of a policeman, who had taken refuge with her family in the St Clement's Caves at West Hill, once allegedly the haunt of smugglers but now well equipped as a shelter with 'electric light . . . washing facilities . . . a canteen and bunks', remembers how 'an air of mystery' spread among the shelterers about the aircraft passing over, which deepened when, instead of being obliged as usual to move out by 9 o'clock, 'messages came to us in the morning that we were not to leave the caves, but stay put.'

No section of the community more readily left home that morning that teenage schoolboys, eager to discuss the exciting events of the night. At one school in Croydon the new aircraft, already greeted with delight as an intriguing novelty, soared to new heights of popularity when the boys were told that due to its appearance they were immediately to go home. At Ashford Grammar School 'We knowledgeable ones were confused,' confesses the member of the Aircraft Spotters Club previously quoted. 'Many ideas were put forward, but none of us thought of Hitler's much-vaunted secret weapon.'

That morning even the staff of some government departments were still in the dark. At the Ministry of Supply – ironically enough Duncan Sandys' department – work virtually ceased as the senior warden insisted on sending all the staff

---

*This flying-bomb had, by chance, hit a genuinely military objective, a concrete gun-post – fortunately empty – on the cliff between St Leonards and Bexhill.

down to the basement, as one woman statistician remembers:

We sat on the bunks and chatted or wandered round to meet others from the building, some making light of it, others apprehensive. As the day wore on our bewilderment increased. . . . How long was it going to last, this mysterious emergency? . . . As the canteen was also in the basement the prospect could have been worse.

The attempt to conceal the arrival of the first flying-bombs was abandoned that morning. When the House of Commons assembled Herbert Morrison rose to make a statement which ended all speculation:

It has been known for some time that the enemy was making preparations for the use of pilotless aircraft against this country, and he has now started to use this much-vaunted new weapon. A small number of these missiles were used in the raids of Tuesday morning, and their fall was scattered over a wide area; a larger number was used last night and this morning. . . .

It is important not to give the enemy any information which would help him. Therefore it has been decided that, for the present, information published about air raids in Southern England, that is south of a line from the Wash to the Bristol Channel, will not give any indication where the air raid has taken place, beyond saying that it had occurred in Southern England. . . . All possible steps are, of course, being taken to frustrate the enemy's attempt. Meanwhile the nation should carry on with its normal business.

Morrison then went along to the Prime Minister's room to give the War Cabinet a fuller account of the night's events:

The Home Secretary said that the attack had been much heavier than that made on the night of the 12 June. First reports showed that about 50 persons had been killed and 400 injured, but later reports would probably show a larger number of casualties. . . . While it is [sic] true that the attacks were no worse than the air raids of last February, undoubtedly their nuisance value was high, and he urged that everything possible should be done to minimise them by dealing with the sites from which they were launched.

Then it was the turn of Air Marshal Sir Douglas Evill, the Vice-Chief of the Air Staff, who was surprisingly optimistic. '150 aircraft, 50 of which had fallen in the Greater London area,' he reported, had taken part in the attack, from 'about 40 sites. . . . The aircraft appeared to fly from 1,000 to 4,000 feet, so that they were well within range of light anti-aircraft guns or balloons, and their speed made them very vulnerable to fighter attack. Preliminary reports suggested that about 11 had been shot down by fighters and 12 by anti-aircraft guns.' General Pile, Commander-in-Chief, Anti-Aircraft, who spoke next had an equally cheerful tale to tell. 'According to present information 29 aircraft had been claimed as brought down by anti-aircraft fire.' On the results of the previous night he was convinced that it was 'desirable . . . to continue to use anti-aircraft guns against pilotless aircraft . . . despite the risk of bringing down in the built-up area aircraft which might otherwise pass over.'

Rather surprisingly, this advice went unchallenged, but already the civilian ministers were showing a more realistic appreciation of the danger than their military advisers.

The Minister of Aircraft Production pointed out that the unusual nature of the attacks had led to a certain amount of uneasiness among the workers in war factories. . . . It would be necessary for the Ministry of Information to do what they could to encourage workers to continue full production.

The Prime Minister stressed the importance of avoiding the suggestion that work should be interrupted because of the attacks. . . . The siren should be regarded only as an alert and . . . it was important that the public should be given guidance in that sense.

At 12.15, while the Cabinet was still in session, Admiral Thompson had issued to the press a 'Private and Confidential Memorandum' formally laying down the stricter censorship rules previously discussed. 'Do not,' editors were told, 'publish the report of the sounding of an air raid warning in the London area. . . . Do not publish the shooting down or the crashing of an aircraft whether pilotless or piloted without submission to censorship.' Obituary notices for people killed by enemy action were rationed to 'not . . . more than three . . . from the same postal district . . . in any one issue' and a ban was imposed on reporting without permission the 'change of address of any persons or firms' in 'Southern England'.

The nation learned of the new attack from the BBC One O'clock News. True to the policy of playing down what was happening, the BBC led the bulletin with the unexciting news that 'No big change in Normandy is reported this morning' and the major story of the day followed a routine item about an RAF raid on Boulogne.

The enemy has started using pilot-less aircraft against this country. A few were over Southern England in the early hours of Tuesday morning, and more were over last night and this morning. Mr. Herbert Morrison has made a statement about them in Parliament.

Very few people had access to a radio at work and most gained their first knowledge of this new complication in their lives from the evening newspapers, which 'led' their front pages with it. 'London under attack by pilotless aircraft' ran a typical headline. One stop press report, however, must have puzzled the Ministry of Information, for it asserted categorically that the flying-bombs were radio-controlled. The explanation was revealed thirty years later. A reporter on the *Bournemouth Evening Echo*, having inspected 'on the untidy outskirts of London . . . a smoking hole where lots of bits and pieces . . . and wire . . . lay entangled around the scene of the explosion,' had failed to notice that the wire 'had come from adjacent telegraph poles destroyed in the explosion'.

The imposingly entitled, but pointless, Staff Conference held while lesser citizens were enjoying their tea seems to have been Churchill's own idea. Neither a meeting of the War Cabinet, nor of the Chiefs of Staff, it achieved nothing except to make further demands, at a busy moment, on the time of Air Chief Marshall Tedder, Air Chief Marshal Hill and General Pile. The future Lord Alanbrooke, who had had to endure Churchill's time-wasting loquacity on many previous occasions over the years, was not impressed. 'Very few real decisions were arrived at,' he wrote in his diary. 'In my mind three essentials stand out: (a) attacks by what can be spared from Overlord on launching sites; (b) barriers of fighters, guns and balloons in succession south of London; (c) no sirens and no guns in London. We shall, I hope, eventually get there but it will take time.'

What the nation's commanders got instead was a four-point plan not even sent out by the Air Ministry till the following day:

At Staff Conference held yesterday by Prime Minister it was agreed:

Target 42: London

(a) To request the Supreme Commander, Allied Expeditionary Force, to take all possible steps to neutralise the supply and launching sites, subject to no interference with the essential requirements of the Battle in France.

(b) That the air raid warning should not be sounded on the approach of a single pilotless aircraft. At night, the sounding of the siren should be reduced to the minimum and the warning should be sounded only on the approach of the first 'covey'.

(c) That, for the time being, pending further experience, the anti-aircraft guns, both inside and outside the London area, should continue to engage pilotless aircraft.

(d) That the Air Marshal commanding A.D.G.B. in consultation with the G.O.C. in C., Anti-Aircraft Command, should redistribute the gun, searchlight and balloon defences, as necessary, to counter the attacks.

(e) That the Air Marshal commanding A.D.G.B. should consider the use of armed cables on those balloons deployed against pilotless aircraft.*

Long before the Air Ministry signal belatedly confirming these decisions was dispatched, they had already been put into action. Hill had already 'given orders for the deployment of the Diver defences to begin' and thanks to his foresight and Pile's energy the first guns were already on Friday evening moving south through the summer darkness, while overhead, between banks of thick cloud, officially described as '10/10ths at 2,000 feet with a further layer of 10/10th cloud at 5,900 feet,' Göring's new toys still roared and rattled towards London. At Brasted, midway between Sevenoaks, where one of the first four flying-bombs had landed, and Churchill's country house at Westerham, a conscientious head warden noted in his logbook that the cloud had broken up into 'occasional banks', between which one could glimpse 'a bright starlit night'. His last entry for Friday, 16 June, recorded a final all clear at around 9.40 p.m., but at 0045 on the morning of Saturday, 17 June, a new entry reported the sounding of the first siren of the new day and the arrival of six new PACs, the first of a whole series to pass overhead between then and dawn. This, though no one had yet fully realized the fact, was to be the pattern of life in the Garden of England for many weeks to come.

---

*For an explanation of this instruction see page 426.

10

THE GUARDS CHAPEL

*I was still in bed working at my boxes when my wife returned.
'The battery has been in action,' she said, 'and the Guards
Chapel is destroyed.'*

Winston Churchill, recalling Sunday, 18 June 1944

The first weekend of the flying-bombs was also the worst,
Saturday was still a working day for most people and as they
waited for their trains weary, sleep-starved citizens in the great
commuter belt to the south and east of London smiled at
Vicky's 'Weekend Fantasia' in the *News Chronicle* which
showed two German airmen suspended on a cloud over the
caption 'Planeless pilots'. The *Daily Mail* had also tried to raise
its readers' spirits with a cartoon entitled 'The Stable's Last
Hope', showing a radio-controlled horse identified as 'Pilotless
Plane, by Lack of Manpower out of Desperation'. On the
whole, however, these well-meaning efforts had little effect;
'Hitler's secret weapon', so long a joke, had already turned
out to be anything but amusing.

The newspapers also carried that morning a note of guidance
from the Ministry of Home Security:

For the general public the advice is that if they see or hear one of
these things, or hear gunfire near, then they should keep under cover.
When the engine of the pilotless aircraft stops and the light at the
end of the machine is seen to go out it may mean that explosion will
soon follow, perhaps in five to fifteen seconds. . . . So take refuge
from blast. Those indoors should keep out of the way of blast and
use the most solid protection immediately available. There is no
reason to think that raids by this weapon will be worse than, or
indeed as heavy as, the raids with which the people of this country
are already familiar and have borne so bravely.

The weather was grey and close, creating an oppressive atmosphere that depressed the spirits, and life everywhere in

London and Kent that afternoon was dominated by the new menace. The writer Mrs Robert Henrey, who had deserted her flat in Mayfair to visit friends near Sevenoaks, watched the 'flying bombs thundering towards London . . . just above the treetops at over three hundred miles an hour. In two and a half minutes,' she reflected, 'they would be crashing down on the capital.' But it was not only London which was suffering, as she soon discovered.

We had walked across a lawn golden with buttercups and shaded with copper beeches and into a wood where hazels grew . . . when we suddenly noticed the undergrowth strewn with green leaves . . . nearly a foot in depth . . . not brown and curly as in autumn, but young and tender in all their strength. . . . They might have been blown there by some giant, puffing with all his might. . . . Then we came upon what was once a coppice, but now looking . . . like a stretch of burned heath . . . and in the centre of it lay a young rabbit without a head. . . . Down the hill . . . at the bottom, we came upon some twisted metal – all that remained of a flying-bomb which, during the night, had whistled over the roof of the big house. . . . A few minutes later [we] came on a cottage . . . ripped open by blast. The head of an iron bedstead and a child's toy lay in the front garden amongst the flaming peonies.

Mrs Henrey was glad on her return journey to be sharing the carriage with two 'young Guards Officers – mere boys – who were to attend morning service the next day at the Guards Chapel in Wellington Barracks.'

For people living in South London it had been an even less peaceful Saturday. At 4 o'clock, just as Mrs Henrey was having tea with friends of her hosts at Ightam Mote, a flying-bomb had dropped on the busy shopping centre of St John's Hill, near Clapham Junction, while the weekly shopping rush was at its height. The first message, from Lavender Hill Police Station, reporting the explosion of a 'glider plane', reached Battersea Control at 4.04 p.m. A call for ambulances and rescue parties followed a minute later. The missile had landed in the road, badly damaging the Surrey Hounds public house, wrecking two passing trolley buses with heavy casualties, demolished three properties and partly destroyed a whole row of shops. With the road blocked, the effects were felt over a wide area, and the final casualty toll was the worst so far; twenty-four killed and twenty-five seriously injured, although these figures were not released until three months later.

That Saturday Charles Graves's wife, Jane Gordon, had a few hours off from the Paddington hospital where she worked:

Sister and I sallied forth to see David Niven's new film [*The Way Ahead*] at the Odeon, Leicester Square. There were five alerts and five All Clears during the performance. . . . We came home by bus and by a coincidence sat behind Dick and Rosemary. 'Dick has got his majority,' I whispered to Sister, and pointed out the crowns on his shoulders which he had sported for the first time on Thursday when we played bridge. The four of us had a little talk and laughed about the alerts. They had been to see Danny Kaye at the Empire [in *Up in Arms*, which had opened there that day], and told us that he was very funny.

Also at the pictures that afternoon was Vere Hodgson, a voluntary social worker who lived in Ladbroke Road, Notting Hill. 'All through we had across the screen "Air Raid Warning",' she wrote in her diary that night, 'then "All Clear". Three times. But the audience was in a light-hearted mood and laughed aloud. We had not learned then to take the robots seriously.' On leaving the cinema and hearing that 'something had fallen on St Mary Abbot's Hospital . . . went along Marloes Road. . . . Great piles of glass marked the route. Heavy rescue lorries were driving in and out gathering up the debris. All one roof of the hospital gone . . . about 4 a.m. Saturday. . . . One woman said twelve children were brought out dead. . . . Many nurses [said to be] killed.* Heard another had fallen at Marble Arch, and in Putney.' Already the frivolous attitude she had observed that afternoon was vanishing. 'London,' she decided, 'is in a chastened mood.'

In Berlin, and at the headquarters of LXV Corps in France, the atmosphere was very different. Colonel Wachtel, his reputation vindicated, sent a self-congratulatory telegram to the High Command: 'May our triumph,' he wrote piously, 'justify all the expectations which Front and Fatherland have bestowed upon our weapon.' Hitler, paying a surprise visit to his forward headquarters at Margival, was also in unwontedly genial spirits. He congratulated General Heinemann and Colonel Walter,

---

*See p. 234 for a fuller account of this incident.

and declared himself proud that Germany was 'fighting with
such weapons'. On no account, he ordered Heinemann, must
flying-bombs be used against any other target than London,
and once back at Berchtesgaden, the Führer ordered Speer to
increase flying-bomb output, even at the expense of the rocket.
'The Führer decides,' Speer noted, 'that A.4 production is to
be only one hundred and fifty a month until further notice.
The labour and materials thus released are to be used . . . for
peak production of "cherry-stones".'

The Allied commanders, by contrast, found little about
which to feel cheerful in the report circulated by the Director
of Operations at the Air Ministry on that morning's
bombardment:

The attack by pilotless aircraft continued. Some 120/140 are estimated
to have been launched during the night of which 80/90 were plotted
over this country. Activity started at 0040 hours and continued until
0610 hours. . . .

The target was the Greater London area which received approximately 50% of the P.A. which crossed the coast. The remainder
impacted in KENT, SUSSEX and SURREY, and compared with the previous night, there were fewer impacts to the North of London. An
isolated P.A., however, exploded near BILLERICAY in ESSEX. . . .
There was a greater concentration than on the previous night, particularly in the area South of LONDON.

There were also disturbing signs that the Germans were beginning to improve their aim:

Home Security report that 14 London Boroughs were struck by P.A.
The most serious instances occurred at CAMBERWELL, at KENSING-
TON, where St. Mary Abbotts Hospital received a direct hit, at LEW-
ISHAM and in SUTTON. 7 of the P.A. exploded in the Borough of
CROYDON. Total casualties reported up to 0600 hours 17 June were
18 killed, 166 seriously and 83 slightly injured.

The defences' response had so far been only modest:

A total of 27 night fighters and 10 Intruders were operating . . . the
latter off the French coast. . . . Claims so far are:

  3 P.A. and 1 Me. 410 destroyed by night fighters.
  4 P.A. destroyed by Intruders.

A.A. Command claim 22 P.A. destroyed. Although a number of

these were blown up in the air, it has not yet been confirmed whether all the remainder were in fact due to A.A. fire or whether they had merely reached the end of their run.

For the moment the initiative clearly lay with the Germans and all through Saturday evening and on into the hours of darkness the launching sites were busy. Already the south-eastern boroughs, and especially Croydon, Wandsworth and Battersea, were coming off worst. Streatham, a closely built-up part of Wandsworth, a borough with a pre-war population of just over 350,000, was already taking on the appearance of a front-line outpost. After a forty-eight-hour lull, following the Globe cinema incident, it suffered on Sunday morning from three flying-bombs in twenty-five minutes. The night was pitch dark. As the ARP workers stumbled about their demanding tasks – one alone ushered 150 people into a rest centre* – the guns kept up an incessant barrage at the stream of intruders roaring overhead. But the casualties were mercifully light: even in the worst incident only two people were killed and thirty-eight badly hurt. But the damage was enormous. A later count revealed that the three missiles between them had damaged 3000 properties; one alone had affected 1671. Many of the houses still habitable lacked cooking facilities and that afternoon the LCC meals service opened up in a local hall, while the homeless were removed to a rest centre in Green Line coaches.

In place of their customary Sunday morning parade the Home Guard that day came to the aid of the civil power, helping to clear the debris, and though a civic service was held as planned the noise of further aerial intruders in the distance made embarrassingly clear that victory was as yet far from won. It was 10 p.m. that night before the last of the Streatham incidents was declared 'Closed'.

Battersea suffered three incidents that day: at 5.30 a.m. when three people were killed, at 8.45, when a flying-bomb came down in a cemetery, disturbing only the dead, and, far more seriously, around 12.45, when many people were enjoying a pre-dinner drink. The first message to reach Battersea

---

*This was Miss Windyridge, known affectionately as 'Windy', who was something of a local celebrity.

Control about this last said simply 'Casualties, Big Incident', which was no exaggeration. When the books were finally closed it was found that nineteen residents of Battersea had died that Sunday lunchtime, at least thirty-five had been seriously injured and another eighty-four slightly hurt. From the borough records one can still recapture some of the grim flavour of that bloody Sabbath. 'Y Post report the finding of a hand at 24 Tennyson Street,' reads one surviving message. 'Have they', asks another addressed to the mortuary from K post, 'a female unidentified body, aged 76, inclined to stoutness, grey hair, 5 feet 5 inches height?'

Just about the time of the Tennyson Street bomb, another, even more disastrous, landed on Putney, which for ARP purposes was part of Wandsworth. The official report on what became known as the Quill Bridge bomb, described it as a 'direct hit on shop premises at the junction with Charlwood Road,' which 'caused the collapse of several shops and major damage to house property on the north side of the Southern Railway and temporary blockage of [the] permanent way by debris.' This brief, unemotional account gave, however, little inkling of what had happened in this peaceful suburban street. The rubble from the wrecked property slid down into the cutting while four heavy rescue and nine light rescue parties struggled to find and remove the families buried beneath the ruins of their homes. A week later, with twelve bodies and twenty-five seriously injured people already recovered, the full toll was still uncertain, but sixteen people remained unaccounted for and a WVS inquiry point was still busy close by at the 'junction of Gwendolen Avenue with Upper Richmond Road'.

On the far side of the Thames it had also been a noisy night and morning. 'Hour by hour,' wrote Jane Gordon of events in Gloucester Place, Marylebone, 'the noise of the raid increased and at dawn there was such a racket that . . . we went out in our dressing gowns to see what we could see and met most of our neighbours.' Jane Gordon learned that 'the flying-bomb had fallen . . . on the convent in Bayswater Road' and 'sauntered out to look. . . . Edgware Road and Connaught Square was strewn with glass. Bayswater Road was a shambles.'

A mile further south, near Piccadilly, Mrs Robert Henrey

had been listening to 'flying-bombs . . . droning away in the distance, each ending with a muffled explosion':

At first we took no notice but just after eleven o'clock when the church bells had stopped ringing, the roar of one of these pilotless planes came ominously near, growing in intensity every second. I . . . ran out into the passage. The noise was now deafening. . . . The missile appeared to be headed straight for the roof. . . . There was a terrific crash and the building shook. Then a heart-rending silence which lasted about thirty seconds, quickly followed by the sound of people running in the street.

Until that Sunday morning, although humbler boroughs to the south and east had already suffered from several missiles, not a single one had landed within the City of Westminster, which contained not merely the Houses of Parliament and 10 Downing Street, but almost all the major government departments. Then in the early hours of Sunday Westminster's first flying-bomb had landed on Hungerford Bridge, which carried railway lines across the Thames between Charing Cross and Waterloo, damaging the track but hurting no one. At about ten to nine it had received its second bomb, 'when', wrote the novelist William Sansom, a wartime fireman and Westminster's future historian, 'there rose into the air above the rooftops the first giant plume of dust that was to be the mark of these explosions.' The dust came from the ruins of Carey Mansions, a block of flats in Rutherford Street but though the explosion killed ten, and seriously injured fifty-two people, 'the incident as a whole,' wrote Sansom, 'presented no particular difficulties.'

Westminster's third flying-bomb, and about the 500th to be fired by Colonel Wachtel's minions 130 miles away, was very different, and many people observed the last few tragic seconds of its flight as it appeared to hover 'over the high black shape of Queen Anne's Mansions', in Queen Anne's Gate, then used as naval offices. One Wren remembers how little attention the warning had attracted; most people had not yet seen what a flying-bomb could do. 'I personally did not hurry,' this informant remembers, 'but put on my jacket and strolled out into the corridor – just in time.'

The bomb was heard, but not seen, by Dr R. V. Jones, in the MI6 headquarters at 55 Broadway:

I was in my office talking to one of my sources on the telephone when a flying-bomb came over and the engine cut out and I said to him, 'It is going to be pretty near, we are just getting under our desks, wait for it!' There was an enormous explosion . . . and I rushed out of the office to find out what had happened.

The Guards Chapel was, like other well-loved buildings, to acquire after its destruction merits it had never possessed in its life. The original interior, dating from 1838, had been considered by the *Household Brigade Magazine* 'chiefly remarkable for its sheer ugliness', but in 1875 it had been transformed through lavish redecoration 'in the Lombardo-Byzantine style', which included a mosaic presented by Queen Victoria: 'Be thou faithful unto death and I will give thee a crown of life.' Below 'stood the band galleries,' wrote one visitor 'where . . . played the bands of the various regiments of His Majesty's Footguards.' Here, in peacetime, 'in solemn grandeur hung their colours, some shrouded in net, dating back to the days of the Crimea'. The colours had been removed, thus surviving when the wooden roof was burned by incendiary bombs in 1940; the roof had since been replaced by fire-resistant, but far weightier, brick and stone.

Sunday morning matins at the Guards Chapel was a fashionable occasion, but not restricted to what was later called 'the Establishment'. The nurses of St Giles Hospital, Camberwell, frequently joined the congregation though that morning they were too busy coping with flying-bomb casualties. The Chaplain General to the Forces had preached there two months earlier on Easter Sunday. Many of the congregation had noticed that 'his voice shook a little as he spoke to them of "our loved chapel" ' and afterwards he had 'confided to a friend, his impression of a strange unfamiliar sadness and doom overshadowing the sacred precincts.'

Among those present on the morning of Sunday, 18 June 1944, was a young ATS subaltern, Elizabeth Sheppard-Jones, who had walked across the park to the service with a girlfriend.

We sat near the back of the chapel and watched the people come in . . . I . . . remember some of the people I saw, in particular a young

Canadian Lieutenant who eagerly surveyed his surroundings as if to memorize the details that he might write them down in his next letter home. . . . In the gallery . . . a band of Guardsmen began to play . . . instead of an organ. . . . We sang the opening hymn. My mind must have wandered during the reading of the first lesson . . . I dare say I was thinking about my forthcoming leave. . . . 'Here endeth the first lesson,' the Guards' colonel who had been reading it must have said. The congregation rose to its feet. In the distance hummed faintly the engine of a flying bomb. 'We praise thee, O God: we acknowledge Thee to be the Lord,' we, the congregation, sang. The dull buzz became a roar, through which our voices could now only faintly be heard. 'All the earth doth worship Thee: the Father everlasting.' The roar stopped abruptly as the engine cut out. . . . The *Te Deum* soared again into the silence. 'To Thee all Angels cry aloud, the Heavens, and all the Powers therein.' Then there was a noise so loud it was as if all the waters and the winds in the world had come together in mighty conflict and the Guards' Chapel collapsed upon us in a bellow of bricks and mortar . . . One moment I was singing the *Te Deum* and the next I lay in dust and blackness, aware of one thing only – that I had to go on breathing.

While Miss Sheppard-Jones was struggling to free herself, Dr R. V. Jones was hurrying to the site down Birdcage Walk.

I had . . . been used to the flying bomb. I knew its warhead was going to be about a ton. I knew what a ton of high explosive could do. . . . [But] it struck me then how very different the academic appreciation of explosions was from the actuality. The Guards Chapel was about 150 yards from my office and by the time I'd got down to the . . . Chapel they were just carrying out the first dead. . . . One lasting impression I had was the whole of Birdcage Walk was a sea of fresh pine tree leaves, the trees had all been stripped and you could hardly see a speck of asphalt for hundreds of yards.

Also rapidly on the scene was the Chief Warden of Westminster, who had been nearby at the Rutherford Street incident:

The whole floor was covered by debris, which blocked the portico entrance; on both sides the debris rose to 10 ft, lessening in the centre. Apart from some movement at the east (altar) end there was a ghostly stillness over the whole scene. I appreciated at once that the incident was a rescue job from first to last. Doubling the length of the barrack square to the officers' mess, I spoke over the telephone to the Deputy Heavy Rescue Officer at Control, gave him a word picture of the scene and suggested Heavy and Light Rescue Parties, mobile cranes and ambulances. Two senior Rescue Officers with parties, ambulances and cranes were quickly on the scene and rescue operations then put in hand continued without a break for 48 hours.

So far the casualties at most incidents had proved less than expected – but not this time, as William Sansom graphically described:

To a first aid party that soon arrived the scene in its subsiding dust looked vast and boxlike, impenetrable; sloping masses of the grey walls and roof shut in the wounded; the doors were blocked; the roof crammed down; it was difficult to find any entrance; but there was one – behind the altar. From then on it became a matter for nurses and doctors to scramble up and down and in between the large intractable slopes and walls of chunked concrete – the same as in a low-tide rock formation, but here gritty and powdered everywhere with the lung-choking dust. These rocks of material had to be man-handled off casualties. While doctors were plugging morphia, and nurses and first aid personnel were feeding bicarbonate solution and wrapping on . . . dressings, all rescue services, together with soldiers from the barracks . . . the King's Guard had just been dismounted and were waiting for dismissal in the barrack square . . . began prising up the debris-blocks and carrying out those freed.

Among those still lying beneath the debris was Elizabeth Sheppard-Jones:

I felt no pain, I was scarcely aware of the chunks of massed grey concrete that had piled on top of me, nor did I realize that this was why breathing was so difficult. My whole being was concentrated in the one tremendous effort of taking in long struggling breaths and then letting them struggle out again. It may have been an hour later, perhaps two or three or more, that . . . I was suddenly aware that somewhere far above me, above the black emptiness, there were people, living helpful people whose voices reached me, dim and disembodied as in a dream. 'Please, please, I'm here,' I said, and I went on saying it until my voice was hoarse and my throat ached with the dust that poured down it. . . . Someone frantically scraped away the rubble from around my head. . . . Somewhere not far away from me someone was screaming, screaming, screaming, like an animal caught in a trap. . . . My eyes rested with horror on a blood-stained body that, had my hands been free, I could have reached out and touched . . . the body of a young soldier whose eyes stared unseeingly at the sky. . . . I tried to convince myself that this was truly a nightmare, one from which I was bound soon to wake up. I think I must have been given a morphia injection for I still felt no pain, but I did begin to have an inkling that I was badly injured. I turned my freed head towards a Guardsman who was helping with the rescue work, and hysterically I cried out: 'How do I look? Tell me how I look!' . . . 'Madam,' he said, 'you look wonderful to me!'

Much later, at St Mary's Hospital, Miss Sheppard-Jones learned the truth. 'My spine was fractured and my spinal cord damaged . . . I was paralysed from the waist down.' That morning's walk across St James's Park had been the last she was ever to take. It was even longer before she knew the fate of her friend, whose father after a long search, found his daughter's body 'on a mortuary slab. . . . Her neck had been broken, probably by the same piece of masonry that had broken my back.'

Sensibly enough, lunch was served as usual in the officers' mess, but in at atmosphere of deep gloom. 'One was so anxiously looking all the time at the door to see who was coming in,' remembers one man who had missed the service, thanks to an unexpected duty. He waited in vain for the friend beside whom he should have sat in chapel. 'No one had seen him that morning. . . . Had he been there? He had.' Long before the final casualty figures were known, news of the disaster had spread through London. The Prime Minister had spent the morning in bed at Chequers working on his boxes, but his wife, who had been to London to visit their daughter Mary, serving with an anti-aircraft battery in Hyde Park, returned with the sad news. 'The battery has been in action,' Mrs Churchill told her husband, 'and the Guards Chapel is destroyed.' 'I gave orders at once,' Churchill later wrote, 'that the Commons should retire again to the Church House, whose modern steel structure offered somewhat more protection than the Palace of Westminster.' Others were equally alarmed by what had happened. Every top civil servant or society hostess knew someone in the Brigade who might have been at Wellington Barracks that morning. Mrs Robert Henrey, remembering the two young officers she had met on the train from Sevenoaks the previous evening, observed how 'the news of this catastrophe . . . cast a gloom over London for it was the first major tragedy occasioned by this new weapon in the heart of the town.' 'All day,' wrote Jane Gordon, 'we kept hearing of more people we knew who had been killed,' and around 2.30 she was telephoned by the distraught wife of the young officer, so proud of being promoted major, with whom they had played bridge only two nights before. Her reaction, even after visiting Wellington Barracks for herself, was incredulity. 'This couldn't have happened to Dick. Why . . . we four had shared so many Blitz evenings. . . . It was only yesterday we were laughing on top of a bus.' But happened it had, for at last on Tuesday night their dead friend's body was recovered, one of the last bodies to be dragged from the rubble.

The Guards Chapel incident was by far the worst of the whole flying-bomb campaign. One hundred and nineteen people, mainly servicemen, were killed, and 102 seriously injured, some of whom later died; 39 others escaped with minor injuries.

Everyone agreed that the Civil Defence services had worked superbly well, and there had been no interruption from curious passers-by or anxious relations, since, as the chief warden of Westminster explained a year later in *ARP Review*, 'the barrack railings and Military Guard formed an effective barrier against the crowds which collected . . . and the barrack square was an ideal place for parking vehicles and loading casualties.' Civilians and military had worked side by side in harmony. 'The Incident Officer's headquarters and later the Incident Enquiry Point . . . were set up in the Guardroom and during darkness Royal Engineers and N.F.S. supplied lighting over the whole incident.'

Among those who heard of the destruction of the Guards Chapel late that day was the writer James Lees-Milne, who was told of it by a friend at his club.

After dining we walked through Queen Anne's Gate, where a lot of windows with old crinkly blown glass panes had been broken. In St. James's Park crowds of people were looking at the Guards Chapel across Birdcage Walk, now roped off. I could see nothing but gaunt walls standing, and gaping windows. No roof at all. While I watched four stretcher bearers carry a body under a blanket, the siren went, and everyone scattered. I felt suddenly sick. Then a rage of fury welled inside me. For sheer damnable devilry what could be worse than this awful instrument?'

11

IN THE FRONT LINE

Flying bombs have again put us in the front line.
Diary of Lord Alanbrooke, Monday, 19 June 1944

On Monday, 19 June, people in London and the South-East settled down to a new way of life. Already there seemed to be damage everywhere. The Chief of the Imperial General Staff, Sir Alan Brooke, later Lord Alanbrooke, observed with irritation in his diary that Monday morning that 'most of the windows of the War Office' had been 'blown in again'. The shadow of the Guards Chapel also hung heavy over Whitehall. 'On my writing-table,' he noted, recording his 'great grief' at the death there of an officer friend, 'was a letter from him written on Saturday. I cannot get him and poor Blanche out of my mind.'

In one respect Monday was quieter than Sunday. Alan Brooke had not been alone in concluding that it made no sense to shoot pilotless aircraft down on to London. The Chief Censor had made the same suggestion to Herbert Morrison to be told, 'Admiral, great minds think alike,' and the Civil Defence Committee minutes on Monday duly recorded that the guns in London would refrain from firing 'for the time being'. In fact they stayed silent for good, since it had become clear that fewer missiles than hoped were being exploded in the air.

The decision, though clearly the right one, left many people feeling uneasy, among them James Lees-Milne.

Whereas previously I cursed the guns for the ceaseless noise they made throughout the night, now I find that without them I am more frightened. Quite irrationally I feel let down. The lack of guns strikes me as an admission of failure in defence. Instead I lie awake for hours and hours, my ears waiting for the sound of rocket planes. Here in Cheyne Walk we have distant trams, trains, motor vehicles and river traffic which one mistakes at first for a plane. This night I was awake until five.

Another change agreed by the Civil Defence Committee that Monday morning was more valuable to morale. 'Pilotless aircraft', argued Herbert Morrison, was an unsatisfactory name for the new weapon, since it implied a mechanical monster impervious to human interference. 'Flying-bomb' was both more accurate and less alarming – and so, at least in Whitehall, 'flying-bomb' it became.

Curiously enough the Guards Chapel incident was not mentioned at that meeting but the casualty figures laid before the committee were still alarming enough. Already, with the attack only three days old, 499 people had been killed – a number bound to rise as more bodies were recovered – 2051 had been seriously injured, 2028 had been slightly injured and a further 633 people had suffered wounds of unknown severity, a grand total of more than 5000. The damage done was vast: 137,000 buildings needed repairs of some kind and 20,000 men had been diverted to this unproductive task, while another 3000 were on their way to London. All this had been done by the 647 bombs which had so far crossed the coast, of which not all had reached London. The Civil Defence services were already under strain. 'The wardens,' warned Sir Ernest Gowers, the regional commissioner for London, 'were on duty for very long hours and becoming over-tired.' The answer, the committee agreed, was to invite part-time volunteers to become full-time professionals. On the credit side, Sir Ernest Gowers reported that there was little demand for evacuation, or for deep shelters, though more people were sleeping in the tubes. Only in that old problem centre, the Chislehurst Caves, to which the cowardly tended to flock from all over London, was the white feather in evidence, with shelterers expecting meals to be brought to them even during the day – a practice, the committee agreed, which should be firmly discouraged.

What troubled Herbert Morrison and his colleagues most was the possibility of another major disaster from a single missile. It was decided to discourage large gatherings, to consider limiting greyhound racing, and to tackle urgently the problem of schools with inadequate shelters.

The committee were also apprehensive about what might happen if a flying-bomb pierced the underground railway tunnels beneath the Thames, though shutting off the affected lines at Charing Cross (now Embankment) and Waterloo whenever . the alert sounded caused widespread disruption. After an expert had testified that 'the flying bomb was very sensitive and would probably explode on hitting water', it was agreed to keep the tubes open though the decision was soon afterwards reversed.

At 5 p.m. that day the Prime Minister assembled his military advisers for another discussion followed by a Cabinet meeting at which Sir Alan Brooke observed: 'Winston was in very good form, quite ten years younger, all due to the fact that the flying bombs have again put us into the front line.'

This meeting in Churchill's underground war room below Storey's Gate endorsed all the decisions taken earlier by Morrison's Civil Defence Committee. The casualty figures he had quoted earlier had already risen, to 5856, of whom 526 had died. The Cabinet agreed, however, that even though there would be much criticism if a school were hit there should be no official evacuation, and that the tube should continue to run during a raid. The Cabinet was more concerned over the threat to industry, which came less from the flying-bombs – though already 'the roofing of over 100 aircraft factories had been damaged' – than from time lost through taking shelter. Government offices set a particularly bad example; one woman statistician at the Ministry of Supply in Tothill Street, Westminster, found herself making a dozen trips to the shelter in a single morning, while an official at the Air Ministry in Aldwych 'counted over thirty alarms' on a single day, though he, as others were soon to do, merely ducked beneath his desk when danger approached. 'Suspense and relief,' he noted, 'were the alternate emotions all day long, until lunch time, when we hurried to a buffet below ground-level where we could eat sandwiches and drink beer in comparative safety. On the way to and fro our eyes searched for doorways or basements into which we might dive.'

Among ordinary citizens, as the first excitement wore off,

spirits undoubtedly dropped. 'The effect of the new weapons,' commented General Eisenhower, who had not yet moved his headquarters across the Channel, 'was very noticeable upon morale. When in June the allies landed successfully on the Normandy coast, the citizens unquestionably experienced a great sense of relief . . . in the hope of gaining some insurance against future bombings. When the new weapons began to come over London in considerable numbers their hopes were dashed.' William Sansom, observing reactions in Westminster, agreed. 'The mood of London,' he wrote of late June and early July, 'sank low.' The 'close wet cloudy weather', which 'punctured the spirit's resilience', almost seemed to suggest 'some comprehensive German control of the elements,' and it also provided 'cover for those winged stiletto-like missiles that evaded thus our gunfire and our eyes.'

In these first days . . . the sound of a flying-bomb approached like a straight line, so that everybody in the half-circle of its fanning-forward sound attached the bomb to themselves and knew that without any particular reason it could drop at any time and any place. . . . The air echoed constantly to the threat of the bombs' approaching sound . . . and the Westminster day was ominous with those frequent explosions beyond the southern bank of the Thames.

A comment by a fictional character in Evelyn Waugh's novel *Unconditional Surrender* aptly caught the prevailing mood. It was, she remarked, 'as though the city were infested with enormous, venomous insects . . . as impersonal as the plague.' Even the practically minded Air Chief Marshal Hill was moved to an almost literary metaphor. 'An intermittent drizzle of malignant robots,' he commented, 'seemed harder to bear than the storm and thunder of the Blitz.' 'The sky was leaden,' wrote Jane Gordon of one morning in Marylebone at this time. 'There were several bursts of thunder and enormous hailstones clattered down. At the same time a flying bomb chugged overhead and crashed not far away. I thought to myself that the world would probably end on such a day as this.'

The city and its suburbs had never seemed, indeed had never been, so empty. A woman seeking a flat in Ladbroke Grove found an embarrassment of choice: 'Half the houses were empty so we could take our pick', their choice falling on a self-contained five-room apartment 'for thirty shillings a week, including rates'. A road in Kingston Vale, remembers another woman, contained only two occupied houses, her own and one occupied by a family bombed-out elsewhere – and soon also she left.

Wherever one looked there was little to inspire cheerful thoughts. That old Etonian champion of the proletariat, George Orwell, grumbled in the *Partisan Review* about 'disgusting scenes in the Tube stations' with 'sordid piles of bedding cluttering up the passage ways and hordes of dirty-faced children, playing round the platforms.' Mrs Robert Henrey, living among the rich in Mayfair, attributed the 'general air of despondency' to the sight of taxis loaded with luggage, as other wealthy residents made for safer quarters. The prevailing gloom was compounded by the censorship, which denied people in the blitzed districts the masochistic pleasure of seeing their own locality identified in print. 'Nothing is said on the wireless or in the papers except . . . Southern England!' wrote Vere Hodgson of Notting Hill in her diary. 'That is us – and we are all fed up.' 'Often did I wish . . .' wrote one man living in Welling, Kent, 'that the country could have been turned round like the pedestal globe in the schoolroom, so that each part in turn would have brought home to it the real meaning of modern war's bestiality. The press . . . played down the severity of the new form of air attack and played up the supposed *sang-froid* of the victims, who were pictured . . . as supremely indifferent to smashed homes and the daily toll of sudden death and hideous maiming which was their lot.'

Since the end of the Blitz in May 1941 London had been visibly tidied up. Now it began again to assume the scarred and battered look so familiar to all who had lived through those noisy months. On all sides there was mute evidence of the number of flying-bombs getting through. Hardly a well-known store or hotel or block of flats escaped at least minor damage and public buildings suffered with the rest. The Log Book of the City of Westminster Plotting Officer covering the whole centre of London, from the edge of the City to the far side of Victoria station, contained by the end of the summer a list of forty-eight incidents caused by flying-bombs, landing inside or just outside its boundaries. It included West End clubs and

fashionable blocks of flats like Sloane Court in Lower Sloane
Street, and St James Court in Buckingham Gate, 'smart' addresses like Berkeley Square, humbler ones like Peabody
Buildings, Drury Lane, and more than once the Victoria Embankment, the home of the down-and-outs. The frontage of
aristocratic Harrods was blasted, along with the little one-man
businesses of the Horseferry Road. The flying-bombs dropped
with democratic impartiality on the 'royals' in St James Palace,
the barristers in the Law Courts and Lincolns Inn, the porters
of Billingsgate Market, the telegraphists of Electra House, and
the accountants of the Bankruptcy Buildings in Carey Street.
The civil servants in the reinforced Rotunda near Monck
Street, in the requisitioned Queen Anne's Mansions and in
Lansdowne House, all felt the force of the enemy's malice; so,
too did, the nuns in Tyburn Convent in the Bayswater Road,
the soapbox orators of Hyde Park Corner, and the animals in
the zoo. Eighty-four hospitals or similar institutions such as old
people's homes, and 111 churches were damaged, some more
than once. St George's (Roman Catholic) Cathedral, Southwark was blasted three times beween 17 June and 3 July, St
Michael's Paternoster Royal in College Street, Dick Whitting-
ton's church, rebuilt by Wren after being burned down in the
Great Fire, was now totally wrecked by Colonel Wachtel. Only
St Paul's Cathedral seemed to bear a charmed life, though one
flying-bomb, according to the watchers on its roof, 'made an
almost complete circle round the cathedral and another missed
one of the west towers by . . . only a few feet.'

Among non-ecclesiastic buildings, the most important to be
damaged was probably Staple Inn, 'the most impressive surviving example', according to Nikolaus Pevsner, 'of timber
buildings in London', with a magnificent Tudor Hall. The most
famous literary figure to suffer was Dr Johnson, whose house
in Gough Square, just off Fleet Street, was badly damaged.
Happily the relics associated with him were safe in the country,
which he had despised.

Hardly a single other tourist attraction escaped damage. The
Tate Gallery in Pimlico, the Natural History Museum in South
Kensington, the British Museum in Bloomsbury and the Royal
Observatory in Greenwich all acquired honourable scars. The
most famous home in London, Buckingham Palace, was twice

damaged, by a bomb on Constitution Hill, on 21 June, which
wrecked a seventy-five-yard stretch of wall, and by another, on
26 June, which hit a tree in the grounds, destroying the King's
tennis court, and shattering many of the Palace windows. But
the royal family did not leave London. 'A change in the daily
routine will be needed,' the King acknowledged in his diary,
and moved his customary Tuesday luncheon with the Prime
Minister to the Palace shelter. Shocked by the death of so
many friends in the Guards Chapel, the King cancelled the
usual investitures, holding some instead at the RAF stations
he visited. His wife voiced her royal displeasure in a letter to
her mother-in-law, Queen Mary. 'There is,' she observed severely, 'something very inhuman about death-dealing missiles
being launched in such an indiscriminate manner.'

As the damage being done became increasingly obvious on
all sides, Members of Parliament became more and more res-
tive, although Herbert Morrison, on 23 June, assured MPs that
the number of people killed on the last five nights of conventional raids, in February, had been larger than those who had
died 'during the first five nights of the attack by flying bombs'.
As for their other effects, 'if the enemy's intention was to upset
the morale of our people he has,' boasted Morrison, 'signally
failed. The morale of the British takes a lot of upsetting.'

An equally reassuring note was struck in a talk on the BBC
Home Service on the evening of 26 June by 'A Wing Commander', in fact the desk-bound airman John Strachey. Strachey admitted that the bombs were 'beastly, vicious things' but
claimed that, thanks to the RAF, 'the attack was delayed for
over a year and now . . . is on much less than a half of the
scale on which the Germans originally planned it.' As for
morale, the people of Southern England were, he assured
listeners in other parts of the country, 'steadiness itself'.

Behind the scenes Morrison felt a good deal less complacent.
On the evening of the following day, Tuesday, 27 June, he
reminded the War Cabinet that within less than two weeks,
'about 1,600 people had been killed, 4,500 had been seriously
injured and nearly 5,000 slightly injured. . . . Over 200,000
houses had been damaged to a greater or less extent.'

The attacks had led to a serious loss of sleep and the fact that they went on continously meant that there was no relaxation of the strain. . . . After five years of war the civil population were not as capable of standing the strains of air attack as they had been during the winter of 1940–41. . . . The effects of the attacks could not be brushed aside lightly, but must be treated as a major element in the strategy of the war.

Morrison's plea received powerful support from his Labour colleagues. Clement Attlee, MP for Stepney and Lord President of the Council, 'supported the view that the continuous nature of the flying bomb attacks was imposing a particularly heavy strain on the civilian population. Even in the worst period of the winter of 1940–1 there had been considerable breaks during which the population had had a chance to recover.' Sir Stafford Cripps, as Minister of Aircraft Production, added his warning. The raids were already having a significant effect on output, with 'a marked increase in absenteeism among married women.' Ernest Bevin, Minister of Labour, urged 'that . . . homeless persons should be removed from rest centres to more comfortable quarters as soon as possible. . . . The repair of damaged houses should be executed as quickly as possible and workers from other areas should, if necessary, be brought to London for this purpose.'

This unanimity of opinion seems, as the minutes reveal, to have impressed even the Prime Minister.

He realised that the civil population were under a considerable strain. . . . Everything possible should be done to provide for the victims of the attacks and nothing should be allowed to stand in the way of the repair of damaged houses and the provision of alternative accommodation and emergency feeding for the people who lost their homes. . . . He attached great importance to encouraging the people to use shelters, particularly at night, so that they could sleep undisturbed, and steps should be taken to improve the sleeping accommodation and general amenities of public shelters. He was not afraid that the civil population would lose their morale provided they were satisfied that everything had been done to help those who had suffered.

The Cabinet duly supported all these proposals and agreed 'that the Civil Defence Committee should consider further what steps could be taken to mitigate the effect of the attacks on the civil population,' including reviewing 'plans for the evacuation of priority classes . . . to ensure that they could, if necessary, be operated at short notice.'

If ministers were satisfied, Members of Parliament were not. The flying-bombs were descending upon constituencies of every type, from the Conservative strongholds of rural Kent to the close-packed Labour heartlands of South London, and united back-benchers of all parties in trying to secure from the government both more information and more energetic action. The oddest suggestion came from the Independent, and Anglo-Catholic, MP, Tom Driberg, who wanted Anthony Eden to seek if not divine intervention at least that of the Pope. 'Could it not be put to him respectfully,' suggested Driberg, 'that condemnation by him of this particularly barbarous weapon would carry great weight with the German Catholic hierarchy, and, through them, with their flocks?' The Foreign Secretary dealt curtly with this plea. 'His Holiness the Pope,' he replied, 'is no doubt already aware of the use . . . being made by the Germans of these pilotless aircraft.'

On the following day Herbert Morrison and the Ministry of Information spokesman had a far rougher passage, when several MPs urged him to identify the areas affected, on the grounds that, as one put it, 'public morale is very much . . . lowered, not so much by the bombs themselves, as by the secrecy which prevails about them.' Morrison refused on the not very convincing grounds that 'there are very valid reasons for the present policy.'

Behind the scenes the Civil Defence Committee was preparing for things to get worse. That same day, 29 June, it had heard from Morrison's Parliamentary Secretary, Ellen Wilkinson, that 20,000 additional Morrison shelters had already been issued and a further 4000 a week were being distributed. Adding to the number of Andersons was more and more difficult, due to lack of men for the heavy digging required. Seventy to seventy-five thousand people a night were finding shelter in the tubes, but the Home Office opposed opening up other deep shelters, even to accommodate building workers, fearing the general public might also demand to use them. Already 68 per cent of shelters provided bunks. The post-raid services were, it appeared, operating smoothly. The rest centres, vastly improved since 1940, had proved able to cope with all comers, and criticism passed on by Ernest Bevin about 'the arrangements for emergency feeding in the Borough of Wandsworth' had proved unfounded. Herbert Morrison had, however, changed his mind about the underground and 'reached the conclusion that . . . tube flood gates at Charing Cross ought to be closed' during alerts.

A long discussion took place about evacuation. After Morrison had pointed out that 'considerable numbers of people were . . . moving out of London under private arrangements, the Committee decided that 'The time had not come to put into effect the plans for organised evacuation,' though noting that finding billets need no longer be a problem, since anywhere outside the South-East was safe, including previously 'evacuable areas in the North-East and the Midlands.' Nor need transport prove a problem, for the Ministry of War Transport 'could, if the need arose, provide . . . at short notice' for 10,000 extra travellers a day, and 'the railway timetables for the organised evacuation plans could be put into operation immediately.'

Of all the subjects discussed that day the most contentious was publicity. So far it had not been admitted that the capital was the sole target and Morrison suggested that 'with a view to keeping up morale in London, it might soon be necessary to allow the press to publish the fact that London, was bearing part of the attack.'* There would have, however, 'to be a careful control on what was published and it . . . would also . . . be important not to minimise the damage caused in smaller places, where the effect of a single flying-bomb might be relatively great.'

The Ministry of Information representative revealed that he would that day be answering a parliamentary question with the statement that 'for the time being there would be no change in the practice of referring to . . . Southern England', but Morrison remained unhappy about the situation and on the following day circulated a long memorandum arguing that since the Cabinet had laid down the 'Southern England' rule the situation had changed. The ban then in force 'on the sending of

---

*In the original typescript minute 'part of' appears as 'the brunt of'. It was later amended in ink.

diplomatic communications by cipher and on the movement of foreign diplomats out of the country,' introduced before D-Day, had been lifted, and 'information . . . that a material proportion of his missiles have hit London' must by now have reached the enemy; it was in any case becoming impossible to hush up the effect of the flying-bombs.

The toll of death, injury and damage to property from these attacks on London is far heavier than is generally appreciated. Though the proportion of persons killed to other casualties is less than in the raids of 1940–41 the total casualties in London for a month of flying-bomb attack would, if the present rate of casualties continues, be equal to those of September 1940, the worst month of the Blitz period. In September 1940, 5,546 persons were killed and 7,167 seriously injured in the London Region. In 14 days and nights of attacks by flying-bombs up to the morning of the 29 June, 1,679 persons have been killed and about 5,000 seriously injured in the London Region. In this period a total of nearly 270,000 houses in London have been damaged, of which over 7,000 have been destroyed. . . . If damage continues at the present rate for two months, as many London houses will have suffered damage in that period as . . . for the nine months of the Blitz. The attacks, though intermittent, go on day and night and the strain upon the people of London is severe. They . . . are bearing it admirably, but it would be of the greatest help to the maintenance of their morale . . . to give to Londoners what is their due and let them and the country know that we are proud of them.

Morrison's proposal was for 'continuing the restriction limiting references to location to "Southern England" while allowing some references to the attacks on London'; there would still be a strict ban on saying how many flying-bombs reached London, or on what dates, but stories about individual incidents would be allowed if submitted for censorship. The new rules, clearly sensible, were endorsed by the Cabinet on 3 July, perhaps from sheer exhaustion, for Sir Alan Brooke noted in his diary that this was 'the record longest Cabinet meeting', lasting from 5.30 till 9.15 p.m., 'Winston wasted hours, and when we got on to flying-bombs . . . he ran short of time. However, the threat is assuming dimensions . . . likely to encroach on our war effort if we are not careful.'

The minutes of the meeting reveal good reason for Brooke's exasperation, for every factual statement which called for some positive decision was followed by a vague and irrelevant dissertation from the Prime Minister. The information laid before the weary Cabinet was alarming. Herbert Morrison reported that 'the weight of high explosive dropped in London in the two weeks ended 29 June was 650 tons,' not much short of the '770 tons dropped . . . from aircraft in the worst fortnight of the 1940–41 raids.' The backlog of houses needing repairs was daily growing worse. 'The attacks,' the Minister of Aircraft Production reported, 'were having a serious effect on output,' and the Minister of War Transport confirmed that already ammunition ships were having to be diverted from the London docks. Duncan Sandys had little to offer for his colleagues' comfort. The best that could be hoped was that 'if we maintained an active offensive against . . . factories, supply depots and launching sites, we might be able to keep the number of bombs launched down to about the present average.' As for those getting through, if the defences could bring down 50 per cent instead of the existing 41 per cent of bombs launched, 'we might reduce the weight of the explosive dropped in London from 50 tons to 30 tons a day. But,' warned Duncan Sandys, in the absence of Allied bombing the enemy 'would be able to increase the scale of his attacks over the next few weeks.' The Cabinet's response was to instruct the Minister of Health 'to arrange for the transfer on the largest possible scale of casualties from hospitals in the London to . . . other parts of the country' and to see what could be done to speed up the evacuation of the priority classes* from London and the South.

The Cabinet had suggested at its meeting on 3 July that the Prime Minister should deliver a frank situation report to the nation, via the House of Commons, and on the following day Anthony Eden, as Leader of the House, promised a statement in two days' time. The House, with letters from irate constituents arriving by every post, was far from content. Why had they got to wait so long? asked one member, warning that 'the profoundest dissatisfaction will be felt by those in the areas affected.'

Another MP called on the government 'to consider opening those big underground shelters' and another made the extraor-

*See page 68 for an explanation of this term.

dinary allegation that 'the flying-bomb was developed through facilities offered by Franco.'

When, on Thursday, 6 July, the promised day at last arrived, Herbert Morrison was subjected to a further barrage of questions on the warning system and the censorship policy until Winston Churchill at last rose to answer the criticisms, open and covert, which for the past three weeks had been directed at his government.

Churchill was always at his best in moments of adversity, national or parliamentary, and his opening sentences made clear that he was not in an apologetic mood:

I consider that His Majesty's Government were right in not giving out a great deal of information about the flying bombs until we knew more about them and were able to measure their effects. . . . The time has come, however, when a fuller account is required and a wider field of discussion should be opened. . . .

Let me say at the outset that it would be a mistake to under-rate the serious character of this particular form of attack. It has never been under-rated in the secret circles of the government.

If it had not been for our bombing operations in France and Germany, . . . the bombardment of London would . . . have started perhaps six months earlier and on a very much heavier scale. . . . There has . . . been in progress for a year past an unseen battle into which great resources have been poured by both sides. This invisible battle has now flashed into the open, and we shall be able, and indeed obliged, to watch its progress at fairly close quarters. . . .

Between 100 and 150 flying bombs, each weighing about one ton, are being discharged daily, and . . . a very large proportion of these have either failed to cross the Channel or have been shot down. . . . The House will, I think, be favourably surprised to learn that the total number of flying bombs launched . . . have killed almost exactly one person per bomb . . . the latest figures are 2,754 flying bombs launched and 2,752 fatal casualties sustained . . . up to six o'clock this morning. . . . The total number of injured detained in hospital is about 8,000. . . .

Penicillin, which up to now has had to be restricted to military uses, will be available for the treatment of all flying bomb casualties.

Churchill assured the House that the damage to property, which every Londoner could see for himself, was also being dealt with by bringing in 'copious reinforcements' of building workers, and went on to touch briefly on the vexed question of publicity and on the prospects of retaliation:

A very high proportion of these casualties I have mentioned . . . have fallen upon London, which presents to the enemy – now I have mentioned it the phrase 'Southern England' passes out of currency – a target 18 miles wide by . . . over 20 miles deep and it is, therefore, the unique target of the world for the use of a weapon of such gross inaccuracy. The flying bomb is a weapon literally and essentially indiscriminate in its nature, purpose and effect. The introduction by the Germans of such a weapon obviously raises some grave questions upon which I do not propose to trench today.

The speech – a vintage Churchillian performance, skillfully blending fact and sentiment – ended with an equally typical peroration.

When I visited various scenes of bomb explosions on Saturday only one man . . . asked a question . . . 'What are you going to do about it?' I replied, 'Everything in human power, and we have never failed yet.' He seemed contented with the reply. That is the only promise I can make. . . . There can be no question of allowing the slightest weakening of the battle in order to diminish in scale injuries which, while they may inflict grievous suffering on many people and change to some extent the normal, regular life and industry of London, will never stand between the British nation and their duty in the van of a victorious and avenging world. It may be a comfort to some to feel that they are sharing in no small degree the perils of our soldiers overseas and that the blows which fall on them diminish those which in other forms would have smitten our fighting men and their allies. But I am sure of one thing, that London will never be conquered and will never fail and that her renown, triumphing over every ordeal, will long shine among men.

12

A BOMBY AFTERNOON

It was a rather 'bomby' afternoon

Diary of a Thornton Heath woman, Sunday, 30 July 1944

Churchill's speech in Parliament cleared the air and largely disarmed the government's critics. But for no one did it come as a greater relief than the Chief Censor. 'This speech,' wrote Admiral Thompson, 'made things much easier for the censors, for the fact that the flying bombs were landing in London was no longer banned from the newspapers and at last Mrs. Jones of London could now describe to a reporter what she had felt like when bombs were falling, though she could not refer to the damage done to her house during "a recent attack". I was also able to help matters by releasing officially after a few days reports of damage to buildings of public interest and of incidents which had aroused great public feeling throughout the country.' In this way, on Monday, 10 July, the general public learned for the first time of the destruction of the Guards Chapel three weeks before; minor incidents could be reported on the same day, provided the location was left imprecise. 'The press . . . were not allowed to refer to more than twelve casualties in any incident,' though the total figures were released once a month.

The summer of 1944 soon acquired a character all of its own, unlike any before or since. To one woman, who stayed on in Thornton Heath to drive an ambulance while her husband was with the Ministry of Aircraft Production in Harrogate, it seemed a 'very eerie' period, living alone with the windows blacked out, the carpets up, and everywhere the all pervading smell of dust. It is 'the horrible smell of powdered brickwork' which brings this period back to a man who worked at Woolwich Arsenal, and another distinctive odour was of fresh sap, as the blast stripped the bark from trees in the streets and parks for hundreds of yards around. The season possessed too its own sounds, of newly shattered glass crunching underfoot and boards covered with 'glass substitute' rattling in damaged window frames. It had its own distinctive sights; the smoke-like plume of dust hanging in the air where a missile had fallen, the leafless branches in roads and gardens as if winter had returned six months too soon. South of the river one passed through street after street swarming with building workers and of houses with roofs draped in tarpaulins, often an incongrous red, yellow or green, as they had been requisitioned from stocks normally used to cover some farmer's haystack.

One man who worked on building invasion barges on the Chelsea Embankment remembers how 'every morning as we went from the World's End bus stop to the river we walked through blasted streets', with 'the glass lying over the road. . . . Almost every day valuable furniture, riddled with glass splinters, and household goods which had been damaged . . . were dumped into the barges of Kensington Borough Council Wharf to be taken down river.' A woman who travelled into London from Upper Hackney, in the north-east, to her job as a shorthand typist for English Electric in Kingsway – recalls other signs of the strange times:

The smell of burning, damp sandbags, crushing glass under our feet, the sight of a half-bombed house or flat with someone's precious suit or coat flapping from a wardrobe or cupboard, even a torn and stained wedding-dress fluttering from a fourth floor flat where no one could reach it. Someone's home cut up in slices like a giant's cake and eaten.

As blocks of flats, then streets, and finally whole districts lost most of their population, life for the few who remained became unusually solitary, though sometimes a new togetherness flourished. One woman, then aged sixteen, can recall seeing the housewives in her road in Cockfosters shed their suburban separateness. After each explosion they would hurry out to discuss 'where that one landed and to say "I hope it was in the fields, don't you?" ' A Catford housewife remembers studying

141

with interest the piles of glass on the pavement outside each front gate. 'If they got bigger you knew you were near a scene of desolation.' But even in the areas which suffered from daily, or more than daily, doodlebugs, women still took pride in their homes. A Sydenham woman honours the memory of 'gallant old ladies still brushing away the glass and scrubbing their doorsteps even when the steps were cracked all over.'

A few people managed to detach themselves from the prevailing tension. A man living in West Central London, 'working terribly hard at a daytime war job and Home Guard duties at night,' started reading astronomy, his wife remembers, 'being so steeped in this that he began to feel that the happenings of our insignificant universe mattered . . . very little.' Equally effective, if less escapist, was the hobby of a man living in South Norwood and his neighbour, who 'between them,' the daughter of one of them remembers, 'ran the war from the back steps of our houses.' So absorbed were they in 'their maps and flags' that they were always loath to abandon them to take shelter, bitterly complaining that the Germans were interfering with the real war. A Tunbridge Wells woman, devoted to the ballet, took refuge in working out the choreography of a highly topical performance. The male lead, in Germanic black and yellow stripes, would dance his way forward through the corps de ballet, dressed as smoke puffs, to the tune of *Flight of the Bumble Bee* until intercepted by the prima ballerina, in Air Force blue.

Social life, of a kind, flourished. One Clapham woman remembers her hostess inviting her to listen for flying-bombs as she made the dinner since she could not hear them over the noise of the gas stove. A draughtsman in Lee started giving 'buzz-bomb parties', which lasted from midday Saturday until Monday morning. The idea, one guest observed, was 'that if today is to be your last, then make it worthwhile.'

Although, throughout late June and early July, a hundred flying-bombs a day were being directed at London, daily life remained remarkably unaffected. Postmen, milkmen and other tradesmen arrived as punctually as in the Blitz. One roundsman who delivered milk in bulk remembers the plea from his customers to unload his churns more peacefully: their clattering was wreaking havoc on bomb-stretched nerves. On one occasion, in Peckham, there seemed to be something slowing his vehicle down. The reason became obvious at his next stop: 'The back of my lorry had loads of rubble in it and also a piece of a bomb, still hot.'

The flying-bombs, sinister though they were, became a fruitful source of jokes. A popular catchphrase was 'Don't forget the Diver!' borrowed from the radio comedy programme 'ITMA' – short for 'It's That Man Again'. An old story, popular in the Blitz, was heard again, of the man who pulled the lavatory chain just as a flying-bomb brought the house down, and remarked 'These jerry-built houses!' A Crowhurst woman admired her brother's spontaneous witticism as they crouched beneath a heavy table: 'Who said Hitler would never bring us to our knees?' An Epsom mother coined the phrase, of an untidy son, 'His bedroom looked as if a flying-bomb had hit it.' There were also many cartoons such as the one which showed a bird addressing the cat lying beneath its perch: 'Purr if you must, but for heaven's sake don't cut out suddenly.' Deafness, no fun for those who suffered it, also prompted many an anecdote. A wartime WAAF remembers how her severely deaf mother-in-law spent the day hurrying into the shelter when the all clear sounded, emerging again on the alert.

Many stories, some true, some apochryphal, illustrated British stoicism. The *Outpost*, written for London-based Americans, told one about a hairdresser who remarked that she had been lucky. Her patrons had been 'under the dryers . . . when the ceiling fell down, so their hair didn't get dirty.'

One woman living near Trafalgar Square remembers that her cleaner always carried with her an enlarged twenty-first birthday portrait of her daughter. 'Hitler,' its owner explained, 'isn't going to get my Gladys!'

The extent to which the flying-bombs became part of one's daily life is illustrated by the diary of a woman then living in Thornton Heath, which she had started as a convenient way of keeping a record of the number of eggs laid by the family hens each day:

Sunday 2 July 3 eggs
Another lot of bombs! Annie has been bombed. A bomb dropped at

the bottom of her garden. All her windows are out and ceilings are down and furniture damaged.

Monday 10 July 2 eggs

A 'bomby' day. I did some washing. I tried to rest this afternoon but some bombs came over.

Sunday 30 July 2 eggs

I made a nice cherry tart. In the afternoon we had a bomb drop on the Electricity Works. It was a rather 'bomby' afternoon.

At this time a day, or even part of a day, without flying-bombs was worthy of recording. 'We were ALL CLEAR in Hackney from 2 p.m. until midnight,' noted the daughter of a Congregational clergyman. 'I helped father in our "Dig for Victory" campaign in the Manse garden. It was a real blessing to have an afternoon and evening free from anxiety.'

Because it was so difficult to remember if an alert was in force or not, many households adopted a private warning system. The woman just quoted, arriving home at Hackney after taking her finals as a would-be teacher at Homerton College, Cambridge, found her mother 'turning over a large green card saying ALL CLEAR to the red side saying ALERT.' An Isleworth family had a home made 'clock', with one hand pointing to the alert or all clear mark, and Vere Hodgson, in Notting Hill, learned of a man who undid a particular button on his waistcoat when he heard the warning, refastening it for the all clear. The systems worked perfectly until one morning he dressed in haste leaving one button over – and could not remember whether he was supposed to be 'alert' or not.

Many households acquired a private roof-spotter. A man living in Pinner would climb into the loft and watch through the skylight towards Harrow Hill. When the light of a distant missile appeared he would call down to his pregnant wife, 'Here it comes,' *before* the noise could be heard to prevent her being startled and perhaps losing her baby. One fifteen-year-old in West Fulham would post himself on top of the Anderson 'armed with a loud whistle' and 'people who lived around us' would come 'hurrying out of their homes and into the garden shelters' when he blew it. The youngest such 'spotter' seems to have been the two-and-half-year-old daughter of a post warden at Carshalton. Whenever she heard the familiar drone she would shout, 'Doodlebug, mummy!' and rush indoors to the Morrison.

It was widely believed that the Germans concentrated their efforts around breakfast-time and lunch-time, though in fact flying-bombs arrived at all hours. In Bexhill-on-Sea the saying was, one man remembers, 'that Hitler wanted us to miss the one o'clock news.' Sundays were not a day of rest for the launching crews and one man living in Grays remembers how 'it became customary for the family to transfer the lunch from the kitchen to the shelter in one easy and highly efficient operation.' With rations small and damaged food irreplaceable, many informants still mourn the meals that never were, like the 'pork chop', a whole week's meat ration, 'covered in soot and glass' when actually in the frying pan in Wimbledon and the 'precious butter' ruined by dust in a similar incident in Leyton. One East London housewife began to buy lump sugar instead of granulated, as the dust could be removed from it more easily. A Gravesend man recalls his wife's dilemma during jam-making. 'When she heard a doodle she'd dive for the shelter, only to find when she emerged that the kitchen had been invaded by wasps. What with alternating attacks by wasps and doodlebugs she had a very nerve-racking morning.'

Many housewives now discovered for the first time just how much noise the ordinary domestic chores created. Running taps, simmering pans, and – worst of all – the loud buzzing of a vacuum cleaner, all could deny one those precious few seconds of warning. A Morden man's favourite breakfast, a great wartime treat, of bacon and eggs was ruined for him as their sizzling in the frying pan made an approaching flying-bomb inaudible. 'We tried never to be undressed more than a few minutes at a time, day or night,' recalls the wife of a Plaistow headmaster. 'Often we had to run to the shelter, wet and wrapped in a towel, carrying clothes in a bundle.' An East London woman did her washing in instalments. 'Top wash. Get dressed. Wait, and if the siren did not go, finish and get dressed. It was done in five minutes flat.' The mother of a Sydenham baby adopted a similar routine, 'topping' him in one session, by washing his face and upper half, and 'tailing' him later.

Worst of all was having a bath, for one felt in every sense

exposed and there was always the prospect of confronting the rescue men naked. The girls of one firm in the West End, housed in former flats, decided for some mysterious reason that it was safer to bathe in working hours, and were allowed to stop work for the purpose. A woman in Pimlico developed the habit of putting her favourite shampoo on after one explosion and rinsing it off as the next pilotless plane approached.

Every family had some particularly precious possession which it was determined to preserve. For a Wandsworth woman it was her 'bottom drawer' consisting of 'linen, china and glass . . . collected throughout the war', which was packed into two trunks and allotted the place of safety under the stairs. A Crayford woman entrusted her valuables to a leather bag suspended on the clothes line which ran from the back door to the shelter. Her son enjoyed seeing her 'haring from the house, grabbing the bag from the clothes line as she dashed toward shelter.' A National Fire Service staff officer in Kent moved his 'treasured grandfather clock . . . from a hazardous position near the front door,' but 'the Old Man resented the change and refused to function with his normal complete reliability until restored to his normal position.' And the same man learned the danger of rashly expressing a wish. When planting two new apple trees, he had 'been bewailing the fact that we had no broken crocks to provide drainage at the bottom of the holes. . . . Within a few days a V-1 gave us half our tiled roof.'

Hundreds of thousands of homes in Southern England contained at least one pet, and their reactions proved as varied as those of human beings. 'Our dog soon realized that the sound might well culminate in a bang and appeared to listen anxiously,' found a woman living in Meopham ['Meppam'] five miles from Gravesend. 'The cat appeared to take no notice whatever.' Kim, a Bedlington terrier in Shirley, 'used to get most distressed,' her owner remembers, 'when we just had to carry on with our lives and ignore the doodlebugs until the moment of cut-out'.

Other canines adopted an 'every dog for himself' attitude. 'Mickey', an Airedale puppy in a Dovercourt family, 'was always first under the table shelter' while the black Labrador of an Esher woman disdained such precautions but as soon as the family were safe in the cupboard under the stairs, seized

146

the chance to climb into a forbidden armchair. A saddle-back collie, Mickie, in Shepherds Bush who 'was usually first into the Anderson shelter' put on a great display of courage once the danger was past, dashing out the moment the all clear sounded and barking boastfully. Sometimes a dog found the whole experience too much, like a Scotch terrier in Neasden, who had always been first into the Morrison and the last to leave, until 'towards the end of this period they were coming . . . fast and furious,' and 'the dog got quite confused and started going into the shelter on the all clear.' Some felt the need of company, like a Biggin Hill dog, who after one noisy near miss, not merely 'found his way into the bed' with his owner, 'but brought his mate, my in-laws' dog, with him.'

At the other end of the courage scale was the small Scottie of one family living on the outskirts of London which 'caused more worry than the rest of the family put together' to his owner, then a schoolgirl, 'by parading along the grass dome of our shelter, barking at every doodlebug that came by.' In Woodford a crossbred Irish terrier, also no giant, ran the whole length of the road in hot pursuit of *his* first flying-bomb. Bob, an eight-year-old Airedale from Finsbury Park, equally courageous, stood in the garden snarling at the aerial intruders.

What proud owners frequently claimed as their pet's 'sixth sense' in warning of approaching missiles was due in reality to the exceptionally acute hearing they enjoyed, which registered sounds too highly pitched to be heard by human ears. Dawn, an Eastbourne elkhound, would prick up her ears, emit a shrill bark, and then her duty done, make for safety under the stairs. Benjamin, a springer spaniel in Sevenoaks, 'would suddenly wake, stand in the middle of the room and "point",' which gave his owners 'time to make our way into the glassless hall.' A New Malden man still remembers with gratitude the morning when their golden labrador rushed straight into the house and into the shelter. 'We had heard nothing,' he remembers, 'but . . . also dived into the shelter' – just before a flying-bomb demolished a nearby bungalow.

The old adage that animals became attached to places as much as to people was also frequently demonstrated that summer. A Heston woman remembers her son-in-law's dog 'going missing' after his home had been bombed, but when the family returned to the ruins a day or so later, they heard a whining sound beneath the rubble and the animal was dug out, 'very thin and covered in bits of glass, which he was licking out, but he recovered.' A Wandsworth woman, whose house had been wrecked on 22 June, heard whimpering, inaudible to everyone else, until a warden tunnelled through the ruins and there, 'cowering under some debris, very nervous' but still alive was her dog, Karlo, though it was months before he became his old, boisterous self. One mongrel, robbed of its owners, fixed itself up with a new home by climbing onto an NFS pump in Leyton. The animal became the pampered pet of the whole station and far from being frightened, developed a positive enthusiasm for 'attending' at incidents, and was always first on the appliance when 'the bells went down'.

Cats have always been better than dogs at foraging for themselves and usually preferred, in the official phrase, 'to make their own arrangements' for shelter. Tim, a large tomcat in South-West London, favoured the cellar. Ginger, in Ashford, the pet of a nurse, thought the sideboard was far enough to go. Timothy, at Rush Green, Romford, took refuge in the coal-bin. The cat belonging to a Muswell Hill shopowner found her private 'safe spot' beneath a nest of biscuit tins. Whimsy, living in an old house at Stratford St Mary in Essex, would seek safety inside the huge brick Tudor fireplace. Tibby, belonging to a Charlton girl, dug out an 'Anderson' of his own, behind the family one, and in Norbury a neighbour's cat would run in from the next-door garden and cringe beneath a pyracantha bush, presumably reasoning that its prickly foliage would deter attackers.

Although less reliable than dogs, cats, too, sometimes provided an advance warning of approaching danger. One woman, then a young girl at Rotherfield in Sussex, remembers her cat, Binkie, acting as 'a doodlebug meter' when she and her sister played table-tennis on top of the Morrison, 'looking rather like a Wimbledon spectator as he followed . . . the landing ball. . . . Whenever my sister and I saw him dive under the shelter we would follow and sure enough seconds later the ominous droning would be heard.' Equally trustworthy was Sandy, in Eastbourne, who one day 'refused to come out' from the cupboard under the stairs after a V-1 had passed over.

Sandy's owner then looked outside 'only to see another dood-lebug almost overhead, its engine stopped.'

More pets were killed by their owners than by the Germans, for bombed-out people frequently decided that they could not cope with them while searching for a new home. One woman living in Merton Park stood, the day after her house was damaged, 'in a long, long line of white-faced women to have my cat destroyed because the kennels were blasted out.' Ronnie, the 'completely black' pet of an Uxbridge family, 'returned home the afternoon of the next day' after their house was blasted. 'We had been distressed at losing him, but . . . we . . . took him to the veterinary surgeon and he was put pain-lessly to sleep. After all, we were having to depend on friends for a night's shelter ourselves and Ronnie had led a very happy life.'

Caged birds often died of shock when a house was damaged, even if they were not visibly harmed, but those left in their natural surroundings stood up well to the flying-bombs, and for one district nurse the strangeness of the times was epitom-ized by the sight of a peacock 'walking down Church Street . . . with no feathers' after a flying-bomb had liberated the inmates of the aviary in Clissold Park, Stoke Newington. One species actually seemed to enjoy the bombing for it had only appeared in London since the Blitz. 'The black redstarts,' noted the historian of Birkbeck College after an explosion only 150 yards away in mid-August, 'were behaving as if nothing unusual had happened.' A Catford 'clippie' remembers think-ing 'it's an ill wind' at the sight of sparrows stripping the feather-bed blown from some wrecked house and carrying the contents off to line their nests.

Geese, as in ancient Rome, proved useful at raising the alarm. Those kept in their orchard by a family at Watton-at-Stone in Hertfordshire always squawked at the approach of danger. For a Bromley family an Aylesbury duck, Tessa, proved equally valuable. 'As soon as she heard a doodlebug coming over the coast, she would come up the path, clucking away, to our back door. . . . She never let us down . . . day or night.'

Many back gardens in 1944 contained a chicken run and there was often a mass escape when a blast blew down a fence.

A Balham woman remembers her sister 'knocking on every door in Alderbrook Road asking, 'Have you seen our dad's chickens?' Amazingly, 'all were recovered and none the worse for their fright.'

In Welling, one twelve-year-old schoolgirl observed, the family's birds reacted vigorously to being 'bombed out'.

Whereas previously they had all been on strike, our chickens, as soon as the doodlebug dropped, all started cackling and laying eggs in unlikely places, for they, too, had lost their 'home'. They were darting about all over the place. Eggs were rationed and like gold-dust. As rescuers and helpers were picking their way towards us. . . . I remember my mother saying, 'That's all right, we'll manage, now mind where you go and don't tread on any of our chickens and most important, *the eggs*!'

The male of the species was, by contrast, singularly cowed by the same experience:

We also possessed a very fractious cockerel and I distinctly remember my mother asking an air-raid warden to find this bird before it attacked anyone. He found it sheltering in our windowless greenhouse. It was unscathed and very subdued and surrendered to our warden without a murmur. 'There you are, madam,' he said to my mother, 'all in a day's work, and you've still got your Christmas dinner left, if nothing else.'

The London Zoo suffered less than in the Blitz, though it had several near misses. Chessington Zoo, to the south, was less fortunate. Here one large animal, slumbering peacefully in its pit, was rudely awakened and mildly burned by an explosion that did no other damage, adding to the statistics of animal casualties one unusual entry: Slightly injured, one bear with a scorched behind.

13

ADDITIONAL NOISES OFF

A few doodlebugs . . . tried to assist the timpani.

Entry in an Enfield woman's diary about a Promenade
Concert, 19 June 1944

For many people that summer the arts provided a means of
escape. One of the earliest casualties of the flying-bombs was
the 'Jubilee' series of Sir Henry Wood Promenade Concerts,
first staged in 1895, and broadcast since 1927. The first Prom
had taken place as usual, on 10 June, but by 16 June arrangements were already being discussed to cancel the concerts and,
on 21 June, at an inter-departmental meeting, the Home Office
representative expressed further alarm. 'There were only two
places of indoor entertainment in London which could be regarded as vulnerable,' he explained, 'viz, the Albert Hall and
the National Gallery, which had glass roofs. At the former, the
attendance last Saturday was 4,000 (capacity 7,000),* but at
the latter . . . used for lunch-time concerts, the attendance had
not varied from the normal of about 1,000.' The Assistant
Commissioner of Police, however, 'did not feel that at present
there was a case for requiring any restriction.'

Among keen Prom-goers that June was a young woman civil
servant working in South Kensington:

It was possible to get into the Promenade without too much
queuing. . . . A green light shone while everything was 'All Clear',
a red one remained on during the air-raid warning, but the orchestra
continued playing. . . . A habit of mine was to eat sandwiches sitting
on the floor during the interval and once I visited a milkbar for a
coffee where a young air force boy talked to me about the

---

*The last pre-flying-bomb attendance had been 6000. By 26 June the
audience was rising again, to 4500.

concert. . . . We arranged to meet in the Prom next evening and he saw me home afterwards.

Alas, the meeting never took place, for, from 30 June onwards, people arriving to claim their seats found the Albert Hall deserted. On 8 July the BBC announced that the Proms had 'been suspended for the time being' but promised that the series would continue from a BBC studio – it was in fact in Bedford – with the same works and artists as originally planned.

The pressure for restrictions on theatre attendance came from the theatre managers, faced by a calamitous drop in takings. The impresario, Jack Hylton, and another theatre manager actually urged the Home Office, as one civil servant noted on 23 June, to close down all the West End theatres to give managements an excuse for cancelling all their existing contracts with performers and back-stage staff. The Home Office refused. The remedy, suggested the official responsible, lay in the management's own hands. They could close down if they liked, but the government was not going to solve their problems for them.

The official line at this time was that audiences at public events would decline without any restrictions being needed. Some already existed: in the area 'South and East of a line Barnstaple/Tonbridge/Kings Lynn,' which included the whole area threatened by the flying-bombs, the maximum number allowed was '8,000 or half the capacity of the ground whichever was less,' though the Chief Constable had discretion 'to allow 15,000 for grounds having a capacity of 60,000.'

The same meeting at the Home Office heard that for 'cinema and other places of indoor entertainment . . . there is no restriction on numbers but the police are empowered to prohibit or restrict the use of premises as they consider necessary to minimise risk of loss of life.' Two specific events were discussed. A race meeting at Windsor on 1 July could, it was agreed, go ahead, but a boxing tournament at Tottenham Hotspur's football ground, on 9 July, which was expected to draw a crowd of 40,000, would have to be re-staged outside London. As for greyhound racing, it was decided that 'as in 1940–41 the matter would settle itself by the discretion of the public'; if they thought attendance dangerous they would stay away.

The government was particularly apprehensive about Saturday morning cinema matinees for children. Urgent inquiries, made by teleprinter on 27 June, were reassuring – except for juvenile cinema-goers – for it was learned that only in four places in Kent and London, and a few in Essex, were such performances still being held. The risk of one of these being hit, the committee agreed, was small enough to be accepted.

A great feature of previous wartime summers had been 'Holidays at Home'. As early as 19 June the town clerk of Lewisham asked for guidance from the Home Office about its planned programme of open air 'concerts, dances, sports, circuses, displays and street parties.' The Home Office temporized but was no doubt relieved to learn, on 8 July, that Lewisham had now abandoned all these events. Another twenty-five boroughs had, it was learned, 'cancelled or postponed . . . all or most of the entertainments' they had planned while attendances had dropped even at those which had gone ahead.

The official policy of not issuing formal restrictions was vindicated by events. No disaster occurred as a result of a V-1 striking a crowded cinema or theatre, and a report to the Home Office by the Assistant Commissioner of Police on 28 June showing comparative attendances at theatres and cinemas throughout Greater London on the last pre-doodlebug Monday, 12 June, and the two subsequent Mondays, 19 and 26 June, spoke for itself. At the Comedy – where potential patrons were invited to 'spend an exciting evening with Sonia Dresdel in *This Was a Woman*' – 435 of the 700 seats had been filled on 12 June, 222 a week later, and 181 by 26 June. At the Globe, 732 had turned up, in a building seating 960, to see the great comedy hit, Terence Rattigan's *While the Sun Shines*, on 12 June, but only 487 and 333 on the subsequent two Mondays. At His Majesty's, offering *The Lilac Domino*, 927 of its 1319 seats had been filled on 12 June, compared to 619 and 492 on the subsequent Mondays. Even that least demanding of entertainments, intimate revue, had suffered. *Sweeter and Lower*, with Hermione Gingold, had had the 'House Full' notices up at the *Ambassadors* before the V-1s came, with all its 430 seats occupied, but by 19 June attendance was down to 323 and a week later the audience numbered only 260. Only one establishment offering live entertainment defied the prevailing trend, the famous Windmill, with its motionless nudes and highly animated comedians. On 26 June after a drop to 180 in the intervening week, the number of seats occupied, 239, was slightly up on the 225 filled two weeks earlier.

Just before the first flying-bombs arrived the London theatre had been flourishing but Jack Hylton's forebodings about their effect on takings proved well founded. At the beginning of July, twenty-five leading theatres were still open. On Saturday, 8 July, the total was down to seventeen and ten days later, on 18 July, to eight. Then, very slowly, the tide began to turn. The *New Yorker*'s London correspondent, Molly Panter-Downes, reported to her readers on 23 July that 'most of the ten theatres still open report that receipts are looking up' and about the same time the Open Air Theatre, in Regent's Park, began to offer *Twelfth Night* to those prepared to brave doodle-bugs, as well as the customary chill winds.

On 1 August Wyndhams reopened with the inappropriately titled, *Quiet Weekend*, followed a week later by a more aptly named revue, *Keep Going*, but it was not until well into the autumn that the West End offered anything like the usual choice of plays.

Few companies, however, can have operated under greater difficulties that damp and noisy summer than the Open Air Theatre in Regent's Park. One man then living in Deal was present at a memorable performance one Saturday afternoon:

It began to drizzle and a delicate little old lady appeared on stage to announce that, in view of the weather, the play would be performed in the adjacent marquee. . . . All settled in the dry, the musicians continued their efforts when a flying-bomb's engine cut out very close indeed. The swishing crescendo of its descent was so near that some of the audience, panicking, jumped up. An authoritative voice yelled, 'Lie down,' which all did with alacrity and the bomb swept over, landing close enough to shake the marquee violently. . . . Shame-facedly we regained our seats, rubbing mud from hands and knees whilst the ruffled musicians recommenced playing. Almost immediately the little old lady reappeared and announced nonchalantly, 'Ladies and gentlemen, the rain has now stopped, so please be so kind as to resume your seats . . . outdoors.' Not a word about the flying-bomb which had just landed about two hundred yards away.

Actors who stayed in the West End, instead of discovering pressing reasons to join a provincial tour, were rewarded by exceptionally enthusiastic, if sparse, audiences. The experience of a woman from Pimlico who 'joined two friends in a box for a Noel Coward play' – probably *Blithe Spirit* – was typical. 'The business on stage was punctuated . . . by the sinister buzz and sound of distant crashes. The actors remained imperturbable. No one took cover and the play was much enjoyed.' In variety shows an actor might take such interruptions as the cue for an apposite *ad lib*. A Barnet man recalls Tommy Trinder commenting 'One of ours' when the customary drone was heard approaching the London Palladium, hastily amending it to 'Famous last words' after an explosion had demonstrated the contrary.

Amateur companies who had spent weeks rehearsing were also not to be cheated of their few nights of glory. One woman appearing in J. B. Priestley's *Dangerous Corner* in Balham remembers reflecting that even the title was appropriate. 'The first flying-bombs interrupted the two performances and between the afternoon and evening performances all the windows of the hall were blown in. We had to speak above the drone of the bombs and the lines spoken by Freda and Olwen in the play:

"Things are quite mad, aren't they?"
"Quite mad, and rapidly getting madder."

were very apposite.'

For ENSA – the often unjustly criticized Entertainments National Service Association, which provided stage shows for the forces and for war workers – the flying-bombs provided just one more impediment to add to the notorious uncertainties involved in going on tour. One flute player then in her twenties remembers an incident on the Hog's Back, near Guildford, one evening:

We were on our way back to base after the performance, travelling in the small ENSA bus. From the back seat went up the cry 'Engine trouble!' which meant that someone needed to spend a penny. . . .

Having cued the driver, our Czech manager, the conjuror in the show, turned round to say reassuringly: 'Buzz is stopping. . . .' His foreign pronunciation was appropriately prophetic. The bus drew up on this very high spot and as we stumbled out sleepily in search of discreet bushes, our purpose was deflected by a sudden perfect view across the valley of a buzz-bomb looking just like a lighted cigar cutting through the black velvet sky, making its loud jarring noise. It seemed to be hurtling along at breakneck speed. Then the abrupt cessation of sound; the terrifying silence before explosive crash and flash.

With their films already booked, all fifteen West End cinemas stayed open although this was not a vintage season for the moviegoer. The earlier enthusiasm for war films had now faded, but at the Odeon, Leicester Square, David Niven was starring in *The Way Ahead*, the Army's answer to Noel Coward's *In Which We Serve*. This had disappeared into the remoter provincial circuits, but Coward's *This Happy Breed* was now drawing the crowds – or what passed for them that summer – to the Marble Arch Pavilion. One Wrotham woman who went to see it found herself one of an audience of five. Molly Panter-Downes noticed the same phenomenon. 'Hardy souls who take in a cinema,' she told the readers of the *New Yorker* on 9 July, 'are apt to feel like moving over and talking to the gentleman fifty-seven seats away for company.'

Outside the West End, since the occupation rate had always varied from week to week, the trend was less marked though still serious. Nearly everywhere there had been a sharp drop in the first week, but in some places the queues began to form again after a fortnight, and where a particularly popular film was showing, attendance two weeks after the flying-bombs had started was sometimes higher than before the first one arrived.

By now the timorous had gone and those still in London were not going to allow the flying-bombs to interfere with their weekly – or sometimes twice- or thrice-weekly – addiction. 'We'd rather have died watching our favourite film stars than stay at home,' remembers one woman then aged fourteen and living in Wood Green. 'They used to put up a notice to say that the siren had gone but nobody ever left.' 'I used to slide down a bit in my seat, put my hands over my ears and wait for the engine to cut out,' remembers a former fifteen-year-old from Greenwich. 'Then would come the explosion and I would carry on watching the film.'

People's private thoughts on such occasions varied. 'I remember wondering whether Gary Cooper would be so tough if he was sitting where I was,' admits one wartime schoolboy from Croydon, as the V-1s passed over during *For Whom the Bell Tolls*. Another informant, aged fifteen, was at the Princess cinema in Dagenham watching 'the exciting climax' to *The Fighting Seabees*, when 'we . . . became collectively aware that there were menacing background noises *outside* the cinema.' He remembers two thoughts passed through his mind. One was that 'it certainly seemed a safer thing to make a film like *The Fighting Seabees* in California than to watch it in Dagenham' and the other was a most untimely recollection of reading about 'a blitzed cinema in an East End back street with the audience still sitting in the cheaper seats with their heads blown off.'

One title stands out in the reminiscences of filmgoers, *Gone with the Wind*, which was still on general release. Even the V-1s could not dislodge the queues waiting to see this already legendary epic, although sitting through its full four hours demanded exceptional concentration. One woman, then living in Welling, had dressed up for the great occasion in her 'beautiful new blouse and . . . one and only matching skirt and jacket' – only to find herself involved at lunchtime in a V-1 incident near her office.

My beautiful new blouse . . . looked a complete mess and . . . my mother was furious and I had a long lecture about my thoughtlessness. . . . It slowly became apparent that the sound track of the battle scenes was having a little help from outside but we became enthralled in the story and Clark Gable. I have since seen the film several times, but that performance was never surpassed.

Although this was the most curious summer in London since the Great Plague of 1665, the cultural life of the capital continued. 'There was a strange, almost magical, atmosphere about the deserted city with its empty streets and playgrounds, its rows of unoccupied houses,' felt one woman living in Pimlico. She particularly remembers the 'tremendous, exotic literary life to be found in the vicinity of the Fitzroy Tavern' on the Bloomsbury edge of Soho.

The diary of a seventeen-year-old schoolgirl living in Enfield accurately captures the feel of that June and July. Her response to the announcement of the flying-bombs' existence had been forthright: 'I wasn't,' she wrote on 16 June of a visit to the Proms, 'going to let the Germans' secret weapon stop my hearing Beethoven,' and as long as the concerts continued she eagerly supported them.

19 June I wore my pink silk frock and camel coat to the Proms. I managed to get on to the rail but along the cellos' side. It wasn't very full. Henry Wood conducted *The Flying Dutchman* overture and it was superb, only he stopped the orchestra in the middle so that a voice on the radio could announce that there was an air raid on. A few doodlebugs certainly tried to assist the timpani.

Even with the Proms banished to Bedford, there were other artistic diversions, of equal calibre:

13 July . . . Rushed off to the New Theatre and managed to get two stalls for this evening. Whoopee! *Sylphides* was lovely. I greatly enjoyed this evening although there were many warnings (announced by an illuminated sign by the footlights). . . . But what a shock for Fokine if he had seen the high spot of the grande valse – the man kneeling, the sylphide doing an arabesque holding his hand, right at the front of the stage, and an illuminated ALERT a few inches beneath them.

Although the Proms were an early casualty of the V-1s the lunchtime recitals at the National Gallery, about which the Home Office had also been particularly concerned, were reprieved. Held in the very heart of the embattled city, with a mixed audience of servicemen, Civil Defence workers and civilians, they became one of the great sights of wartime London. One AA gunner remembers a particularly inspiring occasion.

We were listening to one of Bach's unaccompanied partitas for violin. During this we heard the sound of an approaching V-1. As it came nearer, the audience became tense but the violinist kept on playing, quite unmoved. . . . There was a terrific contrast – the throb of the V-1 engine above us, with its deep menacing notes, and against this the thin beautiful melody of the violin. . . . The audience was held absolutely still and silent. . . . As the sound of the V-1 died away, the violin seemed to be playing away triumphantly. I have never heard Bach's music sound so powerful. I turned over two themes in my mind: the battle between good and evil, with the former triumphant; the opposition of great German music of the past to the sound of the contemporary evil regime we were fighting.

Few outdoor activities in Southern England in the summer of 1944 escaped some interruption by the doodlebugs. 'Not a bite,' remembers a wartime Royal Signals driver who had earmarked a rare day off duty for a few hours' fishing in Elstree Reservoir. 'I saw the greatest number of V-1s that day,' and the constant noise and vibration, he believed, kept the fish well away from the shore. 'I found it very difficult to get my ball through a hoop with one eye firmly fixed on the sky,' confessed a former Women's Land Army organizer of an evening spent playing croquet with some of her charges at a Land Army Club in Eltham.

A few V-1s arrived during the football season and a former member of a Tottenham team, then aged sixteen, remembers the simple rule his club introduced. On the referee blowing three short blasts on his whistle the players must immediately drop to the ground. Another boy, two years younger, in South Norwood, found that the training sessions at his local cycle racing track continued but 'if a V-1 started to dive near us we would all jump off our bikes and lie down with our arms shrouding our heads in the approved manner. After impact, we would remount and resume racing.'

Keeping an eye open for V-1s when playing tennis was exceptionally difficult and sometimes games had to be abandoned. Golfers, by contrast had ready-made shelters on hand. One Barnet warden, playing a round with three colleagues, remembers how a V-1 dived to earth ahead of them. 'Fortunately the bunker protected us but . . . we were very shocked and I yelled out the golf phrase: "It is as we lie, fellows" ' – meaning each ball must be played where it has fallen.

Some cricket teams nominated special 'doodlebug-watchers', like the Malden Wanderers, who on Sunday, 18 June, were playing an Australian service side and posted four players on the boundary to shout a warning. 'We seemed to spend a long time flat on the grass, keeping our fingers crossed,' one player remembers, and 'because of the many stoppages, the match ended in a draw.'

So far as is known, no scorebook actually records how many V-1s passed over, but one fifteen-year-old schoolboy in Wimbledon saw six during a house cricket match at West Barnes in early July. In response to the first the boys merely 'retreated to the edge of the field, where there was a dry ditch,' though they did not get into it for fear of dirtying their white flannels. By the fifth 'the standard of cricket was deteriorating. One batsman claimed that he should not have been given out because his attention was distracted and there was an argument about how many balls had been in the last over. The game was settled by a further V-1. . . . This one came directly overhead . . . dived . . . and . . . hit a group of houses just beyond the edge of the playing fields.'

The Eton and Harrow match in July was moved, for safety's sake, to Harrow and, to the delight of Harrovians, demonstrated the differing response of those accustomed to V-1s from those who seldom heard them. 'Whenever one appeared or was heard approaching, the Etonians threw themselves to the ground,' while 'the Harrovians stood up and waited for the game to continue.'

Similar hardihood was shown at an unspecified ground, probably Lords, on 29 July. 'Spectators sought cover on hearing the bomb,' reported *Reynolds News* next day, under the headline 'Fly-Bomb "Extra" ', 'but the players continued until there was a terrific explosion. They flung themselves on the turf to avoid the blast. The ground has never seen so many "ducks". But almost as quickly they were on their feet again on the cheers of the crowd and went on with the match. Even Göring's "fast one" could not get them out.'

At all the eighteen greyhound racing tracks in London there was some drop in numbers between the last pre-V-1 meetings, on 10 June, and those on the two subsequent Saturdays, but it was in most cases significantly less than at indoor amusements. Overall the total gates went down between 10 June and 27 June from around 116,000 to just under 90,000, a total drop of 22.6 per cent, or less than half that experienced by cinema and theatre owners.

A popular wartime recreation was 'digging for victory' and

sometimes the Germans assisted in harvesting one's crop. 'The allotment looked as though a bulldozer had run over it,' a Richmond woman recalls. 'I had a large crop of shallots and they were blasted all over the place, but luckily without much harm coming to them. I decided to gather as many as I could and ended up going home with a pram full of shallots and the baby perched on top of them.'

Many gardeners observed how the flying-bombs seemed to have upset the seasons. 'It was August, but winter arrived with that V-1,' remembers a Catford woman of one local explosion. 'Every leaf from the trees, every plant, every blade of grass over a wide area had gone. Everywhere was a grey waste, no colour to be seen at all.' 'At the . . . end of the garden . . . we had an apple tree . . . well laden with apples,' remembers an Edgware man of another incident the same month. 'The blast from the flying-bomb blew every apple off the tree and also completely stripped it of every leaf. A few weeks later in the autumn the tree came into full bloom again as though it had experienced two springtimes in one year.'

The perils of the times did not lead to any sudden increase in piety, but for existing churchgoers their religion often gained a new relevance. The daughter of a Congregational minister in Hackney was conscious of an 'inflowing of spiritual help' as her mother, at their customary evening prayers, 'recited the 91st Psalm: "Thou shalt not be afraid for the terror by night, nor for the arrow that flieth by day, nor for the destruction that wasteth at noonday".' 'Duckie,' a woman in Charlton told the rector's wife, 'there is one text in the Psalms that always comforts me. . . . "A thousand shall fall beside thee and ten thousand at thy right hand, but it shall not come nigh thee." ' 'I could not think of anything less comforting,' comments the recipient of this confidence.

In this parish, the parishioners did not let their faith in divine protection lead them to neglect more worldly precautions. The rector's wife was present when the parochial church council 'as one person dived under the table' as the rector was saying prayers, 'while he stood placidly surveying the feet of his PCC. But the menace went over . . . we rose rather sheepishly to our feet and my husband continued the prayers.'

Churches, as the Guards Chapel incident had demonstrated,

enjoyed no special immunity,* and flying-bombs seemed positively to seek them out, because they were often the highest buildings for miles around. Some of the London churches affected have already been mentioned. The most famous rural church to be totally destroyed was Saint Mary of the Holy Rood at Little Chart in Kent, built by loving and pious Norman hands in 1240 and demolished by German high explosives and malice on 15 August 1944. H. E. Bates saw the missile responsible, 'which on a beautiful . . . evening floated over my house, cut out half a mile away and . . . ended its flight on the top of the church tower under which . . . so many years before . . . I had paused to watch a flock of sheep safely graze.'

For a churchgoer the destruction of a much-loved place of worship could be almost as shattering as the loss of his home. One woman living in Raynes Park remembers looking from her front doorway towards a local landmark, St Matthew's church, and suddenly realizing that 'the spire . . . which . . . used to thrust itself darkly upwards against the sky was no longer there.'

I ran up the road to where the church had stood for upwards of sixty years. Nothing was left but a mass of bricks and rubble and one wall. People stood about the ruins in loose groups. Some were crying quietly and others whispering among themselves. . . . One of the sights which hurt me most was that of Miss F., our indefatigable volunteer verger, leaving the scene in a most uncharacteristically dishevelled state. She had kept the floors polished, the brasses shining and everything in spotless order, including herself, always dressed in neat tailor-mades and never a hair out of place. There she was, head bent, tears streaking down her blackened face, her grey hair half up and half down as she went across the road to her damaged home. I guessed that she felt heart-broken. . . . It seemed that the crowd respected and understood her grief, for no one spoke to her, and she looked at no one. The spire in falling had knocked the bottom out of her dedicated life.

Never before had the peace of an early morning communion service contrasted more strikingly with the tumult and danger outside. One Roman Catholic found himself deeply refreshed by attending early mass at a local convent, for not one of the

---

*For details of this particularly tragic incident see page 125.

Belgian nuns present 'showed any sign that they had even heard' the flying-bombs overhead, displaying instead an 'implicit faith . . . that God would protect them. Although houses were demolished all round . . . the convent came through unscathed.' An Anglican worshipper, in Sevenoaks, 'saw the vicar, who . . . was in the act of holding aloft the chalice, pause for an almost imperceptible moment and then continue quietly with the service, when, after an explosion, the church seemed actually to rise and fall again. . . . We found the doodlebug had fallen into a garden on the further side of the road, completely demolishing the church hall.'

One of the most famous stories of the First World War concerned the 'angels of Mons', supposed to have appeared in the sky over the retreating British forces in 1914, but a similar claim, in Peckham in 1944, attracted less attention. When it was reported that a cloud shaped like an angel had appeared in an otherwise clear sky before one particularly bad raid the locals were unimpressed. 'You might have hoped,' the vicar of St Luke's told a local newspaper, 'that the people who had seen such a wonder might have been moved to give thanks . . . to God in His holy church. But, unfortunately, not a bit of it.'

In spite of all discouragement church activities continued. 'We could not help feeling what a brave set of youth and children we had,' remembers the former vicar of St George and St Ethelbert, East Ham. 'The young were not deterred from attending the weekly youth club and neither were choristers discouraged or frightened from coming to take their part in choral weddings.' The afternoon Ladies Meeting held by the Congregationalists of Lower Clapton in Hackney also continued. Among twenty-three women gathered, despite the warning and three V-1s, at three o'clock on the afternoon of Wednesday, 5 July, was an old lady of ninety-five who had arrived alone, by trolley-bus. 'I asked her if she minded the bombs,' the minister's daughter remembers, 'and she replied "Oh no, duck, I can't hear anything." '

Doodlebugs or not, birthdays and other celebrations also came round. Few people needed a break more than the rector of Charlton and his wife, and when their silver wedding arrived they did their best to celebrate it.

The Doodlebugs

I do not think anyone could have had a more dismal day. There had been a raid the night before . . . and we had no post on our great day except funeral notices. We decided to go out into the country for a walk and took a train . . . to Westerham. We came to a place where a bomb had fallen a few days before and several children had been killed. It was an absolute ruin.* . . . Much depressed and saddened we went home and prepared a small tea party . . . when a doodle came over. . . . Our windows blew in from the blast and one of our friends was rung up to be told her house was badly damaged.

With demobilization surely not far off, this seemed a good time to get married. Among that summer's 'doodlebug brides' was a twenty-year-old Tottenham woman who helped to build De Havilland Mosquitoes. The date she had chosen was 1 July 1944, and it seemed a good omen when 'the all clear went just as the vicar said, "I now pronounce you man and wife!" ' The first warning of her married life came twenty minutes later, during the wedding breakfast while 'our three-day honeymoon was completely governed by the doodlebugs. . . . My airman husband, stationed where there were no flying-bombs, couldn't understand why I kept diving under the table and later under the bedclothes.'

A girl living in Leytonstone planned to marry on Saturday, 8 July, the end of the worst week of the whole flying-bomb offensive.

I never thought I would live to see my wedding day. Mother and I went to the Anderson shelter about 10.30 p.m. and . . . they were coming over . . . about every twenty minutes. . . . My mother was plying me with brandy . . . but I did not sleep. . . . However my wedding day dawned and I was feeling terrible, because I had invited people to my wedding from safe areas. . . . My main fear . . . was that one would hit St John's church with all my loved ones round me.

Smartly dressed in her 'blue two-piece with navy accessories and . . . a spray of white stephanotis', she duly got to church. 'At 6 p.m. all the guests departed and still not one V-1. At 8 p.m., they resumed' – the start of a classic family joke that she must be 'in league with Hitler'.

An airman, living at Swanscombe in Kent, has equally uncomfortable memories of his wedding to his childhood sweet-

---

See pages 224–5.

heart, then in the ATS, at St John's Church, Southend. 'The only music we had to accompany the service was the sound of gunfire and the thud of doodlebugs landing in the mud. On our return to the reception, an anti-aircraft shell case landed in front of the car as we were travelling along the sea front at Thorpe Bay.'

'My wife's sister managed to get some tins of Spam for our wedding reception. . . . My wife decided not to get married in a white dress she could have borrowed' because 'she was afraid she would not be able to run in it' – these are the chief memories of a Hackney builder who married a local aircraft factory worker at the height of the attack. He was relieved when she appeared beside him 'at two minutes to two', for a flying-bomb had landed near her home that morning, but soon discovered that, whatever his bride's other virtues, heroism was not among them:

As the vicar started the service . . . the warning sounded. I held my wife's hand. . . . She was already trembling with fear. The vicar . . . read the service faster and faster. . . . It took nine minutes . . . a record. . . . We moved very smartly into the vestry to sign the book. . . . The vicar said to us 'Hurry up . . . and get out of the church as the steeple is very dangerous. The blast of a V-1 could bring it down easily.' That did it! My wife flew out of the church with me running after her. . . . The taxi . . . was waiting outside. She jumped into it and by the time I got there it was well down the road and I was running alongside it. My wife opened the door and dragged me in. . . . When we got to her house she was out first and dived into the Anderson shelter. It was already full up. The blast of the V-1 that had dropped in the morning had made dust settle all over our wedding dinner. My wife cried, but we still ate it.

14

INCIDENT ON THE LINE

*We were all horrified to see this huge lethal object dipping . . .
towards the train.*

Woman from Barking recalling journey on the
District Line, July 1944

'The train coming in on platform five is the Brighton train, stopping only at Redhill. A flying-bomb is approaching platform six.' Many people claim to have heard this famous announcement at London Bridge, though it is probably apocryphal, but there is nothing mythical about the 1940 notice which now reappeared. 'Trains are being delayed due to an INCIDENT on the line.'

All told 1074 V-1s fell on, or near, railway property. The number which affected the different companies accurately reflects the varying weight of the attack in different parts of the country. The Great Western suffered a mere forty-five; the London Midland and Scottish Railway 126; the London and North Eastern Railway 226; and the Southern Railway no fewer than 528. London Transport's 149 seems light, but was heaviest of all in relation to its length of track above ground.

The very first flying-bomb to reach London had, as described earlier, disrupted services to the east from Liverpool Street. Five days later, on Sunday, 18 June, the first to reach Westminster tore up the track on the bridge outside Charing Cross, interrupting travel to the south-eastern suburbs. The same area suffered again when a bridge at Merstham, followed by a signal cabin at Tulse Hill, were wrecked in turn and the latter meant trains being diverted for almost a month. Even worse was what a railway historian described as the 'demoniacally and doubly effective' missile which landed at 7.30 p.m. on Thursday, 13 July, at Cow Lane Bridge, east of Peckham Rye station where 'the double line of the Old Chatham and Dover from Holborn

Viaduct' was 'carried over . . . what was once the London, Brighton and South Coast', a nodal point on the whole South London network. Blowing up the remains of the old bridge caused a girder to collapse on the track and it was ten days before a brand-new temporary bridge was in use.

The nightmare that haunted every railwayman was the des-truction of a bridge while a train was crossing it and the worst railway incident occurred in precisely this way on Wednesday, 16 August. It was observed by a Sittingbourne man stacking barley in a nearby field, who had watched a fighter pursuing a flying-bomb. 'Eventually the fighter drew level and with his wing tip threw the weapon over. It then dived and exploded under a railway bridge over the road that leads to Upchurch.'

Just at this moment the 3.35 p.m. from Victoria to Ramsgate was approaching the bridge, about three-quarters of a mile from Rainham. To the driver's horror the bridge exploded in front of him and a wide gap appeared in the track. Although he instantly slammed on his emergency brakes, the engine crashed down into the gap and overturned, before rolling down the adjoining embankment. The second and third coaches land-ed in the gap, 'sticking up in the air like a letter "V" ', as one man who passed the scene on a relief bus two hours later recalls.

Among those on board was a young woman from Turnham Green, in West London, on her way to spend a few peaceful days on the coast. She still remembers the 'almighty swaying' of the train and her mother's reaction – 'What cheek!' – when another passenger put his arm round her to steady her. When the train finally stopped the same helpful male helped her to climb down. 'My mother,' she remembers, 'got to work at once among the casualties, but, apart from giving my scarf for a sling, I didn't do much. . . . We were in that beautiful Kentish glade for what seemed a very long time. Then non-casualties were taken to the nearest station by car. I remember how grateful I was for tea in the buffet. Eventually we got a train and arrived at my cousin's house. She said we looked like ghosts, white with dust, and weak at the knees.'

A woman from Norbury, travelling with her children, aged two and four, had an even narrower escape:

We were in the second coach which was overhanging the gap, and I can vividly remember all the water from the tanks in the toilets overflowing into the coach. We were helped from the wreckage by two soldiers and my main concern was to get away from the noise of escaping steam and the engine's whistle which had got jammed. We had to crawl beneath the coach to get down the embankment and the wheels were still revolving. Having scrambled down the bank, one of the soldiers stopped a lorry and asked the driver to take us to Sittingbourne station. In the confusion at Sittingbourne, I mislaid my handbag with all my money and papers. I therefore had no money to continue my journey to Sheerness. A kindly ticket collector gave me a ten-shilling note and a very welcome cup of tea. My handbag was eventually returned to me three weeks later by the police. It was intact and in fact some 'good Samaritan' had put some money in my daughter's little beaded purse.

In this incident eight people were killed and sixteen seriously injured, a mercifully light casualty list in the circumstances. By prodigious efforts, a temporary bridge was rapidly erected and trains were running over the line again within sixty-six hours.

Freight services also suffered. One train received a direct hit on 17 June as it was crossing a bridge between the Elephant and Castle and Loughborough Junction, and a bad accident to another on the Ramsgate line was only avoided when a pilot who had shot down a flying-bomb was able to attract the attention of the driver before he ran into the debris thrown across the track.

Damage to railway property which only affected freight traffic – as, for example, the great GWR goods depot at the Minories – attracted little public attention. Even minor damage visible to passengers, by contrast, set tongues wagging, as at Wimbledon station, while Forest Hill station was knocked out and had to be closed. Among the buildings destroyed was 'the former power-house of the Old Croydon Atmospheric Railway', a monument to one of the great scientific dead-ends of the nineteenth century.*

Destruction further out of London was usually caused by missiles which had been shot down, for bridges and railway-

---

*The atmospheric railway made use of a vacuum in an adjoining tube to propel the train forward. It was a promising idea which in practice failed to work.

lines could be found in even the most 'empty' landscape. One particularly bad incident occurred at Maidstone West, observed by a young signalman from his box overlooking the scene.

The windows exploded in on me, like sheets of rain. The telephone board containing eight phones was blown off the wall, knocking me to the floor. I crawled to the door and the steps leading to the ground where I was met by my rescuers climbing the stairs to help me. . . . I was eventually taken to the West Kent Hospital. . . . I had glass in my hand, face and back, my clothes were ruined. . . . I was off work for fifteen days before returning to the box, which had been repaired. . . . Seven people died. . . . Two were coalmen who were unloading trucks. . . . Two of Fremlins', the brewers, beautiful grey horses were killed. One had his head blown off, the other a foreleg and had to be shot . . . by the Railway Home Guard.

Even more talked about, though it involved fewer casualties, was the havoc caused at Ashford. One fifteen-year-old railwayman was waiting on board a train there to travel home to Folkestone:

Suddenly we heard cannon fire . . . and we dived out to the corridor window and looked out towards Folkestone. It was a new Gloster Meteor jet chasing a doodlebug. . . . Someone yelled, 'It's coming down!' so we all dived under the seats, when there was a terrific bang and dust and bits of compartment were floating about and a real downpour of wooden boxes dropping all over the tracks. . . . It had dropped on a goods train in a siding. The boxes all over the line were ammunition boxes but empty, luckily.

Had a V-1 come down on one of the main-line stations crowded with would-be evacuees the carnage would have been enormous. As it was, two main-line terminuses were hit, but both were carrying only normal traffic. At Victoria on 27 June a direct hit damaged the booking office and other premises near one of the departure platforms, leaving fourteen people dead and sixty-eight injured, and a little later Waterloo was affected by a bomb which landed in York Road, just outside. This is a very well-remembered incident, for it occurred during the morning rush hour. The then editor of *Woman's Own*, who had just left the station, remembers, how 'hundreds of us, in a stream stretching right across Waterloo Bridge, fell flat on our faces.' Another passenger was an employee of the Charing Cross Hotel.

The warning sounded just as the train ran into platform 21. We all piled out into the platform and had just passed through the gate when the imminent danger warning was sounded over the speakers. Everyone started to run for the underground. My colleague and I ran to the slope leading down to the tube, he . . . a little ahead of me. I had just started down the top of the slope when the world for me suddenly erupted into a roar like an express train, everything became one great flash of blue, red and orange light and then, just as suddenly, silence and complete darkness. At first I thought that I must be dead, then the smoke and dust began to clear and I found that I was no longer at the top of the slope but at the bottom on my knees with part of the roof of the tunnel on my back, luckily for me mostly wood and small rubble. I tried to move but my legs wouldn't budge. . . . I began to hear sounds in the silence around me, first coughing then moaning. My friend came running back through the rubble to find me. . . . He lifted the wood planks off my back, got me onto my feet and helped me towards the lower tunnel. When we reached the lower booking hall, there were books and papers everywhere from W. H. Smith's bookstall, which had been demolished by the blast, and all the metal ticket machines were lying around the floor as if thrown by some giant hand. . . . We eventually got to the Charing Cross Hotel. When we saw ourselves in the mirror we looked like minstrels, our faces were black with white-ringed eyes and mouths, my hair was full of dust, bits of glass and twisted pieces of wire, rivulets of blood ran down my legs from tiny glass cuts, my precious stockings ruined . . . my skirt was ripped, in fact I was a sorry sight. I eventually got home that night to the suburbs and my own doctor was called in to me. I never returned to work in London again, my nerves had gone completely.

To regular passengers it often seemed that the flying-bombs were pursuing a train and even more unpleasant was being on an elevated line and seeing a V-1 apparently about to hit one's train broadside on. The tension for men on the footplate was continuous. 'It was frightening, especially at night in the black-out wondering whether you would run into a bomb crater or a heap of debris,' admits a railway fireman, who stoked the boilers of the steam engines running between Chingford and Liverpool Street. He particularly disliked the stretch on a viaduct between Hackney Downs and Bethnal Green, partly because of the depressing views this vantage point afforded. 'Each day the scene would change. A fresh street of houses was now a heap of rubble or a small block of flats had been sliced in half.'

If the trains had stopped whenever an alert was in force the transport service in the South-East would have been paralysed. In the worst week, between 3 and 9 July, there were ninety-eight alerts, covering 60 per cent of the whole period, while in the twelve weeks up to 3 September 1944 'red' warnings covered central London for 646 hours, or nearly a third of the time the trains were running. In a single three-and-a-half-hour period on the evening of 24 August, the busiest time of the day for forwarding goods from London, the railways received thirteen 'imminent danger' warnings. Since the crews might not know if the siren had sounded, on the LNER 'whenever a train approached a box during an alert, the signal man would lean out of the window and point upwards into the sky with his right forefinger.' Later 'a board, about two feet long, with an arrow painted on it . . . pointing upwards' was hung outside to warn 'the driver to expect trouble'.

The flying-bombs provided a rich new source of material for travellers' tales. A man then living in Lee, who worked at Fort Halstead in Essex, remembers the day another man in the compartment, seeing a flying-bomb 'just over the train . . . panicked and pulled the communication cord,' to the great annoyance of the regulars playing 'blind brag'. 'There was £2 in the kitty . . . and the resulting jolt put everything on the floor. One player claimed he had a running flush. It was there all right, but whether in one hand or not we never knew.' A schoolboy of seventeen lays claim to the oddest wound inflicted by a V-1, 'frost bite of both big toes', caused by a ninety-minute wait outside Three Bridges station in an unheated train en route to Horsham after the line had been blocked by bomb damage. The experience cost him four days in bed.

A former naval petty officer recalls his reflections when his train stopped on a bridge as a flying-bomb began its descent. If, he mused, he were to be thrown into the river, would he be described as 'Lost at sea', 'Missing in action', or less heroically, 'Lost on the Thames in a Southern Railway train'?

Never had the London Underground been more popular and

many a passenger heaved a sigh of relief as his train plunged back into the security of a tunnel. But the tradition of reserve died hard, as one woman travelling above ground from Wembley station discovered on hearing 'a loud noise':

'It *is* a bomb,' I wanted to shout. Suddenly I flung myself on to the floor of the train as the engine did its customary cut-out. A tremendous explosion came at once. Then silence. I stood up and . . . saw that everybody was doing the same, brushing themselves down, settling to their newspapers again and awaiting the train's departure. . . . In typical English fashion, nobody spoke, the doors of the train closed and off we all went to the West End or the City.

The Underground suffered scores of lesser incidents involving damage to trains or some injury to passengers, and six major ones, which affected traffic: at Essex Road in East London; Ravenscourt Park to the west; Aldersgate, in the City; Walham Green, near Fulham; and West Brompton and South Kensington in the inner south-west districts. Hardly rating a mention in the official histories was this incident, witnessed by a young woman war worker returning from the West End after seeing *The Lisbon Story*:

As the train left East Ham and was approaching Barking, it ground to a halt and we could all hear the droning of a doodlebug. . . . Someone yelled, 'There it is!' and we were all horrified to see this huge lethal object dipping and bearing towards the train. The lines ran between fields here, and on the other side stood huge gasometers. . . . 'Hit the deck!' someone cried, and we all crouched down.
   A strange man flung himself over me to protect me, and miraculously the bomb skimmed the rooftops of the train and for a moment it appeared that it was heading straight for the gasometers. . . . However, it exploded into the ground. . . . Glass from doors and windows of the train shattered and flew in all directions, doors flew open, and the whole train seemed to lift up and land again. The relief after our escape was great and everyone was in a jocular mood. A man whose face was spattered with blood from flying glass was being given first aid by other passengers, and some wit yelled, 'Ma! He's been at the jam again. That's all our ration gorn this month!'

During the opening stages of the offensive a flow of reports of damage to buses or tubes, or both, constantly reached London Transport headquarters and during the first fortnight of July the number soared to more than twenty a day, or almost one an hour. Between 16 June and 31 August London Transport was affected by 270 separate incidents, of which fifty-three caused serious damage. Road services were more affected than the Underground. The flying-bomb on York Road, Waterloo, already mentioned, left two double-deckers with their tops neatly sliced off. In Lambeth a V-1 at the junction of Clapham Road and Kennington Triangle, near the Oval, blew to pieces two trams and two buses crammed with people going home from work. The highest death toll in Battersea occurred when a V-1 hit a lorry on Lavender Hill at lunchtime, and killed fourteen of the twenty people on a No. 77 that was passing; another fourteen people died in the street and the surrounding buildings.

The main damage to vehicles occurred when a whole fleet was caught by a single explosion. One flying-bomb which landed forty yards away from one convoy, fortunately empty, assembled to carry troops to the docks, at Snaresbrook Road, Wanstead, destroyed fifteen buses. The trams suffered badly when a bomb landed in Troutbeck Road near the New Cross tram depot, while Battersea bus garage was damaged three times in a fortnight. Camberwell surpassed it, with four flying-bombs plus others on the tram depot and electricity sub-station. By far the worst such incident, however occurred at Elmers End in Beckenham on 18 July. To one local woman the V-1 responsible appeared to descend as purposefully as 'a plane going into a hangar'. The tragic results were described by London Transport's historian:

It was a fine summer evening, and a dozen of the staff were in the entrance to the garage, when they heard a doodlebug. Suddenly it cut off and . . . could be seen diving straight for the building.

Everyone scattered. . . . Six who went to the kit room were killed instantly. The doodlebug, . . . exploding against the near side of the main entrance, wrecked the traffic office, the ticket department, the canteen, the A.R.P. stores, the cleaners' room, the inside-staff mess-room, as well as the kit room. The depot inspector was taking cash at the time from a woman conductor. . . . He threw himself to the floor . . . near the safes. The woman was killed. Within a few minutes the garage was alight. The N.F.S. hurriedly appeared on the scene, but one petrol tank after another of the parked buses exploded. The tyres smouldered and smelled horribly. Debris was scattered everywhere. The inspector set up an office in a damaged bus inside the nearby cemetery so that returning crews could pay in.

That night urgent telephone calls to various garages enabled the Elmers End Garage to borrow omnibuses and tickets so that next morning the run-out was exactly acording to schedule – except for two buses which started a few minutes late. . . . Some of the buses were windowless, while others had no destination blinds. But the services went on, in spite of the fact that twenty-seven double-deckers, two single-deckers, and ten ambulances had been completely put out of action.

One advantage – or disadvantage – of bus travel at this time was that one rarely knew what was happening outside, for the windows were covered in anti-splinter netting, except for a small diamond-shaped 'porthole' in the centre. One City office worker, on a bus which had stopped on Westminster Bridge, remembers gazing 'out of the window, fascinated to see every-one in the street running from the Parliament side across the road to the tube entrance, exactly like wind across a field of corn'. Often a 'clippie' – a wartime innovation in this previously all-male job – could be seen on the platform of her vehicle scanning the skies like a ship's look-out.

The official advice to drivers was to stop at the approach of danger, and to lie on the floor with the passengers, but this was rarely possible and for bus-crews it was the worst period of the war. One conductress remembers her bus sliding into a shallow, newly opened crater as it approached the depot off the Archway Road. 'I was flung the full length of the bus, hitting my head against the driver's cabin. The money that fell out of my bag was lost and, to add insult to injury, I had to make good the loss on my next pay day.' Another conductress, from Catford, heard a flying-bomb approaching as she reached 'Woolwich' while winding the destination blind. She became apprehensive for this was a place notorious for attracting them. A moment later the bomb exploded:

I was blown up the bus between the seats and . . . cut by some bits of glass. One piece went into my wrist and the blood poured into my hand. . . . I walked over to the first aid post but only the front was left. . . . My driver who had been bombed out . . . had just been issued with a new uniform and he picked up his new cap and, in

174

disgust, said, 'Look what that b——— done. Made a cut in my new cap!'

Many people felt a special affection for the surviving trams, but their popularity dwindled rapidly that summer, for not merely were they exceptionally noisy and one felt especially vulnerable, but they ran through many of the worst-bombed districts. One Croydon man observed that by the end of June almost all the No. 16s and No. 42s had had their internal screens and outside windows removed. 'A thirty-mile-hour gale through the tram was much to be preferred to a hail of glass splinters.' Some people gave up travelling by tram and one student engineer observed how 'often trams would stop short of the terminus at Wimbledon before returning eastwards'. But such a reaction was untypical. A woman personnel officer in a Camden Town factory found that lack of transport was never given as an excuse for lateness. 'We all had to get to our jobs. If there was a fear . . . it was of being unpunctual.'

Trolley-buses were also still in use in 1944, and were exceptionally quiet. One East Finchley woman remembers how when 'the vehicle suddenly stopped halfway between the recognized stops with one accord all the passengers, myself included, dropped to the floor and wriggled under the seats. We felt rather abashed when the conductor . . . called out "You can all get up. It is only the trolley arm come off!" ' There were some incidents involving trolley-buses, however, like that experienced in West Ham Lane by a seventeen-year-old girl from Silvertown, on her way with a girlfriend to the East Ham Premier to see Arthur Askey in *Up in Annie's Room*.

I remember a man pushing me down . . . a big red light, no noise or explosion of any sort, and then thick black dust and smoke. The doodlebug had landed right on top of the pub opposite and the bus had caught a lot of the blast. I was smothered in blood, which belonged mostly to the man who had pushed me down. He was badly cut about the face, while I had cuts on my hands . . . and a torn muscle in my right leg where I was sandwiched between the seats. People were helping each other to get down the stairs, what was left of them. . . . A first-aid man sat me on a bench and . . . put a label around my neck. Our conductress was lying on the ground with a hole right through her middle and the driver was hunched over his wheel, both dead. Some of the downstairs passengers were also dead.

175

The Doodlebugs

My friend and I were taken to St Mary's Hospital, Stratford, which was only a few minutes away. My hands were stitched and I was given an injection for shock. . . . I . . . wouldn't mention about my leg as I was at the age when I couldn't take off my slacks in front of other people. . . . When I arrived home my coat was smothered in blood and I had one arm in a sling.

Driving a car or trade vehicle in London presented similar problems to operating a bus, but the unluckiest drivers of all were surely those responsible for delivering petrol. One such man who worked in Croydon remembers that when he tried to take shelter he was 'not at all welcome. The nearest house promptly said, "Don't stop here with that tanker." '

15

SUDDENLY, WHILE SHOPPING

We are happy to report that nothing has occurred to prevent our giving our usual efficient and courteous service in all departments.

Advertisement by department store in the *South London Press*, 1 September 1944

The danger under which everyone in London now lived had one welcome result: the queues suddenly thinned and long-forgotten goods appeared on the shelves of the shops. 'We asked for our meat ration and the butcher offered as much more,' remembers a man from South Norwood. 'The queues at greengrocers and fishmongers almost disappeared,' found a woman in Maida Vale. 'At the grocers it became easier to get . . . goods on "points", biscuits, raisins, etc., and there might even be an extra egg or orange available.' A housewife living near Regent's Park was astounded to be offered a chicken; 'West End customers', who usually monopolized such luxuries, had gone to the country.

'The shopkeepers were suddenly very cordial. The customer was coming back into his own,' discovered Mrs Robert Henrey in Mayfair. 'London was becoming the city of the brave and the few.' That August Mrs Henrey heard, incredulously, a customer in Fortnums being told she could have as many bottles of orangeade as she wanted, and that her order would be *delivered* if required. 'London wine merchants were suddenly offering clarets and Burgundies which their customers never knew existed. . . . People who had paid £10 for a bottle of Grand Marnier a few months earlier were no longer likely to repeat this folly.'

Some queues did still occur and their reaction to danger was an accurate index of an item's scarcity. The *South London Press* described how not a woman moved when 'danger klaxons sounded' while 'there was a queue for cherries at a stall' though the crowd did disperse in disorder a few minutes later. 'The cause of the panic? A mouse.' A man in Lee remembers his mother telling him how she had stood firm when a flying-bomb was heard. 'It was worth it. I got half a pound of pig's liver.' Fish, also not on coupons, was another great prize. One Sydenham man remembers seeing a fish queue that 'had dashed off into the shuttered shop', reassembling after the crucial explosion.

The first words I heard were:
    'Oh, no mate, she was first and you were about last.'
    'Oh no, I wasn't.'
    'Oh yes, you b——— well was and what's more if you don't get back in the queue I'll get that copper to arrest you.'

The reluctance of determined shoppers to take shelter embarrassed conscientious shopkeepers. One fish and chip shop owner in Walthamstow would emerge from behind the counter blowing a whistle if the waiting crowd was slow to disperse. Others provided their own refuge. One of the earliest memories of a five-year-old boy living in Streatham Vale is of a local butcher, who 'with great aplomb, left his chopping and calmly ushered all the ladies, and me, into his steel-lined cold room.' Mrs Robert Henrey saw two customers of one Central London fishmonger crouching 'under the slab on which he had been cutting the hake,' while in an Honor Oak florist's the stone trough in which the plants were watered saved the lives of two assistants. A customer, who refused to join them for fear of laddering her stockings, was killed.

Many hitherto scarce services also became plentiful. The editor of *Woman's Own* found that she could get her hair washed and set without an appointment for 'an enterprising hairdresser' set up in business in the magazine's basement shelter and she 'chatted, or read manuscripts or wrote editorials' while under the drier. Above ground it was less easy to relax especially while receiving a permanent wave, which involved being tethered by a head-full of rollers to an electric heater. 'I was under this machine when the hairdresser informed me the "imminent danger" warning had gone and asked did I want to "come off", which would ruin the perm,

178

or stay,' remembers one woman from Chingford. 'I decided on the latter.'

An occasional meal out was in 1944 a necessity, for the ration scale was based on the assumption that it would be supplemented by people eating in factory canteens or restaurants. 'The approach of a doodlebug had a markedly freezing effect on conversation at the luncheon or dinner-table,' wrote the literary journalist, John Lehmann, recalling 'a luncheon . . . arranged at the Savoy,' an unpopular location because of its exposed position over-looking the Thames.

I was deep in conversation with Kenneth Clark about the war-artists. . . . At that moment the familiar splutter began to be audible in the distance; as it grew louder, we all became a little more thoughtful; conversation faltered, dried up here and there for some seconds though the thread was never entirely lost; gestures were inhibited, not a fork was lifted to a mouth for the brief span of time that seemed an eternity. When the machine had evidently veered away again, it was satisfactory to observe that no members of the party had actually disappeared under the table.

The editor of *Woman's Own* found the underground grill room of the Strand Palace Hotel ideal for working lunches and in humbler establishments above ground, window seats, normally the most popular, were now the last to be filled. One Women's Land Army organizer, who occupied one in a café in Tenterden, found herself advised to move, 'as the High Street was being peppered by shrapnel.'

A café in East Finchley posted a look-out at the door, ready to blow a whistle. One woman who lunched there remembers glancing up from her newspaper 'to see every table completely empty, though gradually the rest of the customers emerged and continued their meals.'

The flying-bombs added a new dimension of horror to going to the dentist. One woman living in Bromley who was having all her teeth extracted at a clinic remembers how 'eight were pulled and the ninth was nearly out when a doodlebug could be heard coming our way.' At this the staff 'all downed tools and went below for safety,' except for the one attending her, who urged her to take shelter. 'I told him to finish the job as the tooth was hanging by a thread. . . . He did, but the expression on his face I'll remember for the rest of my life.'

In theory, beer should have been plentiful, due to evacuation, but in fact there was a shortage, at least of the bottled variety, because workers in the bottling plants objected to their splinter-prone surroundings. The stern, unyielding British spirit was not much in evidence either among the brewers' draymen, who delivered to one Wimbledon pub:

The delivery men from the East End were very jumpy . . . and though they received extra pay for coming into the district . . . they would hurry off before the order had been completed. On one occasion . . . my father was accused of only thinking of himself when he not only insisted that the full order was left in the cellar, but that the draymen 'fined' the beer, a normal part of their duties which only took a few minutes anyway.

A pub in Marylebone was said to have lost its staff because they considered working among bottles and glass panels too dangerous, but though, by the end of August, 112 public houses had been damaged, the number of serious incidents was surprisingly few. The worst occurred in Southwark, when two adjoining public houses in Great Guildford Street were destroyed. Both were crowded, with a darts match in progress, and it was days before all those trapped could be rescued: the death roll remains uncertain. A fourteen-year-old in South Norwood witnessed the destruction of his family's local, the Albert, one Sunday evening, when ten customers died:

After the initial dust had subsided, I joined a chain of neighbours passing debris, brick by brick, to gain access to several people trapped below. . . . Their only problem was that of rubble falling onto their heads. I remember passing my steel helmet through a hole to one man. . . . I never did get the helmet back, and I'd only borrowed it from my father, a firewatcher.

London in 1944, as now, possessed two major shopping thoroughfares to which people came from miles around, Oxford Street and Kensington High Street. The former escaped without a direct hit, though several V-1s landed very near to it, but Kensington was less fortunate. Its ordeal had begun, as already described, with the disastrous St Mary Abbot's incident, before dawn on Saturday, 17 June, and this was followed by two others at twenty-four-hour intervals, in one of which, Clydesdale Road, twenty-one people were killed. So far the main shopping area had escaped, but this immunity ended when the borough's fourth flying-bomb landed, at the height of the dinner hour, at 12.48 p.m. on Monday, 19 June. The Civil Defence services knew it as the 'Winchester Court' incident, from the nearby block of flats and shops, but the public called it 'the Kensington Church Street bomb', after the road which connects Notting Hill to Kensington High Street. The *Kensington News*, writing in September, called the casualties 'remarkably light': six dead, twenty-two seriously injured and thirty minor casualties; but the affair occurring on a famous thoroughfare familiar to everyone made a deep impression none the less.

Even more famous was Piccadilly Circus, where every Saturday night on 'In Town Tonight', the BBC apparently 'stopped the roar of London's traffic' and silenced the Cockney street vendor offering 'Sweet violets!' The Germans almost succeeding in stopping the traffic and silencing the flower-seller once and for all just after midday on Friday, 30 June, when they landed a flying-bomb on the Regent Palace Hotel, or, more precisely, on its main annexe in Brewer Street, part of that rabbit warren of little streets, which marks the south-west corner of Soho.

Although the whole top storey of the annexe was demolished, and there was serious damage to the sixth and seventh floors directly below, the overwhelming reaction of most Civil Defence workers was 'It might have been worse', for nowhere is emptier at midday on a Friday than the bedroom corridors of a hotel. As it was, only one person, a chambermaid, was killed, though 168, largely in the surrounding streets, were injured, some badly. Almost miraculously, many others in that close-packed, crowded area escaped unhurt, among them a West Norwood woman, several hundred yards away in Regent Street, who watched unbelievingly one plate-glass window of Dickins and Jones 'bulge in and out and then vibrate less and less as it settled back into place.'

Few London streets could have been more different from Piccadilly Circus than Aldwych, a mile and a half due east of it, a wide crescent-shaped thoroughfare, linking the Strand, Fleet Street and Kingsway, and overlooking the northern end of Waterloo Bridge. The office blocks in the area, developed between the wars, were largely modern, steel-framed buildings. Among them was Aldwych House, accommodating the Legal and General Assurance Company, Bush House, containing the BBC External Services, and on the far side of the Strand, Australia House, that country's large and imposing 'shop window' in London.

Unusually for that summer it had been a fine day and two girls working in Australia House were enjoying the lunchtime break:

We sat at the open window in the Cable Office . . . situated on the first floor in the corner . . . facing the Strand at the St Clement's Dane end.

There were two spotters on the roof opposite. They started 'flirting' with us, turning their binoculars on us. We were having great fun when suddenly one of the men grabbed the other pointing at something . . . excitedly. They turned to us and indicated we should leave the window. We caught on quickly and flew under the large cipher table in the corner of the office. . . . There was a terrible explosion and the sound of breaking glass, falling plaster, concrete and marble and the splitting and tearing of wood. Then a sickening, choking smell of cordite. Then utter complete silence for a second or so. The doodlebug had come down on the opposite corner of Australia House on the Aldwych side, between our building and the Air Ministry in Kingsway. The two of us under the table were filthy dirty and I remember we hugged each other, laughing and repeating over and over again, 'We're alive.'

A few floors below them, climbing the staircase, was a man with an administrative post with the Australian Army.

The building . . . swayed from side to side as if the whole structure was airborne in a storm. Glass crashed down from the dome above and it seemed as if the whole building must collapse, crushing all to pulp. But, to my amazement, the building defied all the laws of nature and remained upright.

As in the Regent Palace incident an hour before, most of the casualties occurred among pedestrians in the open, and few people can have had a narrower escape that a fifteen-year-old BBC employee who 'after the usual ghastly canteen meal' had gone for a short walk with a friend.

As we crossed the Strand . . . the engine cut out. We waited for an explosion; none came and by now we were in the eastern courtyard of Bush House, a few yards from the side entrance. Some instinct made me uneasy and I glanced upwards. The sight I saw is burned into my memory, for diving upon us was the bomb which . . . had been gliding towards us. I shouted a warning, pointed and flung myself to the ground. . . . The explosion came almost at once. The blast felt as though I was being compressed from all sides. . . . Thoughts flashed through my mind; I was alive, felt no pain. . . . I tried to squeeze smaller and tensed myself for the stone which I felt must be crashing down. But none came. The sounds of falling glass and debris died away and I cautiously raised my head. My companion did likewise and we scrambled to our feet looking wonderingly and speechlessly at each other. . . .

We ran instinctively toward the steps which led into Aldwych. It was as though a foggy November evening had materialized at the throw of a switch. Through the dust of smoke the casement of the bomb lay burning on the corner of the Kingsway; three victims lay unmoving at the top of the steps only thirty yards from where we had crouched and huddled figures were scattered over the road. . . . The corner of the building had shielded us from the direct path of the explosion.

According to the official report, the flying-bomb had landed in the roadway, sixty feet from the east wing of Bush House and only forty feet from the Air Ministry headquarters in Adastral House. A ten-foot-high blast wall, designed to protect the latter, was demolished but saved the building from serious damage, although some WAAFs, attracted to the window by the sound of the approaching bomb, were sucked out into the street by the vacuum which followed the explosion. In Aldwych House there were several serious casualties. 'A young woman I knew who worked on the fourth floor was naked and dead, stripped and killed by the blast,' remembers the supervisor of the first aid room. 'Another I knew came into the building helped by a friend – blood spurting from her wrist and a deep gash in one eye. . . . From approximately 2.15 to 5.15 we were treating casualties.'

Aldwych lies within the City of Westminster and a mobile unit was on its way while the tell-tale column of dust and smoke still hung in the summer air. The City's historian described the scene:

The Flying Column despatched straightway to the Aldwych arrived on a scene of terrible slaughter. A light mist lifted to unveil those wide pavements littered with shapes of the dead and wounded. In the canyon of the Aldwych's white masonry they were scattered like the victims of a massacre in some spacious curved arena. And this freshly daylit, terrible scene was further confounded by odd wreckages – the twisted frames of a line of buses parked there, and on the pavement and the road a pathetic snow of currency notes.

Although Westminster Control sent thirteen ambulances to ferry the injured to hospital they had to be supplemented by a fleet of Army lorries parked nearby; identifying the dead and injured proved particularly difficult, as so many were passers-by. The final death toll, after the last grey mortuary van had carried away its unmoving cargo, and the firemen had washed the pavements clear of blood, proved to be forty-six, making this second only to the Guards Chapel in the number of fatal casualties. The number of seriously injured was far higher: 399. Another 200 injured were able to go home after treatment.

The 30th of June, with two major incidents within minutes of each other, had been a 'black Friday' for the citizens of London. Exactly four weeks later they were to experience another. It was 1.30 p.m. on Friday, 28 July, when South Kensington's fourteenth V-1 landed in the heart of the royal borough, at the junction of Earls Court Road and Kensington High Street. 'Lyons, the Wooden Horse Restaurant, the Aerated Bread Company and another café [over Lavell's, the confectioners] were packed with diners,' wrote the *Kensington News* six weeks later, and there were many shoppers in the streets outside. Eventually, when the usual tragic aftermath of disaster had been cleared, forty-five people were found to be dead, fifty-four seriously injured and 116 slightly injured – by far the largest toll of all Kensington's twenty V-1s.

Among those on the scene – she had been lunching in a nearby milkbar after calling at a local stationers where she had chatted with the girl assistants – was a young woman civil servant. Her 'greatest wish', feeling she was missing out on an important personal experience, had been to see a doodlebug fall. Now her desire had been satisfied – to her horror.

The stationers shop was completely destroyed, although the outside walls remained standing to hold the two top floors intact. Some people were looking out of an upstairs window awaiting rescue. I tried to shout across to ask them if the young girls underneath had taken cover. . . . No one heard me. The road was a crater with a sea of mud, rubble and glass everywhere. A policeman stood guard and . . . asked us to move on: 'Have you nothing better to do than stare at all this?' . . . I felt extremely guilty.

Even more destructive and lethal than the Kensington High Street bomb was one which had landed four hours before, at 0941 hours, on the street market in Lewisham. A Home Office report, compiled that night, gave the bare facts of the story:

Fly, gliding after stalling, by a direct hit on a reinforced concrete below-ground shelter below the open area in front of shops on the west side of High Street, detonated on the surface and pierced the concrete roof. Blast caused demolition of about 20 shop premises and damage beyond repair to approximately 30 others (including the General Post Office). Major damage to about 20 other shops and minor damage to premises about 600 yards from point of detonation. . . . Blast effect appears to be considerably higher than that found in previous Flys.

This is how a former WAAF, then aged twenty-two and stationed at a balloon centre near her home, remembers the Lewisham market bomb:

Mum was nervous to shop far from home alone, but I wanted to take my spare uniform . . . to the cleaners, so we decided to be very brave and go to shop in Lewisham. . . . It was a dullish morning – clouds very low – and, being a Friday, Lewisham was busy. We went to 'our' cleaners, which was next to the C & A shop and as we left, mum called out 'Keep Dodging!' to the girls there. . . . We crossed to the other side of the main road, past the Times Furnishing Co. and then mum said, 'Come on, let's get home, but first we'll pop across to the market and see if Granny Lettuce has any mushrooms.' The market stalls were lined up outside Marks and Spencer, Woolworths, Sainsburys, etc., and 'Granny Lettuce' was about seventy, had a salad stall outside M and S – she was quite a character with her black school-type velour turned up at the back to let her bun sit comfortably and her blue and gold ear-rings. . . . We were almost opposite Marks and Spencer . . . when . . . I suddenly heard a queer sound – a sort of cracking noise. . . . I instinctively looked up at the very low clouds and there it was, right over the top of us, like a huge black whale's head, coming through the white cloud almost at roof level, and as I shouted, 'Get down, mum!' and tried to push her to the ground I saw it fall on Marks and Spencer and explode. . . . We were thrown into the air and blown about like bits of paper or leaves and there was dust and screams all round and then awful silence and we were lying on the ground with our heads towards the scene of the explosion. . . . I noticed mum's white summer coat covered in blood and she was moaning, and . . . we could only lie there and wait for help.

Presently ARP workers came running up, took one look at us and said, 'Oh! there are worse across the road,' which was true, and went racing off. . . . The priest from St Saviours, where I was baptized . . . wandered along and vicars from other churches murmuring prayers over us, then on to the next victim. Then a young RAF aircrew boy came and knelt by me and stayed until the ambulance came. . . . He was kind and reassuring, telling me he had had his back damaged in a flying incident and was back on duty in two months. He promised to inform my unit of my whereabouts, but . . . they never got the message.

Another WAAF eye-witness of the Lewisham market bomb was the driver of a Bedford truck, who noticed that while the police were busy 'sorting out the injured and the dead, oranges . . . strewn all over the road', and normally reserved for the 'priority' classes like pregnant women, 'were being picked up by people who immediately made off.'

Immediately afterwards her vehicle was pressed into service 'to take the casualties to Orpington Hospital'; they rode alongside the remains of another flying-bomb, which she had been transporting from Biggin Hill to Hounslow.

Frustratingly for the families affected, the *Lewisham Journal* was only able in its next issue to publish a brief account of the incident.

The bomb fell near a store in which many female employees were engaged and which caught fire. . . . Heavy mobile cranes were sent to the scene to lift the debris and firemen and rescue workers endeavoured to reach shop girls and customers who were buried. The store had a café at the back of the premises and it is feared that a large number of people were caught there. Some in the street had their clothes set alight; others had their clothes blown off and were knocked unconscious. . . . For a considerable time smoke burst from heaps of wreckage and spread a pall over the area. . . . Women who were out on shopping expeditions . . . discovered in many instances that their usual shops had been closed . . . and the search for rations became difficult. . . . Loud speakers from police vans called on people not immediately concerned with the rescue work to keep away from the affected area and soldiers in khaki were regulating passing traffic. Work to clear the debris from the site was continued throughout the weekend and by Monday general conditions were much improved.

The final casualty figures, released in September, gave the death roll at fifty-one, with a further 124 seriously injured and 189 able to go home after treatment at first aid posts. One Home Guard who helped to guard the ruins remembers rumours that far more people had died than officially admitted. It was said that 'dozens and dozens of bodies' had been brought out of the basement café in Woolworths, among them 'a young girl black as Newgate's knocker', rescued on Monday evening, who 'asked . . . "Is it still Sunday?" '

The Lewisham High Street incident strikingly indicated the risk of not sounding the siren for a single flying-bomb; the warning had been given only after the bomb had landed. In fact, mercifully, it proved by far the worst of the 'shopping' incidents that summer.* Among the most serious of these was a lunchtime bomb on Acre Lane, Brixton, which wrecked the information centre where bombed-out people were seeking help. Eighteen people were killed and eighty-one others dug out of the ruins alive, among them a seventy-one-year-old woman, whose daughter had waited all night for her to be rescued. 'They fell into each other's arms', but five minutes later the mother suddenly died. Equally distressing was the destruction of a group of shops in Lordship Lane, Camberwell, for no one had any idea how many customers might be buried. Eventually twenty-three bodies were found, while forty-two people were badly injured, and nineteen less seriously.

The centre of the Lordship Lane explosion was the local branch of the Co-op, and the Germans sometimes seemed to be conducting a special vendetta against this institution. A typical 'Co-op incident', in Woolwich Road, Charlton, was observed by the manager of its footwear department, whose

---

*When, a year later, Morrison stood as Labour candidate for Lewisham, a 'smear campaign', blaming him for the policy of not sounding an alarm, proved a total failure. He won the seat with a huge majority.

home in Clapham had already been destroyed.* His son describes what happened:

Just before the shop opened at 8.30 the spotter on the roof of a nearby factory . . . sounded their warning bells. . . . Dad and one of the girls from the shop went into the brick shelter in the yard. Seconds later, the doodlebug demolished the shop. The shelter withstood the blast, but the brickwork was split from top to bottom. Dad and the girl were slammed across to the far wall but, apart from cuts and scratches, were unhurt. However the blast . . . blew almost every stitch of clothing off the girl. The fact that he was still wearing his raincoat saved Dad from a similar embarrassing fate. The coat was ripped to ribbons . . . almost as if someone had slashed it all over with a razor – dozens of little cuts. The girl was bleeding from superficial cuts and, as Dad helped her out of the shelter, bloodstains got on to the coat with, of course, the usual debris dust.

This coat, 'a good quality garbardine raincoat . . . presented by the Ladies War Committee of Montreal', had been issued to its new owner by the Whitstable WVS after he had lost his own wardrobe in Clapham.

The WVS lady was quite astonished when Dad called on her and asked, rather diffidently, whether he could have another raincoat. When he produced the old one he was given a replacement without question. The WVS took the old coat and . . . sent it back to the donating organization in Canada, where it was put on show in a Montreal shop window to advertise a further appeal.

Although South London suffered most, shops in every part of the capital were damaged in a vast variety of ways. One man remembers how 'those in Station Road and Pinner Road, North Harrow, presented the appearance of a French town sacked by armed troops.' Another observer waiting at a shopping precinct on the North Circular Road, 'saw the blast push the windows . . . into fantastic bows. . . . As the blast sucked back into the vacuum it had created, the windows broke and fell away from the frames leaving neat arched bridges of glass along the whole parade.' A woman who came up to work each day from Biggin Hill became hardened to finding the shops near Waterloo Bridge she had passed going home gone by next

---

*See page 280. This man, living with relations in Whitstable, had to catch a train at 5.30 a.m. to get to work.

morning, and, back in Kent, 'a landmark . . . gone while you had been at work.' Another woman remembers calling at three post offices in the City of London in succession one morning to find them all closed by damage during the night.

For shopkeepers and shop assistants it was a nerve-racking time. 'When the sirens went, I did not know what to do first, have a drink, go to the loo or dive in the cellar,' admits the manageress of an off-licence in Chiswick. A sixteen-year-old with a Saturday job at Bentalls in Kingston found her pleasure at being assigned to the coveted cosmetic counter blunted on realizing that it 'had a lot more glass display cabinets than the other counters.' A wartime waitress at Lyons in Chancery Lane remembers when the windows caved in and plaster showered down on the cakes just put on display. 'We spent the rest of the morning clearing up the mess.'

But, from first to last, it was the inner suburbs south of the river which suffered most. One can sympathize with the Catford newagent whom a customer remembers 'shaking his head dolefully and saying he couldn't stand it much longer,' a remark she remembers because his name, 'a misnomer if you like', was Mr Gay. One large store at Clapham Junction thought its mere survival worth announcing, in prose neatly calculated to get past the censor. 'We are happy to report,' ran an advertisement by Messrs Arding and Hobbs Ltd in the *South London Press* of 1 September, 'that nothing has occurred to prevent our giving our usual efficient and courteous service in all departments.'

16

A DEAFENING SILENCE

I still think of it as a deafening silence when the engine cut out.

Isle of Wight woman, then aged twelve, recalling the summer of 1944

The noise is what everyone remembers best: the distant hum, growing to a raucous and deafening rattle, which either diminished as the aircraft disappeared into the distance, or jerked

'It's ridiculous to say these flying-bombs have affected people in *any* way'
Daily Express cartoon, 11 July 1944

abruptly to a stop, to be followed by an explosion. It was this interval which was hardest to bear. It seemed interminable, but from the numerous recordings made at the time – one unsung hero of the summer spent his time on the roof of Broadcasting House holding a microphone towards any approaching flying-bomb – it is clear that it was actually about twelve seconds. When the engine stopped it seemed that everything stopped 'It was,' thought one twelve-year-old girl in East Ham, 'as if the world stood and held its breath.'

Many attempts have been made to find the right adjective for those vital, and sometimes fatal, few moments. An 'ominous silence', felt one woman, who first heard it while taking her bull terrier for a walk on Chipperfield Common in Hertfordshire. A 'dread silence' suggests her husband whom it had caused to order 'the examinees to fall flat on their faces in the aisles between the desks' during a school certificate examination at Kilburn Grammar School. A 'terrifying silence' considers one from Sidcup. But probably the best choice of all was that of a schoolgirl from Lake on the Isle of Wight, conscious of 'a deafening silence when the engine cut out'.

Equally varied have been the attempts to render in words the flying-bomb's distinctive sound. A sixteen-year-old boy in dockland was reminded of 'a thousand rattles at a football match', a girl in East Grinstead of 'a load of biscuit tins rattling', a seven-year-old boy in Southborough of a stick being drawn 'along a corrugated iron fence'. A publisher living in Haslemere privately felt that the sound resembled 'a giant raspberry blown from obscene great lips', but his six-year-old daughter took a different view. He recalls her sitting up in bed and remarking 'Daddy, how perfectly *beautiful*!'

The most accurate descriptions relate this novel sound to familiar machinery: 'a heavy old motor-boat', 'a cross between a motor bike and a lawn-mower', 'a very powerful sawmill', 'a huge clockwork toy'. The commonest comparison is with a motor bicycle, notably 'the old Scott Squirrel two-stroke', 'a Rudge-Multi engine of the late twenties . . . without a silencer', 'a slightly off-beat 250 cc engine' and a '350 cc BSA'. 'An express train gone rusty' thought a Penge woman; 'a train trundling over a wooden bridge' suggested one in Dovercourt. But a Forest Gate girl who remarked that the flying-bomb sounded like a steam train going up an incline, was sternly reproved by her engine-driver father. No self-respecting British train, he assured her, would ever make such a noise.

The sensitive ear of a woman then studying the flute at the Royal College of Music can still hear the flying-bomb 'as though it were yesterday':

It was loud, heavy, a grating, gritty, rattly sound. Aggressive. Ugly. The nearest parallel I can find is with the largest size dental needle in the pre-high-speed-drill era . . . and with the sound, vibration and sensation of heaviness inside one's mouth when this road-drill type was in operation.

Sudden noises were unpopular that summer. Motorcycles, lorries, even bees, all caused people to rush for shelter. One WVS driver watched the traffic parting before her and the pavements emptying as she drove through Forest Hill: there were 250 metal 'Incident Inquiry Point' signs rattling in the back of the lorry. Everywhere it was a time of listening. The cartoonist Giles reflected the prevailing obsession in the *Daily Express* of 11 July 1944. Above a caption claiming that people were carrying on as normal appeared a street scene showing everyone with one outsize ear, including the dog with its head poking through the railings of the adjoining square.

When it first noisily appeared in the skies over England the Germans' latest invention was known as a 'pilotless aircraft' or 'PAC', varied in official reports to 'Diver' or 'Fly'. Among ordinary people 'buzz bomb' had a vogue for a time and the newspapers briefly used the term 'P plane', but this never caught on. 'Robot' or 'rocket' was often used in private diaries but was officially discouraged, as making the weapon seem – as indeed it was – inhuman and remorseless and the government decided on Monday, 19 June, as already described,* to use the term 'flying-bomb'. In popular usage it was immediately ousted by another for on the following day, an RAF flight-lieutenant remarked in the BBC broadcast that 'It was my luck to be the first pilot to get a doodlebug.' The new name, with its overtones of ineffectual, bumbling progress, at once became overwhelmingly popular. As a then ten-year-old boy in Tun-

---

*See page 127.

bridge Wells explains, it had 'a faintly derisory ring which seemed to indicate that if this was all that that ridiculous Hitler could think up as a secret weapon then he needed to think again.' 'A brilliant piece of psychology, which . . . helped the civilian population enormously,' considers a woman then living in Welling. 'After all who could be frightened of a silly-sounding thing like that?' By August 1944 'doodlebug' had become respectable enough to appear in *Aeronautics* magazine, though one London scientist refused to use the term, considering it 'falsely affectionate' and in a socially sensitive tennis club in the south-eastern suburbs it was considered distinctly vulgar. At a school in Brighton 'doodlebug' was reserved for conversation with one's friends; more formal names, like 'buzz-bomb', were employed when talking to the masters.

Effectively, however, 'doodlebug' it became, sometimes shortened to 'doodle'. 'When doodles dive, don't dawdle' urged one exhortatory slogan coined that summer, and on the wall of a 'Gents' in much-blitzed Forest Hill appeared a highly topical graffito: 'When the doodle dawdles – duck'. A Kent policeman recalls a *Punch* cartoon which gave a new twist to the old theme of judicial remoteness from ordinary life. 'And what is a doodlebug?' a bewigged judge is asking, as everyone else cowers below their seats.

What indeed *was* a doodlebug? Curiously, no one at the time seems to have inquired into the word's history, which bore no relation to its new meaning. A 'doodle-bug' was in fact an American tiger-beetle supposed to have almost magical properties. One American author, in 1866, had referred to the difficulty of trying to 'call doodle-bugs out of their holes' and Tom Sawyer, in Mark Twain's book of that name, in 1876, had pleaded, 'Doodle-bug, doodle-bug, tell me what I want to know.' The doodle-bug had the reputation of being able to locate buried treasure, and by the 1920s the name had been transferred to the instrument used by Canadian mineral prospectors. In everyday parlance it had by now acquired a pejorative meaning. 'You blamed doodle bug, yu!' one character told another in an American novel of 1908, and ten years later in *The Man from Bar-20*, presumably a 'Western', two slow-witted characters were upbraided as 'a fine pair of doodlebugs'. The last pre-war appearance of the word was in an Ellery Queen crime novel in 1939.

The comical name given to this far from humorous object encouraged a whole crop of jokes, some of a distinctly coarse kind. One was the suggestion that flying-bombs should be called 'Hitler's Virgins' – 'They've never had a man inside them.' A young woman at WVS headquarters in Westminster referred in her letters home to 'FFs', which stood for 'Farting Fannies', while one clerical warden in Kent showed his broad-mindedness by referring to 'Farting Phillip'.

The flaming wake which trailed behind the missile also inspired many a humorist. 'Why are you in such a hurry?' a fighter pilot was supposed to have asked the V-1 he was pursuing, to be told 'You'd be in a hurry, too, if your backside was on fire.' The daughter of a Norfolk clergyman remembers her brother privately passing on a similar witticism. 'They run on a completely new type of fuel,' he assured her. 'It's called Arselite.' One London man still wonders whether to admire the mother he heard reproving her small son for asking, 'Mummy, why is that thing's bum on fire?' 'You mustn't say that, you must say "behind",' she told him firmly. She was, this informant comments, perfectly right, but 'what a time to choose!'

To the Germans, who had always found the English sense of humour puzzling, such responses would have been particularly annoying, for on 7 July they dropped the weapon's original name, 'flying-bomb', in favour of 'V-1', short for *Vergeltungswaffe Eins*, or 'Revenge Weapon Number One'. This was in line with their insistence that it was a direct reprisal for attacks on German cities – and effectively hinted at worse horrors to come. The name had been suggested by a journalist on Goebbels's staff, but once Hitler had approved it, Goebbels claimed the credit for himself.

It was when the light behind a V-1 went out, and the noise of the motor stopped, that one's real anxieties began, and a mingled wave of fear, profanity and piety spread out like a ripple among those below. In Stepney one married couple, both wardens, would shout 'Keep going, old boy.' ' "Keep going, you bastard!" – I wonder how often that expression was used?' remarks a Tulse Hill man. A GWR roof spotter and his colleague at Old Oak Common, as they stood watch over the locomotive sheds and goods yards, would shout 'like a punter at the racecourse, urging his horse, to "Keep going, you beauty", but we shouted "you bugger!".' A factory worker in Willesden, watching with friends from the roof of the half-built canteen, remembers them singing 'Praise the Lord and keep the engine running.'

Was one really entitled to hope that someone else, rather than oneself, would suffer? This was a question that troubled the consciences of the sensitive. 'The relief when one heard the explosion elsewhere,' acknowledges a woman then aged twenty-three and recovering from an operation on the top floor of the Westminster Hospital, 'was always followed by a shaft of guilt, as if one really had willed the engine to keep going until safely over someone else.'

'A Model Prayer for a Model Citizen', by A. P. Herbert, appeared in a Sunday newspaper:

> Stop, noise, immediately that I
> And not some other chap may die.

Most petitions addressed to the Almighty that summer were less selfless. 'Everybody was looking and silently and even out loud saying "Please pass over",' remembers a woman then living in East Ham. 'Even the vicar used to pray that these things would . . . fall on somebody else and often had his leg pulled about it.' Another clergyman, who reproved a parishioner for a similar prayer, remarking 'That's a bit hard on the next people, isn't it?' was given a robust, and theologically sound, answer. 'I don't care about that; they must pray harder and push it on a bit further!'

Others overcame the qualms of conscience by qualifying their prayers. 'Please, God, don't let it explode here, but please don't let it do too much damage when it does explode,' was the formula devised by one Croydon woman. The family of a Congregational minister produced one even more acceptable, praying daily 'that the launching sites for these deadly weapons would soon be overcome by the Allied advance.'

One's first sight of a V-1 was a traumatic experience, but for keen aircraft-spotters an immensely satisfying one. One man, then aged fourteen and living in South Norwood, can still remember his 'first sighting . . . one evening coming home from a youth club,' an event 'enthusiastically recorded after the suffering of several days, knowing that something was about but I personally had not seen it.' Older people were moved to amazement or near lyricism at the sight. 'A huge lump of iron . . . sailing along quite low', 'a huge eagle', 'an enormous crow', 'a great beetle, all shining silver', 'a sinister black cross', 'like a black dagger flung through the sky', 'just like a dead bird' – these are some of the other images recollected by observers. One nine-year-old at Crayford was reminded of 'a number of dustbins welded together,' like 'the Tin Man in *The Wizard of Oz.*'

An airman walking from the RAF station at Chigwell to the YMCA on an afternoon of 'very heavy low cloud', whose attention was attracted by a 'swishing noise' overhead and looked up to find a silent V-1 travelling so low he 'could have jumped up and touched it', thought of 'some giant prehistoric monster', but, happily, one not quite extinct, for 'the engine miraculously found another vital drop of fuel, spluttered into life and . . . was gone.'

One's first view of a flying-bomb after dark was even more unforgettable. A student nurse in a North London hospital felt, on the night the bombardment began in earnest, that she 'had become part of the front cover of some futuristic horror novel' and 'the balls of fire . . . travelling northwards above the house-tops . . . seemed to be devilish intruders from another planet.' A housewife in Wrotham, Kent, decided that a V-1 in flight 'against the glowing sky, accompanied by the fiendish noise' was like 'a ghost riding the clouds'. Less fanciful images included 'a painter's blowlamp', 'a flaming torch' and – from a South-East London boy – 'hot-tailed tadpole'. To see a whole series in line abreast or astern was particularly impressive. A soldier stationed at Purfleet found it 'a fascinating sight to see the dotted lines of flames, each dot a doodlebug, advancing towards us across the marshes.' A Streatham woman thought of 'fairy lights', a fireman in Whitechapel of 'trains with lighted windows . . . travelling as if coupled together', while the aristocratic Harold Nicolson compared the procession of missiles which rattled over Sissinghurst Castle, to 'illuminated little launches at a regatta'. For some children this sight is the earliest they can remember. The youngest person still living to recall seeing a V-1 is probably a man who was then a ten-month-old infant in Croydon. Years later he told his mother of having 'a clear picture' of lying in her arms and 'watching an aeroplane on fire in the sky.'

Whether or not the V-1s were harder to bear than other forms of attack was a question much debated. In 'Hell-fire corner' there was no doubt that they were better than shells. 'Flying-bombs came and went,' sums up a former editor of the *Folkestone and Hythe Herald*. 'You could never know when shelling would begin or end.' Comparison with conventional bombs produces a more mixed verdict. The general opinion in Hither Green, one local man believes, was that the doodlebugs were an improvement on ordinary bombers, 'because they could be trusted to keep straight on until the engine stopped and . . . only dropped one bomb.' 'If the engine did cut out,' remarks a woman then living in Leigh-on-Sea, 'you at least seemed to have a sporting chance. It gave you time to lie down on the pavement . . . rather like Russian roulette.' This 'lottery' aspect also struck an airman stationed at Sawbridgeworth. 'Death by robot,' he felt, 'had something of the jokey terrifying menace of the Tarot card.'

For some people, however, the prospect of being killed by a robot increased their natural fear. 'The thought that there was nobody inside was the thing I could never swallow,' remarks a woman then living in Purley. 'It just didn't belong to this earth.' It was 'the relentlessness of the thing' which horrified a young woman living in East Ham. A woman filing clerk living near Haslemere also found the V-1 'inexplicably unnerving. Before, one had been aimed at, however inaccurately, by a man in a plane. This new thing . . . travelled blindly and killed blindly.'

The usual 'little old ladies' also contributed their own, distinctive, opinions. One Fighter Command intelligence officer heard of one who objected that the new weapons 'lacked the personal touch'. A West Hampstead woman confessed a preference for the 'old-fashioned type of bomb'.

Although, as will be described later, the numbers killed or injured by V-1s dropped rapidly as the public became accustomed to them, on the whole as the novelty wore off people found them harder. 'The stages were so prolonged,' explains a Kensington woman, then aged thirty-three. 'First, the sirens and one knew they were about. Second . . . that sinister throbbing drone, and, third, the "stop" and tense, terrible seconds of suspense, waiting to know whether it was overhead.' 'At first,' remembers a former fifteen-year-old schoolboy in Dagenham, 'it was a bit of a laugh. We'd joined the ranks of front-line heroes, but . . . as the bombardment wore on it began to take on the dimensions of a permanent nightmare.'

By 1944 nothing could alter the outcome of the war, but this made matters worse. There was something particularly hard to accept about 'being killed by the last bomb' and if, in 1940, the mood had been one of sacrifice the general feeling now was that the whole business should long ago have been over. 'The majority were sick of the whole procedure,' believes one man then living in Chelsea, 'losing their loved ones, their homes, rationing, the sleepless nights.'

'Most Londoners grew nonchalant about manned raids, but few did about flying-bombs,' believes a woman who was then a twenty-three-year-old student. Earlier in the war she had cheerfully held 'a fierce shouting match . . . about the correct tempo for the Slow [movement] in Beethoven Four' while fire-watching on the roof of the Royal College of Music. 'Came the V-1s and I'd lie awake listening with every molecule, like cats listen, with all their fur.'

When I rejoined ENSA, my nerves were really bad. We were billeted in Hastings, Sussex, for a week, doing the camps and air bases in a wide area around, and at night the stream of V-1s seemed constant. . . . I couldn't sleep much, but lay awake tense and rigid, heart racing, cold sweat trickling. Almost I got paranoic, convinced that each visitation was going to get me, and only me. I remember the digs very clearly, because the two elderly sisters, very ladylike, taking in 'Ensas' just for their war effort, kept a few secret hens and not only did we have eggs for breakfast . . . but eggy puddings with meringue tops, or soufflé dishes frothing to the ceiling. . . . But not even such rare magic as that could compensate for the dread of the night visitors.

For a man working at Fords of Dagenham and his wife, who lived with him in Barkingside, the V-1s provided the last, unbearable straw.

A Deafening Silence

My wife was near to breaking point. She could not bath the children, could not prepare proper meals. All she could do was listen for the cut-out and then bury the children's heads in pillows and just wait for the crash. . . . My nerves were so bad, I was making silly and dangerous mistakes on the V.8 engine assembly line. One day I found myself chasing a . . . chargehand with a four-pound hammer in my hand.

A fifteen-year-old schoolboy, living in Dagenham, found that his behaviour in the face of danger was very different from that of his fictional hero, Biggles:

My own reactions to the V-1s could best be described as initially bravado, subsequently, terror, and finally numbness. . . . I am an abject coward by nature. I heard every V-1 that was coming . . . and indeed a few that were not. All the bombs that were proceeding in my general direction were directed at me personally . . . labelled with my name. I imagined what it would be like to fall on your back and embrace in your arms one ton of high explosives falling diagonally at 45° from 500 feet, the little propeller at the front . . . boring intimate revolutions in one's chest wall.

By an agreeable irony this non-hero eventually acquired a novel war injury, 'a sort of slipped disc condition', induced by rapid descents into the Anderson or lingering reluctant departures from it.

A Bromley household also presented a somewhat different picture from that conjured up by the 'London can take it' message of the newsreel with the daughter of the house the least courageous of all:

She would shout at anyone who ventured out of the kitchen and practically wept if we tried to go upstairs. My husband shook with nerves and I felt as if my head was being squeezed by a vice. The fact that we could see the doodlebugs coming seemed to make things worse. . . . If they had come in groups like the ordinary bombs, we could have coped with them, but the weight of numbers shattered even the stout hearted.

17

LIKE SOME GRISLY TRANSPORT SERVICE

It was like some grisly transport service, with occasional gaps in the schedule when one had been shot down.

Kent woman, recalling the summer of 1944

Few supposedly 'secret' weapons can have been heard and seen by so many people as the flying-bomb and within a few days of its first arrival the British public was able to fill in the gaps in its knowledge, gained painfully at first hand, from the details of its performance which appeared, on 20 June, in the newspapers. Later postwar studies have added little though all have confirmed the technical novelty and brilliance of the original concept.

As a handbook later prepared by the US War Department in Washington DC pointed out, the missile had been designed 'for the greatest possible ease of production' with 'each of the component parts . . . of the simplest form, even at the expense of additional weight.' Basically it consisted of four sections, the main fuselage, the propulsion unit and the two wings, which were removed for transport and only attached again just before firing. The fuselage was 2 ft 8¼ in [0·82 metres] wide, and 21 ft 10 in [6·65 metres long], or 25 ft 4½ in [7·73 metres] when the cigar-shaped impulse duct engine was added. Of the overall weight of about two tons [4800 lbs or 2371 kilos] nearly one ton [1870 lbs or 849 kilos] consisted of Amatol, a powerful mixture of TNT and Ammonium Nitrate capable of withstanding considerable shock while in transport.

In front of the warhead was the master compass, which could keep the aircraft on course within an accuracy of half a degree. Behind it were four other sections: the 130 gallon (591 litre) fuel tank, between the wings; two large wirebound globes,

200

containing compressed air; the automatic pilot, and finally a pneumatic master gyro, operated by compressed air. The machine's course was pre-set beforehand and if the machine deviated from its intended path two servo motors adjusted the rudder, at the tail, or the elevators, on the wings, to correct the error. Height was controlled by an aneroid barometer, and the distance travelled by a milometer pre-set to a certain number of revolutions, and operated by a small propeller, like a child's toy 'windmill', in the nose. When the pre-set distance, usually about 140 miles, was reached, a circuit was closed, which caused two detonators to be fired. These lowered two flaps, which put the machine into a dive, and operated a guillotine which cut the air-leads to the automatic-pilot, so that it did not correct the downward movement. By that time, the bomb would have used up almost all its fuel – low-grade 80 octane petrol – and as it tipped downwards the supply to the engine was cut off, causing it to stop with a loud and characteristic 'jerk'. The pulse-jet engine was basically the same as the prewar versions already described. The machine was driven forward by a series of about forty-five explosions a second, producing a thrust of about 600 lb (296 kilo) roughly that of a conventional 600 horsepower aero-engine.

Most V-1s crossed the coast at a speed of about 340 m.p.h. but they speeded up as their fuel was burned, reaching, Air Chief Marshal Hill discovered, '400 m.p.h. or thereabouts', though a later version with a much smaller warhead (1000 lb) and larger wing span was said to have reached 480 m.p.h. The height-controlling device also proved very effective, with almost all the missiles crossing the coast, as intended, around 2500 feet [762 metres], at which height they looked from the ground about half the size of a Spitfire – their actual wing-span being only 17 ft 6 in [5·33 metres].

The basic design changed slightly during the campaign. The first missiles had a tapering wing, but later versions had a 'constant chord', i.e. were straight, being 3 ft 7 in [1·13 metres] wide. There was, too, a change in the material used. The earlier versions had consisted entirely, except for the nose cone, of welded sheet steel, but subsequently even cheaper plywood was used for the wings.

While waiting to be used the bombs were 'parked' beneath

201

the trees around each modified site, and then manhandled on a four-wheeled trailer into position for firing. Each was taken to the checking-out platform, where the wings were added and the warhead armed, then trundled on to the waiting platform, for final examination, and then to the non-magnetic 'direction building' or *Richthaus*, where it was revolved on a turntable to the same alignment as the launching platform and the gyroscopic controls were set.

The bomb was then fuelled and wheeled to the foot of the ramp which was 150 feet [45.7 metres] long, and 16 feet [4.87 metres] high, where it rested on twin guide rails, with its tail separately supported on a sledge. Below the rails was a tube containing a piston which fitted into a metal housing beneath the bomb. The launching catapult was powered by burning hydrogen peroxide. As the pressure in the tube built up the launching trolley was held back by a bolt embedded in the foot of the ramp, until finally this fractured and the trolley then leapt forward, hurling the missile into the air, just as its engine provided sufficient thrust to keep it airborne. The piston and sledge were hurled two or three hundred yards, but could be retrieved and used again.

With the firing sequence completed, the ramp was washed down with potassium permanganate as a safety precaution and the whole process was restarted. It had been estimated that a good experienced crew could fire a V-1 every half hour, and one site actually managed to discharge eighteen in a single night, but the normal maximum proved to be around fifteen per site per day and of these some 8–10 per cent immediately fell to earth.

The collection of fragments from the first V-1s to arrive confirmed that the machine was not radio-controlled, though a few did carry radios to assist the Germans to plot where they landed. The chief mystery still unravelled was its fusing system for as the leading British bomb disposal expert, Major A. B. Hartley, commented, 'from the point of view of the bomb disposer German security had by no means been ineffective.' The first relatively intact V-1 was a prize eagerly awaited, but 'compared with an ordinary H.E. bomb . . . it was of frail construction', so that when one did crash without exploding, at Battle near Hastings on 23 June, 'fragments were scattered over a wide area'. Luckily the warhead survived and 'was eventually steamed out and the fuses recovered.'

Other unexploded, though badly damaged, V-1s were reported soon afterwards from Staplecross in Sussex, Down, Welling and Tunbridge Wells in Kent, and Sandhurst in Surrey. They yielded invaluable information.

It was discovered that three fuse-pockets were fitted and three different types of fuse used. . . . Down the middle of the warhead, which was about four feet long and shaped like a truncated cone, ran a steel tube designed to ensure the satisfactory detonation of the main filling. At the forward end of this tube was the forward pocket; the other two were sunk laterally into the warhead at right-angles to the exploder-tube.

Just to make things more difficult for the bomb disposal men, not all the fuses were present in every V-1, but all gave remarkable proof of German ingenuity. The main fuse, known as the 80-A, 'contained a number of spring-loaded strikers, each of which could fire a small initiating charge' so 'that the action went off on impact regardless of the position in which the machine hit the ground.' This was supplemented by a 106-X, another impact fuse, which was activated by a battery charged in flight, and, occasionally, by a third, clockwork-operated device, designed as a reserve, to explode the bomb two hours after impact.

What was still needed to devise a proper procedure for dealing with unexploded V-1s was a machine that had not broken up on landing, and on 28 July one was at last reported from a smallholding at Southborough near Tunbridge Wells. The machine dropped while the male owner of the land and a landgirl were feeding chickens. They had heard it coming, but not seen it land, having taken cover, and the landgirl 'eventually raised her head to see to her utter horror a large black doodlebug sitting tangled up in chicken wire.'

Knowing all the imponderables the two Royal Engineer officers sent to Southborough must have approached the assignment with mixed feelings:

On arrival they were met by the police who informed them that one thousand five hundred people had had to be evacuated from their homes. . . . The two officers carefully and closely examined the wrecked machine and having discovered the boss of an 80-A fuse realised that this must be immunised without delay. . . . The warhead might go off at any time causing very widespread material damage. . . . Accordingly [Lieutenant] Sivil . . . injected a quantity of urea-formaldehyde resin into the 80-A and successfully blocked the mechanical action within. He then returned to the examination of the other two fuse-pockets; one contained a 106-X, the other was closed with an unmarked bakelite disc. . . .

The jammed 80-A fuse was withdrawn by remote control without mishap. Sivil had formed the opinion that there was no fuse behind the blank bakelite cap on the forward pocket. He slowly undid the locking-ring, pressing down on the cap with his finger to counter any spring-movement concealed behind it. When the ring was loosened he cautiously eased this pressure. . . . It still did not move and he breathed more easily. It was in fact a dummy. . . .

The fuse in the third pocket, the 106-X was, because of the wiring connecting it with the batteries and airscrew generator, a more complicated task. With the help of two sappers, Sivil traced and severed the leads after which he was able to extract it safely. The first complete unexploded flying-bomb was now a harmless hulk.

By September UX Divers, to use the official term, were becoming common enough for there to be arguments about their ownership. One woman who was then an eighteen-year-old typist in Tunbridge Wells remembers the ferocious controversy which occurred in her home village of High Brooms, after one had come peacefully to earth on some allotments:

Everyone in the surrounding houses was evacuated. . . . Then a new 'war' broke out, between the Bomb Disposal Squad (housed in a commandeered garage in the village) and the RAF. . . . The disposal squad wanted the V-1 if they successfully defused it. 'No,' said the RAF. 'It has wings, so it is a plane and therefore ours.'. . . In the meantime it had to be defused. . . . At that time it was the practice to pour wax into the fuse mechanism and when it had hardened they set about taking out the fuse. . . . The waiting period was whiled away drinking cups of tea and playing cards in my father's café, quite unconcerned about the 'legal' battle going on. At last the bomb was safe; defused and the battle was eventually won by the RAF, who, feeling elated with their first V-1 prize, turned up with . . . a 'Queen Mary', a long trailer used for recovering crashed aircraft, and away went our flying bomb. I understand it eventually ended up in America. After this, the apple tree that the 'plane' knocked down in its glide was cut into pieces and Mr B. [the warden involved], my

204

father and mother and I . . . put on the date, varnished them and in a drilled hole threaded red, white and blue tricolour ribbon to hang them up. They were sold for war charities. Out of the smaller branches Mr B. made a model doodlebug and mounted it. . . . I was asked to take it to the office of the Bomb Disposal Squad and . . . handed it very quietly to the sergeant in charge as our 'thank you' for saving our homes.

Even civilians soon realized that since the missiles were fired from fixed ramps at a stationary target an invisible link connected the two. Some might, from mechanical error or damage inflicted by the defences, deviate from that path, but the vast majority behaved in a predictable way. 'If you happened to be at the end of a straight line between their London landing spot and their launching pad, the effect of their approach was quite different on the ears, the nerves, your every sensation, than [of] those bombs which buzzed north, south-east or west of you,' remembers a woman living in Wembley. To a woman who occupied a top floor flat in Forest Hill it seemed as if the flying-bomb kept to three routes, as if on tramlines laid through the sky. The various 'lanes' pointing to West Croydon, one resident remembers, were known as 'traps', like the starting gates on a greyhound track. 'Number Three Trap was ours.' A War Reserve policeman in Folkestone identified three lanes, one 'toward the hills, one right over Cheriton . . . and another one further out over the Romney Marsh.' People in Eastbourne also detected three, 'right over the town . . . a little to the west and one to the east almost over the radar station at Wartling near Pevensey.' A family living at Rhodes Minnis, Kent, were so plagued by the one directly above their home that they travelled several miles each night to sleep in a farmhouse well to one side of it.

On 29 June, only two weeks after the attack had started, Colonel Wachtel's regiment launched its 2000th flying-bomb. At least 1300 of these had crossed the English coast, an average of around a hundred a day. At first some people kept a record of the numbers they had seen. 'A little quieter today,' noted a Hastings man in his diary for 19 June. 'Julia [his wife] counted seventeen go past.' Within ten days however, he had given up bothering with such details. 'Flying-bombs all day long,' ran the entry for 20 June. 'Counted 12 lanes.' No prizes were offered for the largest number of sightings but among non-professionals a Croydon schoolboy's record must stand high. He claimed a total of 142 sightings during the summer, of which 135 occurred between 16 June and 6 August. A Dagenham schoolboy saw 163, though his largest number on a single day was eight, in contrast to the Croydon contender's eleven. Professional sky-watchers exceeded even these figures. One ROC man at Bromley believes he must have seen more than 200, while an NFS observation post in Bayswater – not manned continuously by the same man – logged more than 800 within sight or earshot, of which 'over 50' came during one forty-eight-hour period. A West Hampstead warden collected thirty-five ticks in her log-book, one for each V-1 she heard, during a six-hour spell of night duty; a Kent farmworker saw 'more than 50' during the afternoon he spent carting and stacking wheat sheaves near Rye, though no doubt many of these were promptly shot down.

Another version of the collecting 'game' was to see how many V-1s one could spot in the air simultaneously. A lorry-driver in a repair 'flying squad' saw nine 'almost in formation' over Orpington, and the spotter on the roof of an arms factory near Willesden Junction identified twelve at once, but he was using field-glasses. One woman living in Streatham, who sometimes joined her fireman husband in an NFS look-out on a hill in Norwood, found it 'rather frightening to see many bombs in the air at the same time, like a huge hand with fingers outspread. . . . I must admit to being a bit shaken to see the flaming jets of two V-1s flying side by side. . . . As they disappeared across the sky they sounded like two old gossips, complaining about their neighbours.'

Although the official records do not bear out the widely held belief that the Germans concentrated their fire at certain fixed times of the day, they certainly tended to fire the V-1s in groups or 'coveys', as some reports described them. 'During the height of the bombardment,' observed the wife of an Army instructor at Hurstpierpoint, 'they were launched at more or less specific times – a batch at about 6.30 p.m., then a break and so on throughout the twenty-four hours.' 'We saw the things with monotonous regularity,' agrees a woman living at

Meopham. 'It was like some grisly transport service, with occasional gaps in the schedule when one had been shot down.'

Programmed as they were to fly a fixed distance on a pre-set course, the V-1s rapidly refuted the comforting superstition that lightning never struck twice in the same place. A Tooting woman recalls a series of V-1s, each dropping nearer than the last, until finally one landed in the road next to her own. At Morden Hill, in South-East London, one flying-bomb landed close enough to where another had fallen eight hours before to kill rescue workers searching for the earlier bomb's victims, while two V-1s hit the same North London factory within twenty-four hours of each other.*

Those V-1s that did not behave as expected were much resented. Colourful rumours spread that the antics of 'rogue' V-1s were due to conscripted workers deliberately sabotaging the components, but the true explanation usually lay in the guidance system having been hit by a bullet or shell fragment. As a result of such damage many V-1s performed impressive aerobatics. A Maidstone woman remembers one engaging in what looked uncannily like a dog-fight with a British fighter. A woman living near Sevenoaks, watching the sky with the local rector, was equally fascinated by a V-1 which 'rushed round in figures of eight.' When, finally, it crashed we both found ourselves laughing – it looked so alive . . . and even rather beautiful, as it twisted and turned in the air.' A former landgirl still wonders what happened to the flying-bomb she watched one afternoon near Rochester, climbing steadily upwards. 'I watched it go up and up into the clear summer sky . . . until I couldn't see the tiny dot any more. Where could it have gone?'

V-1s which apparently could not make up their minds when to drop caused much annoyance. One WAAF living in Shepherds Bush recalls heaving a sigh of relief when a V-1 passed over, but it then turned back and circled round twice, causing the family to wonder 'if it was looking for the number on our door'. At a Camberwell hospital it had become an obsession among the younger nurses to watch the V-1s from the hospital roof, until one afternoon one 'suddenly turned a

*See page 313.

complete circle and headed straight back towards us. I do not think our feet touched anything until we were four floors down.' Another 'chose to use us as the centre of its circle,' remembers a man then working in the heavy gun shop at Woolwich Arsenal. 'As it went up river those who lived at Greenwich and Deptford came out to watch, down river brought out those from Abbey Wood and Erith. When it came overhead we *all* watched it.'

Among the knowledgeable a whole new vocabulary developed. As well as 'circlers', a man then stationed at the Central Ordnance Depot in Feltham remembers, there were 'twisters', 'turners' and 'divers', the last-named being the most detested of all, since they plunged to earth with their engine still running. Almost as bad, however, were 'floaters', which prematurely ran out of fuel and glided silently for miles.

Suddenly to be confronted with a gliding V-1 was an unnerving experience. A man then living in Ilford remembers one which 'was very low and . . . seemed to fill the whole sky as it wobbled unstably directly overhead.' The accompanying noise was almost as frightening as the normal raucous tumult. An opthalmic optician in Mitcham recollects a 'soft rustling . . . like a small sailing boat, where the wind was making the sails flutter.' To a Croydon woman, more fancifully inclined, it seemed like 'the breathing of some enormous giant or the gentle flapping of a fabulous creature's wings.'

An official report, based on 205 incidents during July, and compiled for the American government, showed that nonconforming V-1s were very much more common than generally believed. Four per cent of the dives were 'power dives to impact', and in no fewer than 44 per cent of cases there were 'glides of more than 10 seconds'. The longest recorded was 202 seconds, i.e. more than three minutes, sufficient for a machine still travelling at, say, 200 m.p.h. to cover another ten miles after the engine had stopped.

Only one person refused to acknowledge that he had been taken unawares by any aspect of the flying-bomb's behaviour – Lord Cherwell, who had only belatedly accepted that such a weapon existed at all. On 28 June, somewhat mischievously, the Prime Minister returned to Cherwell a minute the latter had prepared on 23 December 1943 predicting its performance.

'You might care,' wrote Churchill, 'to look this over again and see how events and your present ideas fit in with it.' Two days later Cherwell submitted a detailed table, set out under two headings 'Forecast – December 1943' and 'Actuality – June 1944', which, with extraordinary effrontery, claimed that he had been right about everything, except the V-1's engine and the number of casualties each missile would cause. His December estimate of '2–4 persons' had, he now explained, 'obviously' meant *fatal* casualties only. As for his forecast that the attack would be 'comparatively insignificant', he had meant in comparison with the 'predicted casualties from the giant rocket then under discussion.'

Cherwell, who was, after all, employed to get such forecasts right, had in fact got everything disastrously wrong. But to Churchill, his court favourite could do no wrong. 'It is,' he minuted to his private office on 10 July on Cherwell's note, 'a very fine record. I feel it my duty to give an account to the Cabinet, who will be surprised at the many predictions which have come true.' Secretly, however, he may have felt uneasy for he instructed one of his most senior assistants, the future Major-General Sir Ian Jacob, to check the facts. Jacob's response was courageous: Cherwell's forecasts were, Jacob admitted, accurate enough in most respects, but so were everyone else's, since 'exactly the same information . . . was available to all parties'. Where there was disagreement, as on the probable scale of attack, the military authorities had been right and Cherwell wrong.

Most improperly, Churchill showed this private note to Lord Cherwell, who on 20 July responded with another long memo. 'I am,' it began, 'most reluctant to waste your time (or my own) in arguing to what degree on past occasions I was right or not,' and then went on to do precisely that. No doubt with an eye to the future he would not commit himself to 'a view on the likelihood of attacks in the near future by long-range rockets . . . not having been shown all the secret evidence,' a blatant lie, as Ian Jacob pointed out to the Prime Minister. 'No secret information,' he replied to Churchill's angry inquiry on 25 August, 'is withheld from Lord Cherwell.' So that alibi, at least, was exposed. Prudently, recalling Cherwell's confident prediction, back in October 1943, that 'at the end of the war

The Doodlebugs

. . . we should find that the rocket was a mare's nest,' Churchill's staff went on quietly preparing for it to arrive.

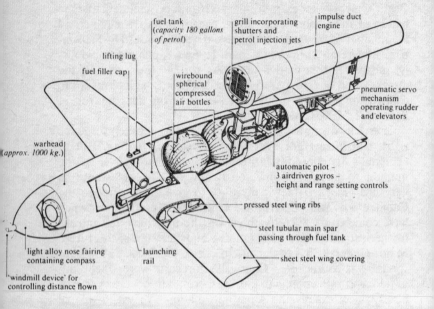

How the flying-bomb worked. The above drawing is based on one issued at the time by the Government, and widely reproduced in the press.

18

LIKE HEAVEN AFTER LONDON

It was like heaven after London.

Ealing woman who moved to Scotland, recalling July 1944

By March 1944 the number of 'official evacuees' who had left the cities under government schemes had reached the lowest level of the whole war, 319,400. By September it had soared to 1,012,200, not far short of the peak reached early in 1941. That increase – and the even vaster one in 'unofficial' evacuees – was a measure of the V-1s' success in making life in the South unpleasant. While their normal residents were drifting back to places like Manchester and Birmingham, London and the South-East were emptying. In relation to the areas affected the great flight from June to August 1944 was the largest of the whole war.

On the whole the civilian ministries had prepared at least as efficiently as the service departments for the arrival of the flying-bombs, but over evacuation the government hesitated and fumbled. As late as 27 June, the Cabinet decided against re-introducing formal schemes for the four priority classes: mothers with infants under five; children of school age; expectant mothers; and the old and infirm. Then rising public dissatisfaction forced an abrupt change of attitude. On 1 July orders went out to the London County Council, which also acted as the agent for neighbouring counties, to start registering mothers with young families, and children of school age, who wished to be sent away, and on 3 July the first parties were dispatched. Thus in his major speech in the House of Commons on 6 July Churchill could boast of what was being done:

Children are already being sent at their parents' wish out of the danger areas and, in all cases, mothers with small children or pregnant women, will be given full facilities by the State. And we do not propose to separate the mother from the children except by her wish. . . . I hope . . . with our growing strength, reserves and facilities for removal, we shall be able to say to a mother with three or four children, 'If you wish to leave, it is perfectly possible. Arrangements will be made to take you into the country with your children. If you wish them to go by themselves and you wish to stay here with your husband, or because of your job, then arrangements can be made that way too.'

At the same time, no doubt aware that many thousands had already gone, Churchill gave other non-essential citizens a powerful hint to leave as well:

As to evacuation . . . everybody must remain at his post and discharge his daily duty. This House would be affronted if any suggestion were made to it that it should change its location from London. Here we began the war, and here we will see it ended. We are not, however, discouraging people who have no essential work to do from leaving London at their own expense if they feel inclined to do so by the arrangements they make. In fact, they assist our affairs by taking such action at their own expense. We do not need more people in London than are required for business purposes of peace and war. For people of small means who are not engaged in war work and wish to leave, registers have been opened and arrangements will be made for their transfer as speedily as possible to safer areas.

This invitation was widely accepted, although in fact no one received any official help unless he or she was in one of the priority categories or belonged to the large and rapidly growing number who had been bombed out. By 17 July it was estimated that 530,000 'private' evacuees had left London, compared to 170,000 'official' ones, though another 37,000 of the latter had registered and were waiting to leave. Thereafter the numbers rose sharply. Between 5 July and 7 September 307,000 mothers and children were evacuated in organized parties, and 140,000 expectant mothers, children from residential nurseries and other small groups with special needs; 552,000 people, including many family units and old people and homeless, went as 'aided' evacuees, making their own arrangements, but being given free railway warrants and billeting certificates, which entitled them to a weekly allowance. Many others moved without official help of any kind. The lowest estimate for all who left the V-1 affected areas is 1,450,000, while the Post Office knew of 1,110,000 'removals out' of London in the period July to September, compared to only 236,000 in the preceding quarter and 374,000 in the one which followed.

So many people had unhappy memories of that earlier evacuation back in 1939 that there was often a half-hearted response to the re-opening of the official schemes. In Beckenham, for example, which had already had more than its share of V-1s, the number at first registering was meagre, but the first party finally got away to Huddersfield from one local school on 7 July, 'all very bright and cheerful' as a teacher noted. 'It was the parents who wanted cheering up.' A Sutton woman, allowed to travel with her school-age child as she also had a younger one, remembers as the most miserable morning of the war the time she spent between 9 a.m., when the party assembled in the playground of a local school, with luggage and gas masks, and 1 p.m., when they finally got away on buses for King's Cross – they ended up in Oldham. 'The flying bombs kept coming over in great numbers, more than ever before. I counted fourteen. They followed on each other and we all had to keep running to the shelters.' In Penge, the worst-bombed place for its size in the whole country, one resident remembers 'heartbreaking scenes . . . as little mites clung to mothers and fathers' before being coaxed on to the buses carrying them to Euston, en route for the Midlands. (The sad effort was justified: 'A month after they went, the schools were there no longer . . . and the mums and dads were housed in tin huts.')

About that flight from London, usually under grey skies and accompanied by periodic explosions and a sinister rattle in the distance, there was often a nightmare quality. 'I vividly recollect the day of departure,' writes a Folkestone woman who, with a bed already booked for her forthcoming confinement, reluctantly left her home town to travel to Bushey in Hertfordshire. 'It was a dull misty morning . . . and we had only gone a short distance when a doodlebug came down quite close . . . causing a few broken panes of glass on the coach. . . . We carried on with our journey regardless.' Independent 'aided' travel could be equally terrifying. A West Hampstead woman remembers setting off with her daughter, not yet two, and a neighbour's son, aged eight, 'to walk to St Pancras, through back streets and odd byways . . . Bruce . . . sharing the pram with Susan, who thought it great fun.' The little party included the least perturbed evacuees to leave London that day, a 'jar of snails' given to the small boy by the even smaller girl to distract him after being bombed out. No present could have been more successful and he hugged it to himself as a talisman as they wearily tramped the long North London streets towards the main-line terminus that was the gateway to safety.

When we arrived at St Pancras station we wondered what had hit us. People queued at all the ticket offices . . . platforms were crowded with people and luggage. I realized for the first time how very infectious and dangerous panic is. I felt quite sick, I wanted very much to go back home but John [her husband] insisted we went, just until they had put a temporary roof on and boarded up the windows, otherwise we would have to go with the rest of the people into a schoolroom or somewhere.

A widespread fear was of being killed while waiting for the train to safety. 'So near and yet so far,' was the reaction of one woman civil servant, as she waited at Euston for the train carrying her to her new post in Scotland. 'I had my first horrible feeling I would not make it.' 'What a cheer went up when at long last the train started to move,' remarks a man working at Fords of Dagenham who had managed to get a transfer to a factory in Newcastle-upon-Tyne. 'It seemed as if the train would never come,' felt a hospital administrator from Hounslow, waiting at Liverpool Street to take his wife and children to Norfolk. 'We waited huddled in two or three lines at the platform edge. The rain was pouring down and cascading on to the platform through large gaps in the glass roof. Alarm bells kept ringing but no one seemed to know what they indicated. As the sound of an approaching V-1 intensified, everyone stiffened with humped shoulders and bent heads.'

All the great main-line terminuses were affected, except Charing Cross and Victoria, which served Kent and Sussex: no one wanted to go there. At King's Cross one journalist noted a sign of the times – a guards van jammed with prams; already, he was told, the station had handled more than 1000. But the

worst of all was Paddington, which served not only Wales and
the West Country but large parts of the Midlands: safe areas
all. One had, after all, to go only as far as Reading to be
reasonably secure and only to Oxford to be among people who
had never heard a flying-bomb. Conditions at Paddington, despite the best efforts of the station staff, became notorious.
One woman first-aider, escorting a hospital patient to Cardiff
on 22 June, found 'crowds far worse than ever I saw. . . .
Everybody was . . . harassed, irritable and thoroughly uncivil.'
An NFS roof-spotter, working in Bayswater, horrified at the
rumours he had heard, also went to see for himself.

My uniform got me past the barrier. The station was a solid mass of
people. The platform was barricaded with seats, barrows or anything
that would pile up. A train on No. 3 platform was packed and still
people were trying to get on. Another train was pulling in to one of
the other platforms and people were climbing over the barricades to
get on. An old lady with three small children was standing near and
was then joined by a young woman. I can still recall the expression
on the young woman's face – fatigue, desperation and fear. I overheard her remark. 'It's no use. We can't get away.' The young woman
was crying as they walked away.

On 2 August, one MP raised the subject in the House of
Commons. Was the minister aware, he inquired, of the 'chaos
at Paddington' on the preceding Saturday, and that, even when
they had boarded a train, 'expectant mothers had to stand up
in the corridor for as much as eight hours?' The minister was
aware, but unconcerned. It was true, the government spokesman admitted, that at least twenty people had required first
aid after fainting in the crush on the day mentioned, but sixteen
relief trains had been run and 'if expectant mothers left London
under the organised evacuation scheme . . . they . . . would
have conditions suitable to their requirements.'

   Special trains or not, the number of seats available was never
adequate to the number of would-be evacuees. The Ford
worker from Dagenham, quoted earlier, recalls that 'We were
crushed into the train like sardines in a tin' and 'when the train
arrived at Newcastle Centre we must have looked like scare-
crows. All were hungry, having had nothing to eat or drink
since midday the previous day.' 'I'm sure the family remembers
that journey,' remarks a man who sent his wife and children

away to Wells-on-Sea in Norfolk. 'It took over twelve hours to do the 150 miles.'

A woman travelling from Marylebone to Quorn in Leicestershire with her small daughter found that her first-class fare merely earned them standing room 'jammed into a corridor with not even room to sit on the floor.' 'There were seventeen of us packed in the small lavatory,' remembers a Chingford woman, of her journey from Paddington to Bridgwater. 'It was so hot we could hardly breathe, let alone move. One enterprising gent had a screwdriver and took the window right off.'

The easiest passengers to handle were 'unaccompanied infants' – who travelled under the competent and kindly care of the WVS and other volunteer escorts. By 7 July, 16,500 children had already left, mainly for the Midlands and North, and on that Monday alone 2400 arrived in Blackpool. Mothers with small children in organized parties were also well looked after. Four WVS travelled on each evacuation train, equipped with 'urns of tea, hot and cold water, biscuits, sweets, baby food, babies' bottles and other comforts,' as the movement's historian recorded, while 'WVS mobile canteen staffs ran a base kitchen in Savile Row where work started at 5.45 each morning. . . . On the peak day, 11 July, 95 five-gallon urns of tea and 92 urns of boiling water . . . were sent out.'

By 18 July Wales alone had already received 28,000 'official' mother and child evacuees, and on the whole reception arrangements worked smoothly. The real problem came from 'unofficial' evacuees, who often arrived first and absorbed accommodation earmarked for later official arrivals. One town in Wales received 230 families the day before the 'official' party was due, and another 1000 'unofficials' on the day itself. As in the past, mothers with babies proved far harder to place than unaccompanied children and presented other difficulties, such as a tendency to get separated from their prams and their luggage. No case is recorded of a mother mislaying her baby, but so many discovered on arrival that their luggage had gone to another destination and their prams to a third that the Ministry of Health set up a special lost property office to straighten out such tangles.

On the whole the evacuees had an enthusiastic reception, especially in 'neutral' areas, not previously called on to absorb outsiders. These were the experiences of a woman teacher from Islington, who acted as an escort on 12 July 1944:

I remember going through the grand old entrance of Euston Station, then moving with relief under the arches, where one felt more safe. . . . The journey up north with Cockney mums, and lively babes, was not dull, as the wriggly youngsters were mixed up with bottles of milk, baskets and bundles. The climax came when we arrived at Bolton. The north-country welcome was superb. I was staggering up the stairs on the arrival platform with a bouncing eighteen-month-old babe in my arms, among other things, in a crowd of lively and perspiring humans. Crowded on the down side of the stairs were lots of friendly local people to meet us, all talking with the popular 'George Formby' accent. . . . One little man was leaning over the stair rail, with a strawberry basket scooping out handfuls of fruit for the children. My wriggly charge, sticky and still cheerful, grabbed the strawberries. Before I was able to remove the green haulm, the lot was stuffed into the sticky little mouth and the buoyant little green-grocer continued on his way, pressing the juicy fruit into the mouths of the poppets gaping like hungry birds.

A Neasden woman, travelling in a crowded special train with her four small children, felt equally grateful for their reception. 'After hanging around all day we reached Leicester at about 7 p.m. and were taken to the High School, where they gave us a marvellous welcome and a huge salad tea. When I asked, one of the staff very kindly took me to the science room, where I could wash myself and feed my baby in peace.'

The 'slave market' method of allocation, so resented in 1939, was still practised in some places, including Birmingham, to which a woman from Cricklewood was evacuated with her two sons:

We were taken to a rest centre where we slept on mattresses on the floor so close together that it was impossible to sleep as one would get a kick from the next person. I got up at five o'clock and we had a bath, then some breakfast. We went outside, lined up against a wall, and people chose their evacuees. Luck was with me as we were chosen to live with an elderly man and his housekeeper. . . . My colleagues were not so lucky. I used to see them as I went past the school, still standing to attention, hoping to be chosen. They said they felt like cattle waiting to be sold.

One woman, then aged fourteen, and the oldest evacuee in her party from Edgware, found it 'humiliating . . . being looked over by the ladies of Whitley Bay to see who they would like to take in', and ultimately she and her sister were left to spend the night 'on the floor of a schoolroom', though they found an excellent foster home next day with 'an extremely kind Scottish lady with . . . a husband who was an executive with a ship-builders' in Wallsend.' One woman from Brentford found her first night with her young family at Rotherham on the floor of a hall distinctly uncomfortable and next morning her real problems began:

I was the last one to go. . . . I think that people who saw three little boys, of two, four and six years, thought that they might be a handful, but in fact my boys were quiet and well-behaved. We were at last offered a place, the people seemed kind, though a bit unkempt. . . . A couple of US soldiers offered to take us all and our luggage . . . in an American jeep. . . . I thought we would at any moment get dashed to pieces. However, we arrived OK and . . . were shown to a room and a double bed, which had no sheets or pillow-cases on it. We had to spread two dish towels on the very dirty pillows, as the bed was far from clean. . . . Next morning, we felt a bit refreshed and . . . were taken to a kitchen and given cups of tea from very dirty old cups. I confess I was afraid to let my children drink out of them. We had some bread and butter . . . not much else, as it was evident that the people were very poor. We went out for a little walk and . . . went back for some dinner, which . . . was quite nice. . . . The Yorkshire pudding was very good. We went back into our bare looking room, we had only the bed and an old wash stand, on which stood a big bowl. . . . I then noticed that there was a big hole in the floor, undoubtedly a rat hole. I was then very scared, especially when the children went to bed, I sat up to watch, in case a rat came out. I then had the idea to put the big bowl over the hole and somehow I got some sleep, but in the morning I vowed to look for some better, cleaner accommodation.

A Lee Green mother, who had for a long time been too scared even to leave the house to make arrangements for evacuation, found her courage rapidly returning after being found rooms in a back-to-back house in Nottingham:

The shock on seeing this place was almost as bad as the V-1s. The place was alive with bugs that came out of the walls at night. My clean little children were covered in great lumps. I went to the billeting officer who eventually found me the exact opposite home, very smart, with a little servant girl. I spent my evenings sitting in the kitchen and my children were expected to be out of sight in bed at 5.30 to 6 p.m. This situation proved impossible after a while, and I came home.

A similar combination of homesickness and discomfort caused many other families to return. A South Croydon man found that within three months his 'wife and children were getting fed up with the quiet of Studley', a village in Wiltshire, and 'with the cramped conditions and difficult shopping . . . the oil lamps and cooking' and 'toilets . . . at the bottom of the garden' of the farm cottage where they were billeted. A woman from Kensington, although staying with 'kind friends' with her new-born son, found life 'in the depths of the country' in Worcestershire hard to hear:

I do not think I have ever felt quite so desolate . . . so cut-off and lonely. This produced feeding problems for the baby. One occasion seems imprinted on my mind for ever. My husband had come on a flying visit and I said goodbye to him when beginning the 6 p.m. feed. I could not stop crying all the way through. I can remember the tears falling all over the baby's head and face. *He* cried all that evening and night.

For some people the absence of danger made up for all inconveniences. 'It was like heaven after London,' felt an Ealing woman who had retreated to a village in Scotland. 'The peace of the Lancashire countryside was like a magic new world to me,' recalls a woman from Forest Gate. 'I just could not believe there were no doodlebugs there.' 'Sheer bliss' is how a Gravesend woman describes her six weeks in Wales. 'No barrage balloons, no searchlights, no guns and above all no aircraft. We could go to bed every night and, what is more, *stay* in bed every night, with no disturbance at all.'

Children commonly adapted even more readily. One Carshalton boy, aged thirteen, was among a party of fifty who left Paddington for an unknown destination:

We finally alighted at Caerphilly, Glamorgan, in what was to us another world. With a hospitable family and glorious weather, we had a marvellous time among the hills and valleys of South Wales. Even at school in Pontypridd we seemed to have a bonus; evacuees were excused from Welsh lessons.

The Doodlebugs

A thirteen-year-old boy from Addiscombe, indignant at being sent to Dunchurch, near Rugby, and thus missing all the excitement at home, speedily made the best of things. 'I consoled myself with fish and chips, watching a loose Horsa glider . . . glide into a field, visiting Leamington Spa by steam train, being treated to a *Stars in Battledress* revue (adult jokes and all), tramping round the ruins of Coventry cathedral and seeing Rita Hayworth in *Cover Girl* in a Rugby cinema.' And one unfortunate woman, born while her mother was in Cheshire, still cannot forget her family's evacuation, as her sister explains: 'She was blessed with the middle name Wirral, which she dislikes.'

So successful had been the government's 'playing down' policy, that few people in the reception areas had the faintest conception of what the new arrivals had endured, and one woman from Forest Gate hardly knew whether to be outraged or amused when 'our landlord asked my father', who had come for a weekend visit, ' "Have you ever seen one of these doodlebug things?" ' 'It was no use telling your particular bomb story. They didn't believe you,' agrees a woman from Harold Park, near Romford, of the people of Leicester. Such reactions help to explain why people from the South often felt uneasy away from it. 'All was so peaceful,' observed a Tulse Hill man who had taken his son to Barrow-on-Soar near Leicester; there was 'a strange feeling of not belonging. I could not get back to London fast enough.'

To the general rule of welcoming the refugees there were some unhappy exceptions. 'Evacuees, a sort of lesser breed, weren't too welcome up there,' a Norbury woman found in Lincolnshire. ' "Keep your flying-bombs down south. We don't want them here," they said. I missed the good comradeship of the south and . . . was rather ashamed of the general attitude of the folk there.' A doctor from Colindale, visiting his wife and child, was shocked to see 'Notices at Northampton station saying "No evacuees accepted during the water shortage".'

Only one place was so unwelcoming as to be publicly denounced in the *South London Press*, which had become unofficial spokesman for the worst afflicted areas. On 11 August 1944 it delivered a stinging front page attack under the headline:

220

Like Heaven After London

The smug city of Bath

South London Press reporters who have visited South Wales and the West Country, say that whilst the Welsh people showed the greatest sympathy with evacuees, the people of Bath were, and are, extremely selfish.

After describing how the reporter who had visited Wales had heard of women who 'went in dozens to the station with milk for the children and . . . opened their houses freely,' it printed the chilling account from a second reporter who had been instead to Bath:

I noticed a disregard for affairs not directly concerning the town, and complete apathy towards those who had been compelled to leave their homes and seek refuge here. They are looked upon as a burden on the resources of the town.

There are 8,000 of them – not a large number – but they are blamed for the shortage of food and for the decreased bus services.

One grocer in a village nearby put a notice in his window:

EVACUEES WILL NOT BE SERVED BEFORE 11 a.m.

What evacuees have endured by bombing has not impressed the dwellers in this lucky spot. . . . Most of them . . . so safe and so smug, feel that war cannot touch them. . . .

One woman objected to 'fat women from London pushing babes in prams about the streets'.

. . . We are fighting for 'freedom and democracy'. What does this cover? Does it mean that safe areas should be left free and that the effect of bombs should only be felt by those near the bomb installations across the Channel?

The following week a reply from the mayor of Bath was, with admirable fairness, given equal prominence in the paper. A number of wardens from Bath had, he pointed out, volunteered to give up their holidays to 'help their fellow wardens in the blitzed districts', and Bath had also sent its quota of building repair workers to the capital. As for the main charges, the mayor rejected them as 'most unjust aspersions', blaming the complaints on people who 'arrived . . . without having made any arrangements. . . . We are,' he insisted 'jealous of the reputation of our city for hospitality and . . . I sincerely believe that, with very few exceptions, the people from the bombed areas are very glad to find a temporary home in Bath.'

The *South London Press* remained unrepentant, pointedly quoting an appreciative telegram from the mayor of Camberwell to a very different borough: 'Bradford,' His Worship had wired, 'is doing a magnificent job for our evacuees and everybody is happy.'

19

MORE BOMBS THAN PUPILS

Nine children present. Fifteen flying-bombs sent at once.
Diary of Beckenham schoolteacher, 7 July 1944

'There was one occasion when I found my little girl of four underneath the dining-room table . . . on all fours, absolutely shaking. . . . It was dreadful to see such a little girl so frightened and be unable to make her safe.' This recollection of a woman then living in Purley will bring back for many mothers one of the recurring nightmares of the V-1 period: that even if their children did not suffer actual injury they might be mentally scarred for life by living in an atmosphere of fear.

Some adults devised elaborate fictions to explain away the martial noises outside. One man, then aged three, can remember his grandfather taking him to his bedroom in Hastings to 'watch the fireworks', as the guns bombarded approaching V-1s. Even more ingenious was the explanation which a Tottenham woman overheard a mother giving to her small son. 'I've just about had enough of that man with his noisy motorbike. The police don't seem to be doing anything. I think I'll try to catch him myself.'

On the whole the experience of living under fire left remarkably little lasting mark on young children. A Gidea Park woman was impressed when a small boy in a neighbouring garden 'called out at the very top of his little voice, as if to inform everybody in earshot, "Gone off!" then returned to his play.' A Hastings man recorded in his diary on 27 July an example of his small daughter's *sang-froid*:

Planted fifty more cabbage plants. Susan came round the corner of

the house and said, 'Come on in, dad, the buggers are here again.'
She must be receiving her primary education from the gardeners next
door.

Some children, knowing no better, positively welcomed the
flying-bombs. 'I shocked the grown-ups by gleefully crying,
"Oh, good bomb!" ' remembers one man who was then a
toddler in Bayswater. 'It was so exciting to find the landscape
changing overnight.' And the prize for the most embarrassing
remark that summer must go to the small boy overheard in a
queue at Victoria saying loudly to his mother as a V-1 cut out
overhead: 'Ooh, mum, I hope it falls. I've never seen one fall.'
One North London teacher remembers a small boy in her
nursery class who, when given bricks to play with, 'piled them
up and said, "Now wait for it, here it comes. . . . Listen for
the bang." Then he'd knock them all down with a crash.'

Two seven-year-old boys in Hadley Wood composed, and,
happily, dated, this topical version of a nursery rhyme, on 1
July 1944:

> Doodlebug, doodlebug,
> Where have you been?
> I've been to London
> To bomb the Queen.
>
> Doodlebug, doodlebug,
> What saw you there?
> Why, I saw the Queen
> Who didn't turn a hair.

By the end of June, just before official evacuation began, 231
boys or girls under the age of sixteen had already been killed,
and another 493 had been detained in hospital. Many were
mere babies. The worst single incident affecting children below
school age occurred at Crockham Hill, near Westerham, in
Kent, in an isolated building, Weald House, originally earmarked as a reserve headquarters for the Kent County Council.
The chances of this isolated building, in thinly populated open
country, being struck by a V-1 were tiny, but this was just what
happened, in the early hours of Friday, 30 June. The whole
building collapsed upon the sleeping infants below, leaving, as
the *Daily Express* reported next morning, 'only a crazy chimney

stack and the shell of the gardener's cottage' still standing. As the rescuers arrived they found 'the fine avenue of lime trees . . . white with the dust of pulverised plaster.' And, nearer still, 'the garden was a shambles of twisted metal cots, baby shoes, sheets and small blue blankets . . . prams, a broken rocking horse, toys.' 'One by one,' the *News Chronicle* reported, 'the tiny victims were recovered. A dark-haired baby boy in blue knitted bed jacket – a fair-haired girl in pink – others just as they had been dressed and tucked in for the night. They were identified by little labels tied to their ankles.'

Twenty-two of the thirty children, all aged under five, were killed or died later, twelve of whom had, tragically, only just been sent there 'for safety'. Eight out of the eleven nurses and domestic staff were also killed, and almost all the other occupants were seriously injured. It is hard not to echo still the question asked by anguished rescuers that sad midsummer morning: 'Why did it have to hit this hostel with so much waste land around?'

It was fears of just such a tragedy which caused some mothers to keep their children by them. A Purley mother remembers how nerve-racking it was to be in charge of several vulnerable toddlers, her own family being aged four, three and one:

I had the dining room table fitted up [i.e. a Morrison shelter installed] and the children were told that that was where they must go if they heard this noise. I went round . . . like a clucking hen . . . gathering them all together . . . under the . . . table and . . . tried to keep conversation going so that they would not be frightened. The children were put in there every night and . . . I used to go in and peep at them through the wire netting and . . . they looked just like rabbits in a hutch.

The mother of one small boy, aged two and a half, who had taken him to live with her parents at St Helens, an isolated spot four miles from Ryde, on the Isle of Wight, relieved her feelings by writing her infant son a long letter that July.

Every night a nightmare, Tristram John. Every night . . . I have to take you from your warm bed and . . . as we go down, I find myself saying, 'Filthy brutes, filthy brutes', over and over again and my heart racing like a bird crazy with fright, fluttering furiously against the bars of its cage. . . . From nine or ten o'clock until six or seven next

225

morning we lie curled up in the cupboard under the stairs. When this
house was built, close on a hundred years ago, they designed this
huge cupboard running the whole length under the stairs to hold the
brooms and the brushes . . . never dreaming that in this year of Our
Lord 1944 it would contain one drop-side cot, four chairs, a small
table, gas-masks, torches, first-aid equipment, spades, hatchets and
pick-axes (in case we have a chance to dig ourselves out), water and
chocolate, and three or four adults and a baby while, outside, the
guns blaze, the searchlights sweep the night sky and the damn doodlebugs roar across the garden.

The authentic flavour of that summer is also accurately captured in this surviving entry of the diary of a thirteen-year-old
schoolgirl in North-West London:

Daddy is in Egypt. We miss him. Colindale Hospital has been hit by
a bomb.* We went to the pictures to see *Princess O'Rourke* with
Olivia de Haviland and we had three alerts and three all clears. It
was a good picture. When we came home our windows were all
broken, there was no gas and no water so we had some lemonade
and went to bed in our shelter.

Aircraft spotting had long been the great hobby of wartime
schoolboys and the V-1 rapidly eclipsed all its piloted prede-
cessors as a subject of study. As one of those affected by the
mania, then a sixteen-year-old at Ashford Grammar School,
explained, 'The doodlebug was something which had been in-
vented – unlike the piloted aeroplane – in our lifetime. Here
was something we could become ready-made experts at.'

No issue of the *Aeroplane Spotter*, the bible of such enthusiasts, published fortnightly, price threepence, was more eagerly
awaited than the first to appear after the V-1s had arrived. The
magazine did not let its devoted readers down. On 29 June,
another of them remembers, 'the front page bore two hazy
photographs of "doodlebugs" (a phrase we refused to use),
and inside were silhouettes of types 1, 2 and 3, together with
an article describing the V-1 in detail [and] naming it very
correctly as "The German Reaction Propelled Explosive-Car-
rying Pilotless Aeroplane". We read it avidly.'

Thanks to the *Aeroplane Spotter* it was often possible to
identify the fragments which littered the countryside after every

---

*See page 239 for an account of this incident.

explosion. One seventeen-year-old apprentice in the GPO Engineering Department, living in Colchester, eventually collected components from thirty-two different flying-bombs and everywhere that summer a constant undeclared war was waged between such enthusiasts and the police. 'My bedroom gradually became the home of a large collection of mangled pieces of V-1,' remembers one of that expert group of aerophiles, the Spotters' Club at Ashford Grammar School, 'and eventually I was able to stagger home with an entire fin, wrapped in a sack to prevent prying eyes and possible confiscation by authority.'

Everyday artefacts like the 'great lengths of coiled steel wire always around a V-1's crater' were soon regarded by serious collectors as hardly worth acquiring, but identifiable components retained their value. 'The coveted prize was the single Bosch sparking plug, used once at the launching site to ignite the first charge of fuel in the impulse jet unit. I was the first to find one in the crater left by a downed bomb and was the envy of my compatriots.'

In retrospect it seems remarkable that few injuries occurred during the ruthless hunt for such trophies. At a school in Wimbledon one boy was the proud possessor of a 'lump of explosive taken from an unexploded bomb which had split open', while a member of the Aero Spotters Club at Ashford Grammar School also had a narrow escape:

One day our own special bush telegraph reported that a doodlebug had come down almost intact on the outskirts of town . . . sitting in the middle of a field, unexploded and begging for visitors. Out came the bikes and away we went. . . . There it was . . . a gorgeous sight, with, wonder of wonders, no one guarding it. Had they been there and defused it, or had they not yet arrived? We didn't stop to ponder. . . . We approached pretty warily, me heading for the tail . . . [and] the small detonators in the tailplanes . . . I . . . found them! It was the work of a few seconds to unscrew them and secrete them in my saddle-bag. Halfway home, I told the others what I'd got and we all got off our bikes and examined the small objects with some awe. We got back on and continued cycling, though somewhat slower now, as the wisdom of keeping them on us was discussed. Not long before, one of our schoolfriends had lost two of his fingers trying to prise the detonator out of a 13-mm cannon shell with a bradawl and it made us a little more choosy about the nature of our booty. In the end, I bowed to the majority verdict and very reluctantly threw them over a hedge.

To be a teacher in Southern England was to have all the anxieties of a parent on a large scale. By the end of August 149 schools had been damaged by flying-bombs and from mid-June others had been emptied by evacuation. A Sidcup schoolmistress remembers teaching in a tent vacated by a searchlight unit and having 'to give the children brown paper and charcoal for their lessons.' Eventually the class was 'rained out' from even these temporary quarters. In Thornton Heath the rustling of the temporary windows, made of canvas, proved a constant distraction and when these were blown out one night the pupils were sent home until September. In Carshalton, one wartime pupil remembers, 'a scheme was devised whereby work was collected and taken home to do' and in various places there were 'cottage schools' in pupils' homes. 'The house where I went,' remembers another wartime pupil, then a girl aged twelve in Welling, 'had a parrot and it used to say "Blast! Blast! Blast!" ' The children tried to enlarge the bird's vocabulary by teaching it to say 'doodlebug' but it proved a slow learner.

Those schools that stayed open found attendances dwindling. One Beckenham teacher noted that only eleven children in her class were present on Tuesday, 20 June, and on the following Monday, 26 June, only six. Numbers then picked up again, until the departure of the first evacuation parties, to Huddersfield and Doncaster on Friday, 7 July, until on Wednesday, 12 July, she was recording more V-1s than pupils: '9 children present. 15 flying-bombs sent at once.'

A 'spotter' system was introduced in many schools. One Barkingside man remembers passing a school playground in Ilford, supervised by two patrolling teachers. When a V-1 cut out 'a teacher blew her whistle and the children went over to the school wall, waiting quite calmly until the doodlebug exploded. . . . The teacher's whistle sounded again and the children resumed their play as if nothing had happened.'

If children had private fears these were rarely in evidence. 'They were always calm, never made a fuss, developed no peculiar behaviour problems, in fact were children to be proud of,' remembered a woman teaching at a primary school in Crayford. A teacher in Norbury found that her class never grumbled and cheerfully played 'the most grisly games'. Their response to an approaching flying-bomb was to start singing 'Ten Green Bottles' in the hope that 'one would accidentally fall' just as the missile exploded.

Even a near miss in school hours was accepted as all in the day's work, as the headmistress of a small village school near Pulborough, which relied for protection on 'good, solid old-fashioned dual desks', discovered:

In the middle of July at about 10 o'clock my class were busy with their arithmetic. All was quiet and peaceful when suddenly there was a shattering explosion which rocked the building and brought down plaster and shattered windows. In the twinkling of an eye every child had disappeared . . . under their desks. As the danger was over I called out, 'You can come up now,' and up they all popped. . . . One local mum (an evacuee) came dashing round and offered to sweep up so we all flocked into the playground and left her with the mess. . . . [When she had finished] I blew the whistle and we all marched back into school. . . . When I asked the children what they would like to write about they all said, 'The flying-bomb.' Once again there was peace and quiet but I had to give out a fresh supply of nibs. All their nibs were crossed. . . . At twelve o'clock most of the children went home for their dinner. . . . Afternoon school commenced at 1.15 p.m. and every single child was present.

For tens of thousands of fifth- and sixth-formers a far more immediate terror than the flying-bombs was the School Certificate examination, due to start a week after the first V-1 arrived. 'Revising the Franchise Acts came a poor second to a doodlebug,' remembers a then sixteen-year-old, living in Northwood, who felt 'somewhat less prepared' for the coming examination 'than Britain had been for war in 1939', but the days he had earmarked for last-minute revision were spent largely in the shelters.

Apart from this distraction, and loss of sleep at a vital moment, there was also the risk of the examination itself being interrupted. Because many school halls were high-roofed, vulnerable buildings, with large windows, many head teachers preferred their candidates to endure discomfort rather than disturbance. At Plaistow Grammar School 'an air-raid shelter was fitted up with desks' and 'the unfortunate candidates' – the headmaster's wife recalls – 'were doomed to sit and work in faint artificial light, through repeated alarms and . . . the continual risk of the light failing altogether.' At Putney High School the examination room was a basement cloakroom, and at a school in Westminster one reinforced with concrete, 'so dark and chilly that we wore our winter coats.'

When the examination was held above ground parents were often required to sign a letter agreeing to their children taking cover only when the 'imminent danger' alarm was sounded. In the worst affected areas the number of such interruptions was enormous. A girl taking her matriculation exam in Croydon between Friday, 23 June, and Wednesday, 5 July, remembers up to five per paper, signalled by the porter ringing the school bell. Things were not much better at Leytonstone. 'The English literature examination was the worst. We were up and down like Jack-in-the-boxes,' remembers one. 'The ear tests of the music examination which should have taken forty-five minutes took three hours.'

These were the experiences of an Enfield schoolgirl taking her School Certificate, on 27 June 1944:

There were air raids nearly all day and we had to keep hopping under our desk when the doodlebugs came along. I couldn't concentrate. The French unseen wasn't bad but the prose was not very good and I wrote an idiotic essay. . . . I had sandwiches at school . . . sitting in the cloakroom because an alert was on.

Conditions next day, when this girl 'wrote absolute nonsense' in her English language essay, were even worse, and 'we lost so much time getting under the desks . . . we were allowed ten minutes extra.' In addition to such concessions, a special report was sent to the examining board so that extra marks could be added for the 'disturbance factor'. Sometimes what had happened almost spoke for itself. 'During the art examination,' remembers a woman then taking her School Certificate at Southborough in Kent, 'the complete art room window was blown in. . . . When we rose from the floor all our paintings were smudged and covered with broken glass. We did our best to remove the damage and . . . a note was sent in with the papers to explain what had occurred.' When taking other papers the candidates also organized a little unofficial compensation of their own. 'There were more than a few whispered queries as to "What is the answer to No. 5?" and "What have you done for Question 6?" while we crouched under the desks.'

Thanks to the allowances made by the examination boards, almost all the informants quoted here managed at least to scrape through this vital test. As the headmaster of the Beckenham and Penge Grammar School candidly told his audience at the next speech day, 'When one considers the tomb-like conditions in which the examinations were worked, it was surprising that twenty candidates passed the Higher School Certificate and fifty-five the General School.' But pass they did and few careers seem to have been permanently blighted by the V-1s.

By 1944 only the favoured few – foreigners, females, scientists, the medically unfit – were able to attend university, and as even their exemption was liable to be withdrawn if they failed an examination, 'finals' and 'intermediates' had never loomed larger in students' lives. The V-1s only affected London University, and not all of that, for most colleges were still evacuated, but those back in London suffered severe distraction for their examinations started on the day the V-1s arrived in strength. 'The university,' one academic has recorded, 'decided that candidates should have the choice of postponing their entries, until the next examination.' Those who did sit them could 'during . . . alerts . . . continue work or go to shelter without penalty, being put on their honour not to discuss the examinations meanwhile.'

This privilege does not seem to have been abused. One young Roman Catholic curate from Northampton, sent down to the basement from the examination hall, remembers 'what a wonderful discussion we had' with 'a young Jesuit from overseas. . . . On returning at the end of the morning we were told to write "Air Raid in Progress" on our unfinished papers.' The university's policy proved sound, as one college's historian has recorded. 'During all the examinations of London University no one was killed . . . thereat . . . and there was but slight injury,' though one candidate was killed by the Aldwych bomb between examinations.

The university institution most affected was Birkbeck College, which catered for extra-mural and part-time students and was situated between Fleet Street and Holborn. With 358 students taking examinations Birkbeck had no option except to carry on, though it squeezed as many as possible into the section of the lecture hall 'safeguarded by the balcony and gallery', and came to an understanding with its less academic neighbour, the *Daily Mirror*, to receive the imminent danger signal from its roof-spotters. 'The second ringing of the bell,' explained the college's historian, 'became known popularly as "Divo" because it meant "Danger Imminent Vertically Overhead". . . . The coined word suggested, with no feeling of panic, the need for seeking sudden shelter at once,' perhaps beneath a table, 'thereby offering to the foe a fitting end.'

Birkbeck was damaged on several occasions, and finally, at 3.07 a.m. on Wednesday, 19 July, so destructively, by a bomb which had landed on the corner of Fetter Lane and Breams Buildings, that the opening of the next academic year had to be postponed for a month, leaving the harassed staff to send out 'well over one thousand letters . . . to inform students of the delay.' This V-1 demonstrated once again how every explosion could present different problems, for it was followed by 'a steady flow of liquid acid descending the stone steps' from broken bottles and accumulators in an upstairs laboratory and 'a fire . . . due to a bottle of phosphorus', which had burst into flames when the water in which it was immersed had drained away after its container had been smashed. The fears of what might happen if a V-1 landed during an examination were also proved well founded for 'the theatre was partly wrecked' and 'desks and chairs in it, where students had sat . . . were smashed to matchwood.' Everywhere 'apparatus and other equipment . . . was broken or thrown into utter confusion; cabinets were burst open, neat holes drilled through glass fronts, and fireplaces were dislodged. . . . Every window in the college's main building was shattered', prompting one remark that was to pass into college legend. The college accountant, on 'rising from his divan . . . covered from head to foot with soot, dust and thousands of fragments of broken glass,' took one look at the shattered panes and shouted, 'Cancel the window-cleaning contract!'

20

A HOSPITAL WAS HIT

Injured doctor crawls to own operating theatre.

Headline in *Daily Express*, 22 June 1944

'The regularity with which hospitals suffered throughout the flying-bomb ordeal was remarkable.' In these words the official historian of the Emergency Medical Services gave formal recognition to the fact that the V-1s seemed to seek out the sick and helpless. Several hospitals were hit during the first week and by the end of October a hundred had suffered varying degrees of damage, seventy-six of them in London itself, involving the permanent loss of 2600 beds and the temporary loss of another 6000. All told 138 patients were killed in hospital and 1155 injured, many of them casualties from earlier incidents. Hospital staff escaped more lightly, but twenty-four lost their lives and 146 were injured.

The strain upon nurses and doctors everywhere in Greater London was incessant. In one twenty-four-hour period, for example, the Middlesex Hospital, in the very heart of London, between Oxford Street and the Marylebone Road, had 190 signals of imminent danger, on hearing which doctors and nurses were 'instructed to jump away from windows and go to the nearest place of comparative safety' – sound advice but impossible to obey.

The Emergency Medical Service, set up on the outbreak of war, embraced both the great 'voluntary' hospitals, which were independent charitable institutions, and the local authority hospitals, wholly supported from public funds. Hardly one of the famous voluntary hospitals escaped, while London County Council hospitals were damaged, including V-2 incidents, on

233

138 occasions. Seven hospitals had for a time to be completely evacuated: Mile End, Lambeth, St Olave's, St Francis's, St Nicholas's, St Clements, and, first and worst, St Mary Abbotts in Kensington.

The St Mary Abbotts flying-bomb struck at 4.05 in the morning of Saturday, 17 June, the very start of the offensive, and scored a direct hit in the middle of the close-packed complex of buildings, totally destroying the children's isolation block, the central block of the main nurses' home, and partly demolishing four blocks of wards. The damage was such that the whole hospital had to be closed, with the loss of 832 beds, and the patients and staff were sent elsewhere. Thirteen patients, largely children, were killed and five of the staff. A handwritten message, scribbled in pencil at 7.10 the following Sunday evening, by a warden from the nearby Post 23, which survives in the former Royal Borough of Kensington archives, sums up the Germans' achievement:

1 child's body recovered. All missing now accounted for. Total casualties now 51. 18 bodies sent to public mortuary. 33 injured evacuated to hospital. Remainder of patients and staff evacuated. Gas and water cut off at hospital. All services returned to depots. . . . Incident closed.

What happened at St Mary Abbotts was soon being repeated on the south side of the Thames. Six days later, another LCC Hospital, St Olave's Bermondsey, was hit, and after another incident on 13 August, it also had to be evacuated. Inevitably, the hospitals which were needed most were most liable to be damaged. Croydon General Hospital, for example, was badly affected by the solitary V-1 which came down close to it, though it stayed in action and handled 2000 flying-bomb casualties. The Mayday Hospital, in the same borough, having evacuated its ordinary patients to Scotland, was able to cope with 485 admissions from flying-bomb casualties and to treat another 248 as out-patients. The Norwood District Hospital was knocked out on 29 June, while 'walking wounded' from an earlier incident were still being treated, and on re-opening in August its first in-patients were injured Home Guards. The Croydon Borough Sanatorium, at North Cheam, had *its* bomb on 12 July, when a kitchen was wrecked, and the Croydon

Isolation Hospital had a ward destroyed on 16 August. Mercifully, St Mary's Maternity Hospital, where the new-born babies spent their first days tucked up in specially made boxes fitted side by side in Morrison shelters, escaped with minor damage. Not a single infant was as much as scratched; one local man remembers seeing a nurse hurrying down the corridor after the siren had sounded with a baby tucked securely under each arm.

The vast peacetime mental hospitals a little further out – mainly in 1944 being used for ordinary patients – also attracted many bombs. The huge Warlingham Park Hospital suffered several hits, but remained open; so, too, did the famous Bethlem Royal, at Shirley, though no fewer than seven V-1s landed in its grounds, costing the hospital its farm buildings, the use of five wards, its research unit and 'almost every door and window' in several other buildings.

Midway between Croydon and Sutton was the St Helier Hospital at Carshalton. The first of its two V-1s landed early on the morning of Thursday, 21 June, and was the subject of a graphic account – though the hospital was not identified – in the following morning's *Daily Express* under the headline: 'Injured doctor crawls to own operating theatre':

When rescue workers arrived at a hospital hit by a flying-bomb yesterday they found the medical superintendent's house demolished. They could not discover the doctor at first – till they found that, although seriously injured, he had crawled to the operating theatre he knew so well. There he had an operation on his head. No one was killed. The bomb blasted the nurses' home and seriously injured twelve nurses.

Among the latter was night sister, Verna Kingdom, who had just come off duty after a 'hectic night' coping with an influx of flying-bomb casualties.

I checked the day staff on duty and went to call nurses who had overslept – thirteen in all – leaving them to have a snack in the dining room. I went to the fourth floor to check a Red Cross nurse, Rosemary G., who had not arrived. She was there and greeted me by saying that . . . the bus windows had been blown out. At that moment, about 7 a.m., a flying-bomb landed between the front of the nurses home and Dr Eric Brooke's, the medical superintendent's, house. I remember whirling round like a spinning top and was later

235

told the corners of the room opened and closed. . . . Mercifully the blast hurled us inside instead of sucking us out. . . . After a moment I realized I was blinded, and hearing nothing from Rosemary knew she must be unconscious. I also realized blood was pumping from my head, so I used my apron as a tourniquet. . . . Knowing that no one knew I had come upstairs and that I was carrying most of the drug keys I groped my way to a telephone and dialled. . . . I was tracked by my bloodstains and . . . I realized my facial injuries were severe because colleagues and friends did not recognize me when searching among the casualties. I lost consciousness for a few minutes while being carried down from the fourth floor head first. I felt an insane desire to laugh on hearing the doctor's voice, whom I repeatedly had called out during the night. Then we were taken to the wards . . . Rosemary G. was in the next bed.

Among the less seriously injured was a twenty-two-year-old student nurse, who also remembers every detail of that memorable morning:

It was just after breakfast. I was in the cloakroom, opposite [the medical superintendent's] house, just a minute before his home was hit. I had been putting on my cap and apron and went out of the door when the cloakroom was wrecked. Nearly everybody received some injury. I only had a slight cut on my arm from flying glass. My two friends were bombed out of their rooms. We moved one nurse's bed into my room and slept three to two beds.

Six days later, on 27 June, the St Helier was hit again, by a bomb which arrived while no warning was in force and, in the words of the *Sutton Times*, landed 'between two wings of the hospital, damaging several wards and setting fire to a store of bedding and linoleum.' The blaze was fed from the hospital's own petrol tanks and Sister Kingdom, now a patient in her own hospital, can still recapture 'the horror of being blind and just listening to the roar of flames as the petrol pumps went up.' The student nurse who had escaped with a scratch from the previous explosion also witnessed this incident, in which two people were fatally injured and two killed outright, among them a child recently dug out from the ruins of her wrecked home:

I was late coming off duty at 9 p.m. as I had to admit an injured, unconscious air-raid warden with a broken thigh. I pressed the button of the lift for the fourth floor, but when it arrived I decided to walk down the stairs. As soon as I reached the second floor the doodlebug hit the hospital. The whole building shook for several seconds. Everything crashed. The lift smashed down and broke, windows, doors, part of the ceiling fell. I heard screams all around me. Then I smelt burning. I followed the smoke and found that the ward hit was reserved for air-raid casualties. As soon as I opened the door I saw the dead girl, twelve-year-old Constance B., lying on the floor. In the bed next to the door my friend was standing next to the bed of a two-year-old boy, holding his severed ear and wondering if it could be stitched on again. I asked the sister what I could do to help and was directed to help in a chain of nurses to move the hospital's stores away from the fire.

The other person killed was a male nurse who had been sent on an errand and died between two hospital blocks. He could only be identified by his watch. We all were either slightly or seriously injured. I escaped with a bruised shoulder. Next day we had to evacuate the hospital with all our patients. . . . We were split up to different hospitals all over Surrey. I went to Warren Street Hospital, Guildford. The nurses were billeted with people living in the town. The wards were terribly overcrowded. I hated it and volunteered to return to St Helier Hospital as soon as two wards were reopened on 9 July.

Sister Kingdom had meanwhile been moved with other patients to Ashridge Park in Hertfordshire:

We arrived early in the morning and one incident caused great hilarity. The only possessions sent with us were flowers – no toilet articles, clothes or money. We were later told by astounded civilian patients they thought a ghastly funeral procession was passing through the ward. The flowers were laid on top of us. . . . We all survived. I had an eye removed three weeks later, was blind for some weeks and partially sighted for some months. Dr Brooke, who had had an eye removed also came over every day, reading to us and writing letters. . . . After more surgery at East Grinstead, under Mr IcIndoe, where I met many burned airmen, I returned in February 1945 to St Helier.*

At Kingston Hospital a new class of eighteen-year-olds had just started the training course for nurses when the first V-1s arrived.

---

*The legendary Archibald McIndoe was later knighted for his pioneering work in plastic surgery. When this informant wrote to me, in 1976, she was in her forty-second year of nursing, thirty-four of them spent in the St Helier.

We were doing some study in a large sunroom attached to Gloucester Lodge [their residential hostel] when another one came over and cut out. This time there was no doubt about how near it was and one of us said, 'Get out of here,' and without question we did, sheltering in the large but almost windowless hall, behind chairs, etc. I and another nurse ducked down by the big fireplace and then it landed, not on our house but very near. . . . The first reaction was to find out if we were all unhurt. We were, although one nurse . . . hurried to the downstairs lavatory to reappear saying, 'I'm dying to spend a penny and it's all broken.' I'm afraid we all laughed. Next we went to see what had happened and on going out passed through the sunroom we had been using. The table with our work books laid on it and the chairs were covered in jagged pieces of glass. . . . The main hospital had been hit and although screened by trees and hedges we could see thick smoke rising above them. . . . We ran to find the doodlebug had landed on the nurses home. . . . One nurse . . . said, 'If all my clothes are gone, I wish I'd gone too.'

Hours later, after helping to move patients from the wrecked wards into those still habitable, these young girls were able to think again about their own situation, with 'nowhere to sleep except the main hospital shelter':

I . . . went with another nurse who was going home for the night. She lived outside the town, too far to walk and the last bus had gone so we went for a taxi, and on finding one were grumbled at by the driver – something about 'young girls gadding about at night'. That finished us. We really turned on him and told him . . . what we had been doing, and he . . . rushed us to where we wanted to go, I think for nothing. The next day was spent moving patients into ambulances to be taken to other hospitals. . . . The nurses in training school were sent to another hospital and, on the way, the sister in charge of us complained about the state of my uniform. . . . It *was* dirty . . . from soot . . . from . . . general dirt from the clearing and blood from small cuts from the broken glass we were clearing.

Hardly one of the famous central London hospitals escaped unscathed and those not badly damaged were regularly flooded out with casualties. The Middlesex in Mortimer Street, for example, where Florence Nightingale had once worked, had to handle 'more than two hundred casualties' in 'not much more than half an hour' after a V-1 had 'landed in Whitfield Street, which was crowded with lunchtime shoppers.' St George's, at Hyde Park Corner, was also comparatively fortunate, but received so many casualties that one junior nurse found herself regularly allocated the most unpopular job: cutting away the patient's filthy and blood-stained clothing and washing the exposed flesh to enable the extent of his injuries to be seen. The Royal Free Hospital, then in Gray's Inn Road, was hit twice in two days, the second occasion very seriously, when, on a mild summer evening, Wednesday, 5 July, a V-1 dived on to one of its central buildings, killing two staff and three patients and making necessary the evacuation of 140 more.

Of all the great voluntary hospitals St Thomas's, just across the river from the Houses of Parliament, came off worst. On 4 July its first flying-bomb caused relatively minor damage, but the second, on 15 July, scored 'a direct hit on the Adelaide ward theatre in block II' and seriously damaged three of the great red-brick blocks that were a feature of the riverside scene. St Thomas's did not close, but the nurses' preliminary training school was evacuated in Edinburgh and the medical school, instead of returning to London, stayed in rural Godalming.

Even hospitals in North and North-West London did not escape occasional flying-bombs and one of the worst incidents of the whole campaign was at Colindale where 350 beds were earmarked for air-raid casualties and other patients evacuated from central London. The medical superintendent, Dr W. E. Snell, recorded in his diary on 16 June his first V-1 'going north and being shot at.' By 26 June, he heard 'V-1s exploding at intervals,' spent the nights in the strengthened cellar of his house where 'one could not hear most of the V-1s passing over.' Eventually, on Saturday, 1 July, one did not pass over but landed 'with a great explosion':

A silence followed . . . and I scrambled into clothes and went out through our back garden door which led towards the main hospital, some fifty yards distant. Dawn was just breaking and it . . . had been recently raining and the path was covered with slippery clay. . . . I reached the south entrance to the hospital, adjoining wards 7 and 8, and was horrified to see that they were now just a pile of bricks. . . . The V-1 had fallen in the earth a few feet from the south side of the two-storey block, which had open balconies at the side. The upper ward, 8, housed some 30 men being treated for pulmonary tuberculosis, of whom 5 on the adjoining open air balcony lost their lives. In some amazing way nearly all the remainder managed to crawl out of, or were rescued from, the wreckage with comparatively minor injuries. In the ground-floor ward, 7, were some five or six WAAFs from Hendon Aerodrome. . . . Of these four were killed, and one nurse, whose bodies were not found until late that day.

Doctors and nurses, whatever their reputation off duty, were expected to be imperturbable while at work but appearances could be deceptive. Sister Kingdom recalls that until the St Helier had been hit the staff 'were not frightened' but 'each V-1 afterwards was frightful and both staff and patients were unnerved.' The student nurse from Kingston quoted earlier reacted similarly. 'I had a real moment of fear,' she confesses, when a second V-1 flew over while she was helping to clear up after the first, 'thinking "Oh God, not another, not yet." '

Fear was perhaps the most natural and least destructive response to being in a situation where others' safety always had to come first. 'A "doodlebug cult" seemed to develop,' remembers a woman from a North London hospital. 'Hospital staffs swapped casualty figures. . . . Sometimes one would miss an incident whilst on leave and was never sure whether to be glad or sorry.' A medical secretary in a West London hospital became conscious of the cumulative effects of danger and loss of sleep:

All the heroism that we showed during the first years of the war, when we fancied we were Florence Nightingale and Edith Cavell rolled into one, disappeared. We were all so tired and were 'taking it out' on one another. Petty jealousies were showing and I remember losing my temper with one of the best of our nurses. Indeed, I screamed at her for no reason. There is a limit of human resistance and . . . those of us who had been in it from the beginning had really had enough. Both I and some of the medical staff were incapable of walking with our two feet firmly on the ground. We were suffering from what a brochure from County Hall called 'effort syndrome'. In our own words we were 'bomb drunk', and not much use to anybody.

The record of the London hospitals that summer contradicts this depressing conclusion. Every nurse learned during her training the importance of tackling every task, however novel, systematically and soon even this unprecedented challenge was being met. A woman then working in a North London hospital remembers what happened when a V-1 had been heard to explode nearby:

We quickly swung into the well-known routine. . . . The first to arrive were the less severely wounded, requiring . . . treatment for shock. The more serious cases spent some time in the operating theatre before reaching the wards . . . usually unconscious. It was in the interval between the two groups that we would glean some information as to the whereabouts of the incident and the extent of the damage. Later in the day would come the most harrowing part . . . when bewildered survivors looking for missing relatives trekked round the wards and hospitals until they found their loved ones or were persuaded it was better to leave it to the rest centre staff to link them up.

Another discovery made by every student as soon as she was allowed on the wards was that patients' possessions were often more trouble than their illness and this familiar problem now reached new heights. One former student nurse, working in a large teaching hospital in South-East London, remembers the remarkable sight in Casualty after a V-1 had devastated a terrace of small houses. 'The old folk had brought their beloved pets with them, and amongst the collection of birds, cats and dogs there was even an unperturbed tortoise.' A woman admitted to hospital after an incident in Horseferry Road remembers the constant pleas of a fellow patient, an old lady, to be reunited with her umbrella, although she was black from head to foot: she had been sheltering in a coal-cellar. Once 'it was with her in bed she was happy' – with good reason; it contained her life savings.

Large-scale evacuation brought a sudden influx of hospital patients from London to places destined barely to hear a siren, let alone a V-1. The first to arrive were the children. Beginning in mid-July parties from children's hospitals in Carshalton, Sutton and Swanley were sent to places as distant as Knaresborough in Yorkshire, Dryburn in Durham, Manchester and Liverpool. On 31 July the Ministry of Health ordered that various categories of adult patients unlikely to be discharged in the near future should also be sent away from London. Evacuation of 'acute' cases, i.e. the seriously ill, began on 4 August, followed by the 'chronic sick', i.e. those with long-term ailments, and sufferers from tuberculosis, still a common category. Most were found beds in emergency, wartime-only hospitals specially opened for the purpose. The male inmates of Colindale Hospital, for example, found themselves at Kinmel Hall, Abergele, in North Wales. All told 8700 patients were evacuated from LCC hospitals alone, though some categories were left behind – sufferers from VD and the mentally ill among them – and in September the general evacuation of hospitals ceased altogether.

The biggest effect of all was felt in the maternity hospitals. Pregnant women had always been one of the 'priority' classes for evacuation and the number of confinements in London maternity wards in 1944 was the lowest since 1934, although the maternal mortality rate of 1·91 per thousand births in 1944 compared very favourably with the 2·67 of 1943. The figures were all the more satisfactory because the wartime system of ante-natal care had largely been disrupted. In one hospital alone the number of mothers-to-be who had not previously booked a bed for their confinement rose from 10 per cent to 40 per cent because, as the LCC's own medical officer explained, 'insistence on evacuation . . . deterred women from booking until they were in labour.' Another phenomenon was that 'A number of other expectant mothers went into the country under the official evacuation scheme, but returned to London unannounced just before their confinement.' Clearly many women wished to have their baby born a Londoner whatever the Germans did.

Women expecting a baby when the doodlebugs started had no choice about evacuation. Among such mothers was one whose son's birthday still provides an 'annual reminder' of them, for he arrived at midday on 15 June in Westminster Hospital, a few hours before the bombardment really began:

Early the next morning the hospital was evacuated, except for us, the maternity patients, and left available only for D-Day wounded and flying-bomb casualties. We were moved down to a floor in the centre of the hospital and all put together in one ward. . . . The babies' cots were placed in a corridor, in order to be away from windows – the two at either end . . . were covered with mattresses – but there were unexpected draughts which caused some sore eyes. I have a vivid recollection of tiny purple-eyed babies brought to us for feeding, as they had been treated with gentian violet. . . . At night our dear night sister started to walk the length of the ward when an engine was first heard. My bed was right at the end and she always seemed to reach me as the explosion was heard. She said I always asked her the time and then went to sleep again.

Almost worse than being in Westminster was being in the middle of the gun-belt, which happened to another mother who had booked a bed in an emergency maternity home, 'a large detached house in the midst of a thickly wooded area a few hundred yards' from her home in Hastings.

My daughter was born in the early evening of 6 July 1944, and five weeks early. My room-mate had her daughter in the early hours of the following morning. In those days mothers weren't allowed to get out of bed until the eighth day, but as a special concession we were permitted to swing our legs over the edge of the bed so that we did not lose muscle power and could walk in an emergency.

Eventually, we were moved downstairs for greater safety and were put in the drawing-room of the house. There was a magnificent chandelier in the centre and our beds were at either end of the room. When the guns opened up and a doodlebug was very near the vibration would set the chandelier swinging, first towards my bed and then towards that of my companion. Matron would appear, expecting to find us alarmed, only to find us in fits of laughter and making bets on whose bed it would land on.*

Despite all the perils, natural and Germanic, of their occupants' situation, the maternity wards seem often to have been a place of laughter that summer. A woman then in Forest Gate Hospital remembers another in the same ward who 'moaned and complained all the time', until finally when 'her baby was born and I heard the sister say, "My word! You have a beautiful little boy here. Oh, he's a darling." The girl started to wail, "Oh no! I wanted a girl!" To my surprise, the sister said, "Well we're not b——— well putting it back now." ' A woman from Pinner was delighted by the novel prayer uttered by a 'dear old Irish nurse'. She would come down in the night, 'wrapped in a voluminous dressing grown' and fervently beseech the Almighty to 'Let this one pass over for the sake of Mrs ———'s milk.'

---

*This informant adds: 'My "doodlebug baby" now has a PhD in biochemistry, so her first hazardous weeks had no permanent effect on her.'

21

DEATH IN CIRCLE GARDENS

*8½ year old AIR RAID CASUALTY with amputated leg
needs DUNGAREES and TROUSERS (girls'),
night dresses or pyjamas.*

Advertisement quoted in *The Outpost*, September 1944

The flying-bombs were intended to spread terror by killing and maiming British civilians and though the toll of suffering they inflicted was trivial by German standards, it was still vast enough. More than 5000 families felt the pains of bereavement; more than 50,000 people were crippled, blinded or savagely hurt. Happily, as the offensive went on, the casualty rate per bomb declined. In the first week alone 723 people lost their lives; by 15 July, after a month's bombardment, the death roll was about 3600; by the end of August 5476. The number of seriously injured, defined as those kept in hospital, showed a similar pattern. In the first week 2610; by 15 July about 10,000; by the end of August just under 16,000. The slightly-injured, sent home after first aid treatment – though some never fully recovered from the shock of being exposed to violence – numbered 12,000 by mid-July, almost 26,000 by the end of August.

As always, it was London – i.e. the London Civil Defence Region, which included the south-eastern suburbs and parts of Essex and Surrey – which came off worst. The 2224 V-1s that dropped there killed 5126 people, an average of 2·3 per bomb. The 2789 which landed outside London caused only 350 deaths, or 0·1 per bomb. The figures for serious injury were similar: 14,712, 6·6 per bomb, in the London Region but only 1206, 0·4 per bomb, outside it. The slightly injured amounted to 25,893 in London, or 11·6 per bomb, and 3,829, 1·4 per bomb, outside it. Overall, between June and August, the combined casualty rate was 51,206, or roughly ten per bomb, and the figure of one death per bomb, quoted by the Prime Minister on 6 July, remained valid. It cost the Germans about £150 to kill a British civilian with a V-1, and about £15 to kill or injure one; Hitler, and his eager tools, like Colonel Wachtel, were on to a military bargain.

The opinion was widely expressed that the V-1s, because they arrived at all hours and in all weathers, were worse than the Blitz, and in terms of casualties this was true. Conventional bombs, in the nine months up to May 1941, had killed 0·83 people per metric ton and seriously injured 0·93. Each flying-bomb warhead, of roughly the same weight, killed 1·1 people and seriously injured 3·1. Luckily, however, the experts' most pessimistic estimates proved wrong. They had predicted that in a densely built-up area about twenty people were likely to be killed or seriously injured for every V-1 that landed by day, and about half that number at night. (The number of killed alone, it was expected, would be about five per bomb by day, and two and a half at night.) The actual casualty rate by the end of September was 8·5 per incident, of which 28·5 per cent proved fatal.

How did the flying-bomb victims die? Every ARP worker had horror stories of finding groups of people, apparently un-harmed, sitting around the family tea-table, or along a shelter bench, dead from blast, which was believed to shock the system into immobility and to paralyse the lungs. Such deaths were in fact rare. 'I have found nothing to suggest that "true blast casualties" . . . ,' wrote the author of an article in the *ARP and NFS Review* in August, 'have increased in number. On the other hand the proportion of casualties in which blast has *originated* the chain of events terminating in injury definitely goes up. The fly-bomb's blast hurls victims against obstacles, crashes them into walls, knocks them down violently.' In an Emergency Medical Service hospital injuries of this kind ac-counted for 20 per cent of all admissions and 50 per cent of all those who died. Six deaths in this small hospital, which admit-ted altogether 259 flying-bomb casualties, were due to a frac-tured skull. Injuries from flying glass accounted for 40 per cent of admissions, though only one death. A larger survey, based on an analysis of the injured (excluding those who subsequently died) from 122 incidents, found that 30 per cent were due to glass, 20 per cent to other flying debris and 50 per cent to other causes. Of these last 15 per cent had suffered compound fractures, 30 per cent simple fractures, 19 per cent eye injuries, 26 per cent lacerations and 10 per cent other injuries.

Almost anything could cause a serious injury if hurled with sufficient force – and the explosive power of a bursting V-1 was enormous. On many people's memories is implanted the sight of some hideous injury caused in this way. A fire-watcher in Wanstead can still remember the face of a woman covered with brick dust and looking 'as though she been scalped.' 'John had an eye and part of his face smashed by a chair,' remembers a woman then living in Streatham of her brother, injured while seated in his dining-room. A nurse in a North London hospital found herself treating a young girl who had been standing outside her home thinking about her forthcoming wedding:

She had been standing on a gravel pathway [and] was covered with embedded gravel on face, arms and legs, giving her a strange grey rough-cast surface when we had washed away the dust and dirt. I can remember that on the following day, Sunday, anyone who had any spare minutes would try to get a few more pieces of gravel out of her skin. Many were the ingenious ideas tried before she was presentable, if not quite smooth, again.

Children were not immune from such injuries or being confronted by such sights. A West Ham boy of fourteen watched a young woman being carried along on an old door, 'covered with blood. At her head the rescue workers had placed a very young baby.' Another victim was a small boy admitted to the Central Middlesex Hospital in Park Royal. 'My dad,' he explained, 'had just finished making my mum a nice new kitchen dresser when that naughty Mr Hitler sent one of his bombs and smashed it all to pieces.' 'He didn't,' comments the nurse concerned, 'seem nearly so concerned about his poor eye, which . . . later had to be removed.'

A single incident could produce a whole range of different injuries. One man in Abbey Wood recorded what happened when a V-1 demolished his home:

My wife, Audrey: multiple wounds around her head and body.
My elder son, Jim: wounded in the eye.
My younger son, Geoff: glass sticking through his thigh.
My daughter Peggy: in shock.

And all had escaped lightly compared to a neighbour, taken to hospital with his false teeth protruding from his neck, where the force of the bomb had driven them. 'He died that same night.'

Apart from those killed or blinded, the worst sufferers were the people who lost limbs, blown off by the explosion or, more commonly, irremediably crushed by falling debris. There was a wealth of tragedy – and a reminder that a poor family did not cease being poor simply because one of their number was maimed – in the small advertisement which appeared in a London newspaper and was reprinted in an American magazine. '8½ year old AIR RAID CASUALTY with amputated leg,' it read, 'needs good DUNGAREES and TROUSERS (girl's), night dresses or pyjamas, blouses and woollies. Good prices given if condition good.'

As the attack went on the nature of the injuries changed. 'The proportion of glass injuries dropped as the importance of taking adequate cover was realised,' reported a resident surgical officer from one EMS hospital, almost certainly in Lewisham, in the *British Medical Journal* on 25 November, 'while the percentage of crush injuries increased from being trapped by falling masonry.'

All told this hospital admitted 259 flying-bomb casualties, while a further 222 received out-patient treatment. Of the 259 more serious cases eighteen died and eighty-three needed surgery in the operating theatre, a proportion which 'remained fairly constant throughout the series'. Its 'peak period' began during a night in July, when twenty-four cases were admitted, but far worse was to follow next morning, with 'a flying-bomb dropped in a nearby market-place' – no doubt the Lewisham High Street incident already described.*

We admitted 74 to the wards and dealt with over 90 in the Casualty Department. At one time we had ambulances evacuating the night's casualties, waiting their turn with ambulances bringing fresh wounded. In twenty-four hours over 100 patients were warded. As we could not deal with all the cases in our single theatre in reasonable time we re-evacuated 35 patients after rest, cleaning and first-aid attention,

---

*See page 185 for an account of this incident and pages 250–51 for a description of the experiences of one of those seriously injured in it.

and 15 more who had had minor operations. The most gravely injured we retained. . . . [On another occasion] we admitted 32 patients from a neighbouring hospital which had been hit, only to send them on in a few hours, to the great grief of the nursing staff, who had just succeeded in disentangling prostatic tubes from false teeth and restoring order out of chaos. . . . Some of our bizarre cases presented interesting problems. Not the least was a poor soul who had been blown into a tank of dirty industrial oil and appeared in the midst of a rush of casualties; we used our gas-decontamination centre for the first – and we hoped the last – time.

Glass remained the biggest single cause of injuries and even the most experienced Civil Defence workers were horrified to discover what damage it could do when flung by a flying-bomb. One ARP instructor who helped in an incident at Thornton Heath was astonished on shining his torch on the back of the head of one man who had asked for a plaster to cover 'a sore patch . . . to see two rows of little pieces of glass sparkling away, similar to a couple of ladies' ornamental combs.' An Eastbourne woman was shocked at the appearance of a neighbour who had been sitting in the sun-parlour of her house, for the flesh of her face was hanging down 'like the skin of a banana'. The daughter of a woman living in Byfleet, who looked out to see if the children from the adjoining houses had taken shelter just as the window was blown in, remembers that 'many small pieces were impregnated in her face and back as she turned round'. Such injuries, especially when someone was bleeding badly, perhaps from a cut artery, presented unexperienced helpers with a tricky problem, for the *ARP and NFS Review* had advised its readers, 'If glass is embedded in a wound do not remove it. It may be acting as a valuable plug and . . . the possibility of . . . increased bleeding due to extraction is too serious for first-aiders to gamble with.'

Frequently the fragments visible on the surface merely masked more serious injury within. One student nurse at Edgware Hospital found that often what looked like 'superficial cuts . . . would later be found to be the entrance to a tunnel running along the flesh at the end of which, when operating, the surgeon would find glass fragments of an infinite variety of shapes and sizes.'

A particularly tragic feature of such cases was that so many affected the eyes, for reasons that the doctor previously quoted explains:

Most of the injuries were above the nipple line, chiefly of the face and neck: a large proportion were received when looking out of windows. . . . We had five cases of perforating wounds of both eyes and ten perforating wounds of one eye. The globe was usually completely destroyed.

A substantial number of people lost their sight. A voluntary nurse at Clapham Women's Hospital helped to treat one who had been in the bathroom when the V-1 fell. 'She was really a pitiful sight; her body was pitted with glass . . . and . . . she had been blinded.' Many others had a narrow escape from the same fate. 'My face was like a pepper pot and unfortunately, after three weeks of treatment I finally lost my right eye,' remembers a woman who had been staying at a public house in Horseferry Road when it was wrecked.

But if the flying-bombs posed new problems for doctors and nurses the latter also possessed an invaluable new weapon in their fight to save life, as one nurse then working in North London rapidly realized:

By now penicillin had become a fact of life and we were progressing from the rather clumsy continuous intra-muscular drip technique . . . to the more laborious method of frequent small doses throughout the twenty-four hours.

What did it feel like to become a flying-bomb casualty? Typical of that large group of people slightly injured was a young mother who was peacefully breast-feeding her two-week-old son at her home in Shaftesbury Avenue, Harrow, at 2.30 in the afternoon of Monday, 26 June 1944:

I remember my husband . . . who had been allowed a weekend compassionate leave to see his new son . . . going to the window and looking up at the sky just as the doodlebug landed almost opposite our flat. . . . The noise almost burst our eardrums. My strongest recollection is of the few seconds' dead silence which followed the crash before the screams and groans of trapped victims were heard, plus the bells of approaching ambulances and fire engines. . . .

My husband was stretched out on the floor wrapped in three layers of curtains – net, brocade and black-out fabric – and when he had recovered enough to disentangle himself I saw that his face was a mass of superficial cuts and he had glass in one eye.

I was pitted with glass all over my chest and blood streamed from wounds in my head and leg. The baby on my lap was soaked to the skin with my blood, but when the rescuers came and took him from me I could not be convinced that he was alive and only very slightly cut about the head and that it was my blood which was all over him. Hubby and I were taken to Harrow hospital and a tourniquet was put on my leg on route. . . . I remember being . . . taken to a small private room where . . . my wounds were cleaned up, but it was not until after midnight that a weary doctor was able to come and stitch the fairly deep wound in my leg. . . . I still have a small scar to show for it.

Much more badly hurt – it was to be eight weeks before he could return home – was a young schoolboy who had been playing in the garden of his home in Reperton Road, Fulham, when a flying-bomb hit the house opposite;

All I remember is choking dust and blood running down my face. The next thing . . . was someone picking me up and saying, 'All right, son, this is Sandy Pearson, you will be all right now.' He lived at the end of our road and was home on leave from the Navy. I was taken to the end of the road and placed on a stretcher to await the ambulance. . . . I was eventually taken to Fulham Hospital, New Kings Road, Hammersmith . . . where my eyes were bathed and cleaned although I could not see out of my left eye, and then taken to the operating theatre and stitches inserted round my left eye, left arm and hand. (I still carry the scars.) From there I was taken to Windsor Hospital with my mother, who had suffered cuts and bruises. My father stayed at Fulham Hospital (broken hip and cuts) with my grandfather (cuts). . . . My eye . . . had to be bathed twice a day until eventually I could see out of it.

Many V-1 casualties were caught in the open, among them this twenty-two-year-old WAAF, a victim, as already mentioned, of the Lewisham High Street bomb:*

We were put into an ambulance and next to me was a man lying moaning faintly. He appeared to be around forty, but . . . one could not distinguish features; it was as though all the skin had been torn off, his face was red and raw. . . . The ambulance took us to St John's Hospital. . . . The ground floor wards were full of injured; some

*See p. 185.

having blood transfusions on the spot. We were brought cups of tea and given injections . . . and then I was wheeled into the theatre as I was – uniform and all. I can see now the bright lights and the doctors all standing round the table and I could just see their eyes and . . . I wondered what the dickens they were going to do and then, blissfully, I was anaesthetized, and when I woke up it was evening I was in bed in one of the wards and sporting a huge plaster from toe to thigh, smeared with blood on the outside. . . . That first night in the hospital was a bad one. . . .

I felt very uncomfortable and couldn't turn over in bed. When matron came along with a sister during the night, she helped to turn me over and the doctor kept coming round to see me. I had a compound fracture of the fibula and tibia and the usual cuts and bruises. All night I could hear a young voice in the next ward, calling out loudly. . . . He was obviously from the market where the bomb fell, he was calling out his wares and it was heartbreaking to hear. . . . A woman in the next bed to me had been waiting to be served in Williamsons, the cake shop. . . . The shop had fallen on her and she had escaped with . . . terrible bruises, she was black and blue all over. . . . There was a young girl from the post office who was badly burnt. . . . There was an elderly lady, badly burnt on the face; cheerful but dreaded the change of dressings. She had been sitting on a bus just past Marks and Spencer and on her lap she had a basket containing two packets of sugar she . . . was taking to a friend. The sugar burst into flames. People kept coming in to see me. My poor dad [was] worried because he said he must warn me my leg might have to come off. But, somehow, nothing seemed to worry me just then. . . . Then my Aunts Rose and Grace [came] and Aunt Grace said, 'Well, anyway, you can be thankful your face hasn't been injured,' and they said goodbye and went away.*

From Lewisham, her leg having been saved, this young woman was sent to Maidstone and then to South Wales, before being 'discharged from hospital and the service' in October 1945. 'That,' she remarks, 'is the story of "my" bomb.'

The dead cannot tell their stories, but their loved-ones can. Among them was a woman then aged fifteen, who can remember every detail of the last few moments before her happy family life, in Winchmore Hill, North London, was shattered for ever.

---

*This informant adds: 'Aunt Grace was killed in November by a rocket, and her face wasn't marked either.'

The Doodlebugs

On 24 June 1944 I was in bed with my younger sister, Iris, who was aged twelve years, when the siren sounded. . . . Almost before it ceased we could hear the throbbing engine of the doodlebug. Dad must have looked out of the window, as he called out to mum something I could not hear. . . . By now . . . the whole house was vibrating, even the bed was jumping up and down. This is it, [I thought] this one is ours. . . . I managed to push my sister to the edge of the bed, I had one leg over her . . . when the bomb exploded. I learnt afterwards that . . . it had tipped the chimney on the other side of the road and dived straight into our house. The explosion was deafening. I felt as if I was sailing up in the air, full of wind, my head felt like a balloon. I was buried with my legs upright, almost in a horizontal position. I tried to open my eyes and a searing pain shot through them. I closed them again and thought I was blinded. As I moved a beam fell on my chest, crushing me even more. I remember feeling quite calm, in fact resigned, that I was possibly dying. . . .

Eventually I heard voices and a man said, 'It's all right, Mary, we have got you.' They then tied my ankles behind somebody's neck, whilst others were freeing my top half. During this time I could not speak or move, although I was aware of what was happening. I was laid out on the ground . . . with other dead people. . . . Luckily a doctor who had come to the scene, looked at me and said there were still signs of life. It was like a nightmare, knowing I was alive, even feeling spots of water dropping on my face – was it raining? – and not being able to give a signal of any kind. . . .

It was several weeks before I really became aware of . . . the extent of my injuries which were so multiple that even a broken ankle was not noticed at the time and an operation was required two years later. My mother and father were killed and my young sister, Iris, lost both of her legs.*

Death came in many ways and many guises that summer, to people of all ages and backgrounds. Sometimes it left its victims looking peaceful. 'Bomb this side of Tulse Hill Bridge. Saw my first dead – a girl. . . . She was quite unmarked but dead,' noted one young woman in her diary for 29 July 1944, after accompanying her doctor father to an incident.

---

*This story ended as well as such a tragic experience could. This woman later joined the Land Army by falsifying her age, married a young man who had given her a lift on his motorcycle, and lived happily ever after. 'I feel that I missed out on my younger years,' she writes, 'but have compensated in later years.'

Sometimes the results were hideous, like the sight which confronted a Lewisham man who joined in removing the debris from a wrecked Home Guard Post.

Eventually I saw a body being removed and laid on a sheet of corrugated iron. It was a headless, limbless torso, all the clothes having been blown off. Someone . . . drew a rescue man's attention to a solitary hand which had been uncovered. He took his penknife out, cut off a square from the blanket covering the remains, wrapped the hand in it and tucked it underneath the blanket.

Sometimes the scene was bizarre. A fourteen-year-old boy in Catford who had also gone to help after an explosion 'suddenly became aware of the figure of a person against the wall, the covering of dust effectively blending in with the brickwork – a poor old lady who must have been killed instantly by the blast.'

The predominant emotion on such occasions was a sense of outrage. In the Blitz, the gunfire and the sirens had prepared one for the eruption of violence. The V-1s dropped out of a clear sky, into hitherto peaceful streets, transforming them in a moment into a blood-stained battlefield. This was how one young man, aged sixteen, reacted when a V-1 landed while he was attending an ATC aircraft recognition course in Wimbledon, 'one lovely summer evening':

I made a dash in the direction of the smoke. I went up Dorset Road, turned right into Poplar Road, I could see it had come down in Circle Gardens, at the end of Poplar Road, a beautiful road of lovely houses and gardens. . . . When I got there, the first thing I saw was a body lying in the grass verge covered with a grey blanket. A pair of stockinged feet were sticking out from under the blanket. At that moment the local vicar arrived. He knelt down beside the body to look at the face, then covered it over again. I remembered seeing a similar scene a short while ago in a newsreel at the local cinema, only that was on the beaches of Normandy on D-Day. But this was Circle Gardens, Merton Park, a quiet suburban road.

'All we did was attend funerals.' That is the melancholy recollection of one housewife living in Penge and if this is an exaggeration it *is* true that several mass 'war graves' were dug and that the dead overflowed the regular mortuaries. The chapel of Otford Palace in Kent was pressed into service for the purpose, its first regular use since the sixteenth century, and

253

another temporary mortuary was set up in the east stand of the Tottenham Hotspur's football ground. The delivery and removal of the dead was done discreetly, often in the early morning, but did not escape the eye of a sixteen-year-old schoolboy, doing a newspaper round. 'On many occasions . . . vans loaded with coffins were arriving while others were already unloading. I used to pass by on the other side of the road and cycle fast towards Park Lane.' It was difficult, since every major incident produced a crop of rumours, not to take an almost morbid interest in the number of deaths. One soldier in the Royal Army Pay Corps used to study the list of casualties in the borough in the previous twenty-four hours posted each day outside St Marylebone town hall. The highest he observed ran to over a hundred, including one particularly ironic death: a sailor home on leave from convoy duty who had been killed in a rowing boat on the lake in Regent's Park.

As during the Blitz, funeral expenses were paid for those whose relatives agreed to their being interred in communal graves. Among them were two young sisters then working in the Land Army at Kingsclere in Hampshire, who were called home to Dulwich to find that their mother had been injured by a V-1 on their home and their younger sister, brother and father had all been killed:

We found we could not afford to bury three of our family, so it was decided to have them buried together in Camberwell New Cemetery in Honor Oak. . . . It was a very hot day – the 12th July 1944. We walked up the hill from the tiny chapel to the graveside. I hardly remember much but the gigantic hole that was to engulf my family. We stood while the vicar talked on, not hearing him really, then more coffins came up the hill from the church . . . draped with a Union Jack.

22

TAKE COVER!

*The government have considered the desirability of
introducing a special warning in the London area . . . to
indicate the near approach of a flying-bomb.*

Herbert Morrison in the House of Commons, 1 August 1944

To warn or not to warn. This was the dilemma confronting the
government, when it rapidly became clear that far more damage was being done to the war effort by people taking shelter
unnecessarily than by the V-1s themselves. Before the offensive
began Herbert Morrison's Civil Defence Committee had (as
he recalled in a Cabinet paper on 5 July) 'decided that public
warnings for the flying bomb . . . should be given by means of
the siren in the same way as for ordinary aircraft, unless and
until experience of the new weapon showed this decision to be
wrong.'

Already, in fact, modifications had been introduced, as he
went on to explain, by ignoring single flying-bombs, not sounding an all clear until 6 a.m. after a warning during the night,
and not giving warnings for 'flying-bombs passing over' en
route to London. These changes had not gone far enough to
satisfy everyone, for some critics argued that 'the sirens make
the populace "nervy" and that they sound so frequently that
. . . people take no notice.' The Home Secretary was, however,
strongly opposed to abolishing the warning system and he attached copies of four letters which had appeared in the press
that morning, following the announcement that a Conservative
MP – for a constituency in Newcastle, which had never heard
a V-1 – was to ask a parliamentary question calling for the
sirens to be silenced. 'A suggestion of superlative stupidity,'
thought one outspoken citizen. 'Please spare us our "Alerts"
and "All Clears" as at present,' wrote a housewife. 'To the
"tough" folk they may seem a nuisance, but to us nervous

ones, even a short "All Clear" comes as a blessed relief from
the tensions of listening while cooking, . . . etc.'

To suspect that Morrison's ministry had itself 'planted' these
timely letters would be unfair but they made a powerful appendix to his paper, which even received the support of his
inveterate opponent, Ernest Bevin. 'I agree with the Home
Secretary', Bevin's paper, circulated on the same day, began,
though he went on to urge an additional 'warning of imminent
danger . . . in the London Region: What I would propose is
that guns should be fired' – 'blank rounds,' Bevan added comfortingly, 'should suffice' – 'in the areas on the line along which
the bomb will pass.'

Whether salvoes of guns would really have encouraged
'greater confidence' seems doubtful, but while the government
dithered one hitherto obscure borough acted, Heston and
Isleworth, a built-up area containing numerous factories strung
along the Great West Road. Heston had been hit by its first
V-1 as early as 19 June in a typical incident in which three
people were killed and 1000 houses were damaged; several
others, with a heavier casualty list, followed. The borough
council rapidly realized that people not working in large factories, which received a private imminent danger signal, either
had to take unnecessary risks or spend hours 'confined to their
shelters'. The borough thereupon decided to introduce its own
system, making use of the fact that it was 'its own electricity
authority'. The borough electrical engineer was instructed to
instal a small siren on each electricity sub-station, controlled
from the central electricity works at Hounslow, which received
an industrial warning. If this arrived between 6 a.m. and 11
p.m. the citizens of Hounslow would be warned to take cover
by 'three short blasts' and resume working on hearing 'one
long blast' which meant that the danger had passed.

Moving faster than the government, the council announced
that it was ready to mount a full-scale test on the morning of
Sunday, 23 July. 'They don't worry when the alert goes at
Heston (Middlesex) now,' proclaimed the *Sunday Pictorial* that
Sunday morning. 'They know it's all right till the second warnings sound – and then they duck for cover.' The government
was furious. A police inspector visited the council official concerned to warn him that he would be breaking the law – it

being an offence to sound sirens or whistles without authority
– but rather spoiled the effect by adding that he 'personally
thought it was a good idea'. Then Scotland Yard telephoned
dramatically in the early hours of the morning and finally – the
ultimate deterrent – a senior civil servant at the Home Office.
All to no avail. The trial went ahead, the council set up
thirty-two sirens 'well spread out' which 'covered the whole of
the borough' and congratulatory messages flowed in from local
shopkeepers. The government sensibly did not convert the
Heston Hampdens into martyrs and let the matter drop. The
scheme must have saved many lives and much avoidable frustration, for between late July and October seven more bombs
fell in the borough, bringing the total to sixteen, which damaged more than 7000 houses but killed only thirty-seven people
and seriously injured 119.

The rebellious councillors had the satisfaction of claiming
that what Heston Borough Council did today the Cabinet did
tomorrow, for on 1 August Herbert Morrison announced the
government's decision to introduce in the London area a 'danger warning' of 'two-second blasts on a klaxon or other suitable
instrument at intervals of two seconds' followed by 'the release
. . . a continuous blast lasting six seconds.' It was hoped to
give 'about one and a half minutes' warning by this means.
The 'unofficial' systems which had sprung up would be required
to conform to the new pattern or be dropped as would all
'visible signals' which were considered liable to cause accidents
by distracting drivers' attention.

Detailed instructions were issued to local authorities on 3
August, suggesting the use of 'steam or compressed air whistles
or klaxons' linked to the existing 'industrial warning system',
which alerted factories connected to seventy-six 'Control Point
Establishments' when a flying-bomb was 'about fifteen miles
distant on the direct line of approach'. The signal was designed
to be audible for up to half a mile, and with scrupulous regard
for the public purse the civil servants concerned laid down that
the factories involved should still pay the GPO the regular
rental of '£7 10s p.a. for each bell on the industrial warning
scheme.' However – who should say that Whitehall could not
be open-handed? – no rental would be charged to the owners
of ' "Klaxon Points" . . . who join the scheme solely for the

purpose of giving the public warning.' Recipients were required to render a detailed return of their response to it, in, of course, triplicate, by 15 August.

But by now the 'unofficial' systems so much disliked by the Home Office were not to be ousted. Typical was an aircraft components factory in Burnt Oak, Edgware. Its roof-spotter patrolled the roof of the adjoining cinema and watched the flagstaff on the top of the De Havilland aircraft factory, which received an official warning. When a white cone was hoisted there, he raised a red flag and sounded his own firm's alarm. At WVS headquarters in Westminster people watched to see a red barrel raised above a neighbouring rooftop, while the occupants of City offices around Guildhall listened for whistles blown by look-outs on its roof.

The industrial warning system was also by now well established. One woman who worked at the Port of London Authority headquarters in the City helped to operate it. In the protected watchroom in the basement was 'a map of South-East England divided into four squares, and these [were] divided into a graph 0–9 down and 0–9 across.' Information about the approach of a V-1 was given by a telephone message quoting the map reference and, to arouse those in the immediate vicinity, 'we had a sort of horn which we blew.'

The traditional British alarm signal was still a bell, but in noisy factories coloured lights were used instead. Those at J. Lyons and Co. at Cadby Hall in Hammersmith resembled traffic lights, 'yellow for "enemy sighted", red for danger and green for all clear.' An engineering factory in Mitcham, a former apprentice recalls, displayed 'Yellow for alert, when the public sirens went off, blue for danger heading our way and red for take cover, at which signal the factory siren went and everybody had to run for shelter – all, except the team of millwrights, who had to run around turning off the main motors.'

At a clothing factory in north London making officers' uniforms, the alarm was given, one woman remembers, by a flashing red bulb.

When we saw this, we had to switch off our machines and get on the floor in a crouching position. . . . The main shaft . . . wasn't switched off, so we were under the machines . . . gazing at the shaft revolving round and round in front of our eyes. . . . One big Irish woman . . . was under the table, saying her prayers with her rosary, with a huge green bottom and tops of bare fat legs which her stockings couldn't reach. At the time it wasn't funny as the poor woman was so scared . . . but we would laugh at it afterwards. Another little woman would get into the box they put the finisher's work in and cover her head with an overall.

The bigger the plant the more sophisticated its warning arrangements. At Fords of Dagenham, which covered sixty-six acres beside the Thames, there was a 'six-pip' system indicating danger in the locality, and a 'three-pip' 'imminent danger' signal which 'meant that those who heard it had about one minute in which to get into shelter.' At a factory in Park Royal, making modifications to armoured vehicles, a single blast on the klaxon was the sign that a flying-bomb was approaching and 'an urgent alternating sound called the "Crash-dive" . . . meant that the bomb was now dangerously close.' At Napier and Co. in Acton the servicing of Sabre engines used in the Hawker Typhoon and Hawker Tempest at first suffered from constant interruptions. Then 'all of us on urgent work,' one craftsman remembers, 'were asked to volunteer to work after the "Alert" had gone and were given a badge with "Carry On" on it. If a bomb was coming in our direction the spotter would sound the klaxon . . . and we had thirty seconds to get under cover.'

Small establishments had at first no prior warning and their staff had to rely on their own ears. In the installation room of the electricity supply department of Ilford Borough Council, one apprentice observed, the only reaction to the siren was that the 'foremen came out from their offices', which were partitioned-off wood and glass cubicles, 'to sit at the main benches,' but 'it was noticeable how much quieter it became. Everyone stopped talking and those writing sat with poised pens and pencils.'

The time wasted in government offices had been one of the factors which finally goaded the government into action and here there was a spectacular improvement. At the Ministry of Aircraft Production, on the Embankment, when the alarm bells sounded, the staff on the upper floors now merely adjourned to the corridors. At the Ministry of Supply offices in Tothill Street, a woman statistician remembers, one visitor 'rather sheepishly climbed under the deputy-director's table while a doodlebug flew over. Shamefaced, he said he was "not used to it" as we were.' Another woman then working in the head office of the National Provincial Bank in the City recalls a senior colleague's equally unheroic response to the imminent danger buzzer. ' "Women and children first" was not in his book,' she discovered. 'He shot under my desk and left me to run to and fro in search of an unoccupied hole. I suppose there was something in his contention . . . that he was my superior officer and therefore had a prior lien on the refuge.'

The imminent danger warning was not always unwelcome. At an RAF maintenance unit at Kidbrooke one observer remembers. 'Certain pairs of men and women dived for the furthest surface shelters for reasons of their own', while the men trooped into the nearest washroom to play cards or sit in the lavatories 'sorting out winners'. At Woolwich Arsenal the shelters assigned to the borers employed on heavy gun manufacture, who had, perhaps unjustly, a reputation for being in no hurry to get back to work, were known as 'The abodes of love'.

One immediate response to the flying-bombs was a rapid increase in the numbers sleeping in the London Underground. During the first two weeks these reached a peak of 73,600, but by 9 August, an official report revealed, the figure had dropped, 'to little more than half the number'.

Some tube-dwellers were there because they had been bombed out. Others seemed to do little else except shelter like the old ladies a soldier on a training course in South-East London observed clustered round the station entrance. 'They seemed to spend all day at their posts and . . . only went home now and again to fetch some food.' The largest group were probably people like one woman civil servant from Kensington who was, she admits, simply 'scared. . . . The passengers from the last trains had passed out into the night of death. They became very brave people in my eyes.'

Even before the war began there had been a campaign for deep shelters, which the government had always been unwilling to provide, partly on grounds of cost, but chiefly because of the fear that a large part of the population would disappear into them and refuse to re-emerge. When the flying-bombs arrived the Ministry of Home Security was at first unwilling even to convert into shelters some tunnels built for other purposes. At the Civil Defence Committee on 29 June Herbert Morrison was still wondering about saving them up for the rockets – Why? one can only wonder – but, as so often, a decision reached after hours of argument was quietly reversed under the pressure of events. The *South London Press* informed its readers on Tuesday, 11 July, that 'The first of London's deep bomb-proof shelters, 130 feet below ground, opened on Sunday night at Stockwell tube station and yesterday 4,000 South Londoners were looking forward to another night's sleep after three weeks' strain. . . . "This is a thousand times better than the tubes," ' one occupant was quoted as saying. ' "It's all clean and new, and there are canteens, not to mention washing facilities. They even send your laundry away for you if you like." '

A second deep shelter was opened on 13 July and a third, the House of Commons was told that day, was to be brought into use shortly. Already the available places were over-subscribed, and the very popularity of the new shelters rapidly proved an embarrassment to the government. As the press controller explained in a confidential note to editors on 13 July, the five deep shelters only had room for 40,000 people between them, while all told the government had provided 7,250,000 places in all types of shelter, to cater for an average night population estimated at only 6,750,000.

To over-emphasise them in the treatment of news and photographs, would therefore be to give the wrong impression to our own people, to the enemy and to the rest of the world . . . of the way in which the average Londoner is adjusting himself to these attacks. Sufficient deep shelters of this new type are not available to meet the demand which might arise if there were to be created any widespread 'deep shelter mentality.'

The press was not to be dissuaded. Two hundred reporters clamoured for permission to visit them, and found they faced a wait of a month or more. Meanwhile, the *South London Press*, that excellent and enterprising local newspaper, 'scooped' its Fleet Street contemporaries by infiltrating a reporter on a borrowed ticket, as it proudly reported on Friday, 14 July:

I slept, on Wednesday night, in the first deep shelter to be opened in Stockwell, an underground city for 8,000 people, 150 feet down.

About 4,000 people are sleeping here each night and thousands more are queuing, hours at a time, for tickets which do not arrive. . . .

Built on a tube planned for post-war development, it stretches for miles below South London, a system of tunnels criss-crossing main tunnels, well-lit, air-conditioned, warm . . . white-painted. . . .

I showed my ticket to the warden at the entrance and went down 200 steps. Notices directed shelterers to their sections and I soon found my bunk, part of a 'family' section of two double and one single bunks. I left my coat and blankets and followed signposts to the canteen. A shilling's worth of tickets from the paybox gave me supper and breakfast. Prices are low – tea, 2d, cake, 2d, sandwiches, 2d, cocoa, 2d.

At 10.40 a warden called 'Lights out in five minutes'. At 10.50 four out of every five lights went out and five minutes later the remaining lights were dimmed. By 11.15 everyone had settled down. The only sounds were the padding of patrols of wardens (all voluntary) and the rumbling of Tube trains . . . faint overhead.

Places like Stockwell were the Ritzes and Savoys of the shelter world. Most public shelters were repellent places. I found one night in one in Mecklenburgh Square, Bloomsbury – lights on all night and noisy prostitutes wandering round in search of customers – more than enough. 'It was sheer bedlam,' found a Sydenham woman of another shelter, which she also deserted after a single night. There were 'no toilet facilities or water for heating up to make my baby's milk feed. . . . Adults were smoking, talking and moving in and out all night.' Primitive toilet facilities could also prove disagreeable. One ARP instructor in Southampton recalls 'a plain wooden seat covering a galvanised bucket. When a person made for this particular spot, popular songs would commence and increase in volume so as to avoid embarrassment.'

Many families tried shelter after shelter until they found one that suited them. A fifteen-year-old girl in Mitcham disliked most the small church hall opposite her home containing wooden three-tier bunks:

I wasn't often lucky enough to get the middle one, which I preferred, as the bottom one was suffocating with the great bulge of someone lying above, [and] the top bunk gave me acute claustrophobia, with the . . . concrete roof only inches from my nose. . . . Another surface shelter I went to . . . contained a whole family . . . and every morning the father would breeze in bearing a tray of tea and crying 'Wakey, wakey, rise and shine.'

Young women of gregarious tastes found shelter life more to their taste, like this fourteen-year-old:

Pam, my friend, lived in Westbeech Road [Wood Green], the next road to where I live. When we left each other on the corner after the pictures, we used to say 'See you later in the shelter.'

First of all, when I got home I would change into my shelter clothes . . . old clothes kept specially for this purpose. We used to put our hair in curlers and then put on a snood, a crocheted hair net made with wool which all the girls wore.

The shelter had three-tiered wooden bunks and Pam and I had the top ones next to each other. We brought our blankets and pillows and we really enjoyed it and we talked and laughed until we were told to go to sleep by everybody else.

The comfortably off, as always, came off best as in the Shepherd Market block of flats where Mrs Robert Henrey lived, which seemed to her to resemble 'a giant liner tied up behind Piccadilly':

In the bowels of the vessel . . . American accents blended with the soft speech of men and women from our market, increasing the trans-atlantic atmosphere. . . . The uniformed porters passed along the corridors with the authority of petty officers. . . . One expected to feel the whole building swing to starboard taking evasive action when the [alarm] bell rang. . . . Our nights were comparatively calm, though from time to time we heard, half asleep, the thud of nearby explosions like depth charges. The vessel would rock slightly but the throb of the engines continued. . . . My own family slept in a corner. . . . Next to us was an American girl . . . who told us all the latest news, from America, including what shows were worth seeing, and we felt inclined to book seats at the end of the night's journey.

Often the regulars in a shelter formed a close-knit community into which acceptance was by no means automatic. One woman civil servant, who finally settled on a public shelter near her lodgings in Barnes, found herself regarded by her shelter-mates as one of themselves because she took with her a book 'called *The Figure of Beatrice*', which her companions assumed was 'some good lurid novel'. It was in fact about Dante's *Inferno*. Another woman, left alone in a house in Pimlico, also found her circle of acquantance unexpectedly widened. 'I found myself among a collection of very dubious characters. There was talk of the "rozzers" and of elderly acquaintances "doing time".'

One could, given long enough, adjust to other human beings. What women in particular found more difficult was in coming to terms with the vermin and insects which tried to reassert their prior claims to their natural habitat. One wartime WAAF, 'sleeping out' at her home near Kidbrooke, remembers the residents in the cellar of the public house opposite:

I quite enjoyed the company of our various neighbours – one had a baby, one a dog. One woman used to come with her deckchair, smelling of gorgeous perfume, beautifully dressed and made up, and more than sixty years old. Other Service people would come, some on leave, and by dawn they were up and away to see what damage had been done to their homes. Of course one could only doze, not sleep and one night I was quite put off the place by the sight of several very large rats slinking silently along a ledge at the rear of the cellar just above the heads of several ladies sitting happily chatting, and quite unaware of the horrors.

A few people came to terms with such intruders. 'I had to share the bed with a fat toad who insisted on sitting at the end . . . each night,' remembers a Warlingham woman. 'I got quite used to him and, as he was living there before I came, I couldn't expect him to go.' People suffering from phobias about particular insects were less tolerant. A Winchmore Hill family battled in vain against the black beetles which infested the cupboard under their stairs. 'I honestly think,' remarks the daughter of the house, then aged fifteen, 'I was more frightened of the beetles than the bombs.'

Apart from the faithful cupboard under the stairs – though one woman has still not forgotten the 'searing pain as if a thousand spikes were sticking in my legs' when she incautiously knelt 'on an upturned hard broom head' – solid furniture of every kind was pressed into service to provide protection. A Willesden couple barricaded themselves in between the sideboard and bookcase, placed against the internal wall. A Croydon family slept below the billiard table, piling mattresses on top of it for extra protection. In Muswell Hill the family 'lay in state' below a huge, oblong dining-room table, which, to retain some semblance of civilized living, was covered with a dark red cloth and decorated with a vase of flowers.

The flying-bombs proved once again the excellence of the government-issued Anderson, which resembled a small metal bicycle shed buried half underground. Time after time people emerged unharmed when their houses a few yards away were in ruins. Families with small children often moved into their Anderson soon after their evening meal, equipped with cards, books, games and – in the case of a Wallington family – 'sandwiches . . . the babies' bottles and a flask of tea.'

The summer of 1944 also proved the finest hour for the Morrison table shelter, which was so strong and well designed that it offered excellent protection against flying glass and masonry; even if the house collapsed on top of it the occupants might still crawl out untouched. Six feet six inches long, by four feet wide, and two feet nine inches high, the Morrison was a tight squeeze for more than two people, but a woman from Rotherfield, Sussex, has vivid memories of sleeping with her family four abreast 'like a Mabel Lucy Atwell postcard. This left, so I thought, our toes all sticking out. . . . Often I would wake my far from grateful parents and sister and entreat them to draw up their feet lest we all be toeless in the morning.'

The Morrison's low metal roof also magnified every sound. A woman then living in Ilford dreaded the heavy breathing of her mother, who suffered from asthma. 'We used to say, "Hush, mother, hold your breath," just in case it was one and then laugh because it was her chest.'

Brick surface shelters had always been more unpopular than other types, but against the flying-bombs they proved remarkably effective. Although there were two direct hits on such shelters in which more than twenty people were killed – in a St Pancras street and in a factory at Hayes – surface shelters saved many lives. A detailed survey prepared by the London Region technical intelligence officer on 28 August quoted several cases of near misses which had produced cracks 'sufficient to admit daylight' in surface shelters from which the occupants had walked away unhurt. There had also been one remarkable piece of luck. One flying-bomb had hit a standard carrying trolley-bus wires at Highbury Corner, Islington, and bounced onto the roof of a similiar shelter totally destroying it – but it had been empty.

On 9 August the regional commissioner for the London Region was able to assure the Ministry of Home Security that the 'well-justified faith in Andersons and Morrisons' now also extended to this hitherto despised type of refuge:

The most striking fact on the shelter side is that the street surface shelter has at last come into its own. It has stood up to blast wonderfully and is universally and deservedly popular. . . . Probably because there is no longer gunfire, and because the penetration of the missiles is so small, there seems to be no longer any great urge to get deep underground. In short, in shelter habits as in many other ways . . . this experience has provided one more illustration of the truth that the public at large can be trusted to do the sensible thing if they are given the facilities for doing it and then left alone and not preached at.

23

SAFER IN THE DESERT

It's bloody safer fighting the Germans in the desert.

Remark by Eighth Army soldier, on leave in Streatham, July
1944

Because the flying-bomb was essentially an anti-civilian
weapon, very little was written at the time, or has appeared
since, about the incidents in which most of the victims were
members of the Forces. Even the number of such casualties is
hard to discover and most statistics exclude them altogether,
as though a man's life were of less account because he was
wearing uniform. In fact the highest single death roll, at the
Guards Chapel on Sunday, 19 June, was almost exclusively
military, and a week later, in the early morning of 24 June,
fifty-one soldiers serving with the 7 (Guards) Tank Brigade
Workshop REME were killed, and an unknown number
wounded, when a flying-bomb was shot down on to their quarters at Newlands, near Charing in Kent, while the unit was
waiting to embark for Normandy. No account of the incident
appears to have been published, but memorial gates to the
cemetery, made in the REME workshop at Ashford, were
unveiled in 1964 and an annual act of remembrance is held in
the nearby village of Lenham.

Other service incidents singled out for mention in the weekly
Ministry of Home Security Report included one on a block of
flats, Thurloe Court in Chelsea, where four servicemen died
and sixty-five were seriously injured, and another on Friday,
29 June, when nine soldiers, caught in the open during a sports
meeting organized by the Welch Guards at Imber Court, Esher, were killed and another sixty seriously injured. Eleven
soldiers were killed, and eight injured when a flying-bomb
landed at Marden, Kent, at 3 a.m. on 3 July, and two more

perished at Watford from another early morning bomb on the 30th.

On another occasion a V-1 hit a Nissen hut near Gravesend, killing all twelve of the occupants and the dog they had adopted. 'Their bodies and clothing were scattered all over the fields and trees,' one local resident remembers, 'and the rest of the soldiers were searching for days to recover them.' The last soldier recorded as being killed by a V-1 in England died on Christmas Eve. On the whole, however, because they were trained to take cover and not many were stationed in London, fewer soldiers became V-1 casualties than civilians. Jokes about it being safer to be a soldier than an ordinary citizen were that summer literally true. In any case being in the Forces was regarded by most servicemen as such a disaster in itself, that the risk from the enemy seemed almost trivial by comparison. In my unit, apart from two timid warriors who bolted for the air-raid shelter immediately the day's work ended, the V-1s were ignored. Other members of the Forces reacted in the same way. One woman then serving in the ATS can recall sitting in the NAAFI at Croydon Barracks 'with the walls behaving like a concertina' with everyone 'taking not the slightest notice', while the girls of another ATS unit, at Woolwich, 'would dance the hokey-cokey on top of an emergency water tank while on night watch duty', indifferent to V-1s passing overhead. A man stationed with the Royal West Kent Regiment at Maidstone confesses that 'We were more frightened of the sergeant-major than the doodlebugs.' When one morning, during an unexpected rifle inspection, a V-1 appeared overhead and 'started to come down, we broke ranks and rushed for our "bivvies" [i.e. bivouacs], not . . . for shelter but to grab a rag . . . find the pull-through and clean the rifle.'

Some soldiers in non-combatant units were less courageous. One man then working in the Central Ordnance Depot at Feltham recalls that after a V-1 dropped so close to a newly arrived group of soldiers during morning roll call that 'the blast blew all their hats off . . . many wanted to return to the peace of Catterick' – normally a highly unpopular posting. The same unwelcome sound would also see the cookhouses emptying as the kitchen staff, dressed in their 'whites', came racing out to dive in the nearest slit trench. 'There were a lot of muttered oaths and foul language in the darkness as I heard them floundering about in the muddy water.'

When the depot, working day and night dispatching cases of motor transport stores to Normandy, was hit the results reflected little credit on anyone:

In the depot was a detachment of Army Fire Service with fire engine and trailer pumps to handle any emergency. . . . The blast buckled the doors of the fire station and the appliances could not be got out. Pandemonium reigned. Untrained ATS couldn't move the hydrants and were trying to put out the fire with stirrup pumps. . . . The civilian fire service eventually came. By then the shed and contents were burnt out.

Providing less military supplies was the Services Central Book Depot in Fieldgate Street, Whitechapel, which supplied textbooks to servicemen following correspondence courses. One ATS NCO, in charge of twenty-five servicemen and women, felt that the results of the one really close explosion typified the pointless destructiveness of war. Not merely was her 'lovely shoulder bag', a costly birthday present from her mother, ruined by glass splinters, but the 'precious new windows' in 'the dark gloomy building', which had just been installed after earlier bomb-damage, were 'shattered, never to be replaced', plunging the occupants back into semi-darkness.

One great compensation for the flying-bombs to men and women in the Forces was that some whose homes were in London were now given sleeping-out passes. For one member of the ATS home was a road in Streatham in which every one of two hundred houses had been damaged, including her own, so that she was far more at risk off duty than on. 'I was terrified when I went home to Cricklewood,' admits another ex-ATS girl, then a radar operator in an AA battery. 'Whereas . . . the V-1s had mainly been flying over at Sheerness, here they were coming down all the time.'

A soldier, on compassionate leave in Streatham from the Eighth Army, who woke to find himself covered in soot blown down the chimney, would clearly have agreed. 'It's bloody safer fighting the Germans in the desert,' he told his future brother-in-law.

The arrival of the flying-bombs introduced a new element

into the complex relationship, part-admiring, part-amused, that existed between British civilians and American servicemen, of whom, despite the rapid drop in numbers since D-Day, several hundred thousand were still concentrated in Southern England. For most GIs the V-1s provided a baptism of fire, and their initial response vindicated the scepticism expressed by battle-hardened Britons about the value of their numerous medal ribbons. One man then living in much-bombed Southfields, who was passing a camp near Slough as a V-1 approached, watched in amusement as the huts' coloured occupants 'started to pour out into the fields with their cigars, gesticulating and eyeballs rolling, seeking shelter behind trees and hedges until the coast was clear.' White 'Yanks' regularly expressed contempt for their black comrades in arms, but were no more heroic. Those stationed near Coggeshall near Colchester, one woman living there observed, would 'dive under the table' at the most distant sound of a pulse-jet. Another British girl, working in the airfield canteen at Great Ashfield in Suffolk, could not believe her eyes at what happened when a V-1 'started to splutter' overhead:

Suddenly there was panic. About 1000 men in the canteen tried to get out as even more tried to get in. . . . By the time the thing had gone over and come down some distance away there wasn't a chair or table left whole, china was smashed, doors and windows torn down and injured men lying everywhere, blood on the floors and walls, it looked like a battlefield. . . . We dived under the counters as they tore over the top of us and prayed the tops wouldn't give way under the weight of men.

Not having been inoculated to danger by four years of conventional raids, many Americans undoubtedly needed time to become accustomed to being under fire. 'It literally took us days to get used to the idea that somebody was actually trying to kill us,' admits one man from Braddock Heights, Maryland, whose unit had 'not been told one thing about the buzz bombs' and only learned of their existence as their vehicle travelled into London along the Bayswater Road. The US Army daily newspaper, the *Stars and Stripes*, carried on 20 July a good-natured verse reflecting its readers' tendency to be over-cautious:

Safer in the Desert

GI Joe was lying in bed
As a buzz bomb cut out overhead.
He held his breath tight,
For two days and a night,
Then, 'I guess it's passed over,' he said.

On 1 September, a cartoon showed a notice hanging in a typical billet: 'All GIs who volunteer for service in France will be considered cowards.'

Newly arrived Americans had good reason for being taken by surprise for even the usually well-informed American press had been caught off guard. 'Shock, Anger, Sweep Entire Nation,' ran the *Stars and Stripes* headline reporting 'US Reaction to Robot Revelations' on 8 July which showed, incidentally, how little credence anyone in the United States had given to the German stories about London being in ruins.

Prime Minister Churchill's disclosure that the British capital was bearing the brunt of the flying-bomb attacks came as a complete eye-opener to most Americans. The censor's purposely vague reference to 'Southern England' had suggested to most persons that the robots were dropping harmlessly in rural areas, only occasionally causing damage. The Prime Minister's disclosure that 2,752 persons had been killed in three weeks and 8,000 injured won banner headlines and gave most people their first hint that London was in the thick of the battle again. The impact was even greater than in 1940–41, many Americans having relatives serving in London and the United Kingdom.

Amazement marked the faces of the crowd watching the *New York Times* election news sign in Times Square. More than one commented: 'Why, it's as bad as the Blitz.'

Although nowhere within range of the French coast was wholly secure, for once it was the men in the field, scattered in rural camps throughout Southern England, who were safest, and the 'top brass' and other headquarters types concentrated in offices and billets in central London who were in most danger. Not all of them resented this. 'Those of us who served in London during those days took pride in our jobs . . . ,' wrote Colonel Joseph R. Darnall of the US Army Medical Corps in an Army journal a few months later. 'Many an officer from Normandy, on temporary duty in London, voiced the desire to get back to the beachhead where there were no buzz bombs.' Day by day this observer watched the V-1s descending on Mayfair from his vantage point at the Cumberland Hotel at Marble Arch. His top score of explosions heard in a day was twenty-one; and he noted with outrage how even on the Fourth of July 'flying-bombs continued to drop on London', including one on the Cumberland Hotel laundry. 'Many of my fellow officers . . . lost their shirts and drawers in that catastrophe.' The destruction of his former billet in the Coburg Court Hotel in the Bayswater Road made a deep impression, but he was even more struck by the British soldiers who, 'in a drizzly rain', on the night of 28 June, 'stood at the entrance to a bar on Quebec Street beneath my window, and as each new missile approached 'sang boisterously, "*She'll be coming round the mountain, when she comes*!"' '

Apart from those stationed in London it was GIs in East Anglia who saw most of the V-1. One staff-sergeant at Leiston, Suffolk, occupied by the Mustangs of the 357th Fighter Group, found himself beneath the flight-path of missiles launched across the East Coast. 'They flew so low that we felt we could have carved our initials on their silly little fuselages.' Eventually one *did* fly into the camp water tower: 'The water was suddenly cut off and about a dozen GIs in the showers dashed out naked to find out what had happened.'

One refreshing characteristic of the Americans was their readiness to indulge in frank self-examination and a detailed study, by an Army sergeant, of how one group of sixty American soldiers reacted to the flying-bombs appeared in an American psychiatric journal in January 1945.

In the beginning there seemed to be a difference in attitude between the English and the Americans. . . . Not having been subjected to enemy action before we were not battle hardened. . . . The full realisation of the situation, at first, resulted in a feeling of panic and fear. No place seemed safe. Then, slowly the first lesson was learned. . . . It is human nature to run from danger, but running away in this case could mean running into danger. Therefore, since the immediate place was as safe as the next one, it became advisable to remain and hope and pray for the best. . . . To go to sleep at night was . . . another problem to be conquered. . . . Unpleasant thoughts such as being caught in a collapsing building, of being sandwiched between floors, buried alive under debris, or being trapped, were not conducive to slumber. . . . We slept fully clothed in our fatigue clothes and, during heavy night attacks, kept our shoes on in order to get out quickly if necessary.

Churchgoing was then, as now, more common in the US than in Great Britain, and here, too, the sergeant did not shrink from some private study of his comrades' behaviour:

It was not unusual to see some of the boys in prayer. . . . A number of the men had definite religious beliefs and exercised them regularly, such as going to church. Some of them appeared to be stable and did not suffer from these dangerous episodes, while others, outwardly just as religious, went to pieces every time danger was near. They suffered in spite of their praying. This merely bears out the well-known fact that a stable person will be able to go through trying experiences without suffering from a trauma, whereas an already unstable person will suffer more, and more easily become the victim of anxiety attacks.

By now a mutual respect and affection had developed between British civilians and American servicemen and the shared experience of the V-1s strengthened this bond. By 6 July American uniforms were already such a familiar sight after a V-1 had fallen that the Prime Minister included a handsome tribute to their owners in his speech to the House of Commons:

Here I must say a word about our American friends and allies in London from the highest official to the ordinary soldier . . . who have, in every way, made common cause with us. . . . No one can visit a bombed site . . . without seeing how very quickly they are . . . on the scene and running any risk to give a helping hand to anyone in distress. And the same is true of the great headquarters under General Eisenhower, where they are conducting this great battle. . . . It will be another tie, I think, between our two peoples to see something of what we go through in London and to take a generous part in facing this burden.

The speed with which 'the Yanks' appeared on the scene and whisked casualties away to hospital – often without any record of their removal being kept – became an embarrassment to the British authorities. A Home Office circular, *Lessons from Recent Raids*, praised 'the prompt and valuable help of personnel and vehicles of the U.S. Army . . . and their keenness to render the Civil Defence Services assistance,' but warned that this enthusiasm could be self-defeating. 'A "Jeep",' it pointed out 'is not a suitable car for the conveyance of a severely injured patient, especially one who has received no adequate first aid treatment prior to moving.'

Thousands of Londoners still feel grateful to the energetic, warmhearted GIs who rallied to their aid in their hour of need. 'They were great fellows. They never let up.' That is the verdict of one incident officer at Deptford, who found that a single request to a local headquarters would bring a large detachment of GIs under a major to the rescue. 'Having brought their own canteen, complete with blankets, lighting equipment and bull-dozer, they cleared a road so that our ambulance and fire brigade could get to the site. . . . Without those boys we would have been in a very sorry plight.'

A section leader in the NFS paid one detachment an equally generous tribute in the magazine *Fire*:

We were working in a very poor locality, where damage from blast was severe. . . .

Suddenly we were joined by about 20 U.S. soldiers under a non-com, who, when I told him we wanted to lower the height of a mound of debris as soon as possible, said 'Say, let some of these guys with me get at it'. Turning to them, he said, 'Come on, now grab that girder'. About 10 of them lifted a light girder, clambered with it over the mound, and, using the girder like we do a squeegee, took most of the top off the mound.

Then, they began to lift bricks. Those in front stooped down, grabbed bricks, threw them over their heads, those behind caught them. Continuing the motion, these Americans made that mound disappear like water down a drain. I then saw what I thought was the back of an Anderson shelter. We cleared rubble away – and . . . inside, safe and sound, were 12 persons.

A woman then living in Ilford with her nine-year-old daughter also remembers with gratitude the sudden arrival of a horde of American servicemen in lorries – on, as it happened the Fourth of July – after she had emerged from the Anderson to find her home a total wreck:

The wingless body of the bomb lay across the kitchen door and . . . had set the coal shed alight. They put out the flames, then, stripped to the waist, they clambered up (the stairs had gone) and pulled out clothes, bedding, etc., from the rubble. . . . All these were piled up on the lawn, and then they somehow managed to get carpets up from under a mound of debris. They had brought with them long wooden boxes and packed them and then nailed carpets on top, to . . . prevent looting. While this was proceeding there were several more alerts, and I was rather surprised to find the Americans diving into the Anderson, but was told it was as instructed by their officers, not to take risks. . . . We had four hens in a battery, which completely fell apart, but the lads caught the hens, minus a few feathers, put them in a crate, nailing that across, and these went on a van. We went to relations, piled up with bundles and boxes, and the four hens, one obliging by laying an egg.

It was difficult for British civilians to appreciate that, although their homes were safe, the GIs were just as likely as themselves to suffer death or injury. After the pre-D-Day exodus, the American Army's Central Base Section, covering all units permanently stationed in the London area, included more than 18,000 men, while another 15,000 were usually on leave in the capital. A few Americans became casualties at every stage of the campaign. The most minor injury was to a GI who cut his foot on broken glass concealed by leaves when a V-1 landed in Russell Square. The most tragic was that of the driver of a jeep blown to pieces while he was waiting for a companion to emerge from an underground public lavatory. Three Americans, a 'Lieutenant, Transportation Corps' and 'two enlisted men of the 8th Flight Command', according to the official COM Z – Communications Zone – report, died in two separate incidents in Tottenham Court Road on 3 July and on the same day there occurred by far the worst incident affecting Americans of the whole campaign. As so often, this appears in the records, both in London and Washington, under a variety of names, but it is best remembered as the Turks Row bomb, Turks Row being a minor road in Chelsea which runs into Lower Sloane Street, close to Sloane Square. The time was 7.45 a.m. on Monday, 3 July.

The Central Base Section commander described what had happened to a staff conference next day – the least holiday-like Fourth of July that any of those present could remember. The place affected, he explained, had been the 'casual center', used to accommodate various American units, and, by a bitter irony, the men concerned had actually been on their way to help civilians who had suffered from an earlier V-1:

The 103rd Chemical Processing Company, strength 143 men, were in the process of dispatching 100 men to assist the civil defence of Lambrooke Borough [sic]* where an incident had occurred. One officer and 28 enlisted men were loaded in a truck, the remainder of the company were sitting in the street waiting for trucks when the bomb was heard by Captain Smith and he directed the men to scatter. The bomb struck the truck and billet. 43 men were identified as dead . . . 14 are still missing, including one officer.

According to the official Home Office report of the incident that day, 'the front of the buildings on each side of [the] road', including a five-storey block of flats, had 'been destroyed . . . up to a distance of about 25 yards in each direction' from the point of impact, '27 yards S.E. from [the] junction of Turks Row.' It was the falling masonry which caused the heavy casualties, officially totalling seventy-four dead – ten civilian and sixty-four 'service, mainly U.S. personnel', and fifty, apparently all servicemen, seriously injured. Other GIs billeted in the same group of buildings were badly shaken. One who had been on night duty at 'the Peter Robinson building' in Oxford Street remembers how anxiety spread as 'the Americans did not show at work on the allotted hour', until, very late, 'a few drifted in, with dust on their uniforms, white as ghosts.'

The Turks Row incident made upon the American authorities the same deep impact as the destruction of the Guards Chapel had upon the British. At the staff conference next day that Base Section commander announced that orders had been issued to stop 'all formations and detachments marching to work, and inspection during work,' and that 'all training formalities have since been discontinued by order of Headquarters ETOUSA' – European Theatre of Operations, United States Army. But, he concluded, 'We are going to have to take our losses when they come.' Churchill himself could not have put it better.

---

*Presumably 'Lambeth' was meant.

24

BOMBED OUT

A policeman . . . took me to see where my home had been.

Teddington woman, recalling July 1944

The Germans did not care where the V-1s fell, so long as they did damage, and it was ordinary houses which suffered most. Officially the number of houses totally destroyed was by mid-September only 23,000 but many houses originally classed as repairable turned out to be fit only for demolition. In Battersea, for example, only 257 had originally been listed as 'destroyed' but by early October it was clear that another 1974 would have to be pulled down, making a true total of 2231. If this was typical of all the bombed boroughs the number of homes permanently lost cannot have been far short of 180,000. Many, many more families were displaced for weeks or months until their houses were made habitable again. The rehousing bureau for the City of Westminster, which had suffered from a mere thirty-one V-1s, had received by mid-September 4500 inquiries about new accommodation by telephone alone. In Wandsworth, with 126 V-1s, there were 7000 removals, with the furniture in 4200 of them going into store. In Croydon - 140 V-1s – 3000 removals, only half to new homes. Over London as a whole the total was 50,000.

The very first families to be bombed out, on the night of 15 June, literally did not know what had hit them for the first announcement about the flying-bombs was not made till the following day. Among these sufferers was a fifteen-year-old girl in Catford, who had spent the afternoon peacefully making a necklace from macaroni, and painting it, to wear at a dance that evening. She had 'a lovely time' there but what followed

277

was less enjoyable. 'I awoke,' she remembers, 'to hear my mum screaming, "Quick, Bill, the boys are in the front." I opened my eyes to see the sky. . . . My dad got us all out . . . down our broken staircase.' They were never to climb it again.

That was how it started and during the next two weeks, as the attack continued, the V-1s seemed to many people in South-East London to be creeping remorselessly closer. Although they might say, 'It'll be our turn next', no one really expected that his house would be destroyed; the remark was meant as an incantation to ward off possible disaster. All too often, however, it proved an accurate prediction, and a fortnight after the incident just described, it was the turn, on 29 June, of the wife of a naval officer in Brockley, whose previous home had been burned out by an incendiary bomb:

That day a neighbour, who had until then completely ignored me, as I was one of the 'rehoused' people . . . spoke over the garden fence to me saying, 'Isn't it getting awful?' . . . That same evening my sister Nell and her husband Wally had come to spend the night in my Anderson shelter with me. She was too nervous to settle in her own home. . . . My four-year-old daughter, Kay, was tucked up in the shelter . . . when, without any air-raid warning, we heard a doodlebug. . . . It blew out our light and we were in pitch darkness. I thought for a minute or two we were buried alive. The relief to see the daylight again as the dust settled down cannot be described. When we climbed out of the shelter, we could hear screaming. The shelter that almost backed on to ours was completely buried. It seemed in a matter of seconds, the quiet residential area was full of people. . . . The house the other side of me had no shelter. They were digging through the rubble all night; the sound of the whistle blowing for dead silence now and then to listen for any sound was grim indeed.

The V-1 which destroyed the home of another family, in Wallington, arrived during that most peaceful of rituals, teatime, much to the indignation of the nine-year-old daughter of the house, who had been forced to take refuge under the stairs, while her father kept a look-out through the kitchen window:

'Look out! It's coming down!' I heard my father shout. The next moment there was a bright flash of light through the small hall window and then the house crashed down around us. I curled myself into a small ball as the bricks and mortar tumbled down, burying us in a cave. The stairway above us still stood, making a roof. The bricks stopped falling and there was silence except for my father's faint voice calling. (We found out afterwards that he had ducked under the sink. . . .) I sat as still as I could and listened to my sister reciting the Lord's Prayer. I kept thinking about my chocolate cake and wishing that I had eaten it. I wondered what had happened to all those pounds of raspberries that we have been picking all day. . . . Gradually the sound of digging came nearer until I could hear my father's voice calling through the rubble, telling us to sit still. I sat as still as a statue, scarcely breathing. At last there was a light in the hole behind me. Slowly it became bigger until I could see my father's grimy face through it. A few more minutes of shovelling and my father's arms were lifting me out into the daylight. I was passed down the line of men, through the trench of rubble which was all that was left of our home, except for the one chimney which stood up against the sky.

Whenever one left one's home even for a few hours there was always the danger of returning to find that it had disintegrated. This was the experience of a soldier's wife living in Teddington, who on 'a beautiful day' in late July decided to visit her former office, to show off her new baby:

As I came out of my door the lady opposite called me over, to say that . . . any time I felt frightened, I was welcome to come over and share their Anderson shelter. . . . She told me how brave she thought I was to risk going on a bus ride to Weybridge. . . . It was not until I changed buses at Kingston on the way home that I heard how the area of Teddington where I lived had been badly hit. When I turned into Church Road . . . there was a police cordon across it. A policeman said: 'And where do you think you are going?' I said, 'Home. I live at the end of Argyle Road, corner of Somerset Road.' He said: 'You mean, you *did*,' and then told me what had happened. . . . He took me to a rest centre . . . at the Baptist Church. . . . We handed the baby over to a Red Cross nurse there and he took me to see where my home had been. It was a terrible mess, rubble mountains high. . . . I never saw [my neighbour] again. She was killed in her Anderson shelter that day.

Few experiences were more disheartening than to return from working all night to find one's home destroyed. Among the many people who can recall this happening was a man then aged seventeen, who had been on duty at the all-night post office in Leicester Square until 6.30 a.m.:

The Doodlebugs

I knew there was something wrong as soon as I came out of Clapham Common tube station. There was a lot of broken glass about and all the signs of a 'near one' in the night. I recall having some regret that I had missed something.

My little road, Downer's Cottages, was just off the main road. As I approached the corner, I had my hands in my jacket pocket, feeling for my door key. Then, as I turned in past the Cock public house, I saw that the entire street – ten houses – had gone. There was just a huge mass of rubble, chunks of broken brickwork and tangled roof timbers. The whole pile was no more than eight or ten feet high; the whole street had been comprehensively reduced to virtually nothing. I think that I had been expecting something of the sort, because I felt no sense of loss or panic. . . . I did not experience any fears for my parents – I felt sure they were safe. And so it was – there were a few Civil Defence people about and they told me that nobody had been hurt, but all the local people had been taken to a rest centre, a school in Bonneville Road at Clapham South. . . . Later I learned that 'our' buzz bomb had landed just on midnight in our small garden and skidded into the back wall of our house before exploding.

A woman living in Winchmore Hill, North London, had a special reason for remembering the date on which her home was demolished for it was her birthday, 8 July:

The noise woke me before the explosion when a great flame burnt my eyeballs. There was dead silence from cut-out to explosion. . . . The thing caught on the telegraph pole opposite and brought it down, and the whole lot landed in my neighbour's garden. The gas main caught alight which caused a big fire. The upstairs of the house fell on us, bit by bit, also part of the outside wall. The wall seemed to float down like a feather, and yet we had an awful job to get it off the pillows. I started to struggle but my husband pulled me under the quilt with him, drew it over our heads, held my hand tight and said, 'Wait till it stops dropping on us.' So we did, and by this time the children were sitting up and crying. The front door was gone and we were open to the street and noise and fire, which frightened them. So we all sat down under the stairs and waited for someone to come.

When one's family had been injured, but had survived, the sudden disappearance of home and possessions seemed by comparison almost trivial. This is what happened to a woman who returned home from night duty as a cashier at Lyons of Cadby Hall in Hammersmith:

What a nightmare! I reached the top of the road and the barriers were up. There were ambulances, fire engines, police cars and every-one digging like mad to get people or bodies out. It was like a scene from a film. It didn't seem real. No one was allowed down the road. A kind Salvation Army man helped me back to my place of work where they revived me with cups of tea. I had a message about 6 a.m. sent by the police telling me they had rescued my daughter and she was in West London hospital. We lived in a first-floor flat and she was in bed at the time and the bed came through two floors. She was trapped with a beam across her neck and another beam across her ankles and they had to saw through them to get her out. The puppy we had was lying at the foot of the bed and he saved her life as he cried like a baby. . . . Next day I reported to the town hall where I was issued with £8 plus 80 coupons for food and clothing as I had lost everything. . . . When I visited my daughter she was delighted, es-pecially about the coupons, and said, 'Cheer up, Mum! Look how much better off you are now, as last night you had no coupons and now you have 80.'

Many people had a private nightmare about being buried alive and took precautions accordingly. 'My one fear,' confesses a woman then living in Brent, was 'of being trapped by my very long plaits' and she carried everywhere a 'pair of round-bladed scissors' ready to sacrifice her hair if the need arose. In fact, though her house was destroyed, she climbed out unhurt from the Morrison, although it 'sped up and round like a bird cage.' A man living in Stoke Newington kept a whistle in his pocket which helped to save his life when, while having breakfast on the morning of 23 August, he just managed to get downstairs and into the coal cellar before the house collapsed on it:

The staircase . . . was completely blocked with debris, as was also the coal hole, so I was completely trapped. In spite of the choking dust, I managed to get a sound on the whistle, which I now blew repeatedly. I heard a woman screaming from the next door cellar. It was Mrs H., our neighbour . . . and I was able to talk to her and try to calm her fears. . . . The ARP men, who we heard working over-head, must have heard the whistle and were able to locate Mrs H. in her cellar. They started to attack the wall between us with a sledge-hammer but I . . . shouted for them to stop as I was afraid that if the wall was weakened it might cause the ceiling to collapse on me. I also called out that I could see a little daylight below the coalhole and suggested it might be easier to get to me by removing the debris from over the coal hole. This they did, and eventually managed to pull me out through. I was taken to Metropolitan Hospital and remember the nurse remarking as she cleaned the grime from my face, 'You are quite good looking,' which boosted my ego tremendously.

Most people who were bombed-out still retain, imprinted on their minds, one particular image of the scene that greeted them. For one North London woman it was the sight 'as you walked down the street' of 'all the stairs intact, just stairs and stairs all in a row, although there were no houses left.' For a woman in Tooting it was the sound of the wardens' 'feet scrunching over the slates, which looked like a sea of grey waves, with clothes and curtains blown up into the trees. We saw all this without getting out of the Morrison. The walls were down.' What a woman in Eastbourne remembers best, after finding her son still asleep in a cradle piled with soot and glass, is the sight of his teddy bear beside it, 'intact, except that his head was missing.'

Once a bombed-out family had collected themselves and their wits together on the pavement outside the remains of their home, the next stop was to get a roof over their heads, sometimes with friends or neighbours – if they had not been bombed out, too – but usually in a rest centre. London alone had more than 1000, with accommodation for 135,000 people, mainly in converted schools and church halls. In 1940 they had come in for much, well-merited, criticism but by 1944 the lessons of the Blitz had been learned. Although by the beginning of August 95,000 people had passed through the rest centres, they were never stretched to capacity and most people have nothing but praise for the way they were treated.

A homeless Ruislip woman found that 'the WVS turned up in an utterly unselfish way . . . to serve tea and provide makeshift beds. . . . Then dawn came and trestle tables appeared from nowhere and a rough sort of breakfast. . . . Those good ladies put a cheerful face on everything.' Even more evocative are the recollections of an eleven-year-old girl from South-East London. 'Even now I still remember three things very clearly, a smell of disinfectant, the prickle of hairy blankets on the bunks and the awful taste of the watery, but scalding hot, tomato soup they gave us.'

The rest centre was merely the first stop on the long journey to becoming a complete citizen again, for ration books, identity cards, insurance policies and other vital papers had usually vanished along with one's furniture and clothes. Here, too, the procedure had been immensely improved since 1940 and some local authorities, like Battersea, opened 'out-stations' in public libraries, where representatives of all the ministries concerned were brought together under one roof. Another welcome innovation was mobile bath units, with small cubicles curtained off on a school playground or by the roadside. The famous soap firm, Lever Brothers, public-spiritedly provided 'eight mobile laundries', with their own generator, which operated 'two domestic washing machines, rinsing apparatus and electric drier, all mounted on a lorry.'

However efficient the post-raid facilities, being bombed out involved an enormous range of tasks. This was merely the start of the list set out in the *News Chronicle* on 30 June under the heading *What to do if your home is hit*.

1. Go to your nearest Rest Centre, where you will be given a hot meal or drinks and shelter until other accommodation can be found for you. . . .
2. If you have lost all your clothing the WVS will provide enough clothes to take you to work next day.
3. If you are in immediate need of money, the Public Assistance Board will give you a sum to replace your damaged spectacles, false teeth, essential tools or anything else you badly need. . . .

This admirable guide made no mention of the activity which dominated the lives of many homeless people for the first few days of their new life – that of trying to salvage whatever they could from the ruins of the old one. It was easy momentarily to lose all grip on reality. The first thought of one woman in Croydon was to salvage something small enough to fit in her bicycle basket. 'I must,' she now feels, 'have been quite bemused, for when I got to a relations' house where my mother had been taken, all I had was five pairs of knickers.'

For many people searching the rubble of their home became almost an obsession until they found one particularly valued object – an engagement ring, a child's school report – which provided at least some link with the past. Probably no one tackled the job, however, with so much determination – or

283

with so little real result – as the seventeen-year-old post office clerk from Clapham quoted earlier, and his father. Having pooled their resources and sent 'mum' off to stay with relatives in Whitstable, they returned to what they always referred to not 'as "home" or "the house",' but 'just "the site" ':

We had no knowledge of building work – dad was a shop manager – no idea of how to set about it and no tools of any kind. Add to this that we were both small and slight and the whole thing now seems ludicrous but we tried.

Our house and those on either side had had a 'pancake' collapse – the walls supporting the roof and the first floor had been blown outwards so that the roof, ceilings and first floor had crashed down to ground level, more or less in one piece. It was difficult even to locate what had been our house, but we did this by finding small landmarks. . . . We climbed to the top of the rubble pile and found ourselves surrounded by loose slates and roof timbers. There was a small depression . . . which we thought was over the front bedroom and . . . we started our digging there. Even one afternoon convinced us that we were not going to get very far. We cleared an area of about six feet by six feet of loose slates and found ourselves in a tangle of beams, joists and laths, the remains of the roof and bedroom ceilings. The ends of the main beams were jammed under big chunks of masonry and seemed immovable. We tried improvising levers from lengths of timber, but without success. It was going to be a long job.

The local post office having advised this man to 'go sick', the family GP obligingly provided 'a certificate covering two weeks' absence because of "Anxiety State and Nervous Debility".' His father's employer, the Co-op, less generously, allowed him to take his annual fortnight's holiday immediately. What followed, however, was hardly a vacation:

Over the next six days, we continued to dig. On the Monday, we borrowed a pick, crowbar and saw from a local builder, but in the main the work was by hand, pulling, pushing and heaving, clearing a bit at a time. By Wednesday evening we had penetrated to a depth of about three feet, but had found literally nothing we could recognize. Then on Thursday we came upon a solid obstruction, which, when we had cleared away the brick dust, we found to be a sheet of plywood. . . . A combined assault with pick and crowbar splintered the wood, and showed that we were attacking the back of a wardrobe. After our efforts it was like striking gold. We got out my mother's tailored suit and the blouse, shoes, hat and handbag that went with it. These were practically new and came out undamaged. The point of the pick had torn a ragged hole in the back of the jacket of my best suit, but that could be repaired and the trousers were unharmed. There were several dresses and coats of my mother and some bed linen. Not much, but a start. We kept going and uncovered more bedding and some odd clothes from a chest of drawers. There was some furniture, chairs and a table, smashed to pieces and fragments of ornaments and pictures, but nothing worth saving. And that was all – a few clothes and some sheets and blankets – to show for a week of the hardest manual labour of my life.

Although much had been heard earlier in the war of the Lord Mayor of London's Relief Fund, this seems to have been better at accumulating money than disbursing it for none of my informants even mentions it. The real help came from the WVS which was faced with a sudden run on its clothing depots, some of which were themselves destroyed. 'Practically every depot in the Region', its report for the three months ending July recorded, had had to cope with a heavy demand with '200,000 garments . . . sent out from the Regional Store as replenishments.' Many of these had come from Canada and the United States in the form of 'Bundles to Britain', and one WVS member working in central London recalls that 'it was marvellous to see the faces of some of the children who had never seen such lovely clothes. . . . It went a great way to cushion the shock they had undergone.'

In October the WVS also set up a home replacements department to provide blankets and linen, mainly from the other side of the Atlantic, and crockery, cutlery and other essentials, collected following a general appeal in unaffected parts of Great Britain. All told fifty-two places in Greater London and nine on the coast received gifts from this source, benefiting more than 100,000 families. Each was alloted fifty points per household, plus thirty for each member, the gifts being 'pointed' according to value and condition, with a bed 'costing' from thirty to fifty points, a saucepan from eight to ten. This official help was supplemented by private 'whip-rounds' in offices and factories, with everyone donating objects such as a tea-cosy or toasting fork instead of cash.

Cash grants to meet immediate needs were given readily and without too much formality: the Clapham family mentioned earlier, for example, received £15 and – through the good luck of being almost the only bombed-out family there – the free run of the WVS clothing depot at Whitstable. Longer-term help came in three stages. The Public Assistance Board was empowered to provide money for necessities and 'to effect urgent replacements of clothing and furniture.' This was followed by an interim settlement a little later, paid through the Customs and Excise, and a final cheque from the Board of Trade, months, or even years, afterwards, under the provisions of the War Damage Act 1943, which provided compensation for 'private chattels' – house property was dealt with separately – up to fairly rigid limits. The first payments under the scheme were made promptly. Subsequent instalments tended to be much slower.

A Brockley housewife, left with nothing but her engagement ring, when her house was destroyed on 29 June 1944, submitted a claim for £172, which was not finally settled until 5 October 1945. She did, however, receive an interim payment in April 1945, along with a printed note which recaptures the very flavour of wartime life:

> The following documents are enclosed:

Utility Furniture permits:	8 brown units
	– *green units
Docket for curtain material	1
Priority docket for floor-covering	–
Priority dockets for mattresses	–
Priority dockets for blankets	–
Priority dockets for sheets	4

> *Green utility furniture units cannot be used yet. The Board of Trade will make an announcement about them later.

25

WIND AND WEATHER PROOF

*Householders, builders and councils all over South London
are united in a race against time to make houses weatherproof
before winter finally sets in.*

South London Press, 3 October 1944

'The clink, clink, clinkety, clink noise of broken glass being
swept into the gutters . . . will remain in my aural memory for
as long as I live. Even with all the front windows like large
sightless eyes, it was difficult to imagine where so much glass
had come from.' That recollection, by a woman whose house,
along with those of all her neighbours, had its windows blown
out on 28 June, is one which millions of people will share,
since for every house destroyed several hundred were
damaged.

At first, however, a bomb-battered house was a novelty, as
one eight-year-old schoolgirl living in Harrow discovered,
around teatime on Sunday, 18 June.

Having emptied the upteenth bucket [of rubbish and debris] about
three-quarters of an hour later, I suddenly became aware of an unusually large number of people walking along on the other side of
the road. . . . The houses on that side had escaped much of the blast
so their pavement was clear for walking. You couldn't very well walk
along on our side because of the clearing-up operations. I was near
exhaustion by this time and having tipped some of mum's best cups
in the gutter, I stopped and rested for a moment and stared at the
passing crowds. . . . There were lots of girls in pretty dresses, young
men in jackets or short sleeves, mums and dads, all out enjoying a
Sunday stroll. . . . It was as though the road between isolated 'them'
from 'us', the poor so-and-sos who had copped it.

Within a few days in many areas of London to have had one's
house damaged barely merited mention; even to have suffered
three or four times in rapid succession was hardly worthy of

comment. A man then living in Thornton Heath, at the heart of the most battered area, remembers a typical snatch of dialogue between two neighbours. 'Did you get much damage?' one asked the other after a local explosion. 'No, not much,' was the reply. 'Just the front door blown open, some windows broken and another ceiling down!'

The picture given by the newspapers, of a battered population cheerfully enduring each new affliction laid upon them, was false. For the rest of the country in 1944 the scent of victory may have filled the air. For people in London, especially South-East London, it was a drab, depressing time, the hallmarks of which were dirt, dust and damp. There was no eager acceptance of sacrifice, merely an unwilling realization of the need to stick it out. But, few as they were, the occasional excuses for laughter were cherished and they do have their place in the story of those dreary days. A Wood Green woman found it hard not to smile at her father's distinctly unheroic, though no doubt painful, wound: 'a big bruise on his leg, where the chamber pot had shot across the room,' and suffered an outright fit of the giggles at the sight of 'our neighbour on her hands and knees looking through the broken panel at the bottom of the door . . . in her flannelette nightdress and hairnet.' A North London woman remembers how her two-year-old nephew was covered in a thick, dark red liquid. 'He was screaming and . . . everybody was rushing around getting hot water and bandages, when it was discovered that the so-called blood was cough-mixture. A bottle had burst and emptied its contents onto the boy's head.' A warden in Highgate recalls seeing 'a gentleman climbing down a ladder from his much-damaged house, clad in a top-hat, tails and pyjama trousers to the cheers of the assembled services. . . . The motley garments had been blasted out of his wardrobe.' One woman living in West Hampstead explains why she failed to appear in a morale-boosting picture after a V-1 had caught her while bathing:

I rushed like mad out of the bath and barely had I carried my daughter out of harm's reach than the glass of the bathroom window shattered leaving only a V-shaped piece intact. I dried myself and phoned the newspapers. Would they care to come and see this beautiful omen of victory?. . . A *Daily Mirror* man came along and was prepared to

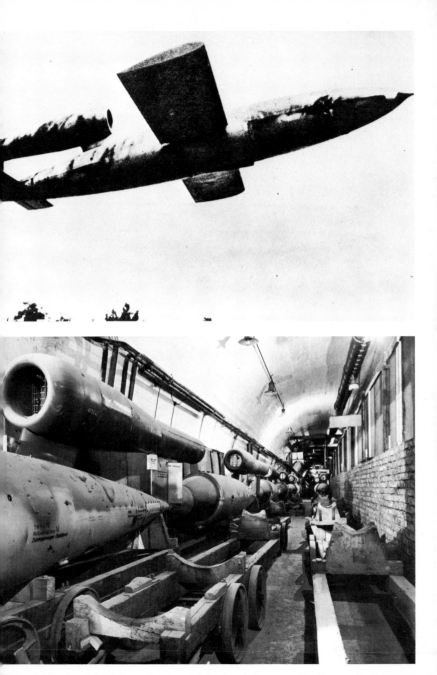

Top: Flying-bomb in flight   2 *Above:* Flying-bomb factory at Nordhausen in Germany

3 Field-Marshal Erhard Milch, the driving
force behind the flying-bomb project

4 Colonel Max Wachtel, Commander
Flak Regiment 155 (W)

5 Nazi leaders watching a weapons' trial, 1943. On the right, with armband,
is Albert Speer, in the centre, shielding eyes, Josef Goebbels

6 *Left:* Danesfield, Medmenham, home of the Photographic Interpretation Unit
7 *Below:* Constance Babington Smith, who first detected a flying-bomb on a reconnaissance photograph

A launching ramp at Peenemünde, complete with flying-bomb (arrowed)

9 Flying-bomb launching site in France under attack by heavy bombers

10 A V-1 being removed from a bunker tail first to be prepared for firing

11 A launching ramp in action. The propulsion unit of the missile is heating up before it develops sufficient thrust to break the retaining bolts holding the firing trolley to the base of the ramp

12 *Top:* Light AA guns deployed against V-1s on the South Coast

13 *Above:* Heavy AA guns in action on the South Coast. In foreground is the Prime Minister

14 *Top:* A Spitfire chasing a
flying-bomb before attempting to tip it
up

15 *Above:* A Hawker Tempest, the
most successful type of fighter used
against the flying-bomb

16 *Above right:* A P.51 Mustang
fighter, extensively used against the
flying bomb

17 *Right:* A De Havilland Mosquito,
used as a night-fighter against the
flying-bomb

18 *Above:* The balloon barrage over Kent and Surrey

19 *Below:* A barrage balloon on the ground. In foreground is the crew's tent and a building damaged by a V-1 brought down by a balloon at the start of the campaign

The British commanders

20 *Top:* Air Marshal Sir Roderic Hill, Commander, Air Defence of Great Britain
21 *Top right:* Air Vice-Marshal W.C.C. Gell, Air Officer Commanding, Balloon Command

22 *Above:* General Sir Frederick Pile, General Officer Commanding, Anti-Aircraft Command, with 'Z battery' rocket projector, manned by Home Guard

'ourney's end

3 *Top:* V-1 diving to earth, after being
hot down, at Brenzett, Kent

4 *Top right:* V-1 which evaded the
efences dropping on Central London. It
landed close to Drury Lane, this picture
being taken from a roof in Fleet Street

25 *Above:* Remains of a V-1 shot down,
apparently without exploding, in Southern
England

26 *Above:* The Guards Chapel, after most
of the debris had been cleared

27 *Below:* The scene in Aldwych, 30 June 1

28&29 Flying-bomb victims in Aldwych

30 *Below:* A typical incident in the suburbs. The Civil Defence workers are searching the ruins for any items of the family's possessions which may have survived

Men against the bomb

Above (from left)

31 Herbert Morrison, Minister of Home Security, inspecting flying-bomb damage

32 Duncan Sandys, Parliamentary Secretary, Ministry of Supply and Minister responsible for coordinating anti-flying-bomb preparations

33 Lord Cherwell, Scientific Adviser to the Prime Minister. (This picture was taken when, as Professor Lindemann, he was first summoned to 10 Downing Street in 1940)

34 *Below:* A street in Islington destroyed by a V-1. Note that the surface shelters are intact

Victims of the bomb
35 *Left:* Old man being
comforted on returning from a
walk to find his house destroyed,
in South London
36 *Below:* Small girl being
carried to safety after an
'incident' in Leytonstone

Opposite page
Targets for the bomb
37 *Top:* Ward C2, St Helier Hospital, Carshalton, Surrey
38 *Bottom:* London Transport Bus Garage, Elmers End, London SE20

This page
Clearing up
39 *Top:* Members of the National Fire Service removing a pet from bomb-damaged property. (Note the typical damaged houses on the far side of the road)
40 *Bottom:* Emergency Repair Squad at work, patching roofs and windows until they can be properly replaced

41 *Top:* A piloted V-1. This type was never used in action

42 *Middle:* A launching site in Holland after capture by Canadian soldiers

43 *Bottom:* V-1 captured intact by members of the United States Air Force in France

photograph the V-sign window pane provided I posed nude by the bath or alternatively, if my little daughter would make the V sign. I refused and my daughter was not in the mood to comply.

If the prevailing sound of the summer – the V-1s themselves excluded – was one of glass being tramped on or swept up, the prevailing smell was of brick dust, but sometimes there were other odours, too, to bring the scene vividly back to mind years later. For a man then living in Barkingside this trigger to unleash the past is provided by the smell of roast pork, which hung in the air after one of the early missiles 'crashed on to a pig farm and had burst into flames.' For the then headmaster of Plaistow Grammar School it was herbs. During the spring he had 'filled the garden with herbs – alecost, thyme, rosemary, lovage, savory, bergamot and . . . dwarf lavender. . . . In the confusion,' when his house was wrecked, 'all this had been trodden into the ground by rescue workers, ARP and our own pupils. The scent, among all that devastation, was unforgettable.'

The sheer amount of destruction caused by the V-1s took everyone by surprise and the mounting arrears of damage featured constantly in Cabinet discussions from 19 June onwards. Already by that Monday morning Herbert Morrison was reporting that 137,000 buildings of various kinds had been 'damaged in varying degrees.' By 27 June the position was visibly deteriorating. 'Over 200,000 houses had been damaged to a greater or less extent,' he told his colleagues, 'and . . . the Ministry of Works . . . were finding it difficult to keep up with the damage caused. Two days later, on 29 June, the Minister of Health described 'the repair of damaged houses' as 'the biggest civil problem arising from the . . . flying-bombs' and said that 'the average number of houses damaged in each twenty-four hours was 22,000,' with arrears piling up at the rate of 12,000 a day. On 17 July he informed his colleagues that already 554,000 houses, out of 2,250,000 in London – about one in five – had been damaged, of which 182,000 were still awaiting repair. So far 14,000 had been totally destroyed. By 30 July the totals were 17,540 destroyed, and almost 800,000 damaged, of which 611,847 had been 'rendered habitable', at least temporarily, but 180,684 were still awaiting attention.

Nearly two weeks later a Ministry of Home Security memorandum, *Lessons from Recent Air Raids*, circulated on 11 August, warned local authorities throughout the country that 'probably the most difficult problem to be faced is that of competing with the first-aid repairs to houses. . . . One flying-bomb may damage in one way or another 1,000 houses.'

Considering the other demands being made on the building industry, including repairs to factories, the government did remarkably well to accomplish as much as it did. But the existence of thousands of battered houses, lacking windows and even roofs, provided a convenient focus for the general indignation in South-East London that the offensive had ever been allowed to develop at all. From late July onwards local authorities and newspapers vied with each other in the bitterness of their reproaches. 'We don't count,' one councillor in an unidentified local borough was quoted as saying in the *South London Press* on 28 July, while another councillor urged his colleagues – a little unnecessarily – not 'to whitewash' the ministries concerned 'for the inertia that has allowed things to get into the position they are. . . . We have,' he declared, strikingly but unjustly, 'had organised chaos.' The bad weather had made matters worse, rendering uninhabitable houses which had escaped relatively lightly. 'For the first three weeks the most we could muster was about 1,200 tarpaulins.'

Most repairs were carried out by private building firms, organized by the local authority. The system worked well, especially in places which had only suffered from the odd 'over-shoot', like Windsor, where a solitary off-course V-1 had left 'five hundred houses . . . in a bad way', and others with lesser damage up to a mile from the point of impact. But in places like Balham and Battersea where such incidents were a twice- or thrice-daily occurrence, to concentrate on one incident at a time was not possible. Apart from the lack of materials and building operatives – 'We have been crying out for them for five weeks,' complained one councillor – the main complaint was about money. The system was in theory simple. The local authority reclaimed the cost of all work undertaken from the War Damage Commission. Repairs costing up to £10 could be undertaken without prior authority and those up to £100 were approved almost automatically. Above this amount the procedure was more complicated, since a building licence was required. The Commission, which, like everyone else, had suffered from blitzed offices and bombed-out staff, seems to have functioned well, but it made an even more obvious target for criticism than Whitehall, which one South London councillor was not slow to deliver:

Describing the Commission's officers as 'criminally negligent' in their failure to make blitzed houses habitable, the councillor said: 'In Germany and Russia such men would have been shot. They are old men, brought back from retirement, and they sit in their offices and smoke their pipes. . . .

'They make a grant of £100 and no more for repairs, and if the building needs another £10 or £20 to make it habitable again they will not pay, but rather let the building go. They say, "Leave it, and the people concerned may be killed and we shan't have to do anything about it." '

The Government was well aware of the mounting tide of discontent and on 2 August the Prime Minister made no effort to minimize the seriousness of the situation when he gave one of his periodic progress reports to the House of Commons:

By our calculations . . . 5,735 of these robots have been launched upon us. . . . The result has been a . . . wholesale destruction of homes, with all the difficult circumstances attaching to that for the people who have lost all the little articles on which their memories and affections centre.

Once the real nature of the V-1s had been realized the best local authorities responded vigorously to their challenge. Often within minutes of a bomb falling a squad of workmen would be on the scene, frequently at the expense of people elsewhere, who tended to find the men working on *their* houses being removed just as they were about to make lasting repairs. 'Squads would be drawn off,' explains the then manager of a Woodford building firm, 'and taken, with tarpaulins, ropes and sandbags to the new incident. The tarpaulins would be manhandled onto and across the damaged roofs, anchored by tying where possible, and the sandbags filled with broken tiles were fastened on to the eyelets in the tarpaulins . . . to keep the wind from lifting them.'

This done, the next task was patching up the windows, with

two-ply roofing felt, and often a dump of this useful material was set up at the roadside, with a box of clout nails, for handyman householders to help themselves. Where felt was not available linoleum, black-out paper and even newspaper were pressed into service, though the latter two, while they kept the light in, usually failed to keep the rain out. 'It made the rooms dark and gloomy,' remembers a then ten-year-old girl in Thornton Heath. 'It stayed that way for weeks and I strained my eyes trying to read *Girls' Crystal* magazines.' If one were lucky a translucent fabric, resembling present-day plastic, which let in the light but was not transparent, might be used on at least some windows. Another universal nuisance was fallen plaster, to replace which plaster board was nailed in place, but it was not always appreciated. 'You're not bringing that b——— stuff into this house!' one builder recalls being told by an irate householder on entering a house in Lambeth to replace the loose sections of the damaged ceiling. 'Needless to say,' comments this informant, 'he had to have it,' not merely because there was no time for traditional plastering, but 'because, with so many people killed and injured by the ceilings falling on them while in bed, . . . it had been proved time and again that it was much safer than the old lath and plaster.'

Once 'first-aid' had been provided the householder had to wait for 'second stage' repairs, with tiles replacing tarpaulins and 'R' glass, coarse, unpolished and almost opaque, replacing the earlier substitutes. Ordinary glass was a luxury, to be used sparingly. A common arrangement, as in Croydon, was to fit 'R' glass in the bedrooms and ordinary glass in the living-rooms, while in Woodford clear glass was used in the centre panes of a downstairs bow window, but 'R' glass at the sides. (The manager previously quoted remembers a complaint from one woman that she could no longer 'see what the neighbours were up to'.) Often there was a long wait before any glazing was done. A Willesden woman remembers a 'devilish draughty . . . winter', for her sash windows remained linen-covered till the end of the war. An East London woman found it 'very queer . . . only seeing white linen, like living in a big box.' This temporary fabric, observed a Hadley Wood man, 'flapped like a sail or tent in the wind' – as he had ample time to discover between 23 August, when his windows were smashed and 27 December, when they were finally replaced. A Streatham family, having used a garden spade to lever a heavy frame back into position, could not, the woman of the house remembers, get it out again 'so the almost complete spade was sticking out into the room. . . . We got used to it.'

A damaged roof was even more inconvenient and one man living in Streatham Hill, whose house had suffered four times in ten weeks, recalls 'on a day in August . . . lying in the bath and watching the clouds drifting across the sky through the wrecked ceiling.' As summer gave way to autumn and autumn to winter such experiences lost their appeal. The changing attitudes of the family of a young nurse in Balham were typical:

The relief of being alive and uninjured left the usual feeling of almost hilarity. We . . . knew that it wouldn't last! The dirt was the worst part at first. We were covered in plaster and soot. . . . The next few days were a nightmare of clearing the rubble into the road. . . . Next . . . it started to rain, and it seemed to rain for ever. And we were so dreadfully cold . . . I just could not stop shivering. . . . We were boxed in for months, and I still recall the misery of not being able to see out of any of the rooms. It was almost claustrophobic. The rain came in everywhere, and the few things that were not bomb damaged were destroyed by the never-ending downpour.

The sudden call for building workers brought men pouring into London from all over the country. 'It is only now that I am older that I realize how very hard it must have been for him,' remarks one woman, whose father, a glazier, found himself at fifty-six sent to London for eight months to live 'in a hostel' where the men 'had seventy-two stairs to climb to their room. He didn't complain . . . but how he looked forward to his weekends (one in three) at home.' The Ministry of Home Security having, for reasons already discussed, vetoed the use of deep shelters as billets, other accommodation had to be found, often in church halls and technical colleges. This presented one member of the staff of the Evening Institute at Richmond with the oddest type of 'war work' on record. As the men filed past the art room on their way upstairs each evening, she had to rush out and veil the nude model posing for the 'life class'.

Not all the imported workers took to being under fire. The

residents of Shirley noted with cynical amusement how a contingent of workers from the Midlands 'decided it was much too dangerous' in Croydon 'and took themselves off back to their homes.' 'Many seemed to be drunk and some had a tendency to help themselves from damaged houses,' remembers one builder of a 'mixed lot' of Welshmen sent to Ilford. 'Women complained that some men lay on the beds in the peoples' houses, still with their boots or dirty clothes on and the foreman or police had to remove unwelcome visitors.' Another building worker remembers a group of Irish workers observed in a street near the Royal Docks in West Ham 'stripped to the waist, lying on the roof sunbathing. . . . One of the tenants called to them to get working and he received some nasty replies, so he brought out an old double-barrel shot gun, and, taking aim, called out, "I'll give you one minute." You never saw such a stampede down ladders and pipes. Of course it was not loaded but it did the trick'.

For the conscientious craftsman life that summer was hard. One who worked for a small building firm employed in the Wanstead and Woodford area remembers nine months of exhausting work, seven days a week, from dawn to dusk – and dusk under double summer time came very late. To a carpenter from Hornchurch, assigned to Stepney, the period seems 'one continuous nightmare . . . working twelve hours a day, seven days a week,' with 'fire-watching at night' thrown in.

The life of a building worker in Lewisham or Lambeth could also be distinctly dangerous, for even a distant explosion could easily dislodge the remaining tiles on a damaged roof, and anyone working on it. 'At first,' remembers one man, then a sixteen-year-old tiler's mate, 'we favoured the pole ladder as this enabled us just to wrap our arms and legs round it and reach the ground in seconds,' but eventually they decided to stay where they were. His own worst moment came when, with a V-1 diving nearby, he simply 'clung on to the exposed rafters. . . . The roof jumped about six inches in the air, hundreds of tiles slithered down . . . and I had sore ribs for a week.'

For servicemen, patching up civilian homes provided a welcome break from the dull routine of camp or barracks, even though skilled craftsmen in uniform found themselves working alongside unskilled civilians earning four or five times as much.

At first unwilling to release men from their normal duties, the service ministries were soon boasting of the contribution they had made. 'Homes for 8,500 – thanks to the Marines,' ran the headlines of an Admiralty press release, which claimed that a special battalion, 700 strong, with headquarters at Sydenham, had given 'first-aid' to more than 4000 houses by the end of August 1944. The Army and RAF had done at least as much. The recollections of a woman living near Croydon, whose house had been damaged while she was out, are typical. 'I came home from shopping . . . to find soldiers swarming all over the place, patching roofs and reglazing windows. The whole thing became something of a party, with endless cups of tea being sloshed from hand to hand, and much laughter and badinage.'

In spite of the critical stories appearing in local newspapers it was not until mid-September that the nation as a whole learned of the real dimensions of the problem. At a press conference on 15 September the Minister of Reconstruction, Lord Woolton, disclosed that when the first V-1s arrived a backlog of 142,000 houses waiting repair already existed. Since then the V-1s had destroyed 23,000 houses – an underestimate in fact, as explained earlier – and damaged 1,104,000, of which 700,000 had received first-aid repairs but needed 'further work to make them habitable'. With no hope of building new houses in the numbers needed, the government was relying on requisitioning empty property – already 51,000 people had been rehoused in this way – and on building '10,000 huts of various designs'. The real remedy lay, however, in repairing damaged houses. '150,000 tiles and slates, 2,000 million square feet of ceiling and wallboard and 50 million square feet of glass' were needed, but even harder to find was an adequate supply of labour, although already '57,000 London workers, 21,000 men brought into London and 5,000 members of the services' were at work. These figures must have come as a shock to people outside London. As *The Times* explained, 'hitherto it had not been thought wise to let the country know the magnitude of the problem, lest the knowledge should give help to the enemy who was now probably too busy licking his own wounds to take comfort from ours.'

Lord Woolton's speech unbarred the floodgates of publicity.

'Fly bombs were worse than the Blitz,' ran a typical headline in the *South London Press*, for 26 September. The paper revealed to the citizens of Camberwell that it had been struck by eighty-one flying-bombs, 'a density of 11·57 bombs per square mile', the heaviest in London, and that 'over three and half times as many houses were seriously damaged in the eleven weeks as during nine months of the Blitz.' A week later, on 3 October, the paper pointed out that three boroughs alone, Battersea, Wandsworth and Lambeth, needed between them nine million square feet of glass, enough 'to completely cover Clapham Common'. As for craftsmen, the number of tilers and slaters available could only 'repair . . . 400 to 450 roofs a week' but Battersea alone had 15,000 waiting attention. The *South London Press* painted a grim picture of worse to come:

Householders, builders and councils all over South London are uniting in a race against time to make houses weatherproof before winter finally sets in. Warnings have been given that bad weather in London's fly-bombed boroughs may start an influenza epidemic equal to that which followed the last war and the repair armies are therefore working not only for South Londoners' comfort alone but possibly also for lives.

Although no credit for it was ever given to the government, a great deal was done to cope with the accommodation crisis. A *South London Press* reporter returned highly impressed from a visit to the Battersea Borough Engineer, who was coping with the problems created by 2231 houses destroyed or needing demolition, 1605 'seriously damaged but partly habitable' and 22,538 more 'slightly damaged':

In the control office I was shown large-scale maps of the borough, coloured and dotted with pins like a map of military manoeuvres, . . . the position of every building firm working on repairs being marked by a pin. . . . There are forty-four contractors working in Battersea at present, employing some 1,500 men, each of whom works a 72½ hour week. . . . 19,277 houses have already been made 'wind and weathertight' and 5,233 of them have been finished to a more comfortable standard.

Another success story was provided by West Ham which had just caught up with the damage left behind by the Blitz when the first of its fifty-seven V-1s arrived. By the autumn, as the

London evening newspaper the *Star*, described on 9 October, it was back where it had started, with 900 houses destroyed and 25,000 damaged:

There are houses which are roofless and seem but shells, yet with 'Still Occupied' or 'Still Living here' scrawled in chalk over the bell push lest the postman and callers disbelieve. Houses definitely classified as uninhabitable continue to have occupants. There is nowhere else for the people to go.

But, the *Star* made clear, an enormous amount had been achieved, thanks largely to 'the redoubtable H. G. Clinch, Chief Sanitary Inspector', in charge of the rehousing programme, 'an intense man with determination and drive. His target is a temporary roof on every habitable house before bad weather and shrinking daylight can hold up his men.'

Morale, so high in the perilous summer of 1940, reached rock bottom in the grim grey winter of 1944, when victory was obviously assured. A leading article in the *North London Press* on Friday, 3 November – although its circulation area, covering Hornsey, Tottenham, Holloway and Islington had got off lightly compared to the boroughs south of the river – struck a grudging note typical of the period. The recent speeding-up in repair work, it claimed, was caused solely by a public outcry, but the average Londoner still 'faced . . . a winter of draught and despair'.

The summer has passed and the bitter winds of approaching winter have howled round his semi-repaired dwelling. He and his family find themselves suffering from rheumatism, coughs, colds and all kinds of ailments, due to dampness and draught, while he waits for his claim to be paid and a licence for further essential work. . . . It is a blessing for Britain and her allies that those who are responsible for the strategy of the war are gifted with more drive and initiative than those whose job it is to care for the bombed and blasted homes of the civil population.

This gloomy picture was not only true of people in London. This is how a woman living at Sandling near Maidstone remembers those chilly months:

It was late January and early February and very cold and frosty before it was possible to spare men and material to plaster our walls and ceilings. I was down with flu and in the only room at the rear of the building which was intact. After some days in bed I got up and sat by the fire with many degrees of frost outside. The men were struggling to mix plaster and cement. The front door had to be open all the time. The wind blew through the building, under my door and took the heat up the chimney. As soon as I felt fit enough to get on my legs, I put on my ski suit, left over from pre-war holidays, a pull-on hat, scarf and gloves and took my skates and went to the lake, the original Dingley Dell of Dickens fame. The remains of the doodle which caused all our misery still lay there, a twisted, rusting piece of broken machinery.

26
AT THE FACTORY GATE

*Total loss of production, both direct and indirect, in
Greater London, amounts to some 15–20% of the total
man hours worked.*

Minister of Production to the Prime Minister, 20 July 1944

The flying-bomb was not, and never could be, aimed at individual factories, but its effect upon war production was far more serious than anyone had foreseen. On 19 June, only three days after the first salvoes had arrived, the Minister of Aircraft Production warned the Prime Minister that a hundred factories – presumably in the aircraft industry alone – had been damaged and five had suffered direct hits. The radio industry had come off particularly badly. The Mullard factory at Mitcham would be out of action for a month, meaning the loss of half a million valves – a return almost sufficient by itself to justify the cost to the Germans of the whole flying-bomb campaign.

The situation rapidly grew worse. The Ministry of Home Security *Weekly Appreciation* for the seven days ending 5 July reported serious damage to seven factories, all of them vital to the war effort, spread over a wide area. On a single day, 1 July, V-1s had reduced production of aero-engine components at a plant in Greenwich by 50 per cent and had stopped altogether aero-engine repairs at Redwing Aircraft in Thornton Heath, and the manufacture of flares and other pyrotechnics in a Dartford works. On the following day a Wimbledon firm making electrical items had lost three-quarters of its capacity, and production of balloon fabric and rubber components had been halted in another on Streatham Common. Callenders Cables, at Belvedere in Kent, had suffered severe damage, and the week had ended with the instrument makers, Negretti and Zambra, having to stop production of oil pressure gauges and thermostats in Islington. At Supreme Headquarters these achievements were viewed with dismay. 'A large number of vital services and installations were damaged in the week's attacks,' acknowledged a report circulated on 5 July. In 900 incidents in London, and 850 outside it, the targets of military importance hit had included twenty factories, two docks and three wharves, and a number of public utilities including a power station. For an indiscriminate 'terror' weapon this was no negligible achievement.

On 20 July, Oliver Lyttleton, Minister of Production, sent a formal warning to the Prime Minister. 'Total loss of production, both direct and indirect, in Greater London,' he wrote, 'amounts to some 15-20 per cent of the total man hours worked. This is as much as 5% of the whole national production.' The radio industry, largely concentrated in London, was again the chief cause of anxiety. Production of radio valves made in London was down 20 per cent and that of other 'radio equipments' 25 per cent. More than 1000 factories, in industry as a whole, had suffered some damage. The real threat, however came from 'increased absenteeism', estimated at 'a loss of man-hours amounting to 3·5 per cent of the total worked in London,' from the 'distinct lowering in the efficiency of workers in the factories,' and, above all, from 'time spent in the shelters,' amounting in one case to '50% of total working time'.

Lord Cherwell, however, when Churchill invited him to comment on these facts, refused to be alarmed. A sixth of all the man-hours normally worked in London had, he agreed on 20 July, indeed been lost, but fewer than one London factory in fifty had suffered a direct hit. As for the drop in output, 'it may well be that the easing off of the bombing and our improved organisation will shortly result in more reassuring figures.' So often wrong, Cherwell proved on this occasion to be right. The general introduction of the 'imminent danger' system, already described, did sharply reduce the loss of working time, although the V-1s kept on coming, and hitting worthwhile targets.

Every type of industrial property was affected, from the small back-street workshop to the vast factory complex, but perhaps the most spectacular incidents were those involving gasometers, then a prominent feature of the skyline in every built-up area. A man then living in Cranleigh still remembers the 'five o-clock' bomb which, early one evening, he watched run 'smack into the largest of the gasometers at the west end' of the town. 'Bits of the gasometer were blown everywhere. . . . A whole panel . . . was found behind St Andrew's Church some four or five hundred yards away.' A then twelve-year-old girl living only half that distance away recalls the same incident for two reasons. The blast 'brought down most of the pears from a tall tree in the next garden. Each year it had been an object of our attempts at "scrumping". . . . The metal rivets which held the panels of the gasometer together flew everywhere like bullets and we were prising them out of our bedroom walls ages afterwards.'

The famous gasometer at the Oval, mentioned so often in cricket commentaries, was another victim, when a flying-bomb hit an adjoining pickle factory. 'The top of the gas holder disintegrated,' remembers a Stockwell man V-1 watching from the roof of the flats where he lived, 'and a sheet of flame shot hundreds of feet into the air. I could feel the heat of it on my face. . . . All that was left was the blackened frame of the gas holder and a large cloud of smoke in the sky.' The huge Nine Elms gas works, close to the river in Battersea, was also struck, among the eye witnesses this time being the Secretary of State for Air, who had just set out that day, 15 July, on a tour of bomb damage. 'Thick black clouds of dust hid it from our view and then a sheet of flame shot up,' he wrote to the Prime Minister next day. 'We found that the bomb had hit some retort chambers nearly 100 yards from the gasholder,' but 'the Deputy Chief Engineer told us that . . . the blast of a bomb exploding within a short distance of a gasholder always set it alight.'

Three days earlier a devastating '25 pump fire' had occurred nearby when 'a bomb had hit a boilerhouse belonging to Price's Candles and Night Lights' and the 'oil in the boilerhouse . . . had caught fire and floated out into the river, burning some barges.'

This particular V-1 is also remembered by a man then employed as foreman in a welding team, converting invasion barges at the boatyard on Chelsea Embankment:

There was candle fat floating all over the river, some on fire. The swans swam into this, presumably out of curiosity, and some had to be destroyed by the swan uppers, who were sent for to catch them. These dead birds were thrown into the barges at the Kensington Council's Wharf, but a dustman recovered one or two younger ones for his table. None of our men would take one.*

Fires and explosions in warehouses filled with food had always been liable to produce unexpected results which made dealing with the destruction in a residential street seem easy by comparison. A good example was provided by the flying-bomb which hit a cereal store at Dudin's Wharf, in Bermondsey Wall, leaving the roadway and floors in the houses all around buried in three or four feet of grain. The same bomb had caused a fire and when the firemen played their hoses on it, the grain was washed into the drains, swelled and blocked them. The *South London Press* described on 15 September the resulting misery of the local inhabitants:

A huge dump of tons of grain was formed and because it was not the responsibility of the Borough Council and the various Ministries concerned 'passed the buck' the area has suffered a plague of flies to add to the discomforts of blocked drains, appalling stench and houses unusable because of the depth of grain in them. The matter has now reached Parliament.

No factory in the kingdom was more likely to be hit than Woolwich Arsenal, which occupied a huge, sprawling site close to the river in a borough on which eighty-two flying-bombs landed. So many of the workforce suffered from blasted homes that, as one man then working in the heavy gun shop remembers, 'the time and place of the latest incidents were chalked up as soon as the details were phoned in', thus preventing an anxious rush for the telephone. 'It was depressing to see the board filled and a start made again at the top' and 'the sight of those affected hurrying out did not encourage any cheerfulness in the rest of the shop.' This daily exodus prompted a grim factory joke. 'If your house was demolished you were granted two whole days' leave to arrange for your dependants, while

*They showed good sense. Roast swan, though once a royal delicacy, is said to be tough, with a fishy flavour.

if you were at home and were killed, you were excused phoning in, but your next of kin was expected to do it.'

No fewer than eight V-1s landed on Woolwich Arsenal but only two caused serious damage. One of these hit the tailor's shop, the other landed 'at the road junction by the heavy forge . . . when it was crowded with people' around midday on a Saturday and the workers, after the final shift of their sixty-six-hour week, were streaming out 'for the weekend shopping'. The official figures at the time admitted '17 killed and 100 injured', but this informant and his workmates were sceptical about their acuracy, since 'our ARP swore that they had picked up at least forty dead'.

Some places vital to the war effort escaped altogether, like Ford's of Dagenham, where 34,000 people were employed. Although the plant suffered 635 hours 12 minutes under 'alert' that summer, its sixteen acres of plate-glass roofing suffered not a single cracked pane, though there were some anxious moments. On 18 June a flying-bomb hit by cannon-shells was diving straight towards the factory when a second fighter shot it down into the river, and two weeks later another V-1, after circling over the works, was caught by the guns and also plunged to a harmless, watery death.

The most serious industrial incident in South-East London could hardly have affected a less military target. On 5 August a V-1 devastated a corset factory in Nunhead Lane, Peckham, killing twenty-four people and seriously injuring sixty-four more. By chance, many of the worst factory incidents occurred well to the north or west of London. Only six V-1s, for example, landed on Hayes and Harlington in Middlesex, but one of these hit the EMI factory making radar aids and other precision equipment on a large site between the Uxbridge Road and a canal. One employee, just crossing from one building to another, as he heard the V-1 coming down, remembers the moment well: it was 2.59 p.m. on Friday, 7 July.

I dived to shelter 'A', but it was absolutely full up and I could only just poke my head inside. I felt the air go completely, and the heat was shocking. I then saw . . . it had dropped just past shelter 'B'. I immediately ran down the road and the first thing I saw was the top portion of a girl in a pink jumper. The face and legs were covered very heavily with rubble. Almost the same second I heard a call for help and found it was an old man trapped in the floor of shed 'E'. There were heavy roof boards falling all round and with the help of another man and a door we finally got them out and washed them. Her eyes were full of sand and muck. I saw him into an ambulance and later he recovered.

Factory rumour had it that 'there were twenty-three killed', but for once the death roll was actually higher, thirty-four with another eighteen injured. The heavy casualty rate was due to the concrete roof of a shelter having collapsed.*

Three miles north-east of Hayes was Greenford, where the firm of Glaxo had its laboratories. In addition to its famous baby foods, known to every mother, the company produced a range of 'fine chemicals' important to the war effort. This time fortune was on the staff's side, for the V-1 landed at 10.30 a.m. on a wet and cloudy Sunday morning, when very few people were in the building. One of those few was at his desk, when he looked out and saw the bomb take 'a left turn downwards' followed by 'a loud noise, a wave of intense heat and a shower of various-sized fragments':

I . . . rose and looked around. The Bulk Floor building gaped wide open, and immediately below, the Powder Packing floor was just a tangled mass of destruction. Flames were already coming up from this floor and . . . the chemical stores at the end of the laboratory were also blazing furiously. . . . I re-entered the Analytical Laboratory. The end was open to the sky and both the stores and the spectrograph room had collapsed and were well alight. . . . Everything seemed almost knee-deep in glass and pieces of laboratory.

What everyone remembers best about the incident is what one sufferer describes as the 'typical Manchester weather', and the almost surrealistic atmosphere which combined the worst afflictions of summer and winter.

The wind blew on us and the rain poured in. . . . All the milk powder and glucose had been burned *and* soaked with water, smelling horribly and attracting every wasp and bee within miles. . . . The powder in the basement was . . . salvaged in . . . conditions resembling deep-sea fishing. Water had soaked into the bags of sugar stored here and

---

*This unusual occurrence was mentioned in an official report on such shelters. See page 265.

. . . this sticky mess adhered to every uncovered portion of the body . . . the bees with it, as they evidently couldn't tell the difference. We swore and slapped and the more we slapped the more sugar was deposited and more bees settled.

No one was killed at Glaxo, the worst injuries being a broken leg and some burns, and 'two days after the bomb fell business was again being carried on as usual,' though there was a record crop of colds. But, as the company's house magazine later remarked, 'When all is said and done, everybody was at least alive – and in Southern England last autumn, to be alive was something for which one could be very grateful indeed.'

The last major factory incident was, alas, to be very different; indeed by the test of the combined total of dead and seriously injured – though not the number of dead alone – it was to be the worst incident of the whole campaign. The victims were the employees of Standard Telephones and Cables Ltd at New Southgate, on the northern edge of London, a location usually, but wrongly, described as 'Barnet' or 'East Barnet'.

Everything made at New Southgate was important to the war effort: Bailey bridges, teleprinters, tank and fighter radios, transceivers for RAF air–sea rescue launches and dinghies, blind-landing gear, known by the code-name 'Beechnuts', and radio-operated predictors and automatic fusing devices for AA guns. Although employees could, if they wished, take shelter when the siren sounded, most waited for the imminent danger signal, a continuous 15-second buzz, and the peremptory cry 'Lie down!' over the loudspeakers.

STC Ltd had been described by the Minister then responsible for Civil Defence as 'the most prepared' company in London, but the site so far had been hit only by a few incendiaries and one small HE bomb. The company, now part of the great international concern ITT, was in the words of one employee, 'not only a factory but a family'. Son followed father through the factory gate, and, during the war, wife joined husband.*

The morning of Wednesday, 23 August 1944, was grey and

---

*My appeal for reminiscences in the company's house journal in 1978 brought several letters from married couples, and one from a man with fifty years' service.

gloomy. By 7 a.m. there had already been two alerts and at
7.10 one of the factory look-outs, Reg Smith, was peacefully
shaving while waiting to hand over to his relief at 8 a.m., when
a third 'yellow' warning was received. 'I went quickly to the
control tower and started plotting two V bombs,' Mr Smith
remembers, 'one that had been located over Beachy Head and
the other in the vicinity of Brighton.' Soon afterwards his chief
joined him, and Mr Smith explained that 'the one that had
come across Brighton . . . if it was to proceed without blowing
up or coming down, would go over the Watford area; the one
that had come in via Beachy Head, if it was to keep a direct
line, should go between our two chimney stacks . . . on the
side of building 8.'

This latter remark was, of course, a joke, but 'The bomb
proceeding from Beachy Head gradually came closer . . . and
at 7.50 a.m. we were flashed . . . a red alert,' which meant the
sirens were sounded. 'Visibility,' the official log recorded, 'was
now about 400 yards with very low cloud,' and Mr Smith,
peering south through the murk, was horrified to 'see and hear
through the slot of the control tower the V bomb just short of
our main gate on the corner of Brunswick Park Road' about
300 yards away. He still remembers that moment and his response. 'I shouted over the factory speakers "Lie down! For
God's sake, lie down." ' The official log records what followed:
'A few seconds later the fly bomb broke through the cloud
SSE and descended on building 7 at 45°, cutting out half way.'
The time was 7.59 a.m.

That final frantic shout must have saved many lives. 'The
spotter literally screamed down his mike and we knew he
meant it,' remembers one woman. 'I dived under my bench.'
Her husband, 'putting his glue-pot on' in the 'Woodshop' on
the other side of the same road, 'said to the chap next to him,'
she later learned, ' "He means it! Get under that bench!"
. . . and then the building collapsed on them.'

The bomb had landed at the very heart of the factory, between Building 8, a strong three-storey building of reinforced
concrete, used for the assembly of airborne radio and radar
equipment, and Building 6, a single storey steel-framed and
brick construction which contained 'The Woodwork Shop',
where Bailey bridge parts were being built, and the paint-

spraying and building maintenance departments for the whole factory. The staircase serving Building 8 was in a projecting rectangle and it was this which caught the wing of the V-1 as it dropped, causing it to spin to earth. The explosion blew out a crater four feet deep and twelve feet wide in the road, but the buildings on either side took the main force of the blast. Most of the wood-working shop, according to the official Ministry of Home Security report compiled a week later, was demolished and the contents blown into a vast pile at the far end of the building, though the steel framework remained as a skeleton, stripped of roof and walls. Block 8 'was not seriously damaged structurally . . . but the internal machinery and fixtures were destroyed and blasted in all directions.' It was in this, the stronger building, that many of the casualties occurred, 'for the building was draped . . . in camouflage rope netting which went up in flames. A number of workers who had taken refuge on a stairway were killed by the flames, for which the stairway acted as a chimney.'

For a moment after the explosion everyone was stunned. A then chargehand in the woodwork shop, who had 'dived under the marking-out table' just in time, recalls a confused impression of 'glass, wood, debris of all kinds and dust and dust and dust. Very difficult to get your breath and everything whirling.' When he could speak, he shouted to his brother, who had taken shelter with him, 'You OK?' to receive an unprintable response, for 'a surface plate had been blown off its position on to his rump.' Unharmed except for 'a few bruises and cuts', the two set off, as trained first-aiders, for the first aid post.

On the way . . . through the assembly shop we stopped to try to give a hand to . . . a huge lumberjack type of bloke with a shock of red hair and a beard to match. The explosion had wrecked part of the roof, and a very heavy beam had crashed over a bench, pinning a group of women underneath. To make things worse a gas pipe had been broken, the gas had ignited and the flames were playing all over these women who were in agony, screaming 'Please get us out, we're burning.' The 'lumberjack's coat, trousers and beard were burnt completely off. We tried our utmost . . . before we were driven back for the flames were very severe. I saw the 'lumberjack' later in the surgery foyer whimpering and badly in shock and blaming himself for not having the strength to resue the trapped women.

Also close to the point of impact was a young engineering apprentice, now a senior manager, who had just clocked on for work in the service and maintenance department of Building 6.

I remember it suddenly going dark, due to dust, with a rushing noise . . . then clearing with hissing noise of steam and compressed air escaping and raining particles on the roof and floor. It cleared enough to see the exit, which I made for. My first sight being a poor chap with his jaw hanging down, walking about in a daze. I felt sick and helpless. Another man steered him to the surgery in Building 8.

To eyes unfamiliar with the power of high explosive, the destruction seemed almost unbelievable. 'Pallets of angle iron and sheet metal were blown through the air like playing cards,' noticed a chargehand in the radio assembly shop on the first floor of Building 8. On the ground floor the sight was much worse. 'About halfway along, where the bomb dropped in the roadway, the side of the building was smashed in. A rectangular supporting pillar 2 feet by 3 feet was stripped of concrete, leaving only the reinforcing rods and allowing the first floor to sag.' To another eye-witness the ground floor 'looked like some vast scrap heap, with machinery and benches piled in indescribable confusion. Some of the huge concrete rooflight slabs had been blown right out, others were teetering on the edge ready to fall down at any moment.'

By good fortune the draughtsmen and planning engineers who normally occupied the ground floor were not due in until 8.20* and the rubble from above deluged down onto empty benches. The reinforced shelter in the basement below also withstood the sudden impact laid upon its roof, while in buildings further from the emplosion the 'heavy cotton mesh coated with thick varnish' glued to the windows prevented them flying into lethal fragments. All the effort which STC Ltd had invested in preparing for just such an emergency now paid off and from all over the factory area trained teams of helpers converged on their report centres. The factory Home Guard

---

*Previously published reports, which refer to the V-1 landing at the factory gate during 'clocking on' time, are wrong. It landed in the middle of the factory, though many of the casualties were caught in the open.

unit, for example, was within minutes, 'putting an armed guard round the area to keep off any unauthorized people.'

A feature of industrial incidents was that they were often followed by a fire and at New Southgate several small outbreaks occurred in the Woodshop, and a major one in the radio building, where there were many naked flames. The missile itself probably carried some incendiary bombs, for several suspicious-looking fins were picked up near the point of impact.

An inspector tester, working on the ground floor of Building 8, observed how the fire started, just after the explosion. 'There was a rush of air (no sound), then the departmental partition crashed over the bench . . . I saw a small light like a match, then fire from floor to ceiling in the Component Test Section.' Whatever the cause, the fires added a new dimension of fear and terror to an already grim situation. One woman remembers seeing as she crawled from the debris another with 'part of her clothing on fire . . . ringed round by a number of filing cabinets, full of drawings, so heavy it would have taken a couple of men to have moved one a couple of feet. By some miracle she was given the strength to move several and so got away from the fire and collapsed in my arms.'

Thanks to the highly efficient works fire-brigade the fire in Building 8 'was quickly under control and did not spread to the wood-working shop across the road.' Meanwhile work was proceeding on rescuing those who had been trapped. One Home Guard who returned to his workplace, the woodshop, to be greeted by a 'heavy pall of smoke and red sawdust', remembers with particular satisfaction dragging out a man being 'drowned' by the water from a fractured main flowing into his face. He also rescued another workman with 'a two-inch sprinkler pipe embedded in the lower portion of his anatomy', which he was able to extract.

The young apprentice, quoted earlier, who had at first felt 'sick and helpless', now reported 'to the fire station as . . . a part-time fireman' to be given a task that was emphatically not for the squeamish:

I was put to work digging for people in Building 6, near where the dust extraction plant had stood. I found the remains of three men in the rubble. These parts were put in three 'Woston' boxes, a wood and plywood box, identified where possible by skin and age: young, middle-aged and old.

One inspector/tester, after being rescued from Building 8, was 'told to get everyone I could out to the roadway and up to the top field, for roll-call' like the survivors of a badly-mauled battalion after a battle. The ominous silence which greeted name after name confirmed more eloquently than words the scale of the disaster which had fallen upon the factory.

Like the fire-fighting arrangements the medical services at STC were, in the words of the official report, 'of a high standard under a whole-time doctor with a staff of ten registered nurses and 108 auxiliaries.' The doctor was Dr Pringle, who lived close by and was on the scene within minutes, attending to the most desperate cases as they lay entombed, or were carried to him on the roadway between the two worst affected buildings. The blast from the bomb had swept down this narrow corridor with such ferocity that it moved a massive metal boiler stored in the open a full two feet and left behind a trail of dead and dying. Most of the other victims who had died or been injured in the woodshop had been struck by the rubble and equipment flung about in the radio workshops, or, as already described, had perished on the staircase projecting from the building. One observer remembers a dead woman with merely 'a bruise at the back of her neck where she had been hit by falling masonry.' Others died in ways that even the most bizarre imagination could hardly have conceived, like one man 'thrown into the sawdust bin' in the woodshop, 'and choked to death.'

Two brothers, half of a four-man first-aid party, who reported to the surgery after escaping from the woodshop, found that the first cases they encountered were beyond the reach of help.

We were detailed to assist on the second floor, not so much for applying first-aid treatment but to stop bleeding or immobilize limbs and get the injured back to surgery. . . . Our first task was to separate two young ladies who were on a landing standing up, both pairs of arms embracing one another, dead. . . . On our way back with the corpses I met old Bert who was standing as if to attention upright against the wall. I stopped, asked if he was OK . . . and as I touched him he keeled over, a gaping hole at the back of his skull.

As the bodies were removed from the wreckage they were laid out in rows in the entrance hall, close by the main surgery. A few, killed outright by blast, 'looked,' the sister in charge remembers, 'as if they had just sat down' but some were unrecognizable or badly mutilated. Another observer recalls 'some with very little clothing, their faces . . . caked solid with dirt and dust.' In the paint-spraying department in Building 6 dead and living alike, 'looked ghastly, completely covered in light grey paint.'

The sister in charge of the main surgery was Mrs R. V. Sandwell, who, with two nurses, had been 'attending to a young man with cuts from a machine' when the bomb fell. Within minutes the three women – and two nurses on duty in the other surgery – found themselves confronted by a long procession of badly injured workers, 'cut by glass, burnt, or injured by burning wood.'

The range of injuries was extraordinary. One inspector saw a foreman whose throat had been slashed by a sharp-edged piece of flying debris, a girl with a finger blown off, another with a totally severed leg. In the close-packed radio assembly shop of Building 8 one fireman remembers still the 'horrible sight' of some of the victims sliding off the steel sheets on to which they were loaded, made slippery by blood.

The two first-aiders quoted earlier remember, after bringing in a whole series of casualties, some of whom 'were declared dead, . . . giving assistance in the main hall,' where the injured awaiting attention were laid in rows.

One young lady lying on a stretcher had a brown smock draped over her legs. She said her foot was hurting her. I took the smock off to see what looked like a piece of liver with some almonds on the end. She moved her leg, leaving the foot where it was, which started the blood to pump. She was most distressed when I had to apply digital pressure to her femoral artery. I explained I was married, but I was relieved when one of the nurses took over. . . . Our last task was a check out right through the workshops . . . and there was a middle-aged chap . . . from the carpenter's shop hobbling along with a large piece of wood through his thigh. He had sawed a piece off it whilst it was still in his leg, to enable him to walk.

Even in the surgery there were lighter moments. Among them was the sudden arrival of one 'boiler houseman', who 'rushed

311

in hysterically saying it wasn't his boiler that had blown up the building' – the 'then plant manager' had regularly warned him that he 'one day would blow the place up' by 'over-stoking'.

Directly the bomb had fallen the main gates had been closed, mainly to prevent people arriving for the 8.30 shift from entering, but soon a crowd of relatives clamouring for news formed outside, as in so many newsreels of pit disasters. Around 10 a.m. all those who had worked in the two damaged buildings and were not busy on post-raid duties were ordered to go home, while the members of the personnel department helped the nursing staff to label every body before it left the factory and to remove the contents of the pockets for safe keeping. Then came the melancholy duty of tracing the next of kin of the dead and injured – a time-consuming business with so many families evacuated. It was 10.30 p.m. that night before the wife of one man deafened by blast, who was living with relations in Bedford, learned what had happened to him and not till next day that another employee was asked to identify the body of a friend whose wife and family lived in Ireland. He found the mortuary in Lyonsdown Road besieged by 'a crowd of distressed people making inquiries about their relatives' and 'the officials . . . very painstaking in the execution of their duties.'

The New Southgate flying-bomb cost the lives of thirty-three people, twenty-one of whom died on the spot, and caused serious injury to about 200 others – the government figures and company records disagree slightly as to the total – making the total of dead and seriously injured 233, the highest of the whole campaign. The public knew little of what had happened, for the *Barnet Press* reported merely that some lives had been lost, when 'a works' had been hit and within two or three days production had been re-started even in the worst damaged buildings.

True to its tradition as a 'caring' company, STC Ltd set up a special committee, which included union representatives, to give both an immediate cash grant and long-term help to the injured and bereaved. It soon became clear – paralleling German experience – that the death and injury of their workmates had merely strengthened the resolve of the survivors. When the men from the two affected buildings returned to work and were asked to help with the clearing up, not one voice protested that he was a craftsman, not a labourer; and when the siren sounded thereafter, people throughout the factory were even more reluctant than before to desert their benches for a single moment.

The tragedy which occurred on the morning of 23 August nearly had a sequel the following evening. At 6.50 p.m. on 24 August another flying-bomb, no doubt fired from the same ramp, was reported approaching from the same direction. This time, however, it landed on the sports field to the north, 'causing only superficial damage to the main buildings and partially destroying a test hut.' The enemy did not trouble Standard Telephones and Cables again.

27

THE WARDENS WERE WONDERFUL

The working of all the Civil Defence services, men and women, has been a model.

Winston Churchill in the House of Commons,
2 August 1944

'The working of the Service has been uniformly admirable.' This assessment by the senior Civil Defence regional commissioner for London, Sir Ernest Gowers, submitted to the Home Secretary on 9 August 1944, was one which hundreds of thousands of bombed-out or injured Londoners would have echoed. Refreshed by the long lull since the Blitz, reinvigorated by new equipment, improved training and better organization, the performance of the ARP services in the summer of 1944 surpassed all expectations, 'in spite of the release of the younger men and many of the younger women to the forces or industry.'

There were, thought Sir Ernest, many reasons why the ARP services had 'never shown up better', including the provision of proper uniforms and badges of rank, with pay to match, 'the conversion of the old Rescue and Stretcher Parties into a composite rescue service' and some timely reinforcement from outside. Three hundred and sixty former full-time wardens who had been directed into industry had been brought back; 167 part-time wardens had become paid full-timers; 400 full-time heavy rescue workers had been transferred 'from other Regions to the L.C.C.' and 1000 wardens in the provinces, chafing at their inactivity, had volunteered for a period of service in London, providing help by 3 August for forty-three of the ninety-five local authorities in the London region. 'The scheme has . . . ,' Sir Ernest reported, 'been an unqualified success.'

The nature of the offensive had also made it easier to cope

with than conventional bombing. Although, as Sir Ernest pointed out, 'fourteen hours is so far the longest lull' and 'as many as fifteen have been known to arrive in the London Region almost simultaneously', the flying-bombs were spread over the whole area and throughout the day and night. 'The largest number to fall in any 24 hour period was 98 on the 2nd/3rd August.' This was bad enough, but the number of incidents had rarely been beyond any local authority's resources to deal with, much less that of any group, the organizational unit midway between the borough and the region, which held reserves of specialist manpower and heavy equipment.

The front line of the nation's Civil Defence forces were the local wardens' posts, beyond which lay 'control', often in the borough town hall, group, and then region, which reported to the Ministry of Home Security War Room. This was housed in the 'Rotunda' in Horseferry Road, near Millbank, which passers-by often assumed to be part of the capital's military defences for reasons which William Sansom made clear:

From street level this stronghold looks like a low, circular pillbox of immense proportion and constructed of thick concrete. On its dark flat roof the seagulls strutted in winter, finding a beached solace in the pebbles laid there against incendiary attack. But beneath, a dramatic edifice burrowed its way down into the earth, an arrangement of passages and offices and chartrooms, lit throughout by whitish-greyish fluorescent bars that are . . . a kind of daylight, the bleakest February daylight. This cylinder of concrete was built in the foundation pit of an ancient gasometer. It was concrete, air-conditioned; stocked with the necessities of a siege, a modern place whose passages were lined with grey pneumatic tubes and . . . grey cables.

From this bleakly utilitarian building orders went out to the headquarters of the three regions affected by the V-1 attacks, No. 4 centred on Cambridge and reaching to the Thames estuary from the Wash, No. 12 at Tunbridge Wells, covering the south-eastern counties and No. 5, the London Region itself.

London Region headquarters were housed in a building far removed from the purposes of modern war, the Geological Museum in South Kensington. This 'fine modern building, admirably adapted and lighted to display the wonderful collection of minerals, gems and stones . . .', wrote the region's chief administrative officer, 'served excellently as an office', but the actual control room was in a 'fortified rectangular pillbox' in the garden of the National History Museum, and was linked to it by an underground passage. 'On one side of the room a big map on which every incident was plotted. . . . At a glance you could see what roads were blocked . . . and other vital information. On the other side . . . the tallyboard . . . showed the number of men and machines available in stretcher, rescue and ambulance parties.' As time passed, the invading Home Security staff – they eventually numbered 800 – spread through the Museum, producing some curious spectacles. The headquarters canteen was dominated by a huge stuffed elephant, while one woman who paid a visit there that summer observed how 'the skeletons of great beasts still looked down imperturbably at the tiny figures in blue Civil Defence uniforms scattered among lines of school desks among a chaos of telephone wires. The contrast between the arches of bone of the bigger dinosaurs and the people struggling with "incidents" was overpowering.'

London was unique in having two regional commissioners. The real head of the region was a highly competent career civil servant, Sir Ernest Gowers, still remembered for his book *Plain Words*, but the public saw more of the 'outdoor commissioner', 'Evans of the *Broke*'. Admiral Lord Mountevans had earned the nickname after a daring naval engagement in the Channel in 1916 and he approached his new duties in the same bold spirit. 'I can't be bothered with all those damned circulars,' he would say, brushing the files on his desk aside. The cry 'The admiral's here' – he invariably wore his naval uniform, to the annoyance of his civilian colleagues – raised spirits. 'The effect of his presence,' his chief administrative officer admitted, 'was electric.' Evans visited 126 flying-bomb incidents and his departure from his post was characteristic. 'I'm off,' he remarked to his chief staff officer, handing over to him a pile of unread papers fourteen inches high. 'Will you stay and clear up?'

One visible sign of the Civil Defence services' efficiency was the speed with which the first helpers arrived, due to the twin networks of observation posts, set up by the National Fire Service and by the local authorities. The result was a keen rivalry to be first on the scene. Usually the fire service won, partly because its hose-drying towers provided excellent look-out posts. This, for example, was what happened at Streatham:

The location of the station on high ground, plus a further fifty feet of tower, gave an excellent vantage point for several miles . . . We hit just one snag. . . . A large oak tree and a church steeple were in direct line with the usual approach route of the bombs. We quickly had the tops of both obstructions removed. . . . Immediately a bomb landed, the lonely man up the tower would telephone his message, say, 'Due South, one and a quarter miles', control room would in-terpret the instructions and within seconds appliances were on their way.

For the fire service the flying-bomb posed fewer problems than the Blitz. H. E. Bates explained the reasons:

Out of 2,299 incidents in the London area, there were . . . 933 fires; small fires begun by broken gas-pipes; spectacular fires like the great riverside burning of a candle factory; difficult fires like the burning of a tar distillation plant where burning tar ran like black lava down the streets; fires at paint works, gas-works, fuel research works, garages. All these fires were widely distributed. The concentrated firing of a city, as in December 1940, never again became a possibility.

The 55,000 members of the London Fire Brigade, of whom 26,000 were part-timers, proved 'more than necessary for deal-ing with the fires of the doodlebug.' But there were still, in the words of one official report, 'some nasty ones', a common cause being unconsumed fuel scattered and set alight when a V-1 exploded. One of the worst outbreaks was at a warehouse in Great Eastern Street, observed by a fireman who had seen the V-1 responsible dive to earth from the roof of his fire-station in Whitechapel:

The cloud of smoke, dust and flying debris seemed to shoot skywards for some hundred feet or more a fraction of a second before I heard the bang. . . . I had just started to move towards the first pole hole to slide to the first floor when the bells started their urgent ringing. . . . I jumped on to the TL [turntable ladder] as it started moving out. . . . I remember that feeling of exhilaration as we sped across Aldgate and down towards Great Eastern Street, the traffic opening up a clear lane for us, our bell clanging. . . . As we came within sight of the incident . . . the police were keeping a lane clear through the spectators and putting rope barriers in position. Glass, slate and other small debris was cracking and crunching under our wheels as we moved in to the control point. . . . The tower had been of three or four floors but now had no roof or windows and parts of the upper walls were missing. Flames were shooting out of most windows with thick black smoke trying to blot out everything. . . . We were soon at work with our jet which I was directing down into what looked like a little bit of hell. Beneath me was swirling, curling smoke, black, brown and other colours and, like all smoke, dirty and stinking. Flames were leaping everywhere and seemed to be doing their best to reach me on the ladder. Intermittently a drum of paint or spirit would explode and shower coloured flames everywhere. . . . The railway line from Liverpool Street ran past the back of the building and, looking down as a train passed, I could just see every window facing the fire had its full quota of faces peering at the scene and lapping up a story to be told when they arrived at their destinations.

Small NFS detachments were distributed throughout the docks, and one man remembers many uneasy moments 'working . . . beside great mounds of filled petrol cans' and 'ships loading ammunition and flying the usual red flag.'

When not in the docks, such firemen might still face the call to action at any moment:

One evening . . . we were passing the time at the station in Wellclose Square [off Cable Street, in Stepney] when, at about ten o'clock, when it was almost dark, the bells went down and we rushed for our appliance. . . . As we leaped on the machine the officer in charge sang out to the driver, 'London Hospital.' We sped down the Mile End Road with . . . traffic giving way, and people scattering. . . . In the courtyard bricks and rubbish were lying everywhere and we made our way into the building through the remains of a window in the basement. We were in almost pitch darkness, just torches to help us, and we were already wading in water about a foot deep. In this water were lying large numbers of cardboard boxes containing lovely blackcurrant juice and I could not help thinking what a waste it was. We found that one end of the hospital had been sheared right down, about five floors.

Once I had to go up to the top floor and had to walk right through one of the women's wards, which at one end was a sheer five floor drop to the debris beneath. Those wonderful East End women were all sitting propped up in their beds smiling and joking. 'Nice to see yer, duck!' they would call out.

The pressure on the fire service was continuous. One NFS officer stationed in Epsom, not one of the worst-hit boroughs, found himself called to almost fifty incidents. In others the total must have been even higher and the customary twenty-four hours off duty was sometimes cut to twelve. But comparatively little of the time spent 'in attendance' at incidents, to use the official term, was devoted to actual fire-fighting. Many firemen had been trained in rescue work, which demanded, as a writer in the *ARP and NFS Review* pointed out in October 1944, not merely 'a very different technique' from 'the rescue of people trapped in burning buildings', but also 'carefulness and patience . . . as contrasted with the quick wit and dash that is so often called for at a fire.'

These comments, perhaps prompted by personal experience, were perceptive. The patient removal, brick by brick, of a dusty mound of debris, 'amid groans and cries of pain and in the presence of mutilated bodies and limbs,' made a deep impression on many firemen. A leading firewoman from Watford retains a clear picture of one row of wrecked houses. 'When we arrived, a cold dawn was just breaking and I shall never forget the desolation of the road, piles of bricks which had been homes, fire service hoses and water everywhere, and an unearthly silence. . . . One house had been blown open and we could look at a table with everything set for a meal.'

The wife of a fireman who rescued a woman buried under a block of flats on Streatham Hill remembers the impact the experience made on her husband:

She had a fearsome wound in her back but was bright and alert. As it was difficult to get the stretcher round some bends . . . my husband used his lanyard to tie round her legs and the stretcher so she would not fall. She kept assuring them she was all right but when they got out to the ambulance she had quietly died. My husband was very much affected by this courageous woman's untimely death. When reporting back to the fire station . . . for 'mislaying' the lanyard he was charged ninepence!

Although the fire brigade usually got there first, the other Civil Defence services were never far behind. To rival the NFS's system of look-out posts the City of Westminster set up a network of observation posts on tall buildings such as the tower of the Victoria Coach Station, the London Transport offices in Broadway and the Regent Palace Hotel, near Piccadilly, and the moment an incident was reported a mobile column, containing an ambulance and a light rescue party, was sent to the scene. Other boroughs were equally efficient, well meriting the Prime Minister's tribute in his major speech of 2 August, that 'the working of all the Civil Defence services, men and women, has been a model.'

The very keenness of all concerned led to some absurd 'boundary disputes' and on at least one occasion, the *ARP News* reported, a casualty had had 'to wait whilst an argument went on as to whether he should be conveyed in that ambulance or taken out of it and put in another ambulance belonging to the opposite area.' On the whole, however, cooperation between the different branches of Civil Defence was excellent and the NFS, after hours of patient labour, would readily hand over to the experts of the Heavy Rescue Squads the privilege of finally extricating some trapped casualty. The rescue men, civilians to the core, usually uneducated and fiercely independent, were a race apart from the highly disciplined firemen, and were held in enormous affection by the public. Admiral Evans knew many of them by their nicknames and referred to these 'big, heavy, bold chested men drawn from the National Union of Building Operatives as his "special pets".' Their work, his biographer commented, called for great physical strength, 'moving steel girders, shifting great blocks of masonry, tunnelling through debris,' but also patience and delicacy of touch, and an intuitive understanding of how a damaged building was likely to behave.

All too often an incautious movement, or a mere shifting of the rubble, let loose a fatal deluge of debris. A senior fire guard in Paddington witnessed a particularly sad case in Westbourne Square, where, after hearing a child's cry from the basement, the wardens tore frantically at the ruins of a house until more earth and timber fell into the space below, followed by silence. 'The father of the missing girl went berserk and attacked the nearest person to him, . . . a newspaper reporter . . . taking a picture of someone holding a Union Jack on a mound of rubble. . . . The small girl was his only child.'

Many rescue stories had happier endings. One wartime sol-

dier from Morden feels eternally grateful to an extraordinarily
small rescue man who dragged out his wife 'trapped for seven
to eight hours from the waist down. . . . The only way to get
through was no wider or rounder than a sewer pipe' but a
volunteer 'only about four and a half feet tall and thin' was
found, and succeeded in bringing her out alive. The Streatham
fireman mentioned earlier remembers another woman 'rescued
from a perfect personal shelter, an upside-down bath with her
still in it, which we found under a mound of bricks.' And every
Civil Defence worker could tell of someone who had taken
absurd risks – or, more commonly, expected someone else to
take them – to regain some comparatively trivial possession.
One fire guard remembers yielding to the pleas of a woman in
Paddington to retrieve a bottle she had been saving for a
victory celebration. 'I managed,' he remembers, 'to get so far
up the stairs, but saw the floor in the room was so rickety that
. . . I decided that my life was worth more than a bottle of
port.'

The commonest type of rescue operation involved people
trapped in the fallen ruins of a house, but occasionally families
were marooned on the upper storeys of tall buildings, when a
flying-bomb had hit them above ground level. A typical instance occurred in Battersea just after 7 o'clock on the morning
of 5 August when, in the words of the post warden's 'Incident
Report', a V-1 'exploded on the roof of Albert Palace Mansions, Blocks 81–90 and 91–100 causing a number of casualties
and damage . . . making it difficult for occupants to get out of
the flats.'

With a good muster of wardens and police I despatched to the outer
perimeter of the incident wardens to search all property and this area
was soon cleared of casualties and uninjured people sent to Rest
Centre, leaving the Rescue Parties and N.F.S. to rescue the trapped
casualties at the main seat of damage. Two splendid jobs were done.
Mr and Mrs F. of 95 Albert Palace Mansions were trapped and badly
injured on the 3rd floor with the staircase gone, they had to be got
down by ladder, also the lowering of a stretcher case from the top
floor by the block and fall of the N.F.S. turntable ladders. . . . All
services had worked with the very best of co-operation so that all
casualties were cleared in about two hours from the fall of bomb. . . .
One outstanding incident was the work of Dr Elsie Boynton . . . who

after attending casualties in and out of debris, went up the turntable ladder to the top of the five storey building to aid a badly injured casualty, which I consider a splendid feat for a lady.*

Undoubtedly there was a good deal of looting of damaged premises. One South-East London man recalls a relation of a man who had been killed recognizing his watch being offered for sale, and it was said in the district that the rescue men took it in turns to be sent to bombed public houses because of the pickings to be gained. 'One leader of a rescue squad opened up an antique shop shortly after the war. Tongues wagged.' A fourteen-year-old boy living at Woodford Bridge, who was visiting some damaged houses, was embarrassed to come 'face to face with a special constable stuffing a handful of the old white £5 notes into his pocket. He said, "What the bloody hell are you up to?" I said "Nothing", turned round and ran.'

Protecting bomb-damaged premises briefly provided the Home Guard with a useful occupation. His unit, remembers one man who was then an engineering student in Surrey, spent much of its time 'guarding bombed premises against looters and the police, while the police guarded the same premises against looters and the Home Guard. Relations were rather strained between the two forces and we did hear tales of them coming to blows near Clapham Junction.'

If the firemen were usually first at an incident, the police were seldom far behind, and, just as in peacetime, they tended to get landed with the disagreeable jobs which had defeated other civilians. The official history of *The Metropolitan Police at War* singled out 'as an illustration of the odd things that happened' an occasion in a south-eastern suburb when blast blew over four hives of bees, which attacked an old man lying cut by glass from his wrecked greenhouse. 'Various people tried to go to his assistance, but they were all driven back by the bees. Then arrived a police sergeant.' He 'went straight out in the garden, lifted the old man (by now unconscious) on to his shoulder and carried him to the nearest road. In the hospital . . . 132 bee stings were removed from the sergeant . . . The old man, unhappily, died.'

---

*Dr Boynton later received the MBE 'for gallantry at flying bomb incidents'. Her heroism that morning is still remembered locally.

The Wardens Were Wonderful

'The wardens were wonderful.' This tribute, given in almost identical words by many people whose homes were damaged, speaks for itself. Grumbled about in the past as officious enforcers of the black-out, these maids-of-all-work of the Civil Defence services now rapidly regained, and retained, the respect and affection of their neighbours. From the very beginning the wardens' service, on which all the others depended, coped admirably with the new challenge. A schoolgirl in Harrow, whose home was damaged on the very first Sunday of the attack, as already described, was deeply impressed at the practical help that was rapidly forthcoming:

A couple of ARP men came along . . . asking at each house if there was anybody injured needing treatment. They came in and examined my grandpa and about half an hour later an ambulance called for him and also a lady ten houses away. . . .*

The ARP men came back again, this time with a loudhailer announcing that a meeting was to be held in three-quarters of an hour at the bottom of the road. . . . At the meeting . . . the ARP man with the loudhailer climbed onto a kitchen table that had been carried into the road. He said that everything was being done to reconnect gas and electricity supplies and it was hoped repairs would be finished by black-out time. He then asked for a show of hands indicating elderly or disabled people who could not sleep in the surface shelter bunks. Then he formed a group of volunteers from reasonably undamaged homes to offer accommodation.

This was precisely the type of help the wardens' service had been designed to provide. Commonsense and good humour were the essential qualities required, not expert knowledge, though some skill as a handyman did not come amiss. One warden in Orpington remembers seeing notices on display at the local railway stations, 'Wardens with hammers', which meant that any who were free were needed to patch up damaged houses. His own speciality was isolating gas mains in such property, his record being 'some thirty houses . . . disconnected in one road in one night's shift.'

---

*This informant's grandfather had to walk with a stick ever afterwards. The woman neighbour lost the sight of an eye. For a fuller account of the incident, in which 270 homes were damaged and two people killed, see page 287.

One of the most time-consuming tasks was tracing missing people, and here the wardens received invaluable help from the Women's Voluntary Services, which early in 1944 had introduced a system of incident inquiry points near the site of every major incident. The IIP was set up in the nearest available premises with a telephone, often a bombed-out shop, but if necessary operated on the pavement. It was usually in operation within half an hour, with two or three trained WVS collating the 'location cards' listing residents in the affected houses with the records of casualties sent to hospitals or known to be safe. One person in each team tended to specialize in breaking the news to inquirers that a friend or relation was dead. 'The usual reaction . . .' the WVS's historian discovered, 'was dazed disbelief.'

By the end of August, 778 incident inquiry points had been set up in London alone; Streatham had at one time seven in use simultaneously. After the 'shopping' incident at Lewisham Market,* which caused 361 known casualties, the local WVS had an IIP in operation within ten minutes on a table borrowed from a coffee stall, but eleven days later some of the fifty-nine dead were still not identified, including several Irish labourers known, even to their foreman, only by their first names. Here, as at other places, the WVS had the infuriating experience of trying to trace 'casualties' who had simply gone away. One couple turned up, bronzed and cheerful, eight days after the rescue men had started to dig for them, from a holiday at Bournemouth.

The points tended, too, to be used as unofficial safety-deposits for valuables, and as sources of help of all kind. One WVS, in the East End, was asked urgently for a blanket for a policeman, stripped naked by blast, who 'was hiding behind a wall clad only in his boots.' A piano-dealer in Greenwich was particularly anxious about his stock. 'At his special request, two hefty members of the WVS lowered him through a window, holding him by his legs while he tried to play "God Save the King" on each piano to see whether it still worked.'

The flying-bombs presented the WVS, and other organizations which provided emergency catering, with new problems.

*See page 185.

324

Partly because of the fear of looting, most families moved back into their damaged homes even when these lacked cooking facilities, so that the emphasis was now placed on taking food to those affected by bombing rather than catering for them communally. The Queen's Messenger convoys, designed to feed a whole blitzed city, were now split up into smaller units and the WVS also 'distributed meals in urns and insulated containers carried in box tricycles or even prams.' The conventional mobile canteen was still in great demand, especially to provide refreshments for ARP workers; indeed the scale of attack on any district could almost have been measured out if not in coffee spoons then by teacups. In Beckenham alone the WVS served 101,407 cups of tea, an average of nearly 1500 per flying-bomb. One WVS member from Kensington regularly took shelter still clutching her teacloth. 'Have you got your cloth, Missie?' the rescue men would call, as she dived for cover.

Other canteen drivers and helpers were employed by local authorities, like those honoured at a Civil Defence 'supper and social' at Sidcup in late August. Here the driver of the mobile canteen was presented by the rescue men with 'a plaque made from a piece of wood recovered from a bombed site, upon which the following verse had been inscribed':

> Rescue work in broken soil,
> And dust like smoke of Hades,
> Refreshing tea renewed our toil –
> 'Thank you, Canteen Ladies!'

28

A CHORUS OF VEHEMENT GLOATING

The German press . . . became a wild chorus of vehement gloating.

H. E. Bates, in unpublished history of the flying-bomb, written *c*. October 1944

'Morale has reached a new low, such as has not been observed since the outbreak of war. Among the masses sayings are common, such as "The wagon has gone off the track. It got stuck in the mud".' That report, submitted in March 1944 by the Nazi security service in Munich, illustrated well enough why the Nazi leaders needed to demonstrate that victory was still attainable. By now so often had the Germans been promised *Wunderwaffe* – wonder weapons – that the term had been shortened in conversation to *Wuwa*. Increasingly, however, as month followed month, the public wondered if they would ever arrive. Goebbels, as the minister responsible for assistance to the bombed cities, had, he told a subordinate, received 'hundreds of letters which often contained the one question only: "Where is the retaliation?" ' Even the legend of the 'Miracle of the Führer', which in his other capacity as promoter of propaganda Goebbels had sedulously fostered, was by the summer of 1944 wearing thin.

Now at last the doubters had their answer. At 3 p.m. on Friday, 16 June, a communiqué from Hitler's headquarters announced that 'Last night and this morning Southern England and the built-up area of London were subjected to a new type of explosive missile with a heavy charge.' The Berlin evening newspapers welcomed the news, the German overseas press service reported, 'with headlines of gigantic dimensions which, in the case of *Nachtausgabe* cover one third of the whole front

page. . . . "We give in, in this hour," ' declared the newspaper,
' "to feelings of hatred and retaliation against the enemy, who
wanted to destroy the Germans by terror and unscrupulous
barbarity.' The rival paper, *DAZ* (*Deutsche Allgemeine Zeitung*) was equally emphatic. 'The Führer had said often and
plainly enough that retaliation would come for crimes committed against German civilians. . . . First reports from Britain
indicate terrified surprise at the coming of the punishment.'

The Germans had always regarded broadcasting as an even
more important medium of propaganda than the press and all
through the afternoon of Friday, 16 June, listeners were promised a major announcement at 7.30 that evening. This proved
to be a ten-minute talk by Hans Fritzsche, the Director-General of the German radio information service. After quoting Morrison's statement, Fritzsche went on:

The German people are following with intense interest the unfolding
of an action for which they have worked and waited so long. . . . We
know the enemy professed that he did not believe in the employment
of new weapons. Here it must be recalled that Goebbels repeatedly
declared that retribution was no mere propaganda bluff, but a hard
military fact of the future. Many a man in Germany may have doubted
this statement; many a man may have been glum or impatient in these
long months of trial, but the German High Command has never
allowed itself to be guided in its decision by consideration of such
displeasure or prestige. . . . The German Command has . . . found
the right moment for the exploitation of at least one of the fruits of
the German inventive spirit. . . . Since we are speaking from Berlin
. . . we cannot refrain from giving expression . . . to the satisfaction
which fills us Germans. . . . After months of enduring and suffering,
we proudly note the fact . . . that we can also hit back.

The argument that the Germans had been forced to use the
new weapon by British brutality, dominated all the broadcasts
that evening from German-controlled transmitters. 'The fundamentally good-hearted and morally inspired Führer,' Oslo
Radio told the oppressed Norwegians, had wanted 'to attack
only military objectives. . . . It is not our Führer's fault that in
the present deadly crisis he has no other choice but to resort
to this weapon. . . . Tens of thousands of German civilian dead
cry for revenge from their graves.'

Lord Haw-Haw, broadcasting to Great Britain in English at

10.30 p.m., was in sparkling form. His British listeners, he said confidently, were not discussing the battle in Normandy that evening, but a very different subject. 'It is hardly possible to treat a weapon of this kind as an indecent expression which is not to be mentioned in polite society.' They should remember 'that it was not Germany who started the bombing war and . . . any complaint that they have to make must be addressed to 10 Downing Street, and nowhere else.'

At lunchtime on Saturday, 17 June, the German public were treated for the first time to the sound of a flying-bomb in flight, recorded, so it was said, by 'an ear-witness' on the Channel coast, but what the Propaganda Ministry really needed was hard news of the damage and casualties caused in Great Britain. In the absence of such facts the German press and radio had to rely on their imagination, some of their wilder flights of fancy being derisively reprinted in the British press. 'German radio,' reported the *Daily Mail* on its front page on Saturday, 17 June, 'said last night that dense smoke clouds cover wide stretches of Southern England . . . reported by German reconnaissance planes.'

Those 'dense smoke clouds' were to prove invaluable in the next few weeks as no aerial photographs appeared in the German press. On Tuesday, 20 June, *The Times* informed its surprised readers that, according to the Germans, 'The roads leading from London to the country are choked with refugees. Only few have motors. Most take their pots and pans with them on hand-drawn carts and other improvised vehicles.' Only occasionally did a news story contain a grain of truth. Big Ben, it was announced on 18 June, was no longer being broadcast 'live', which was true enough, but not because it had been knocked out by a V-1 four days earlier. The true reason was that the microphones sited there would pick up explosions in the vicinity. So many waterworks had been destroyed, the Germans also claimed, that the use of hosepipes for watering gardens was forbidden. This latter statement too, was true, though the real explanation lay not in the V-1s but in the drought. It must have come as an even greater relief to the German Propaganda Ministry than to British editors when it became possible for the latter to publish details of recent incidents, providing the Germans at last with a factual basis for their fictions.

Since the British Ministry of Information was so often criticized, and Goebbels's Ministry of Propaganda has usually been considered superlatively efficient, it is worth remarking here that from the first the British won the propaganda battle of the V-1s, as ultimately they won the military battle, hands down. An essentially impressive story, which reflected enormous credit on German scientific ingenuity and production capacity, was ruined by ridiculous overstatement and totally unnecessary falsehood which merely enabled British editors to provide light relief to what was at first a grim tale of military defeat. The Germans committed the cardinal fault of telling lies that were easily disprovable. The London *Daily Telegraph* reported, for instance, on 6 July how the German Overseas News Agency had quoted a leading war reporter who claimed to have flown over London. 'A dome of searchlights goes up over the sea of houses and the guns roar out in fury against the flying death.' All very impressive except that the capital's guns had ceased to fire a whole fortnight before, so that the description merely confirmed the Germans' lack of informants in England.

Another interesting example of the Germans' lack of understanding of the British came when they failed to realize that to criticize the royal family, and especially the King, was bound to be counter-productive. On 18 June listeners to the German service in English to North America were told that Buckingham Palace had been badly damaged and that 'the Royal Family suffered no injury because they had been evacuated to the safety of a secluded castle in Scotland.' The departure of the King himself had already been reported in a dramatic news flash, stating that 'It has just been revealed that King George . . . has left London, for reasons of personal safety. His destination is not known.'* Three weeks later, on 5 July, the Nazi Party newspaper, the *Völkischer Beobachter (People's Observer)* declared that the King had advised his subjects: 'The only thing to do when one sees a robot bomb is to throw

---

*For a correct account of one of the King's experiences at this period, see page 132.

oneself flat on the ground and await the result' – sensible advice, presumably delivered from his Scottish retreat.

People in the occupied countries were subjected to an equal torrent of lies. 'In London,' a speaker on Radio Paris told his listeners on 19 June, 'life has practically come to a standstill. . . . The rain of explosive meteors is continuing almost without interruption.' The Belgian Home Service, in French, on 24 June, painted an equally lurid picture. 'Since the "ghost planes" began to shower on Southern England . . . the roads to the north and eastern countryside have been choked with panic-stricken evacuees. Seven million Londoners are today forced to resort to camping.'

Audiences outside Europe were subjected to an equal torrent of lies. Of twenty-three items broadcast by 'Station Debunk', a German 'black' transmitter masquerading as an impartial neutral, to North America in a seventeen-minute news bulletin on 18 June, all but two concerned the V-1s. 'Panic and consternation reign in the city,' it was claimed. 'In one section of London . . . not a single building is standing. A high-ranking staff officer admitted to our Scout that the German pilotless aircraft have thrown the entire supply system of the invasion out of gear.'

The real aim of such broadcasts was clearly to make American families feel uneasy about their 'boys' serving in Europe:

The night before last the U.S. Army suffered the heaviest casualties so far. . . . One of the robot machines crashed into the railroad station in London and exploded just when the station was crowded with U.S. soldiers. It is estimated that between 3,000 and 4,000 U.S. soldiers were killed. . . . American Red Cross nurses informed our Scout that some of the U. S. soldiers were torn to pieces so badly . . . that they could not be identified . . . Soldiers of the U.S. army stationed in London complain bitterly that they are ordered to go out and rescue English civilians while German pilotless aircraft are exploding overhead.

Equally outrageous lies were broadcast to other parts of the world and the further from England the target audience the more outrageous the exaggerations tended to become: the Indians, for example, were told that 'There are fires everywhere between Kingston and Bromley' and 'Smoke miles high over Southampton and Portsmouth.'

A Chorus of Vehement Gloating

The flying-bombs also offered the Germans a last-minute chance to convince neutral countries that Germany might after all win the war. Picture displays were arranged in German information offices in neutral capitals, though fatally handicapped by the lack of reconnaissance photographs; even the picture magazine, *Illustrierte Beobachter* was reduced to printing an artist's impression of a V-1 striking a London railway terminus. In this visual publicity battle the honours again went to Great Britain. According to *The Times* of 6 July, a German display of such drawings in Lisbon was attracting far smaller crowds than a rival British exhibition of photographs of German targets wrecked by Bomber Command, with captions stressing that these were the result of aimed bombing, not the 'blind bombardment of the entire countryside'.

In mid-July, a party of twenty neutral journalists was taken on a tour of the launching sites, but the result was merely to remind their governments of the need to disclaim any responsibility for the damage. Already on 5 July the Spanish government had been at pains to deny Russian accusations that Hitler's secret weapons were produced in Spanish factories; a leading Swedish newspaper expressed fears that a report that a German missile (probably a rocket) which had exploded near Kalmar had contained ball-bearings inscribed 'Made in Sweden' might lead to reprisals by the United States.

The spearhead of the attack on British morale was Lord Haw-Haw, supported by the 'black' radio stations supposedly operated by dissident Britons, though no one apart from the BBC's Monitoring Service could actually hear them. This was an opening shot, of the New British Broadcasting Station, at 10.30 p.m. on Saturday, 17 June:

There is a general and very natural feeling among the people that the government has failed seriously in an emergency which ought to have been foreseen. At least Mr Morrison should have been able to state a clear policy in the matter of sirens, although it seems to be a characteristic of this government that it can't state a clear policy on any subject. Mr Churchill ought not only to have foreseen that the Germans would make use of some such weapon, but should also have made sure of adequate counter-measures.

When, on 6 July, Churchill's speech lifted the veil of secrecy on the V-1s' effects, Radio National, another 'black' station, shrewdly picked on another point where the government was vulnerable, its delay in introducing evacuation:

From his [Churchill's] statement we learn that it is only now – three weeks after the first flying bombs fell on London – that an attempt is being made to help those who have nothing to keep them in the danger zone to leave it. It is quite obvious that had these measures been taken from the first, a number of those who are among the 11,000 casualties would have escaped death or injury. Indeed, as Churchill admits that he was fully aware of the danger last October, it becomes even more extraordinary that no measures for the civil population's security were taken until three weeks after the beginning of the attacks.

The Germans' third 'black' station, Workers' Challenge, claimed to speak for the poorer part of the population. This talk, delivered in a proletarian accent on 24 July, was a fair specimen of its output:

The bosses have their houses in the country, outside the present range of the new weapons. They haven't to worry about the problem of evacuation and, what's more, they've been allowed to draw plenty of petrol for the purpose of moving themselves and their goods out of the danger zone. You notice there's no more talk about the buzz-bomb being a propaganda weapon. Now all over the country people are saying that Morrison created false hopes. He's rather a hard nut to crack. But while at the beginning of the war he was pretty popular with a large section of the workers, he is now one of the most unpopular men in the country.

By far the most important target for Goebbels and his minions was the German people itself, as the Air Ministry's historian of the flying-bomb, H. E. Bates, pointed out later that year:

It was meant not only to blast and discourage the enemy but to comfort and encourage the friend . . . to inject spirit into a German national morale that had grown flabby under long defeat. . . . It was the weapon of hope; of 'hang on a little longer and we will give you victory'. All this was clearly shown by the instantaneous reaction of the German press. It at once went mad with national excitement. It became a wild chorus of vehement gloating.

Perhaps because, in his heart of hearts, he knew the war was lost, Goebbels showed a curious lack of assurance in presenting the V-1 to the German people, apparently uncertain whether to play up the weapon's significance, or to damp down the enthusiasm it was bound to create. On the minister's personal insistence the first reference to the flying-bomb had consisted solely of a single 'throwaway' sentence in the routine daily communiqué. 'The mere fact in its very sobriety . . . is going to create an extraordinary effect on the German people,' he told his regular morning conference that day. At this stage he even discouraged talk of *Vergeltung*, and warned against arousing premature hopes that, contrary to all expectation, victory was again in sight.

But all attempts at restraint were soon abandoned, and on 23 June German radio for the first time referred to the new weapon as the V-1, which henceforward became its official name. Some rather heavy-handed Germanic jokes followed, as to whether Churchill would continue to make the 'V' sign on visiting devastated areas. (The British riposte was to report that German soldiers were saying that 'V-1' stood for '*Versager Eins*' 'Dud No.1'.)

Even when 'revenge' had become respectable, Goebbels's uncertainty led to some notable muddles. On 27 June a highly coloured description of operations on a V-1 site issued by the German Telegraph Service was hurriedly withdrawn. The reason was not, it seems likely, the appalling opening sentence – ' "You devilish hell-hound", said Lieut. P., patting the nozzle of the explosive missile, "do your job thoroughly and blow right into their china shop" ' – but the closing passage, describing the secrecy enforced during training: 'To have to go home to a demolished town, stand before your own burnt-out house, your wife and children and not be able to say a word of all that was being done in answer – this enforced silence was harder than the work.' The censor who killed the story was surely well advised. There was not much here to raise anyone's morale.

Such mistakes apart, launching-site stories continued to be popular with the Germans and in July a graphic account of the launching of a missile, complete with 'actuality' sound, was broadcast over German radio. 'The hour of retribution has arrived,' proclaimed the commentator in solemn tones, and proceeded to give a step-by-step account of the firing procedure, punctuated with the noise of the rocket motor being fired. By the end of July similar scenes were appearing on German newsreels.

What effect *did* the launching of the flying-bomb offensive have on German public opinion? Those already hostile to the Nazis were unimpressed. 'Well, the secret weapon didn't shake a thing,' commented one Berlin woman in her diary on Sunday, 18 June. 'It hasn't even upset the programme of dance music from the Savoy Hotel in London.'

Among those loyal to the Nazis, however, the results were all that Goebbels had hoped. This was the reaction of one thirty-seven-year-old former clerk who in 1944 was serving in the army in Denmark:

We were almost crazy with joy when we heard that this first secret weapon . . . was at last being used against Britain. We saw again how the Führer had kept his word. It was now only a matter of his wonderful intuition when the final onslaught was going to take place to force the proud British on to their knees and make a vast desert out of their country. The morale of the whole people was lifted tremendously.

Even more important was the effect on German troops in contact with the enemy. 'All the time new evidence reached us that the rise in German morale was being maintained,' one of those then engaged in directing the Allies' psychological warfare campaign has written. 'Fantastic rumours circulated among German soldiers on the fighting fronts. In Italy, as the questioning of prisoners revealed, . . . troops heard that London had been turned into an inferno, that two and a half million Britons had been killed and that Britain would soon have to capitulate.' Even in Normandy, where the troops were struggling to contain the Allied build-up, the V-1s made a great impression. 'It cannot be doubted,' wrote General Eisenhower, 'that the governmental propaganda on V-weapons had a considerable effect in strengthening morale in these early stages of the campaign.'

What interested the German commanders was the flying-bomb's military potential and at a conference at Hitler's advanced headquarters at Margival near Soissons, on 17 June, both Field-Marshal von Rundstedt, Commander-in-Chief in the West, and his immediate subordinate, Field-Marshal Rommel, urged that the attack should be re-directed against the Allied bridgehead and the invasion ports. Their pleas fell on deaf ears. Hitler rambled off into a long monologue, repeating that by bombarding London he could 'make it eager for peace'. General Heinemann, who was also present, had to admit that the flying-bomb's accuracy, within nine to twelve miles, was inadequate for military purposes, an opinion strikingly confirmed soon after Hitler had left, when a defective flying-bomb landed near the Führer's air-raid shelter. The German commanders seem rapidly to have recognized that the flying-bomb was a military irrelevance, which could irritate the enemy but not defeat him. When, on 20 July, General von Kluge, commanding Army Group B, received a signal from Berlin reporting Hitler's death, his response was prompt. 'I would like to order a cessation of the V-1s immediately.' But Hitler had escaped once again, and next day Goebbels broadcast on 'The Question of Retaliation'. At first, he declared, the British government had dishonestly minimized the effect of the V-1s; now it was 'dramatising things in a sentimental manner in order to evoke pity from the world.'

In the following month, August, the Germans began to use the V-1 as, quite literally, a propaganda vehicle, by fitting some machines with a load of pamphlets and an explosive device which scattered them as the missile approached the end of its journey. Such leaflets are now very rare as they were collected up by the police, not because of their possible effect – though they were skilfully written and persuasive – but because references to their arrival in the press might have given the Germans a clue where particular V-1s had landed.

The first such leaflets known to have reached this country turned up at Stone and Smarden in Kent in August 1944. A third crop was found at Frant, in Sussex, on 5 November, one – just as the government had anticipated – being reproduced in the *News Chronicle* two days later. A fourth set was reported from Great Bentley, Essex, on 25 November, and many copies of a special 'Christmas edition' were gathered up in Lancashire on 24 December. Apart from this last, which will be described later,* the leaflets, though their detailed contents varied, had

*See page 460

the same format, consisting of four pages, about eight inches by six, and were clearly modelled on the language and layout of a leaflet dropped by Bomber Command on German cities, which showed Hitler standing smiling among a sea of corpses. The first leaflet found at Stone carried a photograph of air-raid victims in Berlin, following an RAF raid of November 1943, with the caption: 'Do you like that? You may not, in a few months' time.' The Smarden leaflet, discovered on 28 August, was equally gruesome, containing a series of photographs taken in Cologne and Hamburg in June and July 1943, and placing the whole blame for the escalation of the air war against civilians on the British government:

As early as 1933 and several times in 1934 Adolf Hitler suggested an international pact with a view to make an air war on the civilian population impossible. The British government turned down his proposals. On May 10, 1940, the RAF began the air war against civilians with a raid on the open town of Freiburg, although the German air force had never carried out a single raid on a town in the British Isles . . .* After that more and more German towns were bombed by the Bomber Command.

As late as November the Germans were still using variations on the original leaflet. They also produced an even more ambitious version, 'The Other Side', which crammed into its four pages a mixture of easily digestible news items, photographs, cartoons and even an editorial. Like the earlier pamphlets 'The Other Side' was almost a carbon copy of a propaganda magazine with the same title dropped from Allied bombers since September 1942.

The leaflet made the most of the military and economic advantages of the V-1, pointing out it cost £600 to make a flying-bomb against £60,000 to build a Lancaster,** so that 'For the price of one Lancaster Germany can send over to England 100 V-1s.'

The final touch was provided by 'The V Puzzle' which exploited the British love of crosswords:

---

*This reference must have caused much amusement in the German Air Ministry. Freiburg had been bombed, as the Germans well knew, by the Luftwaffe after an embarrassing navigational error.

**These figures were not quite accurate. See page 474.

A Chorus of Vehement Gloating

The V Puzzle

Clues, across: 1. He is your enemy, too. 7 V 1 is so fast, that it is hard to this. 8. Partly a beverage. 10. This is the beginning of a German victory. 11. We hear that this is a rare commodity in England. 13. This is in Latin. 14. He wants all you've got.

Down: 1. In the case of the air war, he has been bit by V 1. 2. Money but no pence. 3. Men and material intended for Normandy very often finish at the bottom of this. 4. V 1 contains this. 5. Britain has none at inter-Allied conferences. 6. At Tehran, Churchill practically did this before Stalin. 9. First person singular. 10. Two reprisals with nothing in between. 12. Warmongers must this, if England is to be saved. 13. That man.

1		2	3	4		5		6
		7						
8	9					10		
11		12		13				
14								

V 1 is a puzzle for the British Government, and this puzzle is in the form of V 1. If you choose to regard the cross-word merely as an entertainment, no doubt you will get some fun out of it. If you take it seriously you will get more than that – you will find that it contains some very useful advice!

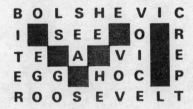

```
B O L S H E V I C
I   S E E   O   R
T E   A   V I   E
E G G   H O C   P
R O O S E V E L T
```

No. 1 of 'The Other Side' was circulated to his colleagues by Herbert Morrison on 11 November. The first known copy of No. 2 was found on 19 November, while others turned up at Radlett, in Hertfordshire, where an eyewitness claimed to have seen a whole 'brown paper parcel' of them, which then mysteriously disappeared. This edition included the usual horrifying pictures of mutilated corpses, but this time they were

337

allegedly the victims of the Russians who had occupied their village. At least four more issues were produced, although it is not certain whether they were dropped on Great Britain, and in all of them the menace from the east had become the dominant theme. One included a cartoon showing English and American soldiers pulling into position a huge shrouded statue labelled 'Freedom'. When unveiled, it revealed an ape-like Stalin, brandishing a pistol.

29

AN EYE FOR AN EYE

*Vansittartism is sweeping Britain and the Old Testament
demand, an eye for an eye, is heard on every hand.*

West London Press, 7 July 1944

'The flying bomb is a weapon literally and essentially indiscriminate in its nature, purpose and effect. The introduction by the Germans of such a weapon obviously raises some grave questions, upon which I do not propose to trench today.' This was the only reference to the prospect of retaliation during the Prime Minister's speech to the House of Commons on 6 July, but it masked a vigorous controversy behind the scenes.

The theme of reprisals, revealed one Member of Parliament in the debate which followed Churchill's statement, was a recurrent one in letters from his constituents, and behind the scenes, Herbert Morrison, so often the spokesman for the ordinary civilian, was raising the same question. In a paper circulated to his Cabinet colleagues on 27 June the Home Secretary frankly confessed his anxieties about the threat to morale.

The public have so far withstood pretty well the growing loss of life and property and general inconvenience of flying bomb attacks. They may have been buoyed up by the belief that . . . in a short period the RAF would have destroyed the sources of mischief. This is proving a slow and doubtful process. . . . This is not 1940–41 . . . and . . . people are asking, 'Where is this air superiority they talk about?' . . . I have done and will do everything to hold up their courage and spirit – but there is a limit, and the limit will come. . . .

There has not yet been time to judge the effects on our soldiers overseas . . . but . . . jeering references to the impotence of the greatest military alliance in history to destroy . . . a menace almost within sight of the capital which it is in process of annihilating . . .

and a growing uncertainty as to the fate of those at home are, in combination, calculated to have a bad effect on the morale of the troops. . . .

The citizens of London have had their full share of this war's troubles: they are entitled to every active protection we can give them.

So much for the problem. But what was the answer? Morrison pointedly recalled 'The Prime Minister's threat of a year ago to "drench the enemy with gas" if he began the use of that method of attack. . . . The knowledge that this was not an idle threat,' commented the Home Secretary, 'may explain why, so far, there has been no gas warfare.' Was there not here a lesson for the present emergency?

I would ask for consideration of the following possibilities . . .

1. The maximum action to destroy the platforms, supply sites, sources of production and transportation.
2. Harrassing bombing over the area of firing by day and night; also naval bombardment.
3. Military action in the Pas de Calais and Dieppe areas with a view to killing the evil at its source; commando raids.
4. A threat to Germany to bomb to destruction as and when opportunity offers their smaller towns, if this utterly indiscriminate bombing does not cease; or the use of gas.

The Prime Minister can hardly have had time to consider Herbert Morrison's paper when, on 1 July, he circulated an even franker note of his own:

1. I am by no means sure that our guns, airplanes and balloons will be able to prevent a steady stream of projectiles, growing bigger and faster, from falling on London and other parts of Southern England for many months to come. In wet and cloudy weather all our defences are largely negligible . . . Accordingly I suggest that we should address ourselves to the question of reprisals. . . .
2. I suggest that a list should be prepared of 100 German towns of between two and five thousand inhabitants, well spread over the whole of Germany; that ten of these towns should be destroyed to begin with, and that thereafter one should be destroyed each day for every day's continuance of the present flying-bomb attacks. The inhabitants of all the towns would have standing notice to quit their inhabitations, otherwise we could take no

responsibility for their suffering injury. If the weather prevented action for two or three days, the account should be made level as soon as possible. These small townships are probably ill-equipped with shelters, flak and fire brigades.

At the 'longest-ever' Cabinet meeting on 3 July, already described, the Prime Minister repeated what he had already said in his circulated paper and 'there was general agreement that the question raised by the Prime Minister should be considered.' The only speaker whose contribution was recorded was, however, emphatically opposed to retaliation. 'The Secretary of State for Air,' summed up the Cabinet Secretary, 'pointed out that already 50% of our air strength was being used to counter the flying-bomb attacks and it would be extremely difficult to spare additional resources from the Battle of France. Again, . . . there was grave risk that attacks of the kind indicated by the Prime Minister would lead to . . . the shooting of any air crews who fell into German hands.'

On the following day, when the Cabinet met again, Churchill returned to the subject, pointing out 'that a considerable proportion of the letters received from the general public urged that counter measures should be taken against Germany', and later that day Herbert Morrison sent a personal note to the Prime Minister. This suggested five possible alternatives, which included using 'flak from landing craft to bring the flying-bombs down on their way across the Channel', employing 'oil and phosphorous bombs' against the launching sites, flooding the areas which contained them or aiming at them 'gliders filled with bombs and high explosives'. Morrison's own favourite, however, seems to have been his fifth alternative, held in reserve ever since 1940:

Gas: Would it be wise to saturate and resaturate the Pas de Calais area concerned with gas? There are two possible objections –

(a)   There may be some French there: my answer would be that they ought not to be there; and

(b)   – This is more serious – the Germans might retaliate by filling the flying bombs with gas, and this would be annoying to our civilian population.

Morrison's list of countermeasures perhaps confirmed the admission in his previous note that he was no 'expert on military affairs', but he undoubtedly understood better than his colleagues what the ordinary family was feeling. Once, like Churchill, he had been cheered when visiting bombed areas. Now, even on his native heath, in South London, he was, his biographers have recorded, 'often on the receiving end of public anger and loud abuse,' an experience reflected in the final remark in his paper: 'On all sides I have confirmed my hunch that the people are by no means in a good temper.' Churchill, however, merely passed Morrison's paper for comment to Duncan Sandys, who submitted his observations, promptly and concisely, on the following day. 'Flak from landing craft,' he advised, was not on, since land-based guns were more accurate, and 'better results would be obtained by continuing the present practice of leaving the fighters a completely free run over the Channel.' 'Oil and Phosphorus Bombs' were already 'being considered by the Scientific Crossbow Sub-Committee'. 'Flooding' was impracticable, as 'many of the firing points appear to have been sited on high ground' and 'Gliders Filled with High Explosive' were unlikely to be accurate enough, especially against the smaller sites, though 'the possibility of attacking the large sites by means of radio-controlled, heavy bombers, loaded with high explosive, is being considered.' Finally 'The Joint Planning Staff,' Sandys confirmed, 'were yesterday asked to re-examine and report on the use of gas; (i) as a weapon against Crossbow installations, (ii) as a measure of retaliation against Germany. When their report is received, it will be considered by the Chiefs of Staff.'

Here, for practical purposes, the matter rested. At a meeting of the Crossbow Committee, on 18 July, the Prime Minister stated that 'if rocket attacks should develop, he was prepared, after consultation with the United States and the USSR to threaten the enemy with large scale gas attacks in retaliation should such a course appear practicable,' but so far as the V-1 was concerned the idea seems already to have been dropped.

If the government *had* decided to use gas, however, public opinion would overwhelmingly have supported it. William Sansom observed the mood in Westminster. 'The people saw this as destruction at its most wanton. . . . Homes, women, children and old people were openly the slaughter-toys of the

German. So a grim fury was generated that to an extent must have recuperated the shocked spirits of a people who now, after all they had suffered, were faced with renewed and fierce attack . . . and an unpredictable future.' The former librarian of the House of Commons, Hilary St George Saunders, writing in the American magazine *Life*, went even further. 'The flying-bomb,' he declared, 'has accomplished one thing. It has revived the hatred which died away after the Blitz. Now the feeling is back again and the people know that justice without mercy is the only hope of a better world.'

In the House of Commons there was a demand by a Conservative MP for the United Nations to 'regard as war criminals those scientists who have been decorated by Hitler for their skill in devising the flying bomb,' but the Foreign Secretary, Anthony Eden, was made of feebler stuff than his leader. 'I have,' he weakly replied, 'no statement to make on this subject.'

By now, as Churchill's private secretary later admitted, a flood of letters demanding reprisals, many of them 'anonymous and abusive', were reaching the Prime Minister. When on 5 July one Tory knight put down a question suggesting 'giving the German government an ultimatum that unless their latest method of terrorism, the robot plane, ceases within say forty-eight hours, steps will be taken, systematically, immediately, to destroy undefended German towns,' it was, without explanation, withdrawn. It was not till five months later, when, for good or ill, the government had finally set its face against reprisals, that it allowed a similar question, from another Conservative, to appear on the order paper. Hansard records the results:

To ask the Prime Minister, whether he will notify Germany that while they continue their war on our civilians by robots and rockets, we shall bomb German cities such as Dresden, Breslau, Magdeburg and elsewhere.
Mr. Eden: As my Hon. Friend has already been informed, the principle on which our targets in Germany are selected is that of destroying as quickly as possible Germany's power to wage war. There really is no comparison between what they are able to do to us and what we are doing to them.

343

Although MPs regularly pleaded for a secret session, the government insisted that any general discussion of the military aspects of the offensive would not be in the national interest. Frustrated backbenchers from flying-bomb constituencies had to content themselves with harassing ministers on the supply of window-substitute and meeting an unofficial committee of ministers to discuss housing and welfare matters. For once the soap-box orators at Hyde Park, who themselves had a narrow escape from the V-1 which roared across Speakers' Corner before damaging Tyburn Convent at Marble Arch, better reflected popular opinion than MPs. Angry crowds roared approval as they called on the government to pay Germany back in its own coin.

The press, too, was eloquent where Parliament was silent. The *West London Press*, serving by no means the most badly affected part of Greater London, published an outspoken editorial on Friday, 7 July:

The flying bomb is a boomerang. It has driven out any mercy that there might have been in the hearts of people in Southern England. It has steeled them to a fanaticism that bodes ill for the defeated Hun. Vansittartism is sweeping Britain, and the Old Testament demand, an eye for an eye, is heard on every hand. Hitler in very truth has sown a breeze which shall return to him as a whirlwind.

'Vansittartism' was the doctrine that the Germans were by nature a warlike aggressive people, as advanced in Lord Vansittart's book *Black Record* in 1941, when the naive illusion that Germany was populated by 'good Germans' led astray by a few vicious Nazis was still widespread. The *West London Press* at least was immune from such misconceptions. If Germany were treated leniently, the paper warned its readers in a further editorial the following week, she would assuredly threaten world peace for a third time in another twenty-five years. 'The obvious solution to the problem is to sterilise the youthful Germans so that in due time this militaristic race will be extinct as the Dodo.'

Such ideas, fantastic as they may seem now, were openly discussed by otherwise humane people in 1944, so effectively had the Germans succeeded in dragging their opponents down to their own degraded level. And even those who might not have supported so drastic a reaction favoured tougher measures than the government was taking. In Tottenham, at the request of an alderman, a special council meeting was convened for Tuesday, 18 July, to consider a firmly unequivocal motion:

Re Flying Bombs

That having regard to the unceasing menace to the lives and homes of the people of this Borough – occasioned by the avowedly indiscriminate bombing being pursued by the German enemy – this Council hereby urges upon the Government to at once notify Germany's Rulers and Peoples, that so long as this indiscriminate bombing continues the British Air Forces will, each day, effect the complete destruction of such number of German Towns, Cities and Villages, as seems to the British Government appropriate to the occasion. That copies of this Resolution be sent to the Prime Minister, the Deputy Prime Minister, the Secretary of State for Foreign Affairs, the Leader of the Opposition and the National Press.

Although the motion's sponsor claimed, in a letter to the mayor that 'The feeling throughout the District – indeed the Country – is obviously intensely in favour of such a policy,' the motion was defeated, perhaps because Tottenham had so far suffered only two minor incidents and two civilians killed.

As so often, the civilians in 1944 were a good deal more bloodthirsty than the soldiers. The hostility of the Supreme Commander, General Eisenhower, to a policy of reprisals never wavered and he was horrified at the idea of using gas against the launching sites. 'Let's, for God's sake,' he told his deputy, Sir Arthur Tedder, 'keep our eyes on the ball and use some sense.' Eisenhower was under no illusions, however, about the danger the V-1s presented to his men:

The effect of the new weapons was very noticeable upon morale. . . . When in June the allies landed successfully on the Normandy coast, the citizens unquestionably experienced a great sense of relief . . . in the hope of gaining some insurance against future bombings. When the new weapons began to come over London in considerable numbers their hopes were dashed. Indeed the depressing effect of the bombs was not confined to the civilian population; soldiers at the front began again to worry about friends and loved ones at home, and many American soldiers asked me in worried tones whether I could give them any news about particular towns where they had previously been stationed in southern England.

The allocation of Allied air power at this time rested with Air Chief Marshal Tedder and he entirely shared Eisenhower's opinion.

I advised strongly against the idea of reprisals, with which the Prime Minister was toying. Portal [Chief of the Air Staff], too, was disturbed by a proposal for a public announcement that if attacks by flying-bombs persisted, we would retaliate by wiping out certain named towns in Germany. He thought it would be a mistake to enter into what would amount to negotiation with the enemy, for such a course would provide the Germans with invaluable proof that the flying-bombs were achieving success. . . . He did not think that the Germans would alter their decision out of consideration for the population of towns which had no important part to play in the war effort. More-over, to bomb German towns on such a scale would represent a very serious diversion of effort from those objectives connected with Germany's power to sustain the war. The Chiefs of Staff therefore decided [on 5 July] on no immediate action. On reading the record of this discussion, Eisenhowever minuted to me: 'As I have before indicated, I am opposed to retaliation as a method of stopping this business – at least, until every other thing has been tried and failed. Please continue to oppose.'

Retaliation having been rejected as a policy, the British government, rather desperately, turned to diplomacy. Napoleon's famous question 'How many divisions has the Pope?' was conveniently forgotten in the Foreign Office which now set its sights on securing a papal condemnation of the flying-bombs. The British envoy at the Vatican duly translated and sent to London a promising article which appeared in *Osservatore Romano*, on 22 June:

What we are dealing with is an application of the air-arm which accentuates its inherent defects, owing to which its use is regrettably indiscriminate to the detriment of the civilian population. The target area of any piloted plane is never precise, so that the environment of a military objective up to about half a kilometre is endangered, and the civilian, rather than military, area, often received a share of bombing tragedies. . . . The use of this weapon is represented as a symbol of the increasing ferocity of the war, in which the final end – the fraternal reconciliation of the warring nations and co-operation in rebuilding the ruins – has been forgotten.

This tepid contribution to the debate on the morality of the

V-1 was read with little enthusiasm in the Foreign Office. 'Very "fence-sitting",' minuted one official on the file. 'In fact it is more a condemnation of piloted bombing than of pilotless.' It is hard to believe that anyone can really have imagined that the Pope, who had failed to condemn the massacre of millions of Jews, would have been much concerned about the fate of a few thousand British Protestants, but the diplomats persevered. On instructions from London, the British ambassador to the Vatican met the papal under secretary on 10 July, though the results, as he reported, were not very encouraging:

The Under Secretary stated that the Pope was considering whether there was anything he could do, but felt that he had already on various occasions in the past condemned inhuman methods of warfare. I said that . . . the matter was one for the Pope's own decision but his past utterances . . . had little bearing on this latest outrage. The Under Secretary observed that a papal protest would not have the slightest effect on the Germans. I agreed but pointed out that [it] would have an effect on world opinion. I did not, however, urge that the Pope should speak. It is . . . up to him to decide.

Further exchanges proved equally unprofitable, the final one, on 20 July, prompting the disillusioned note by one diplomat: 'The Pope's strictures are like the flying-bomb in their indiscriminate application, and like it are both irritating and ineffective.'

While the Pope failed to speak out, at least one neutral – perhaps with an eye to the future – bravely offered to do so. On 11 July the Venezualan minister in London offered to invite his government to protest against the V-1s on the grounds of their inhumanity, but the Permanent Under Secretary, Sir Alexander Cadogan, regretfully concluded on the following day that such a measure would have little practical effect. Even had it gone ahead it seems sadly unlikely, however, that the German government would have spared British civilians rather than quail before the weight of Venezuela's disapprobation.

30

THE ONLY ANSWER

*The only real and effective answer to the flying bomb . . . in
Harris's view, was to increase the weight of the offensive
against Germany.*

Marshal of the RAF, Lord Tedder, recalling August 1944

To the general public, as Herbert Morrison had pointed out to
the Cabinet, it seemed inconceivable that the Allies, with their
overwhelming strength, could not readily dispose of a hundred
missile launching sites, situated only just across the Channel.
The commanders viewed the situation very differently. Having
got their armies safely ashore, they refused to contemplate any
diversion from a plan drawn up over so many months. Even
Air Chief Marshal Tedder, the 'Morrison' of Supreme Headquarters, with a more sensitive ear for public opinion than his
colleagues, at first misjudged the situation. 'When the first
reports came in, we were inclined at S.H.A.E.F. to treat them
with some detachment,' he later wrote, and the military representatives did not disagree when, at the grandiosely named
staff conference on 16 June, 'Churchill refused to allow these
developments to upset our concentration on the battle in
Normandy.'

On this occasion somewhat contradictory instructions were
in fact given to the commanders concerned, the Supreme Commander, Allied Expeditionary Force, being requested, but not
ordered 'to take all possible steps to neutralise the supply and
launching sites, but only subject to no interference with the
essential requirements of the Battle in France.' This qualifi-
cation in practice left General Eisenhower free to do what he
wished, as he recognized. 'Never once,' he later wrote admir-
ingly, 'did . . . the British leaders urge me to vary any detail
of my planned operations merely for the purpose of eliminating
this scourge.'

At this time there was probably not much that the Allied armies *could* have done, for the forces nearest to the main launching area were bogged down around Caen, 120 miles from Wachtel's headquarters at Saleux and at least seventy from the nearest cluster of sites. In practice, therefore, offensive-defensive measures rested on the light bombers of the Tactical Air Forces, whose primary role was to assist the armies on the ground, and the heavies of the Strategic Bomber Force, whose commanders contended that they were wasted on attacking tiny targets like launching sites, and that the war could be won more quickly by bombing German cities. No one in high places in either the RAF or the USA Air Force, really wanted to know about flying-bomb targets, on which an enormous amount of effort had been expended in the past six months with so little result. Air Chief Marshal Sir Trafford Leigh-Mallory, in command of the two Tactical Air Forces, Air Chief Marshal Sir Arthur Harris, C-in-C of Bomber Command, and his American opposite number, Lieutenant-General Spaatz, had had their disagreements in the past, but on this they were agreed, presenting a united front to Air Chief Marshal Tedder. Tedder, however, was well aware of the need for some response.

By the morning of Friday 18 June the situation was more serious. Eisenhower ruled that the air forces' first priority must now be *Crossbow*. He minuted to me later that day: 'These targets are to take first priority over everything except the urgent requirements of the battle; this priority to obtain until we can be certain that we have definitely gotten the upper hand of this particular menace.'

Even with this authority, little, thanks to 'the vile weather of mid-June', could at first be done, but, wrote Tedder, 'from 23 June the offensive went forward with full vigour . . . though . . . I advised that air action could reduce, but not exterminate, the menace,' since bombing the sites was 'using a sledgehammer for a tintack.' Identifying possible targets was at least easier, however, than it had been before the attack started. Many ramps were in the open and reconnaissance photographs, it was noticed on 20 June, showed 'intermittent scarrings of the ground' for several hundred yards wherever a V-1 had been fired, caused by the steel piston below the missile scraping the

349

ground beneath the launching rails. Other tell-tale signs had been discovered by 4 July, such as 'the blast marks caused by a misfire, when a bomb landed in front of the ramp', a 'clover-leaf scorch mark caused by the gases, which had propelled the piston, escaping from the front and sides of the tube', and 'lorry tracks . . . seen leading from the road, across the fields to the end of the ground scarrings.' Flying-bombs themselves were rarely spotted on the ground, the first on an operational site, at Bellow sur Somme, not being discovered until 28 June.

Finding sites was one thing, destroying them quite another, but whenever the weather permitted, the reconnaissance Mustangs and Mosquitoes ranged far and wide during July over Belgium and South Holland, for fear that the forests and hedgerows of these, too, might house ramps ready to burst into life when those in France were overrun. In France itself two great concentrations of sites were identified, in the area enclosed between the Seine and the Somme, seaward of an imaginary line between Rouen and Amiens, and between the Somme and the Belgian border, in a rough rectangle bounded by Amiens and Lille. A few sites, threatened by the American armies advancing towards Cherbourg, were situated in the Côtentin peninsula and aligned on Plymouth or Bristol, and about a dozen were scattered over Normany between Caen and Rouen, pointing towards Portsmouth and Southampton. Even after the bombardment had began, the Germans continued with their building programme. By late August, in France alone 314 places were being subjected to routine reconnaissance, from once a fortnight to twice a week, and another fifty-four areas were being reported on 'whenever they were covered incidentally'.

Although the method of firing of a V-1 was still not fully understood, it soon became clear that the actual bombardment was coming from the modified sites, known to the interpreters as the Belhamelin sites, after the first one to be identified. Ultimately the Germans constructed 135 of these, of which seventy-seven actually fired V-1s, the rest being bombed or abandoned before they could be used. The interpreters also had to keep watch on the original Bois Carré type ski sites, of which ninety-six were ultimately built, though never used. The

Germans also built five sites code-named 'Hottot' by the Allies, rapidly and correctly assessed as dummies, and a variety of other installations identified by British intelligence as dumps, used for storage, heavy sites, suspected to be both firing points and supply depots, supply sites, believed to hold the immediate reserves of V-1s, and many other structures, identified merely as 'experimental' or 'miscellaneous'.

The obvious targets seemed the modified sites but the Chief of the Air Staff, Air Chief Marshal Sir Charles Portal, realized that knocking them out would be an enormous job and opted instead, with the support of Air Chief Marshal Leigh-Mallory, for bombing the four most vulnerable supply sites. Lord Cherwell, who pointed out that the supply sites had been left unrepaired when attacked earlier, was overruled, and, with the agreement of the War Cabinet, between 13 and 15 June the US Eighth Air Force dropped thousands of bombs on the supply sites in heavy daylight raids. On the following two nights Bomber Command took over, and Air Chief Marshal Harris sent heavy forces to all four targets. Then he rebelled, making the same point as Lord Cherwell: that no proof existed that the Germans were actually using these vast installations. The modified sites, of which seventy had been located by 18 June, were, he believed, worth knocking out, although a really large-scale attack would be needed. In the end both the supply sites and the modified launching sites were attacked, though with no significant effect. This was hardly surprising. We now know, from Colonel Wachtel's War Diary, that by 1 July, only two modified sites had been destroyed, though twenty-two had suffered heavy damage and eighteen some damage. In the next fortnight, another two sites were silenced, sixteen badly damaged, and twenty-one more lightly damaged – a poor return for the 3300 sorties by then flown.

Colonel Wachtel's operations were never restricted by an overall shortage of missiles or ramps but by the fact that the flying-bombs he needed were rarely in the right place. This was a by-product of the Tactical Air Forces' attack on transport: the 'communications' enthusiasts, who held that railway repair sheds and road junctions were worthwhile targets, were proved right. The modified sites, consisting solely of a ramp and square building, had no storage capacity for V-1s, unlike the original ski sites, and constantly had to be supplied by rail or lorry; with Allied fighter bombers shooting at everything that moved, neither trains nor trucks arrived on time. In theory each of Wachtel's modified sites could launch a missile every half-hour. In practice the delay, averaged over the whole regiment, was three times as long, the shortfall being, according to Wachtel, 20 per cent due to 'servicing difficulties', and 80 per cent to shortage of supplies – including vital chemicals, like hydrogen peroxide, as well as of the flying-bombs themselves.

Living in Richmond, and working in Westminster, Dr R. V. Jones hardly needed the reports reaching his desk in the Air Ministry to know that the bombing of the supply sites and the launching sites had failed to reduce the number of V-1s reaching London, and reports arriving from French sources soon confirmed that the 'supply sites' had long ago ceased to merit the name. Wachtel's batteries were, it appeared, being supplied from three large new underground depots, one in a railway tunnel, at Rilly-la-Montagne, south of Rheims, a second in limestone caves at Nucourt, about twenty miles north-west of Paris, and the third and largest, at St Leu d'Esserent, in the valley of the River Oise, about the same distance to the north. Both the last two were heavily attacked by the US Eighth Air Force in the last week of June. At Nucourt, it was later learned, 241 V-1s were buried beyond recovery by the collapse of the cavern's roof, and another fifty-seven were badly damaged. Rilly-la-Montagne was also attacked, by Bomber Command, on 31 July, when the entrance caved in, rendering it useless. The really important target was St Leu. Its caves had been a source of building material for centuries and had given to the surrounding district something of the soft, honey-coloured look of the villages of the English Cotswolds. The caves in the hills on the north side of the flat, mile-wide valley, were still used for stone quarrying, while those to the south had been used before the Germans came for growing mushrooms.

H. E. Bates admirably described the importance of the site:

In the caves of St Leu, the Germans found the perfect home for their flying bomb supply. Over a period of nearly two years, they proceeded to adapt these caves with the greatest efficiency. They built branch-tracks up from the main railway to the cave entrances and even into the caves themselves. . . . They floored the caves, throughout their ten kilometres breadth and depth, with concrete. They built inside them canteens, sleeping and living quarters, and storage compartments for bombs. Outside, at the natural entrances they shored up fissures in the rock with vast structures of reinforced concrete and walls of stone. They piped in water supplies and wired in electric light.

This vast effort involved a wholesale employment of French labour, and members of the Resistance, infiltrated into the work gangs, were able to send back to London detailed plans of the storage galleries. Information also arrived that thirty-seven train loads of flying-bombs had been seen to enter the caves on a single day, and as a single train might – though few did – carry as many as 200, this made a potential total of 7400 missiles accumulated in only twenty-four hours.

The first attack on St Leu was made by the US Eighth Air Force at the end of June, when a good deal of damage was done to the road, river and railway track which ran along the valley; the caves themselves were not seriously affected. To R. V. Jones this seemed 'an ideal case for "Tallboy", the big streamlined bomb developed by Barnes Wallis,' which weighed 12,000 pounds and had such powers of penetration that, only a few days before, one dropped by the famous 617 Squadron, under Wing-Commander Leonard Cheshire, VC, had, in the words of Wallis's biographer, 'bored its way through eighty feet of earth' to block a railway tunnel. At St Leu exceptional accuracy was going to be needed if the solid limestone over the main entrance tunnel were to be pierced and Dr Jones drove out to High Wycombe to discuss the mission with Air Chief Marshal Harris in person. 'For ten minutes or so,' Dr Jones has since written, 'he spoke sheer good sense, saying that he had ordered a raid that same night, and then asked for my comments. I replied that what he had said to me was exactly what I had come to say to him and suggested that the aiming point should be moved some 200 yards south-east.' To this Harris readily agreed and the result of the raid, on the night of 4/5 July, was an awesome demonstration of air power. The main tunnel was blocked, several others collapsed, and those bombs that missed the main target rendered the approach roads impassable. Colonel Wachtel's old adversary, Colonel Walter, Chief of Staff to LXV Army Corps, later described what life was like in the St Leu caves when the bombers had gone. 'You could,' he wrote, 'hear a constant rumbling overhead, and began to feel that the very mountain was on the move and might collapse at any moment. It was asking too much of any man's nerves to expect him to hold out in caves like that.'

The results outside were equally impressive. H. E. Bates, driving two months later 'along the road from Creil to St Leu and on to Crecy,' found that the 'road, the railway running beside it, the branch tracks, the concrete by-ways, the blockhouses, the gantries and everything else had . . . been blown to hell. All that remained, for miles and miles, was something like a huge river bed of mud and rocks from which a torrent had swept practically everything else away.' How many V-1s were buried remains uncertain. Allied Intelligence estimated that the caves 'could have been holding 2,000', and the raid was, Dr Jones believed, directly responsible for 'the reduced rate of fire against London which fell from an average of 100 a day before 7 July to fewer than 70 a day for the next ten days.'

On the whole, however, considering the weight of bombs dropped, Allied countermeasures were remarkably ineffective. Probably too much was attempted. On 21 July a special Joint Crossbow Target Priorities Committee, representing both British and American Bomber Forces, was set up. It rapidly decided that, along with storage depots like St Leu, seven 'industrial and production centres' should be attacked, including Peenemünde and the main factory at Fallersleben, followed by fifty-seven modified launching sites. Between 16 and 18 July Nucourt, Rilly-La-Montagne and Peenemünde were all attacked again, but in the next week the bombers switched back to the launching sites, on which 2723 tons of bombs were dropped, against less than 800 on the 'first priority' targets, although another 1400 tons were aimed at 'large sites', and other suspect places. In the following week, 2019 tons out of a total of 2798, were directed at the storage depots, with the launching sites attracting a mere 700, and on 29 July two possible fuel dumps were added to the list.

However many bombs were dropped, so long as the V-1s continued to arrive the British public remained dissatisfied and on 28 July Sir Arthur Tedder was warned by the Chief of the Air Staff that 'the Air Ministry was coming under heavy fire from . . . "certain not too well informed quarters of the government" about the percentage of bomber effort being devoted to *Crossbow*.' On 6 August Tedder sent his reply, explaining that the reason more bomber effort had not been devoted to *Crossbow* was due to 'a combination of the weather . . . and lack of useful targets' and that until 'our intelligence improved . . . our efforts were bound to be rather piecemeal and unsatisfactory.' Behind the scenes, however, the Deputy Supreme Commander was pressing for Bomber Command to do more, and early in August a plan was drawn up for a major blow against Crossbow targets concentrated into twenty-four hours. The US Eighth Air Force was to fly 1500 sorties, against Peenemünde and Fallersleben, two hydrogen peroxide plants at Ober Raderach and Düsseldorf, as well as attacking two suspected storage depots and twenty launching sites. Bomber Command would meanwhile lay on 1000 sorties against three other suspected depots and twenty-two sites, and the two Tactical Air Forces, the US Ninth and the British Second, were to fly 400 sorties against forty launching sites, so that every one known or believed to have fired recently would be hit.

Bad weather, as so often that summer, frustrated the Allies' hopes. Far from being completed within a single day, the whole programme was not even finished within a week, though between 2 and 9 August 15,000 tons were dropped on Crossbow targets of all kinds, bringing the total for the whole two months between mid-June and 16 August to 73,000 tons, of which 26,000 had been delivered against the launching sites alone.

This vast expenditure of high explosive and petrol had not stopped the flying-bombs arriving, but it *had* crippled other Allied air operations, as the chief advocate of strategic bombing made clear to Sir Arthur Tedder on 18 August:

Air Chief Marshal Harris pointed out . . . the extreme difficulty of bombing accurately the flying-bomb and rocket installations. Against these targets Bomber Command had already carried out nearly ten thousand sorties, losing the better part of 100 aircraft and 650 personnel. Nearly 36,000 tons of bombs had been dropped, quite apart from the vast effort made against the same targets by the Americans. Harris did not think that we had achieved a result commensurate with the effort. On the other hand, this scale of attack, combined with the needs of the battle, had caused us to take virtually the whole of Bomber Command, and much of the American effort away from German targets for some three and a half months. . . . The only real and effective answer to the flying-bomb and rocket, in Harris's view, was to increase the weight of the offensive against Germany.

Whatever view one took of 'Bomber' Harris's conclusion, his premise was sound, but, with reprisals ruled out, counter-attacking from the air was all the Allies could do, and during the third week of August another 1200 tons of bombs rained down on suspected storage depots and fuel dumps, on modified sites, and – a new target, of which more will be said later – on airfields suspected of being used for loading air-launched V-1s. By now anxiety about the rocket was beginning to overshadow even the campaign against the flying-bomb. A new list issued by the Crossbow Targets Priorities Committee on 13 August offered to the planning staffs of the various commands a be-wildering choice of 122 different targets, in fourteen separate classes, with seven different degrees of priority and ten sub-categories. The next document it produced was even more elaborate, listing 130 targets, with eight different degrees of priority. Luckily for Air Chief Marshal Harris and his Ameri-can counterparts, the list included many general industrial ob-jectives, such as factories making sheet steel and fuel plants, so that they were able to comply while not abandoning that longer-term campaign on which their hearts were set.

Both the Volkswagen works at Fallersleben, north of Bruns-wick, and the Opel factory at Rüsselheim, also suspected of being used for V-1 assembly, were bombed again, and all told, in the last week of August, of nearly 2800 tons of bombs dropped by Bomber Command on flying-bomb targets, 1800 were aimed at 'industrial and production centres' and about 850 at 'modified' sites, with the balance, 150 tons, directed at aerodromes.

Up to nightfall on 1 September the Allied air forces dropped 98,000 tons of bombs on targets solely, or mainly, concerned with the flying-bomb. Of this vast total, more than 74,000 tons had been delivered since mid-June, making an average of near-ly 1000 tons a day. Including operations against the rocket – and a single raid might well affect both secret weapons – the

Allies had dropped in just over a year, since the sirens sounded at Peenemünde on the night of 12 August 1943, 118,000 tons of bombs, to deliver which had meant the loss of nearly 450 aircraft. An unknown number of French civilians and slave labourers, probably running into hundreds, had been killed by British and American bombs, or had died at the hands of the German firing squads when caught smuggling out information. The German losses were by contrast insignificant. Including, it is believed, accidental casualties during launching, the total number killed was only 146, plus thirty-nine missing – presumably blown to pieces – a total of 185 dead, with another 246 wounded. This was a tiny price to pay for killing, as already described, 5000 British civilians, and seriously injuring 17,000 more, and for claiming the lives of 2900 Allied airmen, of whom nearly 1500 died in the period after D-Day alone. Three hundred and eighty of them belonged to the US Eighth Air Force, which between June and September lost forty-one air- craft in these operations: another 1082 names were added to the already long roll of honour of Bomber Command, from 156 Lancasters, Halifaxes and Mosquitoes shot down or fatally damaged. In terms of lives lost the ground-launched V-1 cam- paign was an outstanding German victory.

The flying-bomb campaign also had one unforeseen result in revealing not merely that the enemy had found a highly econ- omical method of delivering high explosive, but also that the explosive itself was far more efficient that that produced by British chemists. Public mutterings on the subject of the enor- mous amount of damage which a single V-1 could inflict, al- though the Germans seemed able to survive year after year a far heavier weight of British bombs, reached the Prime Min- ister, who, on 13 July, addressed a polite but pointed minute to the Secretary of State for Air. 'It is,' he wrote, 'a puzzle to me and to many others how, with perhaps 30 or 40 tons of bombs, including containers, dropped over London by the Robot, such very noticeable damage occurs; whereas there may well be 2 or 3,000 tons dropped over Berlin or Munich, and yet the German people seem to get away with it all right. . . . We wonder why the effect is so severe here, or whether *per contra* very much less hitting and useful effect is done in Germany.'

Underlying Churchill's note was the nation's growing disillusionment with the whole bomber offensive, as no doubt Sir Archibald Sinclair realized, and his reply was prompt. 'There are,' he explained on the following day, 'certain points in favour of the flying bomb – particularly the continuity of the attack, which has a serious morale effect on factory workers, already fatigued by four years of war exertion, and is reflected in a loss of production.' However, a detailed study on the whole subject was being made by the Commander-in-Chief of Bomber Command. Churchill's answering memo on 18 July, though courteous, carried a sting in its tail:

Thank you very much. You will I am sure admit it is rather uncomfortable that these robots, carrying HE into London at the rate of 30 or 40 tons a day, should do damage and create situations which give the Germans a fair retort for the terrific damage we have cast upon them by aeroplane. This robot bomb is in its infancy. One must expect it to increase in speed and power and above all in range. It is undoubtedly a great reflection on our inventive science that we did not develop this idea . . . apparently so simple and easy to make.

About another, even sharper comment, Churchill had second thoughts. 'If we had started four years ago on a plan of this kind,' he had written in the original draft, 'we might by now be able to make great economies in our bombing force and save a great many lives in good crews and pilots.' Before the note was sent, however, this sentence was crossed out.

No hesitation marked the response of Air Chief Marshal Sir Arthur Harris. On 19 July he submitted to the Air Ministry a typically robust letter which declared uncompromisingly that his claims about the damage done to Germany rested 'on proven fact which, being based upon actual photographs, is incontrovertible' and disproved 'the statement by the Prime Minister that the flying bomb caused 8 to 10 times the damage caused by a comparable weight of our bombs.' Two and a half thousand tons of British bombs on Berlin had 'demolished or irretrievably damaged' 142,000 houses, or fifty-seven per ton, the 1400 tons of high explosive which had landed on London up to 16 July had destroyed only 13,000 houses, a mere eleven per ton. As for the embarrassing question 'why, in view of the great destruction . . . caused in Germany the enemy have been able to carry on, especially when one considers the effect of the comparatively light scale flying-bomb attacks on this country', Sir Arthur had his answer ready. Bomber Command had failed to bring Germany to its knees because of 'the rigid control of the Gestapo' which 'precluded the possibility of any revolution from below' and the 'skilful propaganda' of Josef Goebbels which 'had instilled hopes that victory would be achieved when the . . . secret weapons were employed.'

31

NO SYMPATHY FOR SOUTHAMPTON

I would press you to consider the possibility of commiserating with a 'South Coast town' on the heavy losses sustained.

Lord Cherwell to Herbert Morrison, 14 July 1944

The Germans had originally hoped to disrupt, and perhaps even to delay, the invasion of France by bombarding the Allied assembly areas in Southern England, and the discovery that various launching ramps were aligned on Southampton had greatly troubled the Allied high command. By noon on Friday, 16 June, 244 flying-bombs were believed to have been aimed at London, but another fifty, which had landed well to the south of the main flight path, were assumed to have been intended for Southampton, although none had come down anywhere near it. Accordingly, in the hope of encouraging this continued waste of effort, a report was sent back to Germany, via British-controlled agents, around 22 June, that already there was 'considerable damage' in that town. Since London had so far been the sole target, the news that some V-1s had landed eighty miles away caused embarrassment at the head-quarters of LXV Army Corps, which decided to attribute the supposed damage, if anyone spotted it, to a conventional air-raid. It also, however, revived an idea put forward by Colonel Wachtel in March for bombarding the main British ports, and it was decided, on 26 June, actually to fire an experimental salvo of a dozen or so missiles at Southampton. The experiment ended abruptly, however. First Field Marshal von Rundstedt ordered that it be abandoned, and then on the following day, 27 June, Hitler himself ruled that Colonel Wachtel's sole target should be London. It must therefore have been highly frustrating for the colonel and his superiors when, on 3 July, they received further information from an agent – also, of course, controlled by MI5 – that the few missiles they had been allowed to fire had driven a fighter squadron to retreat from Southampton to another airfield.

So encouraging did these reports seem to the Germans that, though its letter was observed, the spirit of the Führer's order was now ignored, for the squadron of Heinkels equipped to launch flying-bombs from the air was ordered to fire a covey at Southampton. A major attack was delivered on 11 July, when the Civil Defence control room at Hamble was kept busy plotting the fall of twenty-nine V-1s, and there was another flurry of activity on 14 and 15 July, with twenty-seven more recorded. Few of these went anywhere near Southampton, and some came to earth as far inland as Winchester and Andover, but the area worst affected was the Isle of Wight, which lay directly in the line of fire. By 1 July only five V-1s had actually landed on the island, but several had come down in the sea just off shore, and the rest had made a noisy passage overhead. Among those disturbed was the young army officer's wife staying with her parents near Ryde, whose daily diary in the form of a letter to her infant son has already been quoted:*

The first time they came over we didn't know what on earth was happening. The sirens went at about nine o'clock when I was in the kitchen with granny making tea before going to bed. Immediately after the siren ceased wailing there was a roar like an express train outside and a plane . . . came roaring over the house at tremendous speed and flying very low . . . It was followed by a second one right on its tail. My heart gave an almighty jump and . . . I dropped the kettle of boiling water which luckily missed my feet and poured all over the floor. Granny dropped the tray with all the teacups, the milk, the precious sugar and the china, in a thousand pieces, joined my kettle on the floor. . . . There was a loud 'bang' in the distance and then silence. I ran upstairs as fast as I could and brought you down to your cot in the cupboard. You were still sound asleep, for which I was very thankful. About five minutes later another plane could be heard coming more slowly this time and not directly overhead . . . The plane kept well out over the sea heading to our left and passed inland over Nodes Fort towards Portsmouth. . . . Plane after plane appeared at regular intervals chugging across the sea

*See page 225.

towards Portsmouth . . . and sometime after they had vanished in the distance we would hear a series of explosions . . . The next morning . . . we learnt the truth. These were the flying-bombs that up till now we had escaped.

Knowing the truth was little consolation. More comforting was the arrival of visible human assistance.

And now the guns have come. It is a great relief having the soldiers round us. Seven guns, two Bofors and five Oerlikons . . . are installed along the sea wall in front of this house. Before the guns came we were alone down here, the other two houses solitary and empty. It was a horrid feeling. The wailing of the siren would cut through the darkness and only the sea-gulls answered, circling 'the dark sea with shrill cries' of terror. . . . Now it is much better. When the siren goes one hears the soldiers running from the house beside us, their heavy boots ringing on the tiled pathway, their laughter and their voices breaking the silence and dispelling the feeling of devilment abroad.

For this woman's two-year-old son the presence of the Army converted what could have been a memory-scarring experience into a cheerful novelty:

The searchlight is here, too. Behind us on the golf-links. Each man a personal friend of yours . . . Patsy and Jock and also here, the mongrel dogs, their pets and our devoted companions.

Every morning after breakfast you sally forth, a tiny, upright figure carrying the newspapers that I give to the crew each day. Out of the garden gate . . . across the narrow road, over the links to the light. I hear their voices welcoming you, I see them take the papers from you and then swing you up into the light itself. I see you perched inside it, a doll in a big glass box. They give you a duster and you carefully dust inside the light. . . . Every day you do this, and, when it is finished, you have tea with them or cocoa and eat cakes and biscuits. One day, pay day, they put a cap on your head, gave you a paybook and lined you up with the others to receive your pay. You saluted the officer smartly and received the sum of twopence which you returned later, as I had instilled into you that you must not take money from the soldiers, who were only too inclined to fill your pockets with pennies. . . .

I am a mass of contradictions just now . . . one moment praying as I hear the doodlebug approaching, 'Get it, Get it, shoot it down, don't let it get away,' and then in the next breath, 'Dear God, don't let them get it, don't let them shoot it down.'

Like people living under the main flight path, those on the 'Solent route' rapidly became aware of any change in the firing pattern.

For a time the bombs came in two directions. Standing on our front lawn we could see them appearing from behind Bembridge Lifeboat Station, some right towards Sandown and Shanklin. Now they have changed course and come directly over the roof of the Royal Spithead Hotel at Bembridge and straight for this house.

The vast majority of the V-1s which disturbed the Isle of Wight arrived at night, forcing this family to rearrange its daily routine:

We have an early lunch and then retire to our rooms and sleep solidly from about 2 p.m. until 5 or even 6 p.m. It is the sleep of exhaustion. . . . Night is a nightmare. As soon as the shadows of evening begin to fall we begin to count the hours till 'Doodlebug Time'. Four hours to go. Three hours. Two and one. Just as we lie down on our beds the long, shuddering notes of the siren cause us to leap up again and get ready to go through another night of ceaseless noise and anxiety.

These noisy weeks also remain in the memory of a twelve-year-old girl who attended Sandown Grammar School, a three-mile walk from her home at Lake, midway between Sandown and Shanklin, on the east coast of the island. She especially recalls 'one night in August':

I remember peering through the mesh sides of the Morrison table shelter and seeing the window come in towards me, and the curtains flying across the room with chairs and cushions following. . . . I remember the doggy smell of the blankets and hugging . . . our crossbred golden Labrador, named Drifter, because he drifted off . . . telling him not to be scared. He growled and his hackles rose . . . I realized that we were still alive and wondered why.

The greenhouse had a vine of purple grapes. That disintegrated with the blast from the doodlebug and the vine died. The next morning I found that the art master's house was no longer there, some few streets away. . . . Still etched in my mind is the sight of hundreds of tubes of oil paint, squashed and bleeding on the ground, with a kaleidoscope of colour, in contrast to the gaping crater and blackened ground.

Experience confirmed that Lord Cherwell – so often accurate

in small things while wrong about major ones – had been right in predicting that the V-1s fired against the invasion ports would have no effect whatever on the build-up in Normandy. An Air Ministry map showing the fall of shot on the nights of 10/11 and 11/12 July, when Southampton and Portsmouth had been the intended target, revealed that some missiles had fallen well to the west, as far away as Brockenhurst, ten miles from Southampton, and others were scattered well to the north and east of the city, four of them between Winchester and Basingstoke nearly thirty miles away. The mean point of impact for the first night had been well outside the city limits, near the river Hamble. The Germans' aim on the second night had been marginally better for length but still poor for direction, being well to the west of the main built-up area, towards Eastleigh.

Sporadic salvoes of flying-bombs were directed towards Southampton later in July but only two landed inside the borough boundaries, both of them in the Bitterne and Sholing area. The first, at 1 a.m. in the morning of 12 July, left ten houses needing demolition, and badly damaged 139 more. The casualty list was short; five people badly injured and four slightly hurt. Three days later, at about the same time, Southampton's second V-1, in much the same area, had even less effect: sixteen houses required extensive repairs, and 137 minor ones, while six people were injured, one seriously. By chance, however, some of the houses blasted that morning had already suffered three days earlier, so that, as the former ARP control officer of Folland Aircraft Ltd at Hamble remembers, 'several employees of Folland were bombed out twice in three days.' The result was that the residents of Southampton developed a healthy respect for the V-1. Previously, when a missile appeared, 'almost every employee left his or her workbench to gaze up into the sky'; now many people slept in shelters like 'the old vaults . . . under business premises in the lower part' of the town.

So widely dispersed were the flying-bombs aimed at Southampton that the British government assumed that some of them had been intended for Portsmouth, which had a remarkably similar experience, with only two V-1s landing within the borough. The first, on the night of 25/26 June, caused nineteen minor casualties, and sixteen more serious ones, close to the point of impact in Locksway Road. The second, in the early hours of 15 July, was considerably worse, leaving behind it sixty-three minor casualties, thirty-five major ones and fifteen people dead, including several children. The V-1 landed in Newcomen Road, and is recalled by a woman then living nearby, whose house was among those damaged:

The siren sounded about 2 a.m. It was a very dark night with no moon. I was in bed in the front bedroom with my four-year-old son. My mother and father were asleep in the back of the house. I . . . got up on a box under the sash window . . . and looked out. . . . This doodlebug was coming across the sky over the spire of St Saviour's church at the top of Jervis Road. . . . When it got opposite our house about three roads up, the engine stopped . . . a dreadful wait, and then it exploded. . . . About 6 a.m. my Cousin Harry, who lived where the bomb had gone off, came to our house covered in blood.

One result of the bombardment of Portsmouth and Southampton, ineffective though it was, was to give London a breathing space, and for several nights on end during the second week in July no V-1s arrived over the capital during the night. The significance of this was not lost on Lord Cherwell. 'I would press you,' he wrote to Herbert Morrison on 14 July, 'to consider the possibility of commiserating with a "South Coast town" on the heavy losses sustained, or in some other way indicating that the attack had been a success.'

The proposal made no appeal, however, to the Home Secretary, for somewhat curious reasons. Sacrificing people in Portsmouth and Southampton to save lives in London would, he replied on 17 July, be 'politically . . . dangerous in the extreme', while such remarks 'would soon be known to be untrue and doubts would be cast upon the accuracy of government statements generally.'

Undeterred by, or perhaps not knowing of, these objections, the Chiefs of Staff on the following day called for a detailed examination of the possibility of encouraging more attacks on Portsmouth which, like Cherwell, they had assumed to be the Germans' target, and on 22 July a paper by the Chairman of the Home Defence Executive, Sir Findlater Stewart, entitled 'Crossbow Deception – Intensification of Attacks on Portsmouth', was laid before them. The Home Defence Executive was a body with somewhat vague responsibilities, while Stewart himself was a career civil servant who represented the Ministry of Home Security on the Twenty Committee and was generally supposed to be 'Morrison's man'. He carefully weighed up the arguments for and against Cherwell's proposal:

There can be no doubt that, in terms of production and morale, the advantage of decreasing the amount of effort directed against London, particularly if we were able to get more alert-free nights, would outweigh the effects of an intensification of the present attacks on Southampton. . . . We could also hope for a substantial saving of life, since . . . the proportion of deaths in London to bombs launched against London is in the region of one half in comparison with a figure of about one-tenth of this for Portsmouth and Southampton. Even if the number of serious incidents increased . . . the balance of advantage would still be on the side of increasing the Southampton attacks.

The case against attracting more V-1s towards the South Coast ports was, however, even stronger.

Any substantial increase in the number of bombs aimed at Portsmouth and Southampton, whether or not they succeeded in causing serious damage or casualties, would, in the opinion of the Ministry of Home Security and the Air Ministry, give rise to a public demand for protection which it would be difficult to resist. . . . The provision of additional defences for Portsmouth/Southampton would entail a diversion of defensive effort from London. . . . Intensification to any important extent of the present attack, even though it did not interfere directly with the build-up of OVERLORD, might well result in a lowering of the morale of workers in the docks, and certainly a loss of working time. . . .

 The enemy must be presumed to know within narrow limits what would be the spread of his bombs in any given area, and it is very doubtful whether by our special means [i.e. the use of 'turned' agents] we could persuade him that his bombs are achieving results which are completely inconsistent with this knowledge. . . . If we attempted a major deception we should have to put over a large amount of first-hand (eye-witness) intelligence and this would involve manoeuvring agents to the area. S.H.A.E.F. would be opposed to this, since, without danger of compromising them, we could not refrain from giving the agents concerned reports on military movements and dispositions; at the present delicate stage, this might seriously effect plan

FORTITUDE.* Any considerable increase in the hits scored on Portsmouth/Southampton might impose a serious strain on the local civil defence services whose services are not comparable with those of London. . . . If we tell the enemy that he is achieving considerable success in his military attacks on Southampton, we present him with propaganda material which may be of good value in boosting German morale.

How convincing these arguments were must be a matter of opinion. Why, it might have been asked, should the morale of dock workers in Southampton be expected to crack under a far lighter attack than those in East London were experiencing? And how could the claims made by German press and radio for the effects of the V-1 become more outrageous than they already were? But, rightly, or wrongly, the paper reached an emphatically Morrisonian conclusion:

In the face of these arguments we consider that no attempt ought to be made to *increase* the scale of attack on Southampton and Portsmouth. Nevertheless . . . it is clear that a continuance of the present scale of attack would be to our advantage, and we have considered whether our special means would be usefully employed in ensuring this. . . .

 In deciding to attack Southampton and Portsmouth the enemy appears to have persuaded himself, either that his weapon is so accurate that it will produce worthwhile results . . ., or that the importance of hampering the build-up of OVERLORD is important enough to warrant the diversion of effort from an efficient use on a large target to an inefficient use on a small one. . . . If he has not already done so, he must begin shortly to wonder whether his effort is worthwhile. If, therefore, we begin now to pass across a carefully balanced picture, showing that by a few chance hits he has imposed an appreciable delay on port operations, we may persuade him to go on.

After 15 July no more V-1s landed on either Portsmouth or Southampton, though others apparently intended for them came down further round the coast, at Emsworth and Selsey Bill. By the end of August ninety flying-bombs had apparently been aimed at the two great Hampshire ports, but ten of them missed the county altogether and landed in Sussex or Surrey,

---

*The deception plan designed to keep German troops awaiting a second invasion in the Pas de Calais.

while many of the remainder roared inland to fall in the depths of the New Forest, near Lyndhurst and close to such peaceful small towns as Micheldever and Alresford.

Few did any damage, indeed a V-1 in the vicinity gave hitherto quiet areas a not unwelcome kudos. There were, however, a few more serious rural incidents as at Goodworth Clatford, a village of a few hundred inhabitants, thirty miles from the coast and about three from Andover. Until then, acknowledges one then electrical engineer at a local factory which had turned over from making farm equipment to 'Queen Mary' trailers for the RAF, this part of Hampshire had had 'a comparatively quiet war'. Then, early in the morning of 15 July, it was this village's turn to be the recipient of an 'over' from the midnight salvo fired at Southampton:

At 1.05 a.m. a doodlebug fell and exploded between the Royal Oak public house and the village school. Both were completely demolished and also a terrace of four cottages and a private house, 'The Thatch'. About thirty others received varying damage. Six people were killed . . . among them a young mother and child who that afternoon had caught a train from Waterloo to Andover to get out of London. A friendly ticket collector directed them to Goodworth Clatford for lodgings . . . in the terrace of four completely destroyed.

For the Home Guard it was to prove an unusually busy weekend.

My platoon did anti-looting patrol on Sunday, 16th, and Monday, 17th. . . . I was platoon sergeant with a corporal and four men [and] remember that night among the ruins. We had some bunks in the 'Little Thatch' and some tea-making equipment, plus 'haversack rations'. The centre of the village had to be evacuated – no electricity yet back on – everywhere rubble and destruction and ghostly in a near full moon. The 'Little Thatch' was a typical 'chalk pize' constructed house, walls 18 inches thick, and it had been lifted bodily from about 12 inches above ground and put down about two feet further over. The old oak frame of the building held but it was severely strained and every breeze during the night caused it to creak and groan.

A single V-1 on a village often had a greater effect than a whole series on a town and Goodworth Clatford's left it without a school and without a pub. The former need was easily met, for the neighbouring village, Upper Clatford, came to the rescue, providing room in its Church of England school (after some urgent amendment of the trust deeds) for children from its demolished neighbour. The displaced drinkers from the Royal Oak found their way, without too much difficulty, to the Crook and Shears in the neighbouring village. Within two weeks Goodworth Clatford was more or less back to normal.

To this incident there was one unforeseen sequel, for the building workers sent to work on the wrecked thatched cottages 'would come home simply alive with fleas', as the daughter of one of them, who lived in Andover, remembers:

He and my mother seemed to spend most of the night 'big game hunting' as they called it. They never could sleep properly and dad used to say that, while at work, whichever room you went into, one or more of his workmates were always there in a state of undress, flea hunting. He really was a most conscientious man, but I think even he was quite relieved when he had a plank fall on his foot and was off work for a while.

32

WHO ARE WE TO ACT AS GOD?

It appeared that the general sense of the War Cabinet was that it would be a serious matter to assume any direct degree of responsibility for action which would affect the areas against which flying bombs were aimed.

'*TOP SECRET*' annexe to War Cabinet Minutes, 27 July 1944

The discussion about whether or not to try to attract flying-bombs towards Southampton was merely a pale echo of the continuing debate about trying to affect the distribution of the missiles within the London area itself. The British had been remarkably successful in denying to Colonel Wachtel any accurate information about where his missiles were landing, and considering that they had no aerial reconnaissance to assist them and were in effect firing blind the launching crews were not in fact doing badly, especially in direction. Their principal aiming point was Tower Bridge and a little later one V-1 was actually to score a bull's-eye on one of its supporting towers. Many others landed slightly to right or left of the intended flight path, but the Germans considered this acceptable since they knew that these were still bound to drop on a built-up area and thus help to spread terror and damage. Where they had failed was in underestimating the range of their target. The vast majority of flying-bombs landed in the mainly residential areas south of the River Thames instead of in the business and governmental quarters to the north. By 27 June three-quarters of all the V-1s which had reached the London Civil Defence region had landed on the 'wrong' side of the river and the worst-bombed borough, throughout the whole campaign, was Croydon, nine miles short of Tower Bridge, followed by Wandsworth, above five miles to the south-east. Then came Lewisham, four miles from the aiming point, Woolwich, about seven miles from it, and, closest of all, Camber-

370

well, barely two. Lambeth and Battersea, to either side of Wandsworth, were also badly affected, and, like Wandsworth, may have collected 'unders' intended for the Germans' secondary targets, the main-line stations. Here, too, Flak Regiment 155 (W) achieved some remarkable results. Victoria, as already described, suffered a direct hit, Waterloo a very near miss, and Charing Cross was put temporarily out of action by a V-1 knocking out Hungerford Bridge. As for 'grouping', the concentration of successive shots in a small area, a whole succession of V-1s, presumably from the same ramp or group of ramps, repeatedly came down close to each other.

If this relatively high degree of accuracy could have been combined, as the Germans had originally planned, with a really heavy rate of fire, life in London could have become intolerable. As it was the V-1s presented, at the very least, an extremely serious nuisance. In the first twenty-four hours of the main attack about 200 had been launched, of which 144 had 'come within range of the defences,' i.e. had crossed the coast, and seventy-three had, in the common phrase, 'got through to London' and landed somewhere within the London Civil Defence region. It was this last statistic which provided the index of success or failure of the defences. By mid-July, in spite of all their efforts, including the bombing of the launching sites, about a hundred V-1s a day were being launched, of which twenty-five to thirty were reaching the capital, and many of the rest were falling on the towns and villages between London and the coast.

Thanks to the work of the Air Intelligence branch, almost as much was known about the behaviour of the V-1s test-fired during May as of those launched in anger from mid-June onwards, and a chart of the former, showing the same distances flown and the same 'scatter' on landing, was now superimposed on a map of the British Isles. Abbeville, at the centre of the launching area, replaced Peenemünde, and Charing Cross – at that time assumed to be the Germans' aiming point – Bornholm as their general destination. The results were striking. The mean point of impact of the 'trial' bombs, calculated by joining up the sites of the various incidents on the map and seeing where the lines crossed, was almost identical with that of the real ones, both being in Dulwich, about four miles short of Charing Cross.

While MI6 had some cause for satisfaction, since fewer bombs were arriving than expected and most of these were falling short, their German counterparts were suffering a frenzy of frustration. At the end of June* their star agent, Fritz, alias Eddie Chapman, a former safe-breaker, released from gaol in Jersey to spy for the Germans, was dropped by parachute near Cambridge with, according to his own story, £6000 in his pocket and a promise of another 800,000 Reichsmarks (about £100,000) in return for accurate information about where the V-1s were falling. He was, as on his earlier visits, met by representatives of the Twenty (or Doublecross) Committee, which operated turned-round German agents, with whom he had long been in touch and immediately presented them with a troublesome problem. What the Germans wanted to know could easily be discovered by anyone with a sharp pair of eyes and in the absence of plausible reports the Germans were bound to smell a rat, as they would if the details provided by Chapman and other agents were later contradicted by aerial reconnaissance. There was a further complication. Since they had accurate records of when every V-1 had been fired, the authorities in Berlin knew *when* they should have landed, so that the times of incidents signalled to them must appear genuine, whatever else was false.

The problem was brought, like so many others before it, to Dr R. V. Jones:

We were faced with a dilemma. Because if the agents provided false information . . . it would reveal that the agents were false and . . . the whole system would be blown. If on the other hand we allowed the agents to know the truth about fall of shot and damage done, we would be providing the Germans with valuable information. . . . I knew that agents were very unreliable as regards the details of incidents, such as timing and so forth, but were usually pretty accurate about pin points. . . . Therefore, we would have to be right in the places. But there was a chance we could be wrong in the time, without the Germans being able to spot it. . . . For some reason or other

---

*Chapman says July, but J. C. Masterman (see sources) gives the date as the end of June, which seems more likely.

most of the shots seemed to fall rather short, in the southern suburbs of London and even further south than that. And so if we could keep the centre of the pattern there, or, even better, make them put it back still further, they would in fact do less damage. So what I advised M.I.5 to do was to report falls of shot tending to the north and west of London but to give the times of those shots as one which we knew in fact had fallen distinctly short of the centre. . . . If the Germans tried to do any correlation at all they would find . . . that even the shots that they believed were going under range were in fact going over and that . . . they would therefore try and shorten the range rather than increase it.

With this neat and ingenious solution to a difficult conundrum everyone 'in the know' was happy, including the Chiefs of Staff. The inhabitants of Streatham and Carshalton would no doubt have been less enthusiastic, since they would now receive V-1s which would otherwise have descended on Hampstead or Holborn, but they were not consulted. Even the Germans were happy, for they were receiving a flow of apparently reliable information, and when the evidence of the radio transmitters fitted to a number of flying-bombs showed that they were falling short, they assumed this must be wrong. Fortune also favoured the British in other ways. An uncontrolled German agent in Spain, prompted by mere greed, supplied a steady flow of totally false reports which, by mere chance, confirmed what the Germans were hearing from their spies in Britain. And when, on 10 September 1944, a German reconnaissance plane – the new and fast twin-jet Me.262 – did at last fly a reconnaissance mission over London it took back photographs of impressive damage north of the Thames, in the Edgware Road area – caused in fact by conventional bombs three years before. South London, pitted with recent bomb sites, was invisible under heavy cloud. The Germans also ignored the true meaning of such scanty clues as the British press afforded them. A report in the *South London Observer*, on 14 July, admitting that a V-1 had destroyed several buildings at Dulwich College, causing the vital summer examinations to be taken elsewhere, was followed two weeks later by a boast in a German newspaper that the college had deliberately been aimed at as a temporary military headquarters. The significance of at least one flying-bomb having landed four miles short was totally missed.

The proposal to 'attempt to induce the enemy to shorten the range of his flying-bombs' had first been considered by the Chiefs of Staff as early as 7 July, and reports on it had been prepared on 5 and 16 July by Sir Findlater Stewart, secretary to the Chiefs of Staff Committee. Up to now the deception plan had been regarded as essentially a military matter, but on 19 July, General, later Lord, Ismay, who was Chief of Staff to Churchill in his capacity of Minister of Defence, sent him a detailed report of what was being done. Subsequently the whole subject was thrashed out in detail in a paper by Sir Findlater Stewart, dated 24 July, and regarded as so sensitive that the copies were numbered and seen only by the very highest ministers and officials.

The evidence in the paper was set out with scrupulous fairness:

In order to illustrate as accurately as possible the effect of the proposed deception, I have had two charts prepared . . . compiled from an analaysis of the points of impact of 1,076 bombs falling within the period 22 June to 14 July; bombs . . . falling more than 30 miles from London are excluded. The grid on the first map . . . shows in green figures the existing statistical average density of bombs per square mile . . . while the red figures give the densities which would be obtained if the mean point of impact were shifted six miles south-east to Beckenham. . . . It is apparent . . . that overall . . . a successful deception on the lines proposed would move a good deal of the enemy's effort to points outside built-up areas.

The coloured charts and attached table showed the effects, in bombs per square mile, of moving back the mean point of impact, at present in Dulwich, by six miles. The 'bomb density' of Dulwich itself would immediately drop from 3·9 to only 1·9. Lambeth and Southwark would receive respectively 1 and 1·1 bombs instead of 3·2 and 3·4. Whitehall would be spectacularly better off, with a density of 2·8 dropping to only 0·7. So would the City, with an almost identical improvement. The number of bombs falling on Wandsworth would be halved, from 2·5 to 1·1, and Shoreditch and Stepney would do even better, dropping from 2·3–2·8 to 0·6–0·9. Another working-class area north of the river, Islington, would also benefit, with 0·4 bombs

where now it received 1·6, and even Lewisham would be slightly better off, with a figure of 3·3–3·1 giving way to one of 2·8–
2·6. The situation in Croydon was more complicated. The more
northerly parts – Norbury and Thornton Heath (3·0 down to
2·5) and Norwood (3·4 to 2·9) would enjoy some improvement,
but South Croydon would be slightly worse off, with a bomb
density of 3·1 instead of 2·5, Bromley much worse off with 3·6
bombs in place of 1·7, and Bexley spectacularly worse off with
2·3 in place of 0·7. The unluckiest district of all would be
Orpington. Its 0·6 flying-bombs would, if the Germans swal-
lowed the bait being offered them, rise to 2·6.

But these figures alone did not tell the whole story. All the
outer suburbs were less built up, and had a far lower density
of population than the districts nearer in while the flying-bombs
that would otherwise have landed on them, would now, it was
hoped, land even further out, on open, or almost open, country. As Sir Findlater Stewart commented:

In general terms the charts show that the (relatively few) built-up
areas with heavy population densities towards the southern fringes of
Greater London would not be materially worsened by the proposal,
but that the lot of the large aggregations of population north and
south of the river would be considerably improved.

So far, so good, the advocates of the deception policy may
have argued. But in his next few paragraphs Sir Findlater
Stewart candidly acknowledged the opposition to the Chiefs of
Staff view:

The Ministry of Home Security do not accept these arguments. They
are not satisfied that any substantial saving of life would be effected,
even if the deception were completely successful, and they express
themselves as very doubtful about the possibility of achieving success.
They feel moreover that the public have become used to the present
incidence of attack and . . . they doubt whether the Civil Defence
Services on the outskirts . . . could be expected to cope with the
heavier attack to which they might be exposed, as efficiently as the
Services in the existing areas. . . . On balance, therefore, they would
not desire to see the present pattern shifted.

Herbert Morrison had also found an important ally:

The Ministry of Production take much the same general view. Physical damage to factories has been small so far and is not likely to be increased by a shift of incidence, and the Ministry are concerned mainly about the effects which the proposal might have on work people. . . . The present high rates [of absenteeism] in the South are considered to be due mainly to lack of sleep, damage to workers' houses, evacuation of families and like domestic causes, and the Ministry of Production would not accept the argument that a shift of incidence from areas of production, e.g. Wandsworth, Croydon and Deptford, would necessarily have a good effect on absenteeism, since workers are now often drawn from areas remote from their work. They fear that any change in the weight of attack might upset such stability as has been obtained.

Having presented the case against their own proposal the Chiefs of Staff now proceeded to demolish it:

We must take serious note of these arguments, but it is material to point out that both departments appear to assume a *sudden* shift of incidence of attack. No doubt if Beckenham, from tomorrow, began to get a density of 3·9 instead of the present 1·9 the effect on the casualty rate and the Civil Defence might be considerable; although as pointed out above, since Beckenham is less built up than Peckham, from which the weight would have been shifted, instead of an average of one casualty per bomb we might hope for lower averages. But it would be contrary to all our experience for the enemy to make a sudden and complete change of plan solely on the evidence coming to him from our special sources. It is much more likely that any shift would be effected gradually, as we succeeded in influencing his mind against his judgement of the inherent accuracy of his weapon, and possibly also against the evidence of his radio devices. . . . Unless however we can impose some control on his appreciation of the results he is achieving, the enemy may well soon detect his error and there is general agreement that a shift to the north might create a serious situation.

The paper then considered, and rejected, various other alternatives, such as trying to confuse the Germans by transmitting details of 'a haphazard selection of incidents with no bias in any particular direction', finally reaching the unequivocal conclusion 'the policy of moving the mean point of impact to the South East . . . is the most advantageous course open to us.'

Few cases can have been so persuasively argued, but the Cabinet was not convinced, least of all Herbert Morrison, the minister most directly concerned. 'He seemed to think,' Dr

Jones discovered, 'that the attempt to keep the aiming point short was an effort by government officials and others in Westminster, Belgravia and Mayfair, to keep the bombs off themselves at the expense of the proletariat in South London,' the area with which Morrison felt a close affinity.

The minutes of the Cabinet meeting of 27 July recorded the results of the Home Secretary's opposition:

It appeared that the general sense of the War Cabinet was that it would be a serious matter to assume any direct degree of responsibility for action which would affect the areas against which flying bombs were aimed.

The Cabinet opted instead for the Chiefs of Staff's second-best solution, 'the deception authorities' being 'invited . . . to arrange that the "information" conveyed to the enemy as regards the point of impact and the timing of arrival of flying bombs was such as would create confusion in his mind and present him with an inaccurate picture.' Clearly, however, MI5 was not wholly trusted for an unusual codicil was added: 'The draft of any instructions to be issued on this matter should be submitted to the Prime Minister for approval before issue.'

So secret was the matter considered that the War Cabinet's decision was recorded only in a 'Top Secret' annexe to the minutes labelled 'No circulation' – leading to pained notes from some of the usual recipients complaining that they were being kept in the dark. Far more indignant, however, was the response of the members of the intelligence departments, supported by Lord Cherwell and Duncan Sandys. Cherwell's statisticians were set to calculate the effects if the Germans, in the absence of false information, discovered the true facts and moved the mean point of impact forward from Dulwich to Charing Cross, and alternatively, what would happen if they could be persuaded to lower their aim by a further six miles, so that the centre of the bombardment crept six miles further back to Shirley and West Wickham. They calculated that 500 more people would be killed, 1500 more be seriously injured and 2,000 more be slightly injured for each month that the Germans corrected their aim while 1600 fewer than now would be killed, 4600 fewer be badly injured, and 5000 fewer be slightly injured for every month they could be induced to shorten it. The contrast between the two situations was expressed in a single line of figures:

Killed	Seriously injured	Slightly injured	Total
−2100	−6100	−7800	−16,000

This was attached by Mr Duncan Sandys to an eloquent note which on 2 August he addressed to the Prime Minister:

If, as is now proposed, we confine ourselves to feeding the enemy with information of a confused and inconclusive nature, we shall run the risk that he may try other means to find out where his bombs are now falling. . . . On the other hand, our chance of preventing him discovering the true facts will be greatly increased if, instead of merely trying to withhold information, we were to seek positively to mislead him. . . .

In the circumstances I submit that no avoidable risk should be taken and that, accordingly, instead of attempting vaguely to confuse the enemy a positive deception plan should be adopted.

Duncan Sandys had, very properly, sent a copy of this letter to the Home Secretary, who two days later hit back with a rival memo. Merely confusing the enemy was, thought Herbert Morrison, acceptable – but that was all.

To go further and to divert the enemy's attention from certain sections of the population to other sections . . . is a responsibility which ministers ought not to take without the most serious consideration, and I hope that you will not decide in favour of it without reference to the War Cabinet as a whole. Apart altogether from the gravity of the responsibility, if what was being done should ever come out, there might be most serious political consequences.

Such a plea could hardly be ignored. The Cabinet Office was forbidden to circulate Duncan Sandys's note and it was instead tabled at the next Cabinet meeting, with the copies being collected up afterwards. No conclusion was reached on it when the Cabinet met on 9 August, but on 11 August the paper *was* discussed, and the now familiar ground was traversed again at great length.

The result was a partial victory for the 'deception' party, who managed once again to stave off a final decision, as the minutes make clear:

No conclusion was reached. It was decided that the policy pursued hitherto [i.e. that of giving the enemy the impression that he was achieving a mean point of impact at Charing Cross] should be maintained for the present and that the War Cabinet should resume consideration of the matter later.

This further consideration came four days later, on 15 August. By then the Prime Minister was in the Mediterranean, leaving Clement Attlee, as Deputy Prime Minister, in the chair. What was said at that meeting was not recorded in writing due to the sensitivity of the subject, but those involved soon learned what had happened. True to his conviction that nothing should be done to increase the chance of one man rather than another being killed, Herbert Morrison, Dr Jones and his colleagues discovered, had delivered a passionate attack on the whole deception policy, ending his remarks with a dramatic, rhetorical question, all the more impressive because it was totally out of character: 'Who are we to act as God?'

After the meeting Attlee reported the Cabinet's decision to Churchill in a message endorsed – despite its guarded language – 'Top Secret cypher telegram – to be sent on one-time-pad', though the text still survives in the Public Record Office.

The Cabinet reconsidered Sandys' proposal on home security, the discussion of which was adjourned for further consideration. There was agreement that the direction should be to work for the maintenance of the present position with a bias towards a shift of emphasis as suggested.

This distinctly ambiguous decision was, with Attlee's approval, passed on to Sir Findlater Stewart, by the Cabinet secretariat, in terms little more precise.

At the Conference today at which further consideration was given to the Crossbow deception plan, it was agreed that your object should be to ensure that there is no deterioration in the position and that the enemy does not shift the pattern of his bombs towards the north west. With this in view you should continue to convey to the enemy information which will confirm his belief that he has no need to lengthen his range. You are also at liberty, within limits, to take such steps as you may judge safe to intensify this belief.

What, it may be asked, did the War Cabinet actually intend? Had it come down in favour of the 'confusion' policy favoured

by Morrison, or the 'deliberate deception' policy advocated by
the service departments? A properly written minute would, or
should, have made the matter plain, but most exceptionally no
record of the discussion existed. Years later the reason came
to light. The Air Secretary of the War Cabinet, a group captain,
had found its decision so extraordinary that he had persuaded
them that it was too delicate a matter to put on paper, knowing
that his colleagues in the Air Ministry and MI5 would take the
hint, as they did. When his MI5 contact asked Dr Jones what
they should do now, the latter's response was robust: 'I remarked,' Dr Jones has written, 'that I had not been present at
the meeting and the decision was so incredible that I would
only believe it if I received instructions in writing.' Since these
never arrived, the policy of trying to push the bombardment
further south continued.

One possible source of truthful information remained open
to the Germans – the obituary columns of the newspapers. On
20 July, rather tactlessly, one MP had drawn attention in the
House of Commons to the possibility that the enemy could
'ascertain that a particular borough has been attacked by reading the death notices in *The Times* and other papers,' though
Churchill's reply was evasive: 'There are not so very many
death notices in *The Times*.' There was a good reason for this;
three days earlier, all editors had been asked 'not to publish in
any issue more than three notices *re* persons killed by enemy
action from the same postal district in the South of England.'

Even so, the constant reappearance of the same place names
in the obituary columns of the national newspapers troubled
Lord Cherwell, who assigned a statitistician to plot on a map
the addresses given in a series of seventy 'enemy action'
obituaries in *The Times* and eighty in the *Daily Telegraph*. 'The
results,' he told Sir Findlater Stewart in a memo of 20 July,
were 'dangerously near the truth', for the mean point of impact
deduced from the addresses in *The Times* was Streatham Hill;
the *Daily Telegraph* casualties came a little lower down the
social scale; the mean point of impact for the flying-bombs
which had killed them was Clapham Junction. Cherwell suggested the creation of a whole army of 'men who never were',
with 'the inclusion of a score or so of misleading entries', but
the idea does not seem to have been followed up. Obituary

notices remained rationed by the Ministry of Information's rules, but were not falsified.

The obituary notices might in fact have given the Germans some help if they had use of them, for an 'After Action Report', compiled by the Scientific Intelligence Branch of the Air Ministry in December 1945, revealed that the mean point of impact based on obituary notices in *The Times* and *Daily Telegraph* for the whole flying-bomb period would have been Brixton church, only about one and a half miles north-north-west of its real location.

As for the general deception policy, the Germans' actual records, captured after the war, confirmed that the enemy believed he had achieved a mean point of impact 'just East of Waterloo Bridge', i.e. very close to the intended one. In fact this was 'about four miles north north west of the true M.P.I. It would appear,' the Air Ministry concluded with justifiable pride, 'that the counter intelligence measures were extremely effective.'

33

IN DOODLEBUG ALLEY

*It was somebody's home . . . somebody's life, taken
to save London.*

Alderman Oak-Rhind, Chairman of the Civil Defence
Committee of Kent County Council, 14 September 1944

'London will not soon forget the courage and spirit which the
people of the "Alley" have shown during the past few months
. . . and London is grateful.' In those words, delivered to an
audience of Civil Defence workers at Battle on 18 September,
during a thank-you tour of Kent and Sussex, Herbert Morrison
put into words what many people had for a long time felt and
he went on to make a perceptive point: 'There is an important
psychological difference between suffering directly at the hands
of the enemy and suffering, as "Bomb Alley" did, in proportion to the extent to which our defences were able to bring the
enemy missiles down on their way to London.' While the capital, in other words, got the worst of the flying-bombs, people
in the southern counties had the peculiarly unpleasant knowledge that they might be killed as a result of the efforts of their
own side.

Kent, Sussex and parts of Surrey were, in H. E. Bates's
phrase, 'the graveyard' for intercepted doodlebugs – but a
graveyard that was populated by the living.

A shot down bug was not, of course, a dead bug; as it hit the earth
whether in cornfield, village street, meadow or churchyard, it exploded just the same, all too often with fatal results. . . . On my own
piece of pastoral England more than 3,000 of these intercepted bugs
fell in a few weeks, so that a map showing each fallen bug looks like
a settlement of dead flies on a dead carcass. . . .*

*Such a map was in fact prepared and published, as described later in
this chapter (see page 385).

382

The people of doodlebug alley were . . . never free. In eighty days and nights they had every chance to see and hear practically everything a flying-bomb could do. They saw it fall on their ancient and beloved churches, on schools and hospitals, on some of the loveliest villages . . . in . . . the world. They saw the monuments and landmarks of centuries go down in dust. They never knew from one moment to another whether the meal they were eating, the glass of beer they were drinking, or the dart they held poised in their hand ready to throw at the saloon-bar board might not be their last. They said goodbye to their children as they went to school in the morning and never knew if they would see them again. The Battle of Britain, which they had been thrilled and proud to see with their own eyes . . . was a memory without fear. The Battle of the Doodlebug . . . was a time entirely without thrill or pride. They hated it.

Even when the V-1s did not come down, it was impossible to ignore them.

The doodlebug could be heard from a long way off. It came out of the clear summer distance or out of the rain or the dark July cloud with a low level roar that could be heard about thirty miles away. . . . As many as half a dozen would come roaring over together in parallel tracks separated by about a mile. The noise was fantastic. Crows in the field rose up with their own terrified explosion of wings and in houses dogs and cats cowered in their own secret place for shelters.

After dark, life in the Kentish countryside was even worse:

By day the people of Kent and Sussex could stop their work in hayfields or cherry-orchard or shop or factory . . . and calculate the behaviour of the bomb by what they would see and hear. But at night it was rather different. . . . Thousands and thousands of sturdy English country citizens every night for about eighty nights lay in bed and listened to the bombs travelling up on their courses from the coast; they listened to the sound of night-fighters firing and they listened too for the worst sound of all; the sound of silence.

In these strange circumstances, the delights of rural life could become a burden. One woman, then living at Ightam near Sevenoaks, remembers how, as soon as her small daughter had fallen asleep, 'one of the beastly things would come and the cocks and pheasants would crow and the nightingales would start singing. Lovely as the Kent nightingales were, I fear I didn't love them just then.'

The Kent County Council, to its credit, never tried to change the government's policy, but the chairman of its Civil Defence Committee, Alderman E. S. Oak-Rhind, did permit himself some wry comments about it in a long statement in mid-September:

Much has been said about shooting the flying-bomb down over 'open country'.

What is this 'open country?' Our coastal towns, miles of countryside dotted with villages, cottages, farms and houses. Here and there some big town.

A flying bomb exploding in the air, let alone on the ground, will strip the roof, bring down the ceilings, shatter the windows of all beneath, whether it be a cottage or 500 houses – and whether it be a cottage or a house, it was somebody's home. . . . So often [it was] somebody's life, taken to save London.

All told, Alderman Oak-Rhind revealed, '1,388 flying bombs were shot down on Kentish soil' and '1,000 or more shot down into the sea from her coast,' causing '152 dead, 1,716 injured and vast material damage.' And the attack, though it had cost comparatively few lives, had been unrelenting. Twenty-six were 'shot down over Kent during the first 24 hours. . . . During the first week 101.' During July flying-bombs were reported on every single day, and 50 per cent of those landing in the South-East Civil Defence Region came down in Kent, with 40 per cent in Sussex and 10 per cent in Surrey. In August they arrived on every day but one, the 26th, and Kent provided the graveyard for 68 per cent of the 800 shot down.

The government rapidly acknowledged that much of Kent was now a danger area. Previously most of the county had not qualified to receive Morrison shelters, but on 11 July, thanks to energetic lobbying by the regional commissioner, they began to be generally distributed. Parts of the county, such as Gillingham and Rochester, already qualified for evacuation, and during the next fortnight the formerly neutral areas, Bromley, Chislehurst, Sidcup and Orpington, were added to the list, to be followed by several former reception areas, including Sevenoaks, Tenterden and Tunbridge Wells.

When in a headline spread across eight columns the *Kent Messenger* proudly claimed, after the battle was over, 'Kent had 2,400 flying-bombs: 100 more than London' it was not exaggerating. During the first week alone 101 were shot down onto the county and thereafter incidents occurred, on average, at the rate of twenty a day. Four hundred and forty-eight separate communities reported some damage and many suffered time after time. Among the forty-one administrative units – boroughs, rural districts and urban districts – which made up the county, the unenviable honour of heading the list went to Tenterden, with 238. It was followed by Ashford, with 184, New Romney, with 149 and Sevenoaks rural district – the urban district escaped with a mere five – with 137. Others with a sizeable number of V-1s were Malling rural district with 97, Tonbridge rural district, with 95, Hollingbourne rural district with 81, Dartford rural district with 76, Egham rural district with 64 and Maidstone rural district with 63. No other local authority area received more than 35. Several, like Whitstable, Broadstairs, Herne Bay and Northfleet, escaped with under five, but only six had no incidents at all.

If uncomplaining, people in Kent were still intensely interested in their own, and their neighbours', ordeal. When, on 15 September 1944, the *Kent Messenger* published a map showing where every V-1 in the county had landed the day's issue was instantly sold out. (One newsagent, tired of explaining that she had no copies left, hung a notice to this effect round her neck.) Within two weeks, orders for 100,000 copies of the map had been received. It is still a treasured relic in countless homes and a framed copy hangs on the wall of at least one country pub.*

Kent had by far the most to endure of all the south-eastern counties, with 1444 V-1s, a total which rises to 2622 if one includes the 294 in that part of the county included, for Civil Defence purposes, within the London area, and those 'drowned' in the sea off its shores. Sussex came next, with 886, Essex third, with 512; and Surrey fourth with 295, excluding that part of it 'belonging' to London. These were the places which made up 'doodlebug alley', to live in which was soon a matter of pride, though one woman whose family had retreated from

---

*When I appealed for reminiscences for the present book I was inundated with offers of this famous map. The 'one pub' referred to is the Dog and Duck at Warnham, near Horsham, in Sussex.

London to the heart of rural Sussex can still smile at her mother's initial reaction. 'The Germans,' she protested, 'had absolutely no right to fly their nasty machines over our tiny village of Rotherfield.'

About a flying-bomb in the countryside there seemed at first something peculiarly obscene. One woman remembers the 'unearthly . . . smell . . . a mixture of burnt-out wires, trees, bark . . . rubber, explosive, fire, smoke' hanging over a wood after one had dropped at Whitesmith near Lewes, leaving '250 trees destroyed . . . metal work scattered in the trunks of the remaining trees,' and a herd of dead cows with 'their tails . . . blown off.'

The sight of branches and leaves spiralling into the sky in the distance became as familiar as the column of dust in the city and many observers remember the curious sound as a V-1 ploughed its way through the treetops, 'as if the trees were being felled one after another,' in the words of a woman on a Land Army course near Maidstone. Occasionally a tree served the role of a protective rampart, like the stout elm outside the cottage of one farmworker near Leatherhead. Rammed head-on by a V-1, the tree was cut off four feet from the ground, as if severed by a giant axe, but the house was saved. An eleven-year-old boy at Southborough felt that the saplings in a devastated plantation, their bark stripped away, resembled 'bleached bones sticking up out of the ground.'

To a housewife in Eastbourne it seemed as if all the birds, foxes and other small creatures had suddenly disappeared. Farm animals, unable to go underground, soon became hardened to the daily excitement. On a farm near Leatherhead just missed by a V-1, the cows' eyes, one observer remembers, 'were large, almost popping out, but they seemed all right after being calmed down.' A Kent land girl recalls that the cows in her charge, near Rochester, were 'petrified' by the first V-1s and tugged at the chains tethering them, but soon settled down in to their former placidity. Some cows near Pevensey seemed unaffected when a V-1 was shot down nearby but suffered disastrous after-effects from grazing in a field littered with fragments of steel wire. 'You could,' one local man remembers, 'feel the metal and see the lump under their skin. Two of them had to be destroyed.' Horses proved as tough as cows. Two show jumpers, blown clean over a hedge into the next field on a farm near Aylesbury, recovered, though the white coat of the 'grey' had turned black. Hens also, as chicken-owners in towns had discovered, were surprisingly resilient, though a Hasting man who complained to a local farmer that two newly bought pullets 'were not laying as promised', received a topical explanation: ' "It's those bloody doodlebugs . . . The hens don't like he".'

Kent contained many beautiful old houses, and to everyone's surprise, these stood up to blast better than more modern property. 'Throughout the Weald . . . ,' noted one resident, Mr R. H. Goodsall, a retired architect turned farmer who lived between Maidstone and Ashford, 'timber-framed houses shuddered, swayed and then recovered, whereas the apparently more substantial ones of stone, flint or brick collapsed.' Mr Goodsall also noticed how, when a V-1 came down 'in the field adjoining Harrietsham churchyard', where the wheat had been cut the previous day and piled up in stooks, 'we found pieces of doodlebug scattered all over the field but lumps of metal embedded in the shocks of corn had not penetrated right through the straw.'

Just as in town, an explosion could have unexpected, even bizarre, consequences, as in the case of a house at Harrietsham, occupied by an elderly retired couple:

The grounds were delightful for Sinderden spring had been dammed to . . . form a large lake which the proud owner stocked with trout. . . . The explosion of the doodlebug blew out all the water, which fell like rain over a mile or more of the country around. Whilst Mrs R. and her cook brewed tea . . . Mr R made his way down through the plantation of rhododendrons . . . to . . . the valley below. To his horror he found all the surrounding trees festooned with dead or dying fish and the lake empty of water. This shock no doubt contributed to his death a few weeks later.

As those who lived in the cities often found hard to realize, the countryside was also a workplace for hundreds of thousands of men and women. The Kent alderman quoted earlier spoke of watching 'from the Pilgrims Way, near Hollingbourne, the RAF shooting down the bombs over the heads of the land girls and other farm workers. Their work never ceased, but I have seen one of them cry as a bomb escaped and sped London-wards.' Like their counterparts in the towns, rural workers learned to live with the flying-bomb, though as one wartime land girl, then working near Ashford, comments, 'It was as if we had a plague of giant hornets going over all the time.' The real danger came, however, not from the hornets themselves but from those trying to swat them. Another land girl, busy picking cherries in an orchard at Nettlestead, remembers how, when the anti-aircraft guns opened up, 'we used to run for the shelter of the hedge and sit with a wooden fruit box on our heads.' There were, too, dangers unknown in any workshop, such as the constant fear, when one was perched high on a wagon-load of hay, that a sudden explosion might cause the horses to take fright and bolt. For this reason, at the first faint reverberation in the distance she and her workmates would swarm to the ground down a rope. Near the coast the guns were the greater danger. 'The noise was terrific,' remembers one land girl working on Romney Marsh. 'Shrapnel . . . used to fall all around us like rain.' Inland the biggest threat came from friendly aircraft. 'The fighters were a better warning than the sirens,' discovered a woman from Maidstone while cherry-picking at Offham, not far away. 'As soon as they revved up their engines and took to the sky, we scuttled down our ladders and stood up against the tree trunks for shelter from the bullets.' The flying-bombs themselves were a lesser danger, except when 'winged'. 'Frequently we watched them go past and got on with our work only to . . . find one . . . coming straight back for us at treetop height,' remembers the Romney Marsh land girl previously quoted. 'Then no one would move as quickly as we did, practically falling into the ditches, which fortunately were low in water at that time of year.'

The worst job of all was faced by people operating noisy farm machinery. On a farm at Westerham it became standard practice for the tractors to operate in pairs, facing towards each other, so that each driver acted as a look-out for the other. A thirteen-year-old boy at Bexhill acquired a novel duty during harvesting: waving his scarf to attract the attention of the farmhand driving the binder. 'On seeing my signal he would quickly join me under a high hedge or inside a large concrete army pillbox.' On a farm at Tidebrook in Sussex, one wartime schoolboy remembers, the damage done to the cutting blade of the reaping machine by the remains of two 'dead' V-1s was so serious that 'the men cut the wheat with scythes and sickles and tied the sheaves of corn by hand.'

If a wooden-spoon prize had been awarded for the *least* courageous farmworkers that summer, it would surely have been won by the Italian prisoners-of-war who made a colourful addition to the workforce on many farms. One landgirl witnessed what happened when a Spitfire exploded a V-1 in mid-air over a field near Ashford while they were hoeing sugar beet. The girls dropped to the ground, two British soldiers guarding the prisoners stood firm 'but where were the POWs? Not one to be seen. They had fled to the lane to shelter between the high banks and when all was quiet once more they filtered back to the field and their hoeing.'

Among the farm buildings damaged were eighty oast houses, and the flying-bomb bombardment was well under way when the hop season began. By all accounts, 1944 was not a good year for hops and, according to the *Kent Messenger*, at East Farleigh, where the rate of pay was no more than 'a shilling for every three bushels some dissatisfied pickers packed up and went home.' For those who stayed, the 1944 season was not soon forgotten. Thirty years later one woman from Clapton in East London remembered how, after an explosion – when there was no further danger – 'my mother dived under the bin' containing the gathered hops 'and it was ages before she would come out.' A Headcorn woman observed how on her family's farm the 'hoppers' parked their prams permanently in the nearest ditch and joined them there when danger threatened – all but one would-be heroine.

One rather large lady, who wore a big straw hat and Wellington boots, couldn't make it to the ditch on our fifth run that morning. She stood defiant, hoe raised aloft, and shouted, 'Get going you German ———. I'm too big to blow up.' The doodlebug blew up on top of us. No one was hurt but the straw-hatted lady lay in the ditch for the rest of the day, feebly drinking the hot tea I brought to her and moaning that Hitler was out to get her.

Responding to the slogan 'Lend a hand on the land' many

people joined agricultural camps, though these failed to provide the expected break 'away from it all'. One sixteen-year-old from Brighton, in the advance party setting up his school's camp on the village green at Mayfield, on the Kent/Sussex border, recalls that 'we became so used to doodlebugs that we would only stop digging the hole for "the bog", or pitching tents, if a doodlebug was being chased or shot at by ack-ack. . . . There was a doodlebug either coming or going almost all the time.' Eventually the 'teacher in charge decided . . . that we would be safer in the school hall,' and the boys were soon afterwards sent home.

Despite all interruptions, rural recreations, or their wartime equivalent, continued. One man then aged ten particularly enjoyed a National Savings rally on Tunbridge Wells Common, where an unscheduled attraction appeared: two Spitfires in close pursuit of a flying-bomb. 'I vividly remember the sight of the tracer bullets and the crowd, myself among them, going down flat as one man. Afterwards everyone got up and the rally continued.'

Headcorn in Kent (population in 1944 1400, only occupation agriculture and only previous claim to fame 'a venerable oak tree some forty feet in girth') also refused to let twelve flying-bombs within its borders upset its traditional August Bank Holiday sports day on the cricket field. 'Notwithstanding the menace of "doodlebugs",' reported the modestly-entitled local history, *A Record of the Efforts made in the Parish of Headcorn, Kent, to keep the Flag Flying*, 'nearly 2000 visitors' attended, producing a profit of £250 for the Red Cross and £53.16s. for Aid to Russia.

The very essence of rural England, as pictured in innumerable 'cosy' wartime films from *Mrs Miniver* on, was the church fête. A woman then aged eleven, entrusted with a stall with her sister, at Rotherfield in Sussex, still remembers the opening ceremony.

Not a cloud marred the sky as a visiting minister led a large crowd of parishioners in prayer on the lawn. Eyes were devoutly cast down and lips murmured decorously. . . . Then we heard it. Far away at first like a drowsy bumble bee . . . but then more insistent. Eyes flickered upwards, then quickly down, sly peeps between devoutly shielded eyes. . . . Fidgeting broke out in the ranks and anxious skyward glances became more open. Then we saw it! If only that damn parson would stop praying and allow us to run for cover, but still steadily on he ploughed. As it became . . . visible the ranks wavered and finally broke – people streamed for the house, one stall overturned. Audrey and I dived under ours and the lawn was deserted in under two minutes. Almost deserted, that is. Our missionary still prayed, watched by boggling eyes in various directions. Maybe his prayers were answered for the bomb flew harmlessly over, leaving the villagers to emerge sheepishly and try to look as though they had never been missing.

The white cliffs of South-East England had often been romantically referred to as the ramparts of the island fortress and at least six V-1s flew slap into the cliffs between Folkestone and Dover, leaving barely a scar in the chalk. Others came down on the beaches, sometimes colliding with the metal palisades erected against seaborne invaders. The largest single group of V-1s to be destroyed ended their brief and vicious lives in the sea just off the coast, the victims of the fighters patrolling off shore and the massed guns just above high water mark. Six hundred and two plunged into the water off Folkestone alone compared to a mere twenty-six shot down on to, or blown up over, the town itself. Mid-air bursts with nothing to halt the blast wave were often more destructive than explosions on the ground and the damage done by these twenty-six was vast – 14,000 houses were affected. The toll in dead and injured – three killed and twenty-four seriously injured – was miraculously light especially when compared to the effects of shelling from the French coast, which had killed thirty-two people and badly hurt 102. If they had to be under bombardment, the local residents had no doubt that there were far worse types of attack than flying-bombs.

In Hastings, which had never been shelled, the citizens were less philosophic. Many of its residents were retired people, making no contribution to the war effort and enjoying unlimited leisure to complain. The adjutant of a wing of the RAF Regiment stationed in the town observed the chilly reception given to his men:

Some people told me in no uncertain terms that we 'were a bloody nuisance and get to hell out of it'.

The attitude I constantly met was . . . that they did not really care where the flying-bombs came down so long as it was not near them. Pressure was exerted via the civil authorities to get guns moved out of the town and certain deployments were hampered and actually moved to less favourable positions to placate the citizens of a town that had had a very good war. . . . Many appeared unwilling to make any sacrifice in order to save lives in London. Indeed one lady sent a letter demanding that a gun be removed from the vicinity of her house, 'otherwise my cook has threatened to leave!'

No doubt in the hope of generating a little more patriotism among the townsfolk, the military authorities invited the mayor and other dignitaries to tour the gun sites. 'The civil party in their state robes with the mace-bearer carrying the borough's 250 year old mace,' reported the *Hastings and St Leonards Observer* on 5 August 1944, 'were in picturesque contrast to the grim line of heavy guns along the hillside, with the crews standing by ready for instant action.' They were also unfortunately in picturesque contrast to the results of the visit, which proved a public relations disaster. One enterprising journalist from Fleet Street took the opportunity to question the mayor about the townsfolk's by now notorious hostility to the gunners' presence. The resulting story in the following day's *Daily Mail*, under the headline 'Mayor's "I'm Ashamed". People Objected to Guns', exposed the embarrassing facts to the nation. The mayor was quoted as being 'ashamed at the protests of some of the population. . . . Some do not care how many people are killed in London so long as their sleep is not disturbed by the sound of gunfire.'

Inevitably, the mayor's response was to blame the reporter and a flood of letters poured into the local newspaper proclaiming its readers' loyalty. The protesters, declared an 'elderly widow' from St Leonards, 'are the same ones who howled for guns to be brought here when coastal areas had the tip and run raids and every gun was wanted for more important places elsewhere. . . . These protesters are letting the town down. . . . My advice to those people who don't like the noise of gunfire is this: Put some cotton wool in your ears, put your head under the blankets, and go to sleep.' But not everyone took this stalwart view. 'Remarks such as are attributed to the mayor contain the impression that he cares more for the welfare of Londoners than those of his own people and borough,' complained another resident of St Leonards. 'People forget that Hastings endured months of sneak-raiders when London was practically immune from raids of any sort.'

Hastings saw its last V-1 three days later, so the sensitive minority had little more reason to complain. For all the talk of Hastings having had to 'take it' only fifteen V-1s had landed on the town, and its casualty list remained very short: Hastings lost fewer citizens killed and injured during the whole war than many other places suffered in six weeks from the flying-bombs alone.

The truth was that in terms of casualties all the south-eastern counties got off very lightly in comparison to London. The comparison between the more rural part of Kent, which lay in the South-Eastern Civil Defence Region, and the more built-up part of the county, inside the London Region – it included Erith, Crayford, Chislehurst, Sidcup, Orpington, Bromley, Beckenham and Penge – was striking. The 1388 flying-bombs which landed in the former – excluding 'another 1,000 or more shot down into the sea' – produced a casualty list of only 152 dead and 1716 seriously injured: it had taken nearly ten bombs to achieve a single death.* The 294 V-1s on the 'London' part of the county caused by contrast 310 deaths and 3392 cases of serious injury – appreciably more than Churchill's rule of thumb of one fatal casualty per bomb. About the wisdom of what had been done, Kent's Civil Defence chief, Alderman Oak-Rhind, at least, looking back in mid-September, had no doubts:

Was the government right in ordering it [the flying-bomb] to be shot down outside the enormous . . . London boundary? Yes. Of that there is not the faintest doubt. Every analysis to which you can put the known figures answers this question in the affirmative. London could never have won through alone, or if she had her dead would have been numbered at an appalling figure.

---

*The figures given are those quoted at the time. Any discrepancy with those given elsewhere is due to corrections made later as earlier statistics were amended.

34

CHAOS OVER KENT

*Across the middle of Kent and Sussex . . . the noise of
fighters, guns and bombs was . . . an almost continuous
crazy chaos.*

H. E. Bates, unpublished *History of the Flying Bomb*, 1944

The battle against the flying-bombs started badly. After 18
June, when the guns around London fell silent, the V-1s trundled noisily over the capital day after day unmolested by a
single shell. This made good sense, for reasons already explained, but ordinary citizens found the situation humiliating
as General Pile, Commander-in-Chief of Anti-Aircraft Command soon learned. From Clapham, one irate citizen 'wrote to
tell me,' the general later recalled, 'that the anti-aircraft defences were the greatest scandal since Nero, and if I were to go
and spend a couple of hours in his bedroom . . . I would soon
see for myself that there was something wrong with my precious
barrage.' 'Your efforts during the night Blitz were not a great
success and now the flying-bombs get through as they like,'
another candid correspondent reminded the Commander-in-
Chief. 'Isn't it time you went?'

There was much that General Pile might have said in his
defence, for example, that intelligence had been wrong in predicting that the flying-bomb would fly at 5000–6000 feet instead
of that 'thousand feet band, between 2,000 and 3,000 feet
where the effectiveness of anti-aircraft fire was likely to be
small,' and 'that he had been promised a month's warning and
been given two days.' But nonetheless the guns *were* doing
badly. Two officers, sent out from command headquarters at
Northwood on a tour of inspection on Friday, 16 June, returned
on the late evening of 18 June with an alarming report. 'Wherever they went,' H. E. Bates recorded, 'they found their worst
fears justified. The shooting . . . was wild and inaccurate. . . .

394

The tough little flying bomb seemed an almost hopeless target for A.A. guns.'

The original Diver plan, prepared back in December 1943 and January 1944, envisaged, in General Pile's words, 'a series of lines placed across a funnel-shaped area, bounded by the launching sites at the wide end and Greater London at the narrow one.' Some of the lines consisted of fighter patrols, the first out to sea, between Beachy Head and the North Foreland, the second over the coast between Newhaven and Dover, and the third inland, between Haywards Heath and Ashford. Four hundred heavy anti-aircraft guns were, it was agreed, to be established on the seaward side of the North Downs, stretching from East Sussex across Surrey to the Thames Estuary, in a belt about five miles deep. They would be distributed in four rows, 3000 yards apart with a gun site at every 6000 yards, containing eight 3·7-inch guns and a single quick-firing 40-mm. Searchlights were to be distributed every 3000 yards to assist the fighters at night, and along the North Downs a wall of balloons would serve as long-stop to catch any pilotless aircraft that penetrated the other defences. On the afternoon of Friday, 16 June, the planned redeployment began.

Considered as a military manoeuvre it was an outstanding success. The move had been expected to take from eighteen to twenty-five days, though the commanders of five American AA battalions boasted that they would manage it in four. Even they proved wrong. The first guns were installed in their new locations by the early hours of Saturday, in less than eighteen *hours*, and the whole move was completed within five days. By the following Monday evening, 19 June, a far-reaching plan to improve the guns' efficiency had been drawn up and was already being implemented, including intensive training, revised operational 'drills', and, most important of all, re-siting the guns to give them a better view, both visually and by means of radar; the radar sets had originally been placed in hollows, to prevent jamming, which had not materialized. Already experience had shown that the mobile 3·7-inch gun, the command's basic equipment, which had to be traversed by hand, was 'no match for the flying-bomb. . . . So we made up our minds that all AA Command mobile 3·7-inch guns in the Diver defences should be replaced by the static, power-controlled

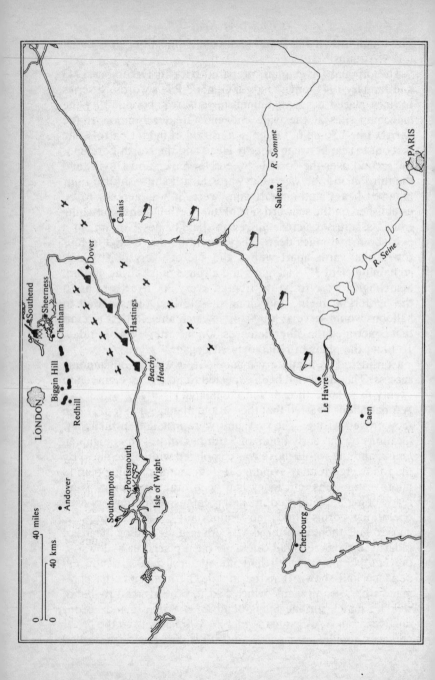

equipment.' This was a heroic decision for the solid concrete base for the static guns 'took months to construct even when one could get the labour to build them.' Necessity, however, proved an effective spur to invention, for the command's engineers devised an ingenious substitute, the 'Pile portable platform' or 'pile mattress', 'a moveable lattice-work of steel rails and sleepers . . . filled with ballast.' Two hundred were built at once in the workshop of the Royal Electrical and Mechanical Engineers, working day and night, and ultimately 720 were made, requiring the collection of '35 miles of railway lines and 22,500 sleepers . . . from 20 different railway depots,' as the press later reported, to provide bases for the 440 static guns now uprooted from all parts of the country and sent south. General Pile also concluded that 'the scattering of 40-mm guns' throughout the defensive zone had been a mistake, 'so we decided we would redeploy them too . . . behind the heavy gun-belt. . . . But, just as we had completed our reconnaissances, the Air Force decided to extend their balloon barrage to occupy the high ground which we had selected for our sites. . . . We had to start all over again and choose some sites to the south of the heavy-gun belt.'

Even without such problems AA Command would have had its hands full with finding, transporting and installing the supplies it needed, including twelve new gun communication rooms for the light guns alone, ton upon ton of hardcore to make marshy sites usable, mile upon mile of metal 'road-substitute', known as Sommerfield Track, plus 13,000 Andersons and three million sandbags to protect the crews engaged in trying to shoot the V-1s down upon themselves. Royal Signals and Post Office engineers sometimes found themselves having to rip out one day the cables and switchboards they had installed the day before. And all the time the rain descended, the clouds lay dank and dismal upon the exposed hillsides of the North Downs and the V-1s roared remorselessly overhead.

No one who relied on the Air Ministry press release issued on Tuesday, 20 June, would have had any suspicion that the defences had so far suffered a defeat:

When the first flying-bomb appeared from the French Coast, Air Marshal Sir Roderic Hill's Command, Air Defence of Great Britain, immediately went into action. The Luftwaffe's new weapon was known to him and his Staff Officers. . . . A.D.G.B.'s plan . . . was at once brought into force. Squadrons of day and night fighters went up, and the Anti-aircraft defences and Royal Observer Corps Units went into action. . . . Many of the flying bombs have been intercepted and destroyed by our fighters over the Channel. . . . A large number have exploded in the air when attacked and others shot down over open country before they could reach built-up areas further inland.

The impression such reports gave was absurdly over-optimistic, except in one respect; the *detection* of flying-bombs, in contrast to their rate of destruction, was better than anyone had dared hope. By 1944 the aircraft reporting system had reached a high level of efficiency. The three Observer Groups chiefly involved had their headquarters at Horsham, Maidstone and Bromley. Three others, Winchester, Watford and Colchester, were also involved though to a lesser degree. As the historian of the Bromley centre later explained:

In comparison with the complicated work of tracking piloted aircraft flying tortuous courses at heights of 15,000 to 30,000 feet . . . the reporting and plotting of flying-bombs was a very simple matter. They travelled low, usually not much above 2,000 feet; and except in rare cases, as when they had hit balloon cables, or passed through electric storms, when they were liable to perform the most peculiar antics, their courses were absolutely straight. At night, the projectiles advertised their presence by the flames streaming from their propulsion ducts . . . enabling their positions to be pin-pointed with absolute precision.

To speed up communications the RAF installed forward air-controllers at Maidstone and Horsham, linked to the main Diver operations room at Biggin Hill, and by a mobile transmitter to the fighters in the air. The radar system which up to now had not coped well with low-flying aircraft was also improved. Borrowed American equipment, known as MEW (Microwave Early-Warning), was installed at Fairlight in Sussex on 29 June, and supplied sighting reports to both Maidstone and Horsham. The existing radar stations also proved able to pick up the V-1s at their regular height of 2000 feet, as the young Typhoon pilot, Richard Hough, temporarily grounded and under training at the radar station at Beachy Head, discovered:

398

I was off watch when the first doodlebugs came in . . . There was an atmosphere of crisis in the dark, stuffy Nissen hut when I got there. 'You can almost see them taking off,' Igoe [a colleague] claimed. 'And, my God, they *go*!'

Then . . . when I had been staring at that stupid tube for a mere hour or two, a smudge appeared a few miles inside France. It gained height with remarkable speed and I watched in consternation as the blips marched across the Channel with a great stride at every sweep.

'Nothing will ever catch that,' I pronounced, and picked up three more blips almost at once from more flying bombs. . . . I vectored a section of Spitfires onto an interception course with a blip that was coming straight for Beachy Head. 'Diver, Diver!' I transmitted. 'Square 27, course. . . .' I ran out of the controller's hut as it approached, and with two or three airmen and a collection of awed WAAFs heard for the first time the off-beat rattle of the . . . primitive engine. It swept overhead with inflexible purposefulness, straight as a ruled line, devastating, implacable.

In these early days of the attack the guns had few successes. The alleged 'morale effect' of anti-aircraft fire in forcing enemy pilots to fly higher was not going to discourage the flying-bombs. But around the end of June three new devices arrived, which, as General Pile remarked, provided between them 'a robot defence against the robot weapon'. The first was the SCR 584 radar set, with a far greater 'pick-up range' than earlier models. Linked to it was the 'M-9 director', or predictor, which solved the basic problem of all anti-aircraft gunnery, i.e. calculating where the target would be when the shell reached it. Marking an even greater breakthrough was the 'VT' – for 'Variable Time' – proximity fuse, which was activated by changes in the magnetic field when within sixty feet of the target. The fuse was so sensitive that it could be set off by flocks of birds and even heavy clouds, or on passing near another shell on the way up. If the self-destroying safety mechanism failed to work, it had a disconcerting habit of exploding as it approached the ground on returning to earth.

Although the idea of this near-miraculous fuse had been conceived by British scientists of EMI and Pye Ltd, development work took place in the United States, where the fuses were tested against a mock-up of a flying-bomb at a US Army testing-ground in New Mexico, and then mass-produced in a peaceful corner of North Carolina. Here 'groups of negroes who sang in unison to the rhythm of the punch presses,' according to an American historian, 'girls who frequently insisted on going barefooted and women of society who had never touched machinery before' mastered the skills needed to make and assemble its intricate mechanism until the factories were turning out 430,000 units a month.

With every service clamouring for new radar sets, predictors and proximity fuses, it was remarkable that Anti-Aircraft Command, which was usually at the end of every queue, should have got so many. The credit lay with General Pile, who had sent the first unexploded V-1 he could lay his hands on to Washington, and with General Marshall, the US Army Chief of Staff, on whose orders 'an immediate allocation of 165 S.C.R. 584s . . . was made, and . . . shipped to England on the very next boat.'

Providing all this new equipment was only the first step, for training sessions in its use now had to be fitted into an already overcrowded day. Between 27 June and 2 July the guns were manned for 108 hours 12 minutes out of 120, and on one day the crews were in their gunpits for the full twenty-four hours. To these exhausted men the arrival of the new-fangled American apparatus caused at first resentment rather than rejoicing. Before they could use the ammunition, the guns needed two hundred modifications and the resulting teething troubles tended to be regarded with relish. ' "This stuff would be ───── good if it worked," ' was, General Pile discovered, a common comment, and in the end 'Strong measures had to be taken . . . to make sure that officers brought the new equipment into action by the time specified.'

Far greater than his troubles with his own men, however, were General Pile's difficulties with his fellow commanders. The ninety miles between Calais and Westminster, and the sixty between the coast and the outskirts of London, had seemed to give adequate room for manoeuvre when the Diver defence plan was drawn up. In practice, since a V-1 could reach London only ten or twelve minutes after passing over Folkestone or Hastings, the three groups of defenders – gunners, airmen and balloon crews – were constantly getting in each others' way. It was, remarked H. E. Bates 'like having two or three boxing matches in a crowded railway carriage'.

Undoubtedly some of the trouble came from ordinary Army units, and trigger-happy Americans. On 11 July the Air Defence of Great Britain headquarters complained that 'an Army vehicle outside Hastings on 28 June 1944 was seen to engage a flying bomb even though a fighter was in close pursuit at the time' and that AA batteries defending airfields had also been engaging in illicit, freelance fire against V-1s. 'Flying bombs do not bear the markings of an enemy Air Force,' pointed out the staff officer concerned, 'nor can they be said to be directly attacking any particular unit over which they pass and therefore troops not trained in AA defence are prohibited from opening fire on them.' Unhappily, however, the sacred requirements of SD 158 Part I – the instructions governing anti-aircraft operations by non AA units – continued to be ignored, and it was General Pile's men who, however unjustly, got the blame.

At this stage RAF fighters constantly found themselves being fired on when about to destroy their target. The CO of one Polish squadron bitterly complained that after a long chase 'our friendly gunners intervened' and 'the wings of both the flying-bomb and the Mustang instantly became so perforated that they could have been used as sieves.' Wing-Commander Roland Beamont, CO of the two squadrons of Tempests engaged in the same battle, was even more incensed that his men had to spend much of their time, 'trying to dodge the shell-bursts of their own side's ack-ack'.

In the first week of the battle two Tempest pilots were shot down by anti-aircraft guns . . . with the result that deputations were sent to the local M.P.s. . . . The Tempest Wing had their own more immediate satisfaction, however, when by a complete coincidence one of them downed a V-1 into the grounds of a country house used as a mess by the gunners. The resulting explosion blew out all the windows in the mess without hurting anybody, just as the gunner officers were having their breakfast. The Tempest pilots were said to have come back from that particular sortie holding their sides.

Air Chief Marshal Hill, as Commander-in-Chief of the Air Defence of Great Britain, was well aware of the dangerous rift developing within his command. As he wrote, 'We could not afford to sacrifice the spirit of co-operation between gunners and pilots,' and a complicated compromise was therefore worked out. Three different possibilities were envisaged, labelled, a little oddly, 'Flabby', 'Fickle' and 'Spouse'. On Flabby days, when perfect weather favoured the fighters, the guns would close down and leave the pilots complete freedom to pursue their prey where they would. In Fickle, or average, weather, the guns would also be free to fire at any targets they spotted, unless a fighter was in close pursuit. When Spouse, or bad visibility and poor weather, prevailed, the guns would have freedom of action up to 8000 feet. All this was fine in theory but most days that June and July were Fickle, with changeable weather, which meant, in H. E. Bates's words, 'guns and fighters mutually interfering with each other' and 'across the middle of Kent and Sussex . . . an almost continuous crazy chaos.'

The results caused deep embarrassment to the adjutant of the wing of the RAF Regiment deployed at Hastings:

Day after day in fine weather Fickle was the code-word laid on from the top and the massed guns had the added experience of watching FBs soar above them – a perfect target – and not being allowed to open fire. The planes were so often conspicuous by their absence. . . . As many of the thousands of gunners had families and friends in London, to see the FBs go through, perhaps to hit their homes, [caused bitter] frustration [which] soon turned to sheer hate of the RAF.

Now it was the gunners' turn to complain. 'Never before,' wrote General Pile, 'had the guns been so forcibly restrained . . . on many days they did not average five rounds apiece.' So vigorously did he protest at inter-service meetings that 'by the middle of July I was hardly on speaking terms with the other members'.

Air Marshal Hill soon realized that the attempt to please both parties had merely made matters disastrously worse. 'I came to the conclusion,' he later explained, 'that the only solution was to give guns and fighters freedom each in their own sphere. On the 10th July, therefore I decided to prohibit fighters from entering the gun-belt, whatever the circumstances, after the 17th July.'

At a conference to discuss the new plan, General Pile suggested that it would be easier to operate if all the guns now on the coast were to be moved back into the main gun-belt and

Hill's senior staff officer, Air Commodore G. H. Ambler, in peacetime a Yorkshire textile merchant, was set to examine the proposal. He carefully set out on paper the pros and cons 'strictly in accordance', an official historian has recorded, 'with the recommended method contained in the War Manual', and reached, on the evening of 12 July, an unexpected conclusion. The intention, in Air Marshal Hill's words, 'to put all the guns together in the place where they could function best' was clearly right, but the proposed method, namely moving them all to the North Downs, was wrong. Logic dictated 'adopting the opposite course, and sending forward the guns already on the Downs to join those on the coast.'

All through Thursday, 13 July, Air Marshal Hill weighed up this proposal, painfully conscious of its implications:

Hundreds of guns, with all their ammunition, were now in position on the Downs. Great reserves of ammunition had been collected there. Thousands of miles of telephone cables had been laid over a period of six months. Accommodation had been found or improvised for the gunners. . . . In short, a small city was spread out between Redhill and the Thames. The proposal was that we should pick up this city bodily and transport it thirty or forty miles further south. On top of this, for the last two weeks men had been busy building permanent emplacements for the guns among the apple orchards and on the slopes of the chalk hills in Kent and Surrey. The organism was still taking root. To transplant it might still be possible but would not long remain so. . . . I decided to think the matter over during the day and hold a conference late that afternoon. . . . My reflections were puncutated by the intermittent clatter of the bombs.

After the Air Officer Commanding No. 11 Group had 'welcomed the proposal' it was the turn of Anti-Aircraft Command.

I then asked General Pile whether he supported the proposal to move all the guns to the coast, leaving the balloons where they were and creating two new areas for fighters, one between the balloons and the new gun-belt, and the other in front of the gun-belt, over the sea. He replied that he was in full agreement with it.

Hill bravely decided that the redeployment should go ahead, but he now faced strong opposition from above. The Air Ministry, in Pile's words, feared that the move would 'increase our successes and decrease the RAF's total' and Hill was made aware that 'the Air Council was very displeased'. Happily, he realized, General Pile commented, 'that . . . the combined efficiency of the defences was of greater importance than the individual glory of one or other Service' and the great move went ahead.

The earlier moves, from London into Kent and Sussex, and from the first sites on the North Downs to others with a better field of fire, rapidly seemed trivial beside the disturbance that now ensued. 'Quite apart from the troops of the various supply services,' wrote General Pile, '23,000 men and women had to be transported forward with all their kit and stores. . . . In this one week the vehicles of a supposedly static Command travelled 2,750,000 miles. All the normal rules went by the board. Routing and movement control were forgotten. One brigade issued no written orders at all; no-one seemed any the worse.' The speed of the move was as astonishing as its scale. The first advance parties had set off for the coast directly after the conference on 13 July; on the following day the move of the heavies began, and by dawn on 17 July they were in action in their new positions. The light guns, left behind to cover the move, were then given the word to leave and by 19 July they, too, were in action. 'It was,' as General Pile justly wrote, 'an extraordinary achievement.'

On 17 July the formal orders went out forbidding the fighters to engage V-1s within the gun-belt, between St Margaret's Bay, to the east of Dover, and Cuckmere Haven, five miles east of Beachy Head. Along this strip of coast, up to 10,000 yards out to sea and 6000 yards inland, the guns could fire at will and any pilot needing to cross it had to do so above 8000 feet, well clear of any shell-bursts. There was no longer any possible room for misunderstanding.

Complete freedom of action against flying bombs will be allowed to AA guns at all times and in all conditions, within the boundaries of the new DIVER Gun Belt. Complete freedom of action against flying bombs will be allowed to fighter aircraft forward of the balloon barrage, but excluding the area of the DIVER Gun Belt.

The new arrangements undoubtedly reduced the grounds for friction between airmen and gunners, but the real test was an increase in the overall number of 'kills'. The first figures seemed to justify the sceptics at the Air Ministry. In the first six days from dawn on 17 July only 269 V-1s had been shot down of 473 that had come within range of the defences, or 57 per cent, 'a substantially lower rate of destruction than . . . during the last week under the old system,' for as Hill observed, 'improved results from the guns . . . had not sufficed to outweigh a sharp decline in the achievement of the fighters.' Hill took comfort, however, from the transformation in the relationship between the two services. 'The mists of suspicion, whose gathering had troubled me so much,' he wrote, 'were dispersed overnight. . . . Pilots and gunners were beginning to understand one another's problems and work together. Unity was restored.'

General Pile, from his forward headquarters near Hastings, noted other benefits. Previously 'in the districts where they [the flying-bombs] fell,' he noted, 'our troops were refused cigarettes in the local shops and even denied access to restaurants.' Everyone, however, could rejoice in the sight of a flying-bomb shot down into the sea and, such black spots as Hastings apart, his men now found themselves popular. 'Their morale was colossal. . . . The percentage of those reporting sick was far below normal. The Sussex Constabulary reported that they had never had so many troops in their area and less trouble with them.'

Guns were now poured into the narrow Diver strip, fifty miles long and less than three miles deep, from all over the country. By the morning of 19 July General Pile had at his disposal 396 heavy and 572 light guns of his own command, plus sixteen heavy 90-mm guns from the US Army Anti-Aircraft artillery, 584 light guns manned by the RAF Regiment (the 'Army' of the RAF, responsible for airfield defence) and twenty-eight from the Royal Armoured Corps, a total of 412 heavy and 1184 light guns. A month later, including the armament round the Thames Estuary which accounted for 208 heavy and 578 light guns, there were 800 heavies in position, 1800 light guns and more than 700 rocket barrels from the so-called 'Z' batteries. Eighty of the heavy guns were American, contributed by General Eisenhower on the grounds that London was an American as well as a British base.

From 8 July onwards the enemy had been making what

General Pile identified as 'a diversionary attack' from the east and during July and August 120 flying-bombs arrived from this direction, mainly coming up the Thames estuary or across Essex. His response was to set up a 'box defence', bounded at the corners by Clacton and Chelmsford to the north, and Whitstable and Rochester to the south. Into this rectangle were fitted another 178 40-mm guns and 402 20-mm, plus 108 rocket barrels. The 'Maunsell forts' were also brought into the scheme, sunken structures resembling a post-war oil rig, erected to guard the sea approaches to London and designed to carry four 3·7-inch guns and two Bofors.

By mid-August the attack on the left flank was visibly increasing, and once again General Pile had to uproot his supposedly static guns, this time to send them north. On 19 August the first ten heavy and five light batteries were dispersed around Ramsgate, Margate and the North Foreland. They were followed two days later by fourteen more heavy batteries and ten light ones, while General Pile's advanced headquarters moved thirty miles east from Hastings to Folkestone. The RAF Regiment batteries and those borrowed from 21st Army Group were left behind. 'We were once more,' wrote General Pile, 'almost entirely on our own,' for though the Diver gun box, as it was known, still contained more than 500 light 20-mm and 40-mm guns manned by 'outsiders', all the 136 3·7-inch heavy guns, plus another seventy-four lighter guns and the single rocket battery came from AA Command itself.

By now it was clear that the redeployment of the defences back in July had been an enormous success. In the first week after their arrival on the coast the guns had shot down only 17 per cent of all V-1s entering the gun-belt. Then week by week the score mounted: 24 per cent, 27 per cent, 40 per cent, 55 per cent, 60 per cent and, in the last week of August, 74 per cent, so that only a quarter of the V-1s which reached the coast survived to be challenged by the fighters inland. On one night during this last week the figure reached 82 per cent, an astonishing achievement.

Almost equally amazing was the harmony which now prevailed between the Army and the RAF. Of this no one was more conscious than Air Marshal Hill, who, as the main campaign was coming to an end, set off to inspect his noisy 'parish':

Chaos over Kent

Flying towards the south coast on the 28 August, I could see over Romney Marsh a wall of black smoke marking the position of the *Diver* barrage. . . . On the far side of the barrage fighters were shooting down flying bombs into the Channel; on the nearer side more fighters waited on its fringe to pounce on the occasional bomb that got so far. The whole was as fine a spectacle of co-operation as any commander could wish to see.

35

ONE SHELL, ONE DOODLEBUG

It soon became one shell, one doodlebug.

Wartime gunner, recalling August 1944

Whatever decisions their commanders made, it was in the end the pilot and ordinary gunner upon whom the defence of the island that dangerous summer rested. For AA Command, whose members had on the whole spent an uneventful war, the shock of being in the front line was especially traumatic, particularly as most gunners had failed to realize what a tough task they faced. The doodlebugs' 'constant height, speed and course' seemed at first 'to make them a gunner's dream ... and we reckoned we would soon "knock 'em for six",' remembers one man then serving with a mobile battery which, instead of being sent to Normany, suddenly found itself translated from Falmouth to Bethersden near Ashford.

It did not take long for the painful truth to dawn, as on a Bofors battery, which had been covering D-Day preparations at Studland Bay in Dorset, and was sent to Lamberhurst near Tunbridge Wells:

We set up our guns immediately in a field just outside the village. It was getting dark and it was cold and raining, with dark scudding low cloud, and we were dirty, tired and hungry. We were told there would be no sleep for us, we were to remain perpetually manned ready for instant action at any hour of the night or day, with no breaks for meals. These were to be brought to us and would be eaten round the gun and abandoned if we had to shoot. Even as we were being briefed, there was a loud rumbling noise, like an aircraft in trouble, and the low clouds were lit up with a flashing sort of light, but we could see nothing. Due to such bad weather, it was to be many nights

408

and days before we got our first sighting and when at last we did, the speed of these things left us gasping! . . . A Bofors maximum aim off speed was only 450 m.p.h. so we had little chance of keeping ahead of a target once it was within range. All we could manage to fire was a dozen rounds at the most. Situated as we were on the low slopes of the Downs, the bomb presented a very tiny target. . . . Nevertheless, after a time we did hit several, only to see our shells bouncing off them due to the rounded armour-plated fuselage.

The experiences of another Bofors unit, at Tenterden, were equally discouraging.

Before many hours passed the flying-bombs were coming over in bulk – three, four, five or six in the sky at one time. . . . We never scored a hit. . . . When the bomb went out of range and we disengaged, one gunner would point his clenched fist in the air and shout 'Bastard!' at the bomb and immediately every man on the site, including the officer, would follow suit. Then we would all look at each other and laugh like hell . . . our way of letting off steam.

Until proper fire discipline was established everyone with a gun in his hand tended to blaze away at will. A former telephonist/plotter in a searchlight battery in the Cranford and Hawkhurst area still remembers letting fly with a machine gun. 'I could see my tracer bullets bouncing off' while 'the Bofors shells were bursting yards behind.' The Head Warden at Brasted in Kent recalls a Bren gun company 'firing away with . . . glorious abandon. A warden on duty had the shock of his life when they opened up for the first time and he heard the bullets whining . . . just over his head.'

A resident of Folkestone watched an unimpressive performance by a Southern Railway Home Guard company:

The gunfire was accompanied by . . . shouts of 'Up a bit', 'Over a bit', etc., but all the bursts of fire missed the flying-bomb. Suddenly about six American Buffalo fighters coming back from a raid over France swooped round to land at Kingsnorth. The American planes were diving in all directions to get out of the way. There was a great shout of 'Trust the Yanks to make us miss.' . . . The flying-bomb . . . got away to London.

The solution to such problems was found, as already explained, in giving the guns and fighters different spheres of activity. This involved a move to the coast by many units, including No.

409 HAA Battery at East Grinstead, which was then expecting important visitors, as one of its warrant officers remembers:

Between calls for action stations during the night, we had to complete the erection and painting of a Nissen hut. . . . We had men painting the inside while others were hammering nails through the outside sheets of corrugated steel.

At 10.30 a.m. the whole unit was paraded and we were told that both the King and Queen were the VIPs. At 12 noon they had not arrived and we stood at ease when, without warning, the motorcade arrived. . . . The battery was put back on parade and the guns and equipment were manned. . . . The Queen charmed us all . . . the King was more interested in the equipment. Immediately the visit terminated the COs apologized for the extra work we had been called upon to do, especially as he had to announce that we were being moved straight away to the coast, where it was expected that . . . we would have more success.

The King left his own account of this visit, on 12 July, after which the party travelled on to Lingfield, where, after lunch in the mess of a 'mixed' HAA Battery, he watched his hosts shooting at six V-1s. Their aim, he recorded in his diary, was 'very level but a bit "behind". . . . I hoped it was not because we were there which had made them nervous.'

The battery from East Grinstead re-established itself at Pevensey Bay, between Eastbourne and Bexhill, where it received '100% reinforcements', which made it possible to work a '24 hours on, 24 hours off' rota, and was re-equipped with 'static guns fixed to railway track', i.e. 'Pile mattresses', and 'special ammunition . . . so short at first we were restricted to a given number of rounds per day', i.e. shells with proximity fuses. 'We had immediate success and morale soared.'

But some military bureaucrat had still not woken up to the urgency of the times:

The fixed 3·7-in guns could not be fired when the angle was below ten degrees . . . a safety measure installed when they were used for the defence of built-up areas. All that was required was the removal of a simple stop. The work was started and then came to a halt. . . . Somebody had ruled that as the guns were the colours of the Royal Regiment of Artillery . . . no modifications could take place without the authority of the Commander-in-Chief, His Majesty King George VI, and this took a week to obtain.

The radar and predictor also presented some problems at first. The same NCO remembers one occasion when 'we found that it had "locked" on the spire of the local church and that we were placing a barrage over that,' while the ATS in a 'mixed' battery at Camber Sands, managed, one of them recalls, 'in our first effort, to have the guns lined up just above hedge height, firing point-blank at any lorries which happened to pass on the road.'

By now the presence of women on the gun sites was universally accepted and no member of AA Command was better known than Mary Churchill, daughter of the Prime Minister, the senior ATS officer of No. 481 Battery, stationed in Hyde Park. One private who served under her remembers Mary Churchill as 'a super person', who lent her 'a lovely red long evening gown' for a camp entertainment. The Prime Minister was a frequent visitor to the site, and this informant remembers that 'we used to smell his cigar before actually seeing him.' No. 481 Battery was now sent south.

At the height of the bombardment we were suddenly told to pack our gear and were moved in big lorries down to . . . West Hill, Hastings. Our command post there was a ladies loo and in about a couple of hours all the porcelain, etc., was taken out and all our maps, telephones, etc., were installed and immediately we were once again in action.

During the first days after the move to the coast the defences were in danger of being swamped by the sheer weight of the attack. One man who rejoined his unit near Lydd on Romney Marsh after a rare weekend away remembers being 'amazed' on his 'return to camp on Sunday evening to find the whole troop on the gun park, draped over the guns or lying in the gun pits fast asleep. . . . They had been in almost continuous action for forty-eight hours and had fired every round and bullet they had.' The supposedly 'weaker sex' were as hard pressed as the men. 'Life was one long rush up and down from the gun park,' remembers a former ATS radar operator with a heavy AA battery at Minster, near Sheerness. 'We had to sleep with our plimsolls on and no sooner did we strip off to have a wash than the alarm bells would sound again.'

Women proved better able than men to fill the tedious

411

periods of waiting in between the frenzied moments of action. On a gun-site close to the river Medway there was a sudden craze for embroidery and one former member of the ATS remembers sitting quietly stitching away, while awaiting the call to action. 'I lost no end of needles jumping up each time the alarm went. Now, thirty-two years later,* I still have not finished one of those tablecloths.'

Although the seaside resorts were full of empty houses, many crews were under canvas. This was August by the sea for an ATS private stationed at Camber Sands in Kent:

Life at the camp was basic. If we weren't on duty we had fatigues to do the same as the men. The loos were just benches and wooden seats. Hot water a luxury, obtained only if we were on cookhouse fatigues. . . . The canteen was in one of the bungalows – jamjars were our cups, but at least there were chairs to sit on. . . . Towards the end of August it started to rain, almost without stopping.

An RAF teleprinter operator, posted to Newchurch in the middle of Romney Marsh on 15 August, recorded in his diary on 23 August his efforts to make daily life more tolerable:

Made a bed from petrol tins and a piece of discarded corrugated iron, with straw palliasse on top, which raises my bed from the ground and provides something to sit on and therefore write, clean one's shoes and buttons, etc., with more comfort.

A tent was no place to sleep with V-1s being shot down all round. One gunner stationed on Romney Marsh remembers 'wishing we were issued with two steel helmets, one to cover our faces and the other for vital organs lower down.' The ATS on Camber Sands, one of them remembers, had 'a series of trenches . . . around the tents for off duty use and a large iron triangle on which to bang a warning. This was only banged once, then . . . everybody stopped running to see what the noise was and the girl doing the banging was cheered loudly and made camp heroine for an hour or so.'

Most servicemen and women were eager to escape from camp when they could. The ATS of No. 566 HAA Battery, who formed part of the Diver 'box' beside the Thames Estuary, faced a long journey since they were separated by the river

---

*My informant was writing in 1976.

Medway from 'the nearest railway station to civilization' in the village of Snodland:

One had to walk down through the cornfields, and across a muddy farm yard and a long-since deserted old churchyard, which led one onto the river bank. Over the other side of this wide river lived the ferry-boat man, the ferry consisting of one rowing boat. (Twopence to cross.) Once at the riverside one had to hail this poor old ferryman, vocally. No good only one ATS trying to shout loud enough: there always had to be at least two of us. . . . Imagine it on a cold, wet windy morning in half-light, trying to make oneself heard against the wind, only, when he did finally arrive, to slip up in the mud getting in his old boat. Finally, when we did arrive at London Bridge Station, we would be picked up by the women military police for having muddy shoes.

On fine days bathing was popular. A warrant officer with 409 HAA Battery at Pevensey remembers 'one Saturday afternoon when . . . we saw a doodlebug which had been winged come down just on the water line. Our instincts were divided between swimming madly out to sea and running back to shore to lie flat.' A civilian at Pevensey Haven watched a gun's crew interrupt their dip 'to man their gun, one of them dressed only in his tin helmet' – surely the classic example of 'being improperly dressed on parade'.

Although many flying-bombs exploded in the air if the warhead or fuel tank was hit, damage to the wings or ailerons could have unpredictable results. 'Some would dive and crash immediately, some would glide on for about a mile,' remembers one gunner, 'whilst others would spiral earthwards until they hit the ground. Still others would tilt and climb upwards before making their death dive. . . . This was tolerable when the sky was clear and one could see them, but when the sky was full of low clouds, as on a wet day, and the doodlebugs could be heard but not seen . . . knowing what acrobatics the bombs were capable of . . . was all very frightening.'

So heavy was the barrage that it was often impossible to make out the noise of an individual flying-bomb above the tumult of the guns, as a Bofors gunner stationed at Camber Sands testifies:

The noise was tremendous. You couldn't hear orders and in fact I had a rope tied to my ankle and whenever you were wanted to stop firing, this was achieved by pulling your foot off the firing pedal. If you were in immediate danger, the sergeant pointed to the slit trench and you dived straight off the gun platform into the trench without waiting to see what was coming at you. . . . The only time I was really frightened was . . . when I counted thirty-two bombs at once coming towards us, and I thought, 'God, we can never cope with this lot.' . . . But as soon as I started firing, my stomach settled and I concentrated on loading and firing as many shells as I could.

The army of weapons finally assembled to greet the V-1s made a deep impression on all who saw it. One man working in a war factory at Rye calculated that between there and Lydd 'were over 1000 Ack-Ack guns of various types,' with 'three batteries within less than a mile.' 'Directly in front of us were 88-mm* guns of the American army, and to the right of these, British 3·7-inch anti-aircraft guns' observed an RAF Regiment gunner, whose own line of Bofors guns was posted 'on high ground at the back of the valley road from Dover to Folkestone. Behind us in the valley were rocket launchers.'

Not far away, in that lively resort Camber Sands, a member of a radar detachment observed with delight the successive lines of defence. 'Aircraft out to sea, tanks on the foreshore, wheel to wheel barrage, batteries of guns every few hundred yards . . . followed by light Ack-Ack with Heavy Ack-Ack as long stops.' Watching on the radar screen, he found it 'a grand sight to see these shells pyramiding up to the target like tracers, the light Ack-Ack rounds bouncing off the V-1s, then the final big reflection as the doodlebug exploded.' A man living at Rhodes Minnis, near Folkestone, was struck by the contrast between the episodes of activity and the peace which preceded and followed them. Long before the V-1 could be seen or heard the AA guns, alerted by their radar, would be probing the air. Then, as the missile came into sight, 'suddenly all hell would be let loose, a veritable pandemonium of gunfire, ending in a ball of fire falling into the sea and a profound, almost eerie, silence.'

AA Command's weapons when the first V-1s arrived were

---

*In fact 90-mm, the nearest Allied equivalent to the famous German '88'.

essentially those it had used throughout the war. Its heaviest gun, the 4·5-inch had proved disappointing and had been modified to fire the same shell as the smaller 3·7-inch gun, which formed the backbone of the defences. This solid, reliable weapon could fire a shell weighing 28 pounds, supposedly with a lethal area of fifty yards, to a height of 32,000 feet, and a skilled crew could loose off ten to twelve rounds a minute, though with its case each projectile weighed 66 pounds. Even the 'mobile' version of the gun itself weighed more than ten tons. The Command's 'light' gun, the Bofors, weighed 2·4 tons and fired clips of five 2-pound shells to a maximum height of 12,000 feet, at a rate of up to 120 rounds a minute, though as they exploded on impact a direct hit was needed to achieve results which could not be guaranteed even then. Sometimes, as already described, the shells merely bounced off again.

The performance of both types of gun was vastly improved by the arrival of the new radar equipment and predictors but the real turning point was the coming of the proximity fuse. One former member remembers the Sunday afternoon when all the available ATS on the site had to fit new nose-cones to their whole stock of shells, the excuse being that the girls' hands were more suitable for doing such delicate turns. 'Mind you, it didn't stop us from having to do manual duties with our dainty sensitive fingers.'

The code-name of the proximity fuse, 'Bonzo', gave nothing away, although its value was soon demonstrated. 'It reached the stage,' claims one gunner, 'where the gun crews took it in turn to "have a go" . . . It soon became one shell, one doodlebug.'

Adding a visually impressive element to such barrages was AA Command's latest acquisition, the rocket-firing 'Z' batteries, which soon became as accurate as the older weapons. 'It was a treat to watch the box barrage of rockets go up and explode every one in turn,' remembers one man who sometimes saw six V-1s at a time heading inland near Folkestone.

From its muddled, unsatisfactory start until its triumphant end, credit for the defeat of the V-1s was never fairly shared out. All along, the public's great heroes were the dashing, photogenic young fighter pilots, complete with topical slang and dazzling row of medals; the sweating, inarticulate gunner in shabby, undecorated khaki came a poor second.

The lack of medals for the gunners was a particularly sore point. 'There was no doubt in my mind,' commented General Pile, 'which needed the greater courage – to stand on a gun-site and fire at a directly approaching flying-bomb with the knowledge that, if you hit it, you will bring it down either on to or near your own site, or to fly an aircraft at a suitable distance behind the bomb and shoot it down.' Any pilot who shot down a large number of V-1s could count on receiving yet another decoration; but 'in the whole of that first phase,' wrote General Pile, 'on not one occasion did the announcements ever say that an anti-aircraft battery had destroyed even a single flying-bomb.' When, late in August, General Pile invited a party of 100 town clerks and ARP controllers to visit the gun belt, so that he could set the record straight, the result was 'a fearful lot of unpleasantness', for he was ordered to send an urgent telegram to his guests forbidding them to pass on any 'specific information . . . regarding the . . . relative effectiveness of the various means of defence.' The RAF continued to get most of the limelight and almost all the glory. A final attempt by General Pile to gain belated recognition for his men also proved unsuccessful. At a lunch at Chequers, in November, after the Prime Minister had congratulated him on the gunners' achievements, General Pile bravely reminded him that they had received precious few medals in return, but 'at that crucial moment Anthony Eden broke in with some other topic, and the subject was dropped.'

36

HURRAH FOR THE BALLOON BOYS!

On Sunday evening, the 18 June, orders came through to fly all the balloons, and up they went.

Air Vice-Marshal Gell, Air Officer Commanding, Balloon
Command, November 1944

Of all the senior officers with the duty of defending London the one with the least glamorous job was Air Vice-Marshal Gell, Air Officer Commanding, Balloon Command. However graceful it might look aloft there was, to civilian eyes, something intrinsically unheroic about a barrage balloon seen at close quarters on the ground. But now Balloon Command's finest hour had come; and these ungainly monsters were visibly to save many lives.

The original defensive plan had called for about 480 balloons to be moved to the twenty-mile-long ridge of high ground between Cobham in Kent and Limpsfield in Surrey, and sites had been selected in good time. One man living at Sidcup was puzzled that January at the sight of 'inexplicable ground sites . . . unostentatiously prepared a few hundred yards apart all over the higher parts of the Downs near Kingsdown. . . . We would see the gateway into a field paved with bricks or wire mesh as if a deal of traffic was expected . . . and . . . somewhere in the field . . . a dozen iron rings screwed into the ground in a circle.' A fifteen-year-old farm worker was singularly intrigued as he cycled to his work near Westerham. 'Openings about twenty feet wide were bulldozed through hedges from the road into fields . . . then an anchorage position was concreted in place and the hole filled in with soil. We had no idea what these sites were for.'

Once the attack began, balloons from all over the country

were sent south to their new location. Near Horniman Park in Forest Hill a balloon affectionately known as 'Daisy' had been moored as long as anyone could remember. 'We used Daisy as a sort of barometer of raids,' remembers one local resident. ' "Daisy's going up!" would mean the siren would shortly sound. The humming of her cable told us the direction of the wind, and we knew when she needed to be refilled with gas, as her fins flapped. Now . . . Daisy was moved down to the Kent edge of London to join hundreds of her sisters.'

The speed with which the balloons were transported, complete with heavy winding-gear and supply lorries, to their new locations was as remarkable an achievement as the redeployment of the guns. Many balloons, lowered before sunset in one location, greeted the dawn of the next day in another. An Observer Corps controller, in New Malden, can recall his astonishment on looking south one morning to see that a complete new barrage, covering a 90° angle from south to east, had appeared overnight in view of his windows.

The flying-bombs had begun to arrive in force on the night of Thursday, 15 June, and by Saturday afternoon the barrage was in its new location, much to the surprise of many of Air Vice-Marshal Gell's men, as he himself described:

The airmen of these squadrons, after over four years spent among shipyards, docks, chemical works and similar targets for enemy bombers, appeared bewildered in their new surroundings. To be deployed into open country . . . amid cornfields and rural surroundings . . . far from obvious targets was a novelty for many who had never served, or perhaps never been outside the Western, Northern and Midland cities. . . . After a journey which in some cases exceeded 400 miles . . . the road between the cornfields emptied and the countryside looked peaceful again. This was at about 1300 hours on the 17 June, and . . . all through the afternoon and evening little silver shapes appeared amid the wooded countryside as balloons were inflated and bedded down pending orders to fly.

At this stage Gell was ordered to keep his balloons grounded to leave the sky clear for the AA and the fighters, and, while they and their guardians slumbered, around 3 a.m. on Sunday morning 'a flying-bomb . . . crashed on a site about thirty yards from the crew's tent, injuring some of the crew and destroying most of the site equipment.' It was not until Sunday evening that, following the Guards Chapel catastrophe, Balloon Command was at last given 'orders . . . to fly all the balloons and up they went.'

The first flying-bomb that was caught came as rather an anti-climax. It arrived at night and exploded on striking the cable. It did not, however, give the information required, namely the distance a bomb would travel after impacting a cable. . . . The answer came a day or two later. . . . Scudding across the sky, directly over one balloon site, appeared a flying-bomb, at about 2,000 feet, which impacted a nearby cable. Everything worked perfectly. The bomb, still spitting furiously, was pulled up, but struggled forward, wriggling its tail from side to side like a fish. After battling for 400 yards it gave up the unequal struggle and power-dived to earth three fields away.

This first success proved an exception. Like everyone else, Balloon Command had underestimated their adversary. Travelling on a fixed path at a predetermined height the flying-bomb seemed an easy opponent, but a great strengthening of the barrage soon proved necessary and this meant more mooring sites. One man directly involved was an RAF corporal, then stationed on a US airfield at Middle Wallop in Hampshire. Within minutes of his CO asking the orderly room to find 'a really bright bod who . . . knows Kent well' he was on his way back to his native county, armed with 'chicken sandwiches and a large tin of peaches', plus instructions that, once given a site to peg out, the ' "pegs must not, repeat not, be altered under any circumstances" '. Among London's unsung defenders this NCO was now to be counted. It was a busy and uncomfortable life, for he set off at dawn 'into the highways and byways' and 'seldom returned in daylight.' Home was soon 'an old Polish landing strip close to Smallfield and Horley,' where under canvas, 'we were all thoroughly wet and miserable.' During the day, however, there was no time to think of anything except the job in hand. One mooring had to be set up 'right in the middle of a farm yard . . . adjoining the milking shed' on a farm at Chelsfield, though the cows placidly accepted its alien presence. More obstructive was a woman resident of Smallfield who 'objected strongly to the balloon flying in the centre of her back garden', despite the men's assurances that it was 'extremely unlikely' that any missile it caught would affect her property.*

The job itself also involved an enormous amount of labour:

An NCO set out with a lorry of airmen and would deposit two . . . at each site. A cross had to be dug, the trenches not less than four feet deep, the bottoms of the trenches to be undercut to enable two railway sleepers to be lowered in and turned not less than their full width. A stout wire cable [was] twice passed round the centre of the sleepers, with a shackle, the double cable being brought up above ground, the trenches then back-filled and consolidated. . . .

Some sites proved very easy, but some with sandstone and even rock presented difficulties. The order was that one pair of men left one anchorage per day ready for the balloon crew. It quite often meant others 'mucking in' to finish off a stubborn anchorage.

Once the urgent need for balloons was realized, the decision was taken to strip the whole country, apart from the Navy's main base at Scapa Flow, of its protective curtain. By the beginning of July the original total of under 500 had already been doubled; a week later, 1750 were floating over the North Downs, the greatest concentration ever assembled. One airman, suddenly posted from a peaceful port, Sunderland in County Durham, to a distinctly noisy village, Hartley in Kent, remembers the brisk and pointed pep talk delivered by the group captain to whom his unit reported. 'Your job', the men were told, 'is to stop these things getting past to London. In other words, you bring them down on top of you. But I want no dead heroes. . . . Fly the balloons between 1000 to 5000 feet; erect your tent and dig a ditch all round it and when you hear these things coming . . . don't stand and watch them – dive for the ditch.'

Like AA Command, Balloon Command now demonstrated that a 'static' command could rapidly become mobile under the pressure of events. Three thousand vehicles assembled supplies and personnel from all over the country, and many drivers did not have their clothes off for days at a time. Five thousand miles of telephone cable were laid to the sites, where WAAFs worked alongside the men on all but the heaviest jobs. There

---

*This house *was* damaged, but 'fortunately with only the loss of glass and tiles.'

was, however, a great deal of manual labour, especially in replacing cables and manhandling gas cylinders. The balloons' appetite for hydrogen seemed insatiable. To inflate it to its full dimensions, 62 feet long and 25 across, each balloon required 19,000 cubic feet; one squadron alone consumed nearly nineteen *million* cubic feet between 17 June and 31 August, as well as 152 miles of 'main cable' and 57 miles of 'light cable', while its transport clocked up more than 120,000 miles.

With a wing-span of 16½ to 18 feet [5 to 5½ metres] the flying-bomb demonstrated an almost uncanny ability to slip between the balloon cables but bringing the balloons closer together increased the risk of cables intertwining. Balloons were also destroyed by thunderstorms and stray bullets, while even success brought its problems as Air Vice-Marshal Gell explained.

Each impact necessitated at least one new balloon and hydrogen to inflate it, and at least one cable to be re-reeved on to a winch. On one occasion, a flying bomb which was brought down necessitated the replacement of two balloons, three main cables and one light cable, and new rigging had to be made and fitted to the balloon by the crew, who also had to salvage the cables carried away from the surrounding woods and fields.

In the past life for most balloon crews had been relatively comfortable and undemanding. Now all was changed. Even the so-called 'parent sites' only contained, as Air Vice-Marshal Gell recorded, 'two bell tents and a paraffin cooking stove', and these were havens of luxury compared to the 'satellites', with only a single tent, and no water supply, so that 'officers and senior NCOs drove round their sites sometimes three times a day, with rations, water, petrol, paraffin and other equipment'. The luckiest crews were those stationed close to civilian homes. One 'Village Beneath the Balloons', as its historian described it, was Farningham, seventeen miles from London on the Maidstone road. The WVS immediately 'opened a canteen', in the village hall, one local couple 'came with dahlias and milk', and the balloon itself flew from a cricket ground 'where in the past ninety years "Kent's best" trod the turf,' justifying its presence by 'catching' four flying-bombs between 26 July and 12 August. Other detachments were in more remote locations. One six-man party found themselves in a cherry orchard near Cobham. 'We had cherry pie till we began to look like one,' one of them remembers. 'We used to get a forty-eight hour pass every fortnight and I used to take bags of cherries home.'

In the early stages of the battle the balloons were lowered on days set aside for the fighters, but this proved impracticable and later the airmen were often frustrated by their presence. 'We felt really sorry for the pilots, having to turn back,' remarks one wartime crew member, stationed in an apple orchard at Hartley. 'They must have felt like hunting men chasing a fox who had "gone to ground".' Although Observer Corps posts were issued with red flares to fire in front of aircraft standing into danger, many airmen came too close to the plantation of cables ahead. One corporal still admires the neat manoeuvre performed by a Typhoon pilot who 'suddenly found himself well into the balloon barrage. He left his quarry by turning with a loop and flying out upside down the same way he came in.'

Lowering or raising a balloon was a tedious process; to bring it down from 5000 feet to its 'close-hauled' altitude of 500 took eleven minutes, to lower it right to earth and tether it appreciably longer. A great deal of maintenance work was also required on the winch and chassis and on the associated engines.

The job of operating a barrage balloon was also more dangerous than outsiders realized. In the early days, 'heavy AA shells bursting low overhead' had provided the chief threat, but after the guns had gone the hazards increased. 'Five sites,' Air Vice-Marshal Gell learned, 'received direct hits' from flying-bombs they had 'netted', though 'the crews had all gone to ground', and another V-1 having circled round and round squadron HQ finally 'crashed some 60 yards from a site, killing twelve rabbits.'

There were also serious incidents. The RAF corporal involved in setting up sites, previously quoted, learned that the first time the balloon was flown from the first site he had built at Brasted, 'the complete crew, one airman and three WAAFs, were killed when a V-1 "ran down" the cable.' Squadron headquarters, encamped 'in the middle of a very dense accumulation of balloons stretching over about half a mile' between Ightam and Horley, seemed 'a real death trap' and he wasted no time in erecting a watch-tower, made of packing cases, from which he could identify 'nine separate lanes of V-1s going over . . . toward London.' Thanks to his alarm whistle and 'a deep ditch that ran through the camp,' the squadron staff during the whole campaign suffered nothing worse than temporarily bruised eardrums from a V-1 that 'seemed as if it would go right through the barrage' but finally 'ran down a cable in the last line, with a terrific explosion,' followed by 'a loud cheer' from the watching airmen. Civilians, too, rejoiced as each V-1 crashed to earth. One YMCA welfare worker in East Kent remembers her reaction after one which had flown over her ended its life in 'a flash and explosion: "Hurrah for the balloon boys!" '

No WAAFs were stationed on the remoter single-tent balloon sites, much, no doubt, to the disappointment of the self-appointed moralists who took a close and prurient interest in 'mixed' AA batteries, but squadron switchboards were often manned by women and many served as nursing orderlies. Among the latter was a leading aircraftwoman posted from the Balloon Command centre at Warrington in Lancashire to Diver headquarters at Biggin Hill, where 'We found that no one was expecting us and that "balloon" was a dirty word to Fighter Command.'

Since Biggin Hill is on a plateau, the doodlebugs were only about 200 feet above us. . . . The group captain in command ordered all those not on duty to sleep in the underground shelters. . . . Apart from the discomfort of trying to sleep in damp blankets on bunks underground, our particular shelter was very near the parking place of the RAF lorries and . . . from our underground dormitories, those Bedford engines sounded just like the V-1s. . . . We had many sleepless hours waiting for the explosion. . . which did not come.

With its later extensions, the Diver balloon barrage ultimately stretched almost from Redhill to Chatham, and covered 260 square miles of countryside, thirty-one miles long at its maximum, and eleven and a half miles deep. In the heart of this area, between Limpsfield and Cobham, there seemed to be balloons everywhere. One head warden, at East Grinstead on the Sussex/Surrey border, counted 250 from his post, while a Women's Land Army organizer, based on Sevenoaks, found that every secluded spot she used 'when "nature called" . . . practically always hid a grinning balloon crew.' Whatever its value, this vast concentration of balloons made a marvellous spectacle and even un-literary citizens combed their vocabularies to find an appropriate metaphor. To a woman at Horniman Park in South-East London 'the myriad balloons all facing one way', which she could see from her front doorstep, looked 'like plump fish waiting to go upstream, flushed rosy in the evening light.' A fifteen-year-old at Grays in Essex compared them to 'huge silver elephants in the sky.' To a Meopham woman they seemed to have 'blossomed forth like airborne mushrooms.'

The best account came from H. E. Bates:

The balloons were the only materially beautiful thing produced by the whole campaign . . . up to two thousand of them glowing in the southern sun, smooth and silver against the blue sky. . . . The erection of so large a barrage as now strung itself out on the chalk slopes or among the great beech woods by the North Downs, had never before been attempted. . . . The result dazzled all of us who saw it. To come up from the south country by train, through the long tunnel in the Downs, and emerge into the clear blue of early summer day and see overhead hundreds and hundreds of sailing white balloons, serene and glistening above the light ground mist of the hills, was the only pleasant experience the doodlebug ever gave.

The balloon barrage was at its most beautiful by moonlight but even on peaceful nights one could not forget its presence for the metal wires became like the reeds or strings of musical instruments. A man then living in Sevenoaks recalls the 'whistling' he heard while firewatching as 6000 cables stirred in the breeze, and another resident of the same town admits that he 'derived some comfort' from the sound. 'If I woke up and couldn't hear them – when the weather was bad the balloons were hauled down – I felt we were much more vulnerable.'

A successful 'catch' also brought problems for the civilians on the ground as the former Westerham farmworker mentioned earlier confirms:

One morning I was awakened at about 5 o'clock by what sounded like very heavy sawing . . . I jumped out of bed to discover, on opening the front door, that the cable from the balloon opposite was across our high tension wires and then caught up in an ash tree, well below the height of the high tension wires. The lads were trying to free it by alternatively paying out a few feet of cable and then hauling a few feet. . . . After a short while the HT wires were severed, causing the cable to whip. This was enough to free the cable from the tree. Apparently . . . a V-1 had been caught by the cable on its starboard wing and had been turned 90° on its course, and crashed a little over a mile away. The lads on the balloon site were most upset . . . they could not claim . . . their 'kill', as it had crashed just inside the Surrey border.

Not every such encounter ended so successfully. 'We found . . .' later acknowledged Air Chief Marshal Hill, 'that in practice the theoretically computed rate of success was not always attained; somehow more bombs slipped through the barrage than should have done so according to the laws of probability.'

This was a judgement that, as already mentioned, many on the ground would have echoed. A man at Brasted saw so many missiles 'weave in and out of the balloons and cables' that he finally decided he must be witnessing 'an optical illusion'. 'Imagination or not,' felt the Land Army organizer from Sevenoaks quoted earlier, 'after a while the doodles appeared to dodge those wires.' A gunner recovering at Swanley after being wounded on a gun site remembers 'standing in the garden of the convalescent home' and watching 'a doodlebug coming through the wires . . . directly for the home, as if a path had been made for it,' to be caught at the last minute by 'a lone sentinel' and brought down 200 yards away.

The toughness of the flying-bomb also came as a disagreeable revelation to the balloon crews. One man stationed in Kent found their capacity to take punishment 'fantastic. I've seen them hit balloon cables, go in and out, turn around and still go on.' A railway worker who enjoyed a splendid vantage point from the signal box at Tonbridge East often saw a V-1 hit a cable, change direction by up to 90° and still fly on. As the *South London Press* commented in September, 'no two kills were the same. Sometimes the cable was cut . . . sometimes the robot exploded on impact. On other occasions a flying bomb's wing was sliced off and the robot spiralled to earth almost immediately.'

Usually a cable-damaged V-1 came down within half a mile but a perpetual anxiety for the defending commanders was that a cable-cutting device might be fitted to the leading edge of its wings, as on some conventional bombers. For evidence of such a development the Balloon Squadron intelligence officers constantly raked through the twisted metal fragments scattered around the fields of Kent and Sussex, but, if ever fitted, it made no difference to the campaign. The defences were in any case one step ahead, thanks to the DPL or 'Double-Parachute-Link'* in use since 1940. This simple but ingenious mechanism was regularly fitted to LZ (i.e. low zone) balloons designed to fly below 5000 feet and consisted of two cutting links installed in the cable just below the balloon and just above the winch. When a fast-moving aircraft struck the cable the links gave way, so that the aircraft flew on trailing the cable behind it. Small, eight-foot diameter parachutes at either end of the severed section simultaneously flew open, exerting a drag of about three tons – six times the engine thrust of a twin-engined bomber, and more than enough, in theory, to bring it tumbling to earth. At the same time a panel on the balloon's underside was torn away, causing it to sink slowly to the ground, to be repaired.

By 21 June all cables previously equipped with the parachute link were again in use, but knowing nothing of what was being done, the amateur inventors had a field day. One obvious idea, published in *Reynolds News* on 30 July, was of wire nets suspended from barrage balloons to trap the bombs like fish, though how they were to be strong enough to stop a two-ton projectile, while light enough to be lifted, was not explained. Another suggestion, sent to the Cabinet Office, was of 'bolas', like those thrown by South American hunters, consisting of metal balls at either end of a rope, to be dropped from an aircraft. Again, the parachute-linked cable was already doing the same job more efficiently and why any fighter close enough

Not, as was sometimes suggested, 'Delayed-Parachute-Landing', though this describes its purpose equally well.

to a V-1 to wrap such a missile round its wing should not simply shoot it down was not explained.

In the end it was not new equipment which made the balloon barrage effective but reinforcement. By mid-July the balloons had already accounted for fifty-five V-1s and in one single twenty-four hour period, from sunset on 20 July, they caught seventeen.* But the more successful they were the more important it was to keep the Germans in the dark about them and on 3 August 1944 the Assistant Chief of the Air Staff asked the Ministry of Information to 'once again stress to editors, very confidentially, the great damage which would be done . . . by any publicity which would draw the attention of the enemy to the successes gained by the balloons.' This plea, and the accompanying censorship, were so effective that it was not until September that people outside the 'balloon belt' learned about the achievements of the men whom, a little later, the *RAF Journal* dubbed 'the goalkeepers of London'. By then one squadron alone was credited with thirty-seven kills, a figure which would have seemed incredible only two months earlier.

---

*See page 440 for an analysis of the number of V-1s brought down by guns, balloons and fighters respectively.

37

A STIFF TASK FOR THE
FIGHTERS

In many respects the fighters had a stiff task.

Air Chief Marshal Roderic Hill, *Air Operations . . . in
Connection with the German Flying-bomb and Rocket
Offensives, 1944–5,* 1948

In 1944, as in 1940, it was the fighters which, in the public's
eye, were the lords of the aerial battlefield. The original plan
had been for the fighters of No. 11 Group to patrol at 12,000
feet on three imaginary lines, twenty miles off shore between
Beachy Head and Dover, directly above the coast between
Newhaven and Dover, and inland between Haywards Heath
and Ashford. When an attack actually developed further
squadrons were to be called upon, to fly a second patrol line
at 6000 feet. At first it was thought that six squadrons of
Spitfires, three of them the latest Mark XIV, would be enough,
plus two squadrons of Tempests, the latest, highly secret,
single-seat fighter. Before long, however, with the fighters
catching only 30 per cent of all bombs fired, it became obvious
that more and faster aircraft were needed. 'Personal experience
convinced me,' Air Chief Marshal Hill wrote in his dispatch
on the campaign, 'that the first problem confronting the fighters
was the speed of the bombs. . . . The fastest aircraft I had
were a wing of Tempest Vs and a wing of Spitfire XIVs. These
could not be everywhere at once. One of my first moves,
therefore, was to obtain the Air Commander-in-Chief's consent
to my borrowing at first a flight and later a wing of Mustang
IIIs from the Second Tactical Air Force.' But even these reinforcements were not enough, and by mid-July, he was using
'a total of thirteen single-engined and nine twin-engined (Mosquito) squadrons against flying-bombs.'

Their new duties were rarely popular with the pilots concerned. At 2000 feet even the Tempest, which could reach 408 m.p.h. in level flight, had only a small margin of speed in hand, while the Mustang, with a maximum of 395 m.p.h. when 'boosted', and the Spitfire XIV, with 375 m.p.h., could barely catch their target. Hitler had been enchanted to see a V-1 under test easily outfly a captured Spitfire. Luckily this was the outmoded Mark V, but Hill discovered that the improved Mark IX Spitfire was barely fast enough, while even the Spitfire XIV and the Tempest enjoyed 'no more than a fractional superiority'. Every mile of extra speed now mattered and he therefore ordered that 'aircraft which were to be used exclusively against flying bombs should be stripped of their armour and all unnecessary external fittings . . . that their paint should be removed and their outer surfaces polished,' while 'the engines were modified to use 150-octane fuel and accept a higher boost than usual.' All this raised the speed of some of the single-engined fighters by as much as 30 m.p.h. but, lacking armour, the modified fighters could no longer safely be used on the far side of the Channel. This meant relying on coastal radar – which gave at most six minutes' warning. Only in the closing stages was the Navy able to set up 'a chain of small craft . . . at three-mile intervals seven miles off the French coast, carrying observers who warned our pilots by means of signal rockets and star-shells that flying-bombs were on their way.'

Upon Hill's judgement more than on any other factor rested the success of the battle against the flying-bomb. A member of his family witnessed his life that summer:

For a month, from the middle of June to the middle of July, he and his staff . . . worked almost literally night and day . . . always seeking improvement. After a day lasting until late in the evening he would often two or three times in the night pick up the telephone beside his bed, then quickly dress. Down below the garage door rolled back in the dark and he went up to the operations room where he stood on the balcony from which three years ago Air Marshal Dowding had watched the Battle of Britain. Night and day the course of the battle filled his mind.

From the start, Hill, a pilot himself, realized that 'in many respects the fighters had a stiff task.'

The majority of the flying-bombs crossed the coast between Cuckmere Haven and St. Margaret's Bay. The distance thence to the southern edge of the gun belt was in most places about thirty miles. The flying-bombs covered this distance in five minutes. Five minutes, then, was the time available to the pilot of an overland fighter to select his target, get within range of it and shoot it down. . . . There was rarely time for a stern chase unless the pursuer started with a substantial advantage in height. On the whole the most effective procedure was to fly on roughly the same course as an approaching bomb, allow it to draw level, and fire deflection shots when it passed, being careful not to fire when it was closer than 200 yards lest it should explode in the air and blow up the attacker. . . . The hot gases emitted by a bomb immediately in front of the fighter made a steady aim difficult, so that short bursts and frequent aiming corrections were required. Usually several bursts were needed to inflict enough damage to explode the bomb or bring it down.

In the front line of the battle was No. 3 Squadron, Fighter Command, one of three which formed 150 Wing, commanded by Wing-Commander Roland Beamont. His wing was the first to be equipped with Tempests and he had chosen its base, Newchurch near Dungeness, because it 'had completely clear approaches in all directions, was on firm, well-drained land and was nearest to France.' The pilots and ground crew, however, had to sleep under canvas and suffered from 'shrapnel falling all over the airfield and going through our tents,' and the squadron's first casualty occurred when 'one P.47 Thunderbolt fired at a V-1 over the airfield . . . the bullet drilling a hole through the hand of one of our airmen lying asleep in his bed.'*

150 Wing was 'scrambled' for its first *Diver* mission at 5.30 a.m. on the morning the main bombardment opened, 16 June, and was immediately successful, though one pilot had a lucky escape:

We had finished our patrol and were going back to Newchurch when

---

*This appears to be the same incident described, more colourfully, by a senior NCO at Newchurch, who says that the wounded airman lost 'one of his symbols of manhood. . . . So concerned were all ranks . . . that an item was included on "Orders" stating that the unfortunate chap was recovering well and that his matrimonial prospects had not been impaired.'

we heard on the radio that there was a V-1 crossing near Ashford. The sky was overcast, but there was a big ray of sunshine coming through a hole in the clouds.

The V-1 broke out in front of me. I was right underneath it, and let fly for two or three seconds. When I was only fifty yards away, it blew up in my face. My wingman saw me disappear in a sheet of flame and shouted, 'You are on fire. Bale out!' I thought I had had it, and I found later that the aeroplane in places was burned and blackened.

By nightfall that day 150 Wing had shot down eight flying-bombs but already its pilots were complaining that they were being hampered not merely by the guns but by other aircraft. One former flight-lieutenant, then stationed at RAF Hawkinge, remembers seeing 'numerous planes . . . circling . . . over the town of Folkestone' each waiting for 'a very sick doodlebug to get clear of the built-up area . . . even the Air Sea Rescue Walrus' – an unbelievably slow flying-boat, powered by a 'pusher' engine. 'Within a few days of the attack beginning,' wrote Wing-Commander Beamont and a co-author later, 'the sky over South-East England was a whirlpool of allied fighters desperately manoeuvring around each other to get in a shot at the invaders and trying to dodge the shell-bursts of their own side's ack-ack.' Beamont flew to Uxbridge to suggest to the Commander-in-Chief of No. 11 Group that the guns should be more strictly controlled and that 'all slow fighters should be withdrawn leaving a clear field for the Tempests, [and] some squadrons of special Spitfires with increased boost.'

This suggestion was to a large extent adopted as was another, that 'Observer Corps posts should be concentrated along that coastline', i.e. the main V-1 arrival area, 'at half-mile intervals and equipped with rockets to be fired towards the position of the V-1 reported on the radar plot.'

Locating a V-1 was often, however, only the start for seen, as it usually was, from the rear, the flying-bomb presented a tiny target and to get nearer was to risk being destroyed in the resulting explosion. the Bomber Command rule was to stay at least 5000 feet [1523 metres] above an exploding 4000 lb [1800 kilo] bomb but, applying the same formula, an attacking fighter would need, when the V-1's 2000-pound warhead blew up, to be nearly half a mile away – an impossible range for even a crack shot. Beamont established the practice of 'harmonising the guns' 200 yards ahead,* so that their shells converged just far enough ahead to prevent the fighter being destroyed, or the pilot suffering more than minor burns 'from the explosion entering the cockpit through the air ventilators'. This he regarded as a legitimate risk of war. 'It was,' he commented dryly, 'certainly impressive, to fly straight through the middle of a 2,000 lb. bomb explosion, but not many pilots were hurt doing it.'

Under Beamont's fearless leadership the Tempest soon proved itself the supreme doodlebug catcher and before long 'most pilots were able to destroy at least one V-1 per sortie . . . and individual scores of two or three V-1s in a day were becoming not uncommon'. The Wing could have done even better if its third squadron could have replaced its Spitfire Vs with additional Tempests. 'The major cause of the delay,' Beamont revealed at a press conference, 'was a strike in the Wing Shop at the Langley factory in the early months of 1944, due to transition from Hurricane production to Tempest production and consequent reduction of piece-rate wages.' Even in wartime no criticism of well-paid manual workers was permitted and Beamont found himself 'at the receiving end of short and sharp messages from Command headquarters,' before the recalcitrant workmen returned to their benches. Despite such difficulties by the end of the summer 150 Wing's establishment of Tempests had been raised from thirty-two to forty-eight though the demands on both ground crews and pilots were remorseless. Instead of the normal 500 to 600 hours a month of operational flying the squadrons were in the air between 900 and 1000 hours and individual pilots flew four or five sorties a day, living and eating close to their dispersal points.

The pressure on the ground crews, especially as engines being operated flat out needed an abnormal amount of maintenance, was even greater. 'For nearly two months,' wrote Beamont's biographer, 'ground crews took time off only for sleep and worked eighteen hours in twenty-four . . . servicing . . . aircraft right round the clock. . . . All leave was can-

---

*This figure appears in Beamont's autobiography. In the book he wrote jointly with another author it is given as 300 yards.

celled. . . . Daily inspection, and minor and major overhauls were staggered to provide the maximum number of machines in the air for an indefinite period.'

One former senior engine fitter with 56 Squadron, to which he had moved from the peaceful inactivity of Scorton in Yorkshire, still remembers that amazing summer:

Newchurch village, a couple of hundred yards from the camp, was the only sign of habitation. The camp itself was a sprawl of tents and hangars adjacent to the aircraft dispersal areas; only HQ claimed the privilege of a tiled roof in a nearby farmhouse. . . . Hammered down across fields, hedgerows and the one road across the camp, were two Sommerfield tracks of steel mesh, which served as runways. . . . Life was bearable for ridge-tent living, apart . . . from the earwigs which . . . made some of the toughest chaps sweat with fear.

This senior NCO remembers being on duty for twenty-seven hours at a stretch, for the Napier Sabre, which powered the Tempest, was 'the most temperamental piston engine ever devised'. But morale was high, thanks largely to their CO, 'a superb fighter pilot with seven and a half enemy aircraft to his credit and eyes in his backside', and by the end of June the two Tempest squadrons had accounted for 232 of the 370 flying-bombs so far destroyed. They were by then shooting down more than 80 per cent of those sighted, double the success rate for the RAF as a whole.

Second only to the Tempests, at least by day, were the Mustang IIIs, American machines powered by British engines and largely flown by Poles. The engineering officer of one Polish squadron, then stationed at Coltishall in Norfolk, remembers that the machine could be given 'the extra speed required to catch a bomb . . . by increasing the boost of the engine', though only for a precious five minutes; after that it suffered damage.

Senior Rolls-Royce representatives arrived with the parts, springs, bolts and nuts, etc. . . . Modification of the engines was carried out in the afternoon and next morning one flight flew to RAF Station West Malling, in Kent, to fight the bombs. . . . I followed with the ground staff and equipment by road. On arrival . . . I found that almost half of the squadron's aeroplanes were unserviceable because of engine failure. The pilots when chasing the bombs and using high boost did not watch their watches.

In noteworthy contrast to the striking fitters at Hawkers, the men from Rolls-Royce rapidly responded to the challenge, and 'three or four came to live more or less on the aerodrome' at West Malling while 'suggestions were telephoned to Derby and modifications carried out on the engine on the test bed.' Equally responsive was Duncan Sandys, who visited the Poles at their advanced landing field at Friston, near Eastbourne, and asked what he could do to help. They told him, and the very next morning 'six retired men arrived with glass paper, polishes and rags and from dusk to dawn were polishing the planes, which were eventually smooth as mirrors. Result: the speed of the aircraft was increased by five to seven miles per hour, and every extra mile helped.'

The Poles' hatred of all things German was legendary and they showed little concern for their own lives in their determination to destroy any V-1 they sighted. One had fallen to a Polish pilot on 16 June, but the main Polish contribution did not begin until 1 July, when 316 'City of Warsaw' Squadron, one of three squadrons in the Polish Wing, arrived at West Malling, under the command of Squadron-Leader Bohdan Arct. Soon afterwards the squadron scored its first victory and 'a large chart was drawn, hung in the disperal barrack and [Sergeant Pilot Henryk] Murkowski's name with a miniature . . . V-1 at the side was written honourably at the top.'

Soon life at West Malling, at Friston, and at Brenzett, where other Polish squadrons were stationed, resembled that of 150 Wing at Newchurch. 'There was no time for days off or leaves,' wrote Arct, 'although our unit contained thirty pilots and twenty Mustangs. . . . We talked exclusively of flying-bombs, discussing and arguing about the best methods of shooting them down.'

The Poles boasted that they would not press the firing button until they 'could see the red-hot ring of the jet engine's exhaust nozzle' and they had hardly started operations when one man had to bale out, having blown the propeller off his Mustang and bent 'the wings . . . to a most peculiar shape.' Squadron-Leader Arct described another typical encounter in his equally typical, if distinctly un-English, prose:

I saw my quarry from a few miles distance . . . flying a couple of thousand feet lower . . . approaching me very quickly, but at a very slight angle.

I pushed forward the throttle and control stick. . . . The hands of the speed indicator moved: 390 . . . 400 . . . then 410 and finally 420 miles per hour. I was now much faster than my target. . . .

It was strange to watch this monstrosity and I could hardly believe that a real, live pilot was not sitting in the fuselage. The dead 'witch' seemed to be alive, locked like some monstrous freak as it flew on in nervous jerks.

When deserted hills and woods spread below, I closed in to 200 yards and pressed the trigger, giving a short burst from my four cannons. . . . I flew on through the hot whirlpool behind its flaming tail. . . . The bomb spat fire like a legendary dragon, slowed down and, turning to the left, ejected fireworks of sparks. The first burst was accurate, the second deadly. With great satisfaction I watched the 'witch' diving to end its infamous life.

Diving on a V-1 while flying in the same direction became the standard method of engaging it, but a new technique became popular, or at all events talked about, after 23 June, when in the words of the official RAF history, 'a Spitfire pilot threw a flying-bomb on its back by tipping it with his wing so that it fell out of control, and on 27 June a Tempest pilot destroyed a bomb by using his slipstream which forced it into a spin.' Soon many other airmen were experimenting with similar methods. As one writer pointed out, any who 'employed the "brute force" method of using their own wing to knock up that of the flying-bomb' were likely to come off worst, 'since the V-1s were skinned in rolled steel and the wing tips of the fighters constructed from far weaker light alloy.' A more sophisticated approach was to place the wing of one's aircraft just above, or more commonly below, that of the enemy machine, which in theory at least, destroyed the 'lift' which kept it airborne.

Reports of this new tactic spread through the squadrons and rapidly captured the imagination of public and pilots alike. Roland Beamont's first such victory came by chance after he had dived across a V-1's path to avoid a collision, but his next was deliberate, when he found himself out of ammunition, and he flew alongside the V-1 at 380 m.p.h., gradually raising his wing until the missile 'heeled over in a dive to earth'. Inevitably the Poles of 316 Squadron embraced the idea with their usual fierce enthusiasm. One of the first to try it found that the flying-bomb swung back with such force that 'the Mustang lost the tip of its wing'. Another Pole, with 'an urge to throw a "witch" out of its bewitching balance', only succeeded at the twelfth attempt 'when . . . happy but perspiring he set course for West Malling'.

Most of the credit for the rising scores of so many pilots belonged to the fighter controllers: those at Maidstone and Horsham, using the new radar at Fairlight, had contributed by the end of August to the destruction of 142 flying-bombs. Even those great individualists, the Poles, acknowledged that 'a controller who knew his business' made all the difference. Richard Hough, confined to the radar hut on top of Beachy Head, found Roland Beamont 'a delight to control, instant in his responses, relying unquestioningly on our information and instructions until he got a "visual", when he quite rightly cut you out of his consideration.' The controllers eventually threw a party at Bexhill for Beamont and his colleagues to celebrate 'the destruction of 500 doodlebugs'. 150 Wing, not to be outdone, gave on 20 July a 'Doodlebug Celebration Dance'.

You are invited to attend the

DOODLE BUG
CELEBRATION DANCE

AT THE

Majestic Hotel, Folkestone,
THURSDAY, 20th JULY,

7.30—11.30 p.m.

Held by 150 Wing, R.A.F., to celebrate their Squadrons'
successes in shooting down flying bombs.

One unsubstantiated legend born that summer was that the tide was turned by the Meteor, the first jet-propelled British aircraft, a twin-engined machine of which later versions reached 600 m.p.h. In reality, although the idea of matching 'jet against jet' appealed to Roderic Hill, only one Squadron, No. 316 based on Manston, was equipped with Meteors, and this did not come into operation until August. The struggle against the highly unconventional V-1 was won by conventional aircraft.

For the victors, unlike the vanquished, it was not a bloodless battle. In the first six weeks alone eighteen fighters were badly damaged and six air-crew killed by exploding V-1s. On 3 August 1944, a twenty-three-year-old French Spitfire pilot, due to marry his English sweetheart a week later, was killed in a desperate attempt to prevent a flying-bomb falling on a hospital near Benenden. A proposal to award him a posthumous VC came to nothing, but his sacrifice is still commemorated in the proud title of his biography: *Jean Maridor, Chasseur de V-1*.

As the nights lengthened, a growing proportion of the flying-bombs arrived after dark. At first the overworked Tempest squadrons at Newchurch found themselves asked to mount another six patrols between 11.30 p.m. and 3 a.m., but 'It was soon apparent,' wrote an officer of the RAF's air-combat university, the Fighter Interception Unit, 'that day-fighter pilots were not sufficiently at home in the dark clouds of night.' Attempts were therefore made 'to see whether night-fighter pilots could more easily convert to the Tempest than day-fighter pilots could convert to all-weather night flying.'

The first two 'guinea-pigs' sent to Newchurch on 25 June suffered some leg-pulling in the bar of the officers' mess tent when 'low cloud and rain prevented flying on the first three nights', but 'on 28 June the clouds lifted a little' and the new boys confounded their sceptical hosts by shooting down four V-1s in three successive sorties. One of the two was drowned after baling out when a V-1 damaged his machine's engine; his replacement was killed after crashing in poor visibility – it was found 'later that Tempest altimeters all over-read at high speed near the ground'; a third man was injured in a collision with a Mosquito. Flying against the V-1s by night soon proved, in fact, more dangerous than by day, and life was even more unpleasant with 'sleep . . . constantly interrupted by the roar of the day-wing taking off'. But some pilots revealed a natural aptitude for the work. The 'Beamont of the night-fighters' was this detachment's commander, Flight-Lieutenant, later Squadron-Leader, Berry. On 23 July he shot down seven flying-bombs in one night and on 10 August he was posted to Manston to convert another Tempest squadron, No. 501, to night-flying Diver operations. By the end of the month its rate of kills had increased tenfold and ultimately Berry became the highest-scoring pilot of all. His end, after the flying-bomb campaign had been won, was in the great tradition; shot down by AA fire over the Dutch coast, he radioed his companions: 'Carry on chaps. I've had it.'

The RAF's main night fighter was by 1944 the famous Mosquito, the 'wooden wonder', delightful to fly, which had proved a success in every role entrusted to it. As a twin-engined, two-seater machine it had room enough for airborne air interception radar (AI), though not all Mosquitoes were yet equipped with it, and an operator. Experiments were also made with Monica, a device designed to warn British bombers of enemy night-fighters. Finding the V-1s in the dark proved, however, far easier than expected, thanks to their flaming jets. Overtaking them was another matter. The Mosquitoes could only intercept a V-1 before it reached the coast if they patrolled at 8000 feet, so that they could dive on the target and were given extra speed by using 150 octane fuel with 'boosted' engines.

Some V-1s were caught at night by Mustangs and Tempests, but Wing-Commander Beamont, one of the few day pilots also successful at night, did not underestimate the difficulties.

With nothing by which to judge distance, except a light which got progressively bigger and more dazzling, it was not easy to get into an effective firing range without suddenly overshooting and possibly even running into the target. I found that the best method was to approach the target from astern until we appeared to be within about 1000 yards and then to descend below it until . . . approximately 100 feet below and 300 yards behind. . . . From this situation, a gentle climb was made into the dead-astern position until . . . the wake of the V-1 was felt in the Tempest. Then, with the gunsight centred directly on the exhaust flame, a long burst was generally enough to deal with it.

For less expert pilots, the range-finding problem was solved by the physicist Sir Thomas Merton, who designed an optical gunsight in which were reflected two images of the flying-bomb's exhaust. When they came together one opened fire. The device was turned out in large numbers by the Royal Aircraft Establishment at Farnborough and, when news of it was released, was dubbed 'the shilling gadget' by the press.

Other techniques were also tried to make life easier for the pilots.

Control had a system of searchlights on the coast between Hastings and Dungeness, with two shining out to sea and two shining upwards. This was the point around which the Tempests were stacked, flying figures of eight, waiting for the V-1s to come over. When the bottom aircraft left the stack, the others would move down. It was an un-popular operation, as it was necessary to fly with navigation lights on to avoid mid-air collisions, and the Germans tried to infiltrate their own aircraft into the pattern. Control would broadcast the code phrase, 'Close your windows' where there was an intruder, as a signal to switch off our navigation lights.

A midshipman, based at Newhaven, has equally uncomfortable memories of an experiment in using two of the 105-feet mine-sweepers in his flotilla as lightships, each being equipped with 'a battleship sized searchlight and . . . serried tiers of 100 and 150 watt lamps.'

The two ships sailed at dusk on alternate nights to a given position in the middle of the flight path, anchored, and switched on. I was . . . in charge of the lighting arrangements, and in between bouts of seasickness, dashed around replacing lamps which . . . blew like machine-gun fire every time a bit of spray broke aboard. We had a grandstand view of the action and each night saw many doodlebugs shot down. . . . There were other excitements too. Our own fighters were supposed to be showing their navigation lights . . . but on successive nights we were circled by an aircraft without lights and first bombed then machine-gunned. . . . I wonder if our anchors are still lying there? We slipped them from their cables in record time and sped off home at our maximum ten knots.

The first, and by far the most important, phase of the battle against the V-1, which had begun on 12 June, ended on 5 September 1944. The first month, until 15 July, was predomi-nantly the fighters' battle. They caught 925 of the V-1s brought down, the guns 261 and the balloons 55, a total of 1241, or

42·3 per cent of the 2934 reported.* From 16 July to 5 September the guns came into their own, disposing of 1199 missiles, compared to the fighters' 847 and the balloons' 176, a total of 2222, 58·6 per cent of the 3791 targets coming within range. All told, between mid-June and early September, the fighters brought down 1772 V-1s, the guns 1460 and the balloons 231, a total of 3463 or 51·5 per cent of all bombs observed by the defences.

Within the RAF the Tempests were easy winners, having claimed 638. The Mosquitoes had accounted for 428, largely at night, Spitfire XIVs 303, Mustangs 232 and the new Meteors, which had come very late on the scene, 13. The remaining 158 doodlebugs which had fallen to the fighters had been caught by slower types: Typhoons and Spitfires Mark V, IX and XII.

150 Wing was, as its commander pointed out with justifiable pride, 'the top scoring unit by a large margin', though his own score, of 32, had been surpassed by one of his officers, a Belgian flying from Newchurch, with 52, and by the CO of 501 Squadron, Squadron-Leader Berry, at Manston, with 61. Polish pilots, mainly from the Polish Wing, disposed of 190 flying-bombs, of which Bodhan Arct's 'City of Warsaw' Squadron, No. 316, was responsible for 74. After the war the Commander-in-Chief of Fighter Command paid the Poles a handsome tribute, which was equally true of all who had fought the battle against the flying-bomb: 'The inhabitants of London and the Southern counties had every reason to bless these men and did so with all their hearts.'

---

*In all the figures given here I have 'rounded-up' or down all the official statistics to the nearest whole number. Where a V-1 was shared between different services or types of aircraft I have 'awarded' it to the higher scoring arm or squadron.

38

AUTUMN IN EAST ANGLIA

Except possibly for a few last shots, the Battle of Londonis over.

Mr Duncan [later Lord] Sandys, 7 September 1944

Towards the end of August the feeling began to spread that it would all soon be over. 'No raid all day and a quiet night. Couldn't believe it,' wrote a Clapham woman in her diary for 25 August. 'Came to the conclusion "they" were stocktaking.' The diary of a thirteen-year-old boy, on holiday at his grandfather's home near Rye, told the same story:

Thursday, 29 August . . . 6 exploded by guns, 6 brought down by guns.
Wednesday, 30 August . . . 1 brought down by guns during darkness.
Thursday, 31 August, and Friday, 1 September . . . No sightings.

Folkestone had its last flying-bomb a little later, at 0014 hours on the Friday morning. Then it, too, was left in peace. In the capital, however, the tension of the last few weeks had left people too weary to celebrate the new tranquillity. London, felt Mrs Robert Henrey, had the 'curious sensation of a city only half alive. Londoners were tired. They felt that the war was beginning to drag.'

On 5 September, after several days without a single V-1, the Air Ministry sent Air Marshal Hill 'warm congratulations' on his 'notable victory'. From Italy came a cable from the Prime Minister to General Pile: 'The guns achieved all that we did hope for them.' On 5 September, rumours swept London that Germany had already capitulated. 'People left their suburban homes,' reported the *Daily Herald*, 'and came to town to join the celebrations. There were taxis full of singing soldiers. . . . And in newspaper offices the telephone never stopped: "Is it true? Is it true?" ' Alas, it was *not* true, but the public was deeply impatient for the war to be over. On 15 September the *Kent Messenger* reported that 'Kent folk have got the Victory Day fever'. A shop in Gravesend which had filled its windows with flags had been 'besieged' by eager buyers.

The growing spirit of optimism in Southern England was encouraged by a press conference on 7 September, where the commanders responsible for defeating the flying-bomb all spoke with cheerful confidence about the future, and none more so than Mr Duncan Sandys. 'Except possibly for a few last shots,' he began his speech, 'the Battle of London is over.' Only *ARP News* stood firm against the prevailing euphoria. 'Robot Bombs may not be confined to Southern England' it reminded its readers in its September issue, adding several pages of practical 'Advice on Preparations in Other Areas'.

Duncan Sandys had mentioned the possibility that now the launching sites were in Allied hands V-1s might be released from aircraft, and the air-launched V-1 was to prove a nuisance, if not a major menace, for the rest of the war. Air-launching had a comparatively long history. The very first flying-bomb had been dropped from an aircraft at Peene-münde, two years before, and late in 1943 experiments in air-launching were resumed, using Heinkel 111s which carried a V-1 suspended below their inner wing between the fuselage and port or starboard engine. On 7 July a specially trained unit, Gruppe III of Kampfgeschwader 3, grandiosely known as Blitz Geschwader or Lightning Wing, was at last ready to open fire. Its first operation was such a fiasco that as mentioned earlier, the British assumed the target to be Portsmouth instead of Southampton. The first air-launched V-1s aimed at London were fired over the North Sea in the early hours of 8 July. They were at first assumed to have come from Belgium, and only after other arrivals from the east, later in the week, all at night, was their true source realized.

Any enthusiasn the men of III KG 3 felt at being posted from Russia to Gilze Ryan in Holland must have waned rapidly. Taking off with a ton of high explosive and petrol slung precariously beneath their aircraft's fuselage was bad enough, but struggling along only 300 feet above the waves to avoid detection by British radar was even worse. A sudden climb to

1500 feet forty miles off shore followed, and then came the most dangerous moments of all, firing the V-1's sparking plugs via the cable linking it to the transporting aircraft. Sometimes the missile proved reluctant to 'unstick'; more often, once its engine was started, it became altogether too boisterous and threatened to send both machines crashing into the sea together.

The results which III KG 3 had achieved by the end of August had barely justified the effort involved. Compared to the 8600 V-1s fired from the ground, about 410 had been launched from the air, of which 300 had been intended for London. Only 160 of these had even reached the coast, and barely fifty had got through to London, mainly afflicting such riverside boroughs as Barking and Woolwich, on the south bank of the Thames, and Bethnal Green and Stepney on the north. Another ninety, with even less success, had been aimed at Portsmouth, and on the night of 30/31 August, presumably in an attempt to cause public alarm, twenty were directed at Gloucester, but none got anywhere near the city and its inhabitants remained unaware that they had been attacked.

Now, however, air-launching seemed likely to come into its own. On 7 August General Heinemann's LXV Corps had warned Flak Regiment 155 (W) that it might soon have to move and in mid-August Colonel Wachtel began to evacuate the launching sites on his left flank, leaving only those in the Pas de Calais in action. As the Allied advance speeded up the orderly retreat became a rout. By late August only one battery of the original four remained in action, and in the early hours of 1 September its last bombs were fired off and the remaining stores and equipment destroyed. In the general confusion some men, perhaps by design, 'went missing', so that only 80 per cent of the regiment reached its temporary camp near Antwerp, from which it moved soon afterwards to Enschede, near Deventer. Wachtel's superior, General Heinemann, and his staff at first moved to Waterloo, and then, on 4 September, joined Wachtel at Deventer, and promptly began a 'witch-hunting' inquiry at corps headquarters into the near-shambles of the recent evacuation. This rapidly established that the main responsibility lay with the corps staff, and no more was heard of it.

Legend:
- searchlights
- air-launched V-1's
- anti-aircraft guns
- launching sites

Scarborough

R. Humber

Oldham
Manchester

Norwich
Great Yarmouth
Orfordness
Saffron Walden
Ipswich
Datchworth
Brightlingsea
Gloucester
LONDON
Bristol
Swanscombe
Southampton
Portsmouth

Zwischenahn
Deventer
The Hague
Delft
Handford-
bei-Münster
Rotterdam
Gilze Ryan
Antwerp
Brussels

| 0 | 100 miles |
| 0 | 100 kms |

The last attack: the launching sites for flying-bombs fired from the ground
from September 1944 to March 1945 and the airfields used by the bombers
which launched V-1s from the air

444

Between 5 and 6 a.m. on 5 September, after a lull of four and a half days, the peace over Southern England was briefly broken when nine V-1s were observed approaching from the east, but on 6 September the Vice-Chiefs of Staff confidently reported that all areas from which flying-bombs, or even rockets, might be aimed at London were already, or soon would be, in Allied hands.

This was true enough so far as ground-fired V-1s were concerned, but the danger of air-launched missiles remained. III KG 3 had been occupied moving to new, and less vulnerable, bases in north-west Germany, at Aalhorn, Varrelbusch, Zwischenahn and Handorf-bei-Munster. Here, just before dawn on 16 September, operations were resumed, though the fifteen aircraft involved only managed to loose off nine bombs between them. The Navy shot down two into the sea, the fighters caught three, off shore or over land, two dived prematurely to earth in open countryside in Essex, and only two landed in London, in Woolwich and Barking. Similar attacks continued, on the same modest scale, on most nights that month, with equally little result except to familiarize many people who had never heard it before with the noise of a V-1. The Germans' fears about the inaccuracy of air-launching were proved well founded, and between 27 and 29 September for example, eight flying-bombs landed in Essex, two in Cambridgeshire, three in Suffolk and one each in Kent, Sussex and Hertfordshire.*

Throughout October, the bombardment, if it merited the name, continued and around the end of the month III KG 3 was reinforced by other aircraft and redesignated I KG 53. During November two additional Gruppen from the same wing, or Geschwader, also came under its control, giving it ultimately an operational strength of 101 aircraft, though the available force on any one night was far smaller.

The new attack was an irritant, rather than a threat, but proved difficult to counter. In mid-October Air Chief Marshal – formerly Air Marshal – Hill had become Air Officer Com-

---

*Only 50 per cent of air-launched missiles fell within a twenty-four-mile radius of the target, compared to 50 per cent within twelve miles of those fired from the ground, and the carrying aircraft proved slow and vulnerable.

manding in Chief, Fighter Command, when the former Air Defence of Great Britain headquarters was dissolved, and though he remained responsible for anti-V-1 measures, he was dependent for bombers on Air Chief Marshal Harris. Harris, having been proved right about the uselessness of bombing the ground launching sites, was even more reluctant to spare bombers to attack the air-launching units' airfields, which were poor targets for heavy bombers at the best of times. A token effort was made. Between 23 September and 7 October, the chief German base, at Handorf, was attacked several times, and in mid-October there were raids on Varrelbusch and Zwischenahn, though the fourth airfield, at Aalhorn, escaped altogether. Little was achieved, and though Bomber Command did agree that, when possible, these last three should be attacked again, they refused to name a date. When Hill appealed to the Deputy Chief of the Air Staff for support in giving further raids priority, it was not forthcoming; his chief ally in the past, Tedder, was now in France. All Hill could do was order intruder sorties to be flown against the airfields housing the air-launching squadrons, but catching enemy aircraft taking off or landing was notoriously difficult; one experienced crew had flown twenty such missions by November without a single success. 'Standing patrols' over the sea were equally unproductive; the same crew spent nearly fifty hours in this way with nothing to show for it.

At first sight no target seemed easier than a lumbering old bomber slowed down still further by carrying a flying-bomb, but intercepting the Heinkels proved remarkably difficult. They were only visible on the coastal radar screens for seven minutes, the time it took them, in the words of one night-fighter pilot, to 'climb to 1,500 feet and open up to the minimum launching speed (150 m.p.h.), release their bomb and turn and dive away again to just above the water.' They were highly vulnerable while climbing, but so slow, 110 m.p.h. that the Mosquito either overshot them or 'fell out of the sky' in a stall if it throttled back to keep them in range.

While the cry a few weeks earlier had been for faster fighters the demand now was for slower ones, and 'somebody in Fighter command suggested bringing Beaufighters out of retirement for the job'. Unfortunately, very few of these almost obsolete

machines possessed the latest Mark IX and Mark X air interception radar sets, which had mainly gone to the new Mosquitoes. It was, however, in a Beaufighter with just such an
out-of-date set that this airman made a typical 'kill' on the
night of 4 November:

Mac [his radar-operator] and I take a Beau with AI Mk VIII to
Coltishall again. This time Hopton CHEL [Chain Home, Extra
Low-looking coastal defence radar station] gives us trade at 1,500
feet, crossing port to starboard. . . . I point the Beau to port a bit
and Mac soon gets a contact at 1½ miles. We let it cross us and I
lower 30° of flap for the approach. We close to a visual quickly and
it is a Heinkel 111 going west at 140 m.p.h., looking for all the world
like a sinister black crow as it prepares to release its flying-bomb from
underneath the right wing. . . . I take aim on the centre of the Hun's
fuselage and hold my thumb on the gun button. Things start happening immediately; a nice big fire breaks out and he nosedives straight
into the drink, complete with flying-bomb, where a pool of burning
fuel spreads briefly on the surface sending flames dancing on the
water.

To reduce the risk of flying into the sea some Mosquitoes and
Beaufighters were fitted with radio altimeters, and a naval
frigate, HMS *Caicos*, was fitted up as a floating radar station
and fighter control centre. Around the end of the year Operation Vapour was also launched, which involved equipping
ancient Wellington bombers with ASV – air to surface vessel
– radar, to pick up the low-flying Heinkels. Neither attempt
had much success, and this crew flew three Vapour sorties
between 2 and 13 January without result.

The principles applied in defending the East Coast were the
same as those which had proved effective further south. Out
at sea the Beaufighters and Mosquitoes had full rein; any V-1s
which reached the coast were at the unfettered mercy of the
guns; and behind the guns were more fighters. Those used
overland were Tempests, flown by night-fighter pilots. They
accounted for some fifty V-1s which crossed the coast, while
the Mosquitoes shot down at least another twenty over the sea;
another ten fell to the guns of the Royal Navy.

The balloons played no part in the battle; it was feared their
metal cables would cause radar interference. The searchlights,
however, now came into their own, being established in a

rough rectangle sixteen to twenty miles wide, stretching for twenty-three miles at the front, from Sudbury to Brightlingsea, and about forty miles at its base between Saffron Walden and Southend. General Pile's original aim had been to create 'a layout . . . capable in the flat countryside of continuously engaging a target flying at 2,000 feet with anything from three to seven beams,' but the air-launched V-1s came in at half that height and it soon proved 'impossible to engage a target continuously with even one beam.' Seven more searchlight batteries were therefore added to the original eleven, and the space between them cut down from 6000 to 3000 yards. General Pile was enthusiastic about the results. 'Although chases at 500 feet were commonplace,' he wrote, 'no fighter was ever lost by dazzle and complaints of lagging beams were few' – while the RAF's 'kills rose in a fortnight from 26% to 33%.' The airmen were, as usual, less pleased. 'So thick a spacing,' concluded Air Marshal Hill, 'tended to dazzle pilots and we altered the interval to the normal 6,000 yards.'

Some searchlights were also used as beacons to assist the night-fighter pilots and a man then living at Whitstable remembers how thousands of starlings joined the innocent victims of the war. Fascinated by the light, they circled the beam endlessly until dropping to the ground, dead from exhaustion.

By early September the area from the Thames Estuary almost to Clacton was well guarded. Like every commander throughout history, however, General Pile was apprehensive about being outflanked, for, as he wrote, 'The enemy might conceivably be able to launch attacks simultaneously from the North Foreland to Yorkshire.' V-1s were already coming in over Suffolk and Norfolk as well as Essex, so that a start was made early in September on moving guns from the South Coast into the eastern counties beyond the Thames Estuary. This time everything went wrong.

All the portable platforms had to be dug up out of the ground before they could be moved. And while the working parties were actually digging them up, their numbers were decimated by a sudden call for labour for the estuary defences. . . . The immediate effect . . . was that many of the 168 10-ton lorries that had been ordered to report at Ashford, Kent . . . were kept standing idle and empty for over a week. . . . Traffic control either broke down or was non-existent. On the narrow, twisting roads of East Anglia . . . convoys of 10-tonners would suddenly encounter head-on convoys of 3-tonners. The subsequent delay and confusion were enormous. . . . Two regiments who arrived at Leiston found that no Army rations had been supplied. Brigadiers who did not even know what troops they were to command arrived at the prearranged rendezvous . . . to find that their guides were missing; they were still reconnoitring the sites or had simply disappeared. . . . From the point of view of the man on the spot, chaos was the only polite word to describe what was going on.

By 2 October the 'four day' operation was still unfinished and it was not until 13 October that the 300 'static' heavy guns were at last in position; by the end of the month, the new gun belt, stretching in a band 5000 yards wide from Great Yarmouth to the Diver 'box' beyond the Thames Estuary, contained 542 heavy guns and 503 of 40-mm calibre. The gunners had to learn a new technique for coping with the exceptionally low-flying air-launched V-1s, and the pressure on them was heavy. One wartime major, commanding a gun site of 489 HAA Battery at Landguard Point, Felixstowe, remembers being in action every night throughout December 1944, during which his men accounted for 'approximately 20 V-1s'. Morale was high. 'We had to snatch forty winks whenever we could,' remembers one man then stationed at Frinton-on-Sea, but 'it was a pleasure to see a V-1 wrecked on account of our accurate firing . . . and we did not mind the overtime we had to put in to bring them down.'

General Pile's troops had hardly started their long vigil when he faced the familiar demand to send several of his best batteries to the Continent, where Antwerp was now under flying-bomb attack. A far greater problem, also not new, was the need to provide adequate living conditions for his men. The East Coast, always the bleakest part of Britain's sea-girt shores, had never been less appealing than in late 1944. 'June,' wrote H. E. Bates, 'was cold and wet. July was if possible colder and wetter; August . . . after a heat-wave became worse than July; September was worse than August, and October far worse than September. . . . It was the earliest and wettest Autumn within living memory.'

Mud, that ancient ally of General Winter, was everywhere, and among those who testified to its effects that autumn was the Speaker of the House of Commons, who visited, though he did not name it, No. 409 HAA Battery at Walton-on-Naze.

My visit to the first battery was made in a driving downpour. . . . It reminded me of Flanders in the last war. . . . No metalled roads run to the coastline and . . . the seashore is mud and not shingle, so everything had to be carried from afar in lorries. . . . The men were on the alert all night . . . so what they had already done . . . by erecting duck-board passages across the mud was, I thought, highly creditable. . . . When you stepped off in the dark you went up to the knees in mud.

Colonel Clifton-Brown also left the gun-site full of admiration for the ATS girls who had 'not merely . . . dried but pressed' his wet trousers. His experiences demonstrated, he thought, the value of mixed batteries. 'The work that women can do . . . in the operational sphere . . .' he concluded, 'is very great and no Victorian fears of the mixing of the sexes are justified by the tests of this war.' Another parliamentary visit to a gun site had less happy results. Tom Driberg, the Independent MP for Maldon, was invited to visit an isolated gun-site in Essex to lecture on 'The Power of the Press to Influence Opinion', with results revealed in Hansard the next day:

Mr Driberg asked the Secretary of State for War if he is aware that A.T.S. personnel in anti-aircraft batteries are still sleeping under canvas on marshy ground at a place which he has been informed; and if he will take immediate steps to transfer them to billets or provide hutments.

Sir James Grigg's response was to claim that all ATS slept under 'double tentage', an assertion which Tom Driberg was immediately able to refute, and poor General Pile found himself blamed. The irate minister telephoned demanding 'to know why we allowed Mr Driberg to lecture at gun-sites and to come away with information which he could use . . . against the government' and, 'the incident . . . very nearly upset our good relations with the War Office.'

In fact the War Office had for once a good case. A month before, on 14 October, it had approved a far-reaching scheme, costing £2 million, to provide, in General Pile's words, 'accommodation (including living-huts, canteens, theatres, mess rooms and the like) sufficient for a town the size of Windsor.'

It proved as good as its word, and by the use of men from within A A Command, especially redundant searchlight crews, the whole project, estimated to take at least six months, was finished in ten weeks.

By then, however, it seemed that the new huts and cook-houses might prove to be in the wrong place. Intelligence reports in mid-October suggested that more air-launching German squadrons were about to come into service, perhaps aiming at the Midlands, Merseyside and industrial Lancashire and Yorkshire. On 2 November a detailed reconnaissance began of the area between Skegness, in Lincolnshire, and Whitby, in the North Riding of Yorkshire, to select sites for gun batteries, ammunition dumps and living quarters. By 18 November a detailed plan had been drawn up, 'suitable accommodation had been earmarked and all the administrative details lined up', though one problem was insuperable. To cover the whole Diver 'Fringe', as it was known, would require fifty-nine batteries, and so many had been sent to Europe that only fifty were available. The best that could be done was to man at least the three central sections of the new line, near Bridlington, in Yorkshire, Louth in Lincolnshire and around both sides of the mouth of the river Humber.

Despite the upheaval of the move to East Anglia, the guns had never performed better than that autumn. Over the whole East Coast phase of the battle the average rate of 'kills' among targets coming within range was 65 per cent and by the end of November it had reached 82 per cent. The 'number of rounds per bird', in Pile's phrase, was only 156, which made the exercise, as he modestly commented, 'a reasonably economic proposition'.

By the standards of Southern England the attack on East Anglia was a very minor affair. Only thirteen flying-bombs landed in Norfolk, for example, including strays during the main attack in the summer, and though they fell on such unprotected communities as Great Cressingham, Stow Bedon and Thwaite St Mary, they injured all told only eleven people and killed no one.

Battle-hardened Londoners who had retreated to these previously peaceful counties felt a strange mixture of indignation and pride like a Mill Hill woman and her husband, staying in

Huntingdon, where one evening they heard 'the old familiar throbbing beat of a buzz bomb'.

I will never forget the look on our friends' faces as George and I . . . scrabbled hastily under the huge kitchen table, shouting at them to get down. The fat old collie dog, Nellie, pricked up her ears and thumped her tail as we joined her at floor level. 'I can't hear anything,' our friend said. Of course he couldn't. The engine had cut out. . . . Apart from a few covered slates that had shattered down the steep roofs there was no damage. The first and last doodlebug in that district had ploughed its way harmlessly into a potato field.

An AFS man, recuperating in Suffolk after an injury, remembers having to 'pinch myself to know whether I was dreaming or not' after a similar experience, and the exchange with the village postman which followed could have come from *Punch*. 'He said, "Mister, do ee come from Lunnon?" to which I replied, "Yes." "Well," he said, "thou 'ad best be going back, 'cos one of they flying-bombs as followed ee." . . . The thing had burst six miles away, in a cornfield.'

For the regular residents of East Anglia, the flying-bombs remained an interesting curiosity. One wartime railwayman still feels pleased at instantly identifying the 'pulsating humming' at 5.30 one morning near his signal box at Oulton Broad, three miles from Lowestoft, as 'the secret weapon . . . I had heard about from several guards on trains from the London area.' On returning home he found 'everybody outside . . . trying to salvage what they could from the garden crops and yarning with each other about the strange "vacuum phenomena" ' that had sucked out their windows. A farm-worker at Steeple Bumpstead in Suffolk climbed on a tractor to get a better view when his first V-1 appeared, while he was in the fields, and was at the pictures when the second was heard. 'Everybody rushed out in the High Street' to see better, he remembers – only to find they were not allowed back to see the end of the film.

Only rarely did the V-1s cause something like panic, as during a dance at the RAF base near Newmarket racecourse:

When the siren went . . . no one took any notice and the band still played, until someone entered and in a very loud voice said, 'Listen! It's a buzz bomb. Can't you hear it?' . . . Everything went dead quiet.

Autumn in East Anglia

The band stopped, even the chink of glasses at the bar ceased. . . . Faces were white and husbands put their arms around their wives. . . . Then suddenly an airman . . . got up and grasped a large plate of sandwiches, shouting, 'Save the sandwiches!' and dived under the table. He saved the situation because somebody laughed and remarked, 'You are a damn fool. It's a good job you didn't grab the blancmange.'

39

CHRISTMAS AT OLDHAM

Dearest, This is an unexpected and extra letter card that we have been permitted to send off with our Xmas greetings.

Letter from British prisoner-of-war dropped by V-1 near Oldham, 24 December 1944

This year it really should have been over by Christmas. Instead, as the days grew darker and the nights longer with fog, drizzle and finally snow rounding off a miserable year, news of the German offensive in the Ardennes arrived to lower spirits still further. The rockets, which had begun to arrive on 8 September, though news of them was suppressed until 10 November, were still pounding down on Greater London several times a day, while the occasional V-1 still arrived across the North Sea. The spirit of the times is reflected in the recollections of a woman then living at Epping Green Corner, Hertfordshire who two days before Christmas was decorating a small Christmas tree with silver milk-bottle tops and anti-radar 'window' for tinsel when the noise of flying-bomb broke into her peaceful occupation. 'Though the explosion was a long way off, the children got very upset. I remember saying, "Let's show them the tree," . . . and in all the "Ohs" and "Ahs" from the children, the bomb was forgotten.'

Christmas 1944 was marked by a last, desperate attempt by the Germans to cause alarm in a part of the country hitherto untouched by the flying-bombs. The assault was planned, just as General Pile had feared, to outflank the East Coast defences, and was delivered at a time when vigilance was likely to be at its lowest – the early hours of the morning of Christmas Eve, Sunday, 24 December. Soon after midnight almost the whole available strength of Kampfgruppe 53, about fifty Heinkels, staggered one by one into the air with their heavy burdens, and set course almost due north. One was caught by a night-fighter, but the rest managed to launch their missiles just off the coast between Skegness in Lincolnshire and Bridlington in Yorkshire, a front of more than seventy miles. As usual with air launches, several missiles crashed almost at once, but thirty survived to cross the coast, between Mablethorpe and Spurn Head. Seven were engaged, unsuccessfully, by the defences around the Humber, and the whole salvo then disappeared into the darkness over Northern England.

Some of the V-1s vanished without trace. One near Mundesley, after its motor had fired, refused to separate from its parent aircraft and both dived together into the North Sea. Another plunged into the mud of the river Humber, with the engine still running, near Reads Island; a third landed innocuously near the Lincolnshire village of Redbourne. A fourth, which also hurt no one, was reported by the Royal Observer Corps post at Dunham-on-Trent; while the Epworth ROC post sent an urgent sighting report to its centre at York: 'The b— engine has stopped and . . . if we go off the air you'll know we've had it.' Luckily they had not, though the crater was near enough to walk to. Evacuees and people who had gone north to spend a bomb-free Christmas with friends and relations also identified the flying-bombs correctly, but faced a sceptical reception. 'Our friends laughed and said she was imagining things,' remembers a Lowestoft woman, staying with her sister-in-law at a village near Worksop in Nottinghamshire, when a fellow guest remarked, 'It's one of those so-and-so doodlebugs.' London children had to tell the local wardens what was happening. 'We shouted "That's a doodlebug",' remembers one man then aged fourteen, evacuated to Hyde in Cheshire. 'I don't think they believed us, but it was.' A teacher from Dartford in Kent 'couldn't believe it' when she woke to the familiar sound during her second night in Darwen. 'Next morning all was great excitement. . . . As someone said, "Eee, they'd a doodlebug at Oswaldtwistle." '

A similar experience gave a ten-year-old girl living at Cheadle, six miles to the south of Manchester, something to boast of to her best friend, an evacuee who 'gave lurid accounts of these V-1s'.

One night the sirens went and, as usual, I was first out of bed. . . .

The Doodlebugs

I heard a droning noise of an engine coming from outside and, looking out, saw a dark, aeroplane-shaped object with a light on it pass a few feet from our house. My sister and I stood clutching one another, too frightened to move. . . . When it had passed, we ran downstairs. My mother was sceptical at first when we told her, until a neighbour across the road ran, screaming hysterically, through our front door saying a V-1 had passed over both our houses. Next day we found out that it had landed about one and a half miles away. When I told my friend from London, 'Humph', she said philosophically, 'your name wasn't on it!'

The first of that night's V-1s to get anywhere near its target came down at Brindle, four miles south-east of Preston, around 5.30 a.m., about twenty-five miles 'wide' to the north-west. Others landed over an area sixty-five miles in diameter: at Beighton, just across the Yorkshire border in Derbyshire and forty miles short of its target; at Buxton, in the same county, about twenty miles south-east of Manchester, at Davenport and Hyde, in Cheshire, eight miles to the south-east, and in a variety of other places in the great Manchester conurbation, including Worsley, Tottington and Radcliffe. Mostly they did comparatively little damage: the one at Didsbury obligingly fell on a golf course. Casualties were caused, however, in Davenport and Hyde, and in Worsley, where a small boy was killed. Three days after the raid the *Manchester Evening News* reported that six people had been killed in one unidentified town when 'some cottages were completely demolished and the nearby village church was damaged,' though 'the vicar carried through the Christmas Day services in the windowless church.' Elsewhere, it was stated, four people were seriously injured, and in a third location a child and an elderly woman had been killed when a farmhouse was hit.

Only when the Germans announced that the attack had been aimed at Manchester was the flying-bombs' objective known for certain; indeed 'few Lancashire people,' the *Manchester Evening News* reported later, 'knew of their arrival till they heard the phrase "Northern England" in the Air Ministry's communiqué.' The whole attack had caused far fewer casualties and much less damage than many single incidents in London. Only one flying-bomb landed within the city limits of Manchester, but six had fallen within ten miles of the centre of the

456

city and eleven more within fifteen miles, while thirty-seven people had been killed and sixty-seven seriously injured, remarkably close to the overall average of one death per bomb. By far the most serious incidents had been at Tottington, where the six deaths reported by the *Manchester Evening News* had occurred, and sixteen people had been seriously injured, and at Oldham, where there had been a near disaster, in which twenty-eight people had lost their lives and thirty-eight been badly hurt.*

Because of the strict censorship rules, the *Oldham Chronicle* in its next issue, on 30 December, could refer only to 'one industrial town' without giving details, though it did report that the dead included four members of a wedding party, several infants, including one only six months old, and an old lady of seventy-nine. Any zealous German intelligence officer scrutinizing the paper could have discovered that at least fourteen people had been killed and at least ten had been injured, but the final figures were not published until 21 April 1945, when a much fuller account revealed that the bomb had fallen in Abbey Hills Road:

The sounding of the sirens shortly before 5.30 a.m. came as a surprise, but notwithstanding that Civil Defence and other personnel had not been standing by at posts and depots for some time there was an excellent response. Wardens and police were quickly on the scene, followed shortly afterwards by ambulances, rescue and casualty services. The Home Guard rescue squads also reported and gave good help. . . . Incident Inquiry Points (staffed by W.V.S. and wardens) were established for the first time in this area and worked very well. It was necessary to open one Rest Centre only. Regional Columns [i.e. outside reinforcements] were called early by the Controller, and their speedy arrival and strenuous efforts were an incentive and valuable aid to our local services. . . . First-aid repairs to property were taken quickly in hand and . . . damaged houses were . . . rapidly made weather-proof. . . . Help by way of labour and materials was afforded by surrounding areas, in particular Manchester.

The regional commissioner for the North-West, Hartley, later Lord, Shawcross, arrived in Oldham within two hours of the

---

*Final casualty figures for the incidents that night never seem to have been agreed.

Christmas Eve attack and returned during Christmas Day to see how the post-raid services were coping and to visit the injured, now at Oldham Royal Infirmary. The *Oldham Chronicle* headlines, 'Magnificent Work Done by A.R.P. Services', 'V-bomb found them ready' were not wholly borne out by the private postmortem held by Hartley Shawcross. 'Incident Control,' he wrote in his report, 'was not good, the Oldham incident being too big for one Incident Officer. . . . I was not impressed with the organisation and leadership of the part time [rescue] parties.' It had, the regional commissioner felt, been fortunate that the attack had come outside working hours, for Civil Defence in the North now had few full-time professionals. At Oldham, where ten parties had assembled, at Stockport, with a further ten, and at Manchester, with eleven the turnout had been good, but 'at Liverpool . . . the response was bad, only 25 men reporting' and 'at Bootle, Birkenhead and Wallasey, the numbers were six men, three parties and three parties respectively.' Even more serious, 'in one or two places the sirens were not sounded, in some others the alert was given little if at all in advance of the fall of bombs.'

At least some local authorities in the North had, it was clear, been caught napping, though the government was largely to blame: it had cut down Civil Defence so drastically that at Oldham the report and control centre was no longer kept open at night, though on Christmas Eve it had been brought into action within a few minutes. The nearest first-aid post to Abbey Hills Road had also been closed though once the incident had occurred everyone had reacted energetically.

Because it had affected an area undisturbed for so long the Oldham incident was later studied in great detail. After the raid a conference had been held between the ARP controller, incident officer and the heads of the various ARP services, and five weeks later other Civil Defence workers were assembled to hear a lecture on the lessons to be learned. The V-1, after approaching from the east, the lecturer explained, had dived to earth at 5.50 a.m., demolishing twenty-three houses – another twelve had to be pulled down later – and damaging 1025 over a three-quarter mile radius. The nearest wardens' post had been only 200 yards away, and though the wardens had not at first identified the incident as due to a V-1, by 6 a.m.

the first reports had reached the newly-opened control centre, by 6.10 the first ambulances were on the scene, and by 8.45 an incident inquiry post had been set up nearby by the WVS. It had later moved to a school, where it had successfully handled 450 inquiries in the first two days alone. As in London, few people had used the rest centre, though twenty-seven had spent Christmas there, but five mobile canteens had been needed. 'Where such complete devastation occurs . . .' commented the speaker, 'fine powdered dust clogs the throat and if only cups of tea can be provided it helps considerably.'

More useful, however, than hearing what had gone right was learning what had gone wrong. There were the usual difficulties from over-zealous 'freelance' helpers; one woman, it was discovered, had treated twenty casualties in her own home unknown to the wardens; communications had been poor, for the telephone kiosk at first used had developed a technical hitch, and the police car radio then used had rapidly run down its batteries. If more ladders and other simple equipment had been on hand, more people not badly trapped could have been got out of the ruins before the rescue parties arrived. Reading between the lines, it was not difficult to picture the nightmare scene which had greeted the first helpers who, with no previous experience of this kind to guide them, had stumbled over the rubble-blocked roadway to reach the column of dust towering over Abbey Hills Road that raw December morning. Houses on both sides of the road had been wrecked, there was a strong smell of gas – due to broken domestic gas pipes, not to a fractured main – and as the wardens and policemen approached the mound of rubble formed by the ruins of more than thirty houses, hearing 'calls for help in almost every direction', they found that the official warden's lamp was almost useless, for it 'had to be carried in one hand and gave a light only to the feet of the personnel carrying it.'

The deficiencies revealed by the sudden foray against Manchester caused a good deal of heart-searching in official circles. On 2 January Hartley Shawcross reminded ARP controllers in his region that ARP part-timers who failed to turn out when the sirens sounded could be prosecuted. The Ministry of Home Security issued a similar warning on 17 January 1945 in a long letter to Civil Defence regions entitled *Air Attacks on Areas which have had Immunity for some Time*.

The recent flying bomb attack on the North, which may well be repeated and may extend to other areas, has emphasised the importance of ensuring that the Civil Defence Services are kept up in a state of operational efficiency. . . . Many Wardens' Posts have been shut and in some areas Wardens' Posts are only opened for a short period in the early evening. . . . Many Depots are now only manned on the siren sounding or enemy action occurring. Telephones should be tested frequently at these Posts to be used for operations. . . . All personnel must be definitely informed of their obligation to turn out on an alert, or on enemy action occurring . . . and of the consequences which may follow a failure to report for duty.

The explosion at Abbey Hills Road, Oldham, was the last serious incident caused by a flying-bomb. But the Manchester raid was also unique, providing the oddest delivery of Christmas greetings in history. The Germans had on several occasions earlier in the year used V-1s to deliver bundles of propaganda, as already described,* and some of the missiles aimed at Manchester included an air-mail version, with a reduced page size, of their forty-page newspaper, *Signal*, designed for circulation in neutral and occupied countries. This particular edition, while maintaining stoutly that Germany would still win, did not conceal that time was growing short. A large clock face on the front page showed the hands standing at five to twelve, a reference to one of Hitler's speeches in which he had criticized the German generals for having surrendered in 1910 'at a quarter to twelve. This time,' he boasted, 'we will lay down our arms at five minutes past twelve' – meaning that the enemy would give in first.

The first copies of *Signal* seem to have been found on Christmas Eve by the ROC post at Epworth, from which one of the two observers ventured out to the still smoking crater nearby to retrieve from it a cardboard box containing three copies of the magazine. While the police were still searching for other copies the Oldham V-1 scattered a far more intriguing and ingenious piece of propaganda, 'V-1 POW Post'. The Oldham police force were ordered to gather up or confiscate every copy

---

*See page 335.

and, as a whole bundle had come down in a cemetery at Lees about three miles away, few, if any, copies seem to have reached those for whom they were intended, the relations of British prisoners of war.

'POW Post' was an ingenious idea. Each leaflet contained several facsimile letters from prisoners of war whose homes were in the area, with reassuring comments from a German official and a covering note:

The finder is requested to cut out or copy the letters printed here and to transmit them to the addresses [sic] so that they receive them as early as possible. The original letters are being sent through the Red Cross in the usual mail channel.

This appeal must have been hard for any kind-hearted person to resist, for the letters were likely to make the intended recipient's Christmas. This, for example, was written by a staff sergeant to his wife in Manchester:

My own darling wife, just a line to let you know I am in the same old place. . . . When my glider got burnt, I received burns on the right hand (now healed) right shoulder (now better) right arm (healing very well), and a large burn on the right leg. . . . I should be able to walk quite well when I am better, so do not worry! Dearest darling I love you always, and can wait for ever if it is necessary.

To this moving letter, the colonel in command of the camp had added a sympathetic postscript:

You can rest assured that regarding the health and welfare of your husband he gets all the attention possible.

A Scotswoman, living near Peebles, must also have been reassured to receive this letter from her absent husband, involuntarily resident in Germany:

Dearest, This is an unexpected and extra letter card that we have been permitted to send off with our Xmas greetings, so I do hope it reaches you in time. Knowing that I am in good hands, dear, and getting on fine and hoping to be with you before so very long, I do hope you will do your best to enjoy Xmas and New Year, difficult though I know it will be! . . . By the time you receive this, dear, I hope to have my plaster cast off. Then I start learning to bend my legs again and so on to walking. I am . . . looking forward to getting on my feet again. My love and regards to you all, dear! Hubby.

461

The Doodlebugs

The Germans had clearly hoped that the recipients when writing to their husbands in Germany would reveal where the V-1 concerned had landed, but they were to be disappointed. At a meeting on 15 January 1945 between the POW Directorate and the Chief Censor it was decided to send on the letters but to warn the recipients not to mention that they had arrived. At least one letter, intended for a woman in Maidstone, *was* sent on by a passer-by, but as the Post Office were opening incoming letters addressed to people named in the leaflets, it too was detected.

The Manchester attack confirmed the need for continued vigilance by AA Command and for the men on the East Coast gun-sites the words 'festive season' had an ironic ring. This was how the holiday is remembered by one gunner, whose battery had already that year moved three times, from Bognor to Edenbridge then to Romney Marsh and finally to Great Oakley in Essex:

The rain had turned the road to the cookhouse into a sea of mud about one foot deep. An improvised snow plough was fitted to the rear of a lorry to try and clear it. To add weight, six of us had to stand on the planks. I was jerked off, going base over apex in that sea of mud. The dining place was a marquee in which the Christmas barrel of beer was placed. It was so cold that the beer formed an icicle on the top.

Many other units had an even worse time, for within a few hours of the attack on Manchester, Air Chief Marshal Hill agreed to thin out the East Coast gun-belt and authorized the immediate move of sixty heavy guns to the Diver 'Fringe' between Filey and Skegness. They were to be followed two days later by four troops of light AA guns and a number of searchlight detachments.

Gunners and ATS who had just settled into their new huts, were now uprooted again. Christmas Day 1943 had found many members of AA Command driving south as part of the initial Diver build-up. Christmas Day 1944 saw many units on the road again, moving north, under far worse conditions, as General Pile described:

The whole deployment took place . . . in terrible weather. On Christmas Day and Boxing Day progress was held up by a thick fog, which was followed by a hard frost, during which the task of emplacing the gun platforms was a difficult one. . . . There were heavy falls of snow along the Yorkshire coast which made roads impassable and which actually isolated two of the sites for three days. . . . At all times movement was difficult over the low-lying and marshy ground south of the Humber. The roads were few and poor. Bridges had to be strengthened. In the weather that we had that Christmas, the move was more of a nightmare than most. . . . But by December 29 it was almost completed and the guns were in position to engage the flying-bombs that never came that way again.

In making the Manchester attacks KG 53 had almost literally shot its last bolt. Very few V-1s were fired from the air during the next few days and the final air-launched V-1 of the whole war landed at Hornsey, in North-East London, at 0213 hours on 14 January 1945. On the following day the launching unit ceased operations, because of the crippling fuel shortage and because it was feared that its bases in north-west Germany would soon become untenable.

The battle of the air-launched V-1s provided a clear victory for the defence. During all the air-launching operations, including those during the summer, the launching units had lost seventy-seven aircraft, against an operational strength, when finally grounded, of 101 – a crippling casualty rate. During the main phase of the air-launching bombardment, between 16 September 1944 and 14 January 1945, losses totalled forty-five, of which four aircraft were destroyed on the ground, sixteen were, it was claimed, shot down by British night-fighters and twenty-five succumbed to accidents of various kinds. As one night-fighter pilot remarked, 'Sir Isaac's influence,' i.e. the law of gravity, 'must have found the extremely low-flying unit a temptation impossible to resist.'

40

THE FINAL SPRING

*ULTRA indicates evacuation about 8 April German Air
Ammunition Depot at Karwitz known to have supplied flying
bombs for London attacks. Destination unknown.*

Message to Air Ministry Intelligence Branch, 23 April 1945

While the fight for Führer and Fatherland was being waged by
the air-launching squadrons of KG 53, Colonel Wachtel and
his men, having been chased out of France, had been sitting
frustratingly on the side lines. Early in September, much
against his wishes, he had been ordered to set up new sites in
the Eiffel area of Germany to bombard Antwerp, now the
major port supplying the British armies. He was also instructed
to bombard Liège, the supply centre for the US First Army.
About 1500 missiles a month were still reaching him and when,
on 16 December 1944, von Rundstedt's troops launched the
Ardennes offensive, they advanced to the comforting rattle of
the flying-bombs overhead. Wachtel's insistence, however, that
the V-1 was simply not accurate enough to provide tactical
support proved well founded. By the time these operations
ceased in March 5960 missiles – including some V-2s – had
fallen within an eight-mile radius of the centre of Antwerp and
302 had landed within the port area. These had sunk one ship,
damaged sixteen others and put a dry dock out of action for
three months – not negligible results, but less than a single raid
by manned bombers might have accomplished. The attack had
also cost the lives of 3470 Belgian civilians and 682 Allied
servicemen and done an enormous amount of damage to property, destroying 6400 houses in greater Antwerp and damaging
another 60,000 and 4300 more had been destroyed and 44,000
damaged in greater Liège.

In January 1945, to Colonel Wachtel's relief, his old adversary Colonel Walter was posted elsewhere and Wachtel was

belatedly given a medal and entrusted with responsibility for planning, as well as directing, flying-bomb operations. By now, however, his command was dwindling. Two of his detachments were converted into light AA regiments, one was sent into reserve east of the Rhine and only one Abteilung continued the task for which it had been trained. Being based in the Fatherland also produced a new complication. The Germans had not cared at all when a V-1 fell short and killed French civilians but they minded very much when this happened to their own people and every V-1 was now subjected to a rigorous safety inspection before firing. This led to 200 out of one stock of 320 bombs being declared unserviceable and slowed down the rate of fire of the remainder.

Apart from strengthening their anti-aircraft artillery in the Low Countries there was not much the Allied commanders could do against this new menace, for the launching ramps proved, as in France, difficult to locate and attack. But, having so often been taken unawares by earlier developments, the British government was no longer inclined to underestimate the prospect of a sudden new attack. As early as 16 October 1944 the War Cabinet in London had been warned that 'over 40 flying-bomb sites were being constructed in the Ruhr,' though it was at first assumed that these were for use against targets in the Low Countries. When fragments of a new type of V-1, with a longer range, were picked up in Belgium new and more alarming possibilities were opened up. On 25 February 1945 the Air Ministry, determined not to be caught napping, formally warned the Chiefs of Staff that the United Kingdom was once more open to flying-bomb attack. On the following day, Hut 3 at Bletchley informed the Air Intelligence Branch, in an Ultra secret dispatch, that 'Introduction of longer range flying bomb must be expected [in the] near future. Trial launching from West coast of Denmark . . . at range of about 230 miles foreseen for week 18–24 February.' Once again, it was not the glamorous Ultra which provided the really important information but the reconnaissance pilots and the photographic interpreters at Medmenham. Both must have felt that old times had returned, as a new survey was ordered of the German-occupied parts of the Low Countries. This time the area to be combed was far smaller than before and two ramps aligned on London, at Ypenburg, near the Hague, and Vlaardingen, near Rotterdam, were discovered almost at once, on 26 February. As they seemed unlikely to be used for several weeks the sites were not bombed, but Anti-Aircraft Command was ordered to move its batteries once again, this time in the reverse direction, to strengthen the Diver 'box' beside the Thames Estuary, and the southern end of the Diver 'strip' in Essex. Twelve batteries, consisting of ninety-six heavy guns, were earmarked for the purpose, though only three-quarters of these actually made the journey.

The defensive strategy which had proved so successful the previous summer should, it was agreed, be adopted again, this time with the advantage of an early-warning radar station in Belgium. By day, three squadrons of Mustangs would try to catch the intruders over the sea, with another three squadrons, plus a squadron of Meteors, patrolling between the coast and London. By night two squadrons of Mosquitoes would maintain the coastal watch, with another squadron of Tempests inland. In the event, the defences were never really stretched, for the new bombs came not from Germany, as at one time feared, but from Holland.

This third and last phase of the V-1 offensive, and the second phase of the land-launched battle, began on 3 March 1945. By earlier standards it was a trivial affair, and the Germans managed only to get occasional bombs into the air. Offensive counter-measures did not begin until 20 March, when fighter-bombers attacked one of the two sites so far discovered at Ypenburg. The turn of the second, at Vlaardingen, came two days later and both were badly damaged. A site near Delft remained undetected and it was from here that the closing shots in the campaign were fired. The three sites between them managed to loose off some 275 bombs, but only 125 got within range of the defences. Of these four were shot down by aircraft, eighty-seven by the guns, including one shared with the Royal Navy, and thirty-four crossed the coast, of which thirteen reached Greater London.

The last full day of the offensive came on 28 March. That morning two V-1s came down at Waltham Cross, about twelve miles north of Tower Bridge, and at Chislehurst, roughly the same distance to the south-east. Around 9.30 that evening the

Germans began their final bombardment. By now all that survived of the once dreaded flying-bomb army was the solitary site at Delft, still gamely but pointlessly catapulting loads of high explosive into the sky. Before it too ceased operations it had fired twenty-one flying-bombs. Of these only one evaded the guns and fighters and dived to earth under its own power, finding a singularly appropriate graveyard, a sewage farm at Datchworth near Hatfield in Hertfordshire, twenty-one miles from London, just before 9 a.m. on 29 March 1945. An hour later the last V-1 of all to land on British soil was shot down by AA fire and exploded harmlessly at Iwade, near Sittingbourne, forty miles short of its target, beside the same main road near which the very first V-1 had exploded, at Swanscombe, nine months before, but twice as far from its intended target. Even this was not quite the end. At 12.43 p.m. that Thursday, 29 March 1945, the last V-1 to approach the British Isles charged towards the shores of Suffolk near Orfordness. It never reached them; the guns caught it and it plunged ignominiously into the sea.

With that solitary splash, it seemed, died Colonel Wachtel's hopes of winning the war for the Fatherland, but the Germans would still not admit that they were beaten. The Air Intelligence Branch in Whitehall had warned its outpost in Hut 3 at Bletchley on 19 March, while occasional V-1s were still reaching London, that the possibility of a longer-range V-1 remained, if the technical problem of the limited life of the 'spring leaf valves in [the] propulsion unit' could be solved. 'This weakness,' the Air Ministry concluded, 'could be easily overcome but [it is] considered that at greater ranges (say 300 miles) [a] general alteration in design would become necessary to avoid [a] considerable reduction in [the] size of [the] warhead.' On 9 April Hut 3 responded with an intercepted message, which revealed that the Germans were trying to bring into use by mid-April a modified V-1, with an increased range of 500 kilometres [310 miles] but a reduced explosive charge of only 400 kilogrammes [882 pounds, against the normal 1840]. 'If modified weapon materialises,' the code-breakers suggested, 'ANTWERP [is] still likely to be [the] main target', with the areas east of the river Weser, well inside Germany, as 'most suitable for launching'.

The next messages from Bletchley revealed, however, that Flak Regiment 155 (W) and its supporting services had reached the end of the road. 'Experimental Abteilung', Hut 3 reported in mid-April, 'had ceased work and was awaiting transport to the front, presumably to fight. This may mean that plans for the 500 kilometre flying-bomb have been shelved.' Finally on 23 April, the postscript was written to this last, despairing German effort: 'ULTRA indicates evacuation about 8 April German Air Force Ammunition Depot at Karwitz [which is] known to have supplied flying-bombs for London attacks. Destination unknown.'

Colonel Wachtel himself had also disappeared, after somewhat pointlessly assuming his old alias of 'Colonel Wolf'. Driven from Holland, as previously from France, he retreated to Luneberg in the north-west corner of Germany and re-formed his surviving troops into infantry to fight the advancing British on the ground. They were no more successful in this new role than in the old one, for on 4 May on nearby Luneberg Heath all the German forces in north-west Germany, including his own, surrendered unconditionally to Field-Marshal Montgomery. Four days later the war in Europe was over. It was an undramatic ending to the long story of the V-1, which was never to be used in action again.

Although the idea of an unmanned missile was to be vigorously pursued after the war and a far more elaborate variety, with a sophisticated terrain-following guidance system is now deployed in the United Kingdom, this really has little in common with the superbly cheap and simple flying-bomb. The V-2, not the V-1, is the true ancestor of most post-war long-range weapons.

One version of the flying-bomb, of which very little has hitherto been written, failed to appear at all; a piloted model which, while exploiting all the machine's strong points, added the one quality it conspicuously lacked, that of accuracy. The idea of using what was virtually a suicide-aircraft to redress the balance of the Allies' visibly growing air superiority seems to have originated spontaneously in several quarters in Germany, long before the first Japanese *Kamikaze* aircraft plunged on to the American fleet in Leyte Gulf on 25 October 1944. The chief driving force behind it, according to her own account,

The Final Spring

was the thirty-year-old Hanna Reitsch, the Amy Johnson of
German aviation. An immensely brave and experienced test
pilot, Hanna Reitsch had test flown the original prototype
flying-bomb, stretched out on the floor of the fuselage and
operating makeshift controls with her hands, when the original
design was giving trouble. By August 1943, however, only a
few months later, Hanna Reitsch, as she subsequently claimed,
had decided that the war was lost and, a little oddly the sceptic
may feel, had concluded that the quickest way to end it was to
make Germany stronger. Over lunch in the Flying Club in
Berlin she courageously – so she said – propounded to two
friends her idea for Operation Suicide.

We believed that the war must be brought to an early end if Germany
were to be saved from disaster and that this could only be secured
through a negotiated peace. To prepare the ground for negotiation,
it would be necessary to weaken considerably the enemy's military
strength. . . . If volunteers were forthcoming to pilot a suitable projectile into the centre of its target, destroying it totally, . . . it should
be possible to deliver, while sparing the enemy civil population, a
rapid succession of devastating blows at generating stations, waterworks, key production centres and, in the event of invasion, at naval
and merchant shipping.

The first response in official quarters was not encouraging, for
Göring's deputy, Field-Marshal Milch, turned the idea down
flat as 'contrary to the German mentality'. The Director of the
Aeronautical Research Institute was more open minded and
'undertook to call a conference of all interested scientists, tech-
nicians and tacticians . . . to consider our plan'. This meeting,
held during the winter of 1944, endorsed the proposal in principle. Hanna Reitsch herself put it to the Führer when summoned to his Austrian retreat, the Berghof, on 28 February
1944 to receive the Iron Cross (First Class). 'Hitler's first reaction,' she later wrote, 'was to reject completely the idea of
suicide missions,' but he admitted the situation might change
and she managed to extract 'permission for us to start experimental work on the type of plane to be used, so that when
Hitler decided that the right moment had arrived . . . the
suicide attacks could be started at once.' Armed with this
authority, the Chief of the Luftwaffe General Staff, General
Korten, formally created a 'Suicide Group' attached to an

existing squadron. Hanna Reitsch was among the first to sign the declaration drawn up for future pilots:

I hereby voluntarily apply to be enrolled in the suicide group as pilot of a human glider-bomb. I fully understand that employment in this capacity will entail my own death.

Although no public appeal was made for volunteers, as news of the project leaked out there proved to be no lack of them.

We found them everywhere. Most of them were married and fathers of families and were robust uncomplicated individuals. As they saw it, the sacrifices of their lives would be as nothing compared with the millions, both soldiers and civilians, who would die if the war was allowed to continue. Moreover, they were convinced that the sacrifice was necessary if their wives and children, and their country, were to be saved. . . . Here was required nothing less than the complete conquest of self.

At this stage the intention was to use as 'a human glider-bomb' a promising new design of fighter, the Messerschmitt 328. When the Messerschmitts failed to appear on schedule the project's sponsors turned again to the V-1. In the same month, April 1944, they received the valuable support of Otto Skorzeny, another pilot of legendary skill, famous for rescuing Mussolini from captivity. Skorzeny's assertion that 'Hitler had vested him with full powers' was powerful enough to open all doors. Within 'four or five days' the first V-1 was converted to its new, piloted role, under the code name *Reichenberg*, abbreviated to 'R'.

Several types of 'R' series flying-bomb were produced. The first piloted version, the Fieseler 103R-I, was equipped with skids and flaps so that it could be landed after test flights; it was followed by the R-II, a two-seater trainer, and the R-III, also equipped with landing gear, but otherwise close to the final, operational version, the R-IV. This looked little different from the ordinary flying-bomb, but the nose was reshaped and space was found for the pilot by removing one of the two large globes containing compressed air, which was no longer needed to operate controls automatically. The other globe was moved to the rear compartment previously occupied by the automatic pilot. The simplest possible instruments and controls for its single, one-way journey were installed: a clock, an airspeed indicator, an altimeter, a joystick and a foot-operated rudder bar. These were needed only to direct the machine, when it had completed its pre-set journey, on to its target. There was no radio, but all the 'R' series V–1s were to be air-launched and the pilot would be in touch through his headphones with the parent Heinkel until the moment of release.

The Luftwaffe experimental station at Lärz at first declined Hanna Reitsch's offer to test fly the piloted V-1s but after two accidents she was allowed to take over, and after some ten uneventful flights had two narrow escapes herself. Once, a sack of sand broke loose, and on another occasion, where water was being used as ballast, the 'draining hole', designed to empty the tank before landing, froze up. 'In a frenzy of desperation,' she later wrote, 'I gripped and clawed at the lever till my fingers were bleeding. . . . At last, with only a few hundred feet to go the lever suddenly moved and there was just time to drain out most of the water.'

These difficulties apart – and they arose from features which would be absent from the operational model – Hanna Reitsch reported that 'though any average pilot could fly the V-1 without difficulty once it was in the air, to land it called for exceptional skill.' But, if they never landed, how were the volunteer pilots to learn to fly it? The first step, to train the instructors who would teach them, proved very difficult and eventually 'of the thousands who had volunteered as suicide-pilots . . . only about seventy were called up.' It was the intention for 'the remainder . . . to be embodied when the technical details had been completed . . . and an officer appointed to command the Group,' but this never happened. The production of the operational model, the R-IV, also proved disappointing. Although an existing flying-bomb assembly plant, code-named *Pulverhof*, was partly turned over to making them, and others were produced in a new factory near Dannenberg, only 250 were ordered, of which about 175 were completed.

By this time the original conception had changed. Instead of being sealed into his cockpit like the Japanese *Kamikaze* pilots, the man flying the V-1 was to be given a chance of life, although the likelihood of his getting clear of the aircraft was very slight. The pilot was expected to steer it manually until the last possible moment, then, in the brief interval left, the cockpit canopy had to hinge back 45° to starboard before it would fall away. Its release mechanism soon proved to be inefficient, and if he did succeed in jettisoning it the pilot was liable to be struck by the pulse-jet cowling as he tried to leave the aircraft. What was needed was a hatch below the fuselage, but this would have meant more extensive modifications, and the Germans perhaps never really expected the pilot to escape. The official name for the would-be V-1 pilots, *Selbstopfermänner* or 'self-sacrifice men', spoke for itself.

By now there seems to have been a lack of enthusiasm for the whole project in the highest Nazi circles. The conception of 'a collection of brave, clear-headed and intelligent Germans who seriously believed . . . that by sacrificing their own lives they might . . . ensure some kind of future for their children' was, Hanna Reitsch believed, 'too cold to kindle the imaginations of Himmler and Goebbels.' Goebbels did at least encourage the group 'by summoning its members to His Ministry and reciting to them a premature panegyric on the theme of heroism. . . . Himmler,' by contrast, 'suggested that the suicide-pilots should be recruited among the incurably diseased, the neurotics and the criminals so that through a voluntary death they might redeem their "honour".' Others, thinking on similar lines, felt that flying the V-1 would be an ideal assignment for pilots suffering from what the RAF called 'lack of moral fibre'. Eventually, around the end of 1944, the whole scheme was quietly abandoned.

41

COUNTING THE COST

The results of the campaign were greatly in the enemy's favour, the estimated ratio of our costs to his being nearly four to one.

Air Ministry report, 4 November 1944

The battle of the flying-bomb was won by the Allies. A mechanical masterpiece, designed, developed and produced with astonishing speed, the V-1 nevertheless failed to delay the landing in Normandy, or to cause the Allies to change their overall plan of campaign. Any effect it had in raising German morale was short lived. It neither staved off defeat, nor secured peace by negotiation.

All this acknowledged, however, and the moral question of the indiscriminate nature of the weapon set aside, it remains a remarkable achievement. The claims made in the German propaganda leaflets – in contrast to the ludicrous boasts of their press and radio – were true; it was an amazingly cheap weapon and cost nothing at all in terms of German life. Just how little the flying-bomb did cost is hard to determine. The writer David Irving acknowledged in 1964 that 'there is an unbridgeable gap between the various estimates for the production costs of the two main German secret weapons,' though he concluded 'that for attacking large targets at medium range the unsophisticated flying-bomb was unrivalled for simplicity, economy and efficiency'. By any test the V-1 was a fantastic bargain. The Royal Aircraft Establishment at Farnborough estimated that a British factory, with a large-scale contract, would have built it for £115 a time. The contract between the German government and its main suppliers Volkswagen, allowed for an average cost of £125, though in the leaflet dropped over England in November 1944, the Germans described it as £600. This seems, however, to have been due to a miscalculation of the exchange rate; in the same document they described the Lancaster as costing £60,000, about four times the figure usually quoted in British National Savings appeals. The true cost of the V-1 was probably around £150 – the extra £25 being accounted for by the expense of modifications to the later models.

In a secret report compiled on 4 November 1944 the Air Ministry set out the unpalatable facts. 'The results of the campaign,' it acknowledged, 'were greatly in the enemy's favour, the estimated ratio of our costs to his being nearly four to one.' The V-1 offensive from 12 June to 1 September alone was estimated to have cost the Allies nearly £48 million, in aircraft and airmen lost, bombs dropped, shells fired and balloons lost, the clearance of damage and the loss of military production. If to this were added the cost of replacing destroyed or damaged housing, estimated by the Ministry of Health early in November to be at least £25 million (including some V-2 damage), the total cost to the Allies, and mainly to the British taxpayer, by the autumn rose to £62 million. Expenditure from then on, with the tailing off of the offensive, was at a much lower rate, but still significant, including £2 million worth of buildings for AA Command in East Anglia and the repair of 1000 houses at Oldham. By the end of the war the V-1s cannot have cost the country much less than £70 million. The cost to the Germans, by contrast, to 1 September 1944, was estimated by the Air Ministry to be £12,600,000 for constructing launching sites, training the crews, and building the missiles themselves. Assuming this had risen to say £14 million by the end of the war, with the loss of some ancient Heinkels, the balance of advantage lay even more in the Germans' favour. For every £1 the V-1 cost the Germans it cost the British (aided to a lesser extent by the American) taxpayer £5.

War, unhappily, involves killing people. Here too the V-1 campaign was a triumph for the Germans. Colonel Wachtel's fatal casualties, by February 1945, numbered only 185, including accidents, while to achieve this total 2900 Allied airmen had died, including those killed in the attack on Peenemünde and in bombing V-2 targets. In addition some hundreds of Allied servicemen were killed by V-1s on the ground. All told 6184 civilians and 2917 servicemen (the latter including V-2 casualties) died during the campaign, while 17,981 civilians and

1939 soldiers, sailors and airmen (including V-2 victims) were seriously injured. Many more mourn the loss of homes, or prized possessions, in the 23,000 houses destroyed and nearly one million damaged.*

Of flying-bomb incidents on land 5823 were reported to the Civil Defence authorities, though the remains of a few V-1s probably lie undetected to this day in lonely woods or desolate marshes; 2242, or 41 per cent of the total, landed in London and a table compiled by the Air Ministry for the period up to the end of August 1944 – with eighty V-1s still to reach Greater London – showed that hardly any part of the capital and its environs had escaped entirely. The Borough of Croydon, with 141, was an easy 'winner', followed by Wandsworth (which included Streatham) with 122, and Lewisham with 114. Camberwell with 80, Woolwich with 77, Greenwich with 73, and Lambeth with 71, all testified to how much the area immediately south of the Thames had suffered, and Beckenham with 70, Orpington with 63, both a little further out, were not far behind. The worst affected borough north of the river was West Ham, with 58, but the next place on the list was a south-eastern suburb, Coulsdon, which suffered from 54. Top of the 'under-fifties' category were two somewhat similar places, Chislehurst, with 45, and Mitcham with 43. Then came fifteen boroughs, again mainly in the south, with between 39 and 30: Poplar, Barking, Bromley, Beddington, East Ham, Hackney, Banstead, Esher, Battersea, Ilford, Sutton, Wimbledon, Bermondsey, Deptford and Stepney; Westminster, Epsom, Dagenham, Twickenham, Carshalton, Bexley, Leyton, Wanstead, Malden, Chigwell, Kensington and Surbiton had been hit by between 29 and 20; St Pancras, Penge (most battered of all in relation to its size), Walthamstow, the City of London, Fulham, Heston, Hornsey (where the very last V-1 to reach London landed), Islington, Willesden, Southwark, Wembley, Hammersmith, Brentford, Hendon, St Marylebone,

---

*These figures are from an Air Ministry report dated 28 October 1944 and hence do not include damage after that date. Unfortunately most figures covering the period bracket V-1 and V-2 damage together. The 'houses destroyed' figure does not include the far larger total of those classed as 'damaged' which later had to be demolished.

Erith, Harrow, Ealing, Crayford, Waltham, Holy Cross, had from 19 to 10 incidents; and the remaining thirty-three boroughs had had fewer than ten, the number tending to drop the further one travelled from Central London, so that Barnes and Bethnal Green, with nine each, followed by Kingston, Richmond and Chingford, with eight, did worse than almost rural Bushey, Friern Barnet and Potters Bar, with only one apiece.

The flying-bombs had also been widely distributed outside London. The counties of 'doodlebug alley' came easily top after London, notably Kent, with 1444, followed by Sussex with 886. Essex, the recipient of most of the air-launched missiles, came a long way behind with 412, followed by Surrey with 295 – largely, no doubt, 'wides' that strayed from the proper flight-path – and, after another long gap, Suffolk with 93, mainly in the autumn and winter, and Hertforshire with 82 – 'overs' which had sailed right across London or V-1s fired from the east. Hampshire's total of 80 had a different explanation, the results of the inept attack on Portsmouth and Southampton. No other county could claim to have experienced the V-1s on a really significant scale, but a large number had at least heard one including the inhabitants of tiny, and now alas vanished, Rutland. Shropshire, Leicestershire, Nottinghamshire and Durham had also had a solitary V-1, while Lincolnshire, Huntingdonshire, Derbyshire, Oxfordshire, Northamptonshire, Cambridgeshire, Cheshire, Yorkshire and Lancashire had suffered from between two and eight and Bedford (10), Berkshire (12) and Norfolk (13) had just attained double figures. All told, excluding London, and counting the Isle of Ely as part of Cambridgeshire, twenty-five of the forty counties of England had endured at least one missile, though Wales, Scotland and Northern Ireland escaped completely.*

Little physical evidence now remains anywhere of the great offensive that was intended to change the whole course of the war. Deep in a forest near Calais one can still find a few V-1 launching ramps, preserved, very properly, as ancient monu-

---

*The figures for flying-bombs landing in the counties, unlike those for the London boroughs, cover the period up till the end of the war, i.e. they include missiles which landed between 1 September 1944 and 29 March 1945.

ments, but the sheep and cattle now graze between the stone pillars that once supported the firing platform. In England a similar memorial is provided by the ruins of the parish church at Little Chart in Kent, preserved following a successful fight by the villagers in 1972, after the diocesan authorities had threatened to clear them. In the Sussex village of Frant, two miles from Wadhurst, a plaque in the church records a memorable deliverance: 'With thanksgiving to God for the preservation of the teachers and the scholars of Tidebrook church school on 4th August 1944, when an enemy flying-bomb shattered the school buildings. Honour and discipline.'

Complete V-1s are not hard to find. There are perfect specimens in both the Science Museum in South Kensington and the Imperial War Museum in Lambeth, and more surprisingly, one rests on a 'V' shaped concrete pillar in the court-house square at Greencastle, Indiana, in the United States. But most reminders of that memorable summer are less obvious. The visitor to Epping Forest has no means of knowing which of the water-filled pools he discovers are craters lefts by V-1s. In one near High Wycombe a Bramley seedling apple tree, planted by a local resident, is still flourishing. In Reading one woman looks proudly on a rockery of stones thrown up by another explosion. The remains of a V-1 are buried to this day in a pond at Steeple Bumpstead in Suffolk, filled in after the missile's fall, while the ebb and flow of the tide of the river Humber near Winterton sometimes reveals the remains of the flying-bomb that landed there on Christmas Eve 1944 and now lies 'covered with river mud . . . near to the eastern end of Reads Island.' In a Kent wood, in 1976, one man of forty-six found that the lighter patch of foliage in the treetops above still betrayed the spot where as a fourteen-year-old schoolboy he had witnessed the explosion of a flying-bomb. An Edgware family, when they look to the end of their garden, are reminded of the August day when five of their neighbours were killed, for one of two Lombardy poplars, 'both now grown to a great height', is for ever 'shorter than the other' since its top was blown off. A timber dealer at Battle in Sussex was probably the last person to suffer financial loss from a flying-bomb; having bought a copse of standing timber around 1970, he found his chain saws ruined by metal still embedded in the trees.

Fragments of many V-1s also survive in other guises. A South London 'clippie' used the wire which once encircled some compressed air bottles to train her rambler roses. The former head warden at Brasted managed to convert one of the hollow metal spars supporting the wing of a V-1 shot down on a local hilltop into a chimney for his kitchen boiler, which 'as it was made of exceptionally hard metal, it is likely to outlive.'

Many families whose treasured possessions were lost when their homes were wrecked are still conscious of the gap in their lives, as though half their history had been wiped out. A Clapham man, then aged seventeen, sums it up well:*

It was not . . . the big items that we missed later on: it was all the trivial things which had little value but which could not be replaced. None of my school reports or prizes survived; we have very few family photographs prior to 1944. . . . Theatre programmes, holiday souvenirs, my autograph album and many other things went as well. . . . I have regretted their loss ever since.

For some families the effects of the flying-bombs can never be wiped out. Their loved ones lie in communal graves, as in Bexley cemetery, or beneath headstones on which only the words 'By enemy action' and the date reveal how they died. Many individuals who were injured bear the scars to this day like Elizabeth Sheppard-Jones, confined to a wheelchair since her backbone was shattered by the falling roof of the Guards Chapel. For many others who lost a limb or their sight, life could never be remotely the same again.

And what of the Germans? None of those who had planned or carried out the V-weapons offensive were tried as war criminals on that account even though their efforts, apart from the 10,000 or so deaths directly attributable to them in England or Belgium, were designed to prolong the war and thus give the monsters in the extermination camps a few more months of happy sadism in which hundreds of thousands died; most of the massacres occurred in the last year of the war. Werner von Braun, a natural survivor, lived comfortably in the United

---

*See page 280 for an account of this incident.

States in the service of the American government until the age of sixty-five when, in 1977, he died of cancer. After the end of the war Colonel Watchtel became a respected figure in the world of peaceful enterprise, the manager of Hamburg airport. Hanna Reitsch, who had cheerfully risked her life to develop the V-1, was released after only one year's imprisonment for other offences and died in 1979. Like so many Germans, her enthusiasm for Hitler had begun to wane when she realized the war was lost, and in her words, which perhaps indicate some belated repentance, one may write the V-1's epitaph. 'Human inventiveness, learning, technical science, can achieve nothing, if heart and soul do not keep pace with the development.

The map shows a scale bar: 0 — 5 miles

1 Bushey **1**	25 Hornsey **15**	49 Hackney **36**	73 Bermondsey **30**
2 Elstree **2**	26 Wood Green **5**	50 Shoreditch **7**	74 Deptford **30**
3 Potters Bar **1**	27 Tottenham **4**	51 Finsbury **5**	75 Greenwich **73**
4 East Barnet **6**	28 Walthamstow **17**	52 Holborn **4**	76 Woolwich **77**
5 Enfield **20**	29 Wanstead **23**	53 The City of London **17**	77 Erith **12**
6 Cheshunt **6**	30 Ilford **34**	54 Stepney **30**	78 Surbiton **20**
7 Waltham Holy Cross **11**	31 Staines **7**	55 Bethnal Green **9**	79 Merton **35**
8 Uxbridge **5**	32 Sunbury **4**	56 Poplar **39**	80 Mitcham **43**
9 Ruislip **4**	33 Feltham **5**	57 Leyton **24**	81 Croydon **141**
10 Ealing **20**	34 Heston **15**	58 West Ham **58**	82 Penge **17**
11 Hendon **13**	35 Twickenham **27**	59 East Ham **36**	83 Beckenham **70**
12 Barnet Urban District **4**	36 Brentford **13**	60 Barking **37**	84 Lewisham **114**
13 Southgate **6**	37 Acton **7**	61 Dagenham **28**	85 Bromley **37**
14 Edmonton **7**	38 Hammersmith **14**	62 Esher **35**	86 Chislehurst **45**
15 Chingford **8**	39 Kensington **20**	63 Kingston **8**	87 Bexley **25**
16 Chigwell **20**	40 Fulham **15**	64 Malden **21**	88 Crayford **11**
17 Yiewsley **3**	41 Chelsea **3**	65 Richmond **8**	89 Epsom **29**
18 Hayes **6**	42 Westminster **29**	66 Barnes **9**	90 Banstead **35**
19 Southall **7**	43 Paddington **5**	67 Wimbledon **33**	91 Sutton **34**
20 Ealing **11**	44 St Marylebone **12**	68 Wandsworth **122**	92 Carshalton **27**
21 Wembley **14**	45 Hampstead **8**	69 Battersea **34**	93 Beddington **36**
22 Willesden **15**	46 St Pancras **19**	70 Lambeth **71**	94 Coulsdon **54**
23 Finchley **6**	47 Islington **15**	71 Camberwell **80**	95 Orpington **63**
24 Friern Barnet **1**	48 Stoke Newington **7**	72 Southwark **14**	

Where the V-1s landed in London. The London Civil Defence Region as it was in June 1944. It included parts of several counties adjoining the County of London. The list shows the number of flying-bombs which landed in each borough or urban district within the Region during the main attack, from 13 June to 1 September 1944.

Where the V-1s landed outside London: all those counties in which flying-bombs landed between 13 June 1944 and 29 March 1945. The names and boundaries are as they were at the time, not as they are today. The map shows the number of flying-bombs in each county, excluding the County of London and those parts of other counties included inside the London Civil Defence Region.

APPENDIX

The Flying-Bomb and the Public

The British public has never, until the publication of the present book, been able to read the full story of the battle which involved those living in the South-East more intimately and more continuously than any other campaign of the whole war. The press accounts published at the time were heavily censored, especially on the subject which interested the reader most, *where* the V-1s had landed. On 15 September 1944 the *Kent Messenger* filled the gap so far as that county was concerned, with the results described earlier, and from 25 September the *Evening News* began to publish each day a map showing the location of all the incidents in each London borough in turn. At No. 14, however, which covered West Ham, on 11 October, the series ceased abruptly, for reasons only revealed thirty years later, when the War Cabinet minutes for 9 October 1944 became open to researchers:

The Minister of Aircraft Production drew attention to the maps appearing in the press giving detailed information as to where flying-bombs had fallen in particular parts of the London Region. It was suggested that such detailed information as to the fall of shot might help the enemy to estimate the accuracy of the weapon, and this [might] be of use in the event of future flying bomb attacks against targets on the Continent. The Chiefs of Staff were invited to consider whether publication of further maps of this description should be permitted.

Given a choice between publishing information and withholding it, few senior officers were likely to hesitate long and a report was laid before the Cabinet on the following Monday, 16 October:

Over forty flying-bomb sites were being constructed in the Ruhr, and . . . there was good reason to suppose that the publication of maps showing the fall of flying-bombs in London Region would enable the enemy to draw deductions which would help him in any future attacks that he might launch. . . . The War Cabinet agreed that any further publication of accurate information as to the fall of flying-bombs in the London Region should be prohibited.

Considering how ill-placed the Germans were to take advantage of any information they did glean from the British press, the government was surely overcautious, and, rather oddly, they decided that such information could be made available to American civilians, following a request from General Marshall to use maps showing where the V-1s had landed in an off-the-record talk to US senators. The reasons he gave did him credit.

It seems to me I could make a profound impression on them in two ways, a real appreciation of the suffering the British nation is now enduring in its homeland and, second, the tragic injustice our writers frequently do the British under the existing circumstances, together with a humiliating appreciation of the furore aroused in this country over incidents or threats of trifling importance by way of comparison.

The request was conveyed by Admiral Somerville to the Chiefs of Staff, who referred it to Air Chief Marshal Bottomley at the Air Ministry. He agreed to supply whatever was wanted about the V-1s, which were now little more than a memory, but to refuse all details of where the V-2s had landed, since these were still a very real menace.

Meanwhile all the British public were allowed to learn came from two propaganda films that winter, both prematurely asserting that victory over the flying-bomb was complete. No team of writers and directors had a higher reputation than the Crown Film unit but *V–1* was not one of their greatest productions and is now forgotten. *The Times'* review of it, on 25 November 1944, was respectful rather than enthusiastic:

V–1 . . . compresses into its 20–minute length something of the ordeal London and the South of England suffered during the 80 days of intense bombardment by this weapon. The guns are shown in action and one flying-bomb at least is seen to blow up in mid-air, but *V-1* gets its most realistic effects through its sound track. The grunt and grinding of the monster as it approaches, the sudden nerve-racking silence, and the crash of the explosion are all recorded with a disturbing perfection.

To single out the sound-track of a film for praise was something of a back-handed compliment and General Pile, who attended a private showing at Chequers, was frankly disappointed. 'There were,' he wrote, 'so many pictures of devastated houses and wounded people being carried out of them that I had my doubts about its effectiveness for propaganda purposes.' Nor was he impressed by another propaganda film shown at the same time, a 22-minute account by Gaumont-British of the work of Anti-Aircraft Command entitled *The Second Battle of London*, which also made no lasting impact. *The Times* reviewer, on 2 December 1944, was again noncommittal. 'The guns,' he wrote, 'are seen bringing down rights and lefts . . . with a satisfying consistency,' but to General Pile the result seemed wretchedly inadequate. 'I was shocked at the way it was put over,' he commented later. 'The sound was just like that of a gramophone which is running down. . . . However, both the P.M. and Mrs Churchill, between whom I sat, seemed to think that it was all right.'

There still remained the possibility, however, that the work of all the defences, including Anti-Aircraft Command, might be recognized in print. It was a threepenny booklet (or sixpence with pictures), *The Battle of Britain*, which had immortalized the RAF's legendary victory. The flying-bomb offensive had hardly begun when, on 29 June 1944, a wing-commander in the PR3 branch of the Air Ministry wrote to the Director of Public Relations suggesting that the same author should be invited to compile a similar account of the RAF's anticipated triumph over the V-1. 'It should be possible, if we start preparing it now,' he suggested, 'to have it on sale within a few weeks of the end of the attack.' The project was approved, and when it was learned that Hilary St George Saunders, who had anonymously written *The Battle of Britain*, was not available, the task was entrusted to Squadron-Leader Bates, better known as the novelist H. E. Bates, the Air Ministry's 'writer in residence'. Bates had enterprisingly been recruited earlier in the war to the Public Relations Branch and had already scored a great success with his stories of the bomber crews, published under the pseudonym 'Flying Officer X'. As usual in large organizations, while one talented man did the work, others with time on their hands created difficulties. The publication, one civil servant warned the Director of Public Relations on 5 September, would take four months to prepare and three more to produce, even if unillustrated. In the meantime a full-scale press conference, complete with maps and photographs, was planned – that held two days later by Duncan Sandys and already described elsewhere – and 'this . . . may satiate the public appetite for this particular subject in these tremendous days'. To this the wing-commander who had originally proposed the idea replied effectively on 8 September, after the press conference had been held. Squadron-Leader Bates, he pointed out, had already gone to France to begin his research on the ground, and – an even more powerful argument – the RAF would benefit by receiving the chief credit in his booklet for defeating the flying-bomb.

By now the original modest plan for a short, 5000-word pamphlet, produced by the RAF and selling at threepence, had been lost sight of as the War Office, the Ministry of Home Security and – most formidable of all, on this particular battle-field – the Ministry of Information all became involved. At a meeting of representatives of all the interested parties, except the author himself, on 11 September, it emerged that a 40,000-word book was now contemplated to be published by the Ministry of Information for His Majesty's Stationery Office. Every department was eager to ensure that its share of the credit was not stolen by a rival. By 13 October the pamphlet's 'founding father' in the Air Ministry was writing a little despairingly to his director to report that even the Ministry of Health – presumably because of their responsibility for housing – were demanding a say in the contents, while two months later poor H. E. Bates, now back from France and hard at work, was encountering opposition even from within his own department. 'There is,' wrote one officer of the Air Intelligence Branch, in response to a very reasonable request for details of the cost of the battle in Allied aircraft, 'strong security objection against publishing the figure of our losses.' By 2 January 1945 – a week after the Christmas raid on Manchester – Bates caused further consternation by requesting details of air-launched V-1s and on 2 March, with the war almost over and not a line yet set in type, came an official ruling that the text must be treated as secret until passed by the censor.

Victory in Europe, so that the last excuse for delay was removed, seems to have passed almost unnoticed by those happily engaged in the controversy over *The Battle of the Flying-Bomb*, as the booklet had been provisionally entitled. By now the argument had developed a momentum of its own and in the files new names and ever more impressive sets of abbreviations blossomed daily as more and more under-employed bureaucrats generated a weight of paper far more voluminous than the work they were discussing. The matter had even reached the War Cabinet which had, not very helpfully, simply instructed the Ministry of Information to issue a book about all the Crossbow operations. Wing-Commander Barker, who had now been fighting this particular battle for nearly a year, promptly asked for guidance from the Ministry of Information. Was Bates's work, he wanted to know, to be used as the basis? Was he to continue to amass information? Or was all his effort to be wasted? No clear answer was forthcoming, for reasons which Barker explained to a superior: 'I gather, confidentially,' he wrote on 11 May 1945, 'that the truth is the Ministry of Information are extremely loath to produce any book at all if they are not to be allowed to explain the Mimoyecques installation, as they feel that, now that the German war is over, to withhold the information would be to deceive the public.'

'The Mimoyecques installation' consisted of a battery of long-range, high-powered guns, unconnected with the flying-bomb and never used in action, and there was therefore every possible ground for ignoring them. They proved, however, a convenient stick to use against a project about which, presumably because it had originated elsewhere, the Ministry had never been enthusiastic. The Ministry of Information believed, explained an internal Air Ministry memorandum of 3 October 1945, 'that unless a chapter on these structures is included the pamphlet will lose much of its appeal to the public' – although the public had not even known they existed.

It was all sadly reminiscent of the rivalry between the German Army and the Luftwaffe which had bedevilled the secret weapons project and why the Ministry of Information, if the guns really were still a danger, did not simply omit all reference to them – as Bates himself wished – is something of a mystery. In the event, however, the arguments for doing nothing prevailed. By an interesting twist of fate, it was left to a future Poet Laureate, C. Day Lewis, to make a final effort to save his fellow writer's work. 'In a letter from Mr. Day Lewis of the Publications Division of the M. of I.,' one officer of the Air Ministry Public Relations Division reported to his superiors on 1 November 1945, 'he says he understands that "the details of the Mimoyecques installations can be described and that all the Chiefs of Staff ask is that there should be formal security review of the actual text". . . . It may well be that the War Office can be persuaded to allow us to use some of the details which M. of I. require.' The final sentence of the same letter made clear, however, that time was finally running out for *The Battle of the Flying-Bomb*, after a struggle which had lasted sixteen months – far longer than the events it described. 'S/Ldr. Bates . . . ,' the writer pointed out, 'is to be demobilised next week.' With his departure into civilian life – followed by that of many of the officers who had fought so valiantly on his behalf in Section PR3, which surely deserves to be remembered among other, more famous formations in the annals of the Royal Air Force – the attempt to tell the story of the V-1s to the British public was finally abandoned. Bates's manuscript, which finally ran to 30,000 words, remains unpublished to this day, although the substantial extracts from it quoted in this book illustrate what a loss its suppression was.

SOURCES

In writing this book I have used the following: published books and pamphlets; contemporary newspapers and other periodicals; articles in a variety of journals; a number of unpublished accounts and histories which exist in typescript or duplicated form; official files in the Public Record Office; miscellaneous contemporary documents, such as letters, diaries, scrapbooks and permits; and specially written contributions from the informants listed later, plus a few others who preferred their names not to appear. The bibliography follows the main categories set out above. The place of publication is normally London, and where the year is not stated, it can be assumed to be 1944. Where I have consulted successive issues of a newspaper or magazine, e.g. the *Daily Express* or *ARP News*, during the relevant period (i.e. June 1944 to May 1945) each reference is not listed separately, but major articles in other magazines, e.g. the *British Medical Journal*, are indexed under the name of the author in the list below. Where I have used several books by the same author, the first title listed is the one quoted unless otherwise indicated in the chapter references. Almost every book which covers 1944 refers to the flying-bombs but those which I used only for background, or from which I drew only a single fact, are not listed here to save space. Quotations and anecdotes not otherwise attributed are from the contributions sent to me by informants. I have also in a few places used material from my script for 'The Summer of the Doodlebugs' first broadcast by BBC Radio 4 on 3 June 1972.

Books, pamphlets and articles

'Air-Raid Damage to Museums', in *Museums' Journal*, vol. 44, no. 10, January 1945

Sources

'Air-Raids on Norfolk', in *Britannia*, no. 29, February 1947

Andreas-Friedrich, Ruth, *Berlin Underground, 1939–45*, Henry Holt New York, 1947

Angell, Joseph Warner, 'Guided Missiles Could Have Won', in *Atlantic Monthly* (Boston, Mass., USA). vol. 189, January 1952

Arnold, C. H., *Global Mission*, Hutchinson, 1951

Arct, Bohdan, *Poles against the V-Weapons*, Interpress Publications, Warsaw, 1972

Artillery Training Volume IV, AA Gunnery, Pamphlet No. 7, War Office, 1944

Auckland, R. G., *Aerial Propaganda over Great Britain* (duplicated), published by the author, 1962

Babington Smith, Constance, *Evidence in Camera. The Story of Photographic Intelligence in World War II*, Chatto and Windus, 1958

Baker, H.A., *The Memoirs of H. A. Baker, 46 Years in the Royal Arsenal*, vol. 1 (typescript), Imperial War Museum

Baker, Michael H. C., *Sussex Villages*, Robert Hale, 1977

Baker, Richard Brown, *The Year of the Buzz Bomb. A Journal of London, 1944*, Exposition Press, New York, 1952

Bates, H. E., *The Battle of the Flying Bomb* (duplicated), unpublished, 1945, in file Air 20/4140 in Public Record Office

Bates, H. E., *The World in Ripeness* [vol. III of his autobiography], Michael Joseph, 1972

Battersea Borough Council, *Report on the Repair of War Damage in Battersea*, 1949

BBC Monitoring Service Reports

Beamont, Roland, *Phoenix into Ashes*, William Kimber, 1968

Beccehamian, The magazine of the County School for Boys, Beckenham and Penge, summer term 1945, vol. VI, no. 7

Bell, R., *History of the British Railways During the War, 1939–45*, Railway Gazette, 1946

Bell, R. C., 'An Analysis of 259 of the Recent Flying-Bomb Casualties', in *British Medical Journal*, 25 November 1944, pp. 689–92. (see also related letter in issue of 16 December 1944, p. 799)

Bergier, Jacques, *Secret Weapons – Secret Agents*, Hurst and Blackett, 1956

Bertrand, Gustave, *Enigma, ou la plus grande Enigme de la Guerre 1939–1945*, Libraire Plon, France, 1973

Berwick Sayers, W. C. (ed.), *Croydon and the Second World War*, Croydon Corporation, 1949

Birkenhead, Earl of, *The Prof. in Two Worlds: The Official Life of Professor F. A. Lindemann, Viscount Cherwell*, Collins, 1961

489

Boyce, Joseph C., *New Weapons for Air Warfare*, Little Brown, Boston, 1947

Bramson, Alan, and Birch, Neville, *The Tiger Moth Story*, Air Review Ltd, Letchworth, 1964

Bramsted, Ernest K., *Goebbels and National Socialist Propaganda 1925–1945*, Cresset Press, 1965

Brookes, A. J., *Photo-Reconnaissance*, Ian Allen, 1975

Bryant, Arthur, *Triumph in the West 1943–1946. Based on the Diaries and Autobiographical Notes of Field Marshal The Viscount Alanbrooke*, Collins, 1959

Bryer (pseud.), *The Days of Mars. A Memoir, 1940–1946*, Calder and Boyars, 1972

Butcher, Harry C., *Three Years with Eisenhower*, Heinemann, 1946

Calder, Angus, *The People's War, Britain 1939–45*, Cape, 1969

Carroll, Wallace, *Persuade or Perish*, Boston, 1948

Carter, Ernest F., *Railways in Wartime*, Fred Miller, 1964

Catalogue of the Science Museum, South Kensington, 1946

Cave Brown, Anthony, *Bodyguard of Lies. The Vital Role of Deceptive Strategy in World War II*, W. H. Allen, 1976

Chaplin, A. W. (ed.), *A Record of the Efforts Made in the Parish of Headcorn, Kent, to Keep the Flag Flying During the War, 1939–1945*, 1948 (manuscript), Imperial War Museum

Childs, Marquis W., 'London wins the Battle' in *National Geographic Magazine*, vol. LXXXVIII, no. 2, Washington DC, August 1945

Churchill, Winston S., *The Second World War*, vol. I, Cassell, 1948; vol. V, Cassell, 1952; vol. VI, Cassell, 1954

Civilian Air Raid Casualties, 1939–April 1945 (typescript), Imperial War Museum, No. KH 9816

Clark, Ronald W., *The Rise of the Boffins*, Phoenix House, 1962

Closterman, Pierre, *The Big Show*, Chatto and Windus, 1972

Collier, Basil, *The Defence of the United Kingdom*, HMSO, 1957

Collier, Basil, *The Battle of the V-Weapons 1944–1945*, Hodder and Stoughton, 1964

Commissioner of Police of the Metropolis for the Year 1944, Report of the, Command 6627, HMSO, 1945

Cookridge, E. H., *Inside SOE*, Arthur Barker, 1966

Cox, Gwladys, *London War Diary 1939–45*, (manuscript), 1950, Imperial War Museum

Crump, Norman, *By Rail to Victory, The Story of the LNER in Wartime*, LNER, 1947

Dainton, Courtney, *The Story of England's Hospitals*, Museum Press, 1961

Sources

Damage and Casualties in London in the Summer of 1944 (duplicated), note in Imperial War Museum file No. 39102, March 1945

Darnall, J. R., 'Buzz-Bomb Assaults on London', in *Military Surgeon* (Washington DC, USA), vol. 100, no. 6, June 1947

Darwin, Bernard, *War on the Line. The Southern Railway in Wartime,* Southern Railway, 1946

'Defeating V-1' in *Flight*, 21 September 1944

Donoughue, Bernard, and Jones, W. G., *Herbert Morrison*, Weidenfeld and Nicolson, 1973

Dornberger, Major-General Walter, *V-2*, Hurst and Blackett Ltd, 1954

Drew, Bernard, *Farningham against Hitler*, Kentish District Times, 1946

Dudeney, Leonard (ed.), *War Came to New Street Square* (i.e. Wyman and Sons Ltd), Wyman and Sons Ltd., n.d. but *c.* 1945

Dunn, C. L., *The Emergency Medical Services*, vol. I, HMSO, 1952

East Barnet Civil Defence Council, *District A Civil Dfence, 1939–1945*, 1945

Eisenhower, Dwight D., *Crusade in Europe,* Heinemann, 1948

'Electric Brain Directs AA Fire', in *Canadian Geographical Journal*, March 1944

Eyre, A. H., *Perpetual Target*, privately published, 1946

Ferguson, Sheila, and Fitzgerald, Hilde, *Studies in the Social Services*, HMSO 1954

Finn, S., *Lincolnshire Air War, 1939–1945*, Aero Litho Co., Lincoln, 1973

Foot, M. R. D., *Resistance*, Eyre Methuen, 1976

Foot, M. R. D., *SOE in France*, HMSO, 1966

Ford, Brian, 'German Secret Weapons: Blueprint for Mars', in *Purnell's History of the Second World War*, Weapons Book no. 5, 1969

Fourth Anniversary of 477 (M) HAA Battery, RA. 11th September 1941 to 1945, The, privately published, n.d.

Front Line Folkestone, The Story in Pictures of Folkestone's Ordeal During Five Years of War, Folkestone Hythe and District Herald, 1945

Galland, Adolf, *The First and the Last*, Methuen, 1959

Garlinski, Jozef, *Hitler's Last Weapons*, Friedmann, 1978

Gell, Air Vice-Marshal, W.C.C., 'Balloons v. Flying Bombs', in *Royal Air Force Journal*, November 1944

German Flying Bombs, National Association of Spotters' Clubs, 1944

'Glaxo Laboratories under Fire – The Story of "Our Buzz Bomb",' in *GL Monthly Bulletin*, May-June 1945

Goodsall, R. H., *A Third Kentish Patchwork*, Stedhill Publications, 1970

Gordon, Jane, *Married to Charles,* Heinemann, 1950

Graves, Charles, *London Transport Carried On*, London Passenger Transport Board, 1947

Graves, Charles, *Women in Green, The Story of the WVS in Wartime*, Heinemann, 1948

Guards Chapel, The, Pitkin Pictorials Ltd, 1971

'Guards' Chapel, The', in *Household Brigade Magazine*, Autumn 1944 and Winter 1945–6

Gwynn, Sir C. S., and Hammerton, Sir J. A., *The Second Great War. A Standard History*, vol. 6 and 7, Amalgamated Press, 1946

Hadley, Sylvia, 'Sylvia's War', in *Adscene* (Canterbury) 15, 23 and 30 April 1946

Hagen, Louis, *Follow My Leader*, Wingate, 1951

Haarer, A. E., *A Cold-Blooded Business*, Staples Press, 1958

Hampstead at War, 1939–1945, Hampstead Borough Council, n.d. but *c.* 1946

Handbook on Guided Missiles of Germany and Japan, War Department, Washington DC, 1946

Hardy, N. W. (ed.), *Eastbourne, 1939–1945*, privately published, n.d. but *c.* 1945

Harmsworth, Cecil, Lord, *Dr Johnson's House, Gough Square*, Trustees of Dr Johnson's House, 1968

Harriss, C. F., *Hotchpot: A Domestic Journal of the War Years from the 1st September 1939 to the 10th May 1945*, vol. 3 (manuscript), Imperial War Museum

Harrods Ltd, *A Story of British Achievement, 1849–1949*, 1949

Hartley, A. B., *Unexploded Bomb, A History of Bomb Disposal*, Cassell, 1958

Hastings and St Leonards in the Front Line, Hastings and St Leonards Observer, n.d. but *c.* 1945.

Helfers, Lieutenant-Colonel M. C., *The Employment of V-Weapons by the Germans During World War II* (duplicated), Department of the Army, Washington DC, n.d.

Henrey, Mrs Robert, *The Siege of London*, Dent, 1946

Henrey, Mrs Robert, *London*, Dent, 1955

Herbert, A. P., *Light the Lights*, Methuen, 1945

Herbert, A.P., *Independent Member*, Howard Baker, 1950

Hewison, Robert, *Under Siege, Literary Life in London 1939–45*, Weidenfeld and Nicolson, 1977

Hill, Prudence, *To Know the Sky, The Life of Air Chief Marshal Sir Roderic Hill*, Kimber, 1962

Sources

Hill, Air Chief Marshal Sir Roderic, *Air Operations by Air Defence of Great Britain and Fighter Command in Connection with the German Flying Bomb and Rocket Offensives, 1944–1945*, published as *Supplement to the London Gazette*, Tuesday, 19 October 1948, no. 38347

History of the Photographic Interpretation Unit (duplicated), September 1945 in File 34/80 in Public Record Office

Hodgson, Vere, *Few Eggs and No Oranges. A Diary Showing How Unimportant People in London and Birmingham Lived Through the War Years, 1940–1945*, Dennis Dobson, 1976

Hogg, I. V., *German Secret Weapons of World War II*, Arms and Armour Press, 1970

Holl, W. E., *Civil Defence Goes Through It. Paddington 1937–1945* (typescript), 1946

Hough, Richard, *One Boy's War*, Heinemann, 1975

Howard-Williams, Jeremy, *Night Intruder. A Personal Account of the Radar War between the Luftwaffe and the RAF Night Fighter Forces*, David and Charles, 1976

Howgrave-Graham, H. M., *The Metropolitan Police at War*, HMSO, 1947

Irving, David, *The Mare's Nest*, William Kimber, 1964

Irving, David, *The Rise and Fall of the Luftwaffe. The Life of Erhard Milch*, Weidenfeld and Nicolson, 1973

Illingworth, Frank, *Flying Bomb*, Citizen Press, n.d. but *c.* 1945

Jackson, Alan, A., *London's Termini*, David and Charles, 1969

Jackson, A. J., *De Havilland Aircraft since 1915*, Putnam, 1962

John, Evan, *Timetable for Victory*, British Railways, 1947

Johnson, Brian, *The Secret War*, BBC, 1978

Jones, R. V., 'Scientific Intelligence', in *RUSI Journal*, vol. XCII, no. 567, August 1947

Jones, R. V., 'Lord Cherwell's Judgement in World War Two', in *Oxford Magazine*, new series, vol. 3, no. 18, 9 May 1963

Jones, R. V., 'Dr Jones's War', three programmes broadcast by BBC Radio 4 on 18 and 25 July and 1 August 1974

Jones, R. V., *Most Secret War, British Scientific Intelligence 1939–45*, Hamish Hamilton, 1978

Jullian, Marcel, *Jean Maridor, Chasseur de V-1*, Amiot-Dumont, Paris, 1954

Kent, William, *The Lost Treasures of London*, Phoenix House, 1947

Keesings Contemporary Archives

Keith, Sir Arthur, *An Autobiography*, Watts, 1950

Klee, Ernst, and Mark, Otto, *The Birth of a Missile*, 1965

Kohan, C. M., *Works and Buildings*, HMSO, 1952

The Doodlebugs

Lambeth Civil Defence (duplicated), Lambeth Civil Defence Association, 1948

Lanchbery, Edward, *Against the Sun*, Cassell, 1955

Lee, Asher, *Blitz on Britain*, Four Square Books, 1960

Lees-Milne, James *Prophesying Peace*, Chatto and Windus, 1977

Lehmann, John, *I Am My Brother*, Longman, 1960

List of Incidents of Fly Bombs and Long Range Rockets Affecting Corporation Property in the City of London and Elsewhere (duplicated), Corporation of London, n.d. but *c.* 1945

Low, Professor, A. M. 'The Origin of the Flying Bomb', in *Aeronautics*, vol. II, no. 2, September 1944

Lusar, Rudolf, *German Secret Weapons of the Second World War*, Neville Spearman, 1959

McInnes, E. M., *St Thomas's Hospital*, Allen and Unwin, 1963

Macmillan, Norman, *The Royal Air Force in the World War*, vol. IV, Harrap, 1950

MacNalty, Sir Arthur Salisbury, and Mellor, W. Franklin, *Medical Services in War*, HMSO, 1968

Martelli, George, *The Man Who Saved London, The Story of Michel Hollard*, Companion Book Club, 1960

Masterman, J. C., *The Doublecross System 1939–1945*, Sphere Books, 1973

Matthews, Very Rev. W. R., *St Paul's Cathedral in Wartime*, Hutchinson, 1946

Mee, Arthur, *London: The City and Westminster*, Hodder and Stoughton, 1975

Montagu, Ewen, *Beyond Top Secret U*, Peter Davies, 1977

Moody, G. T., *Southern Electric*, Ian Allan, 1957

Morpurgo, J. E., *Barnes Wallis*, Longman, 1972

Moyhihan, Michael (ed.), *People at War 1939–1945. Their Own Account of the Conflict – Dunkirk to the Far East and on the Home Front,* David and Charles, 1974

Newman, Bernard, *They Saved London*, Wernie Laurie, 1952

Nicholas, S. W., and Lancaster, K., 'Fieseler Fi.103' in *Air-Britain Digest*, vol. V, no. 2, Februáry 1953

Nicolson, Harold, *Diaries and Letters 1939–45*, Collins, 1967

Norton, Charles, 'An "Incident". The Story of the Guard's Chapel', in *ARP and NFS Review*, June 1945

Oak-Rhind, E.S., 'In "Bomb Alley" the Land Girls Wept When a Doodlebug Got Through', in *Local Government Service*, vol. XXIII, no. 10, October 1944

O'Brien, T. H., *Civil Defence*, HMSO, 1955

Sources

Observer's Tale, The Story of Group 17 of the Royal Observer Corps, Roland Bros., 1950

Orwell, George, 'Letter to *Partisan Review*', 24 July, in *The Collected Essays, Journalism and Letters*, Vol. III, Secker and Warburg, 1968

Owen, Frank, *The Eddie Chapman Story*, Wingate, 1953

Owen, Roderick, *Tedder*, Collins, 1952

Panter-Downes, Mollie, *London War Notes 1939–45*, Longman, 1972

Peters, T. P., *Reminiscences of 1938–1945 by a Head Warden* (privately printed)

Pevsner, Nikolaus, *The Buildings of England. London, Vol. 1: The Cities of London and Westminster*, Penguin, 1962

Pile, General Sir Frederick, *Ack-Ack*, Harrap, 1949

Plastow, Norman, *Safe as Houses. Wimbledon 1939–1945*, John Evelyn Society, 1972

Platts, W. L., *Kent. The County Administration in War, 1939–1945*, Maidstone, 1946

Popov, Dusko, *Spy Counterspy*, Weidenfeld and Nicolson, 1974

Postan, M. M. Hay, D., and Scott, J. D., *Design and Development of Weapons*, HMSO, 1964

Pound, Reginald, *Evans of the Broke*, Oxford University Press, 1963

Pratt Boorman, H. R., 'Folkestone, Front Line Town,' in *The Queen*, 4 January 1950

Pratt Boorman, H. R., *Kent Unconquered*, published by *Kent Messenger*, Ashford, 1951

Price, Alfred, *Spitfire at War*, Ian Allan, 1974

Price, Alfred, *Blitz on Britain, The Bomber Attacks on the United Kingdom, 1939–1945*, Ian Allan, 1977

Pullin, A. H., *The Story of Reporting Post 12* [Southwark], privately published, 1944

Queen's Own Gazette, Journal of the Queen's Own Royal West Kent Regiment, Maidstone, vol. LXV, no. 1, January 1948

Raczynski, Count Edward, *In Allied London*, Weidenfeld and Nicolson, 1962

Reed, Arthur, and Beamont, Roland, *Typhoon and Tempest at War*, Ian Allan, 1974

Reitsch, Hanna, *The Sky My Kingdom*, Bodley Head, 1955

Richards, Denis, and St George Saunders, Hilary, *Royal Air Force 1939–1945*, vol. III, HMSO, 1953

Robot Bombardment, The (Article in Imperial War Museum, source unknown)

St George Saunders, Hilary, 'The Flying Bomb', in *Life*, vol. 17, no. 21, November 1944 (published in United States)

St George Saunders, Hilary, *Ford at War, 1939–45*, privately published, 1946

St George Saunders, Hilary, *The Middlesex Hospital, 1745–1948*, Parrish, 1949

Sansom, William, *Westminster in War*, Faber, 1947

Scott, Sir Harold, *Your Obedient Servant*, Deutsch, 1959

Secrets of the Flying Bomb Revealed, published in aid of NFS Benevolent Fund

Service of Commenoration and the Dedication of Memorial Gates at Lenham, Kent, REME, 29 November 1964

Shepheard-Walwyn, B. W., *Purleigh in Wartime*, Chelmsford, 1946

Sheppard-Jones, Elizabeth, *I Walk on Wheels*, Geoffrey Bles, 1958

Smith, J. R., and Kay, Anthony, *German Aircraft of the Second World War*, Putnam, 1972

Soffner, Max, *Horam and District Under Fire 1939–1945*, Horam Organization Committee, 1945

Speidel, Lieutenant-General Hans, *We Defended Normandy*, Herbert Jenkins, 1951

Standard Telephones and Cables Company, *The Story of Air Raid Precautions, New Southgate* (duplicated), 1945

Stephen, Sir James, *Diaries*, vol. V; *Diary G, 13 March 1943–10 December 1945* (manuscript), Imperial War Museum

Streatham's 41, privately published, n.d. but *c.* 1945

Summary of Damage Caused by Enemy Action Against the United Kingdom (duplicated), Ministry of Information, September 1945, Imperial War Museum, File K 12863

Swanwick, F. W., *ARP (Civil Defence) in the Borough of Heston and Isleworth 1938–1945* (duplicated), 1961

Tedder, Marshal of the RAF, Lord, *With Prejudice*, Cassell, 1966

Thomas, John Oram, *The Giant-Killers*, Michael Joseph, 1975

Thompson, George P., *Blue Pencil Admiral. The Inside Story of the Press Censorship*, Sampson Low, 1947

Thompson, R. J., *Battle over Essex*, Chelmsford, 1946

Thompson, Royce L., *Military Impact of the German V-Weapons 1943–1945* (duplicated), Department of the Army, Washington DC, 1953

Titmuss, R. M., *Problems of Social Policy*, HMSO, 1950

Trevor-Roper, H. R. (ed.), *Hitler's War Directives, 1939–1945*, Sidgwick and Jackson, 1964

Twickenham, Borough of, *Civil Defence, 1939–1945. Salute to the People's Service*, 1945, Imperial War Museum

V-1 Story (typescript), Imperial War Museum

Sources

Vale, George F., *Bethnal Green's Ordeal*, Bethnal Green Borough Council, 1945

Wadsworth, John, *Counter Defensive, Being the Story of a Bank in Battle*, Hodder and Stoughton, 1946

Wandsworth, Metropolitan Borough of, The Official Guide, 1948

Wanless, Alexander, *British People at War, Compiled from the Daily Press*, J. and G. Innes, Cupar, Fife, 1956

War Damage to Buildings in Great Britain, Part II. Schedule of About 100 Bombed Buildings in London and the Provinces Chiefly Selected for Their Historic or Architectural Interest (duplicated), Ministry of Information, June 1946

War Damage to Hospitals (typescript), Imperial War Museum, No. K 17728, 7 May 1945 and 22 May 1945

War in East Sussex, The, Sussex Express and County Herald, n.d. but *c*. 1945

War in Westminster, The. A Summary Report of the work of the City Council's Civil Defence and Related Services, City of Westminster, 1945

Warmington, E. H., *A History of Birkbeck College, University of London, during the Second World War, 1939–1945*, Birkbeck College, 1954

Watkins, J. G., and Leslie, Major Donald, *On Target, The Great Story of Ack Ack Command*, Territorial Publications, 1955

Waugh, Evelyn, *Unconditional Surrender*, Chapman and Hall, 1961

Webster, Sir Charles, and Frankland, Noble, *The Strategic Air Offensive Against Germany, 1939–45*, 4 vols., HMSO, 1961

'Westminster Garrison Battalion', in *Household Brigade Magazine*, Winter 1945–46

Weymouth, Anthony (pseud)., *Journal of the War Years and One Year Later*, vol. II, Littlebury, Worcester, 1948

Wheeler-Bennett, John W., *King George VI, His Life and Reign*, Macmillan, 1958

Wilmot, Chester, *The Struggle for Europe*, Collins, 1952

Wilton, Eric, *Centre Crew, a Memory of the Royal Observer Corps*, privately printed, 1946

Woltman, Sgt Adolf G., 'Life on a Target', in *American Journal of Orthopsychiatry*, (Menasha, Wisconsin, USA) vol. 15, January 1945

Wood, Derek, *Attack Warning Red. The Royal Observer Corps and the Defence of Britain, 1925–1975*, Macdonald and Janes, 1976

Woolf, Arthur L., *The Battle of South London*, Crystal Publications, n.d. but *c*. 1945

Wright, Robert, and Rawnsley, C. F., *Night Fighter*, Collins, 1957

Wykeham, Peter, *Fighter Command*, Putnam, 1960
Wyld, Ross, *The War over Walthamstow, The Story of Civil Defence, 1939–1945*, Walthamstow Borough Council, 1945

Other Periodicals Consulted

Aeroplane
Aeronautics
Aircraft Recognition
ARP and NFS Review
Barnet Press
Birmingham Post
Chelsea, Westminster and Pimlico News
Croydon Advertiser
Daily Express
Daily Herald
Daily Mail
Daily Mirror
Daily Sketch
Daily Telegraph
Folkestone, Hythe and District Herald
Herts Advertiser and St Albans Times
Kensington News
Kentish District Times
Kent Messenger
Lewisham Borough News
London Evening News
London Evening Standard
London Star
Maidenhead Advertiser
Manchester Despatch
Manchester Evening News
News Chronicle
News of the World
Oldham Chronicle
Outpost, The, Published by Committee for defending America by Aiding the Allies, London, September 1944 – July 1945
Portsmouth Evening News
Reynolds News
South London Observer
South London Press
Sunday Graphic

Sources

The Times
Tunbridge Wells Advertiser
Wembley News
Western Mail
West London Press
Westminster and Pimlico News

Detailed References

1 A Weapon which Cannot Be Used Against Us

On the scene in Danzig, see Shirer, p. 174. The German News Agency translation is in Irving, p. 15; British government reaction in Churchill, I, p. 453; Dr Jones's report, *The Hitler Waffe*, dated 11 November 1939, is in the Public Record Office, and he describes his life that winter in *Dr Jones's War*. On the Oslo Report, see Cave Brown p. 199. Collier, *Battle*, pp. 13–15 describes the origins of the pulse-jet. On mishaps with the Bug and the decision not to use it, see Arnold, pp. 64–5 and 157. Irving, pp. 16–17 and 23–5, describes work on the flying-bomb engine and supplies the 'sprouting wings' quotation. On Milch's attitude, see Irving, *Rise*, pp. 174 and 160; on Fieseler's involvement, Wood, p. 66; on the development of the Queen Bee, Bramson and Birch, p. 20, and Jackson, p. 238.

2 Suspicious Erections of Rails or Scaffolding

Most quotations are from Babington Smith, pp. 200–209, and Irving, pp. 35–52 and 124. Jones, pp. 334–5, describes the Sandys' investigation, p. 339, the 'ill-considered questionnaires'; and, in *Dr Jones's War* the detection of the radar companies. The first War Office orders to Medmenham are in Air 34/80 of 13 February 1943 and the Air Ministry instructions are in the same file, for 19 April. Cherwell's minute to the Prime Minister is mentioned by Birkenhead, p. 259, and the full text is in PREM 3/110 of 11 June 1943. The Cabinet Defence Committee minute is in CAB 69/5 for 28 June 1943.

3 All Will Be Revenged

My principal source is Irving: see pp. 25, 72–4, 83–4, 89–94, 119, 161, 179–84, 181. On Milch's contribution, see Irving, *Rise*, pp. 214, 221, 231, 266, 407. On Goebbels, see Bramsted, pp. 317–8; on the raid on

Kassel, Webster and Frankland, II, p. 268. On Flak Regiment 155 (W), see Joubert, pp. 82–6, and Collier, *Battle*, p. 64.

4 Sinister Activities

See Irving, pp. 124–5, 138 and 171; Babington Smith, pp. 209–223; Jones, p. 342, and *Dr Jones's War*. On 'Johnny', see Popov, p. 214; on Hollard, see Martelli, *seriatim*, and, for Churchill's tribute, p. 181. The number of exposures is given in *History of the PIU*, para. 29.

5 Mysterious Targets

Cherwell's letter to Churchill is quoted by Irving, p. 186. Churchill, V, p. 212, mentions the DCAS's warning; Collier, *Battle*, p. 45, the first air attacks; Martelli, p. 185, Hollard's exploit at Auffay. On the changing codenames, see *History of the PIU*. The quotations from Hough are on pp. 115–17. Macmillan, p. 179, describes the setting up of ADGB and, p. 180, the orders to Bomber Command. Angell, p. 58, reports the rumours in the United States and, pp. 58–60, the tests in Florida. Closterman, pp. 77–81, describes attacking launching sites. On Portal, see Irving, p. 187; on the first attacks, Webster and Frankland, II, p. 184; for the Crossbow directive, IV, pp. 164 and 167–9; for the US Bombing Survey, III p. 281. See also Verrier, pp. 269–71; Bates, pp. 10, 41 and 46; and on the losses suffered, Air 20/ 6016 of 28 October.

6 Any Time Now

On Morrison's struggle to protect Civil Defence, see WP (43) 520, 16 November 1943; and on proposals for a new evacuation scheme CDC (43) 35, 28 December 1943. O'Brien p. 640, describes the postponement of the proposed cuts and, pp. 647, 651 and 656, the plans to distribute more Morrison shelters. The plan to give civil servants priority appears in HO 186/1848 of 4 December 1943, 'CDC (43) 16 of 31 December 1943, CDC (44) 1 of 20 January 1944, and O'Brien, p. 651. The changes in code-words are explained in HO 186/1848 of 15 January. For Cherwell's comments, see Irving, pp. 199–202; for censorship plans, Thompson, p. 198. The warning letter to the regional commissioners is in HO 186/2271 of 12 February; the draft instruction to newspaper editors in CDC (44) 5 of 17 February; the decision on the existing warning system in CDC (43) 35 of 28 December 1943; the group captain's standing instruction in HO 186/1848 of 7 March, and the successive letters to ARP controllers are in file HO

186/1848. The letter to the Observer Corps is quoted by Wood, p. 170, and reaction in No. 17 Group is described in *Observer's Tale*, pp. 26–7. The Chiefs of Staff's warning is mentioned by Irving, pp. 211–12; the alarming developments near Belhamelin by Babington Smith, pp. 226–7. Collier, p. 361, Collier, *Battle*, p. 68, and Irving, p. 194, give details of the modified sites. Sydney Camm's admiration of the flying-bomb design is mentioned by Wood, p. 168. The 'other authorities' mentioned in the footnote are Irving, p. 226, and Collier, p. 360. The closing quotation is from Hill, pp. 5590–91.

7 Open Fire!

On events in Germany, see Irving, pp. 193–5, 200, 210–13, 224 and 230, and Irving, *Rise*, p. 266. Goebbels's role is described by Bramsted, pp. 319–20. *Rumpelkammer* is mentioned by Wood, p. 171, Polar Bear by Irving, p. 181. Keitel's instructions are in Trevor-Roper, p. 164–5.

8 Diver!

On the weather, see Meterological Office Daily Weather Report No. 3054 in HO 192/492 of 14 June. Collier, *Battle*, p. 74, describes the shelling; Wood, p. 61 and 127, the organization of the Observer Corps; Hough, pp. 120 and 125–6, the radar station at Beachy Head. The *Sunday Telegraph*, 16 June 1974, carried interviews with the first observers to see a flying-bomb. The censored American messages are in PREM 3/11, p. 512; the Ministry of Home Security reports on the first incident in WO 199/553 and on the fourth incident in WP (44) 320, both of 13 June. Haarer, p. 179, is the bomb disposal officer quoted. The times of the first four incidents are given in Air 20/3684. The report, unsigned and undated, on the Gravesend incident appears in WO 199/553, and reports on the Grove Road incident appear in HO 192/492 and HO 186/2369 for 13 June. Cherwell's jocular reaction is mentioned by Irving, pp. 233–4, and the Chiefs of Staff's response by Hill, p. 5591. The report set before the Cabinet, including Portal's advice, is in WP (44) 320, and the Cabinet's conclusions in WM (44) 320, both of 13 June. The Chief Censor's comments are in Thompson, p. 200. The note circulated on 6 June is in Air 34/80, p. 33. The sending of the Diver signal is mentioned by Babington Smith, pp. 227–8, and the Air Ministry's lack of response by Brookes, p. 199, and Hill, p. 5591.

9 Target 42: London

On Wachtel's escape from a court martial, see Irving, pp. 232–3; on Bates's first sight of a flying-bomb, *The World*, p. 42; on A. P. Herbert's, *Independent*, pp. 312–3; on Saturday evening in Marylebone, Gordon, p. 233; and in Streatham, *Streatham's 41*, p. 6. The Cabinet discussion is in WM (44) 89, and the censorship instruction in Air 20/6016, both for 16 June. On the *Bournemouth Evening Echo*, see that paper for 13 December 1973; on Alanbrooke's reaction, Bryant, p. 220. The Air Ministry dispatch is in Air 20/6016 for 17 June. The Head Warden of Brasted's logbook was privately loaned to me.

10 The Guards Chapel

For the Ministry advice see *The Times*, 17 June; for Mrs Robert Henrey's weekend, pp. 67–72, for Jane Gordon's, pp. 234–7, for Vere Hodgson's, p. 389. The St John's Hill incident is well documented as Incident 1008 in the Borough of Wandsworth records. On the published casualty figures see the *News of the World* for 10 September. Irving, pp. 236–7, describes Hitler's visit to Margival. See Air 20/6016 for 17 June for the Director of Operations' report. On Streatham I used *Streatham's 41*, pp. 9–11; on the Quill Bridge bomb HO 186/2418; on Westminster's first flying-bombs, Sansom, p. 84. On the Guards Chapel incident see *Dr Jones's War*, the *Household Brigade Magazine*, Autumn 1944, pp. 71–3, 105–7, and Winter 1945–6, pp. 161–3, *The Guards Chapel*, the *Daily Sketch* and *Daily Mirror*, 10 July 1944, the *ARP and NFS Review*, June 1945, Sheppard-Jones, p. 187, Churchill, VI, p. 35, Sansom p. 186, and Lees-Milne, p. 80.

11 In the Front Line

On the events of Monday, 19 June, see Bryant, p. 220, G. P. Thompson, p. 201, Lees-Milne, p. 81, and CDC (44) 7 and WM (44) 80 for that date. The Air Ministry official was Haarer, pp. 179–80. For other quotations, see Eisenhower, p. 284, Sansom, p. 189, Hill, p. 5593, Gordon, p. 241–2, *Partisan Review* for 24 July 1944, Henrey, p. 75, and Hodgson, p. 388. The 'man living in Kent' is Eyre, p. 22. The Evelyn Waugh character is in *Unconditional Surrender*, p. 245. The City of Westminster Log Book is in its archives and other material on London buildings destroyed appears in St George Saunders' *Life*, Mee, p. 158, Pevsner, I, p. 328, *The Times* for 7 September 1944, Wheeler-Bennett, p. 610 and the Ministry of Information, *Summary of Damage*, for 23 September 1945 and 17 June 1946. On St Paul's see Matthews, p. 61. Morrison's report to the War Cabinet and the subsequent discussion are in WM (44) 82 of 27 June. Strachey's broadcast is in BBC Sound Archives. Driberg's suggestion is in Hansard, col. 698, for 28 June, and MPs' requests for more publicity in col. 790 for 29 June. For Civil Defence Committee proceedings see CDC (44) 9 for 29 June. Morrison's memorandum on 'Southern England' is in WP (44) 359 of 30 June. Alanbrooke's comments about Churchill are in Bryant, p. 226. On Churchill's speech to the House and the subsequent debate there, see Hansard, col. 1290 and 1322–39 for 6 July.

12   A Bomby Afternoon

On response to Churchill's speech, see Hansard, cited above, and Thompson, p. 202. *Outpost*, September 1944, reported on Londoners' heroism, Hodgson, p. 400, on the 'button' warning system, Warmington, p. 160, on the appearance of the black redstarts. All other quotations are from private informants.

13   Additional Noises Off

On the Proms I used information from the BBC Written Archives Centre; on attendances at theatres in general HO 186/2083 of 23 June; on 'Holidays at Home', the same file for 8 July; on the West End theatres' programmes, *The Times* for 12, 19 and 26 June; on attendances 'picking up', Panter Downes, p. 338; on dog track and cinema attendances, HO 186/2083 of 21 and 28 June; on the Lords' bomb, *Reynolds News*, 30 July; on churches and public houses destroyed, the *Daily Sketch*, 8 September, on Little Chart, information displayed in the new church and Bates, *The World*, p. 43. The mysterious cloud is mentioned by the *South London Observer*, 8 September.

14   Incident on the Line

The 'Platform Five' story is quoted by Lee, p. 152. Carter, pp. 186–9, summarizes the experience of the various networks. Details of the incidents mentioned appear in Moody, pp. 119, and 189, and Darwin (the 'railway historian' mentioned), pp. 86–7, The Victoria incident is described by Sansom, p. 192, and Jackson, p. 294. Bell, p. 56, gives figures for the number of warnings and Crump, p. 170, describes the 'board . . . two feet long'. On London Transport, see Graves *London*, pp. 89–90, and the *South London Press*, 15 September.

The Doodlebugs

15 Suddenly, While Shopping

See Henrey, p. 75, on shopkeepers' cordiality and the sheltering customers and, p. 96, on Fortnums. On the mouse, see *South London Press*, 11 August; on lunch at the Savoy, Lehmann, p. 280; on damage to public houses, the *Daily Sketch* for 8 September and the *South London Press*, 15 September. On South Kensington I used File 940.544 in the Kensington Reference Library and the *Kensington News* for 15 September; on the Regent Palace bomb, Sansom, p. 192; on Aldwych, Sansom, p. 195, and HO 192/545 for 30 June: on the Lewisham incident, HO 186/2405 of 28 July, the *Lewisham Journal*, 4 August, the *Lewisham Borough News*, 12 and 26 September, *The Times House of Commons*, 1945, p. 38. The incidents at Brixton and Camberwell are mentioned in the *South London Press*, 15 September.

16 A Deafening Silence

On the IIP signs, see Graves, p. 223; on the derivation of 'doodlebug', the *Supplement to the Oxford English Dictionary*, vol. I, 1972; on the origins of 'V-1', Bramsted, p. 321; on 'illuminated launches', Nicolson, p. 383. See Herbert for the 'Model Prayer.'

17 Like Some Grisly Transport Service

The technical material in this chapter is drawn from *Handbook*, p. 11.1.1; *Aircraft Recognition*, October 1944, vol. III, no. 2; *How the Flying Bomb Works*; *Air-Britain Digest*, vol. V, no. 2; Smith and Kay, p. 150; and Martelli, p. 177. On unexploded V-1s, see Hartley, pp. 185–8. Figures for V-1s launched appear in Brookes, p. 199, and Air 40/1653, and for 'non-conforming' missiles, in *Handbook*, 11-1–3 (2). Cherwell's attempt at self-justification is revealed in PREM 3/111 of 28 and 30 June and 14 July. The 'mare's nest' quotation is from Irving, title page.

18 Like Heaven After London

The figures quoted are from Titmuss, pp. 413, 430, 427–8, and 562, and O'Brien, p. 655. Churchill's speech is in Hansard, col. 1329–30, 6 July, and the chaos at Paddington is admitted in col. 1370–1, 2 August. The work of the WVS is described by Bates, pp. 38–40, and Graves, pp. 230–33. On Bath, see the *South London Press* for 11 and 18 August.

19   More Bombs than Pupils

The tragedy at Westerham is described by Platts, p. 37, the *Daily Express* and *News Chronicle* for 1 July; the damage to schools by the *Daily Sketch* for 8 September; conditions at Beckenham Grammar School by the *Beccehamian*, Summer Term 1945, vol. VI, no. 7; and at London University, Warmington pp. 71 and 149–62.

20   A Hospital Was Hit

The 'official historian' is MacNalty, p. 299. On the Middlesex Hospital see St George Saunders, *Middlesex*, p. 83; on damage to the various types of hospital, evacuation and the maternal mortality rate, *Medical Officer*, vol. LXXVI, no. 8, 24 August 1946, and Dunn, p. 172; on the death roll at St Mary Abbott's, the Kensington archives; on St Olave's, Dunn, p. 173; on Croydon and Warlingham Park, Berwick-Sayers, pp. 199, and 208; on St Helier, the *Sutton Times*, date uncertain but *c.* 28 June, and the *Daily Express*, 28 June; on central London hospitals, Ministry of Information, *Summary of Damage*, 25 September 1945 and 17 June 1946; on the Royal Free Hospital, Dunn, I, p. 173; on St Thomas's, McInnes, pp. 174–5.

21   Death in Circle Gardens

The first week's casualty figures are in PREM 3/111 of 15 July; casualty figures in general are examined in Dunn, I, pp. 170–71. On 'true blast casualties' see *ARP and NFS Review* for August. The 'resident surgical officer' is R. C. Ball.

22   Take Cover!

Morrison's paper is in WP (44) 377 and Bevin's in WP (44) 378, both of 5 July. Swanwick, pp. 55–6, describes what happened at Heston. Morrison's speech is in Hansard, col. 1172, 1 August, and the instructions to local authorities in HO 186/184B of 3 August. On Fords, see St George Saunders, *Ford*, p. 6; on Woolwich, Baker, p. 210. For the Civil Defence Committee proceedings of 29 June, see CDC (44) 9. The *South London Press* dealt with underground shelters on 11 and 14 July and the censor's reaction is in HO 186/1668 of 13 July. On the 'giant liner' see Henrey, pp. 77–9. For the effects of bombing on shelters, see *The Times*, 8 September, HO 192/1506 of 28 August, and HO 207/85 of 9 August.

The Doodlebugs

23 Safer in the Desert

Details of the Newlands incident appear in Ministry of Home Security War Report No. 210 and of the Imber Court incident in Report No. 211, both in HO 202/10. On the Marden incident, see Air 20/2439 of 22 May 1945. The *Stars and Stripes* verse appeared on 20 July, the cartoon on 1 September and American reaction to the attack on 8 July. Darnall, pp. 469–73, wrote of the reactions of American officers in London, and Woltman is the US sergeant quoted. Churchill's tribute to the Americans is in Hansard, col. 1322–99, 6 July. *Lessons from Recent Raids* is in HO 186/2299, undated. The NFS section leader was quoted in *Outpost*, November 1944, p. 4. The official American response to the V-1s is described by R. Thompson, *Military Impact of the German V Weapons*, Appendix, which gives a full account of the Turk's Row incident. Other details appear in HO 198/ 84 of 3 July and Air 20/3439 of 22 May 1945.

24 Bombed Out

The figures for damage are taken from *The Times*, 16 September, the *South London Press*, 3 October, the *Westminster and Pimlico News*, 22 September, and Bates, pp. 32–3. On rest centres, see Bates, p. 40, and the *News Chronicle*, 30 June, and on other post-raid services, the *ARP and NFS Review*, September 1944. The WVS report quoted is for May–July 1944, p. 4, and is in Air 20/4376. On the War Damage Act, see Titmuss, p. 283.

25 Wind and Weather Proof

On damage at various dates, see WM (44) 80 of 19 June, WM (44) 82 of 27 June, WM (44) 91 of 17 July, WM (44) 99 of 31 July. *Lessons from Recent Air Raids* is in HO 186/2299 of 11 August, and the Secretary of State for Air's letter in PREM 3/111 of 16 July. The figures given by Churchill are in Hansard, col. 1475, of 2 August. *The Times*, 16 September reported and commented on the scale of the problem; the *South London Press*, 26 September, described the local situation, and, 3 October, what was being done in Battersea; the *Star*, 9 October, West Ham's achievements; and the *North London Press*, 3 November, the chilly winter faced by its readers.

26 At the Factory Gate

The Minister of Aircraft Production's Report of 19 June is WM (44) 80. The Ministry of Home Security *Weekly Appreciation* is in WO

202/10. For the Supreme Headquarters' report of 5 July see SHAEF/
16599/ADD. Oliver Lyttleton's warning of 20 July and Lord Cherwell's response, which gives details of the damage to various types of
factories, are in PREM 3/111; the Ministry of Aircraft Production's
figures come from WM (44) 99 of 31 July; and Sinclair's letter is in
PREM 3/111 for 16 July. On the Dudin's Wharf fire see the *South
London Press* for 15 September; for events at Woolwich Arsenal,
Baker, pp. 202–3; for Fords, St George Saunders, *Ford*, pp. 5 and
88. The corset factory incident is mentioned in the *South London
Press*, 15 September, the EMI one in Air 20/3439, 'Comprehensive
Report', undated. The Glaxo incident was described in the *GL
Monthly Bulletin*, May-June 1945, pp. 6–8. On Standard Telephones
beside information from private informants, I used a report by the
senior regional officer in Air 20/4376, 4 September, and documents
provided by the company, particularly 'The Story of Air Raid Precautions, New Southgate', 11 June 1945 and press cuttings from *The
Times* and *Manchester Guardian* for 8 July 1939, and the *Municipal
Journal and Local Government Administrator* for 14 July 1939.

27   The Wardens Were Wonderful

Sir Ernest Gowers' tribute is in HO 207/85 for 9 August. Sansom,
pp. 130–31, describes the Rotunda; Scott, pp. 113, 119 and 137, and
O'Brien, p. 311, the London region headquarters at South Kensington. The visitor quoted was Bryer, p. 35. Scott, pp. 117 and 141, and
Pound, p. 301, describe Evans of the *Broke*. On fires, see Bates, p.
34. The 'nasty ones' quotation is in HO 207/85 of 9 August. The
comparison between a fireman's work and a rescue worker's is in the
ARP and NFS Review, October 1944, pp. 77 and 94. The ARP
observation system is described in HO 186/2299, *Lessons from Recent
Raids*, undated. The Prime Minister's speech is reported in Hansard
for 2 August, col. 1475. The argument over the casualty is mentioned
by *ARP News* for January 1945. On Evans's 'special pets', see Pound,
p. 290; on Albert Palace Mansions the report on Incident 1056 in the
Wandsworth Borough Archives. Howgrave-Graham, p. 39, recounted
the 'bees' incident. The incident inquiry points and other WVS work
are mentioned in Graves, pp. 211, 224–5 and 229–30, and the WVS
Region V Report for May-July is in Air 20/4376. Bates, p. 36, gives
statistics for cups of tea, and the *Kentish Times* for 1 September
reported the Sidcup supper party.

28 A Chorus of Vehement Gloating

On the Nazi Security Service report, see Carroll, p. 198 footnote, on the *Wuwa*, p. 256. Bramsted, p. 321, mentions Goebbels's correspondence. For the Oslo Radio report, see the *Daily Mail*, 17 June; *The Times*, 20 June, quoted the description of roads choked with refugees; the *Daily Telegraph* for 6 July the *Völkischer Beobachter*; *The Times*, 6 July, the Spanish disclaimer and the exhibition in Lisbon; the *Daily Sketch*, 18 July, the tour by neutral journalists. Bates, p. 4, refers to a 'chorus of vehement gloating'; Bramsted, p. 321, to Goebbels's morning conference; the *Star* for 15 August the *Versager Eins* story; the *Evening News* for 28 July the German newsreels. Andreas-Friedric, pp. 114–15 was the Berlin woman quoted; Hagen, p. 36, became 'almost crazy with joy'; Carroll, p. 259, quoted Eisenhower's report. Hitler's conference at Margival is described by Speidel, pp. 108–10; von Kluge's desire to make peace by Wilmot, p. 378; Goebbels's broadcast by Bramsted, p. 323. On leaflet-carrying V-1s and the leaflets themselves, see Auckland, pp. 31–5, and CAB 66/57, 11 November, and HO 199/292. Other quotations are taken from BBC Monitoring Service reports.

29 An Eye for an Eye

For Churchill's speech, see vol. VI, p. 39; for Morrison's response WP (44) 348, 27 June, and PREM 3/111, 1 July. Letters from the public are mentioned in WM (44) 87, 4 July; public hostility by Donoughue and Jones, p. 319. The Joint Planning Staff's assessment is in PREM 3/111, 5 July. Sansom, p. 189, describes the public's 'grim fury'; see also St George Saunders, *Life*. On Eden, see Hansard, 19 July; on the withdrawn question FO 371/39053 C8766; on reprisals generally, the *West London Press*, 7 July and 14 July, and the Tottenham Council minutes for 18 July. Eisenhower's attitude is described by Tedder, pp. 581–2. On the V-1s effect on morale, see Eisenhower, p. 284. Approaches to the papacy are recorded in FO 371/43000 (11162/106/49), FO 371/43000 (W 10925) and W 11173/106/49. Venezuela's noble offer is in FO 371/43000 (W 11057).

30 The Only Answer

On reaction at SHAEF, see Tedder, p. 580, and Eisenhower, p. 284; Tedder's biographer was Owen, pp. 284–5. On the Staff Conference, see Air 20/6016 of 17 June. The problem of locating the launching ramps is set out in Air 34/80, p. 6, par. 33, Bates, p. 56, and *History of the Photographic Intelligence Investigation*, paras. 1, 26, 27, 31, 33.

On the decision to attack the supply sites, see Collier, *Battle*, pp. 78–9; on Harris's response, pp. 82–3. Joubert, p. 96, quotes Wachtel's War Diary and, p. 184 (Appendix by D. W. Kendall), describes the modified sites. On the underground depots, see Jones, pp. 426–7, Bates, pp. 13, 47–8, Brickhill, p. 230, and Morpurgo ('Wallis's biographer'), p. 346. Irving, p. 245, quotes Colonel Walter. Collier, pp. 386–9, describes the Crossbow Priorities Committee; Tedder pp. 582–4, the criticism of Bomber Command. The revised target list is quoted in Webster and Frankland, II, p. 285, and the bombing of suspected factories is recorded in Air 20/6016, paras. 64–6, of 28 October. The last named and Joubert, p. 87, list the casualties suffered. Churchill's scepticism about British bombing and Harris's response are in PREM 3/111, folios 729 and 731–5.

31   No Sympathy for Southampton

On bombs aimed at Southampton, see Collier, p. 371; on the use of British agents, and Hitler's orders to Wachtel, Irving, pp. 251–2. The Air Ministry map is in AVIA 11/60 of 15 July. The list of flying-bombs affecting the Isle of Wight came from a private informant. On casualties I used Dunn, II, p. 402. On Portsmouth see the *Portsmouth Evening News*, 15 July. Irving, p. 252, describes Morrison's objections to the deception proposals, and the Crossbow deception paper is in PREM 3/111, folio 930. The number of bombs launched is given by Collier, p. 389, and O'Brien, p. 682, and in PREM 3/111, Third Report of the Crossbow Committee, 3 July.

32   Who Are We to Act as God?

On the distribution of the early V-1s, and the number destroyed, see Irving, p. 228, Hill, pp. 5592–3, Collier, p. 381, and Jones, p. 416. Chapman's mission is mentioned by Cave Brown, p. 725, and Masterman, p. 172. MI5's dilemma is described by Jones, pp. 422–3, in *Dr Jones's War* and by Masterman, p. 180. The Dulwich College incident is in the *South London Observer* for 14 July and 1 September. Lord Ismay's report of 19 July is in PREM 3/111, Part III, the 'Restricted Circulation' Cabinet paper is in PREM 3/111, 24 July, and the resulting minute in WM 3/111, 24 July, and the resulting minute in WM (44), 97, 27 July. Duncan Sandys's plea is in WM 98, 2 August; Herbert Morrison's response in Prem 3/111 of 4 August; and the Cabinet discussion in WM 104 of 11 August. Irving, p. 257, reveals that Morrison asked 'Who are we to act as God?' The cipher telegram and Cabinet decisions are in PREM 3/111, 15 August. Jones, pp. 422–4, describes how the decision was evaded. The obituary notices are mentioned by Irving, p. 256, and in Air 20/6016 (QR No. K 463) of 16 July 1944. On the effects of the deception plan, see Air 40/4130 SORS/1/97 of 14 December 1945.

33   In Doodlebug Alley

See the *Kent Messenger*, 15 September, for Alderman Oak-Rhind's speech, 22 September for Morrison's, and 29 June 1973 for a post-war summary. The quotations from Bates are from pp. 22–4 and 43 ('a dead bug'). *The Times*, 13 September, reported the number of incidents in Kent; Platts, p. 27, the damage to oast houses and, p. 40, the 'score' of individual places. The Goodsall quotations are on pp. 143–4. On the 'guns' controversy see the *Hastings and St Leonard's Observer*, 5 August 1944 and 19 February 1977.

34   Chaos over Kent

The principal source is Pile and the passages quoted come from pp. 323–4, 328–33, 339–41, 348 and 398. See Bates, p. 7, on the defence plans, pp. 15–16, the 'boxing match in a railway carriage', p. 19 on the inspecting officers' report and the 'crazy chaos'; Hill, p. 5592, describes the guns' first move, as does Bates, p. 20. On the 'Pile mattress' see Watkins and Leslie. The press release quoted is Bulletin No. 14403 in Air 20/6016. On the Royal Observer Corps, see Wood, p. 172, Wilton, pp. 64–5 and Hough, pp. 126–7. The improvements in radar and artillery performance are in Hill, p. 5595, *Flight*, for 21 September 1944, p. 311, Boyce, pp. 104 and 153, Pile, p. 340, Lee, p. 155, and *Artillery Training*, vol. IV, Pamphlet 7. Boyce, pp. 149–54, describes the New Mexico experiment. On the trouble with non-AA units, see WO/199/553, 11 July. Arct criticized 'our friendly gunners' on pp. 91–2. Reed and Beamont, p. 134, and Lanchbery, p. 157, recorded the Tempest Wing's trials. On the move to the coast, see Collier, p. 383, Collier, *Battle*, pp. 91–2, Hill, pp. 5595–9, Pile, pp. 334–45, and WO 199/553 of 17 July.

35   One Shell, One Doodlebug

The King's visit to an AA battery is described in Wheeler-Bennett, p. 611. Details about the 3·7-inch and Bofors gun appear in Postan, pp. 289–90. Extracts from Pile are on pp. 346–7 and 365.

Sources

36 Hurrah for the Balloon Boys!

The principal source throughout is Gell. See also Collier, p. 373, Collier, *Battle*, p. 85, and *Flight*, 21 September 1944, p. 311. Prince, pp. 19–21, and Macmillan, p. 187, provide technical details about the balloons and the DPL. Other quotations are from Bates, pp. 17, and 54, Peters, p. 13, Hill, p. 5595, the *South London Press*, 28 September, *Reynolds News*, 30 July, Air 20/4376, date unstated, on the extent of the barrage, and Air 20/6016, 20 August, on the memo to the Ministry of Information.

37 A Stiff Task for the Fighters

The principal source was Hill, pp. 5589–99 and 5603. Prudence Hill, p. 211, mentions Hill's absorption in the battle. Bates, p. 17, recalls the belief that six squadrons of Spitfires would be adequate. I also used Beamont, p. 70, on the choice of Newchurch, p. 71, on the trouble at Hawkers, and p. 82, on flying through a V-1 explosion. See Reed and Beamont, p. 132, on the injured airman, p. 134, on the Wing's reinforcement and 'the whirlpool of allied fighters', p. 137, on the dance invitation. The quotation from Hough is on p. 128. Beamont, p. 81, mentions a 200-yard safety margin and Reed and Beamont, p. 133, one of 300 yards. See also Lanchbery, p. 157, on the V-1's speed, p. 158, on Beamont's mission to 11 Group and pp. 160–61, Beamont's first 'tip up' victory. On similar attacks see Richards and Saunders, III, p. 165, and Price, *Spitfire* p. 114. On the Poles' contribution, see Arct, pp. 88–92 and 95–6; on Jean Maridor, Bertrand, pp. 218–22, and Jullian, p. 188. On the Tempests' involvement in night-fighting I used Reed and Beamont, pp. 132–5, and Howard-Williams, including p. 30, on Monica, and 122, on boosted engines. The Merton gun sight is mentioned by Collier, p. 391, Reed and Beamont, p. 134, Lanchbery, p. 158, and the *Daily Sketch*, of 8 September 1944. On the success rate of the various squadrons, see Lanchbery, p. 162, Beamont, p. 85, and Arct, pp. 102 and 117.

38 Autumn in East Anglia

London's 'sleepy look' is described by Henrey, p. 91; the Air Ministry's congratulatory telegram is quoted by Prudence Hill, p. 206; and the Prime Minister's by Pile, p. 344. The premature rejoicing on 5 September is mentioned by Wanless, p. 426; and 'Victory Day Fever' by the *Kent Messenger*, 15 September. A verbatim report of the press conference on 7 September appears in Air 20/6016. *Handbook*, 11-1-3 (2) reported the relative inaccuracy of air-launched missiles; *Robot Bombardment*, pp. 142–3, the trials of III KG; Smith and Kay, pp. 670–71, the unit's movements; and Hill, p. 5599, the assumption that the first such missiles came from Belgium. The figures about air launching up to August appear in Air 40/1653, Collier, p. 523, and Pile, p. 369; Wachtel's successive moves are described by Joubert, pp. 97–8, and Collier, p. 389. The Vice-Chiefs of Staff's confidence and the subsequent bombardment are reported by Collier, p. 390, and later operations by *Robot Bombardment*, pp. 142–3, Collier, p. 393, and Bates, p. 58. Intruder operations are mentioned by Howard-Williams, p. 153, interception over the sea, p. 148, the shooting down of a V-1, pp. 151–2, and Operation Vapour p. 157. Collier, p. 390, refers to HMS *Caicos*, and, p. 391, gives the figures for V-1s destroyed. Collier, *Battle*, p. 130, describes the Diver 'Fringe'.

39   Christmas at Oldham

The letter to local authorities of 17 January is in HO 186/2299. A set of V-1-dropped leaflets is in file HO 199/292, which includes the suggested solution to the crossword. Details of the *Signal* leaflet appear in Auckland, p. 33. The Epworth leaflets are mentioned by Finn, pp. 74–5, and the Oldham ones by the *Oldham Chronicle*, 21 April 1945. Collier, p. 392, describes Hill's reluctance to thin out the east coast gun belt; Hill, p. 5602, explains his reasons; *Robot Bombardment*, p. 143, gives the figures of III KG's losses; and Collier, p. 392, and Hill, p. 5602, the end of its operations. Pile, pp. 384–5, describes AA Command's miserable Christmas; and Howard-Williams, p. 150, 'Sir Isaac's influence'.

40   The Final Spring

The epigraph is from Air 40/2114, 23 April 1945. On casualties and damage in Antwerp, see Wilmot, p. 661, and Helfers. Joubert, pp. 98–9, mentions the firing procedures in Germany and Colonel Walter's departure. The warning to the War Cabinet on 16 October appears in WM 137 (44) Minute 3. Collier, p. 394, mentions the fear of a long-range V-1 and the ULTRA dispatch of 26 February 1945 is in Air 40/2114. Collier, *Battle*, p. 33, describes the search for new ramps; Collier, *Defence*, p. 394, the decision to strengthen the Diver 'strip'; Hill, p. 5603, and Collier, *Defence*, p. 395, the closing salvoes. The Datchworth doodlebug was mentioned by a local informant. The Air Ministry's anxieties are recorded in Air 40/2114 of 19 March 1945. Joubert, p. 99, describes Wachtel's last stand. On Operation Suicide, see Reitsch, pp. 188–99, and Smith and Kay, p. 153.

Sources

41   Counting the Cost

See Irving, p. 302, for the epigraph, pp. 302–3, for the cost of the campaign and, p. 314, on the cost of each missile. Bates, p. 67, records the RAF's losses. Overall casualty figures appear in Collier, p. 528, and Helfers, p. 99; the figures for houses destroyed and damaged in Air 20/6016 of 28 October 1944 and Titmuss, p. 329. The number of V-1s in each borough is in Air 20/4127, Appendix I, and in each county in O'Brien, p. 682. The launching ramps near Calais are mentioned in an unidentified, undated, press cutting sent to me. On the ruins of Little Chart church, see the *Kent Messenger*, 29 October 1972; on the plaque at Frant, Baker, p. 166; on the V-1 in the Humber, Finn, p. 75. Von Braun's obituary appeared in the *Daily Telegraph*, 18 June 1977. The closing quotation is from Reitsch, pp. 216–7.

Appendix: The Flying-Bomb and the Public

The War Cabinet minute about the *Evening News* maps is WM 134 (44) 3 of 9 October 1944. General Marshall's request is in Air 20/6016, 16 January 1945, and Air Chief Marshal Bottomley's response is dated 19 January. *The Times* reviewed *V-1* on 25 November 1944 and *The Second Battle of London* on 2 December. For his comments, see Pile, pp. 366–7. The original proposal for the RAF booklet in Air 20/4138, 26 and 29 June; the Civil Servant's comments are added 5 September; the Ministry of Health's reactions 13 October. The objection to publishing RAF losses is in Air 20/4138 of 13 December 1944 and the Ministry of Information's arguments are referred to on 11 May, 8 July and 1 November 1945. The controversy about the Mimoyecques guns can be followed in Air 20/4140 of 3 October and 1 November 1945.

CONTRIBUTORS

Miss I. Abbey, Luncarty, Perthshire; Mrs G. A. Abnett, Exeter, Devon; Peter Abrahams, London, NW3; R. G. Absalom, Southend-on-Sea, Essex; Mrs Doris Adams, Rockland St Mary, Norwich; J. Adams, London, SE8; G. R. Adcock, Watton, Norfolk; Mrs Esme Ahmed, Enfield, Middx; Mrs J. Akerman, Chislehurst, Kent; Mrs Marion E. Alcock, Winchester, Hants; Mrs Eleanor Alldridge, Poole, Dorset; Trevor Allen, London, W8; Mrs Catherine Allwork, Wallington, Surrey; Joe Alton, Sudbury, Suffolk; John Ames, Robertsbridge, Sussex; N. D. Anderson, Eastbourne; Miss Olive R. Anderson, London, N4; Mrs Phyllis E. Anderson, Carnforth, Lancs; W. H. H. Andrews, Kings Langley, Herts; Mrs S. Anstee, Fleet, Hants; H. V. Anthony, Boxhill, Sussex; Mrs E. Argent, Barking, Essex; Mrs E. Armstrong, Bournemouth; Mrs J. Arnett, Norwich, Norfolk; Mrs H. M. B. Ashbury-Smith, London, N16; John Astle, Horton Kirby, Kent; Mrs Mollie Atkinson, Bedford; R. G. Auckland, St Albans, Herts; Giles Auty, Penzance, Cornwall; Mrs Harold Avery, Pevensey, Sussex; H. Avery, London, N17; Alf Ayling, Basildon, Essex; Mrs E. Aylward, Thornton Heath, Surrey; Mrs I. Bagnall, London, SW16; Mr and Mrs Baker, London, E17; C. J. Baker, Bexleyheath, Kent; H. A. Baker, Deal, Kent; Mrs I. E. Baker, Gravesend, Kent; Mrs N. Baker, East Grinstead, Sussex; W. Barcroft, London, W12; J. Bards, Brentwood, Essex; Sister A. Bailey, Maidstone, Kent; C. Stuart Bailey, Purley, Surrey; Mrs V. M. Bailey, Oxford; Mrs Marjorie Baillie, Norwich; J. B. Baird, London, SE2; Miss Gertrude M. Bannister, London, SW2; Victor Barham, Thetford, Norfolk; Dan M. Barker, London, SE18; Mrs Irene Barker, Newhaven, Sussex; Mrs S. E. Barlow, Windsor, Berks; Ken Barnacle, Holt, Norfolk; Mrs Joyce Barnard, Horsham, Sussex; Peter R. Barnard, Ashford, Middx; F/Lt S. P. Barnard, Cheam, Surrey; Mrs Ellen

Contributors

Barnes, South Ockendon, Essex; A. A. Barnett, London, NW9; G. W. Barren, Spilsby, Lincs; F. Barrett, Sidcup, Kent; G. C. Bartle, Tunbridge Wells, Kent; Miss Bartlett, Eastbourne, Sussex; Mrs F. W. Barton, Ashford, Kent; E. L. Basire, Harrow, Middx; Mrs Edith Batchelor, Twineham, Sussex; Mrs Eugenie Bates; Mrs Florence Bates, London, SW16; J. E. Bates, Chigwell, Essex; Thomas M. Bates, London, SW16; Mrs M. K. Baylie, Cheam, Surrey; Miss H. Baylie, West Worthing; Walter C. Beament, Colchester, Essex; Mr Ronald H. Beard, and Mrs Davina R. Beard, Southend-on-Sea, Essex; Mrs Violet Beaulieu, Thorpe-le-Soken, Essex; Stephen J. Beaven, London, SE11; Mr and Mrs Bebbington, Hythe, Kent; R. J. Becket, Reading, Berks; Mrs Marjorie Beechey, Beaminster, Dorset; S. Beer, Waddon; Miss N. O. Belcher, Wallington, Surrey; Mrs E. G. Bell, Tiptree, Essex; L. Bender, London, SE4; Mrs Maude L. Benfield, Eastbourne, Sussex; Mrs Doreen Bennett, Gillingham, Kent; Mrs E. Bennett, Eastbourne, Sussex; Mrs E. G. Bennett, Fareham, Hants; Mrs May Bennett, South Croydon, Surrey; Roy E. Bennett, Sutton Coldfield, West Midlands; Mrs M. Bentley, Edenbridge, Kent; G. H. Benton, Tunbridge Wells, Kent; Major Stuart Bedford, Henfield, Sussex; Mrs Millicent Berks, Herne Bay, Kent; Mrs Esme Berry, Eastbourne, Sussex; E. N. R. Berry, Sunbury-on-Thames, Middx; Mrs Patricia Berry, Seaford, Sussex; Ray Billings, Pinner, Middx; F. C. Billows, Maidenhead, Berks; John Bird, Leigh-on-Sea, Essex; Mrs L. E. Bird, Ramsgate, Kent; Miss E. P. Black, Westcliff on Sea, Essex; Mrs Joyce Blackburn, Doncaster, Yorks; Miss Lorelie Blake, Folkestone, Kent; Mrs D. M. Blanchard, High Wycombe, Bucks; Mrs Clare Bland, Hatfield Heath, Hertfordshire; J. D. Blayney, Romford, Essex; G. Wyverne Blears, Clacton-on-Sea, Essex; Mrs Frances Bleasdale, Aylesbury, Buckinghamshire; Mrs C. R. Blick, Maidenhead, Berkshire; John J. G. Blundell, Orpington, Kent; Mrs V. Bolwell, Chatham, Kent; Miss Cicely M. Botley, Tunbridge Wells, Kent; D. T. Bouchard, Burlesdon, Hampshire; Dan Boulton, Swanscombe, Kent; Arthur W. Bourne, London, SE5; T. J. Bowen, Rayleigh, Essex; E. Bowles, Tunbridge Wells, Kent; Mrs Florence Bowley, Doncaster, Yorks; Mrs Ethel Bowman, Rochester, Kent; Mrs P. R. Bowring, Cuckfield, Sussex; Mrs Pat Bowsell, Broadstairs, Kent; Terry Boxall, Beckenham, Kent; Mrs M. F. Boyd, Arundel, Sussex; J. S. Bradforth, London, E17; Derek Bradley, Loughborough, Leicestershire; George Brailey, Barnet, Hertfordshire; Mrs V. A. D. Brandom, Eastbourne, Sussex; J. A. S. Brasier, Guildford, Surrey; Mrs E. Bray; Mrs Rosetta Brazil, Basildon, Essex; Mrs H. Breeze, Bromley Common, Kent; James J. Breslin, Bromley; T. G. Brett, Whitstable, Kent; R. Brew, London,

E13; F. Bright, Ipswich, Suffolk; Michael Bristow-Smith, Battle, Sussex; Miss Nellie Broad, London, N4; Mrs E. Bromhead, Norwich, Norfolk; Greville Brooke, Bournemouth, Dorset; Roy S. Brooker, Maidstone; Mrs E. Brooks, Dunkirk, Kent; Jim Broom, London, SW2; Mrs Lilian Brotherston, Brentwood, Essex; Mrs D. Brown, Somersham, Hampshire; F. M. Brown, London, W4; F/Lt F. McM. Brown, Chorleywood, Hertfordshire; John B. Brown, Kingston-upon-Thames, Surrey; John Brown, London, W3; R. E. Brown, Wickford, Essex; Mrs R. P. Brown, London, SW12; J. Bruin, Poole, Dorset; Allan Bula, Guildford, Surrey; John E. Bullingham, Barnet, Hertfordshire; Robert Burgess, Pembury, Kent; J. B. Burke, Haywards Heath, Sussex; Miss Muriel J. Burke, London, W12; Eric J. Burman, Bexhill-on-Sea, Sussex; M. J. Burn, Slindon, Sussex; G. M. Burt, Aldershot, Hampshire; W. D. Bush, Ham, Surrey; Mrs Dorothea Bushell, Harlow, Essex; Mrs Elsie Butcher, Clacton-on-Sea, Essex; F. E. Butler, London, N9; J. Butcher, London, E7; Miss Lilian F. Butcher, Broadstairs, Kent; Thomas Butcher, Maidstone, Kent; Mrs Margaret Butler, Ilford, Essex; Mrs Renata Butler, Leigh on Sea, Essex; Mrs K. D. Buxton, Shirley, Croydon; P. Caffarate, Worcester Park, Surrey; Miss Kate Caffrey, Wembley, Middlesex; Mrs L. Cain, Sittingbourne, Kent; Mrs Valerie Caldwell, Leatherhead, Surrey; Mrs J. F. Callaway, Bexhill, Sussex; Mrs Irene Calvert, South Tankerton, Kent; Mrs E. B. Campbell, Box, Wiltshire; Mrs Phyllis R. Campling, Moulsford, Oxfordshire; John L. Cannell, London, E12; Peter N. Cannon, Farnham, Surrey; Edna G. Carr, Gillingham, Kent; Mrs Betty Carrington, Southwick, Sussex; John Carrington, Southampton; Bruce Carter, Eastbourne, Sussex; Mrs Elsie Carter, London, SW16; Mrs Patricia Carter, Pulborough, West Sussex; Richard A. S. Carter, Aylesbury, Bucks; F. C. Carvell, Farnham, Surrey; Mrs J. Cary, Hassocks, Sussex; Mrs Fredi Cawkell, Stansted, Essex; Mrs Penny Chambers, Rochester, Kent; Mrs Joan Chandler, West Byfleet, Surrey; Mrs A. E. Chapman, West Wickham, Kent; Mrs Muriel Chapman, Ferndown, Dorset; Mrs P. M. Charles; Mrs Jean Charman, nee Maclean, Uxbridge, Middlesex; Mrs P. M. Chenery, Cromer, Norfolk; F. K. Cherry, London, N17; W. Cherry, Morden, Surrey; Miss Joan Chinery, Fairseat, Kent; A. Christie, Barnet, Herts; Mrs V. L. Chubb, Woking, Surrey; S. Clapham, Norwich; George B. Clark, Bradwell, Great Yarmouth; John Clark, Rye, Sussex; Mrs Laurette Clark, Sevenoaks, Kent; Mrs M. W. Clark, Eastbourne, Sussex; Robin Clark, Brighton, Sussex; Mrs V. Le Gros Clark, Oxford; Len Clarke, Bournemouth, Dorset; Albert and Joan Clash, Horam, Sussex; B. G. Clay, Romford, Essex; Fred Claydon, Thorpe Bay, Essex; L. E. Claydon, Ulting, Essex;

Contributors

Mrs Joan Claye, Harrow, Middlesex; Rodney F. Clements, and Mrs Catherine Clements, Bracknell, Berks; Robert Cleveland, Eastbourne, Sussex; Mrs F. Cload, St Leonards-on-Sea, Sussex; F. A. Cluett, Gravesend, Kent; Mrs V. P. Cobbett, London, SW17; Geoffrey Cole, New Malden, Surrey; Mrs Irene Cole, Farnham, Surrey; Mrs M. A. Cole, Fleet, Hants; Mrs Pat Cole, West Byfleet, Surrey; Mrs Kitty Coleman, London, NW3; Mrs I. Coles, Offham, Kent; Mrs S. Collier, Eton Wick, Berks; A. G. Collins, Piltdown, E. Sussex; D. H. Collins, Ashford, Middlesex; E. W. Collins, Seaford, Sussex; Mrs G. M. Collins, Sutton, Surrey; Mrs Joan Collins, London, SW17; Mrs M. D. Collins, Tunbridge Wells; Mrs Phyllis E. Collins, Hove, Sussex; David G. Collyer, Deal, Kent; Harold Collyer, Kingsdown, Kent; Albert Cook, London, SW15; Mrs Dora A. V. Cook, Eastbourne; H. Cookson, Ringmer, Sussex; George Cooley, Richmond, Surrey; John Cooper, Rugby, Warwickshire; Miss Rita Cooper, Hanwell, London; W. F. Cooper, Eastbourne, Sussex; F. C. Coppard, East Croydon, Surrey; F. Copperwaite, and Mrs M. E. Copperwaite, London, SE24; Albert Copping, Wycombe Marsh, Bucks; Mrs Hilda Copps, Whitton, Middlesex; Miss E. M. Corben, London, SW17; Peter Cornish, London, SE19; Stephen Corrin, and Mrs Sara Corrin, London, SW1; Mrs K. Couchman, Linton, Kent; Miss Ida M. Coughlan, Princes Risborough, Bucks; Mrs Mary Court, London, NW4; Sid Coveney, Biddenden, Kent; Rev. C. Leslie Craig, Epsom Downs, Surrey; Mrs C. Crain, Southall, Middlesex; Paul Cramer, London, NW4; Lt. P. Creek, Feltham, Middlesex; Miss Emily Bernadine Crellin, London, SW4; Mrs Winifred Crisp, Coventry; Miss N. Crofton Savill, Herongate, Essex; Mrs Betty M. Crook, Ipswich, Suffolk; Mrs Pam Croome, Thaxted, Essex; Mrs Sadie Crothall, Andover, Hants; C. C. Crowhurst, Folkestone, Kent; Vic Cruse, Buckingham; Gordon Cullingham, Windsor, Berks; D. Cummins, Beckenham, Kent; Mrs P. B. Curwood, Romford, Essex; Mrs E. C. M. Cusden, Cheam, Surrey; Miss M. Cutten, London, SE1; Mrs Esther Cutting, London, E17; Mrs D. E. Daddy, Folkestone, Kent; Miss J. Dalgliesh, Ringmer, Sussex; Miss Patricia Daly; Mrs M. R. Dance, Purley, Surrey; Miss Q. R. A. Daniels, Peacehaven, Sussex; Miss S. Dann, West Hoathly, Sussex; Dennis and Joy Darney, Alresford, Hants; George Davey, Lowestoft, Suffolk; Mrs K. C. Davey, Tunbridge Wells; Mrs M. Davis, Holland on Sea, Essex; Mrs Mary G. Davies, Horsell, Surrey; Nicholas Davies, Eythorne, Kent; Mrs Davis, London, SE14; D. W. Davy, Brighton, Sussex; Mrs F. H. Dawn, London, SW11; Mrs Margaret L. Day, Ashford, Middlesex; Mrs Doris Dayan, Boscombe; E. Dean, Crawfordsville, Indiana, USA,; Bert Delaney, Dover; Mrs L. H. Dell, Herne Bay, Kent; John Denby, Burgess Hill,

Sussex; D. G. A. Denman, Tunbridge Wells; Peter Denman, London, SE25; Mrs W. Derham, Lancing, W. Sussex; Mrs G. R. Devereux, Margate; A. Devonshire, West Drayton, Middlesex; S. A. N. Dibbs, Langley, Berks; Alan Dick, Tonbridge, Kent; Mrs M. Dimond, London, N22; P. J. Dixon, Fleet, Hants; Mrs Elizabeth Dodds, Bedford, Beds; Ken Dorman, Hounslow, Middlesex; Mrs Jean M. Dovery, Dorney, Berks; George R. Downing, Horstead, Norfolk; A. R. Drane, London, SW14; T. Drew, Deal, Kent; Mrs Joyce E. Drewett, Wolvercote, Oxford; Mrs Dororthy L. Driscoll, Kingston, Surrey; Mrs Ivy M. Dubois, Purley, Surrey; Cyril D. Ducat, Corfe Castle, Dorset; Mrs I. Glen Dunlop, Sevenoaks, Kent; Mrs W. G. Dunscombe, Horsham, Sussex; Mrs H. M. Dyer, Hounslow, Middlesex; Mrs E. L. Eadon, Broadstairs, Kent; L. Eames-Dixon, London, N10; Mr and Mrs R. East, London, E17; Mrs Anne E. Edington, Hassocks, Sussex; Cyril N. Edwards, Herne Bay, Kent; Mrs Daphne Edwards, Streetly, Sutton Coldfield; Mrs J. P. Edwards, Laxfield, Suffolk; Mrs Maud Edwards, Romney Marsh, Kent; Mrs D. E. Eggleden, Tenterden, Kent; Mrs B. A. Elliott, Brock Hill, Essex; Mrs K. M. Elliott, Battle, Sussex; Mrs J. M. Ellis, Colchester, Essex; Mrs V. Elsden, Exmouth, Devon; W. A. Elsom, North Weald, Essex; Robert Elwig, Crowborough, Sussex; Mrs Hazel V. Escortt, Rayleigh, Essex; Miss B. Evans, Windsor, Berks, Mrs Doreen Evans, Eastbourne, Sussex; Norman L. Evans, Burgess Hill, Sussex; Mrs Ruby Evans, Otham, Kent; Mrs J. Everett, Meopham, Kent; D. Everson, East Barnet, Herts; Gordon R. Everson, West Horndon, Essex; Norman Ezard, London, SE4; Mrs Joan Fairchild; Derek B. Fallon, London, W7; Miss Muriel Fancett, London, NW2; Mrs M. Farham, Eastbourne, Sussex; Mrs Joan Farmer, Pyrford, Surrey; Dr R. H. Farmer, Aylesbury, Bucks; Robert Farrance, Biddenden, Kent; Mrs P. Farrelly, Herne Bay, Kent; Mrs Elsie Farrington, Handcross, Sussex; Neil Farrow, Sedlescombe, Sussex; William Fast, Uxbridge, Middlesex; Supt. K. J. Fayers, Sur, Sultanate of Oman; Andrew Fayle, Heathfield, Sussex; F. A. Felstead, Clerkenwell; Mrs Irene M. Fenton, Milton Keynes, Bucks; A. L. Field, Shirley, Croydon; Cyril Field, St Leonards on Sea, Sussex; E. A. Figg, Haywards Heath, Sussex; Leon D. Figg, Burgess Hill, Sussex; Mrs E. S. File, Woodchurch, Kent; J. P. File, Lyminge, Kent; Leslie Finegold, Hove, Sussex; Miss Margaret Fish, Norwich; John Fisher, Colchester, Essex; Mrs Doreen Filtchett, Eastbourne, Sussex; Mrs Iris N. Fitton, Harleston, Norfolk; Mrs Beryl Fleming, Woodingdean, Sussex; Mrs I. Fonseca, Sutton; Mrs V. L. Ford, Fleet, Hants; Dennis Fordham, and Mrs Barbara Fordham, Gravesend, Kent; S. N. Forster, London, SE19; G. Howard Foster, Shanklin, Isle of Wight; C. J. F. Fox,

Walmer, Kent; John P. Francis, Woking, Surrey; A. W. Gordon Franklin, Northwood, Middlesex; L. J. Franklin, Bishopston, Kent; James Franks, Lewes, Sussex; Mrs Isobel M. Freeborn, Bury St Edmunds, Suffolk; Miss G. M. French, London, W4; Mrs I. Frenette, Hastings, Sussex; Mrs H. Friend, Buckhurst Hill, Essex; Mrs I. Friend, Bournemouth; Mr and Mrs T. Fuller, London, SE3; P. E. Fullick, Haslemere, Surrey; Miss M. C. Gaizelek, Bury St Edmunds; R. J. Gale, Dorking, Surrey; Terence Gallacher, Doddinghurst, Essex; Raymond J. Gambrill, Gillingham, Kent; Mrs Elizabeth E. Gamham, Diss, Norfolk; Mrs Ellen Gardiner, Herne Bay, Kent; Guy Gardiner, New Addington, Surrey; Mrs M. A. Gardner, Hastings, Sussex; Peter Gardner, Horsham, Sussex; John Garlick, London, E17; Mrs H. Garner, Eastwood, Essex; Miss D. Garrard, Leigh-on-Sea, Essex; Mrs Doris Gash, Clifton, Manchester; Patrick Gaskell-Taylor, London, SW6; Mrs C. Geddings, London, W9; Miss Esme E. M. Geering, Tunbridge Wells; E. Geiringer, Sutton, Surrey; Mrs Margaret Gennett, London, E9; Hector Gent, Thornton Heath, Surrey; Mrs L. George, West Wickham, Kent; Mrs M. L. Gibbens, Halesworth, Suffolk; Mrs Marjorie Gibbins, Croydon; Frank S. Gibbons, Worthing, Sussex; Ken Gibbons, London, SW19; C. D. Gilbey, Morden, Surrey; G. R. Gillam, Enfield, Middlesex; Mrs Marian Gilliam, Shirley, Surrey; Mrs T. Gillman, Bexley, Kent; J. M. Glanville, Norwich; Miss E. J. Glen, Bradford, West Yorks; Mrs Gym Glover, Margate, Kent; Mrs M. E. Goddard, Tunbridge Wells; P. H. Godfrey, Norwich; Mrs M. A. Goldsmith, Emmer Green, Berks; Mrs Sylvia Gollings, Worthing, Sussex; Peter Goodall, Mitcham, Surrey; Mrs Doris Goode, Iver Heath, Bucks; Mrs R. Goodenough, Folkestone, Kent; Mrs Beryl Goodge, Otford, Kent; Mrs Florence Gorton, Ilford, Essex; Frederick G. Gould, Hockley, Essex; L. Govey, Bearsted, Kent; L. Gower, Southbourne, Dorset; Mrs Doris Graham, Billericay, Essex; Alick Grant, Brentwood, Essex; Dr Alfred E. Gray, Hazlemere, Bucks; Miss Esther D. Gray, Harold Hill, Essex; Mrs L. Gray, Cuckfield, Sussex; R. G. Gray, Trowse, Norfolk; Andrew M. Green, Robertsbridge, Sussex; Miss Brenda Green, Belvedere, Kent; Mr and Mrs G. W. Green, New Costessey, Norfolk; Roy Green, Cheriton, Kent; Mrs Elsie Greenfield, Storrington, Sussex; J. T. Greenin, Worthing, Sussex; H. S. Greenough, London, E18; Mrs Christine Greenstock, London, SW18; Mrs C. A. Grimes; Mrs G. E. Grist, Rickmansworth, Herts; J. S. Guest, Whitstable, Kent; Douglas J. Gurton, Tollesbury, Essex; Mrs Wilhelmina Gwillim, West Wickham, Kent; Mrs Dorrie Habgood, Thetford, Norfolk; Sylvia Hadley, Westbrook, Kent; Robert A. Hales, Hadlow Down, Sussex; A. D. Halstead, Tonbridge, Kent; A. E. Hammer, London, SE26; R. W.

The Doodlebugs

Hammond, London, N20; Mrs J. Hampson, Keymer, Sussex; Albert Hands, Ilford, Essex; Mrs E. Handscombe, Barnet, Herts; A. W. Hanlon, Harefield, Hants; Bill Harden, Writtle, Essex; Don Harding, Shirley, Croydon; Mrs Brenda Hargreaves, London, SW2; Mrs Christabel Harker, Pinner, Middlesex; Mrs D. Harman-Lewis, Gt. Bookham, Surrey; Mrs Peggy Harmsworth, Riseley, Berks; Mrs Marjorie G. Harper, Fairlight, Sussex; Mrs Harris, Deal, Kent; C. J. C. Harris, London, N8; Mr and Mrs H. W. Hart, Frinton on Sea, Essex; Mike Hasler, Aylesbury, Bucks; Mrs Doris Hatchard, London, E11; Mrs Edith Hawes, London, N22; Doris and Rowland Hawksworth, Bournemouth; Mrs Patricia Hawtin, Chipping Norton, Oxon; Miss Alice M. Hayes, Saltdean, Sussex; E. J. Haynes, Flixton, Suffolk; G. Hayward, Bordon, Hants; Albert E. Hedges, Bishops Stortford, Herts; Fred Hedley, London, SW18; John Hemmings, Cirencester, Gloucestershire; Sidney Hendry, Melton Constable, Norfolk; A. F. Henson, Twickenham, Middlesex; C. Hewett, Margate, Kent; Mrs John E. Hewitt, Windsor, Berks. Mrs Stella Heydon, Eastbourne, Sussex; J. M. Heyes, Southampton; Mrs Violet M. Hibberd, Brook, Hants; G. E. Hibon, Enfield, Middlesex; G. Hickmott, Herne Bay, Kent; C. R. Higgett, London, EC1; Mrs J. W. Higgins, Canterbury, Kent; Joan A. Hill, Eastleigh, Hants; Mrs B. Hills, Eastbourne, Sussex; Cyril A. Hills, Maidenhead, Berks; F. W. Hills, London, N4; V. C. Hinxman, East Preston, Sussex; F/Lt K. B. Hiscock, Billericay, Essex; Sid Hoare, Whitstable, Kent; Mrs S. Hockey, Langley, Berks; Ron Hodges, Polegate, Sussex; Mrs Eileen Hodgkinson, Haywood, Lancs; Mrs D. Hodgson, Byfleet, Surrey; Mrs G. Hogan, London, E1; Ian Hogg, Stanway, Essex; J. K. Holden, Pinner, Middlesex; David R. Hollamby, Hastings, Sussex; W. J. Hollidge, Birehanger, Herts; W. Hollie, Farnborough, Hants; Mrs D. A. Hollister, Winton, Dorset; Mrs A. Holloway, Henley-on-Thames, Oxon; Mrs S. M. Holloway, Maidenhead, Berks; K. Holmes, London, NW5; Bob Holness, Pinner, Middlesex; Miss Constance Holt, London, WC1; Mrs Hilda Hooke, Madeley, Shropshire; Miss Mary Hopley, Gravesend, Kent; Mrs Eve Horne, Marsden Green, Herts; Michael Horovitz, Bisley, Glos; Mrs Doreen Horrocks, London, N21; G. W. Horsham, Harrow, Middlesex; Mrs Betty Hoskins, South Lopham, Norfolk; Mrs Jean Hoskins, Eastbourne, Sussex; C. Hotton, London, N20; Mrs C. A. Hudson, Herne Bay, Kent; Peter J. Hudson, London, SE18; Mrs E. Hughes, Witham, Essex; Mrs I. L. Hughes, Eye, Suffolk; W. G. Hughes, Westham, Sussex; Mrs Ida Hughes-Stanton, Stratford-St-Mary, Essex; Canon Anthony Hulme, Bedford; Charles N. Humphrey, Slough, Berks; Ken Humphreys, Hadleigh, Essex; Roy S. Humphreys, Dover, Kent; Mrs E. Hunnisett, Eastbourne,

Sussex; Mrs A. E. Hunt, East Grinstead, Sussex; the late Iris Violet Hunter, Birchington, Kent; J. Hunter, Tunbridge Wells; H. Hutchinson, Fleet, Hants; Noel A. Igoe, Lisburn, Co Antrim, N. Ireland; Arthur Impey, Wembley, Middlesex; Miss Connie Ives, London, W3; A. J. Jackson; Mr and Mrs S. V. Jacobs; A. James, Southall, Middlesex; Mrs Marina M. James, Ramsgate, Kent; Mrs F. E. Jarvis, Whoberley, Coventry; Mrs Ruth Jenkinson, London, SE14; Barton Johnson, Rochester, Kent; Mrs E. G. Johnson, Gillingham, Kent; Miss Gladys I. Johnson, London, SE11; Mrs M. Johnson, Gayton, Northampton; Mrs Mary Johnson, Gravesend, Kent; Noel Johnson, Twickenham, Middlesex; Mrs Pamela Johnson, Shere, Surrey; R. Johnson, Pinner, Middlesex; Stowers Johnson, Hutton, Essex; S. P. Johnson, Ramsgate, Kent; Mrs Eileen Johnstone, St Day, Cornwall; Alan Jones, Clayhall, Essex; Mrs Annet Jones, Ashendon, Bucks; Mrs B. H. Jones, London, SE11; C. F. L. Jones, London, SW20; Mrs Frances Jones, Perivale, Middlesex; Gerald E. Jones, Stanmore, Middlesex; L. R. Jones, Canterbury, Kent; Peter Jones, Chatham, Kent; R. E. Jones, London, E4; Mrs S. J. Jones, Chertsey, Surrey; E. W. Jordan, New Barnet, Herts; Willie Jordan, Norwich, Norfolk; Miss Phyllis Jordan, Bridge, Kent; Mrs Stephen Joyce, London, SW11; Mrs Lilian Kavanagh, Ramsgate, Kent; Miss Thelma Kay, Brighton, Sussex; William Kearns, Aylesbury, Bucks; Mrs Elizabeth Kelling, Nelson, Motueka, New Zealand; Mrs A. E. Kemp, London, SW16; Mrs D. Kemp, Uxbridge, Middlesex; Mrs Doreen Kemp, Kessingland, Suffolk; A. Kewell, London, E15; Mrs George Kevan, Eastbourne, Sussex; W. Kidger, North Lancing, Sussex; Egbert Kieser and Mrs M. L. Kieser, Whitstable, Kent; Mrs Holly Kindred, London, SE5; Miss Amelia King, Haywards Heath, Sussex; Mrs E. King, Watford, Herts; Mrs Joy King, Thorpe-le-Soken, Essex; Mrs Verna Kingdom, Sutton, Surrey; Mrs N. Kingston, Prittlewell, Essex; Mrs I. V. Kingston-Lynch, London, SW16; Kenneth N. Kirby, St Leonard's-on-Sea, Sussex; Mrs N. Kirk, Littlebourne, Kent; Mrs J. E. Kiss, Orpington, Kent; Leonard J. Kloot, London, NW9; Miss Dorothy Knight, Hailsham, Sussex; John Knight, London, SE5; R. G. Kreamer, Sudbury, Suffolk; Mrs G. Kynaston Nicholas, Epsom, Surrey; Ken Lake, London, E17; D. G. Lane, Orpington, Kent; Philip Lane, Orpington, Kent; W. Langley, Dereham, Norfolk; Russell F. Large, Bury St Edmunds, Suffolk; Mrs Patricia La Trobe, Hythe, Kent; Donald Law, Romford, Essex; Sq. Ldr F. B. Lawless (Rtd) and Mrs Lawless, Point Clear, Essex; Mrs G. Lawrence, Sittingbourne, Kent; Mrs V. G. Lawrence, Prittlewell, Essex; Miss W. E. Lawry, Church Crookham, Hants; Stan Leader, Coulsdon, Surrey; Mrs Patricia Ledsham, Ewell, Surrey; Mrs Lee, Maidenhead, Berks;

The Doodlebugs

Miss D. Lee, Bexleyheath, Kent; Donald Lee, Lindfield, Sussex; Mrs A. M. Leech, Harlow, Essex; the late Mrs Margaret Le Geyt, Emmer Green, Berks; G. A. Le Good, Gillingham, Kent; N. E. Lenney, Otley, Suffolk; Alfred Levy, London, N2; Neville S. Lewis, Semer, Suffolk; S. Lewis, Loughton, Essex; Trevor Lewis, Canterbury, Kent; Miss D. E. Lidbury, Ashford, Middlesex; Tony Lidiard, Bedford; Mrs K. B. Liddle, South Tankerton, Kent; W. Gordon Lilly, Sanderstead, Surrey; L. R. Lincoln, London, NW2; R. V. Ling, London, SE26; Dame Mary Lioba, Worcester; Dr Ian Lockhart, Staines, Middlesex; Mr and Mrs H. Lomas, Worthing, Sussex; Harry Long, Sanderstead, Surrey; R. M. Long, Horsham, Sussex; S. I. E. Long, London, NW6; G. A. Longman, Great Clacton, Essex; W. G. Longman, Westcliffe-on-Sea, Essex; Mrs Lilian Lovelace, St Leonard's, Sussex; G. Lovell, London, E6; Mrs Audrey Lovelock, Basildon, Essex; Mrs M. Selby Lowndes, Mundesley, Norfolk; M. L.; Miss V. E. Maby, Kempston, Bedford; Mrs Betty D. Macey, Bridport, Dorset; Mrs D. Macey, Wallington, Surrey; Dr Hugh C. Maingay, Bergh Apton, Norfolk; Mrs F. M. Mallaburn, Sale, Cheshire; Mrs T. C. Mallik, Sutton-at-Hone, Kent; E. Leslie Mann, Beckenham, Kent; Mrs M. Mann, Maidenhead, Berks; T. Mann, Portslade, Sussex; E. V. Marks, Banstead, Surrey; R. J. Marrion, London, E17; Gordon K. Marriott, S. Ruislip, Middlesex; A. C. Marsh, Aylesbury, Bucks; Miss Evelyn Marsh, and Miss Violet E. Marsh, Hove, Sussex; Mrs Marshall, Stevenage, Herts; Mrs B. Marshall, Colchester, Essex; Mrs Mary Marshall, Westgate-on-Sea, Kent; A. G. Martin, Findon, Sussex; Mrs M. E. Martin, Strood, Kent; W. R. Maskell, Norwich; Mrs J. Mason, Brockfastleigh, Devon; John E. Mason, and Mrs Irene Mason, Farnham, Surrey; Mrs W. M. Mason, London, SE5; Mr and Mrs W. C. Mason, East Grinstead, Sussex; Mrs M. L. Mather, Pulborough, Sussex; Mrs Ada M. Matthews, Bishops Stortford, Herts; Harold Matthews, London, NW5; L. Matthews, West Southbourne, Dorset; Mrs Rose Mathews, Southwater, Sussex; R. Mathieson, Eastwood, Essex; Mrs H. Maunton, Broadstairs, Kent; R. R. May, Ashford, Kent; Mrs V. L. Mayhew, London, E4; Mrs Rona M. Maynard, Maidstone, Kent; Mrs E. McCarthy, Purley, Surrey; Mrs Doris McCartney, Beeston Regis, Norfolk; A. F. McClarty, Westerham Hill, Kent; J. McDermott, London, E6; Dorothy H. McDonald, Slough, Berks; Mrs E. C. McDonald, Hounslow, Middlesex; H. D. McDonald, Brandon, Suffolk; Miss Anne MacDougall, London, W5; John Scanlan McFadden, Polegate, Sussex; Mrs Eileen McGain, Ruislip, Middlesex; Miss Sarah McGough, Blaydon-on-Tyne, Tyne and Wear; J. H. McKay, Ditton, Kent; Mary McMath, Ewhurst, Surrey; Mrs M. F. MacRonald, Croydon; H. H. Meachen, Highfield, Southampton; Mrs Florence L.

Medhurst, Farnham, Surrey; Mrs G. Meekcoms, London, SE5; Chas.
H. Meggs, Dereham, Norfolk; Mrs C. P. Mercer, Colchester., Essex;
P. A. W. Merriton, Rocheville, France; N. E. Metson, Steeple
Bumpstead, Suffolk; Miss Violet A. Middlemiss, St Albans, Herts;
Mrs M. Middleton, Bournemouth; Mrs Violet Mildon, Slough, Berks;
W. T. Miles, and W. J. T. Miles, London, E17; Mrs L. P. Millard,
Pinner, Middlesex; Roderick D. Miller, Rayleigh, Essex; Edward N.
Mills, Hextable, Kent; Mrs Lucy Mills, Guildford, Surrey; A. Milton,
Croxley Green, Herts; Miss H. A. Minns, Guildford, Surrey; H.
Minns, Norwich; Mrs Alice Evelyn Mintrum, Bitterne Park,
Southampton; Mrs Hilda Mirams, Aylesbury, Bucks; Miss M. Miskell,
London, SE25; W. W. Mitchell, Wilmslow, Cheshire; Mrs Naomi
Mitchison, Carradale, Argyll; Mrs W. M. Molden, London, SE9; Karl
G. Molnar, and Mrs Molnar, Birmingham; Miss Audrey Moore,
Watford, Herts; Mrs Ethel Moore, Studd Hill, Kent; Miss F.
M. Moore, London, W9; Frederick E. Moore, Telscombe Cliffs,
Sussex; Richard Moore, Thorpe St Andrew, Norfolk; Mrs C. More-
ton, Norwich; Mrs D. Morrow, West Wickham, Kent; Mrs Chris
Mortimore, Chislehurst, Kent; H. Douglas Moss, Hove, Sussex; Mrs
Violet Mott, Welwyn Garden City, Herts; Mrs M. J. Moya, Woking,
Surrey; Arthur Moyse, London, W14; Brian Mulliner, Alvescot,
Oxon; R. G. Mullinger, London, E11; Ray Munday, Gravesend,
Kent; Mrs Freda Mundon Reid, Brighton, Sussex; A. Murphy, Har-
low, Essex; Miss Pearl Murphy, Oxford; Adrian Murray, New Mal-
den, Surrey; Mrs J. I. M.; Cyril W. Nash, Bolney, Sussex; E. E.
Natali, Woodford Green, Essex; Arthur H. Neall, Bournemouth,
Dorset; Edward Neville, Hullbridge, Essex; Bert Newman, London,
SW4; L. I. Newman, Reepham, Norfolk; Mrs I. Newton, Carshalton,
Surrey; Miss Dorene Nice, Culford, Suffolk; D. F. Nichols, Basildon,
Essex; Mrs H. Nicholls, Greenhithe, Kent; J. O. H. Norman, Ligh-
twater, Surrey; C. W. Norris, London, E9; J. J. North, London, E7;
Don Nowers, Seabrook, Kent; N. Nugent, Clacton on Sea, Essex;
D. N. B. Nutman, Reading, Berks; E. J. Nye, East Peckham, Kent;
Mrs Olive Nye, Hornchurch, Essex; Denis Oakenfull, London, SE22;
Mrs R. Oakley; Patrick O'Brien, Greenford, Middlesex; F. R. Olive,
London, W4; Mrs Sara Oliver, Aylesbury, Bucks; H. R. Olphert,
London, N11; Mrs Ivy Orton, Grays, Essex; A. G. A. Page, Crawley
Down, Sussex; Mrs Catherine Page, London, SW15; Mrs M. Page,
London, NW2; Ralph Page, Guildford, Surrey; Mrs Marion Pain,
Hastings, Sussex; D. Palmer, Bexhill-on-Sea, Sussex; Frank Palmer,
Pinner, Middlesex; Peter E. Parbery, Crowthorne, Berks; C. J. Par-
due, Felmingham, Norfolk; Arthur James Parker, Downham, Kent;
Mrs Ellen Parker, High Wycombe, Bucks; Mrs Mary Parker, Cam-

berley, Surrey; Mrs P. M. Parker, Camberley, Surrey; W. R. Parker, London, NW10; A. W. Parlour, Brightlingsea, Essex; Mrs G. M. Parsons, West Wickham, Kent; Miss Ruth Partington, St Albans, Herts; Mrs E. Partridge, Gillingham, Kent; Miss J. Pascoe, Whitchurch, Hants; Mrs Anne Paterson, Yateley, Surrey; Stanley Patrick, Lakenheath, Suffolk; Mrs B. Patterson, Chessington, Surrey; Major C. A. Paul, High Wycombe, Bucks; R. Paul, Aylesbury, Bucks; Norman Paulding, Galleywood, Essex; A. J. T. Pawlowski, Trimley St Mary, Ipswich; Mrs L. D. Payne, Sutton, Surrey; Mr and Mrs Pearce, Canterbury, Kent; F. C. Pearce, Morden, Surrey; Mrs W. Pearce, London, N12; J. B. Pearson, Thetford, Norfolk; Miss Patricia Peasnell, London, NW10; Mrs J. Pendergast, Strood, Kent; Mrs D. Penfold, Hove, Sussex; Mrs D. Pengelly, London, NW3; Mrs Anne Penton, Shirley, Croydon; Mrs P. M. Perkins, Gravesend, Kent; Ralph Perkins, London, SW4; Mrs M. E. Perrott, Teignmouth, Devon; Mrs Verina Pettigrew, Sawbridgeworth, Herts; A. J. Phelps, Welling, Kent; Clement Phillips, Warlingham, Surrey; Mrs M. R. Phillips, St Leonards, Sussex; P. E. Phillips, Cowbeech, Sussex; A. E. Phipps, Wickford, Essex; R. Pidgeon, Dover, Kent; R. J. Pike, London, E14; Mrs Yvonne S. Pike, Rayleigh, Essex; E. Pilbeam, Ringmere, Sussex; S. Pipe, London, N11; W. H. Pitcher, London, SE6; Mrs Vera L. Plant, London, N13; Norman Plastow, London, SW19; Mrs M. H. Platt, Northampton; Miss Wyn Polley, Bournemouth; Mrs Jean Pollinger, Walton-on-Thames, Surrey; Thomas F. Pond, Ruislip, Middlesex; F. G. Pont and Mrs V. Pont, London, SE19; Mrs Mary Pook, Bury St Edmunds, Suffolk; R. G. Pooley, Haslemere, Surrey; John Pope, Isleworth, Middlesex; Mrs Dorothy Poskitt, Hainault, Essex; F. A. Potter, Kirby le Soken, Essex; Mrs John Potter, Pulborough, Sussex; Capt. R. A. Potts and Mrs Joan Potts, Burpham, Surrey; Mrs G. Powell, Dedham, Essex; Mrs O. S. Powell, Potters Bar, Herts; Mrs E. M. Pratt, Westerham, Kent; Len Prentis, Ruislip, Middx; W. H. Prentis, Mitcham, Surrey; Mrs Kathleen Prescott, Eastbourne, Sussex; Mrs Patricia B. Price, Ramsgate, Kent; Mrs Florence Priestley, Benfleet, Essex; Mrs R. Prior, Northam Rye, Sussex; Miss E. E. Privett, Croydon; Roy Procter, Felixstowe, Suffolk; W. J. T. Proctor, Northfleet, Kent; Mrs Enid G. Prole, High Wycombe, Bucks; Harry Prothero, Ramsgate, Kent; Derek Pruce, West Horndon, Essex; W. C. Pummell, London, E10; Miss B. M. Punter, Uppingham, Rutland; David Purdie, Hailsham, Sussex; Mrs E. M. Putnam, Louse, Kent; Miss Mary Pybus, Bury St Edmunds, Suffolk; W. J. Pyne, Barnet, Herts; Leven Quarterman, London, E10; Mrs Muriel Quigley, Bury St Edmunds, Suffolk; James Ransford, London, SE14; Professor D. D. Raphael and Mrs S. D. Raphael, Petersham, Surrey; Harry Rapp,

London, NW8; Elizabeth Rathbone, Dunton Green, Kent; Mrs Ruth Raybould, Thetford, Norfolk; Mrs J. P. Raynes, Knaphill, Surrey; M. Redshaw, Milton Regis, Kent; J. B. Reed, Broadstairs, Kent; Mrs Nora A. Reed, Bexhill-on-Sea, Sussex; Roy Reed, London, EC3; Fred Rees, Eastbourne, Sussex; Mrs A. Reeves, Crowborough, Sussex; Mrs T. M. Reteer, Chard, Somerset; Rev A. C. and Mrs Reynolds, Harwich, Essex; Gordon Reynolds, Lowestoft, Suffolk; Mrs L. Reynolds, Balcombe, Sussex; Mrs N. Reynolds, Eastbourne, Sussex; Mrs P. M. Reynolds, Winchester, Hants; W. G. Reynolds, Poole, Dorset; Reginald Rham, Whitton, Middlesex; Mrs Marion Richards, Haywards Heath, Sussex; Walter G. Richards, London, SW18; Mrs Richens, London, SE27; Miss F. B. Richter, Sutton, Surrey; Bill Ridgway, London, SE9; Mrs M. I. Ridout, Ramsay, Isle of Man; J. H. Risdon, London, SW19; Mrs K. M. Risk, Andover, Hants; Alan Roberts, Northfleet, Kent; A. T. F. Roberts, Eastbourne, Sussex; Mrs Emily Elizabeth Roberts, Eastbourne, Sussex; Eric Roberts, Reading, Berks; Miss Marjorie Roberts, London, W4; John Robbins, London, EC4; Mrs P. R. Robbins, London, E17; Mrs Eileen Robinson, Crowthorne, Berks; A. G. Roddis, Bournemouth, Dorset; Ian Rodger, Brill, Bucks; Roy Rofe, Paddock Wood, Kent; A. R. Roffey, London, N14; G. W. Rogers, High Wycombe, Bucks; Peter Rogers, Luton, Beds; Alan W. Rolfe, London, SW2; Mrs May Rollins, Leatherhead, Surrey; A. J. Rome, Flitwick, Beds; W. C. Rood, Edgware, Middlesex; Miss J. Roper, Frimley, Surrey; Dennis Rose, Hove, Sussex; Mrs Lily Rose Rose, London, E2; Edwin S. Rosenthal, Witnesham, Suffolk; Miss S. Rossiter, Streatham; Mrs Joan Roth, Sawbridgeworth, Herts; Paul Rotha, Aylesbury, Bucks; L. V. Rowe, Frinton-on-Sea, Essex; F. O. Rowsell, Selsdon, Surrey; Mrs J. M. Rowley, London, N1; for the Stewart family, Mrs Alice V. Ruck, Chartham, Kent; Ernest W. Rumsey, Harrow, Middlesex; Miss Betty Rush, Croydon, Surrey; Mrs Helena Russell, Little Chalfont, Bucks; Mrs Joan Russell, Aylesbury, Bucks; Raymond John Russell, Aylesbury, Bucks; R. J. Rutherford, Edgware, Middlesex; R. A. Salaman, Harpenden, Herts; Fredk. J. Salmon, Edgware, Middlesex; Mrs F. L. Salter, Banstead, Surrey; R. W. Sampson, Watford, Herts; Mrs I. Samson, Bishop's Stortford, Herts; Mrs Givenda Sanders, Haywards Heath, Sussex; Michael Sands, Farnborough, Hants; Mrs S. V. Sandwell, London, N3; Mr and Mrs H. J. Saunders, Worthing, Sussex; Mrs D. Frances Saunders-Veness, Onslow, Guildford; Mrs Joyce Savile, London, SE12; John Saxby, Brantford, Ontario, Canada; P. B. Sayer, Hornchurch, Essex; A. J. Schirn, London, E15; Miss Doris Scott, London, SW18; F. G. Scott, Steeple Aston, Oxford; H. Eric Scott, West Southbourne, Dorset;

Mrs Kathleen Scott, St Albans, Herts; Mrs Loris Seager, Walton-on-the-Naze, Essex; Mrs Kathleen Sharpe, Ickwell, Beds; Mrs Joan Shaw, Mayford, Surrey; Mrs N. Shaw, Bexleyheath, Kent; Mrs Ina Shepard, London, SW16; Joyce Shephard, Strood, Kent; Mrs Iris Shepherd, King's Lynn, Norfolk; Brian C. Sherren, Deal, Kent; A. H, Shipman, Taverham, Norfolk; Mrs Christine Shirvill, Snodland, Kent; Geoffrey Shoosmith, Little Kimble, Bucks; Miss Olive Shorey, Lancing, Sussex; A. R. Simmonds, Brammerton, Norwich; Miss Patricia Simmons, Hastings, Sussex; Roger Simmons, Gravesend, Kent; Allan and Mrs Caroline Sissons, London, SE9; M. W. G. and Mrs B. Skinner, Coulsdon, Surrey; Mrs H. V. Skinner, Southampton, Hants; Mrs B. A. Slade, Ramsgate, Kent; Mrs Alice Smith, Canvey Island, Essex; Bert Smith, London, N6; C. D. Smith, Windsor, Berks; Chris Smith, Westerham, Kent; Mrs D. Smith, Sutton, Norfolk; Donald Smith, Hounslow, Middlesex; Mrs Dorothy Smith, Christchurch, Dorset; Edward R. Smith, Richmond, Surrey; Mrs E. Smith, Ramsgate, Kent; Mr and Mrs Eric Smith, Hoo, Kent; F. Smith, London, W12; F. A. Smith, Chestfield, Kent; G. I. Smith, Pulborough, Sussex; Mrs Joan Smith, Poole, Dorset; Leslie Smith, Mitcham, Surrey; Mrs Miriam Smith, Edgware, Middlesex; Mrs Mabel Smith, Stafford, Staffs; M. L. Smith, Aylesbury, Bucks; Reg Smith, Paignton, Devon; Cdr. R. J. Smith, Eastbourne, Sussex; S. C. Smith, Croydon, Surrey; W. M. Smith, Iver Heath, Bucks; Dr W. E. Snell, Hambleden, Oxon; Rev H. Neal Snelling, Steyning, Sussex; R. B. Somerville, Broadstone, Dorset; Mrs Joan Songhurst, Staines, Middlesex; Mrs Gladys Soper, King's Lyn, Norfolk; E. Y. Sownsend, London, SW12; Miss June Sparey, Camberley, Surrey; F. C. Spencer, Fairlight, Sussex; Victor Spink, Chertsey, Surrey; Mrs I. M. Spinks, Ashford, Kent; Lionel D. Spinks, Rayleigh, Essex; M. T. Stack, London, SW20; Mrs. N. C. Stainton, Southwold, Suffolk; Mrs F. H. Stanbury, Leigh-on-Sea, Essex; G. P. Staniford, London, SE22; Mrs L. Stannard, Colchester, Essex; Mrs E. F. Stanton, Heston, Middlesex; T. A. Stanway, Wallington, Surrey; C. W. Stark, Gravesend, Kent; Mrs A. C. Steel, Pembury, Kent; James Stephen, Poole, Dorset; S. J. Stephen, London, W12; Mrs W. Steward, Ispwich, Suffolk; Mrs Dorothy Frances Stewart, Purley, Surrey; Mrs B. B. Stock, Worthing, Sussex; Mrs Elsie Stockbridge, Hove, Sussex; Henry Stone, Southampton; Mrs J. E. Stone, Northwood, Middlesex; Mrs Katie Stone, Horsham, Sussex; John Stone, Cranleigh, Surrey; I. T. Stratford, Wakes Colne, Essex; Mrs M. Streeter, Hampden Park, Sussex; Mrs P. E. Struthers-Law, Crowborough; Alan Stuart, Caversham Park Village, Berks; Mrs Marion G. Stuart-Hemsley, Eastbourne, Sussex; Mrs Pat Sturgeon, Broadstairs, Kent; Mrs J. S. Stythe, Harrietsham,

Kent; H. E. Sullivan, London, SE13; Miss Margaret Summerton, Etchingham, Sussex; K. D. Sutherland, Sevenoaks, Kent; Mrs Jean Swindell, London, SE7; Mrs Dorothy Sykes, Sutton, Surrey; Mrs Gill Sykes, Alvechurch, Worcs; Alan J. Tann, Prittlewell, Essex; Aubrey Tanner, Harrow, Middlesex; Philip E. Tapp, Milstead, Kent; L. Tapsell, Sittingbourne, Kent; Mrs Sybil Tarr, Pinner, Middlesex; Mrs Mary Tassell, Ashford, Kent; H. R. Tavener, Ryehill, Northants; A. Taylor, London, E17; Mrs D. Taylor, Romford, Essex; Mrs M. C. Taylor, Colchester, Essex; R. B. Taylor, Maidstone, Kent; William and Mrs Norah Taylor, Hadley Wood, Herts; Mrs N. Terry, East Grinstead, Sussex; Dr Jan den Tex, Leusden, Holland; Mr and Mrs Richard Thomas, London, N9; Thomas M. Thorp, Gillingham, Kent; Roger Thurgood, Pinner, Middlesex; Mrs Hettie Thurston, Eastleigh, Hants; James A. Tice, Guildford, Surrey; E. R. Ticehurst, London, SW2; W. P. Timms, Sheerwater, Surrey; Mrs C. Tipper, Hemel Hempstead, Herts; Miss Joyce D. Tobin, Hove, Sussex; Mrs Beatrice M. Todd, Wellingborough; Fred Tolhurst, Woking, Surrey; Mrs Dorothy A. Tompkins, Uxbridge, Middlesex; Mrs M. S. Tompkins, Harrow, Middlesex; Mrs Rhoda Tompkins, London, SW13; Miss E. Towell, Bradford-on-Avon, Wilts; Miss Violet Townshend, Headington, Oxford; Mrs Gwen M. Trash, Burgess Hill, Sussex; T. H. Troughton, Greenford, Middlesex; Miss L. R. Tuck, Englefield Green, Surrey; C. R. Tucker, Wallington, Surrey; Mrs E. Tucker, Northolt, Middlesex; Mrs Mary Turbin, Harleston, Norfolk; Miss D. V. Turner, Westbury, Wilts; J. Alan Turner, Southwold, Suffolk; Miss D. Twyman, Bodle Street Green, Sussex; Miss A. S. Tyler, Yateley, Surrey; Miss Irene Tyler, West Ewell, Surrey; Lawrence Tyrell, Calgary, Alberta, Canada; Derek Underhill, Hounslow, Middlesex; Mrs J. R. Underwood, London, N3; Philip Unwin, Haslemere, Surrey; Clarence Uren, Edgware, Middlesex; Miss E. M. Vinall, Dartford, Kent; Don Vincent, Andover, Hants; Rev G. S. Waghorn, Boston, Lincs; Mrs E. Walker, Glasgow, Scotland; Mrs Audrey Wall, Reading, Berks; David Waller, Bray, Berks; Mrs Marion Walsh, Eastbourne, Sussex; L. V. Walshaw, Selsdon, Surrey; Major C. E. Walter, Worthing, Sussex; Robert Wanden, Maidenhead, Berks; George Wansbrough, Winchester, Hants; Mrs C. A. Warbey, Harlow, Essex; John Warburton, London, SW11; Mrs Patricia Ward, Bishop's Stortford, Herts; Mrs Rose Warden, London, W11; Geoff Warne, Bexley, Kent; Mrs E. Warner, Folkestone, Kent; Brian Warren, Cockfosters, Herts; Frank Warren, Addington, Croydon; G. A. Warwicker, London, N18; Mrs M. Wash, Frinton-on-Sea, Essex; Archie Waters, St Leonards-on-Sea, Sussex; Philip Watling, Manningtree, Essex; Mrs E. Watson, Backworth, Newcastle-on-

Tyne; Ian F. Watts, Richmond, Surrey; Mrs Maud M. Watts, London, N22; Eric Wayman, Bexleyheath, Kent; F. R. Weaver, Cherry Hinton, Cambs; Derek Webb, Colchester, Essex; S. A. C. Webb, London, E12; W. F. Webbe, Bournemouth, Dorset; Harold Webster, Rooklands, Norfolk; Graeme Weir, Sudbury, Suffolk; Mrs Ivy Hannah Weller, London, SE9; Roy Wells, Orpington, Kent; Mrs B. West, London, SE9; W. Westbrook, London, NW1; Ronald A. Westwood, Denver, Colarado, U.S.A.; D. A. Whatman, Staplehurst, Kent; Eric Wheeler, Weybridge, Surrey; F. A. Wheeler, Chatham, Kent; Mrs Harold Whishaw; Mrs Daphne White, Clacton-on-Sea, Essex; Mrs Edith White, Balcombe, Sussex; Mrs June White, London, N1; Mrs Marjorie White, Fetcham, Surrey; Mrs R. White, Thornton Heath, Surrey; Robert J. White, Arundel, Sussex; Mrs Sheila White, St Helens, Isle of Wight; Harry Whiteman, Sheringham, Norfolk; Hugh Whitemore, London, SW11; Noel Whitworth, Woodham Ferrers, Essex; Helen Welch, London, SE27; Mrs Kathleen Wieloch, Mastin Moor, Derbs; C. H. Wilkins, Newick, Sussex; Miss Teresa Wilkins; Mr and Mrs Williams, Ramsgate, Kent; Anthony Williams, Sudbury, Suffolk; Mrs Heather Williams, Lewes, Sussex; Mrs Phyllis V. Williams, Guildford, Surrey; Rex Williams, Burgess Hill, Sussex; Ron Williams, Chelsham, Surrey; Mike Willsmer, Chelmsford, Essex; Mrs Joan M. R. Wilson, Kingsport, Tennessee, USA; Miss Margaret M. M. Wilson, Glasgow, Scotland; R. G. D. Wilson, Worthing, Sussex; Ted Wilson, Harlow, Essex; Mrs V. Wilson, Chatburn, Lancs; Albert Winchester, London, E15; John Tatton Winter, London, SW12; Mrs L. Wiseman, London, SW8; Mrs B. E. Wood, London, SW16; Charles A. Wood, New Barnet, Herts; F. H. Wood, Shipton Gorge, Bridport, Dorset; Mrs Winston Wood, London, WC1; Mrs Cecile Woodford, Polegate, Sussex; Mrs R. Woodford, Bournemouth, Dorset; Mrs Enid Woodgate, Robertsbridge, Sussex; Rev C. G. Woodhead, Hoo, Kent; Mrs Xenia N. Woodthorpe, Etchingham, Sussex; R. W. Noble Woodward, Colchester, Essex; Miss Joyce Woolford, Reading, Berks; Nelson Woolsey, King's Lynn, Norfolk; M. J. Worley, High Wycombe, Bucks; Mrs Joan Wren, Polegate, Sussex; Leslie Wright, London, SW4; Victor Wright, Holt, Norfolk; Bill Wrigley, Epsom, Surrey; D. B. Wyke, Dunston, Staffs; Mrs Christine Wylde, London, SW13; Mrs J. L. Wyley, Shoeburyness, Essex; Mrs Sophie Wyss, Surbiton, Surrey; Mrs A. Yarnell, London, E16; S. V. Yeakes, Dover, Kent; C. E. Young, Potters Bar, Herts; Y. Young, London, E16; Frank H. Ziegler, Haslemere, Surrey.

GENERAL INDEX

accuracy of V–1, 51, 335, 371–4, 376, 445, 464, 468

Air Raid Precautions (ARP),
deficiences in organization, 458–60
Heavy Rescue Squads, 320–22
London Region HQ, Geological Museum, South Kensington, 315–16
Ministry of Home Security War Room, Rotunda, Horseferry Road, 131, 315
rescue operations, 314–25, 458
rest centres, 282–3, 457, 459
Wardens, 314, 315, 321, 323–4
warning system, 113, 255–60

altitude of V–1, operational, 41, 51, 74, 201, 394

Ambler, Air Commodore G. H., 403

Anti-Aircraft Command, 58, 105, 113, 392, 394–416, 484
achievements unrecognized, 415–16
ATS presence, 411–13, 415, 450, 462
chaos with RAF, 401–2; hits on RAF planes, 401
Diver plan, 72, 98, 395–7, 398, 400, 404, 405, 406, 407
guns silenced, 126, 394
radar equipment, 398–400, 415
RAF Regiment batteries, 405, 406, 414

redeployment, 403–6, 448–9, 462–3
Royal Armoured Corps batteries, 405
searchlight batteries, 447–8
US Army batteries, 405, 414
weapons, 414–16

airframe development of pilotless aircraft, 23–4, 26, 27

Allied Expeditionary Air Force, 58, 76

animals, reactions of, 146–9, 386–7

Arct, Squadron-Leader Bohdan, 434–5, 440

Ardennes offensive, 454, 464

Arnold, General, 24–5, 59

Attlee, Clement (later Lord Attlee), 133, 379

Axthelm, Lieutenant-General Walter von, 37, 38, 39, 41, 43, 82

Babington Smith, Section Officer Constance, 30, 32, 34, 48, 52, 54–6

Balloon Command, 58, 72, 111, 395, 397, 417–27
casualties, 422
mobility, 420
parachute link equipment, 426
V–1 victims, 419, 423, 425–7, 440
WAAF involvement, 420, 422, 423

Barker, Wing-Commander, 486

529

ground crews, 432–3; tally of flying-bombs destroyed, 431, 432, 433, 436, 437, 438, 439–40, 447, 448, 466; Tempests, 432, 433, 437, 440, 447, 462; wing-tipping, 435–6.

Mediterranean Air Force, 65

photographic reconnaissance of V–1 build-up, 29–30, 34, 54–6, 76, 349–50, 464

RAF Regiment, 405, 406, 414

Second Tactical Air Force, 355

WAAFs, 420, 422, 423

see also Balloon Command

Royal Aircraft Establishment, Farnborough, 77, 439, 473

Royal Navy

bombs destroyed by gunfire, 445, 447, 466

floating radar station HMS *Caicos*, 447

lightships, 429, 439

Royal Observer Corps, 58, 73–5, 89–91, 107, 206, 398, 418, 422, 431, 455

detection efficiency, 398

Rundstedt, Field-Marshal von, 334, 360, 464

St George Saunders, Hilary, 343, 484

salvaging from the ruins, 283–5

Salvation Army, 281

Sandwell, Mrs R. V., 311

Sandys, Duncan (later Lord Duncan-Sandys, 97, 109, 137, 377, 434, 441, 442, 485

heads Bodyline inquiry into secret weapons, 31–2, 35–6, 49, 52

proposal on home security, 378, 379

reports Bodyline findings to War Cabinet, 32, 35

reprisal reports, 342

Sansom, William, 120, 123, 129, 315, 342–3

Sauckel, Gauleiter, 38

Schmidt, Dr Paul, 24, 27

schools, effect on, 228–32

Ashford Grammar, 105, 109, 226, 227

Beckenham and Penge Grammar, 231

Dulwich College, 373

Goodworth Clatford, 368–9

Kilburn Grammar, 191

Plaistow Grammar, 229–30, 289

Putney High, 230

Sandown Grammar, 363

Tidebrook, 477

Shawcross, Sir Hartley (later Lord Shawcross), 457–8, 459

shelling from the French coast, 391

shelters, 260–66

Anderson, 134, 265, 266, 274, 397

brick surface, 265–6

Chislehurst Caves, 127

deep underground, 134, 137, 260–62

Morrison, 68, 134, 265, 266, 384

plan to give priority to civil servants, 68–9

St Clement's Caves, West Hill, Folkestone, 109

tube stations, 68, 127, 130, 134, 135, 260

Sheppard-Jones, Elizabeth, 121–2, 123–4, 478

Shirer, William, 19

shooting down of V–1s, 384, 385, 398; at sea, 391, 393, 398

shopping incidents, 177–89

shops

Arding and Hobbs Ltd, Clapham Junction, 189

Bentalls, Kingston, 189

Co-op incidents, 187–8

Dickins and Jones, Regent Street, 181

Fortnum and Mason, 177

Harrods, 131

Marks and Spencer, Lewisham, 186, 251

Peter Robinson, Oxford Street, 276

Williamsons, Lewisham, 251

Woolworths, Lewisham, 187

Sinclair, Sir Archibald, 357, 358

Sivil, Lieutenant, 204

Skorzeny, Otto, 470

Smith, Captain, 276

Smith, Reg, 306

INDEX OF PLACE NAMES

Index of Place Names

On the following pages are details of Arrow books that will be of interest.

THE GREAT ESCAPE

Paul Brickhill

There could be no other war book like *The Great Escape*, Paul Brickhill's celebrated, classic account of the heroic and tragic breakout from Stalag Luft III.

'The high-water mark of all active prisoner-of-war books . . . I found myself putting it down almost literally to get my breath. Scattered through its packed and racing pages are a hundred tiny incidents and characters worthy of mention, indelibly etched on a reader's memory' *Daily Telegraph*

'One of the most unputdownable stories of the war' *The Observer*

'A tale of group heroism, determination and ingenuity which gets hold of the reader's nerves and emotions and won't let go' *Sunday Times*

A RUMOR OF WAR

Philip Caputo

A Rumor of War is Pulitzer Prize winner Philip Caputo's account of his own war as a young marine. It is a story of the hell of modern jungle warfare. Of desperate courage and casual brutality. Of what men do in war and of what war does to men.

Hailed as the war classic of our generation, *A Rumor of War* has been compared to *All Quiet on the Western Front* and *The Naked and the Dead*. With this difference – it all happened.

'A singular and marvellous book' *New York Times*

'A classic' *Guardian*

'Brilliant' *William Stryon, New York Review of Books*

THE BERLIN BUNKER

James P. O'Donnell

Never before have the final, desperate days of Hitler and his closest followers been re-created as hauntingly as in *The Berlin Bunker*.

'Superb. Quite simply the most terrifying account of the nightmare and its end I have ever read' *Theodore H. White*

'Quite staggering . . . exciting and riveting reading' *The Bookseller*

BESTSELLING NON-FICTION FROM ARROW

All these books are available from your bookshop or newsagent or you can order them direct. Just tick the titles you want and complete the form below.

☐	THE GREAT ESCAPE	Paul Brickhill	£1.75
☐	A RUMOR OF WAR	Philip Caputo	£2.50
☐	A LITTLE ZIT ON THE SIDE	Jasper Carrott	£1.50
☐	THE ART OF COARSE ACTING	Michael Green	£1.50
☐	THE UNLUCKIEST MAN IN THE WORLD	Mike Harding	£1.75
☐	DIARY OF A SOMEBODY	Christopher Matthew	£1.25
☐	TALES FROM A LONG ROOM	Peter Tinniswood	£1.75
☐	LOVE WITHOUT FEAR	Eustace Chesser	£1.95
☐	NO CHANGE	Wendy Cooper	£1.95
☐	MEN IN LOVE	Nancy Friday	£2.75

Postage

Total

ARROW BOOKS, BOOKSERVICE BY POST, PO BOX 29, DOUGLAS, ISLE OF MAN, BRITISH ISLES

Please enclose a cheque or postal order made out to Arrow Books Ltd for the amount due including 15p per book for postage and packing both for orders within the UK and for overseas orders.

Please print clearly

NAME ....

ADDRESS ....

....

Whilst every effort is made to keep prices down and to keep popular books in print, Arrow Books cannot guarantee that prices will be the same as those advertised here or that the books will be available.